T0316615

THE ROUTLEDGE COMPANION TO INTERNATIONAL HOSPITALITY MANAGEMENT

The hospitality sector has been facing increasing competition and complexity over recent decades in its development towards a global industry. The strategic response to this is still that hospitality companies try to grow outside their traditional territories and domestic markets, while the expansion patterns and M&A activities of international hotel and restaurant chains reflect this phenomenon. Yet, interestingly, the strategies, concepts, and methods of internationalization as well as the managerial and organizational challenges and impacts of globalizing the hospitality business are under-researched in this industry.

While the mainstream research on international management offers an abundance of information and knowledge on topics, players, trends, concepts, frameworks, or methodologies, its ability to produce viable insights for the hospitality industry is limited, as the mainstream research is taking place outside of the service sector. Specific research directions and related cases like the international dimensions of strategy, organization, marketing, sales, staffing, control, culture, and others to the hospitality industry are rarely identifiable so far. The core rationale of this book is therefore to present the newest insights from research and industry in the field of international hospitality, drawing together recent scientific knowledge and state-of-the-art expertise to suggest directions for future work. It is designed to raise awareness of the international factors influencing the strategy and performance of hospitality organizations, while analyzing and discussing the present and future challenges for hospitality firms going or being international.

This book will provide a comprehensive overview and deeper understanding of trends and issues to researchers, practitioners, and students by showing how to master current and future challenges when entering and competing in the global hospitality industry.

Marco A. Gardini is Professor of International Hospitality Management and Marketing, and Vice Dean of the Faculty of Tourism, at Kempten UAS, Germany.

Michael C. Ottenbacher is Head of the Department of Hospitality Management at Kansas State University, USA.

Markus Schuckert is Associate Professor in the School of Hotel and Tourism Management at The Hong Kong Polytechnic University, Hong Kong S.A.R., China.

ROUTLEDGE COMPANIONS IN BUSINESS, MANAGEMENT AND MARKETING

Routledge Companions are prestige volumes which provide an overview of a research field or topic. Surveying the business disciplines, the books in this series incorporate both established and emerging research themes. Compiled and edited by an array of highly regarded scholars, these volumes also benefit from global teams of contributors reflecting disciplinary diversity.

Individually, *Routledge Companions in Business, Management and Marketing* provide impactful one-stop-shop publications. Collectively, they represent a comprehensive learning and research resource for researchers, postgraduate students and practitioners.

Published titles in this series include:

THE ROUTLEDGE COMPANION TO ACCOUNTING HISTORY, 2ND EDITION
Edited by John Richard Edwards and Stephen Walker

THE ROUTLEDGE COMPANION TO MANAGING DIGITAL OUTSOURCING
Edited by Erik Beulen and Pieter Ribbers

THE ROUTLEDGE COMPANION TO HAPPINESS AT WORK
Edited by Joan Marques

THE ROUTLEDGE COMPANION TO ANTHROPOLOGY AND BUSINESS
Edited by Raza Mir and Anne-Laure Fayard

THE ROUTLEDGE COMPANION TO INTERNATIONAL HOSPITALITY MANAGEMENT
Edited by Marco A. Gardini, Michael C. Ottenbacher, and Markus Schuckert

THE ROUTLEDGE HANDBOOK OF CRITICAL FINANCE STUDIES
Edited by Christian Borch and Robert Wosnitzer

For more information about this series, please visit: www.routledge.com/Routledge-Companions-in-Business-Management-and-Marketing/book-series/RCBUS

THE ROUTLEDGE COMPANION TO INTERNATIONAL HOSPITALITY MANAGEMENT

Edited by Marco A. Gardini, Michael C. Ottenbacher, and Markus Schuckert

Routledge
Taylor & Francis Group

NEW YORK AND LONDON

First published 2021
by Routledge
52 Vanderbilt Avenue, New York, NY 10017

and by Routledge
2 Park Square, Milton Park, Abingdon, Oxon, OX14 4RN

Routledge is an imprint of the Taylor & Francis Group, an informa business

Library of Congress Cataloging-in-Publication Data
Names: Gardini, Marco A., 1964– editor. |
Ottenbacher, Michael C., 1966– editor. | Schuckert, Markus, editor.
Title: The Routledge companion to international hospitality management /
edited by Marco A. Gardini, Michael C. Ottenbacher and Markus Schuckert.
Description: New York: Routledge, 2021. |
Series: Routledge companions in business, management and marketing |
Includes bibliographical references and index.
Identifiers: LCCN 2020021049 (print) | LCCN 2020021050 (ebook) |
ISBN 9781138386372 (hardback) | ISBN 9780429426834 (ebook)
Subjects: LCSH: Hospitality industry—Management.
Classification: LCC TX911.3.M27 R67 2021 (print) |
LCC TX911.3.M27 (ebook) | DDC 647.94—dc23
LC record available at https://lccn.loc.gov/2020021049
LC ebook record available at https://lccn.loc.gov/2020021050

ISBN: 978-1-138-38637-2 (hbk)
ISBN: 978-0-429-42683-4 (ebk)

Typeset in Bembo
by codeMantra

CONTENTS

ABOUT THE EDITORS

Marco A. Gardini is Professor of International Hospitality Management and Marketing and Vice Dean of the Faculty of Tourism at Kempten UAS in Germany. Prior to joining Kempten UAS, he was Faculty Head of the Hospitality Department and Professor of Service Management and Marketing at the International University Bad Honnef. He studied international management, marketing, and psychology in Marburg and Gießen and holds a master's degree and doctorate in business administration from the Justus-Liebig University in Gießen, Germany.

Beginning in a family-owned gastronomy business, Professor Gardini's professional marketing, consulting, and training activities in multinational companies and consultancy firms span more than 25 years. To date, his clients have included Accor, Thomas Cook, NH Hotels, Deutsche Hospitality, Design Hotels, Falkensteiner Hotels and Residences, Seetel Hotels, Allgäu Top Hotels, Treugast Solutions Group, and the Austrian Hotel Association (ÖHV). Along with teaching undergraduate, graduate, and executive education courses in German and English, he has served for the past 15 years as a guest lecturer at various German and international universities (i.e., JLU Gießen, WHU Koblenz, FU Bozen, MCI Innsbruck, HWTH Chur, GUTech Oman, and Munich Business School). His primary areas of research are international hospitality management and marketing, service excellence, brand management, customer relationship management, and total quality management.

Professor Gardini is also deputy chairman of the Bavarian Center for Tourism, a board member of the SME Institute at Kempten UAS, and the author and editor of several standard German-language textbooks on tourism, hospitality marketing, and management. Furthermore, he has published numerous articles in refereed journals, as well as various magazines and newspapers.

Michael C. Ottenbacher is the Head of the Department of Hospitality Management and the Mary L. Vanier endowed Professor at Kansas State University. Professor Ottenbacher received his doctorate in marketing from the University of Otago, New Zealand, and his master and bachelor of science degrees in hospitality management from Florida International University, USA. Prior to joining Kansas State University, he taught at Heilbronn University, Germany; San Diego State University, USA; the University of Guelph, Canada; and the University of Surrey, UK. In addition to academia, he has extensive business experience, including at the Savoy Hotel (London, UK), the Ritz Hotel (Paris, France), the Royal Sonesta (New Orleans, USA), and the Steigenberger Hotel (Stuttgart, Germany).

Professor Ottenbacher has published widely in leading journals on hospitality, tourism, and management, as well as serving on the editorial board of several journals, and, since 2013, an co-editor of the *Journal of Hospitality and Tourism Education*. He has also been a visiting professor at the Institute Paul Bocuse in France; the German–Vietnamese University in Ho Chi Minh City, Vietnam; Taylor's University in Kuala Lumpur, Malaysia; and University of Applied Sciences of the Grisons, Switzerland.

Markus Schuckert is currently Associate Professor in the School of Hotel & Tourism Management at The Hong Kong Polytechnic University. Prior to joining SHTM in January 2012, he was Professor of Tourism and Transport Management and Director of the Institute for Tourism and Leisure Research and School of Tourism at the University of Applied Sciences (UAS) HTW Chur, Switzerland. Throughout his academic career, Professor Schuckert been a consultant for many companies, served on various organizational boards, and actively participated in several professional associations. While earning his doctorate in economics and social sciences at Innsbruck University (Austria), he cofounded a consulting company for tourism market research, product development, and change management in tourism organizations and destinations. Currently his research interests span strategic management and marketing aspects of (dis)integrated value chains in tourism, transport, and entrepreneurial networks, including in airlines, airports, theme parks, Hotels & resorts, and destination organizations.

To share his experience, Professor Schuckert has taught courses in related subjects at management schools in Austria, Canada, China, Germany, Hong Kong, South Korea, Switzerland, Taiwan, and the USA at the undergraduate and graduate levels and is currently supervising postgraduate students in Europe, North America, and Asia. Beyond leisure, his work-related visits have taken him to tourism schools around the world. He contributes by publishing in journals on hospitality, tourism, and transport management, speaking at conferences and industry meetings, and editing books on science and industry.

CONTRIBUTORS

Abijith Abraham is a Research Scholar at the Department of Tourism and Hotel Management, North-Eastern Hill University, Shillong, Meghalaya (India). His research interests include Destination Competitiveness, Gastronomic Tourism, Experiential Management and Marketing in the contexts of Tourism and Hospitality. He holds a Bachelor's Degree in Hospitality and Hotel Administration and a Master's Degree in Business Administration (Tourism and Travel Management). He is a recipient of the prestigious Junior Research Fellowship (JRF) awarded by the Union Grants Commission (UGC), New Delhi.

Dr. Oriol Anguera-Torrell is the Director of the Hospitality Research Group at CETT – Universitat de Barcelona, where he also teaches Tourism Research Methods, Tourism Economics, and Revenue Management. His main areas of research are Applied Economics in the Tourism and in the Hospitality industries. He received his Ph.D. in Economics from Universitat Pompeu Fabra in June 2016.

Dr. Wolfgang Georg Arlt is the Founder and Director of COTRI China Outbound Tourism Institute. From 1991–1999, he owned Inbound Tour Operator China-Europe. He is Professor for International Tourism Management at West Coast UAS in Germany (Heide). As visiting professor in several international universities, he is a Fellow of the Royal Geographical Society, Researcher for the Japan Society for the Promotion of Science and Member of the UNTWO Panel of Tourism Experts, Member of Expert Committee of WTCF and Member of Friends of Europe Think tank (Brussels). He serves as Board member of PATA and Vice President Western Europe of ITSA.

Dr. Florian Aubke is Head of Tourism and Hospitality Management study programs at FHWien der WKW, the leading University of Applied Sciences for Management and Communication in Austria. Before joining the FHWien der WKW, Florian played an integral part in the development of the private University Modul, where he was Dean of the Undergraduate School and Director of Non-Degree Programs. He teaches a wide range of subjects in hospitality management, including hotel asset management, revenue management and hotel development. His interests cover relational aspects of creativity, innovation, and organizational design – with a particular application to the hospitality and tourism industry.

Dr. Engin Aytekin is an English Instructor at Afyon Kocatepe University in Turkey. He holds an MA in Tourism and Hospitality Management, and particularly lectured in tourism faculty in

English courses. He graduated with a Ph.D. from Eskişehir Osmangazi University, Department of Tourism and Hospitality Management.

Dr. Ulrich Bauer trained as fitter and mechanic, and traveled widely before studying in his late twenties anthropology, modern history, and linguistics. In a second academic career he studied German philology, geography, and applied linguistics, and did his doctoral thesis on epistemological and hermeneutical questions of understanding other cultures. He has traveled, worked and lived in well over 100 countries altogether, spending 15 years outside Europe. Today he is Professor for Intercultural Communication at Kempten University, Germany, management coach in industry (mechanical engineering, automotive, electrical industry, travel industry, etc.) and living on a farm in the Bavarian Alps.

Yoy Bergs is a lecturer at Breda University of Applied Sciences and a PhD candidate at Nyenrode Business Universiteit. She finished a Master's Degree in both Work, Health & Career and in Work & Organizational Psychology from Maastricht University. For both masters she conducted research on work-family conflict and its influence on specific health outcomes in the working population. Her research interests include image construction, sustainable employability, health & wellbeing, work-family conflict and boundary management.

Dr. Hartwig Bohne is Professor and Head of International Study Programs at SRH Dresden School of Management, and the Managing Director of the Institute of Global Hospitality Research. He started his career with an apprenticeship as hotel specialist at the Kempinski Hotel Dresden, followed by his first job at the Kempinski Hotel Geneva. His studies in Business Administration and Tourism at the University Trier and the EM Strasbourg Business School led him to the German Hotel Association as an adviser. Later he served as the Director Apprenticeship Management & University relations to the corporate head office of Kempinski Hotels.

Dr. Stefano Borzillo is Associate Professor of Organizational Behavior and Associate Dean of Undergraduate Program at Ecole hôtelière de Lausanne. He obtained his Ph.D. in Organizational Behavior from the University of Geneva. His main fields of research are communities of practice, processes of knowledge creation, and best practice transfers in organizations. He has also published in peer-reviewed journals such as European Management Journal, Journal of Business Strategy, Management Learning, Knowledge Management Research & Practice, and Journal of Knowledge Management. Stefano has multiple experiences in Executive Education, and in consulting for SMEs and large organizations.

Hjalte Brøndum Mansa is an Assistant Professor at University College Lillebaelt in Denmark where he teaches Hotel Management, Revenue Management, Local Food Supply Chain Integration, and Employability for AP and BA students. He further manages the local alumni association, facilitates the yearly participation in the European hotel management championships, and is currently the Director of Member Services and Development for EuroCHRIE. Apart from the University teaching and network management, he teaches and facilitates globally, when requested. He studied his BA at UCL in Denmark and Master at Derby in UK, while working at UCL past his studies.

Dr. Elena Cavagnaro is a Professor of Sustainability in Hospitality and Tourism at Stenden University of Applied Sciences. She is visiting professor at the University of Derby (UK) and the University of Macerata and Bergamo (Italy). Elena has consulted several organizations in sectors such as hospitality, retail, and health care on sustainability strategy and implementation. Following her understanding of sustainability as a multi-dimensional and multi-layered concept, her research focuses on issues that run across and connect the social, organizational, and individual layer of sustainability. The 'Three levels of Sustainability' book that she co-authored with G. Curiel is a bestseller.

Dr. Celine Chang is Professor of Human Resources Management at Munich University of Applied Sciences, Department of Tourism. Her research interests include regional HR approaches and HRM in SMEs. She has conducted studies on HRM in the hospitality industry and on job satisfaction of employees working in the hospitality industry. Prior to her professorship, she worked in the consulting industry with a focus on talent management and leadership development as well as in HR departments and Academia. She studied Psychology at the University of Regensburg, Germany, and the University of Queensland, Australia. She holds a doctorate in Psychology from the University of Hildesheim, Germany. She is a certified executive coach and advisor for systemic organizational development.

Dr. Kaye Chon is Dean, Chair Professor, and Walter & Wendy Kwok Family Foundation Professor in International Hospitality Management of the School of Hotel and Tourism Management at The Hong Kong Polytechnic University. Professor Chon previously held academic positions at the University of Houston, University of Nevada, Las Vegas, and Virginia Tech in the United States. In 2011, he was honored by the United Nations World Tourism Organization (UNWTO) with the UNWTO Ulysses Prize. He is currently the Editor-in-Chief of the Journal of Travel & Tourism Marketing and the Asia Pacific Journal of Tourism Research.

Philipp Corradini, MA, is a researcher at the Institute for Regional Development, Eurac Research in Bolzano/Bozen in Italy. He collaborates in different projects in the areas of tourism development and destination management within the regional and international context. Further areas of his work comprise economics and management, resilience, complex system analysis and mobility. Being a passionate tourism professional, he spent most of his working life within the tourism sector. One of his main assets is his tourism affinity and his practical approach towards this sector, which he was able to constantly enhance and hone throughout his professional and academic career.

Dr. Basak Denizci-Guillet is an Professor of Revenue Management at the School of Hotel and Tourism Management at the Hong Kong Polytechnic University. She received a B.S. degree in tourism and hotel management from Bilkent University, an M.S. degree in hotel administration from the University of Massachusetts, Amherst, and a Ph.D. degree in hospitality financial management from the Pennsylvania State University. She worked in the hotel industry as part of the Hilton and Marriot teams. Her academic research interests include hospitality business analytics with an emphasis on financial and revenue management.

Dr. Saurabh Kumar Dixit is an Associate Professor and founding Head of the Department of Tourism and Hotel Management, North - Eastern Hill University, Shillong (Meghalaya), India. His research interests include Consumer Behavior, Gastronomic Tourism, and Experiential Management and Marketing in hospitality and tourism contexts. He has thirteen books to his credit, including The Routledge Handbook of Consumer Behaviour in Hospitality and Tourism (2017), The Routledge Handbook of Gastronomic Tourism (2019), and The Routledge Handbook of Tourism Experience Management and Marketing (2020) and Tourism in Asian Cities (2020). His recent profile can be seen at https://www.routledge.com/authors/i15903-saurabh-dixit.

Nicolas Dubrocard, Director of Audit Diagnostic Solutions Tourism, has been involved in sustainability for the tourism industry for more than 15 years, starting this journey in Morocco where he supported hotels to obtain Green Key certification. He implemented the 'Every Drop

Counts' program for the Travel Foundation to reduce water consumption in hotels. He conducted audits for UNPD in the southern oases to evaluate the type of tourism development possibilities in that area. In 2011 he became the International Director of Green Key and could develop the standards in more than 40 countries. In 2014, Nicolas implemented, on behalf of Kuoni, the Water Champion program in Thailand and started to audit hotels for Green Globe. He has worked with more than 200 hotels in 31 countries.

Katrin Eberhardt is Assistant Catering Manager at Ratiopharm Arena in Ulm/Neu-Ulm, Germany. She is responsible for F&B and human resources management within the scope of big events such as basketball matches, concerts, or business presentations. Before, she was a Research Associate at Munich University of Applied Sciences, Department of Tourism. Her research focused on HR management in health tourism. She holds a master's degree in Hospitality Management from Munich University of Applied Sciences and a Bachelor's degree in Tourism Management from Kempten University of Applied Sciences.

Robert Eller is a Ph.D. candidate at the Department for Strategic Management, Marketing and Tourism at the University of Innsbruck, Austria. After completing an apprenticeship as a machine mechanic and further practical experience primarily in e-commerce business, he studied business and management at MCI Innsbruck and wrote his diploma thesis on certificates in the primary and secondary market. After completing his studies, he spent further years in the private sector before continuing his academic career. His research focuses on digital transformation and SME.

Dr. Desiderio J. García-Almeida is Professor of Management at the Faculty of Economics, Business Administration and Tourism of the University of Las Palmas de Gran Canaria. His research interests focus on knowledge management and innovation, management skills, and tourism and hospitality management. He has published many articles in refereed academic journals. He teaches courses on organization, management skills, strategic management, competitiveness and destination management, and hospitality management.

Dr. Marco A. Gardini is Professor of International Hospitality Management and Marketing and Vice Dean of the Faculty of Tourism at Kempten University in Germany. He holds a master's degree and doctorate in business administration from the Justus-Liebig University in Gießen, Germany. Along with teaching undergraduate, graduate, and executive education courses in German and English, he has served for the past 15 years as a guest lecturer at various German and international universities. Professor Gardini is author and editor of several standard textbooks on tourism, hospitality marketing, and management. Furthermore, he has published numerous articles in refereed journals, as well as various magazines and newspapers.

Dr. Volkan Genc is an Assistant Professor at the School of Tourism and Hotel Management at Batman University. He graduated with a Ph.D. in Tourism Management from Eskisehir Anadolu University in Turkey. He continues to work on emotional and social competence, emotional labor, aesthetic labor, and the role of employee's emotions in resistance to change.

Philippa Golding completed her BSc in Tourism at University of Applied Sciences of the Grisons and is currently studying towards a MSc. B.A. with a Major in Tourism at the same University.

Joselyn Goopio is a lecturer and former Director of the Centre for Tourism and Hospitality at Strathmore University in Nairobi, Kenya. She is the Area Consultant of East Africa for Euro-CHRIE, and the founding member and Vice-Chair of the Tourism Professional Association of

Kenya. Joy obtained the Certification for Hotel Industry Analytics and is recognized as a Certified Hospitality Educator by the AHLEI. She obtained her degree in chemical engineering from the University of San Carlos, Philippines and Master of Home Economics from the University of the Philippines. Joy is currently pursuing a doctoral degree in Hotel and Tourism Management at the Hong Kong Polytechnic University.

Dr. Seray Gulertekin Genc is an Assistant Professor at the School of Tourism and Hotel Management at Batman University. She graduated with a Ph.D. in Tourism Management from Eskisehir Eskisehir Osmangazi University in Turkey, focusing on the aesthetics of destinations.

Dr. Rhonda Hammond is an Assistant Professor in the School of Hospitality Business Management at Washington State University's Carson College of Business. She earned her Ph.D. in Hospitality Administration from Texas Tech University while serving the Texas Wine Marketing Research Institute. Rhonda has also served as faculty in hospitality programs at Kent State University and the University of Arkansas in the areas of beverage management, marketing, food and beverage pairing, human resources, and operations. Her culinary arts background and wine research, particularly regarding underserved market segments, and Millennials, furthers her interest in defining and implementing the art of hospitality.

Dr. Robert J. Harrington, Director and Professor in the School of Hospitality Business Management at Washington State University, received his Ph.D. and MBA from Washington State University, and BBA from Boise State University, USA. Prior to joining WSU-Tri-Cities, he was the 21st century Endowed Chair in Hospitality at the University of Arkansas, faculty member at the University of Guelph, Canada, and Dean of the Chef John Folse Culinary Institute. He has widely published in the areas of hospitality innovation, strategic management, food & wine, and is author of *Food and Wine Pairing: A Sensory Experience*.

Dr. Anders P.F. Herdenstam is an Assistant Professor at the School of Hospitality, Culinary Arts & Meal Science at Örebro University. He has also been appointed in the field of Professional Skill and Technology at the Royal Institute of Technology. Anders is combining analytical sensory evaluation with analogical training in order to develop new methods within the field of sensory science. These methods have been applied in different areas of studies, such as educational training, product development, and multi-sensory meal studies. He also has long experience as an entrepreneur and professional wine taster with special skills in sommelier training and multi-sensory training.

Dr. Jichul Jang is an Associate Professor in the department of hospitality management at Kansas State University. His current research interests include hospitality human resources management and service management. Jichul's primary research interests include leadership, employee retention, supervisor-subordinate relationships and managing employee engagement, and linking employee attitude and behaviors to customer experiences in hospitality organizations using a variety of research methods such as big data analysis, and social network analysis. He has published research articles in such journals as Journal of Service Management, Management Decision, International Journal of Hospitality Management, and International Journal of Contemporary Hospitality Management.

Misun (Sunny) Kim is a second-year master's student in hospitality management at Kansas State University working as a graduate assistant. She graduated from Sookmyung's Women University in Korea with bachelor's degrees in La Cordon Bleu hospitality management. After graduation, she worked for one of the biggest food service companies in Korea as a project manager for three years. She also accumulated her experience at Japanese traditional ryokan located in Fukuoka. Now based on a wide range of work experience, she is endeavoring to learn how to do decent research in organizational behavior.

Dr. Jeffery C. Kreeger is the Director of Tourism and Hospitality Studies at Central Connecticut State University. His research interests include Revenue Management, Shared Economy (e.g., Airbnb), Sustainability, and Sports' impact on Accommodations.

He spent over 20 years in the telecommunications industry utilizing GIS technology for corporate solutions and earned his doctorate in Hospitality Management at the University of South Carolina. He earned an MBA with an emphasis in Marketing from the University of Colorado at Denver and a GIS Certificate (one-half of a master's degree) at the University of Denver, where he teaches GIS courses as an adjunct professor.

Theodor Kubak occupied various executive positions in hotels in Europe, Eastern Europe, and Asia Pacific before founding SERVUS International in Istanbul in 1997. SERVUS assists private and institutional investors and governmental bodies with new investments and the repositioning of existing hotels and leisure facilities. Since 2007, Theodor acted as External Advisor for Union Investment Real Estate, implementing Asset Management Strategies and overseeing transactions internationally. In 2019, Theodor formed a hospitality arm within Arbireo Capital and established a hotel fund to purchase and asset manage Hotel Assets markets. Theodor was also central in founding the Hotel Asset Managers Association Europe.

Dr. Henri Kuokkanen is an Associate Professor at Institut Paul Bocuse, France, with expertise in the fields of corporate social responsibility (CSR) and revenue management. He holds a Ph.D. in CSR from Leeds Beckett University. His industry experience includes treasury and business control management in the global telecoms industry; he has also been a partner in a consulting business aimed at transforming CSR into a strategic tool. His main field of research focuses on the business potential CSR offers from a consumer perspective, and published in Journal of Business Ethics, aims to facilitate transformation toward a responsible model of business.

Dr. Willy Legrand is a Professor of Hospitality Management at the IUBH University of Applied Sciences located in Bad Honnef – Bonn, Germany. He is the lead author of Sustainability in the Hospitality Industry: Principles of Sustainable Operations now in its third edition. He is the co-editor of Sustainable Hospitality and Tourism as Motors for Development: Case Studies from Developing Regions of the World and the co-editor of the Routledge Handbook of Sustainable Food and Gastronomy. Prof. Legrand is the Guest Chief Editor of the Hotel Yearbook Sustainable Hospitality 2018 and 2020 Special Editions.

Dr. Naiqing Lin is an Instructor in the Hospitality Management Department at Kansas State University. He received his Ph.D. and M.S. in Hospitality Management and Dietetics Administration at the Kansas State University, and B.A. in Logistic Management at RMIT Australia. Dr. Lin has published articles at various prestigious journals such as International Journal of Hospitality Management, Food Control, and American Journal of Infection Control. He is a member of Veterans of Foreign Wars and has over eight years of foodservice experiences with senior management services.

Dr. Yimo Liu received her Ph.D. in Genetics from Iowa State University, and her M.B.A. from Washington State University. She is currently a faculty member at Washington State University

Tri-Cities. She teaches general biology and coordinates science teaching laboratories. Prior to joining the faculty at WSU, Yimo worked as a research scientist at Pacific Northwest National Laboratory in Richland, WA.

Dr. Xander Lub is a Research Fellow at Nyenrode Business University and Professor in Hospitality Management and Experience Design in the Academy of Hotel & Facility Management at Breda University of Applied Sciences. He holds an MSc from University of Leiden and a Ph.D from Tilburg University. Trained as a psychologist and an organizational scientist, Xander's research focuses on understanding how people (customers, guests, employees) interpret their changing environment and translate their understanding into action and focuses on the implications this has for business. His research interests include generational differences, psychological contracts, temporal research, design thinking and hospitality management.

Anja Marcher, MA, is a Researcher at the Center for Advanced Studies at Eurac Research in Italy. Previously she was one of three members of the research group "Economy and Labour" located in the Eurac Research Institute for Regional Development. She holds a Master of Arts in Human Geography from the University of Vienna in Austria and started her doctoral study in Geography in 2016 at the Catholic University of Eichstätt-Ingolstadt in Germany. Her academic background is reflected in her main research interests, which include innovation and networks, migration, and tourism.

Dr. Byron Marlowe received his Ph.D. with a concentration in Hospitality Management from Iowa State University. Byron coordinates Washington State University's Wine Beverage Business Management program and is faculty in the Carson College of Business, School of Hospitality Business Management. Byron also holds visiting lecturer/professor positions at University of Applied Sciences, Hochschule Harz, Institute Paul Bocuse, and Castello Sonnino Field Study. Byron's teaching background is from Southern Oregon University where he was previously Sr. Instructor and Hospitality and Tourism Coordinator in their School of Business. Byron is developing his academic literature on wine hospitality and tourism studies.

Dr. Glenn McCartney, MBE, is Associate Professor of International Integrated Resort Management and Associate Dean (Curriculum and Teaching), Faculty of Business Administration, University of Macau. He has worked for many years in different operational, strategic, and consultancy roles within the tourism, hospitality, and gaming industry in Macao and other Asian regional countries, and is an acknowledged global expert on integrated resort, destination marketing and management, including casino and event tourism. In 2016 for his role at British Honorary Consul, Macao, he was awarded an MBE (Member of the Most Excellent Order of the British Empire) by HM Queen Elizabeth II.

Dr. Thorsten Merkle is Professor and Director of Studies in Tourism at University of Applied Sciences of the Grisons. He holds a Ph.D. from the University of Gloucestershire. His research interests lie in consumer behavior studies as well as in Food and Beverage related operations and experiences. Prior to joining the University of Applied Sciences of the Grisons, Thorsten Merkle has been involved professionally in food and beverage-related projects on a global scale.

Dr. Peter O'Connor is Professor of Strategic Management at University of South Australia Business School. His primary research, teaching and consulting interests focus on the use of technology in online retailing and marketing. In addition to authoring two leading textbooks, Peter has published research-based articles in leading academic journals including the Journal of

Marketing, Harvard Business Review, Journal of Retailing and Consumer Services, Tourism Management, the Cornell Quarterly and the International Journal of Hospitality Management, amongst others. Prior to joining the UniSA, Peter founded the Chair in Digital Disruption, sponsored by BNP Paribas, at Essec Business School in Paris France. He has also regularly taught executive education seminars at London Business School; held visiting positions at both the Johnson Graduate Business School and the School of Hotel Administration at Cornell University; as well as worked in a variety of positions in industry in both Europe and the USA.

Dr. Hyunghwa (Rick) Oh is an Assistant Professor at the Ted Rogers School of Hospitality and Tourism Management at Ryerson University in Toronto, Ontario. He teaches revenue management for hospitality and tourism. He received his Ph.D. in Hospitality Management at the Kansas State University, M.S. in Hotel and Restaurant Management at the University of Houston, and B.A. in Tourism Management at Tongmyong University. He has over 13 years of industry experience in both lodging and food service. His research interests include service improvisation, service recovery, team effectiveness, leadership, empowerment, motivation, employee turnover, and job performance.

Dr. Michael C. Ottenbacher is Department Head and Mary L. Vanier Endowed Professor in the Department of Hospitality Management at Kansas State University. He received his Ph.D. in Marketing from the University of Otago, New Zealand. He is on the editorial board of several journals and has been the Co-editor of the Journal of Hospitality and Tourism Education since 2013. Further, Dr. Ottenbacher has been a Visiting Professor at the Institute Paul Bocuse in France, the German-Vietnamese-University in Ho Chi Minh City, Vietnam, Taylor's University in Kuala Lumpur, Malaysia, and University of Applied Sciences of the Grisons, Switzerland.

Tatijana Pantovic is currently employed as Data Analyst und Sales Performance Manager at Swarovski. She graduated at the Megatrend University in Belgrade and finalized her master's degree in Strategic Management at the University of Innsbruck in 2018. Her research interests are SME and social media.

Dr. Harald Pechlaner is Chair Professor in Tourism and Director of the Center for Entrepreneurship at the Catholic University Eichstätt-Ingolstadt in Germany. He is Adjunct Research Professor at Curtin University in Perth/WA (Curtin Business School). Since 2014 he has been President of the International Association of Scientific Experts in Tourism (AIEST). He is Director of the Center for Advanced Studies at the Eurac Research in Bolzano in Italy. Before he was Director of the Institute for Regional Development and Location Management at Eurac Research. His main areas of expertise include sustainable development, tourism and culture, and interdisciplinary analysis and policy.

Dr. Mike Peters is a Professor at the Department for Strategic Management, Marketing and Tourism at the University of Innsbruck, Austria. After completing an apprenticeship as a restaurant specialist and practical years in the hotel business, he studied at the University of Regensburg and Innsbruck. His dissertation dealt with internationalization behavior in the hotel industry, and his habilitation analyzes the growth behavior of small service companies. Further research focuses on destination management and social responsibility in tourism. Currently, he is full professor for SMEs & Tourism at the Faculty of Business and Management and spokesman of the "Research Centre Tourism and Leisure" at the University of Innsbruck.

Dr. Ige Pirnar works as Professor, Head of Department of Business Administration and elected member of University Senate, Yasar University, Turkey. She has published many articles, conference papers, and book chapters, both in English and Turkish. She also authors eight books in

Turkish (three edited and two with co-authors) and one in English. Her areas of expertise are: international business, international marketing management, hospitality marketing, F&B management, and international tourism management.

Dr. Steffen Raub is a Professor of Organizational Behavior at the Ecole Hôtelière de Lausanne. He holds a Ph.D. in Management from the University of Geneva. He held regular faculty positions at the Asian Institute of Technology (AIT) in Bangkok, HEC Lausanne and HEC Geneva, as well as visiting positions at the University of North Carolina, Chapel Hill, USA and the National University of Singapore. His research has appeared in the leading hospitality journals (*Cornell Hospitality Quarterly, International Journal of Hospitality Management, International Journal of Contemporary Hospitality Management*) and in leading academic journals (*Journal of Applied Psychology, Human Relations*).

Dr. Lianping Ren is currently an Assistant Professor at the Macao Institute for Tourism Studies. Dr. Ren holds a doctorate (D.HTM) from the School of Hotel and Tourism Management, the Hong Kong Polytechnic University. Her research areas include strategic management, consumer behavior, and hospitality education.

Laura Schmidt started her career in hotel management with Hilton hotels. After a triannual apprenticeship she studied tourism management (B.A.) and hospitality management (M.A.) at Munich University of Applied Sciences, Faculty of Tourism. Since 2020, she freelances for a renowned German hospitality magazine besides her PhD thesis in the field of knowledge management at Universidad de Las Palmas de Gran Canaria. Laura Schmidt is a lecturer at Munich University, Faculty of Tourism, as well as at Baden-Wuerttemberg Cooperative State University (DHBW) in Ravensburg. Her teaching fields are strategic hotel management and hospitality innovation management. She is author of various hospitality publications.

Dr. Robert Schønrock Nielsen works for the Government of Greenland in the Ministry of Education, Culture and Church. Prior to this, he was Associate Lecturer at the Copenhagen Business Academy (Cphbusiness) located in Denmark. With his research, he hopes to contribute to finding solutions to the many challenges faced by the hospitality industry as well as to explore the role of experience economy within that sector. Dr. Schønrock Nielsen's research draws on a combination of organization science, entrepreneurship, and innovation spiced up with elements from sociology and philosophy.

Dr. Markus Schuckert is Associate Professor at the School of Hotel & Tourism Management. His industry experience is from tourism industry. As an entrepreneur, Markus founded a consulting firm for market research, product development, and change management in Europe. As researcher, Markus is specialized in digital marketing, travel technology, and strategic management. He applies this expertise across the travel and hospitality industry. Markus contributes to top-journals in the field and is educator at international business schools. He is nurturing the next generation of industry leaders by supervising postgraduates and is working on contemporary teaching technologies to make learning more fun.

Dr. Raija Seppälä-Esser is a Professor of Tourism Management at the Kempten University of Applied Sciences. Prior to her professorship, she worked in the advertising industry and in marketing. She has held leading positions in the NTO of Finland for Middle-European, American, and Scandinavian markets. She studied Business Administration at the University of Tampere in Finland, Tourism at the George Washington University (Washington, D.C.), and is Certified

Travel Counselor (The Travel Institute, Boston). She holds a doctorate in Tourism Management from the University of Surrey in Guildford, UK. Her research interests include management and marketing of tourism destinations and customer experience management and design.

Dr. Betsy Bender Stringam is Professor of Hotels and Resorts at New Mexico State University. Dr. Stringam received her Bachelor's degree in Hotel Administration from Cornell University, her Master's in Hotel and Food Service Management from Florida International University, and her doctorate from Northern Arizona University. Dr. Stringam is the author of the book: A Profile of the Hospitality Industry. She serves as the Collection Editor for the Hospitality and Tourism Collection for Business Expert Press. Dr. Stringam conducts research on hotels and resorts. Some of her current projects include strategic management of hotels and resort, and technology in hospitality.

Dr. Michael Volgger is a Senior Lecturer with the School of Marketing, Faculty of Business and Law, at Curtin University in Australia where he is Co-Director of the Tourism Research Cluster. He obtained a doctoral degree in Economics and Business Administration from the Catholic University of Eichstaett-Ingolstadt in Germany. Prior to joining Curtin University, he has been a Senior Research Fellow at the Institute for Regional Development at Eurac Research in Italy. His areas of expertise include tourism destination governance and location management, product development and innovation in tourism, sharing economy, inter-organizational cooperation, and qualitative research.

Dr. Burkhard von Freyberg is Professor of Hospitality Management at the Faculty of Tourism at Munich University of Applied Sciences. He started his career in hotel management at the five star superior Hotel Bayerischer Hof in Munich. Afterwards he studied business administration at the Ludwig-Maximilians-University in Munich and the University of Regensburg. In 2008 he founded Zarges von Freyberg Hotel Consulting, a consulting company focusing on global hotel developments and operations mainly in the leisure segment. He is guest lecturer at various institutions, editor and author of various hospitality text books. Moreover, he is founding partner of different startups in the hospitality industry and in the advisory board of several hotel companies.

Dr. Arthur S.R. Wang holds a D.HTM from The Hong Kong Polytechnic University and obtained a Master and Bachelor degree from Iowa State University and Ohio University. He holds an EMBA from NCCU (Taiwan). He has more than 20 years of international industry and leadership experience in high profile positions such as Director of HR in Penang (Malaysia) at Evergreen Laurel Hotel, Group Director of International Sales for Evergreen Laurel Hotels & Resorts, Group VP and GM in Caesar Park Hotels & Resorts (Taiwan). He is an entrepreneur as Founder and Managing Director of his own consulting firm, restaurant company and a very boutique hotel.

ACKNOWLEDGMENTS

Such a book project stands and falls inevitably with the dedication and enthusiasm of the participants. As ambitious as the project seemed to those of us in between, the numerous spontaneous promises and creative ideas of the scholars addressed motivated us to stick firmly to the project. We would like to thank all the authors for their commitment and willingness to adapt their contributions to the overall concept of the anthology. As editors, we would be delighted if the food for thought contained in this anthology met with a fruitful response and serves as a stimulus for further research. We would like to hear your comments on this edition and are already looking forward to a lively exchange of ideas and information.

We owe a special thanks to Naiqing Lin, Ph.D., Kansas State University, who helped to shape this edition. We also would like to express a word of thanks to all the members of the Routledge editorial, production, and marketing team for their support from the submission of our first proposal to the delivery of the full manuscript. Finally, we would like to thank our families and friends for their patience, support, and encouragement.

Marco A. Gardini
Michael C. Ottenbacher
Markus Schuckert

INTRODUCTION AND HANDBOOK ORGANIZATION

Marco A. Gardini, Michael C. Ottenbacher, and Markus Schuckert

Internationalization and Globalization of the Hospitality Industry

Among the service industries, hospitality represents a thriving sector, based on the consistently growing numbers of travelers, a rising demand for traditional and nontraditional accommodations worldwide, and competition on the supply side to expand to and conquer new markets. The hospitality sector of the 21st century is on its way to becoming a global industry. Even local players and stand-alone hotels are experiencing this internationalization on the demand side, with rising numbers of foreign guests. On the supply side, the competition is growing with the expansion of foreign hotel brands as well as foreign investors buying and managing local properties. The complexity of managing hospitality on an international level is highly relevant for a large target group and enjoys wide readership including hospitality managers, investors, and policy makers at one end of the continuum and academics, researchers, and students from various disciplines at the other.

Global Context	Culture	Paradigms and Business Models	Strategies and Business Operations	Cases
Streams in International Hospitality Management	Customer Experience across Cultures	New Hospitality Paradigms	Merger and Acquisitions	Food and Beverage
Key Players of the Industry	Organizational Culture and Country Culture	Digitalization and Transformation	Internationalization and Growth	Destinations
Trends in International Hospitality Research	Intercultural Competencies and Cultural Standards	Corporate Social Responsibility	Marketing and Branding	Education Sector
Structure and Organization of the Industry	Hospitality Training	Asset Management	Positioning and Identity	Small and medium-sized Hospitality
	Leadership and Culture	Shared-Lodging Economy	Human Resource Management	Corporates, Groups and Chains
		Sustainability	Management and Modes of Operations	Sports and Entertainment Venues
		Emerging Markets	Entrepreneurship	
		Integrated Resorts and Casinos		

Figure I.1 Overview of the Content and Organization of this Book

The editors of the contemporary *Routledge Companion to International Hospitality Management* take a strictly global perspective of this topic. Based on three different continents and with a focus on hospitality management, research, and education, the editors have gathered a unique combination of authors and contributors for this *Routledge Companion to International Hospitality Management*. Thus, the book presents practically relevant and theoretically outstanding contributions by international experts in their fields (Figure I.1). Defined in this book, hospitality is understood beyond the traditional hospitality context and discusses contemporary topics along the value chain including corporate hotels, small- and medium-sized enterprises, and nontraditional supplies from the sharing economy. In addition, several contributions consider topics related to hospitality management such as the food and beverage sector, destinations, and sports and entertainment venues.

Part I: Global Context of International Hospitality Management

For this holistic view on international hospitality management, the book is divided into five parts. Part I is the foundation that sets the stage for the entire book, taking an introductory perspective of the *Global Context of International Hospitality Management* by blending state-of-the-art research with contemporary business analysis. Here, Naiqing Lin and Michael C. Ottenbacher look into *Past and Present Streams in International Hospitality Management* to help the reader understand and structure contemporary issues and topics of industry and practice. An analysis of *Past and Present Key Players in the Hospitality Industry*, by Betsy Bender Stringam, Joselyn Goopio, Basak Denizci-Guillet, and Hjalte Brøndum Mansa aims to analyze the many drivers and key players of the hospitality industry, including hotel and accommodation providers and restaurant and food service operators, from historical, industrial, and technological perspectives. Markus Schuckert turns to *The Role of Internationalization in Hospitality Management* to analyze previous trends and new directions regarding the internationalization of the industry and its resonance in research. This theoretical view of how the hospitality industry has evolved internationally over time is complemented by the contribution of Bender Stringam, Goopio, Denizci-Guillet, and Brøndum Mansa, who provide a contemporary overview of the *Hospitality Industry Structures and Organization*. This is important for understanding the structure and organization regarding the industry, with its diversity in culture, paradigms, and business models as well as management strategies and ways to operate a business.

Part II: Culture and International Hospitality Management

Part II considers the relations and interconnections between *Culture and International Hospitality Management*. Raija Seppälä-Esser takes *A Cross-Cultural Perspective on Customer Experience in Hospitality and Tourism* by looking from the angle of the demand side at the shift from consumption to experience of a growing number of culturally diverse guests and customers. Steffen Raub and Stefano Borzillo take a contrasting view from the supply side, comparing and analyzing *Country Culture vs. Organizational Culture* and the influence of each on hospitality operation and management. With their second contribution, *Organization, Culture, and Leadership,* they extend their analysis and discussion of culture with respect to the leadership and management of hospitality organizations. The contribution of Ulrich Bauer more closely discusses *Intercultural Competencies and Cultural Standards in International Hospitality*, while Robert J. Harrington, Yimo Lin, Rhonda Hammond, Anders P.F. Herdenstam, and Byron Marlowe extend the view on culture and *International Hospitality Development: Training to Enhance the Understanding of 'The Art of Hospitality' Business Model* as a specific business model. They address what is meant by the international hospitality business and whether this concept is shared across geographic locations, especially in regard to training and mentoring the next generation of hospitality practitioners.

Part III: Hospitality Paradigms and Business Models

Part III considers the culture with its underlying concepts and philosophies as a foundation, taking a look at the variety of *Hospitality Paradigms and Business Models*. Here, the contribution by Kaye Chon and Markus Schuckert sets the stage by analyzing and discussing the European paradigm of hospitality and how it differs from the North American paradigm of hospitality. From there, the concept of *Hospitality in Asia* is developed and how it is leading to *The Dawn of a New Paradigm* in the hospitality industry of the 21st century is examined. Peter O'Connor addresses this issue from a technical angle and sheds light on the factor of distribution technology and the related paradigm shift regarding *Digital Transformation: The Blurring of Organizational Boundaries in Hotel Distribution*. This is especially important for a highly traditional hotel industry facing a hyper-dynamic competitive business environment and revolutionizing digital technologies of today. Sustainability and the concept of corporate social responsibility are significant contemporary and important topics in the context of international hospitality management. Here, Henri Kuokkanen takes a longer view, looking into *The Future of CSR in the Hospitality Industry: Next Stop, Global Responsibility?* and Willy Legrand, Elena Cavagnaro, Robert Schønrock Nielsen, and Nicolas Dubrocard discuss *Sustainability without Limits: Strategic and Operational Innovations in the Hospitality Industry*. When other sectors of the service industry, like low-cost carriers, are striving to become lighter regarding their assets – or even asset-free – hospitality companies worldwide are forced to rethink their financial structure and their asset management. Florian Aubke and Theodor Kubak offer insights into *Hotel Asset Management: A Professional Approach and an International Perspective* for the industry. Jeffery C. Kreeger discusses the relationship between *Globalization and the Lodging-Shared Economy*. He draws a comparison between the traditional and nontraditional hospitality sector and offers a contemporary discussion regarding the expansion of the lodging-shared economy, as well as its advantages and disadvantages. Las Vegas and Macau are the hot spots for integrated resorts and casino tourism; however, integrated resorts as well as casinos are not limited to those two destinations but rather are becoming a rising global phenomenon. With his contribution, Glenn McCartney examines the question of *Integrated Resort and Casino Tourism: A Global Hospitality Trend but a Sure Win?* This part concludes with a look at the present and future regarding *New Trends in Chinese Outbound Tourism: Consequences for the International Hospitality Industry*. Wolfgang Georg Arlt places emphasis on the importance of *Chinese Outbound Tourism* and how international hospitality managers can make their staff and properties "China-ready."

Part IV: International Strategies and Business Operations

Part IV, *Internationalization Strategies and Business Operations*, looks at strategies and procedures regarding international hospitality businesses. *The Role of Mergers and Acquisitions as Growth Strategies in the International Hospitality Industry* is the focus of a contribution by Volkan Genc, Seray Gulertekin Genc, and Engin Aytekin. Because not all international expansion can be accomplished by generic growth strategies, mergers and acquisitions are important tools for growing and expanding internationally. The contribution by Oriol Anguera-Torrell highlights, in the context of *Hotel Firms*, the importance of firm-level productivity to answer the question: *Who Internationalizes and How?* The author, based on *Evidence from the Spanish Hotel Industry*, shows that productivity is an essential factor for understanding internationalization patterns in the hotel industry. Marco A. Gardini discusses branding and brand extension, which are becoming major trends in the global hospitality market. Hotel brands have been expanding mostly from the West to the East, but recent developments indicate an increasing reverse push, where Asian hotel brands are heading westward in order to expand into new markets. Gardini sheds light on *Brand Relevance and Relevance of Brands in the Global Hotel Industry: A Look at Research and Practice*.

Saurabh Kumar Dixit and Abijith Abraham continue the theme with their contribution in the area of branding by focusing on *Brand Identity and Positioning in Selected Indian Chain Hotel Companies*. While India is one of the future markets for the international hospitality industry, Lianping Ren takes the reader to the current center of gravity regarding hotel development and internationalization by looking into *The Development of Hotel Management Contracts in China*. With the development of thousands of properties and the expansion of dozens of brands around the world, questions are arising about how to attract, train, and retain the current and future workforce in the sector. With global employee mobility in mind as well as an international demand for talent, Yoy Bergs and Xander Lub look into *International Human Resource Management in the Hospitality Industry* with its current challenges and future perspectives. Ige Pirnar focuses the reader's attention on goals, principal characteristics, process types, and areas of various innovation practices by analyzing and discussing contemporary *Innovation Management in International Hotel Industry*. Arthur S.R. Wang is a successful entrepreneur, restaurateur, consultant, and hotelier. With his background in operating various hospitality businesses across the value chain, he explores and discusses the *Success Factors of SME Hotel Management Companies in China*. His contribution enables the reader to understand and appreciate the complexity of the international hospitality business, especially in culturally rich and highly dynamic business environments like China, based on the viewpoints of small- and medium-sized hotel-management companies.

Part V: International Challenges and Perspectives: A Case Study Approach

Finally, Part V presents a synopsis of this *Routledge Companion to International Hospitality Management. International Challenges and Perspectives: A Case Study Approach* brings industry cases across the hospitality sector into the spotlight of management practices. Its sources include the food and beverage sector; tourism destinations; the education sector; small- and medium-sized hotels as well as corporate hotels, groups, and chains; and sports and entertainment venues. The contribution by Desiderio Juan García-Almeida, Laura Schmidt, and Burkhard von Freyberg takes an example from the food and beverage sector. *Knowledge Replication and Adaptation in the International Growth of Hospitality Firms: The Case of Paulaner* showcases operational strategy and decision-making during the process of international expansion by discussing growth options based on strict standardization or allowing an adaptation to the local environment. *The Special Role of 'Hospitableness' for Customer Satisfaction in South Tyrol* is a case study from Italy by Anja Marcher, Philipp Corradini, Harald Pechlaner, and Michael Volgger. It reveals how successful destinations deliver more than professional service quality by building on additional service elements such as helpfulness, friendliness, or reliability, which the authors summarize as hospitableness, to enhance the competitiveness of the destination. As a result of demographic, social, and economic development and changes, recruiting and retaining staff becomes increasingly important for the hospitality industry. In his contribution *Keys to Success: Connective Structures for Educational Innovations in the Hotel Industry*, Hartwig Bohne operates in the triangle between education providers, the hospitality industry, and students as potential employees. He develops a framework for future-oriented cooperation between industry and education providers for priming and retaining future staff at an early stage. Robert Eller, Mike Peters, and Tatijana Pantovic take an entrepreneurial perspective of the importance of digitalization in the noncorporate small- and medium-sized hospitality sector with their contribution *Owner-Managers' Interpretations of Digitalization Impacts on SME Management Processes: A Qualitative Study of the Hospitality Industry*. The topic of *Sports Stadium Hospitality and Catering: A Global Perspective* is the domain of Thorsten Merkle and Philippa Golding. The authors provide a look into sports and entertainment venues regarding food and beverage operations, branding, public health, service quality, and customer satisfaction. With their contribution *Hotel Market Analysis: The Case of Beijing, China,*

Jichul Jang Misun Kim and Hyunghwa Oh focus on the hotel industry in China, in particular, in the capital of Beijing and analyze contemporary trends and developments to discuss future options of the hotel industry in Beijing and China. Celine Chang and Kathrin Eberhardt developed *A Regional Approach to Attracting and Retaining Employees: A Chance for Small and Medium-sized Hotels?* to effectively counter the skills shortage in the hospitality industry. The authors show that it is important to invest in strategic and professional human resource management, and they conceptualize, based on an empirical case study, how small- and medium-sized enterprises can overcome their human resource shortages based on a regional HR alliance. This last case study closes the list of contributions of conceptual approaches as well as industry-related cases.

International Hospitality Management for the Next Decade

Routledge Companion to International Hospitality Management closes a longstanding gap between the academics and industry. Readers targeting practitioners, managers, educators, researchers, and enthusiasts will find this book unique and contemporary. Specifically, its hybrid approach, blending conceptual contributions with applied examples and cases makes this book a highly relevant source for tertiary educators and researchers in the disciplines of hospitality, tourism, and service management. With this *Routledge Companion to International Hospitality Management*, the authors want to put the spotlight on important yet under researched aspects of the hospitality industry in the area of international entrepreneurship and management on a global scale. It stands as the guidelines of cutting edge research in this emerging field to encourage and inspire current and future researchers.

Kempten
Manhattan (KS)
Hong Kong

Marco A. Gardini
Michael C. Ottenbacher
Markus Schuckert

January 20, 2020

PART I

Global Context of International Hospitality Management

1

PAST AND PRESENT RESEARCH STREAMS IN INTERNATIONAL HOSPITALITY MANAGEMENT

Naiqing Lin and Michael C. Ottenbacher

The Growth of International Hospitality Management: Embrace the Paradigm Shift and the Culture Change

Globalization deeply impacted the hospitality industry, and as a consequence, international hospitality enterprises need to have a comprehensive focus. While the international hospitality industry is traditionally embraced by a large number of small- to medium-sized local operations, we have seen a strong increase of large international hospitality chains recently. The international hospitality management industry has not only been thriving but is a sector that is significantly different to be considered separately from other aspects of management.

In order to discuss the fast-growing international hospitality industry, we first have to understand what consistently describe the international hospitality market. According to the services marketing literature, the hospitality industry often has been only classified as the accommodation service with food and beverage operations (Johns, 1999; Rust and Huang, 2014). However, modern researchers from hospitality management have classified the industry based on possible, aggregate, and profile model approaches, with six core multidimensional concepts like restaurants, hotels, travel, attractions, conventions, and leisure with their constituent and relevant interdependent relationships (Ottenbacher et al., 2009). Regardless of heterogeneous aspects of the hospitality industry, geographically, the hospitality industry is also dispersed, from metropolitan cities to remote rural areas, which can be characterized by multinational structural in natural (Brotherton, 2012).

With the increasing geographical diversity of the hospitality industry, the driving force of this trend includes but not limited to the accelerated communication, advanced transportation, elimination of the political trading barriers, global expansion needs, and financial or political risk aversion. The global hospitality market continued to strive and has become increasingly competitive with the more emerging competitors from new fast-growing economics (Clarke and Chen, 2009). As the hospitality companies become more multinational, the future hospitality managers must be prepared for a globalized competition and should be able to effectively manage the increasingly diverse and multinational teams with swift shifting market demands within a short notice. Thus, the study of international hospitality management becomes more imminent and important. Some of the main reasons to study international hospitality management are as follows:

- The growing world economic market has more emerging needs for high-quality hospitality services and products. Thus, it requires modern-day hospitality managers to incorporate these opportunities for possible international opportunities. For example, Brazil, Russia, India, and

China (BRIC) have an increased demand in hospitality market, thus requiring more specialized talents which can provide cooperation in the new demand (Biggemann and Fam, 2011).
- While globalization continues to expand, and competition continues to rise, hospitality cooperation has increasing demands for aversive risk strategies, such as global investment strategies, product/service diversion, decentralized model of the operation, or to protect themselves
from the risks and uncertainties of the domestic business cycle (Teare and Olsen, 1992). For
example, Chinese companies have an increasing demand for international expansion from
2012 to 2017, as to protect themselves from their domestic market downturns.
- The desire to reduce cost of operation by outsourcing service or production to foreign
companies. A typical move for the production industry in North America, over the past
20 years, has been extending to service industry when outsourcing their service division to
more cheaper countries as a strategic move to reduce cost and increase revenue. Hospitality
cooperation might begin with a licensing or franchising agreement – a standard practice
that provides the know-how to some of the management by exchanging for a fee or royalty.
For example, McDonald's has more international locations than domestic, which adversely
protects them from invasive foreign companies by maintaining competition in the foreign
market (Schmid and Gombert, 2018).

Besides the reasons above, the expanded international operation enables consumers to get a
better variety of services with lower prices. For example, daily meals served by a local restaurant might contain spices that are not prepared or grown locally and fresh produce that's out
of season from an international location, or standardized menu options. With the expansion
of international business models, future hospitality managers require to embrace *The Paradigm
Shift*, and thus develop a deeper understanding of the problems in the market while developing
international managerial strategies that maintain an extensive understanding of the differences
between multiple countries.

Some of the newly emerged managerial challenges can be elucidated but not limited to the
discussion below:

- Increased usage and application of new mobile computing and social network in global cus-
tomer relationship management (Sigala, 2018)
- The growth of environmental pressure and consumer concerns for sustainability practices
(Legrand et al., 2017; McGrady and Cottrell, 2018)
- Strategic development of decentralized business models that support greater flexibility, allow-
ing adaptation at each international hospitality operations (Vaughan and Koh, 2019)
- Branding strategies that decrease national or political identities (Seraphin et al., 2018)
- Increasing concerns in fair trade resourcing, poverty reduction in developing countries, and
cooperate public relationships in an international market (Dada, 2018)
- Smarter international marketing including new media and application of big data analytics
(Xiang et al., 2015)
- Expansion of cross-national human resourcing and international talent management (Sheehan
et al., 2018)

Indubitably, these *New Paradigm Challenges* are interrelated and deserve a closer look at the international level (Ottenbacher et al., 2009). Often, private consulting services and government surveillance data (e.g., department of labor, and national association's forecast) are often used to help
with the critical decision-making process. However, acquiring and investing in empirical data
collection and educating future managers on the issues related to multi-culture and multi-country
management become especially relevant. Therefore, decision making with more risk-awareness

and forecasting has always ensured future profit for sustainable development in hospitality management (Osland, 2003).

Definition and Misperceptions of International Hospitality Management

The definition of *international hospitality* becomes vital in navigating through the literature on international hospitality management, understanding the culture change, and observing how the paradigm shift can relate to practical contemporary managerial problems and stay relevant to the global market. One major issue relates to the phrase itself. In the phrase *international hospitality*, the term hospitality can be defined both as a firm and as an activity (Toyne and Nigh, 1997), which has been a source of confusion. If it is defined as a firm, it can be interpreted as a multinational enterprise; if it is defined as an activity, it is more leaning towards the definition of goods and services. However, the broadly defined term *hospitality* has often caused substantial issues in terms of the external validity of empirical studies, as it often failed to separate hospitality as a term from more general services (Ottenbacher et al., 2009). The unclarified definition of hospitality also causes obscuration when conducting marketing research and, further, results in variational misconception in terms of the constructible boundaries and classifications (Taylor and Edgar, 1996).

Another misperception often includes the association between the phrases *international management* and *global management*. Often the term has been used interchangeably with the appropriate formulation to suit various situational needs, which international hospitality management is often confused with global cooperation, or foreign investment management, as the term is extending itself over borders and begging for a question (Dunning and Rugman, 1985). Additionally, hospitality firms often make foreign investments in other countries with modified nationality, strategically decentralized country-of-operation with global governance; for example, different places of headquarters in the United States, British, or China (Buckley and Casson, 1985). An international hospitality enterprise often involves various macro-structural aspects with micro-operational characteristics, which is more of global governance and the product of continuum globalization (Weiss and Wilkinson, 2014). Therefore, the important concepts need to be defined first, before the discussion.

According to Ottenbacher et al. (2009), modern hospitality management could be defined as classified business management based on six multidimensional core industries like restaurants, hotels, travel, attractions, conventions, and leisure with their constituent and relevant interdependent relationships. Also, international hospitality management often provides a channel for intra-country connections, which is not merely a channel for domestic contracts but more of a multinational internal organization. Therefore, the history of international hospitality management is distinct from the rich and extensive literature on the history of the international business (Wilkins, 1974). But, in more general, works on the development of intra-country hospitality service itself are based on these six core industries (Jones and Pizam, 1993; Ottenbacher et al., 2009).

A Brief History of International Hospitality Management

As old as the civilization and business itself, people have been engaged in hospitality throughout history, whether they are aware of it or not (Wearne and Morrison, 2011). Historical roots of hospitality date back to ancient times. A picture of hospitality can be traced back to the Iliad and the Odyssey (Homer, *Odyssey*, 1176). In both classics, hospitality represents a readiness for reciprocal relationships with strangers (Homer, *Odyssey*, 1176). Hospitality is the traditional translation of the Latin noun *hospitium* (or the adjective *hospitalis*), which in turn derives from *hospes*, meaning both 'guest' and 'host.' However, the brief historical investigation by Oh and Pizam (2008) indicated that hospitality serves more than a guest and host relationship, which indeed offers other meanings like social and commercial transfer. The social and commercial practices provide both social values and economic relationships, which add more values to the already host and guest relationship (Lashley and Morrison, 2000).

However, the rapid growth of *modern* hospitality industry has only begun in the late 20th century (postwar era; Bartels, 1976; Shaw and Tamilia, 2001); the term corresponds to the previous *pre-modern* stage or *institutionalization stage* of hospitality industry (1841 to mid-1950), also known as the *McDonaldization* or *Disneyization stage* of the hospitality industrializations (first defined in Ritzer and Liska, 1997). The postwar stage of hospitality management or modern hospitality industry often involved with the development of mass communications, the development of international commerce, and intercontinental travel by air.

Today according to the pocket factbook provided by U.S. National Restaurant Association (NRA, 2018), there are 1 million restaurant locations in the United States, with more than $825 billion sales in 2018 (2.4% increase compared to the previous year), and about 15.1 million restaurant industry employees counting over 10% of all U.S. workforce (see Figure 1.1).

Approximately at the same time, the growth of the Chinese restaurant market has almost quadrupled the growth rate of U.S. restaurant industry at an average rate of 10% since 2012 (see Figure 1.2 for comparison), at 3.96 billion Chinese Yuan (≈0.59 billion USD).

Restaurant market, which is only one sector of the entire hospitality industry, has inspired guest spending in all hospitality sectors. The massive growth of *modern* hospitality industry comes with the change in culture and adaptive lifestyle. Scarborough (2006) reported that 96% of the U.S. adults dined out at a restaurant at least once in a month, and 40% of the adults visited a Quick Service Restaurant, such as Burger King, McDonald's, or Pizza Hut, six or more times in a month. Another 19% of the U.S. consumers visited a fast-casual restaurant (such as Applebee or Longhorn) at least once in the month. Because there are significant overlaps between sectors of the hospitality industry, such as the foodservice sector in the hotel, or catering with the restaurant, or dining or lodging services in the destination location, data of their interdependent relationships with other hospitality sectors like the travel, clubs, and conventions are hard to gauge.

Taking the independent reports of the American Lodging Association (AHLA, 2018) for example, the U.S. lodging sector has recorded solid growth every year, supports nearly 1.9 million domestic jobs, and has generated $176 billion in gross revenue (Figure 1.3). Given the reliable statistics and history above, we expect the hospitality industry will continue to grow strongly. For example, the U.S. restaurant industry at the end of 2017 grew 4.3% at $799 billion in revenue (Griffith, 2018). The hotel industry has reached a growth rate of 3.7% (adjusted for inflation), and

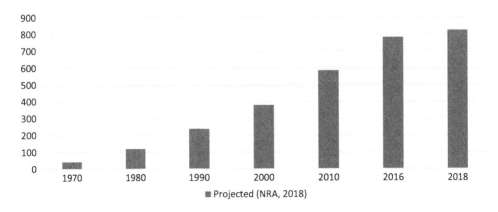

Figure 1.1 U.S. restaurant industry sales (billion, in USD).

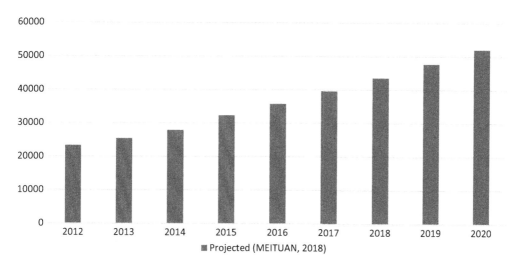

Figure 1.2 P.R. China restaurant industry sales (billion, in Yuan).

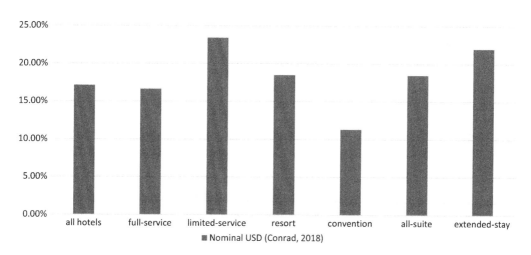

Figure 1.3 U.S. hotel sector operating growth rate (2017).

average around $123.37 per room daily rate, with an expected gross revenue of $208 billion, and continuous growth on all hotel sectors (Conrad, 2018; Figure 1.3).

Overall, the hospitality and tourism enterprises continued to thrive and created a massive amount of employment opportunities to help with the growth of both the domestic economy and overall international industry. However, today's hospitality manager must embrace both challenges and opportunities from international market, as the workforce has become more diversified with multi-cultural, multi-generational background. Also, the modern hospitality managers must also embrace the competition from international market and continue to assure customer service with multinational background. Therefore, there is an increasing need to study international hospitality management, educate future managers on the issues related to multi-culture and multi-country operations, and develop sustainable international strategies to stay relevant to the impact in the market.

The Development of International Hospitality Management

According to the history and statistics provided above, the development of international hospitality management often corresponds to the globalization of the economic systems (Oh and Pizam, 2008). The international hospitality management was first referring to the hospitality industry as the geographical barriers of the current business system, and often time the business operations occurred in one part of the system, was franchised and resolved in a specific contracting company, which stay irrelevant to the other part of the world. However, international hospitality enterprises nowadays have developed and incorporated more multinational management, where the cooperation realized the operations that happen in one country often potentially impact the business system in another part of the world. Alternatively, the business model can often be transferred without considering the geographical barriers (Osland, 2003). For example, the international airline industry had a unique type of global customer. When making a reservation, customers often expect to enjoy a standardized service which encompasses the basis of service quality, service reliability, frequent flier programs, and an international standard of safety. This significance of global strategy also transfers to the food and beverage industries, where development of the global sector has become more evident in recent years. In recent years, the eating habits of the world have also become more convergent. For example, donuts were more embraced in Japan when cinnamon was introduced as a flavoring for donuts in the Japanese market. Today, more of the same recipe for making donuts is being used throughout the world; doing international hospitality management and standardization is more of an immediate need rather than a geographical barrier.

The increasing international activities among hospitality operations, thus, require cooperation to develop management strategies which help develop the cooperate standard and can be or should be applied for multiple purposes, ranging from assisting major fiscal decisions to determining and evaluating potential marketing locations, or modifying specific international hospitality industry standards. Often, a successful business model is also transferred from one part of the world to other parts of the world, to help eliminate the barriers of services, capital movement, transfer of new technologies, and influential cooperate philosophies (Osland, 2003). Therefore, international business research and relevant methodologies to collect data, which ultimately help fine tune the global strategies, are adopted by many international hospitality firms. According to Orbis Research (2018), the global management consulting market continues to grow and will be worth an estimated $5,860 million by 2022. A well-developed global strategy often helps hospitality enterprises position themselves in apprehension in terms of the continuously expanding globalized market. Thus, a considerable volume of the book will help readers to adopt *scientific* methods to systematically collect, analyze, and synthesize information to assist hospitality operations in solving and finalizing global marketing strategies. Therefore, future managers could use the relevant research methodology to develop integrated strategies which combine global marketing research and global strategic management.

Future Marketing Research Trend: Issues and Challenges

Conducting international hospitality management research is expensive, time-consuming, and highly complicated involving many facets which affect its outcome. For interpretation purposes, global marketing research may be defined as a scientific and methodical technique to systematically collect, analyze, and synthesize information to assist hospitality operations in solving and finalizing management strategies.

First, international hospitality management research needs to be *scientific*; in other words, it must follow a sound methodology that is well planned and documented for the replication process. Moreover, pre-validated questions must be supported from a concurrent literature review or theory. Second, the management theories or principles need to support and help extend the existing understanding of the market; thus, these theories principles can be justified by accurate information and help explain and address the current managerial problems (Harrington and Ottenbacher, 2011). Many new management teams have failed to cover a management problem when the information or managerial strategies applied have not contributed to the true state of a given situation. Third, the managerial principles applied with international hospitality management must be supported with evidence, which involves not only collecting raw data and analyses for a meaningful interpretation but also disseminating them, so that they can be applied as new principles for actions. Lastly, the international managemental principles could be used for decision making, which needs all information and data collected to be put to good use to solve practical problems faced by the international hospitality companies and make new venues for significant investments. Specific problems can be discussed in the following sub-bulletins.

Price of Conducting Multinational Research

Conducting international hospitality management research is expensive, and the cost of the research project can vary considerably from country to country. For example, a focus group with industrial panel research can cost as little as 100–500 dollars in China, but with the same panel can cost between $1,000 and $5,000 in the United States depending upon the geographic locations. However, a valid research project is essential in assisting cooperate decision-making process, and it even helps reduce costs and improve operational efficiencies (Jones and Pizam, 1993). Thus, the cost is one of the dearth of reasons for future investigators to be cautious with international hospitality management research, but it should be generally considered as an investment rather than an expense when seeking funding opportunities.

Second, some of the ready familiarized research infrastructures might not be available in many developing countries. For example, in some developing countries, the necessary demographic data might be sparse or even non-existent. Some governments do not have the resources to collect quality, or relevant, reliable data including economic figures and the financial report of the hospitality industry; sometimes even census information is neither readily available nor up-to-date. Cooperate executives in the United States, Britain, and Japan often rely on established industrial originations (e.g., American National Restaurant Associations, American Hotel and Lodging Association) for support with both background and demographic information. However, the lack of research infrastructure and cost-efficient secondary data often makes the international hospitality research much costly and challenging to complete. Therefore, future investigators should seek to collect and verify demographic information from various countries before proceeding to data analysis for international projects.

Variation of the Quality of the Data

International hospitality management research might be under considerable influences for discrepancies in data quality, ethical considerations during data collection, and time allocations for data collection. For example, data collected in the United States might be considered of higher quality due to the considerable involvement of various institutional professionals and the contribution of government-sponsored projects with possible longitudinal data collection methods. Compared to other countries, especially developing countries, the problem with the quality of the data, the trustworthiness of the data, and time allocations for data collection can be subject to scrutiny. The variation of data quality often became a considerable issue, which involves both empirical study and secondary data analysis. The dataset such as population census, industrial turnover rate, national income level, and the unemployment rate might often not be available. Thus, the decision making and data analysis become much more complicated in many instances with international research. Before conducting international hospitality management research, future managers should first get familiarized with local hospitality agencies and corporations to determine whether a formal research partnership can be achieved, or the research activity is based on a certain competitive advantage rather than limitations.

Time Zone/Lead Times for Completing the Investigations

International hospitality management research is indeed conducted internationally, which is across multiple countries with differences in language, culture, business associations, and practices. The coordination of research activity across multiple countries (often more than two) is challenging and may induce problematic and unusable data collection and equivalencies. For example, for an employee working in Korea, to manage one of its data collections in Guangzhou, China, which is just hours away by air, is much easier than managing one of the operations in San Jose, California, which is often more than 12 hours away and across different time zones. However, international research is indeed multinational, encompasses a multitude of operational hospitality activities, and often involves levels of international activities. Each data collection project often involves different operation systems, which in most instances coordinate all research activities between different companies making the decision process miles away from different data collection sites of international projects. In conducting cooperative research internationally, the extent and the method of research methodology may vary tremendously from project to project. In other words, some of the projects require to develop a comparing strategy that is entirely different from that needed when a strategic question is planned across different geographic regions.

Complexity and Language Barriers Involving Validity and Transferability

An entire marketing or management research project in one country requires a fulfilling amount of investment. When the research project is conducted internationally, researchers must recognize that even the standard research steps have their limitations. For example, data collection schedules tend to be longer, collaboration and research meeting tend to be more difficult, and the depths of analysis will be weaker because of the various heterogeneous environments. Even more difficult is controlling the exact design and methodology for each country in a multicounty study (Douglas and Craig, 1992). When the project is international, the dynamic factors that often contribute to the complexity in research design are establishing comparability and equivalency in data collection and analysis, generalization of the study results from one country to another, and variation of decision process involved in the international activities. Therefore, several serious critiques of international management research exist as the types of criticism to international research projects continues (e.g., Boyacigiller and Adler, 1991; Peterson et al., 1995).

Provincialism (Boyacigiller and Adler, 1991): As noted before, culture is often ignored or homogenized in assuming that all research questions will be investigated in westernized industrial model domain. However, a sound research project should not ignore culture in hospitality research; instead, it should compare the model in different domains.

Convenience sample and lack of generalizability (Osland, 2001): The investigation of international management research often relies on the convenience sample, which limits the comparison to inform practice in the future. The managers and sample characters gathered in the United States often lack relevance to the international market, because the United States has a strong economy and represents a westernized viewpoint, where international market can differ tremendously (Thomas, 1996). A review of the literature concludes that international management research projects are often conducted in a small number of western countries and rarely in Japan. On the other side, the managers conducting the research might know very little about samples from the Middle East, Africa, and Latin America.

Reliance on a single method, single level, and cross-sectional studies (Osland, 2001): Most international management research responses to questionnaire design and data collection were completed at a single point of time. The richness of culture and multinational location and multi-organizational hierarchies (managers versus employees) often provide new opportunities for researchers and allow alternative methods. However, the body of the research often ignored these factors and rarely drawn samples from multiple positions and multiple locations of the organization.

The issues discussed reinforce the importance of conducting international hospitality management research. At the same time, they also explicate the difficulties of forming and advising international hospitality management strategies. In the process of conducting international hospitality management research, the extent and the method of confounding problems can vary from situation to situation. Therefore, future managers are engaged in developing more cost-effective research methodologies to overcome the elevated international management issues presented above. Thus, when many existing limitations are levigated, the relevance of research to managers' decision making in global scope can be improved.

Conclusion

International hospitality management should be studied and can be applied for many purposes, ranging from assisting financial and international decision making to formalizing specific marketing strategies. The study and understanding of international hospitality management can help hospitality cooperation to face many problems. Some major factors of the operation are cost of conducting multinational management, variation of the marketing data collection and global decision making, complexity of the global market and competitors, time zone/lead times for completing the multinational business, and complexity and language barriers in involving team members.

Nevertheless, the operations of international hospitality management have become imperative for all hospitality firms engaged in international business regardless of sizes and interest of activities. Therefore, the relevant research and knowledge for understanding international hospitality management are likely to contribute to the existing doctrines and help future hospitality managers develop a new transnational standpoint, equipping hospitality managers with the much-needed informational strategy and operational standpoint in a new global market. Thus, other volumes of this book will help readers to adopt scientific methods to systematically collect, analyze, and synthesize information to assist hospitality operations, and provide understanding and case studies in solving and finalizing global marketing strategies. It will also demonstrate future managers with a new relevant research methodology to conduct international research projects, which ultimately develop integrated strategies to guide global marketing and global strategic management.

This book can help future managers to understand the multinational business behavior and different political, economic, social-cultural, and legal systems for developing an improved decision-making process in the global market. More importantly, it also helps them learn leading scientific methods to deal with daily business operation and global strategic positioning. When hospitality managers are educated on the issues related to multi-culture and multi-country management, future development of the hospitality industry can be expected (Osland, 2003).

References

AHLA. (2018), "Lodging industry profile. Prepared by the American Hotel & Lodging Association", available at: available at: https://www.ahla.com/ (accessed 17 November 2018).

Ayoun, B.M. and Moreo, P.J. (2008), "The influence of the cultural dimension of uncertainty avoidance on business strategy development: A cross-national study of hotel managers", *International Journal of Hospitality Management*, Vol.27, No.1, pp.65–75, https://doi.org/10.1016/j.ijhm.2007.07.008

Bartels, R. (1976), *The History of Marketing Thought*, Publishing Horizons, Bloomington, IN.

Biggemann, S. and Fam, K.S. (2011), "Business marketing in BRIC countries", *Industrial Marketing Management*, Vol.40, No.1, pp.5–7. https://doi.org/10.1016/j.indmarman.2010.09.004.

Boyacigiller, N.A. and Adler, N.J. (1991), "The parochial dinosaur: Organizational science in a global context", *Academy of Management Review*, Vol.16, No.2, pp.262–290. https://doi.org/10.5465/amr .1991.4278936.

Brotherton, B. (2012). *The International Hospitality Industry*, Elsevier, Oxford, UK.

Buckley, P.J. and Casson, M. (1985), *The Economic Theory of the Multinational Enterprise*, Springer, Berlin, Germany. https://doi.org/10.1007/978-1-349-05242-4.

Chen, J., Sloan, P., and Legrand, W. (2010), *Sustainability in the Hospitality Industry*, Routledge, London, UK. https://doi.org/10.4324/9780080941387.

Clarke, A. and Chen, W. (2009), *International Hospitality Management*, Routledge, Abingdon, UK. https://doi.org/10.4324/9780080547312.

Conrad, R.M. (2018), *Annual Global Hotel Rates*, Retrieved from https://www.statista.com/statistics/324/93/annual-growth-in-average-global-hotel-rates/ (accessed December, 2019).

Dada, Z.A. (2018), "Revisiting the discourse on poverty alleviation through tourism: An empirical investigation", *International Journal of Hospitality & Tourism Systems*, Vol.11 p.1.

Douglas, S.P. and Craig, C.S. (1992), "Advances in international marketing", *International Journal of Research in Marketing*, Vol.9, No.4, pp.291–318. https://doi.org/10.1016/0167-8116(92)90002-3.

Dunning, J.H. and Rugman, A.M. (1985), "The influence of Hymer's dissertation on the theory of foreign direct investment", *The American Economic Review*, Vol.75, No 2, pp.228–232.

Griffith. (2018), *2018 Restaurant Trends Industry*, available at: https://www.rewardsnetwork.com/blog/2018-restaurant-trends-industry/ (accessed December, 2019).

Harrington J.R. and Ottenbacher, M.C. (2011), "Strategic management: An analysis of its representation and focus in recent hospitality research", *International Journal of Contemporary Hospitality Management*, Vol.23, No.4, pp.439–462. https://doi.org/10.1108/09596111111129977.

Homer. (1176, 1919). *The Odyssey*, W. Heinemann; G.P. Putnam's Sons, London and New York. https://doi.org/10.4159/DLCL.homer-odyssey.1919.

Huimin, G. and Hobson, P. (2008), "The dragon is roaring... the development of tourism, hospitality & event management education in China", *Journal of Hospitality & Tourism Education*, Vol.20, No.1, pp.20–29. https://doi.org/10.1080/10963758.2008.10696909.

Johns, N. (1999), "What is this thing called service?" *European Journal of Marketing*, Vol.33, No.9/10, pp.958–974. https://doi.org/10.1108/03090569910285959.

Jones, P. and Pizam, A. (1993), *The International Hospitality Industry: Organizational and Operational Issues*, Wiley, Hoboken, NJ.

Lashley, C. and Morrison, A.J. (2000), *In Search of Hospitality: Theoretical Perspectives and Debates*, Routledge, London, UK.

Lee, S., Oh, H., and Hsu, C.H. (2017), "Country-of-operation and brand images: Evidence from the Chinese hotel industry", *International Journal of Contemporary Hospitality Management*, Vol.29, pp.1814–1833. https://doi.org/10.1108/IJCHM-11-2014-0577.

Legrand, W., Sloan, P., and Chen, J.S. (2017), *Sustainability in the Hospitality Industry 3rd Ed: Principles of Sustainable Operations*, Routledge, Abingdon, UK.

Lovelock, C.H. and Wirtz, J. (2004), *Services Marketing: People, Technology, Strategy*, 5th ed., Prentice Hall, Upper Saddle River, NJ.

McGrady, P. and Cottrell, S. (2018), "Factors affecting corporate sustainability among Colorado ski resorts: A mixed methods approach", *Journal of Tourism and Hospitality Management*, Vol.6, No.4, pp.167–186. https://doi.org/10.17265/2328-2169/2018.08.003.

MeiTuan (2017). Mietuan: 2018 restaurant report. Available at www.199it.com/archives/727120.html (accessed December, 2019).

Muhanna, E. (2007), "The contribution of sustainable tourism development in poverty alleviation of local communities in South Africa", *Journal of Human Resources in Hospitality & Tourism*, Vol.6, No.1, pp.37–67. https://doi.org/10.1300/J171v06n01_03.

National Restaurant Association. (NRA, 2018), *National Restaurant Association Fact Book*, NRA, Washington, DC, available at: https://www.restaurant.org/Downloads/PDFs/News-Research (accessed December, 2019).

Nilsson, J.H., Eskilsson, L., and Ek, R. (2010), "Creating cross-border destinations: Interreg programmes and regionalisation in the Baltic sea area", *Scandinavian Journal of Hospitality and Tourism*, Vol.10, No.2, pp.153–172. https://doi.org/10.1080/15022250903561978.

Oh, H. and Pizam, A. (2008), *Handbook of Hospitality Marketing Management*, Elsevier, Oxford, UK. https://doi.org/10.4324/9780080569437.

Orbis Research. (2018), *Global Marketing Consulting Market Size 2018–2022*, available at: https://www.reuters.com/brandfeatures/venture-capital/ (accessed December 2019).

Osland, J.S. (2001), "The quest for transformation: The process of global leadership development", *Developing Global Business Leaders: Policies, Processes and Innovations*, Routledge, Abingdon UK, pp.137–156.

Osland, J.S. (2003), "Broadening the debate: The pros and cons of globalization", *Journal of Management Inquiry*, Vol.10, No.2, pp.137–54. https://doi.org/10.1177/1056492603012002005.

Ottenbacher, M.C. (2007), "Innovation management in the hospitality industry: Different strategies for achieving success", *Journal of Hospitality and Tourism Research*, Vol.31, No.4, pp.431–454. https://doi.org/10.1177/1096348007302352.

Ottenbacher, M.C., Harrington, R., and Parsa, H.G. (2009), "Defining the hospitality discipline: A discussion of pedagogical and research implications", *Journal of Hospitality & Tourism Research*, Vol.33, No.3, pp.263–283. https://doi.org/10.1177/1096348009338675.

Peterson, M.F., Smith, P.B., Akande, A., Ayestaran, S., Bochner, S., Callan, V., … and Hofmann, K. (1995), "Role conflict, ambiguity, and overload: A 21-nation study", *Academy of Management Journal*, Vol.38, No.2, pp.429–452. https://doi.org/10.2307/256687.

Ritzer, G. and Liska, A. (1997), "McDisneyisation'and post-tourism", in Rojek, C. and Urry, J. (Eds.), *Touring Cultures: Transformations of Travel and Theory*, Routledge, London, UK, pp. 96–111.

Rust, R.T. and Huang, M.H. (2014), *Handbook of Service Marketing Research*, Edward Elgar Publishing, Oxford, UK. https://doi.org/10.4337/9780857938855.

Scarborough. (2006), *Restaurant News Resourcea*, available at: https://www.restaurantnewsresource.com/article23120.html (accessed December, 2019).

Schmid, S. and Gombert, A. (2018), "McDonald's: Is the fast food icon reaching the limits of growth?" in *Internationalization of Business*, Springer Nature, Cham Heidelberg, Germany, pp.155–171. https://doi.org/10.1007/978-3-319-74089-8_7.

Seraphin, H., Yallop, A.C. Capatîna, A., and Gowreesunkar, V.G. (2018), "Heritage in tourism organisations' branding strategy: The case of a post-colonial, post-conflict and post-disaster destination", *International Journal of Culture, Tourism and Hospitality Research*, Vol.12, No.1, pp.89–105. https://doi.org/10.1108/IJCTHR-05-2017-0057.

Shaw, E.H. and Tamilia, R.D. (2001), "Robert Bartels and the history of marketing thought", *Journal of Macromarketing,* Vol.21, No.2, pp.156–163, https://doi.org/10.1177/0276146701212006.

Sheehan, M., Grant, K., and Garavan, T. (2018), "Strategic talent management: A macro and micro analysis of current issues in hospitality and tourism", *Worldwide Hospitality and Tourism Themes*, Vol.10, No.1, pp. 28–41. https://doi.org/10.1108/WHATT-10-2017-0062.

Sigala, M. (2005), "Integrating customer relationship management in hotel operations: Managerial and operational implications", *International Journal of Hospitality Management*, Vol.24, No.3, pp.391–413. https://doi.org/10.1016/j.ijhm.2004.08.008.

Sigala, M. (2018), "Implementing social customer relationship management: A process framework and implications in tourism and hospitality", *International Journal of Contemporary Hospitality Management*, Vol.30, No.7, pp. 2698–2726. https://doi.org/10.1108/IJCHM-10-2015-0536.

Talias, M. (2018), "Global governance conceptualization and the case of hotel classification", *International Journal of Hospitality Management*, Vol.72, pp.132–139. https://doi.org/10.1016/j.ijhm.2018.01.012.

Taylor, S. and Edgar, D. (1996), "Hospitality research: The emperor's new clothes?" *International Journal of Hospitality Management*, Vol.15, pp.211–227. https://doi.org/10.1016/S0278-4319(96)00018-7.

Teare, R. and Olsen, M. (1992), *International Hospitality Management*. Wiley, New York, NY.

Thomas, C. (1995). US international transaction in 1994. *Federal Reserve Bulletin., 81*, 407.

Toyne, B. and Nigh, D.W. (1997), *International Business: An Emerging Vision*, Vol.1, University of South Carolina Press, Columbia, SC.

Vaughan, Y. and Koh, Y. (2019), "Role of resource slack in rapid international expansion of restaurant companies", *International Journal of Contemporary Hospitality Management*, Vol.31, No.1, pp.2–20. https://doi.org/10.1108/IJCHM-07-2017-0415.

Wearne, N., Morrison, A. (1996). Hospitality Marketing. London: Routledge, https://doi.org/10.4324/9780080938486.

Weiss, T.G.., & Wilkinson, R. (2014). Rethinking global governance? Complexity, authority, power, change. *International Studies Quarterly, 58*(1), 207–215.

Wilkins, M. (1974), *The Maturing of Multinational Enterprise: American Business Abroad from 1914 to 1970*, Vol.27, Harvard University Press, Cambridge, MA. https://doi.org/10.4159/harvard.9780674863019.

Xiang, Z., Schwartz, Z., Gerdes Jr, J.H., and Uysal, M. (2015), "What can big data and text analytics tell us about hotel guest experience and satisfaction?", *International Journal of Hospitality Management*, Vol.44, pp.120–130. https://doi.org/10.1016/j.ijhm.2014.10.013.

2

PAST AND PRESENT KEY PLAYERS IN THE HOSPITALITY INDUSTRY

Betsy Bender Stringam, Joselyn Goopio, Basak Denizci Guillet, and Hjalte Brøndum Mansa

Key Players

Unlike many industries which were developed by a few key people or organizations, the hospitality industry has traditionally been an entrepreneurial industry with many key players instrumental in its development. To highlight every person and company who has played a key role in the international hospitality industry would take volumes. This chapter seeks to discuss some of the key players who helped to shape the industry and to highlight key organizations in the industry today.

The hospitality industry is generally divided into several segments or industries: travel and tourism, food and beverage, and hotels and lodging.

Travel and Tourism

Thomas Cook is often considered the father of tourism. Credited with inventing modern tourism, Cook introduced concepts such as prepaid inclusive tours, hotel coupons, and traveler's checks. Thomas and his son John developed an extensive travel business with excursions and tours all over the world (Brendon, 1991; Hamilton, 2005). The travel company they developed, Thomas Cook, became one of the world's leading travel companies, with more than 22,000 employees, operating from 16 countries (Thomas Cook, 2019).

A key component of early travel and tourism was travel guidebooks. The first travel guidebooks are attributed to John Murray, Johannes August Klein, and Karl Baedeker. In 1836, Murray wrote his first guidebook, transforming his notes about travel into a "Handbook for Travelers on the Continent." He continued developing additional guidebooks for other areas of the world. His books helped British travelers explore Europe, Asia, and North Africa (Bruce, 2010). Johannes August Klein wrote a similar handbook for travelers in 1828. After Klein's death, Karl Baedeker who had acquired the publishing company for Klein's book published a new edition in which he significantly expanded the travel information. Baedeker's guides were published in German, French, and English and became the standard guidebook for the latter half of the 19th century (Bruce, 2010).

The concept of travel by boat for pleasure was introduced by Albert Ballin, considered the father of cruise ship travel. Ballin's initial success was in shipping, catering to steerage passengers. Rather than competing for who could cross the Atlantic in the shortest time, Ballin sought to attract a wealthier clientele by developing luxurious accommodations on board his ships. Ballin endeavored to make travel by sea a luxury experience rather than a test of endurance. The upper decks of his ships were designed to rival the palatial homes and hotels that were more aristocratic, to which wealthy passengers were accustomed. Ballin went on to develop the concept of a leisure cruise ship. To make use of his ships during the winter months when passenger transport demand was lower due to unfavorable weather in the North Atlantic, Ballin developed the concept of using his ships for pleasure in the Mediterranean. This first trip departed Cuxhaven, Germany on 22 January 1891, traveling for 57 days and visiting over a dozen Mediterranean ports. The cruise offered luxury cabins, first-class cuisine, and shore excursions. The trip was such a success; the company converted three additional ships for cruises and built its first purpose-built cruise ship in 1899. Ballin was also a pioneer in quality improvement. Ballin frequently traveled on his own ships, seeking passenger insight for improvements, implementing their ideas (Grace, 2011).

Food and Beverage

The serving of food has been a part of daily life since the beginning of time. There are mentions and artifacts of foodservice throughout ancient history. Taverns, inns, and caravanserais were noted as far back as ancient Greece and early China, serving food to travelers on the road. For most, foodservice was a necessity and very basic in its preparation and presentation. During the Roman Empire, foodservice began to evolve. The size of the Roman Empire necessitated travel, requiring more meals eaten away from the home and hearth. It was also during this time that foodservice included elaborate preparation, presentation, and service of food and wines (Stringam and Partlow, 2016).

Early foodservice was generally eaten around one table, with little to no selection of menu items. Food was served in communal bowls or troughs. Towns and communities had inns, wine shops, and taverns which served travelers and locals. But, it was not until the late 1700s that free-standing restaurants became popular.

Traditional Restaurants/Culinary

The word restaurant itself comes from a shop in Paris which was serving a restorative broth. In 1765, Boulanger opened a shop serving a soup called "le restaurant divin" or the divine restorative. The broth was a stark contrast to the heavy meals and foods of the time and was thought to help combat a variety of ailments. Boulanger's restaurant was quickly copied with many similar "restaurants" opening across Europe (Lattin et al., 2014; Pillsbury, 1990). The French Revolution helped to expand the concept of freestanding restaurants. The chefs previously employed by the bourgeois were now in need of work. Many of them opened restaurants. Before the French Revolution, there were only about 50 restaurants in Paris, but by 1814, there were more than 3,000 restaurants in Paris (Flandrin and Montanari, 1999).

A discussion of early restaurants and the culinary movements that created them would not be complete without Antoine Careme (1784–1833) and Auguste Escoffier (1846–1935). Both are considered the founders of professional cooking and culinary techniques, skills, and principles (Lattin et al., 2014; Walker, 2013). Careme, a French chef and pastry cook elevated food presentation to an art form with elaborate garnishes, decorative trimmings, and spectacular recipes (Lang, 1988).

Beginning at the Carlton Hotel 1899, Auguste Escoffier created the modern kitchen brigade of chefs that is still the model in most large kitchens. Escoffier introduced a new culinary philosophy of simplifying recipes and preserving the nutrition of foods. Escoffier was also noted for his establishment of sanitation standards in the kitchens. Escoffier was also instrumental in the offering of gourmet food in early luxury hotels, collaborating with Cesar Ritz to run the Savoy in London. Escoffier and Ritz enjoyed a long partnership opening and managing many hotels (Flandrin and Montanari, 1999).

Delmonico's of New York is important in restaurant history as the first symbol of fine dining in the United States (Lattin et al., 2014; Pillsbury, 1990). John and Peter Delmonico opened a bakery and wine shop in 1827, expanding to their first full-service restaurant in 1831. Delmonico's went on to open many other restaurants throughout its history, progressing to larger buildings and more prosperous neighborhoods as the restaurants progressed. While the Delmonico brothers were not the first restauranteurs in America, they were some of the first to capitalize on an undeveloped idea and to expand changing American dining (Mariani, 1991).

Paul Bocuse was a leading chef in the path breaking culinary movement in the late 1960s and early 1970s known as nouvelle cuisine. Bocuse shaped a style of cooking "that stressed fresh ingredients, lighter sauces, unusual flavor combinations, and relentless innovation" (Grimes, 2018). Bocuse was also instrumental in sharing of these new culinary techniques across the globe, bringing changes to traditional cuisine. In modern times, European restaurants have been incremental to the fine dining cuisine development. Ferran Adriá of El Bulli and René Redzepi of Nomaare are two chefs accredited for being the trendsetters in the industry since the turn of this century.

Pioneers of the Quick Service and Fast Casual Industries

Restaurants on a more casual scale became popular during the early 1900s. Roy Allen and Frank Wright pioneered the concept of franchising in the restaurant industry with the first A&W Root Beer Stand in 1919. A&W eventually grew to over 2,500 restaurants (Lattin et al., 2014).

Quick Service

The quick service restaurant industry traces its origins to two pioneering restaurants: White Castle and The Pig Stand. White Castle hamburgers opened in Wichita, Kansas in 1921. Edgar Waldo "Billy" Ingram developed a method for cooking hamburgers by flattening the ground meat and cooking it with onions on a flat griddle, thereby inventing the modern-day hamburger (Nusair and Parsa, 2009; Smith, 2011). Ingram changed the perception of the hamburger from an undesired menu item to the "most preferred menu item in America in the 1940s" (Nusair and Parsa, 2009, p. 157). Jesse Kirby pioneered the drive-in restaurant concept in 1921 in Dallas, Texas. With an eye toward expanding automobile travel, Kirby developed the Pig Stand with carhops racing to serve customers in their automobiles (Summers, 2007).

Many quick service fans point to Harry Snyder who created In-N-Out Burger as another pioneer. Snyder opened In-N-Out Burgers in 1948 in Baldwin Park, California. Snyder is credited with many innovations in the industry to include the first two-way speakerphone for drive-thru restaurants (Perman, 2009).

McDonald's is one of the largest and most well-known quick service giants throughout the globe with over 36,000 restaurants in more than 100 countries (McDonald's, 2019). The original McDonald's concept started in 1940 by the McDonald's brothers, Richard and Maurie in San Bernardino, California. This first McDonald's restaurant was counter service only with no seating. Ray Kroc, a milkshake machine salesman, saw the potential of the McDonald's concept and partnered with the McDonald's brothers to expand the company. Kroc later bought out the McDonald's brothers and expanded and developed the company into the large multinational conglomeration known today (Roberts et al., 2009; Smith, 2011).

The quick service industry had other transforming pioneers. Truett Cathy transformed the quick service industry from a menu based on hamburgers by bringing the boneless chicken sandwich to popularity in 1961. He named the sandwich the Chick-fil-A. Within a few years, he started the quick service restaurant company with the same name (Brizek et al., 2009). Glen Bell introduced America to fast Mexican food with Taco Bell (Pillsbury, 1990). Harland Sanders opened the first Kentucky Fried Chicken in Salt Lake City in 1952 (Yum, 2019), and Dave Thomas began his Wendy's Old Fashioned Hamburgers chain, which he named after his daughter, Melinda "Wendy" Thomas, in 1969 (Wendy's, 2020). Carl Karcher started Carl's Jr. with several hot dog stands (Perman, 2009), and Matthew Burns and Keith Cramer started Burger King in Florida in 1952 (under the name Insta-Burger King).

The hamburger and quick service restaurants still reign today as some of the most popular restaurant concepts. The quick service concept has spread across the globe, with McDonald's, Burger King, Subway, and Kentucky Fried Chicken having restaurants on six of the seven continents. Internationally, most of the quick service restaurants offer small adaptations to the menu such as the addition of sweet and sour sauce or a shrimp burger, but the menus remain largely unchanged. It is projected that quick service makes up more than 25% of total restaurant sales worldwide (Brotherton, 2003).

Fast Casual

Fast Casual is a segment of the restaurant industry that is a cross between table service and quick service. Similar to Quick Service, Fast Casual does not have table service. Food is ordered and delivered over the counter. However, the price point and recipe quality match more closely to table service restaurants. One of the key players in this segment is the founder of Chipotle, Steve Ells. The first Chipotle Mexican Grill restaurant opened in Denver in 1993. Ells never planned to start a new restaurant trend. Lacking the funds for a fine dining restaurant, he opened a small burrito shop in Colorado. His intent was to use the burrito shop to raise the capital for the fine dining restaurant (Whitten, 2017). Today, Chipotle has more than 2,500 restaurants and is one of the most successful restaurant companies ever (Chipotle, 2019). The Fast Casual market is the fastest growing segment of the restaurant industry. Some other U.S. based top Fast Casual restaurants today are Panera Bread, Zaxby's, Five Guys, and Wingstop (Oches, 2018).

Casual Dining

Casual dining is a restaurant concept that is a step up from the fast casual and quick service restaurants. Casual dining allows an affordable menu price, yet still employs sit-down table service. Casual Dining is the second-largest segment of the foodservice industry today, following close behind quick service. There are examples of casual dining early in restaurant history with eateries such as A&W and Hot Shoppes. Norman Brinker is accredited with expanding or contributing to the development and growth of casual dining with chains such as Steak and Ale, Bennigan's, and Chili's restaurants. Brinker founded Steak and Ale in 1966. Building on the success of Steak and Ale, Brinker started Bennigan's restaurant chain in 1976 (Barrows, 2009; Bernstein, 1981). Brinker developed a number of additional restaurant concepts, which he sold to Pillsbury. Brinker bought Chili's restaurants in 1983 and transformed the company from "Hamburger Hippies" into a leading restaurant chain (Brinker, 2019). Today, Brinker International owns, operates or franchises more than 1600 restaurants in 31 countries and two territories.

Managed Foodservice

Managed foodservice, also called contract foodservice, includes dining facilities at education, medical, government, corporate, and sports facilities (Walker, 2013). Aramark, one of the early managed foodservice companies, and one of the largest today, was started in 1936 when an entrepreneurial peanut salesman talked an aircraft plant into putting peanut dispensers on the factory floor. Merging with another vending machine company in 1959, Automatic Retailers of America

(ARA) was formed. During the next decades, ARA expanded into sports arenas and stadiums, followed by corporate dining facilities, hospitals, and schools. ARA later changed its name to Aramark (Summers, 2007). Aramark now serves more than 575 million meals annually and provides managed foodservice, facility management, and uniform services in 22 countries (Aramark, 2019). Sodexo, another key player in managed foodservice, began in 1948 when three World War II veterans were attending Hobart College in Geneva New York under the GI Bill. While attending college, they took over the management of the dining hall. After graduating two years later, they expanded their expertise to other colleges and universities, eventually creating Saga Corporation, one of the first nationwide providers of educational foodservice. Saga was later acquired by Marriott and eventually sold to Sodexo, which is a leading contract foodservice company today (Summers, 2007; Walker, 2013). Sodexo operates in more than 80 countries and serves more than 100 million people every day (Sodexo, 2019).

Hotels and Accommodations

Hotels

The hotel industry like restaurants has many entrepreneurs and key players. Today the global industry is split with about half of the hotels in the world affiliated with a brand and about half are independent.

Transportation often drove early hotel development. Hotels and motels were established along rail lines and newly built roadways. Fred Harvey, one of the early pioneers in the hotel industry, started in by contracting with early railroad companies to provide foodservice along expanding railroads in the United States in 1876 (Lattin et al., 2014). Two years later, Harvey opened his first hotel in Florence, Kansas, again negotiating contracts and exclusive rights for expansion along the rail routes. Harvey employed the same railroad companies to deliver food to his Harvey House restaurants (with no freight charges), thus allowing for expanded menus beyond locally produced food. The lack of shipping costs also allowed Harvey to keep menu prices low, even in isolated locations. Harvey was able to demand better-quality food product at lower prices and to control the distribution processes. Fred Harvey also pioneered vertical integration, or the owning of components of the supply chain, in purchasing large cattle ranches to supply the beef needed for his restaurants. Harvey pioneered the central commissary concept to help standardize and control food quality. Under this concept, some of the food for the restaurants was prepped in central commissaries, and distributed to the restaurants, rather than each restaurant ordering food and products locally (Fried, 2010). Fred Harvey demanded quality in his hotels and restaurants in the product, employees, and service, thus changing the face of the hospitality industry along the rural U.S. frontier. Harvey was also a pioneer in customer service and menu offerings. He developed menu offerings at his restaurants so that patrons traveling with the railroad would not encounter the same food in consecutive meal periods (Stringam and Partlow, 2016).

Ellsworth Statler, considered by many to be the father of the hotel industry, brought the next great transformation in hotel development (Lattin et al., 2014). With the opening of the Buffalo Statler in 1908, Statler was the first to put in private baths, full-length mirrors, and telephones in each room (Vallen and Vallen, 2018). Statler developed a set of standards for service and required his employees to carry the Statler Service Code (Stutts and Wortman, 2006). Statler's vision of hotels shaped the industry for the next 40 years (Barrows et al., 2011).

Many other hotel companies started in the early 1900s. Conrad Hilton acquired his first hotel, the 40 unit Mobley in Cisco, Texas in 1919 (Hilton, 1957). Hilton went on to build a great hotel empire throughout the next century. Hilton contributed to the hotel industry in many ways: pioneering a multi-hotel reservation system in 1948 and pioneering forecasting and control methods.

Hilton had a forecasting committee which met to predict the number of rooms that would be sold for future dates (Hilton, 1957; Stutts and Wortman, 2006). The Caribe Hilton in Puerto Rico was the first international chain hotel to open in the Caribbean opening the competition for resort hotels in that region (Lattin et al., 2014). Hilton Hotels is one of the largest hotel companies today.

As air travel began to develop, hotels were needed to meet the needs of traveling passengers. Juan Trippe, a commercial aviation pioneer, founded Pan American Airways. Trippe determined early on that for Pan American Airways to succeed he would need luxury hotels at the end of every flight (Potter, 1996). Trippe developed Intercontinental Hotels to meet this need and opened his first hotel in Belem Brazil in 1949 (IHG, 2019). InterContinental Hotels was instrumental in the global expansion of the hotel industry.

Many key hoteliers first started in the restaurant industry before expanding into hotels. J. Willard Marriott, founder of the world's largest hotel company, was one of them. Marriott opened a nine-seat root beer stand in Washington D.C. in 1927. Marriott expanded his food-service operations over the next few decades creating Hot Shoppes Restaurants and entering the airline catering market (Marriott and Brown, 2013). In 1957, Marriott opened his first hotel, The Twin Bridges, in Washington D.C. under the management of his son, Bill Marriott. For the next 60 years, Marriott developed many different hotels and expanded across the globe. In 2016 Marriott International acquired Starwood Hotels and Resorts, becoming the world's largest hotel company with more than 6,700 hotels, with more than 1.2 million rooms across 30 brands in over 130 countries (Marriott, 2019; Touyalai, 2018).

Charles Carmine Forte was another successful hotelier who began his career in the foodservice industry managing a milk bar in London in 1935. In 1958, he purchased the ailing Waldorf Hotel in London which was the founding of the Forte Group of hotels. Within 30 years, he was managing one of the world's greatest hotel and catering complexes (Forte, 1987).

AccorHotels is one of the largest multinational hotel companies headquartered outside of the United States. AccorHotels began in 1967 when Paul Dubrule and Gerard Pelisson opened the Lesquin Novotel. Dubrule and Pélisson noted the success of U.S. hotels located in suburban areas and along major highways. They opened their first Novotel hotel outside of Lille. AccorHotels today has more than 4,500 hotels in over 100 countries (AccorHotels, 2019; Sido et al., 2007).

Franchising and Consortia

Kemmons Wilson was one of the key pioneers of the franchise model for the hotel and motel industry as the founder of Holiday Inn hotels. Wilson built his first Holiday Inn in 1952 in Memphis, Tennessee (O'Halloran, 2009; Wilson and Kerr, 1996). Embracing the franchising model, Wilson helped to develop 1,000 Holiday Inns by 1968. Wilson brought key changes to the hotel industry creating a hotel product that was affordable for traveling families allowing children to stay for free and providing family-friendly amenities: swimming pools, air conditioners, free cribs, television, and free parking (IHG, 2019; Stutts and Wortman, 2006). Wilson focused on consistency among his hotels setting the standard for the modern lodging industry (O'Halloran, 2009). He developed a school for his innkeepers to teach them the "Holiday Inn Way" (Stutts and Wortman, 2006). Wilson is said to have changed the hotel industry from fragmented, disorganized, and inconsistent "fleabag" local hotel businesses to standardized properties run by international corporations (Jakle et al., 1996; O'Halloran, 2009; Turkel, 2009).

Hotel consortia or referral systems had an early start as informal networks. Hotels would refer guests to hotels with similar products or quality in other cities. The concept was formalized with Merile Guertin a motel owner from California. Guertin decided to formally associate a group of motels who maintained similar high standards (Go and Pine, 1995). He toured 507 motels and selected 66 to form Western Motels, one of the first referral groups or consortia. Western Motels later changed the name to Best Western (Margolies, 1995; Turkel, 2009).

Boutique Hotels and Resorts

While the large hotel companies focused on brand standards and developing hotels that were similar to one another, another concept was taking route: boutique hotels. Boutique hotels are a hotel concept that focuses on unique architecture, style, decor, and size (Walker, 2013). In 1981, Bill Kimpton was inspired by his European travels to develop hotels which were "more beautiful, livable and stylish" (IHG, 2019). He established Kimpton Hotels and Restaurants. Kimpton is now a part of the IHG Hotels and Resorts.

The boutique concept took hold and developed across the globe. Another key player in the development of boutique hotels and resorts was Adrian Willem Lauw Zecha. Zecha founded Aman Resorts combining boutique and luxury in a resort setting. The first Aman Resort was in Phuket, Thailand. Aman Hotels and Resorts has since expanded to more than 33 properties in 21 different countries across the globe (Aman, 2019). Zecha later sold the assets but maintained a role as CEO for a number of years. Zecha recently founded Azerai hotels focusing on affordable luxury (Sile, 2018).

Luxury Hotels

Because early travelers were often the wealthy, upper-class, luxury hotels have always been a part of the hotel industry. While most large cities had a luxury hotel, very few of the early brands or hotel companies focused their development on luxury hotels. But, this segment had a few key players who led the development of the luxury segment of the hotel industry. One of the first luxury hoteliers was Cesar Ritz. In the 1820s, Cesar Ritz, a Swiss developer, partnered with a prominent French chef, Auguste Escoffier and built the Grand hotel of Monte Carlo, the first to offer luxury accommodations and gourmet dining all under one roof (Flandrin and Montanari, 1999). Ritz opened additional hotels in Paris, London, Madrid, Rome, Lisbon, and Cairo, becoming the first hotel chain (Barr, 2018; Slattery, 2012; Turkel, 2009). Ritz is also often accredited with the first hotel franchise when he licensed the use of the Ritz Carlton name for The Ritz Carlton Hotel in New York City in 1907 (Lattin et al., 2014).

Mohan Singh Oberoi led the development of the luxury hotel industry in much of India, Indonesia, Mauritius, Egypt, Saudi Arabia, and Australia (Chathoth and Chon, 2009; Karkaria, 2003). In 1934 M.S. Oberoi purchased the Clarke Hotel in Simla, India beginning the Oberoi Hotel Group. Today the Oberoi group operates 31 luxury hotels in 6 countries (Oberoi, 2019), and has received many awards and accolades for its luxury hotels.

Another key luxury brand, Dusit International, was established when Thanpuying Chanut opened her first property, the Princess Hotel, in Bangkok, Thailand, in 1949. It was one of the first properties in the city to feature a swimming pool, an elevator, and air conditioning. Chanut's desire to incorporate the Thai culture into the luxury hotel market led to the opening of the flagship Dusit Thani Bangkok, in 1970. Building on the success of this property, Thanpuying Chanut opened many more 5-star hotels in Thailand and other countries. Today Dusit International is a leader in the luxury hotel and resort market (Ngan, 2018).

Another key luxury hotel developer was Isadore Sharpe, an architect. Sharpe built his first Four Seasons hotel in 1961. He had a vision for a new kind of hotel featuring superior design, top-quality amenities and a deep commitment to service. He aimed to make Four Seasons a worldwide brand synonymous with luxury (Sharpe, 2009). Focusing on exceptional service, Four Seasons Hotels and Resorts has become a luxury brand with approximately 100 hotels in 39 countries, all under the single brand name (Four Seasons, 2019).

By 1928 "Leading Hotels of the World," LHW, was established in Europe with a collaborative office in New York, "Hotel Representatives Inc.," HRI. LHW is a consortium of the very best of the independent luxury hotels, with more than 400 hotels across 80 countries (LHW, 2019).

Resorts

Resorts and resort hotels can be traced as far back as the Romans who developed lodging and resorts around ancient baths and spas, and in mountain communities (Mill, 2012). Like other segments of the lodging industry, resorts had many early pioneers and developers.

One of the world's largest all-inclusive destination resort companies, Club Med, was established in 1950 by Gerard Blitz. His first all-inclusive resort was a sports activity destination with 200 tents on Alcudia beach in the Balearics. Club Med today has 80 resort villages on five continents and is still a leader in destination resorts (Club Med, 2019).

Another key resort developer was Sol Kerzner. In 1979, Kerzner developed Sun City, an ambitious resort project in Africa. The project included four hotels, and expansive resort and entertainment amenities including a 6,000-seat multi-purpose arena. Southern Sun Hotels became the most successful hotel and resort company in South Africa and is now part of Tsogo Sun (Tsogo, 2019). Kerzner developed many other resorts and hotels including the Mohegan Sun Casino in Connecticut in the United States, the Atlantis Resort in the Bahamas, The Palm, Dubai, and the Mazagan Beach Resort in El Jadida. Kerzner expanded the concept of resorts with The Atlantis, Bahamas. The Atlantis, a 2,300-room resort, is also home to the world's largest man-made marine habitats and the Caribbean's biggest casino. Kerzner recently developed the Atlantis Sanya on Hainan Island, China. The Atlantis Sanya is even grander with a large aquarium complex, a shopping mall, and more than 21 restaurants (Rosen, 2018).

Luxury resorts were opened across the globe; Ho Kwon Ping, another key resort developer, opened the first Banyan Tree resort in Phuket in 1994. Banyan Tree Hotels and Resorts has now grown into one of the world's leading international operators in the hospitality and spa industry that manages more than 40 resorts and hotels, 60 spas, 80 retail galleries, and three championship golf courses in 28 countries (Banyan Tree (2019).

A discussion of key resort developers would not be complete without the inclusion of Walt Disney. Walt Disney was instrumental in weaving travel and entertainment together. Walt started with movies and animation but went on to create a world of entertainment theme parks and resorts. Disney revolutionized entertainment attractions with the opening of his first theme park, Disneyland Park in California in 1955. Disney was meticulous about cleanliness, service quality, and security, factors not common in theme parks at the time. A master planner Disney wanted to extend the theme park experience to the hotels and restaurants for his theme park guests, leading him to open his first hotel. Within just a few years of opening Disneyland, Disney began planning a theme park in Florida. As a part of those plans, he included a master resort and hotel complex in Walt Disney World. While Disney passed away in 1966 before Walt Disney World was completed, his brother Roy Disney carried on the plans to finish the park and resort complex. Today Walt Disney Parks, Experiences and Consumer Products has more than 52 resorts (Disney, 2019; Shani and Logan, 2010).

Key Organizations

The hospitality industry is very dynamic, constantly evolving. New products are introduced. Hotels and restaurants that are successful are expanded to other parts of the globe. A common process in that expansion in the hospitality industry is for the larger companies to acquire or merge with smaller regional companies. This is true regardless of whether the companies own, manage, or franchise hotels and restaurants. Recent years have seen rapid merger and acquisition activities. As a result, of the constant changes in the industry, any list of key organizations is very fluid and changing almost daily. Additionally, the hospitality industry is comprised of many companies large and small. It is not possible to list all of the current key organizations within the bounds of any single work. Nevertheless, we present several listings of many of the largest key organizations to help outline some of the key players of the industry. It is important to note that within any one region, country, cuisine, amenity, or type of service, there may be other key organizations that are important, which may not be included in these lists. That is some of the beauty of the hospitality industry: despite the large players, there is always room for new entrepreneurs and concepts.

Restaurants and Foodservice

The restaurant industry is still predominantly comprised of many independent restaurants. Most of the largest companies are quick service or managed foodservice (see Table 2.1).

But a key player to the restaurant industry cannot be defined by sales volume alone. Often a key player is a restaurant that is an integral part of a community, or a few restaurants that define cuisine for a region, or an entrepreneur that transports a regional cuisine to a new continent. Each region and country of the world has many key restauranteurs. Table 2.2 presents some of the key restaurant and foodservice companies across the globe.

Hotels and Accommodation

Defining the current key players for the hotels and accommodations industry is equally hard as the industry is very complex. Hotels can be owned, managed, and flagged by separate entities. Some companies only manage or operate hotels, some only franchise, some are a combination of ownership, operations, and flag. Tables 2.3 and 2.4 present the largest hotel companies and a list of key hotel companies worldwide. Table 2.3 was compiled using data from the Hotels 325 Report, 2019 (Weinstein, 2019), and from individual hotel company reports.

Table 2.1 The world's largest public companies, restaurants

Company	Country	2018 Sales	Market Value
McDonald's	United States	$22.3 B	$129.9 B
Starbucks	United States	$23.5 B	$79 B
Compass Group	United Kingdom	$29.8 B	$32.4 B
Restaurant Brands International	Canada	$4.8 B	$26.2 B
Yum! Brands	United States	$5.8 B	$27.4 B
Aramark	United States	$15.2 B	$9.4 B
Yum China Holdings	United States	$8.1 B	$14.5 B
Darden Restaurants	United States	$7.9 B	$11.2 B
Whitbread	United Kingdom	$4.3 B	$10.5 B

Sources: Forbes (2018) and McGrath (2018).

Table 2.2 Key restaurant and foodservice companies worldwide (listed alphabetically)

Restaurant Company	Company Headquarters Location	Restaurant Company	Company Headquarters Location
Al Baik	Saudi Arabia	McDonald's Company	USA
Aramark	USA	Nordsee	Germany
Bloomin' Brands	USA	Oporto	Australia
Brinker International	USA	Quick	France
Burger Ranch	Portugal	Restaurant Brands International	Canada
Compass Group	United Kingdom	Starbucks	USA
Darden Restaurants	USA	Steers	South Africa
Denny's	USA	Subway	USA
Dicos	China	Sukiya	Japan
DineEquity, Inc.	USA	Supermac's	Ireland
Domino's	USA	Telepizza	Spain
Dunkin' Donuts	USA	Teremok	Russia
Giraffas	Brazil	Toast Box	Singapore
Hamburguesas El Corral	Columbia	Wagamama	United Kingdom
IKEA	Netherlands	Wendy's International	USA
Ippudo	Japan	Whitbread	United Kingdom
JD Wetherspoon	United Kingdom	Yum! Brands	USA
Jollibee	Philippines	Yum – China Holdings	China
Kungfu	China		

Sources: Franchise Times (2019); Irvin (2018); and Nation's Restaurant News (2018a, 2018b).

Table 2.3 Largest hotel companies

Hotel Company	Company Headquarters Location	Number of Rooms	Number of Properties
Marriott International	Bethesda, Maryland USA	1,317,368	6,906
Jin Jiang International Holdings Co.	Shanghai, China	941,794	8,715
Hilton	McLean, Virginia, USA	912,960	5,685
IHG (InterContinental Hotels Group)	Denham, Buckinghamshire, England	836,541	5,603
Wyndham Hotel Group	Parsippany, New Jersey, USA	809,900	9,200
AccorHotels	Paris, France	703,806	4,780
Choice Hotels International	Rockville, Maryland USA	569,108	7,021
Oyo Hotels and Home	Gurugram, India	515,144	17,344
Huazhu Group, Ltd	Shanghai, China	422,747	4,230
BTG HomeInns Hotels (Group) Co	Beijing, China	397,561	4,049
Best Western Hotels & Resorts	Phoenix, Arizona, USA	295,849	3,618

(Continued)

Hotel Company	Company Headquarters Location	Number of Rooms	Number of Properties
GreenTree Hospitality Group	Shanghai, China	221,529	2,757
Hyatt Hotels Corp.	Chicago, Illinois USA	208,297	852
Dossen International Group	Guangzhou City, China	199,042	2,247
G6 Hospitality	Carrollton, Texas, USA	123,162	1,122
Qingdao Sunmei Group Co.	Qingdao, China	121,483	2,352
Aimbridge Hospitality	Plano, Texas, USA	102,786	834
Magnuson Worldwide	Spokane, Washington, USA	94,386	1,119
RLH Corp	Spokane, Washington, USA	85,700	1,327
Meliá Hotels International	Palma de Mallorca, Spain	83,253	329
Westmont Hospitality Group	Houston, Texas, USA	82,617	731
Interstate Hotels & Resorts	Arlington, Virginia, USA	80,172	481
Minor International	Bangkok, Thailand	75,219	513
Whitbread	Dunstable, England	74,624	793

Table 2.4 Key hotel companies worldwide (listed alphabetically)

Hotel Company	Company Headquarters Location	Hotel Ccompany	Company Headquarters Location
Aha Hotels & Lodges	South Africa	Leading Hotels of the World	USA
Absolute Hotel Services	Thailand	Loews	USA
AccorHotels	France	Louvre Hotels Group	France
Aimbridge	USA	Magnuson Hotels	USA
AmericInn	USA	Mandarin Oriental Hotel Group	China
AMResorts	USA	Mantra Group	Australia
APA Group	Japan	Marriott International	USA
Archipelago International	Indonesia	Meliá Hotels International	Spain
Ascott	Singapore	MGM Resorts International	USA
B&B Hotel	France	Millennium & Copthorne Hotels	United Kingdom
Banyan Tree Luxury Hotels and Resorts	Singapore	Minor Hotels	Thailand
Barcelo Hotel Group	Spain	Movenpick	Switzerland
Barrière	France	Nacional Inn	Brazil
Best Western Hotels & Resorts	USA	Narada Hotel Group	China
BTG Homeinns Hotels Group	China	New Century Hotels & Resorts	China
Caesars Entertainment.	USA	New World Hotels and Resorts	China
Casa Andina	Peru	NH Hotel Group	Spain
Choice Hotels International	USA	Nobile Hotels	Brazil
City Lodge Hotels	South Africa	Nordic Choice Hotels	Norway
Club Méditerranée	France	Oberoi Hotels	India

Hotel Company	Company Headquarters Location	Hotel Ccompany	Company Headquarters Location
Crescent Hotels and Resorts	USA	Okura-Nikko	Japan
Deutsche Hospitality	Germany	Omni Hotels & Resorts	USA
Dorchester Collection	United Kingdom	One Hotels	Mexico
Dossen International Group	China	Orbis	Poland
Drury Hotels	USA	OYO Hotels and Homes	India
Dusit International	Thailand	Pandox	Sweden
Elegant Hotels Group	Barbados	Prince Hotels and Resorts	Japan
Estelar	Columbia	Pyramid Hotel Group	USA
Extended Stay Hotels	USA	Qingdao Sunmei Group	China
Fattal International Hotels & Resorts	Israel	Red Roof	USA
FIH Regent Group	Taiwan ROC	RIHGA Hotels	South Korea
Four Seasons Hotels and Resorts	Canada	RIU Hotels & Resorts	Spain
Frasers Hospitality	Singapore	RLH Corporation	USA
G6 Hospitality	USA	Rotana	United Arab Emirates
GreenTree Hospitality Group	China	Rydges	Australia
Grupo de Turismo Gaviota	Cuba	Scandic Hotels	Sweden
Grupo Posadas	Mexico	Serena Hotels Group	Kenya
HEI Hotels & Resorts	USA	Shanghai Jinjiang International Hotel Group	China
Highgate	USA	Shangri-La Hotels and Resorts	China
Hilton Worldwide	USA	TFE Hotels	Australia
HK CTS Hotels Co.	China	Tokyo Inn Company	Japan
HNA Hospitality Group	China	Transamerica	Brazil
Hongkong and Shanghai Hotels	China	Travelodge Hotels	United Kingdom
Hotel Okura	Japan	Treebo Hotels	India
Huazhu Group	China	Tsogo Sun	South Africa
Hyatt Hotels Corporation	USA	Tui Group	Germany
Iberostar Hotels & Resorts	Spain	Walt Disney Company	USA
IHG (InterContinental Hotels Group)	United Kingdom	Warwick	France, USA, Lebanon and Viti Levu
Indian Hotels Company Limited	India	Westmont Hospitality Group	USA
InTownSuites	USA	Whitbread	United Kingdom
Jinling Hotels & Resorts	China	Windsor Hotels	Brazil
Jumeirah Group	United Arab Emirates	WoodSpring Hotels	USA
Kempinski	Switzerland	Wyndham Hotel Group	USA
Langham Hospitality Group	Hong Kong	Zhuyou Hotel Group	China

Table 2.5 Key hotel management companies (listed alphabetically)

Key Hotel Management Companies	
AccorHotels	Hotel Equities
Aimbridge Hospitality	Hyatt Hotels Corporation
Benchmark Global Hospitality	IHG (InterContinental Hotel Group)
BTG HomeInns	Interstate Hotels & Resorts
China Lodging Group	Island Hospitality Management
Concord Hospitality Enterprises	Marriott International
Crescent Hotels & Resorts	McKibbon Hospitality
Crestline Hotels & Resorts LLC	ONE Lodging Management
Davidson Hotels & Resorts	OTO Development
Dimension Development	PM Hotel Group
Dossen International Group	Pyramid Hotel Group
Driftwood Hospitality	Real Hospitality Group
GF Hotels & Resorts	Remington Hotels
GreenTree Hospitality Group	Sage Hospitality
HEI Hotels	Sonesta International Hotels Corporation
HHM	TPG Hotel & Resorts
Highgate	Two Roads Hospitality
Hilton	White Lodging Services Corporation

Sources: Weinstein (2019); Hotel Business (2018); Lodging (2018).

Management Companies/Development Companies

Some hotel management companies do not own or license their brand names. Instead, they develop and manage hotels under franchise and management agreements, or as independents. Some companies focus primarily on hotel investment and ownership. Table 2.5 presents Key Third Party Hotel Management Companies. Hotel management companies in the top 25 by sales, number of rooms managed, or number of hotels managed are included.

Future

The hospitality industry has an exciting future. Technology promises many changes, and with those changes we can expect new key players and continuous changes to key organizations. The hospitality industry is one of the largest and most diverse industries in the world. As such there are many key players and organizations. New concepts, cuisines, products, and services are constantly developing. Some of these new elements of the hospitality industry will be through the existing key players and organizations, but many will bring new key players, and organizations.

One key change brought by technology is the introduction of the sharing economy and peer-to-peer accommodations. The sharing economy is changing both the accommodations and the lodging industries. Peer-to-peer accommodations are changing how people travel. Airbnb is the best known of the peer-to-peer accommodations network, but many other companies throughout the world are trying to enter this market. Some of the large hotel companies are starting to offer a form of "home sharing" in their portfolio of brands, and Airbnb is developing its own hotels and resorts to add to its portfolio. How these elements will intertwine is yet to be seen, but promises to bring some changes to the hotel and lodging side of the hospitality industry.

Another player in the sharing economy that will impact restaurants is UberEats, foodpanda and other delivery companies. UberEats is an extension of the ride-sharing company Uber. With UberEats consumers can order food from local restaurants and utilize ride sharing drivers to deliver the food to their home. Many other delivery companies are entering this market. This change in delivery availability has the potential to change the landscape of consumer behavior and convenience in restaurants and foodservice.

Technology

The IoT (Internet of Things) has the potential to change how consumers connect to and consume hospitality products. The opportunity to have a smart device in a home or workplace to select, order, and arrange for the delivery of hospitality products has the potential to change the industry in many directions. Automation and artificial intelligence will change how we deliver, receive, and perceive service. Will the next key players be robots, chats, or a product we have yet to imagine?

Summary

The hospitality industry is vast and diverse. Many key players have contributed to its development. Key players in the travel and tourism sector were instrumental in establishing the first travel agencies, tours information books, and pleasure cruises. The food and beverage industry is perhaps the world's most diverse with many cuisines, cultures, and foods intersecting in communities across the globe. Key players have influenced how food is prepared and served. While the majority of restaurants are independent, some segments such as quick service and fast casual are increasingly branded, with several large prominent corporations. Key players in the hotel and accommodations industry have helped to standardize and upgrade the hotel product, establish franchise and management systems, and develop various hotel markets. Similar to the restaurant industry the hotel and accommodations industry has many independent hotels, yet several large brands dominate the market. The future is bright for the hospitality industry with technology introducing changes to how food and hotel rooms are purchased and consumed. As consumer behavior and technology evolve, the hospitality industry will continue to grow and change, introducing new key players along the way. Perhaps one of the best things about the hospitality industry is many key players are helping to shape foodservice, restaurants, and hotels in each community, region, and market.

References

AccorHotels. (2019), "Our history", *Accorhotels.com*, available at: https://www.accorhotels.group/en/group/who-we-are/our-history (accessed 4 January 2019).

Aman. (2019), "History", *Aman.com*, available at: https://www.aman.com/history (accessed 12 February 2019).

Aramark. (2019), "Company profile", *Aramark.com*, available at: https://aramark.gcs-web.com/company-profile (accessed 12 July 2019).

Banyan Tree. (2019), "Brand story", *Banyanntree.com*, available at: https://www.banyantree.com/en/brand-story (accessed 12 February 2019).

Barr, L. (2018), *Ritz & Escoffier: The Hotelier, the Chef and the Rise of the Leisure Class*, Clarkson Potter Publishers, New York, NY.

Barrows, C. (2009), "A profile of Norman Brinker", in Shea, L. and Roberts, C. (Eds.), *Pioneers of the Hospitality Industry: Lessons from Leaders, Innovators and Visionaries*, International CHRIE, Richmond, VA, pp.139–149.

Barrows, C., Powers, T., and Reynolds, D. (2011), *Introduction to the Hospitality Industry*, John Wiley & Sons, Hoboken, NJ.

Bernstein, C. (1981), *Great Restaurant Innovators*, Lebhar-Friedman Books, New York, NY.

Brendon, P. (1991), *Thomas Cook, 150 Years of Popular Tourism*, Martin Secker & Warburg Ltd, London, UK.

Brinker. (2019), "Our story", *Brinker International*, available at: https://www.brinker.com/company/ourstory.asp (accessed 12 July 2019).

Brizek, M., Partlow, C., and Nguyen, A. (2009), "S. Truett Cathy: From young entrepreneur to a foodservice industry leader", in Shea, L. and Roberts, C. (Eds.), *Pioneers of the Hospitality Industry: Lessons from Leaders, Innovators and Visionaries*, International CHRIE, Richmond, VA, pp.177–185.

Brotherton, B. (2003), *The International Hospitality Industry: Structure Characteristics and Issues*, Jordan Hill, Butterworth-Heinemann, Oxford, UK.

Bruce, D. (2010), "Baedeker: The perceived 'inventor' of the formal guidebook – a Bible for travelers in the 19th century", in Butler, P. and Russel, R. (Eds.), *Giants of Tourism*, CAB International, Oxfordshire, UK.

Chathoth, P. and Chon, K.S. (2009), "Rai Bahadur Mohan Singh Oberoi: Father of the Indian hotel industry", in Shea, L. and Roberts, C. (Eds.), *Pioneers of the Hospitality Industry: Lessons from Leaders, Innovators and Visionaries*, International CHRIE, Richmond, VA, pp.99–107.

Chipotle. (2019), "Chipotle opens 2,500th restaurant, highlighting continued growth", *Chipotle Mexican Grill News Release,* available at: https://ir.chipotle.com/2019-02-08-Chipotle-Opens-2-500th-Restaurant-Highlighting-Continued-Growth (accessed 11 July 2020).

Club Med. (2019), "About Club Med", *ClubMed.com*, available at: http://www.clubmed.com.au/cm/all-inclusive-vacations-all-inclusive-holidays-br-by-club-med-about-club-med_p-14-l-AE-pa-A_PROPOS_DE_CLUB_MED-ac-at.html (accessed 4 January 2019).

Disney. (2019), *Disney Parks, Experiences and Products Fact Sheet*, available at: https://dpep.disney.com/wp-content/uploads/2019/02/fact_sheet_disney_parks_experiences_and_products_2019_Q1.pdf (accessed 25 February 2019).

Flandrin, J.L. and Montanari, M. (1999), *A Culinary History of Food*, Columbia University Press, New York, NY.

Forbes. (2018), "The world's largest public companies: Restaurants", *Forbes*, available at: https://www.forbes.com/global2000/list/#industry:Restaurants (accessed 15 October 2018).

Forte, C. (1987), *Forte: The Autobiography of Charles Forte*, Pan Books, London, UK.

Four Seasons. (2019), "About us: Four Seasons hotels and resorts", *Fourseasons.com*, available at: http://www.fourseasons.com/about_four_seasons/ (accessed 4 January 2019).

Franchise Times. (2019), "Franchise Times Top 200", *Franchise Times*, available at: http://www.franchisetimes.com/Top200 (accessed 4 January 2019).

Fried, S. (2010), *Appetite for America: How Visionary Businessman Fred Harvey Built an Empire that Civilized the West*, Bantam, New York, NY.

Go, F. and Pine, R. (1995), *Globalization Strategy in the Hotel Industry*, Routledge, London, UK.

Grace, M. (2011), "Albert Ballin – Inventor and father of the pleasure cruise", *Cruise Line History*, available at: https://www.cruiselinehistory.com/albert-ballin-inventor-and-father-of-the-pleasure-cruise/ (accessed 11 July 2020).

Grimes, W. (2018), "Paul Bocuse, celebrated French Chef, dies at 91", *New York Times*, available at: https://www.nytimes.com/2018/01/20/obituaries/paul-bocuse-dead.html (accessed 11 July 2020).

Hamilton, J. (2005), *Thomas Cook, The Holiday Maker*, Sutton Publishing, Gloucestershire, UK.

Hilton, C. (1957), *Be My Guest*, Simon & Schuster, New York, NY.

Hotel Business. (2018), "2018 management companies annual ranking", *Hotel Business*, available at: https://togo.hotelbusiness.com/article/2018-management-companies-annual-ranking/ (accessed 11 January 2019).

IHG. (2019), "Our history", *IHG.com*, available at: https://www.ihgplc.com/about-us/our-history (accessed 5 January 2019).

Irvin, D. (2018, 5 March), "Top restaurant group's that dominate the world's dining", available at: https://www.msn.com/en-us/foodanddrink/foodnews/top-restaurant-groups-that-dominate-the-worlds-dining/(accessed 4 December 2018).

Jakle, J., Sculle, K., and Rogers, J. (1996), *The Motel in America*, The Johns Hopkins University Press, Baltimore, MD.

Karkaria, B. (2003), *Dare to Dream: The Life of M.S.Oberoi*, Penguin Books, Australia.

Lattin, G., Lattin, T., and Lattin, J. (2014), *The Lodging and Foodservice Industry*, American Hotel & Lodging Association Educational Institute, Lansing, MI.

Lang, J. (ed.) (1988), *Larousse Gastronomique*, Crown Publishers, New York, NY.

Leading Hotels of the World. (2019, June), "History of Leading Hotels of the World", *LHW.com*, available at: https://www.lhw.com/corporate/company-history (accessed 20 June 2019).

Lodging. (2018), "Guide to management companies", *Lodging*, Vol.43, No.8, pp.39–66.

Margolies, J. (1995), *Home Away from Home: Motels in America*, Bulfinch Press, Boston, MA.

Mariani, J. (1991), *America Eats Out*, William Morrow and Company, Inc., New York, NY.

Marriott. (2019), "About Marriott International", *Marriott.com*, available at: https://www.marriott.com/marriott/aboutmarriott.mi (accessed 6 February 2019).

Marriott, J.W. Jr., and Brown, K.A. (2013), *Without Reservations: How a Family Root Beer Stand Grew into a Global Hotel Company*, Diversion Books: New York, NY.

McDonald's. (2019), "Our history, McDonald's", *Mcdonalds.com*, available at: http://www.mcdonalds.com/us/en/our_story/our_history.html (accessed 4 January 2019).

McGrath, M. (2018), "The largest restaurant companies in the world 2018: McDonald's and Starbucks at top of food chain", *Forbes.com*, available at: https://www.forbes.com/sites/maggiemcgrath/2018/06/06/the-largest-restaurant-companies-in-the-world-2018-mcdonalds-and-starbucks-at-top-of-food-chain/ (accessed 4 December 2018).

Mill, R. (2012), *Resorts Management and Operation*, John Wiley & Sons, Hoboken, NJ.

Nation's Restaurant News. (2018a, 14 November), "2018 International 25: Meet the largest foreign restaurant chains", *Nation's Restaurant News*, available at: https://www.nrn.com/data-research/2018-international-25-meet-largest-foreign-restaurant-chains (accessed 28 November 2018).

Nation's Restaurant News. (2018b, 11 June), "2018 Top 200", *Nation's Restaurant News*, available at: https://www.nrn.com/2018top200 (accessed 4 December 2018).

Ngan, P. (2018, June 25), "Legendary Hotelier Thanpuying Chanut Piyaoui honoured with SHTM lifetime achievement award", *The Hong Kong Polytechnic University*, available at: https://www.polyu.edu.hk/web/en/media/media_releases/index_id_6553.html (accessed 1 February 2019).

Nusair, K. and Parsa, H. (2009), "Contributions of the White Castle and Ingram family to the quick service industry", in Shea, L. and Roberts, C. (Eds.), *Pioneers of the Hospitality Industry: Lessons from Leaders, Innovators and Visionaries*, International CHRIE, Richmond, VA, pp.151–164.

Oberoi. (2019), "The Oberoi Group profile," available at: https://www.oberoihotels.com/about-us/profile (accessed 18 February 2019).

Oches, S. (2018), "The QSR 50, 2008-2018", *QSR Magazine*, available at: https://www.qsrmagazine.com/reports/2018-qsr-50 (accessed 18 February 2019).

O'Halloran, R. (2009), "Kemmons Wilson: An American original", in Shea, L. and Roberts, C. (Eds.), *Pioneers of the Hospitality Industry: Lessons from Leaders, Innovators and Visionaries*, International CHRIE, Richmond, VA, pp.61–84.

Perman, S. (2009), *In-N-Out Burger: A Behind the Counter Look at the Fast-Food Chain That Breaks All the Rules*, Harper, New York, NY.

Pillsbury, R. (1990), *From Boarding House to Bistro: The American Restaurant, Then and Now*, Unwin Hyman, Inc., Boston, MA.

Potter, J. (1996), *A Room with a World View: 50 Years of Intercontinental Hotels and Its People*, Weidenfeld & Nicholson, London, UK.

Roberts, C., Shea, L., and Sasso, S. (2009), "Ray Kroc: A visionary CEO who reshaped an industry", in Shea, L. and Roberts, C. (Eds.), *Pioneers of the Hospitality Industry: Lessons from Leaders, Innovators and Visionaries*, International CHRIE, Richmond, VA, pp.129–137.

Rosen, E. (2018, May 2), "China's newest luxury resort Atlantis Sanya opens on Hainan Island", *Forbes*, available at: https://www.forbes.com/sites/ericrosen/2018/05/02/chinas-newest-luxury-resort-atlantis-sanya-opens-on-hainan-island/#2b1030eb6da0 (accessed 4 February 2019).

Shani, A. and Logan, R. (2010), "Walt Disney's world of entertainment attractions", in Butler, R. and Russell, R. (Eds.), *Giants of Tourism*, CABI, Oxfordshire, UK, pp.155–169.

Sharpe, I. (2009), *Four Seasons: The Story of a Business Philosophy*, Penguin Group, New York, NY.

Sido, V., Morille, S., Felix-Frazao, M., and Sol, A. (Eds.) (2007), *Accor: Reaching for the Impossible 1967–2007*, available at: http://www.accorhotels-group.com/uploads/static/livreaccor/uk/appli.htm (accessed 4 January 2019).

Sile, E. (2018, January 25), "The legendary founder of Aman Resorts discusses his ambitious projects and why age 84 is no time to take a break", *Departures*, available at: https://www.departures.com/travel/aman-resorts-founder-adrian-zecha-azerai-hotels (accessed 4 February 2019).

Slattery, P. (2012), *The Economic Ascent of the Hotel Business*, Goodfellow Publishers, Oxford, UK.

Smith, A. (2011), *Eating History: Turning Points in the Making of American Cuisine*, Columbia University Press, New York, NY.

Sodexo. (2019), "About Us", *Sodexo.com*, available at: https://us.sodexo.com/about-us/overview.html (accessed 12 July 2019).

Stringam, B. and Partlow, C. (2016), *A Profile of the Hospitality Industry*, Business Expert Press, New York, NY.

Stutts, A. and Wortman, J. (2006), *Hotel and Lodging Management*, John Wiley & Sons, Hoboken, NJ.

Summers, B. (2007), *Hospitality Goes Global*, Cornell Hotel Society, Ithaca, NY.

Thomas Cook. (2019), "About Thomas Cook", available at: https://www.thomascook.com/about-us/ (accessed 12 February 2019).

Touyalai, H. (2018), "World's largest hotels 2018: Marriott dominates, Hyatt & Accor rise", *Forbes.com*. available at: https://www.forbes.com/sites/halahtouryalai/2018/06/06/worlds-biggest-hotels-2018 (accessed 4 December 2018).

Tsogo. (2019), "Tsogo Sun corporate profile", *Tsogosunhotels.com*, available at: https://www.tsogosun.com/about-us (accessed 4 January 2019).

Turkel, S. (2009), *Great American Hoteliers. Pioneers of the Hotel Industry*, Authorhouse, Bloomington, IN

Vallen, J. and Vallen G. (2018), *Check-in, Check-out*, Pearson, Upper Saddle River, NJ.

Walker, J.R. (2013), *Introduction to Hospitality Management*, Pearson, Upper Saddle River, NJ.

Weinstein, J. (2019), "Hotels 325", available at: http://cdn.coverstand.com/18556/602570/a8b471b11fbebe-541238139974131341504fcb25.pdf (accessed 7 August 2019).

Wendy's. (2020). Dave Thomas' Legacy. Wendys.com, available at: https://www.wendys.com/daves-legacy (accessed 20 January 2020).

Whitten, S. (2017), "Steve Ells wanted to open a fine-dining restaurant, instead he built a burrito empire", *CNBC*, available at: https://www.cnbc.com/2017/11/29/how-steve-ells-built-chipotle-mexican-grill-into-a-burrito-empire.html (accessed 25 February 2019).

Wilson, K. and Kerr, R. (1996), *Half Luck and Half Brains: The Kemmons Wilson, Holiday Inn Story*, Hambleton-Hill Publishing, Nashville, TN.

3

THE ROLE OF INTERNATIONALIZATION IN HOSPITALITY MANAGEMENT

Previous Trends and New Directions

Markus Schuckert

Introduction

The hospitality industry can be seen as a synonym for internationalization in a highly dynamic and competitive industry environment (Brookes et al., 2011). This internationalization took off when the central European paradigm of hospitality was standardized; the mass-market was proven by American hospitality pioneers; and the globalizing effects of trade, travel, and tourism turned into the drivers for hotel companies, and the hospitality business to become international (Dwyer, 2015). This international growth can be divided into two aspects as Brookes and Becket (2011) put it: (1) internationalization at home in a domestic market environment and (2) internationalization abroad and across borders. The first aspect is about the push of domestic hospitality providers by its international customers to provide hospitality services for a global base of guests. The second aspect is the push by owners and shareholders to go for international growth as well as a pull by international demand abroad to expand businesses and brands beyond domestic operations.

Consequently, this book chapter focuses on the role of academic research regarding the topic of international hospitality management by analyzing published journal articles and research reports. It takes up the discussion from Litteljohn (1997) about the internationalization in hotels with its current aspects and developments (p. 187). Considering the last 24 years, since 1996, in the development of the hospitality business, researchers and practitioners have witnessed a tremendous shift in the traditions, procedures, dynamics, and functionality of this industry (Zervas et al., 2017). This includes the expansion from Western markets (Europe and North America) into the developing Eastern markets (e.g., Thailand, Indonesia, China, and India), structural corrections and strategic moves by merger and acquisitions (e.g., Marriott and Starwood), as well as the entrance of new business formulas and disruptors of the traditional hospitality business from the sharing economy (e.g., Airbnb or Tujia). Subsequently, this chapter goes after the questions of (1) what have been the dominating topics in scientific discussion regarding international hospitality management from 1996 to 2019, and (2) which topics indicate existing gaps, beginning contemporary trends and future new directions?

The objectives of this chapter are clearly to close the gap of the last 24 years as well as to continue writing and documenting the story of research in the context of international hospitality management. Methodologically, the book chapter is based on a contemporary application of constructivist-oriented literature review, sourcing from a data mining in electronic online libraries a content analysis of 74 related articles in the discussion and projection of further research based on Litteljohn (1997)

Methodology

This systematic review of relevant literature follows a constructivist tradition. In opposition to narrative literature reviews, a systematic approach places specific questions in the center of inquiry and follows a generalizable and replicable structure, guiding the researcher in funneling and integrating relevant results (Briner and Walshe, 2014). In the field of tourism and hospitality, systematic literature reviews support the research community into new topical areas or reflect intermediately or conclusively on past research activities like Kwok et al. (2017), Fong et al. (2016), Schuckert et al. (2015), Law et al. (2014), Leung et al. (2013), and Line and Runyan (2012).

According to the structure of Kwok et al. (2017), the subject of research has been identified as internationally renowned hospitality, tourism, and service management journals, exceeding the list of Gursoy and Sandstrom (2016). As a result, the literature research is based on the following journals: *Cornell Hospitality Quarterly, International Journal of Contemporary Hospitality Management, International Journal of Hospitality Management, International Journal of Hospitality Marketing and Management*, and *Hospitality and Society* for the domain of hospitality. Journals merging the domain of hospitality and tourism are represented by the *International Journal of Culture, Tourism, Hospitality Research, International Journal of Hospitality and Tourism Administration*, and the *Journal of Hospitality and Tourism Research*. The *Service Industries Journal* represents broader service industry studies. *Annals of Tourism Research, Current Issues in Tourism, European Journal of Tourism Research, Journal of Sustainable Tourism, Journal of Travel Research, Journal of Travel & Tourism Marketing, Tourism Economics, Tourism Management, Tourism Management Perspectives, Tourism Recreation Research, Tourism Review*, and *Tourism* are journals published studies in tourism.

The methodology for data collection and data analysis adopts Schuckert et al. (2015). Data collection was performed between January and February 2019 and a repeated, confirmatory review took place in May and June 2019, accessing the three largest and most common online databases EBSCOHOST, Google Scholar, and Scopus online. Cross citations have been used to follow back already identified relevant references and in order to discover additional relevant sources. As relevant keywords for the keyword search, the terms "internationalization" in American English as well as in British English spelling, "hotel," "hospitality," and "international" have been identified. 74 journal articles published between 1996 and 2019 have been identified as relevant after three cycles of data collection and subsequent screening. The identification process went through an initial screening of the headline, the keywords given by the author, and an analysis of the abstract. Passing this identification process, relevant publications have been reviewed, analyzed and discussed in-depth, and coded accordingly. The documentation of the intermediate selection results as well as the final list of articles has been cross-checked by an experienced, associated researcher to minimize a potential bias by the author.

The following analyses have been performed: descriptive analysis and topical review, management context used in current literature, synthesizing themes, thematic frameworks, and future research opportunities. The current results have been compared and discussed with the findings of Litteljohn (1997), and a summary of suggested directions for further research has been developed based on the results of this study.

Analysis and Results

Published between 1996 and June of 2019, 74 studies have been identified. Regarding the publications per year over the analyzed outlets, the analysis shows fluctuations between 1996 and 2019 (see Figure 3.1). It seems that the topic of internationalization regarding the hospitality industry has been peaking roughly every third year, while since 2014 the industry gained currently additional attention to global events such as the acquisition of Starwood by Marriott or the sharp rise of Airbnb.

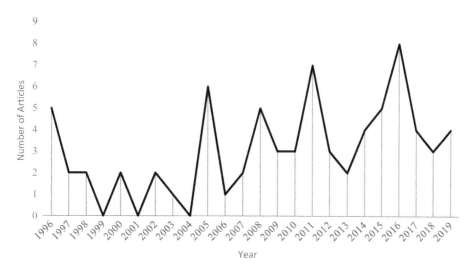

Figure 3.1   Trends of publications of review-related articles.

Regarding the quantity per journal, 21 journals have been analyzed. Out of the 21 journals, 5 (24%) have a pure hospitality focus, 3 (14%) journals cater to both domains, tourism and hospitality, while 12 (57%) journals are tourism centric. One journal is in the wider service industry context. From the 74 as relevant identified papers, 37 (50%) of the relevant publications have been published in pure hospitality journals, followed by 30 (41%) in tourism-centric outlets. Four (5%) of the publications come from the *Service Industries Journal* and three (4%) from the mixed-domains journals. Table 3.1 illustrates the distribution of outlets. Results show that the focus is on internationally renowned, high-impact outlets. Tourism-centric journals as well as mixed mode or low-impact outlets each publish only a fraction of the overall volume. The top three hospitality journals account for 35 (47%) of the relevant publications.

After performing the content analysis of the 74 publications and aggregation of the related codes, 12 topical clusters regarding the internationalization of hospitality management have been found. The clusters and the related number of publications are listed in Table 3.2.

The cluster *Mode of Expansion Market Entry* count is 17 (23%) and the most of the overall number of publications. Research in this area focuses on strategies and entry modes into foreign markets or globally (Andreu et al., 2017; García de Soto-Camacho and Vargas-Sánchez, 2015; Martorell et al., 2013; León-Darder et al. 2011; Rodríguez, 2002; Villar et al., 2012), the expansion of brands across borders or in a global context is also a focus (Dev et al., 2007; Han and Hyun, 2014), as is on location strategies (Johnson and Vanetti, 2005; Puciato, 2016; Marco-Lajara et al., 2017), as well as internationalization by franchising in particular (Alon et al., 2012; Dev et al., 2002; Klonowski et al., 2008; Lee, 2008a; Lee et al., 2018; Miller, 2008).

International Human Resources was identified as the second most active cluster with 11 contributions (15%). Here, skills and training demands and procedures for internationalization are a focus (Burgess, 1996; Jones and McCleary, 2005; Kontogeorgopoulos, 1998; Kriegl 2000; Nickson, 1997; Plog and Sturman, 2005; Velo and Mittaz, 2006), as are changes and challenges in hotel management contracts (Deroos, 2010; Gannon et al., 2010), as well as the challenges of human resource management with internationalization (Chen et al., 2016; Enz, 2009).

The *Operation and Performance* of hotels in an international context accounts for eight (11%) contributions. Internationalization and hotel performance (Assaf et al., 2016, Brida et al., 2016;

Table 3.1 Titles of journals, related domain, and numbers (*n*) of publications

Journal	Domain	*n*
Cornell Hospitality Quarterly	Hospitality	14
Int'l Journal of Contemporary Hospitality Management	Hospitality	12
International Journal of Hospitality Management	Hospitality	9
Tourism Management	Tourism	6
Service Industries Journal	Service	4
Tourism Economics	Tourism	4
Tourism Review	Tourism	3
Annals of Tourism Research	Tourism	2
Journal of Travel and Tourism Marketing	Tourism	2
Current Issues in Tourism	Tourism	2
European Journal of Tourism Research	Tourism	2
Journal of Sustainable Tourism	Tourism	2
Tourism	Tourism	2
Tourism Management Perspectives	Tourism	2
Tourism Recreation Research	Tourism	2
Hospitality & Society	Hospitality	1
Int'l Journal of Culture, Tourism, and Hospitality Research	Hospitality/Tourism	1
Int'l Journal of Hospitality and Tourism Administration	Hospitality/Tourism	1
Journal of Hospitality & Tourism Research	Hospitality/Tourism	1
Journal of Hospitality Marketing and Management	Hospitality	1
Journal of Travel Research	Tourism	1
Sum		**74**

Table 3.2 Overview topical clusters and related numbers (*n*)

Topical cluster	*n*
Mode of Expansion and Market Entry	17
International Human Resources	11
Hotel Operation and Performance in an international context	8
Financial Performance in an international context	7
Growing from Domestic to International	6
Internationalization of the Industry in general	6
Internationalization: West to East	6
Sustainability and Environmental Impact	4
International Strategic Management	3
Demand Side of Internationalization	2
International Marketing Management	2
Internationalization: East to West	2
Sum	**74**

Lee et al., 2014; Sainaghi, 2010; Woo et al., 2019) as well as efficiency indicators and management methods (Golembski, 2007; Parte-Esteban and Alberca-Oliver, 2015; Rushmore and Goldhoff, 1997) have been of interest. *Financial performance in an international context* attracted the attention of seven (9%) contributors, ranging from the influence of the firm on financial characteristics

(Devesa et al., 2009; Menicucci, 2018; Parte-Esteban and Ferrer García, 2014), the growth of accounting (Smeral, 2009) and transaction costs (Lee et al., 2011), as well as the return of investment regarding internationalization (Lee et al., 2014; Hua and Upneja, 2011).

The topic of *Internationalization of the Industry* in general attracted six contributions (8%) by analyzing the internationalization of the hotel industry by the sector (Alexander and Lockwood, 1996), on the regional level (Spain: Brida et al., 2015; China: Gu et al., 2012; Europe: Peters and Frehse, 2005), from an entrepreneurial point of view (de Correia et al., 2019), or from a single-brand perspective (Hilton International: Strand, 1996).

Going from Domestic to International accounts for six papers (8%), focusing on selected questions of going international by leaving the domestic base from a restaurant perspective (Lee et al., 2016), from a hotel perspective (Gross and Huang, 2011; Rogerson, 2016), or regarding for instance knowledge transfer (García-Almeida and Yu, 2015), family involvement (Andreu et al., 2019), or reasons for going international (Rodtook and Altinay, 2013).

The internationalization and expansion from Western hotel companies into European and/or Asian markets attracted six papers 8%, while the focus on China is the most important (Harrison et al., 2005; Kivela and Leung, 2005; Niñerola et al., 2016). Lee (2008b) compares Asian versus European expansion from a US perspective, while McVey and King (2000) analyze India. Czyzewska and Roper (2017) analyze the steps of Hilton in the London market. In the opposite direction, expanding from the Eastern Hemisphere into Western markets (*Internationalization: East to West*) has drawn attention from Gross et al. (2017) and Lam et al. (2015). These two contributions account for 3%. The topic of *Sustainability and Environmental Impact* accounts for four different contributions (5%). De Grosbois and Fennell (2011) look into the carbon footprint of global hotel companies and Bohdanowicz et al. (2011) into the business we care! program. The process of sustainability reporting is analyzed by Guix et al. (2018), while Spenceley (2019) looks into the sustainable tourism certification process of the African hotel industry.

Hwang and Chang (2003), Olsen and Roper (1998), as well as Jansen-Verbeke (1996) analyze issues of strategic management within an international hospitality context (3; 4%). The clusters of *Demand Side of Internationalization* and *International Marketing Management* account for two papers (3%) each. However, the cluster of international marketing management has a strong technological bias with its two papers focusing on e-marketing on the new upcoming Internet in 1996 by Harris, as well as email marketing by international hotel chains, 14 years later by O'Connor (2008). The *Demand Side of Internationalization* is research by the authors de la Peña et al. (2016) and Tirados (2011).

Of the 74 papers, 23 (31%) take the perspective of the value chain with the segments of human resources, finance, marketing, and strategic management. Fourteen contributions (19%) take operations, performance, and sustainability into account. However, 50% of the papers (37) focus on growth and expansion within the context of international hospitality.

Implications and Further Research

The research is published across the available journals, creating a fragmented overview on the topic of international development and hospitality management, when most of the publications are with the top hospitality journals. Probably a wider range of research output would contribute to the topic but cannot be identified based on nonmatching or not indicated keywords.

The research results indicate that most publications take a supply-side perspective along the value chain of hotel management or are output-oriented, looking into selected areas like operations, performance, and sustainability. Most of the research questions are influenced by the philosophy of economic growth, where increasing and extending the capacity abroad prevails. The detected focus of past research can be described as rather narrow and leaves a lot of space for further research.

- The aspects of international growth regarding strategic management and new business models which resonated with diversity of markets and economies remain an important research area. This results from an increasing globalization, growing competition, and new market entrants into the traditional accommodation sector as well as from dynamics coming from non-traditional entrants.

- Airbnb and other accommodation suppliers are disrupting the traditional hospitality formula. Topics around internationalization and sharing economy regarding non-traditional hospitality formulas seem under-researched. Different business models do exist in Western countries, India, or China, where comparative studies may benefit the industry. Topics around trust, reputation, and reviews of such foreign platforms or experiences with competition between international hospitality companies and its sharing economy competitors could contribute as well.

- The aspects of internationalization regarding new information and communication technologies (ICT) and their impact on the hospitality industry were not visible in the pre-1997 and 1997 stage. However, since the last two decades, technology has made huge advances. Reflecting that, different online ecosystems, social media, chat applications, or mobile payment solutions, as well as automatization and robots indicate further research possibilities.

- From a value chain perspective, the aspects of intercultural management and international human relations management are important because the task and requirements for international talents are growing as well as the increasing demand. Generation Y and generation Z are new cohorts of employees entering and sharpening the industry. In addition, aspects of internationalization and organizational behavior, motivation, positive psychology, and performance seem underrepresented in an international context.

- Since the opening of China and the increasing demand by Chinese outbound tourism, Chinese hospitality companies are expanding beyond the domestic territory of the mainland, Hong Kong, and Macau. Here, comparative studies between the mode and management of expansion, the preferred business models, and diverse ownership and operation models can be of interest as well as questions about experiences with the market entry in foreign markets, the coping with cultural differences, as well as studies on management and working culture.

- Regarding the aspects of an experience economy, no papers have been retrieved targeting topics like the development of new market segments, market gaps in niche markets, as well as demand integration on the international level. It seems that related studies may focus on single source markets. Perhaps researchers do not regard their research as influential regarding international growth.

- Similar with experiences, questions regarding the shift towards value creation, customer co-creation, and customer experiences are of increasing importance not only in the hospitality industry.

- In terms of revenue management and related topics, it has been difficult for the current study to identify related papers. This may indicate a need for further studies regarding the international perspectives on revenue management and value drivers in hotels and restaurants. A further array of potential topics and the contribution of F&B outlets to the overall revenue are the duration of hotels across markets and across hotel categories.

- Further keywords may indicate a need for future research regarding international merger and acquisition case studies, a review of experiences regarding international operations and growth, issues on legal and organizational aspects in international hospitality, as well as sustainability and innovation. Especially the fields of corporate social responsibility (CSR), CSR reporting, the implementation and acceptance of sustainability initiatives, as well as coping with different sustainability standards lack attention.

Pre 1997	1997	2019
Internationalization perceived as an explicit organizational feature	Internationalization an explicit feature in organizations	Internationalization an explicit feature in stategy and business model
Value created through strong, vertical links with chosen suppliers	Value added through flexible links with wide numbers of suppliers	Value creation based on customer co-creation processes and regional sourcing
Economies of scale (vertical and horizontal)	Economies of scope and scale	Economies of scope, scale and density
Growth strategies use standardized product/service specfications, altered as little as possible	Growth strategies targeted at international and local markets, susceptible to adaptation	Global growth targeted, diagonal, expansion with outbound toursim flow
International expansion features brands, franchising, management contracts	Expansion through wider variety of means including strategic alliances, joint ventures, loose confederations	Expansion adds mergers and aquisitions as well as new business models from the sharing economy; development towards light assets
Operations focus	Knowledge focus	Technology focus
Internal centre-periphery relationships important in determining management method	Internal and local networks important; greater communication within and across the organization	Density and relevance of networks becomes important, multi-channel
Ethnocentric markets and change agents given priority, often following markets	Market gaps identified	Market gaps and nisches identified
Pricing and competitive focus	New services development and pricing focus	Experience and revenue focus
Markets segmented by purpose, geography, culture	Supersegmentation adds multi-variate groupings to those formerly used	Segmentation adds lifestyle segmentation, lifetime customer value, loyality and key opinion leadership

Figure 3.2 Transcription and extension from 1997 to 2019 based on Litteljohn (1997, p. 191).

The results of this literature review extend Litteljohn's (1997) emphasis on international hospitality. He compared "Old emphasis" versus "New emphasis" (p. 191). Figure 3.2 extends this comparison by transcribing the results of the analysis between 1996 and 2019 into a contemporary view regarding international hospitality management. For this purpose, the column of "Old emphasis" has been designated as "Pre 1997" because it is based on research prior to the publication date of 1997. The column of "New emphasis" has been correlated with "1997" as a result of Litteljohn's analysis. The column of "Post 1997" is the contemporary and consecutive extrapolation of the former columns based on the current literature review.

Conclusion

By reviewing and analyzing the content of 74 related contributions, this book chapter contributes with its analysis and recommendations to the further development of research in the field of international hospitality management and its body of literature. Spanning 24 years and summarizing the document and published research from 1996 to 2019, this contribution is able to advance Litteljohn's (1997) analysis and close the gap since the work has been published.

With the benefits of bibliometric studies and literature reviews, some limitations are coming with this methodical approach chosen, too (Schuckert et al., 2015). Even if the topic of international hospitality management and internationalization of the industry seems relatively broad, the retrieved number of 74 papers can be regarded as a small number for analysis and classification. Regarding the search algorithm, focusing on title, abstract, and keywords may lead to a small number of results if articles focus on the subject of internationalization, but do not use related keywords used in the search. In addition, this analysis focuses on (a) international journals published in English as well as (b) a justified but still selected number of journals from the domains service hospitality and tourism. This automatically limits the number of results regarding other languages as well as the possibility of being published in other outlets than the chosen one. Especially the topic of internationalization from the East to the West with a strong emphasis on China may indicate, that for further studies the examination of articles published in Chinese might be of importance and relevance.

References

Alexander, N. and Lockwood, A. (1996), "Internationalisation: A comparison of the hotel and retail sectors", *Service Industries Journal*, Vol.16, No.4, pp.458–473.

Alon, I., Ni, L., and Wang, Y. (2012), "Examining the determinants of hotel chain expansion through international franchising", *International Journal of Hospitality Management*, Vol.31, No.2, pp.379–386.

Andreu, R., Claver-Cortés, E., Quer, D., and Rienda, L. (2019), "Family involvement and Spanish hotel chains' entry modes abroad", *Current Issues in Tourism*, pp.1–19. doi: 10.1080/13683500.2019.1.

Andreu, R., Claver, E., and Quer, D. (2017), "Foreign market entry mode choice of hotel companies: Determining factors", *International Journal of Hospitality Management*, Vol.62, pp.111–119.

Assaf, A.G., Josiassen, A., and Oh, H. (2016), "Internationalization and hotel performance: The missing pieces", *Tourism Economics*, Vol.22, No.3, pp.572–592.

Bohdanowicz, P., Zientara, P., and Novotna, E. (2011), "International hotel chains and environmental protection: An analysis of Hilton's we care! Programme", *Journal of Sustainable Tourism*, Vol.19, No.7, pp.797–816.

Brida, J.G., Driha, O.M., Ramón-Rodríguez, A.B., and Scuderi, R. (2015), "Dynamics of internationalisation of the hotel industry: The case of Spain", *International Journal of Contemporary Hospitality Management*, Vol.27, No.5, pp.1024–1047.

Brida, J.G., Driha, O., Ramón-Rodriguez, A.B., and Such-Devesa, M.J. (2016), "The inverted-U relationship between the degree of internationalization and the performance: The case of Spanish hotel chains", *Tourism Management Perspectives*, Vol.17, pp.72–81.

Briner, R.B. and Walshe, N.D. (2014), "From passively received wisdom to actively constructed knowledge: Teaching systematic review skills as a foundation of evidence-based management", *Academy of Management Learning & Education*, Vol.13, No.3, pp.415–432.

Brookes, M., Altinay, L., and Gannon, J. (2011), "Editorial: Internationalization of the hospitality industry", *International Journal of Contemporary Hospitality Management*, Vol.23, No.2, pp.147–274.

Brookes, M. and Becket, N. (2011), "Internationalising hospitality management degree programmes", *International Journal of Contemporary Hospitality Management*, Vol.23, No.2, pp.241–260.

Burgess, C.L. (1996), "A profile of the hotel financial controller in the United Kingdom, United States and Hong Kong", *International Journal of Hospitality Management*, Vol.15, No.1, pp.19–28.

Chen, C.M., Chiu, H.H., and Hsu, C.L. (2016), "How does demand uncertainty affect food and beverage capacity in the hotel industry?", *Current Issues in Tourism*, Vol.19, No.13, pp.1288–1294.

Czyzewska, B. and Roper, A. (2017), "A foreign hotel in London – The history of Hilton's negotiation of legitimacy in the swinging sixties", *Hospitality & Society*, Vol.7, No.3, pp.219–244.

De Correia, R.J., Lengler, J., and Mohsin, A. (2019), "Entrepreneurial approaches to the internationalisation of Portugal's hotel industry", *International Journal of Contemporary Hospitality Management*, Vol.31, No.3, pp.1141–1165.

De Grosbois, D. and Fennell, D. (2011), "Carbon footprint of the global hotel companies: Comparison of methodologies and results", *Tourism Recreation Research*, Vol.36, No.3, pp.231–245.

De la Peña, M.R., Núñez-Serrano, J.A., Turrión, J., and Velázquez, F.J. (2016), "Are innovations relevant for consumers in the hospitality industry? A hedonic approach for Cuban hotels", *Tourism Management*, Vol.55, pp.184–196.

Deroos, J.A. (2010), "Hotel management contracts – Past and present", *Cornell Hospitality Quarterly*, Vol.51, No.1, pp.68–80.

Dev, C.S., Brown, J.R., and Zhou, K.Z. (2007), "Global brand expansion: How to select a market entry strategy", *Cornell Hotel and Restaurant Administration Quarterly*, Vol.48, No.1, pp.13–27.

Dev, C.S., Erramilli, M.K., and Agarwal, S. (2002), "Brands across borders: Determining factors in choosing franchising or management contracts for entering international markets", *Cornell Hotel and Restaurant Administration Quarterly*, Vol.43, No.6, pp.91–104.

Devesa, M.J.S., Esteban, L.P., and Martínez, A.G. (2009), "The financial structure of the Spanish hotel industry: Evidence from cluster analysis", *Tourism Economics*, Vol.15, No.1, pp.121–138.

Dwyer, L. (2015), "Globalization of tourism: Drivers and outcomes", *Tourism Recreation Research*, Vol.40, No.3, pp.326–339.

Enz, C.A. (2009), "Human resource management: A troubling issue for the global hotel industry", *Cornell Hospitality Quarterly*, Vol.50, No.4, pp.578–583.

Fong, L.H.N., Law, R., Tang, C.M.F., and Yap, M.H.T. (2016), "Experimental research in hospitality and tourism: A critical review", *International Journal of Contemporary Hospitality Management*, Vol.28, No.2, pp.246–266.

Gannon, J., Roper, A., and Doherty, L. (2010), "The impact of hotel management contracting on IHRM practices: Understanding the bricks and brains split", *International Journal of Contemporary Hospitality Management*, Vol.22, No.5, pp.638–658.

García de Soto-Camacho, E., and Vargas-Sánchez, A. (2015), "Choice of entry mode, strategic flexibility and performance of international strategy in hotel chains: An approach based on real options", *European Journal of Tourism Research*, Vol.9, pp.92–114.

García-Almeida, D.J., and Yu, L. (2015), "Knowledge transfer in hotel firms: Determinants of success in international expansion", *International Journal of Hospitality & Tourism Administration*, Vol.16, No.1, pp.16–39.

Golembski, G. (2007), "The impact of modern management methods on hotel operational performance", *Tourism Review*, Vol.62, No.2, pp.31–36.

González Tirados, R.M. (2011), "Half a century of mass tourism: Evolution and expectations", *Service Industries Journal*, Vol.31, No.10, pp.1589–1601.

Gross, M.J. and Huang, S. (2011), "Exploring the internationalisation prospects of a Chinese domestic hotel firm", *International Journal of Contemporary Hospitality Management*, Vol.23, No.2, pp.261–274.

Gross, M.J., Huang, S., and Ding, Y. (2017), "Chinese hotel firm internationalisation: Jin Jiang's joint venture acquisition", *International Journal of Contemporary Hospitality Management*, Vol.29, No.11, pp.2730–2750.

Gu, H., Ryan, C., and Yu, L. (2012), "The changing structure of the Chinese hotel industry: 1980–2012", *Tourism Management Perspectives*, Vol.4, pp.56–63.

Guix, M., Bonilla-Priego, M.J., and Font, X. (2018), "The process of sustainability reporting in international hotel groups: An analysis of stakeholder inclusiveness, materiality and responsiveness", *Journal of Sustainable Tourism*, Vol.26, No.7, pp.1063–1084.

Gursoy, D. and Sandstrom, J.K. (2016), "An updated ranking of hospitality and tourism journals", *Journal of Hospitality & Tourism Research*, Vol.40, No.1, pp.3–18.

Han, H. and Hyun, S.S. (2014), "Medical hotel in the growth of global medical tourism", *Journal of Travel & Tourism Marketing*, Vol.31, No.3, pp.366–380.

Harris, K.J. (1996), "International hospitality marketing on the Internet: Project 'Interweave' ", *International Journal of Hospitality Management*, Vol.15, No.2, pp.155–163.

Harrison, J.S., Chang, E.Y., Gauthier, C., Joerchel, T., Nevarez, J., and Wang, M. (2005), "Exporting a North American concept to Asia: Starbucks in China", *Cornell Hotel and Restaurant Administration Quarterly*, Vol.46, No.2, pp.275–283.

Hua, N. and Upneja, A. (2011), "Do investors reward restaurant firms that go abroad?", *International Journal of Contemporary Hospitality Management*, Vol.23, No.2, pp.174–188.

Hwang, S.N. and Chang, T.Y. (2003), "Using data envelopment analysis to measure hotel managerial efficiency change in Taiwan", *Tourism Management*, Vol.24, No.4, pp.357–369.

Jansen-Verbeke, M. (1996), "Cross-cultural differences in the practices of hotel managers. A study of Dutch and Belgian hotel managers" *Tourism Management*, Vol.17, No.7, pp.544–548.

Johnson, C. and Vanetti, M. (2005), "Locational strategies of international hotel chains", *Annals of Tourism Research*, Vol.32, No.4, pp.1077–1099.

Jones, D.L. and McCleary, K.W. (2005), "An empirical approach to identifying cross-cultural modifications to international hospitality industry sales training", *Journal of Travel & Tourism Marketing*, Vol.18, No.4, pp.65–81.

Kivela, J. and Leung, L.F.L. (2005), "Doing business in the People's Republic of China", *Cornell Hotel and Restaurant Administration Quarterly*, Vol.46, No.2, pp.125–152.

Klonowski, D., Power, J.L., and Linton, D., (2008), "The development of franchise operations in emerging markets: The case of a Poland-based restaurant operator", *Cornell Hospitality Quarterly*, Vol.49, No.4, pp.436–449.

Kontogeorgopoulos, N. (1998), "Accommodation employment patterns and opportunities", *Annals of Tourism Research*, Vol.25, No.2, pp.314–339.

Kriegl, U. (2000), "International hospitality management: Identifying important skills and effective raining", *Cornell Hotel and Restaurant Administration Quarterly*, Vol.41, No.2, pp.64–71.

Kwok, L., Xie, K.L., and Richards, T. (2017), "Thematic framework of online review research: A systematic analysis of contemporary literature on seven major hospitality and tourism journals", *International Journal of Contemporary Hospitality Management*, Vol.29, No.1, pp.307–354.

Lam, C., Ho, G.K., and Law, R. (2015), "How can Asian hotel companies remain internationally competitive?", *International Journal of Contemporary Hospitality Management*, Vol.27, No.5, pp.827–852.

Law, R., Buhalis, D., and Cobanoglu, C. (2014), "Progress on information and communication technologies in hospitality and tourism", *International Journal of Contemporary Hospitality Management*, Vol.26, No.5, pp.727–750.

Lee, K. (2008a), "Issues for international franchising: Lessons from the case of a Poland-based restaurant operator", *Cornell Hospitality Quarterly*, Vol.49, No.4, pp.454–457.

Lee, S. (2008b), "Internationalization of US multinational hotel companies: Expansion to Asia versus Europe", *International Journal of Hospitality Management*, Vol.27, No.4, pp.657–664.

Lee, S., Koh, Y., and Heo, C.Y. (2011), "Research note: Internationalization of US publicly traded restaurant companies – A transaction cost economics perspective", *Tourism Economics*, Vol.17, No.2, pp.465–471.

Lee, S., Koh, Y., and Xiao, Q. (2014), "Internationalization and financial health in the US hotel industry", *Tourism Economics*, Vol.20, No.1, pp.87–105.

Lee, S., Upneja, A., Özdemir, Ö., and Sun, K.A. (2014), "A synergy effect of internationalization and firm size on performance: US hotel industry", *International Journal of Contemporary Hospitality Management*, Vol.26, No.1, pp.35–49.

Lee, W.S., Choi, C., and Moon, J. (2018), "The upper echelon effect on restaurant franchising: The moderating role of internationalization", *International Journal of Culture, Tourism and Hospitality Research*, Vol.12, No.1, pp.15–28.

Lee, W.S., Kim, I., and Moon, J. (2016), "Determinants of restaurant internationalization: An upper echelons theory perspective", *International Journal of Contemporary Hospitality Management*, Vol.28, No.12, pp.2864–2887.

León-Darder, F., Villar-García, C., and Pla-Barber, J. (2011), "Entry mode choice in the internationalisation of the hotel industry: A holistic approach", *Service Industries Journal*, Vol.31, No.1, pp.107–122.

Leung, D., Law, R., Van Hoof, H., and Buhalis, D. (2013), "Social media in tourism and hospitality: A literature review", *Journal of Travel & Tourism Marketing*, Vol.30, No.1–2, pp.3–22.

Line, N.D. and Runyan, R.C. (2012), "Hospitality marketing research: Recent trends and future directions", *International Journal of Hospitality Management*, Vol.31, No.2, pp.477–488.

Litteljohn, D. (1997), "Internationalization in hotels: Current aspects and developments", *International Journal of Contemporary Hospitality Management*, Vol.9, No.5/6, pp.187–192.

Marco-Lajara, B., Del Carmen Zaragoza-Sáez, P., Claver-Cortés, E., Úbeda-García, M., and García-Lillo, F. (2017), "Tourist districts and internationalization of hotel firms", *Tourism Management*, Vol.61, pp.451–464.

Martorell, O., Mulet, C., and Otero, L. (2013), "Choice of market entry mode by Balearic hotel chains in the Caribbean and Gulf of Mexico", *International Journal of Hospitality Management*, Vol.32, pp.217–227.

Mcvey, M. and King, B. (2000), "A profile of India's hotel sector: Is a giant finally awakening?", *Tourism Recreation Research*, Vol.25, No.2, pp.97–110.

Menicucci, E. (2018), "The influence of firm characteristics on profitability: Evidence from Italian hospitality industry", *International Journal of Contemporary Hospitality Management*, Vol.30, No.8, pp.2845–2868.

Miller, B. (2008), "Using a modular system approach to international franchising: Analyzing the case study of a Poland-based restaurant operator", *Cornell Hospitality Quarterly*, Vol.49, No.4, pp.458–462.

Nickson, D. (1997), "'Colorful stories' or historical insight? – A review of the auto/biographies of Charles Forte, Conrad Hilton, JW Marriott and Kemmons Wilson", *Journal of Hospitality & Tourism Research*, Vol.21, No.1, pp.179–192.

Niñerola, A., Campa-Planas, F., Hernández-Lara, A.B., and Sánchez-Rebull, M.V. (2016), "The experience of Meliá Hotels International in China: A case of internationalisation of a Spanish hotel group", *European Journal of Tourism Research*, Vol.12, p.191.

O'Connor, P. (2008), "E-mail marketing by international hotel chains: An industry-practices update", *Cornell Hospitality Quarterly*, Vol.49, No.1, pp.42–52.

Olsen, M.D. and Roper, A. (1998), "Research in strategic management in the hospitality industry", *International Journal of Hospitality Management*, Vol.17, No.2, pp.111–124.

Oskam, J. and Boswijk, A. (2016), "Airbnb: The future of networked hospitality businesses", *Journal of Tourism Futures*, Vol.2, No.1, pp.22–42.

Parte-Esteban, L. and Alberca-Oliver, P. (2015), "New insights into dynamic efficiency: The effects of firm factors", *International Journal of Contemporary Hospitality Management*, Vol.27, No.1, pp.107–129.

Parte-Esteban, L. and García, C.F. (2014), "The influence of firm characteristics on earnings quality", *International Journal of Hospitality Management*, Vol.42, pp.50–60.

Peters, M. and Frehse, J. (2005), "The internationalization of the European hotel industry in the light of competition theories", *Tourism*, Vol.53, No.1, pp.55–65.

Plog, S.C. and Sturman, M.C. (2005), "The problems and challenges of working in international settings: A special topic issue of the Cornell Quarterly", *Cornell Hotel and Restaurant Administration Quarterly*, Vol.46, No.2, pp.116–124.

Puciato, D. (2016), "Attractiveness of municipalities in South-Western Poland as determinants for hotel chain investments", *Tourism Management*, Vol.57, pp.245–255.

Rodríguez, A.R. (2002), "Determining factors in entry choice for international expansion. The case of the Spanish hotel industry", *Tourism Management*, Vol.23, No.6, pp.597–607.

Rodtook, P. and Altinay, L. (2013), "Reasons for internationalization of domestic hotel chains in Thailand", *Journal of Hospitality Marketing & Management*, Vol.22, No.1, pp.92–115.

Rogerson, J.M. (2016), "Hotel chains of the global South: The internationalization of South African hotel brands", *Turizam*, Vol.64, No.4, pp.445–450.

Rushmore, S. and Goldhoff, G. (1997), "Hotel value trends: Yesterday, today, and tomorrow", *Cornell Hotel and Restaurant Administration Quarterly*, Vol.38, No.6, pp.18–29.

Sainaghi, R. (2010), "A meta-analysis of hotel performance. Continental or worldwide style?", *Tourism Review*, Vol.65, No.3, pp.46–69.

Schuckert, M., Liu, X., and Law, R. (2015), "Hospitality and tourism online reviews: Recent trends and future directions", *Journal of Travel & Tourism Marketing*, Vol.32, No.5, pp.608–621.

Smeral, E. (2009), "Growth accounting for hotel and restaurant industries", *Journal of Travel Research*, Vol.47, No.4, pp.413–424.

Spenceley, A. (2019), "Sustainable tourism certification in the African hotel sector", *Tourism Review*, Vol.74, No.2, pp.179–193.

Strand, C.R. (1996), "Lessons of a lifetime: The development of Hilton International", *Cornell Hotel and Restaurant Administration Quarterly*, Vol.37, No.3, pp.83–95.

Velo, V. and Mittaz, C. (2006), "Breaking into emerging international hotel markets: Skills needed to face this challenge and ways to develop them in hospitality management students", *International Journal of Contemporary Hospitality Management*, Vol.18, No.6, pp.496–508.

Villar, C., Pla-Barber, J., and León-Darder, F. (2012), "Service characteristics as moderators of the entry mode choice: Empirical evidence in the hotel industry", *Service Industries Journal*, Vol.32, No.7, pp.1137–1148.

Woo, L., Assaf, A.G., Josiassen, A., and Kock, F. (2019), "Internationalization and hotel performance: Agglomeration-related moderators", *International Journal of Hospitality Management*, Vol.82, pp.48–58.

Zervas, G., Proserpio, D., and Byers, J.W. (2017), "The rise of the sharing economy: Estimating the impact of Airbnb on the hotel industry" *Journal of Marketing Research*, Vol.54, No.5, pp.687–705.

4

HOSPITALITY INDUSTRY STRUCTURES AND ORGANIZATION

*Betsy Bender Stringam, Joselyn Goopio, Basak Denizci-Guillet,
and Hjalte Brøndum Mansa*

Industry Structure

The hospitality industry was traditionally entrepreneurial, with many small independently operated hotels and restaurants. More than half of the hospitality industry is independently owned and operated. However, the last century has seen a movement toward corporate ownership, consolidation, and branding. The dominant players are large multinational companies. Overall, the hospitality industry is "composed of a relatively small number of large multinationals and a large number of locally operated small and medium-sized enterprises" (Brotherton, 2003, pp. 142–143). The hospitality industry is an incredibly diverse industry with many differences in ownership and management structures. Even within countries and among large corporations, the structures differ vastly.

Organizational Structure within the Industry

In general, the hospitality industry has four main organizational structures: independent ownership, franchise agreements, management contracts, and consortiums or referral groups. Some hospitality businesses utilize more than one of these structures. Hotels are key examples with many independently owned hotels that have a franchise agreement.

Brand Affiliation

Brand or chain affiliation refers to two or more units owned or operated by a company with similar target markets, products, and concepts (Brotherton, 2003). Brand affiliation and chains in the hospitality industry are often further grouped by parent companies. A parent company owns multiple brands. For example, Marriott as a parent company presents many hotel brands to the consumers: Fairfield by Marriott, Courtyard by Marriott, TownePlace Suites by Marriott, etc. The parent company can choose to present the brands in a consolidated manner where the consumer knows they all belong to the same company. Or, they may choose to keep the brands separate or differentiated so that the consumer does not know the brands are part of the same company. For example, Marriott also owns The Ritz Carlton, Luxury Hotels and Resorts brand. Note that this brand name does not include in its name or title "by Marriott" as did those mentioned above. Table 4.1 shows examples of many of the brands affiliated with hotel franchise companies.

Table 4.1 Top Hotel Franchise companies (listed alphabetically)

Top Hotel Franchise companies	Brands
Accor Hotels	Raffles, Fairmont, Banyan Tree, Sofitel Legend, Rixos, So, Sofitel, Onefinestay, Mantis, MGallery, Pullman, Swissôtel, Angsana, 25hours, Art Series, Movenpick, Grand Mercure, HUAZHU, Peppers, The Sebel, Mantra, Novotel, Mercure, Mama Shelter, Adagio, BreakFree, ibis, ibis Styles, ibis budget, JO&JOE, greet, hotelF1, Thalassa sea & spa
BTG Hotels Group	Jianguo Hotel, Tangram, Home Inn, Shindom Inn
Choice Hotels International	Econo Lodge, Rodeway Inn, Suburban, Woodspring Suites, Mainstay Suites, Quality, Sleep Inn, Clarion, Comfort Inn, Comfort Suites, Cambria Hotels and Suites, Ascend Hotel Collection
G6 Hospitality	Motel 6, Studio 6, Hotel 6, Estudio 6
GreenTree Hospitality Group	GreenTree Inn, GreenTree Eastern Hotel, GT Alliance Hotel, GME Hotel, GYA Hotel, VX Hotel, Vatica Hotel, Shell Hotel, Overseas Hotel
Hilton Worldwide	Tru, Home2 Suites, Hampton, Hilton Garden Inn, Hilton Hotels & Resorts, DoubleTree, Homewood Suites, Embassy Suites, Canopy, Conrad, Waldorf Astoria, LXR, Signia, Curio Collection, Tapestry Collection, Motto
InterContinental Hotels Group	Candlewood Suites, Holiday Inn Express, Holiday Inn Hotels and Resorts, Crowne Plaza Hotels and Resorts, EVEN Hotels, Hotel Indigo, Staybridge Suites, InterContinental Hotels and Resorts, Regent, Kimpton, HUALUXE, voco, avid hotels
Jin Jiang International Holdings	J.Hotel, Jin Jiang, Metropolo, Jin Jiang, Radisson, Radisson Red, Radisson Blue, Park Inn, Country Inn & Suites, Park Plaza
Magnuson Worldwide	M Star Hotels, Magnuson Hotels, Magnuson Grand Hotels, By Magnuson Worldwide Collection
Marriott Hotels, Resorts & Suites	Marriott Hotels, Moxy Hotels, Fairfield Inn and Suites by Marriott, TownePlace Suites by Marriott, Aloft, Courtyard by Marriott, Element, Four Points by Sheraton, Residence Inn by Marriott, SpringHill Suites by Marriott, AC Hotels by Marriott, Delta Hotels, Le Meridian, Renaissance, Sheraton, Westin Hotels & Resorts, JW Marriott, BVLGARI Hotels & Resorts, The Ritz-Carlton, St. Regis, W Hotels, EDITION Hotels, The Luxury Collection, Autograph Collection Hotels, Tribute Portfolio, Design Hotels, Gaylord Hotels, Protea Hotels
Qingdao Sunmei Group	Thank Inn Hotel, JUNYI, U Plus Hotel, AA Room, Lano Hotel, Feronia Hotel, Midi Hotels and Resorts
RLH Corporation	Red Lion Hotels, Americas Best Value Inn, Canadas Best Value Inn, Knights Inn, Guesthouse, Signature, Red Lion Inn & Suites, Hotel RL, Lexington
Wyndham Hotel Group	Days Inn, Howard Johnson, Microtel, Super 8, Travelodge, AmericInn, Baymont, Hawthorn Suites, LaQuinta, Ramada, Wingate, TRYP, Wyndham Garden, Wyndham Hotels and Resorts, Wyndham Grand, Dolce, Esplendor Boutique Hotels, Dazzler, Trademark Collection

Sources: Hotels (2019), Lodging (2018), and websites of each hotel company.

The hospitality industry as a whole did not begin to embrace brand affiliation until the mid-1900s (Pillsbury, 1990). In fact, in 1950, there were only a few major hotel chains: Dusit International, Hilton, InterContinental, Peninsula, Sheraton, Statler, and The Oberoi Group (Gee, 2008). The beginnings of the branding concept for restaurants is often traced to the mid-1800s when successful restauranteurs such as Delmonico's of New York and Lovejoy and Brown opened additional restaurants at different locations, using the same name, similar menus, décor, and formats. It was common for a successful restaurant owner to open additional restaurants in the same city. Expansion beyond the local community for restaurants was not common until the 1940s and 1950s when restaurant companies such as A&W Root Beer, Bob's Big Boy, Dairy Queen, White Castle, In-N-Out, and Burger King embraced regional and national expansion. Branded restaurants were initially few in number with only about 4% of all U.S. restaurants affiliated with a chain or brand in 1958 (Pillsbury, 1990). Today restaurants affiliated with a brand or chain comprise almost half of the worldwide restaurants (Statistica, 2019).

Brand affiliation is not as complete through the rest of the world (Fried, 2010; Powell, 2018). Europe, for example, still has more unaffiliated hotels than brand hotels (Slattery, 2012; STR, 2016). Yet, one of the large multinational hotel corporations, AccorHotels, is headquartered in France. Hotels and restaurants in South and Central America have traditionally been independent, but branding is slowly becoming a part of the hospitality industry there as well (Higley, 2015). Some markets see increasing chain affiliations but with smaller regional brands. The Scandinavian countries are a showcase of this, where the market is predominantly run by regional brands with very low penetration of the global dominant hotel brands. Even in the restaurant market, McDonald's is essentially the only major brand that has found a proper market position, in the Scandinavian countries by its franchise operations strategy (Bourget, 2012).

Brand affiliation in emerging markets has been slower. For example, Kentucky Fried Chicken opened its first stores in South Africa in 1971. But its expansion into other areas of Africa was slower. It was not until 2011 when the first KFC started in an affluent area of Nairobi that the company saw positive results in Kenya. The chain now has more than 20 stores in Kenya and is expanding into other countries in Africa. Several other international restaurant franchisors are now turning to "Africa for growth, attracted by rising disposable household incomes, fast economic growth, and a young population" (Mutegi, 2017).

Franchising

Franchising is the process where one company permits another person or another company the right to operate a business under their name or brand, using their name, product, and services in return for fees and or royalties. A common example of this is when a hotel or restaurant is owned independently but operates under a brand name; participating in marketing programs, reservations systems, and other services (Enz, 2010; Vallen and Vallen, 2018; Walker, 2016). Franchising is a common investment practice in the hospitality industry. It reduces economic risk to the international brand while meeting local regulations for national investment funds (Rodriguez, 2002). Franchising can mitigate some of the challenges associated with international expansion. Franchising can help bridge access to reliable local suppliers, and skilled management (Dev, 2012).

Franchising for the hospitality industry originated in Germany and England in early 1900 with taverns and breweries. The first known hospitality franchise is often attributed to the Ritz Development Company franchising the Ritz Carlton name for a hotel in New York City in 1907 (Walker, 2016). Howard Johnsons, A&W, and Dairy Queen Restaurants also entered the franchising arena in the early 1900s, bringing the franchising concept to foodservice and restaurants (Lattin et al., 2013: Mariani, 1991; Summers, 2007). Howard Johnson, known for his orange-roofed restaurants, is also known as the man to take franchising in the restaurant industry to mass deployment (Turkel, 2009). By the 1960s, Howard Johnsons was the "second largest provider of meals outside the home, second only to the U.S. Army" (Miller, 2009, p. 57). Other noted early hospitality franchising endeavors were McDonald's and Holiday Inns (Walker, 2016). McDonald's today is the largest restaurant franchisor and one of the largest foodservice companies worldwide (Franchise Times, 2018; McDonald's 2019)

Table 4.2 Top 20 restaurant franchise brands by worldwide sales

Rank	Brand	Rank	Brand
1	McDonald's	11	Tim Hortons
2	KFC	12	Panera Bread
3	Burger King	13	Dairy Queen
4	Subway	14	Applebee's
5	Domino's	15	Sonic Drive-In
6	Pizza Hut	16	Little Caesars
7	Wendy's	17	Chili's
8	Taco Bell	18	Buffalo Wild Wings
9	Dunkin' Donuts	19	Papa John's
10	Chick-fil-A	20	Arby's

Source: Franchise Times (2018).

Despite the gains of franchising, independent mom-and-pop hotels and motels dominated the lodging industry until well after World War II. The early 1960s found fewer than 2% of U.S. lodging properties associated with a franchise. By the late 1980s, as many as 64% of U.S. lodging properties were associated with a franchise chain (Jakle et al., 1996; Vermillion et al., 2009). Today franchising is abundant across the hotel industry (see Table 4.1). Marriott, with its recent acquisition of Starwood, is considered to be the largest hotel franchisor in the world today. Table 4.1 presents the top hotel franchise companies and their brands. Given the prolific mergers and acquisitions of the industry, this list changes rapidly. Likewise, hotel companies are developing brands at a rapid pace, thus this list is constantly expanding and changing.

The restaurant industry experienced similar franchising growth with the number of franchised restaurants doubling between the years 1960 and 1970 and then doubling again by 1980 (Summers, 2007). Currently, the restaurant industry comprises the largest number of franchises of any industry worldwide, with Subway restaurants as the world's largest franchisor by the number of restaurants, and McDonald's as the largest franchisor by sales volume (see Table 4.2) (Franchise Times, 2018).

Management Contracts

A management contract is an agreement between an owner and a management company by which the owner pays the management company to operate or manage the business (Stringam and Partlow, 2016). A management company can manage an independent hotel or one affiliated with a brand. The hotel industry uses the management contract model more than other industries. Management contracts are more prevalent in the U.S. hotel industry than for other areas of the world (Cunill, 2006). Management contracts are not widely utilized in the restaurant industry.

Management contracts allow major hotel brands to offer management expertise to hotel owners. Just over one-third of hotels utilizing management contracts are associated with a large multinational hotel brand. The other two-thirds of the hotels are managed by other smaller management contract companies, not affiliated with a major brand. It is estimated that there are over 800 hotel management companies managing more than 12,000 hotel properties worldwide (deRoos, 2010). An advantage to management contracts is that it minimizes risk for the operator or management company. Management contracts have the benefit of separating the volatility of the real estate market from hotel operations (Jackson and Naipaul, 2009). Separation of these distinct businesses is particularly advantageous in volatile markets.

The origin of management contracts in the hospitality industry is often disputed. Fred Harvey was one of the pioneers of the management contract system utilizing management contracts for his restaurants and hotels in the expanding railroad eras of the late 1800s (Fried, 2010). Management contracts were also highly utilized by U.S. hotel companies in the 1940s to expand into overseas markets (Summers, 2007). InterContinental ran many of its Latin American hotels under management contracts in the 1950s (Cunill, 2006). Four Seasons was one of the first hotel companies to use solely management contracts, instead of owning any hotels (Jackson and Naipaul, 2009).

Consortiums or Referral Groups

Consortiums or referral groups are used often in hotels, but rarely for restaurants. A consortium or referral group is a group of hotels or restaurants that agree to affiliate to take advantage of economies of scale in marketing, reservation services, purchasing, etc. See Table 4.3 for a list of key hotel consortia companies. Consortiums or referral group appear to be similar to franchising agreements, but the requirements and restrictions of a consortium or management contract are generally fewer, with more autonomy permitted. While restaurants generally do not engage in large consortiums, they may participate in locally based smaller co-ops and small local consortiums.

In a referral group or consortium, independent hotels group together to collectively gain expertise and support services (Margolies, 1995). The key differences between a consortium and franchise are that the consortium typically operates on a cost recovery basis, consortia members pay a membership fee and the hotels stay independently owned and operated (Go and Pine, 1995). Hotels in consortiums typically have more say in the governance of the organization. Standards or requirements for uniform conformity are often more flexible, allowing the independent hotel to still maintain its unique market strengths. Hotels in consortiums gain added credibility for financing and investment processes than an independent hotel, yet maintain independence in operations (Sullivan, 2013). Consortiums and referral groups occur in greater proportion throughout the world than franchising and management contracts which are used more heavily in the United States than other countries (see Table 4.3).

Consortiums started as referral groups, consisting of calls between hotel front desks, helping a guest to gain reservations at similar hotels while they traveled. One of the more well-known of the early referral groups was United Motor Courts, established in 1932 (Margolies, 1995). Consortiums were then established to share in marketing and reservations processes: maintaining reservations call centers, large-scale marketing campaigns, etc. As reservation and marketing processes have moved to the Internet in recent years, the primary advantage of consortiums has moved toward expertise such as revenue management, loyalty programs, quality assurance, and purchasing (Vermillion et al., 2009).

Other Organizational Structures

Sometimes specific countries develop additional or alternative organizational structures. China, for instance, has a complex structure with up to ten types of hotel ownership: state-owned, collective, shareholding cooperative, alliance, limited liability, limited liability shares, privately owned, foreign funded, owned by Hong Kong, Macau, and Taiwan companies, and others (China National Tourism Administration, 2009). State-owned hotels (national, regional, or municipal) account for more than half of the hotels in China (Hung, 2013, Zhang et al., 2005). State ownership brings additional challenges. In addition to the bureaucratic restrictions, most state-owned hotels are operated as independent units. State-owned hotels are usually smaller with an average hotel size of 89 rooms and have a lower occupancy and average daily rate (ADR) than foreign funded and hotels owned by Hong Kong, Macau, and Taiwan. Hotels owned by the special provinces are the largest at an average size of 178 rooms (Zhang et al., 2005).

Table 4.3 Key Hotel Consortia companies (listed alphabetically)

Consortia company	Headquarters location
Amplified Hotels	United Kingdom
Associated Luxury Hotels International	United States
Design Hotels	Germany
Epoque Hotels	United States
Global Hotel Alliance	United Arab Emirates
Historic Hotels of America	United States
Historic Hotels of Europe	France
Historic Hotels Worldwide	United States
Hotel Republic	United Kingdom
HotelREZ Hotels and Resorts	United Kingdom
Hotusa Hotels	Spain
Keytel Hotels	Spain
Logis Hotels	France
Preferred Hotels and Resorts	United States
SEH (Société Européenne d'Hôtellerie)	France
Sercotel Hotels	Spain
Small Luxury Hotels of the World	United Kingdom
Supranational Hotels	United Kingdom
The Leading Hotels of the World	United States

Source: Hotels (2019).

Structure and Strategies of the Hotel Industry

Vertical Disintegration

During the latter part of the 20th century, large corporate hotel companies began to divide into two parts: one that owns and invests in hotel assets and one that manages or franchises properties (Geller, 1998; Watkins, 2013). Hotel companies sold off the real estate or property assets, and concentrated on management contracts and franchise agreements, separating the asset ownership from operations (Bender et al., 2008). In some instances, the companies split into separate companies: one with real estate, and the other with franchises, management contracts, and management leases. Some of the driving force in this separation was that the two separate business models (real estate and hotel operations) were valued very differently on stock markets. The separation was said to allow for more focused investment (Cunill, 2006; Go and Pine, 1995; Summers, 2007).

Dividing the operations from real estate ownership allowed hotel ownership companies to focus on real estate acquisition, project feasibility, and project financing, while hotel management companies focused on the operations of the hotels (Cunill, 2006; Go and Pine, 1995). Marriott is said to have begun this asset-light movement with the sale of its owned hotels in the early 1990s to Host Marriott, emphasizing management rather than ownership of hotels (Jakle et al., 1996; Turkel, 2009). Host later diversified its portfolio, buying a large portion of Starwood's hotel assets and dropping Marriott from the name of the company. Other hotel companies followed suit with many varied forms of divestiture and sale of assets (Cunill, 2006; Turkel, 2009). Most of the large multinational hotel companies today own very little real estate and concentrate on management and contract business (Bender et al., 2008). This asset-light structure is expected to continue.

The hotel industry is unique in its disintegration strategies wherein the ownership of the hotel is separated from the management component. Of the large major brands, most only own a few strategic properties, with the majority of their business as management contracts and franchises. This is called fee for service, or fee-based business. While a few of the large hotel companies still own a number of hotels, some own no real estate and operate only in the fee-based businesses.

Asset Management Company

This separation of the ownership of the hotel asset from hotel operations created a need for asset management. Hotels can be owned by many different types of people, companies, and organizations. Some owners lack hotel expertise to effectively oversee their investment. This creates a need for an asset manager who could provide expertise and align the interests of hotel operators and hotel owners. Asset management companies work with the hotels to create the highest possible return to the owners by helping hotels achieve the highest possible revenue while reducing unnecessary costs, therein achieving the best profit margin possible. Generally, the asset management company serves as a go-between the hotel operations management company and the hotel owner. But, some hotel operations management companies are also asset management companies, or a hotel may have a separate hotel operations management company as well as an asset management company, and some hotel investment companies or owners perform their own asset management (STR, 2016).

An asset management company helps the hotel owner to maximize their investment in the hotel. Essentially the asset managers oversee the hotel investment for the owners, working with the hotel management. Asset management companies oversee the day-to-day operations of the hotels as well as the long-term strategy of the hotel investors. Asset management companies monitor the financial performance of the hotel. Responsibilities of the asset management company vary according to the needs of the owners. They may be involved in site analysis and selection, brand management, selection and compliance, contract and franchise agreements, review of hotel day-to-day operations, property repositioning, capital expenditures, facilities planning revenue management, and strategic decision making (Jackson, 2012; Singh et al., 2012).

Consolidation of the Hotel Industry

Brand Collectors

As the hotel industry has expanded globally, mergers and acquisitions have been a key part of their strategy. Acquisitions can be used to penetrate new markets and new geographical regions (Cunill, 2006). Often when a company expands into a new market, there is a shortage of prime or key locations on which to build hotels or restaurants. Thus, an acquisition or merger provides a process for the company to gain access to strategic locations. Mergers and acquisitions also provide access to local expertise, supply chains, governmental and other key relationships.

While mergers and acquisitions have been occurring at an accelerated pace in recent years, they are not a new concept for the hotel industry. One of the first well-known acquisitions was Associated Hotels of India by the Oberoi Group in 1944 (Chathoth and Chon, 2009). Another well-known early acquisition was the purchase of the Statler chain of hotels by Hilton in 1954. It was considered to be the largest real estate transaction that had ever occurred at that time (Turkel, 2009). Another noted hospitality industry merger of the mid-century was Trust House, which merged with Forte to create Trusthouse Forte Hotels in 1970 (Slattery, 2012). Acquisitions and mergers have continued since. Today the pace is rapid and the process is growing larger. Marriott's acquisition of Starwood and Jin Jiang's acquisition of Radisson have formed the two largest hotel companies in the world. Acquisitions and mergers are predicted to continue creating even larger companies

Sometimes acquisitions are part of international expansion strategies. Companies seeking to expand into new geographic regions and countries are acquiring existing hospitality products in foreign countries in addition to building new hotels or restaurants. Marriott, for example, acquired the Renaissance Hotel Group in 1997. The principal owner of Renaissance was a Chinese national with political ties to the top of the Chinese government and very influential in tourism affairs (Becker, 2013). This acquisition instantly gave Marriott a physical and political presence in China. Marriott's recent purchases of Protea Hospitality Holdings and AC Hotels are other examples of this type of acquisition (Sampson, 2018). These transactions doubled Marriott's hotel presence in Africa and Spain.

Acquisitions of hospitality companies were common in the mid- to late-1900s with many hospitality companies acquired by large corporate conglomerates in various portfolio strategies. Beginning in the 1980s, the hospitality industry experienced unprecedented acquisitions and mergers that some have labeled the era of brand collectors or brand consolidation (Go and Pine, 1995; Rogerson, 2011; Vermillion et al., 2009). Acquisitions in the hotel industry remained prolific, as hotel companies have pursued new markets and new products (Brotherton, 2003). As hospitality companies have sought to expand and grow, smaller regional companies could often be acquired for less capital than it would take to build comparable new hotels. For some markets, this has been particularly true. Due to the overbuilding of luxury hotels, purchase of existing luxury hotel properties has generally been less expensive than the cost to build a new hotel (Kim and Olsen, 1999).

Large multinational companies have developed strategies to expand in various ways. Hotel companies sought to expand the types of hotels offered, to offer a hotel product at every price, purpose, place, and reason to travel (Bender et al., 2008). In addition to acquisitions and mergers hotel companies are developing new brands to target new market segments. But many wonder if brand proliferation has gone too far. It is estimated that there are more than 750 brands worldwide, with the ten largest hotel companies having more than 130 hotel brands between them (see Table 4.1).

Acquisitions also occur because many of the hospitality companies are now publically held companies. Their performance is no longer just about day-to-day operations and property level performance, but also about increasing shareholder value (Summers, 2007). Acquisitions of other hospitality companies allow these companies to increase shareholder value. Mergers and acquisitions in the hotel industry are expected to continue as travel expands globally, with more people traveling to more places.

Structure and Strategies of the Restaurant and Foodservice Industry

The restaurant and foodservice industry is one of the largest industries in the world. The structure of the restaurant industry is very similar to the hotel industry, but with many more independent establishments (Brotherton, 2003; Sturman et al., 2011). Restaurants are typically divided into three structures: (1) independent, (2) chain owned and operated, and (3) franchised (Brotherton, 2003).

Worldwide, most restaurants are still owned and operated by independents (Stringam and Partlow, 2016). Most independent restaurants have a small business structure, typically employing 20 or fewer employees (Brotherton, 2003). Owners of an independent restaurant are generally highly involved in the day-to-day operations. Many independent restaurants are family owned and operated. By the same token, restaurants rely more on local patrons than hotels. Overall, the restaurant industry reports that three in four customers are local, with only one in four customers related to travel (Timothy and Teye, 2009).

Differing from hotel companies, most large restaurant chains both franchise and own restaurant units (Bradach, 1998). Restaurants also sometimes employ a reversal in the franchising ownership arrangement. A restaurant company may initially own the restaurant and then seek both a lease and a franchise agreement with a local operator (Sturman et al., 2011). In some parts of the world, franchising and chain-affiliated restaurants comprise a large portion of the industry. In the United States, just over half of all restaurant revenue is generated by restaurants affiliated with a chain or large company (Barrows and Powers, 2011). Nevertheless, three out of four restaurants are single-unit operations.

Similar to hotels, restaurants outside of the United States are significantly more independent in ownership structure (Sturman et al., 2011). Recent years have seen chain restaurants gaining an increasing share of the market worldwide (Parsa et al., 2011). For example, in East Africa, local restaurant brands started barely 45 years ago when The Tamarind Group opened its first restaurant in Mombasa in 1972. The Tamarind Group owns and operates some of the most successful restaurants and leisure operations in Africa, notably Carnivore and Tamarind Dhow, and recently opened Tamarind Tree Hotel. Local branding concepts became even more pronounced when Java House, founded by Kevin Ashley and John Wagner, opened its first coffee house in Nairobi in 1999. Since then, Java House has become a major chain of coffee houses offering export-quality brewed Kenyan coffee with over 50 branches across East Africa (Kenya, Uganda, and Rwanda) being tagged as "Africa's Starbucks", Africa's largest coffee shop chain. Both, The Tamarind Group and Java House, are chain owned and operated by Africans and do not accept franchise contracts.

In South East Asian countries such as Vietnam, Thailand, Indonesia, and the Philippines, homegrown restaurant brands are in fierce competition with their U.S. rivals such as McDonald's, KFC, and Pizza Hut (Tomiyama, 2015). Jollibee, a large multinational restaurant chain started in the Philippines known as the "McDonald's of the Philippines," is preferred over McDonald's by most Filipinos (Sigalos and Turner, 2018). Another example of a local company succeeding over large international brands is Trung Nguyen Coffee in Vietnam with more than 2,500 restaurants in Vietnam, Thailand, and Singapore. Their specialty is high-quality Vietnamese coffee based on the traditional brewing method of using a steel filter. Coffee culture is deeply rooted in Vietnamese culture, as it was once a French colony.

Consolidation of the Restaurant Industry

There have been many mergers, acquisitions, and minority stock purchases throughout the restaurant industry, with most of the major companies buying and selling over the last three decades (Smith, 2011). Entrepreneurs sold out to larger companies, and large companies began to expand and diversify. Mergers and acquisitions in the restaurant industry mirrored hotel acquisitions, with multinational firms acquiring restaurant companies in other countries as part of the expansion process (Lattin et al., 2013). The history of restaurant acquisitions and mergers has its roots in unrelated diversification. Much of the early consolidation in the restaurant industry was started by large food conglomerates such as General Foods, General Mills, Nestle, Pillsbury, and PepsiCo (Bernstein and Paul, 1994). Mergers and acquisitions remain fluid today for the restaurant industry as companies seek to expand and utilize resources effectively.

International Factors Influencing the Hospitality Industry Structure

Industry structure and organization differ between regions of the world and across economies. Overall, hospitality enterprises in Europe and South America are predominantly independent (Powell, 2018). North America has the most brand affiliation, while Australia, Africa, and Asia are more of a balance of independents and brand affiliation. Franchising has been gaining popularity in China. Strong brand awareness, supportive centralized reservation systems, high returns on investment with relatively low franchisee fees are contributing to franchise growth in China (Xiao et al., 2008).

The franchise model provides international expertise to local developers. In exchange, it also allows a large, remotely located company to employ the local expertise of the franchisee (Bradach, 1998). When the host business environment is highly developed, the franchise model is preferred. In poorly developed markets, the management contract is preferred. An exception to this is for larger luxury hotels for which a management contract is almost always the preferred structure over a franchise (Dev, 2012). A common form of international expansion is the master franchise agreement wherein rights to franchise for a geographic region are granted to an individual or company (Brookes and Roper, 2010; Brotherton, 2003). The master franchise agreement helps bridge the challenges of culture and regional business practices (Summers, 2007).

Developing Countries (Fragile Economic Stability) versus Established Economies

In developing countries or countries with fragile economic stability, hospitality businesses are more likely to be independent or affiliated with small regional companies. Then, as a country's economy improves, there is an increase in international business travelers who then seek higher quality hotels and restaurants (Rogerson, 2011). As the economy expands there is also an increase in foreign interest and investment in the hospitality industry, often resulting in an increased affiliation with brands.

Most brand expansion into developing countries is through franchise arrangements, with local individuals and companies owning and operating the hotels and restaurants. While no equity investment is usually required from hotel management or franchise companies in the United States, most other countries require equity investment in hotel projects (Gee, 2008). Restaurants, in contrast, often require an equity investment by management companies, even in the United States (Bernstein and Paul, 1994).

International brand expansion often brings cultural challenges. Differing countries have diverse cultures which can impact the acceptance of the brand. Africa is an example of this challenge in brand expansion. Africa is such a vast continent that the culture in the East is very different from the West or South. Even within the East African regions, each country has diverse cultural differences. For a chain hotel or restaurant to survive, it has to learn and adjust to each local culture, especially when dealing with employees and local patrons. A chain or brand's best practice in one African country may not work in another African country, so companies have to constantly reinvent themselves every time they open a property in another country.

Another challenge in developing areas of the world is the lack of skilled hospitality staff. In Africa, for example, basic concepts of food sanitation and service culture are not inherent to the labor force. Recruiting and training is more challenging and requires significantly more attention than for other areas of the world. This lack of a trained workforce is common in other developing areas of the world. Other challenges in developing areas, such as Africa, are disrupted and inefficient supply chains, and overreaching governmental regulations. Governments often protect local supply industries, resulting in low quality but high-cost supply chain (Maritz, 2012).

Africa presents additional challenges to global companies. Africa is a fragmented continent with a population of about 1 billion people, in 54 countries resulting in dozens of different legal systems and languages. In the hotel industry in Africa many of those countries are what executives call "one-single place": just one hotel in the capital with little prospect of expansion. Contrast this to China which has roughly the same population with only one legal system and official language (Blitz and Blas, 2014).

China is undisputedly the largest market in Asia. Both domestic and international hotel brands are expanding rapidly in this emerging market (Hung, 2013). In China, the expansion of large international hotel brands has met several challenges: threats of international hotel brands to the local hotel companies, lack of personality of domestic hotel brands, and lack of local brands (Hung 2013). These challenges are not unique to China and indeed summarize most international expansion.

The Balance of Independent Hotels versus Branded Throughout the World

Hotels have a stronger brand affiliation than restaurants. A hotel reservation involves an intangible transaction where guests are making purchases decisions sight unseen. In this market, branding provides a sense of security and affirmation of quality standards to the consumer. While branding is common across the hotel industry there are still more independent hotels worldwide than those affiliated with a brand. Yet, because independently owned and operated hotels are often smaller in size, there are more hotel rooms worldwide affiliated with a brand (Rogerson, 2011). While independent hotels run the gamut from large luxury properties to small economy hotels. Overall, most of the independent hotels are in the economy or lower-priced segment, are in suburban or small-town locations, and typically have 50 rooms or less (STR, 2016).

In the United States, about 30% of hotels today are independent, with the other 70% associated or affiliated with a brand or chain (Dev, 2012). For the remainder of the world, the ratio flips: between 60% and 70% of hotels as independent and only 30–40% associated or affiliated with a brand or chain (STR, 2016), with many countries estimating more than 85% of their hotels to be small independent hotels. Some countries have more independent hotels than others do (see Table 4.4). For example, while in France just over half of the hotels are independent, in Greece 93.6% of the hotels are independent, or not affiliated with a brand or chain.

Many hotels start as an independent or affiliate with small regional companies. In Africa, South America, the Middle East, Scandinavia, and Asia, hotels are often branded via regional hotel chains versus the large international hotel chains. Some of these markets present economic instability, high costs of entry to market, or are culturally very diverse markets as compared to the Western general market. Lease agreements present another favorable alternative and are utilized widely in the Scandinavian market.

Recent years have seen many independent hotels purchased by hotel companies. For example, in Kenya, Fairmont purchased The Norfolk and Mount Kenya Safari Club, which were initially locally owned hotels. Additionally, many regional companies are being acquired by larger multinational companies. A common growth strategy of hotel chains is to purchase small regional chains or independent hotels as a way of gaining strength in markets and countries (Stringam and Partlow, 2016). Another example is the acquisition of Top Star (small-scale brand) by rival Home Inns (larger brand) in China in 2007 (Chen and Fang, 2008). Home Inns & Hotels Management, Inc. is one of the top economy brands in China since its founding in 2002. At the time, Top Star was a popular economy brand with about 26 hotels in 18 cities, which helped Home Inns & Hotels Management, Inc. to expand its portfolio in China. In this respect, these types of mergers and acquisitions, where larger companies are acquired by small-scale brands and independent hotels, are also gaining popularity in China.

Multinational hotel companies can take several forms. Most of the companies engage in franchising and management contracts with little or no ownership involvement. In the United States, the hotel industry is primarily comprised of management contracts, franchise agreements with large multinational companies, and referral systems, all emphasizing the brand. Europe has a more integrated system, with large multinational company owned and operated hotels interspersed among smaller hotel companies and independent hotels (Gee, 2008; Powell, 2018). While branding through large multinational hotel companies is becoming more common in Europe, it is still

Table 4.4 Percentage of hotels independent versus chain affiliation

Region	Country	Percentage of hotels which are independent (%)
Europe	France	54.3
	Germany	82.5
	Greece	93.6
	Italy	89.1
	Norway	49.3
	Romania	85.4
	Spain	66.9
	United Kingdom	63.1
Russia	Russia	81.6
Asia–Pacific	Australia	70.8
	China	54.5
	India	78.3
	Japan	45.2
	Singapore	70.0
	Thailand	71.7
Mideast/Africa	Egypt	65.2
	Morocco	81.5
	South Africa	61.6
	Tunisia	87.2
Americas	Brazil	68.6
	Canada	77.6
	Mexico	80.1
	Panama	62.8
	Peru	77.6
	United States	30.0

Source: (STR, 2016).

the minority and varies by country (Gee, 2008). Europe has many independent hotels and regional hotel companies (Powell, 2018). Strong labor unions and high wages create a barrier for hotel market entry, particularly in Scandinavian hotels (Bourget, 2012). Similar to China, in the Scandinavian hotel market, recent years have seen some of these small regional companies acquired by other companies. Most of the prime real estate has already been developed, so hotel companies seeking a foothold in Europe often do so through acquisitions and mergers (Go and Pine, 1995).

Trends and Issues

With the globalization of travel, more acquisitions and mergers are expected to follow the patterns seen within the United States (Cunill, 2006). The hotel and restaurant industries are both expected to become increasingly affiliated with large companies. Independent hotels and restaurants are finding it increasingly more difficult to remain competitive in the global marketplace, gradually merging with larger international hospitality companies (Timothy and Tye, 2009). The same is true for small regional hotel and restaurant companies who are increasingly consolidating. While there will always be a place for the independent hotel or restaurant, their numbers will continue to decrease as more and more join with the brand.

For the restaurant industry globalization is bringing more diverse cuisine to more regions of the world. While some of the increase in international foods and cuisines will be due to the expansion of global brands, some will also be a result of various cultures migrating to different regions of the world. Alternatively, consumers are also seeking more locally grown, brewed, and produced products, giving strength to independent and locally owned restaurants, breweries, and food and beverage sources. Many of these have grown from single owned enthusiast brands to internationally acclaimed brands, redefining the market. For example, Mikkeller Beer started in 2006 in the kitchen of a math and physics teacher. Now just over ten years later it spans the globe with more than 40 dedicated bars, international Mikkeller beer festivals, and a fan base of dedicated followers that most microbreweries don't even dare dream about (Mikkeller, 2019). Another example is the UK-based BrewDog brewery. In ten years, they went from start up to more than 1,000 employees, 70,000 shareholders, follower-driven funding, their very own hotel (with a dedicated beer tap in every room!) and 46 bars (BrewDog, 2019). One more example is the Danish high-end steak restaurant MASH. Within three years of opening their first restaurant, they have opened their fifth restaurant, as an international restaurant in the very center of London and their expansion is limited only by their own quality assurance demands and a sworn goal of no further expansions in their home country (MASH, 2019).

The sharing economy or peer-to-peer accommodations are increasing as more travelers forgo the traditional hotel room product to rent apartments and rooms in homes. Airbnb has recently begun to expand its business model with the purchase of several resorts, hotels, and apartments. And hotel companies are trying their hand in the peer-to-peer accommodations industries. The growth of these markets is expected to bring changes to the industry structures and organization.

Technology is increasingly changing the hotel and restaurant industries. Beginning with central restaurant commissaries and early hotel reservation centers of a half-century ago, technology continues to shape the nature and organization of the hospitality industry. Cloud-based technologies allow for more integration of products and services. Robots allow for changes to production, and delivery of products and services. The Internet of Things (IoT) is changing consumer behavior. How will these changes impact the organization and structure of hotels and restaurants? While some technologies will allow small independent organizations to compete against large companies, other technologies will require larger investments and more skilled expertise which will favor the large companies. The hotel and restaurant industries are resilient and far-reaching. We have historical records of food and accommodations businesses dating back more than 4,000 years (Stringam and Partlow, 2016). How will the trends of today and the future impact such resilient, dynamic, and resourceful industries?

Conclusion

The hospitality industry is a dynamic industry. Overall, the hospitality industry utilizes four main organizational structures: independent ownership, franchising, management contracts, and consortiums or referral groups. There are more independent hotels and restaurants across the globe than those affiliated with a brand. However, brand affiliation is becoming more prevalent. Brand affiliation is not as significant for the restaurant industry. The hotel industry has experienced vertical disintegration or the separation of the ownership of the hotel asset from the management process. Most of the largest hotel management companies now own very few hotels. Both the hotel and restaurant industries have experienced and are continuing to see significant merger and acquisition activity with larger companies acquiring smaller regional companies. This is a common process for international expansion where large international companies acquire an existing company as a means of entry into a country. Franchising is another means of expansion into international markets, providing expertise, yet minimizing risk for the parent franchisor company. Brand affiliation is not as common in developing countries, where hospitality businesses are more likely to be independent or affiliated with small regional companies. Developing countries bring additional challenges of differing cultures and a lack of skilled employees. Globalization is changing the landscape and organizational structure of the hospitality industry. Regional cuisines have expanded across the globe, while at the same time consumers are seeking more locally sourced products. Technology is also bringing changes to the hospitality industry as hotels and restaurants increasingly adapt to meet the needs of an increasingly technology-driven consumer behavior, and take advantage of improvements in technology delivery. The Internet of Things, cloud-based technologies, artificial intelligence, and robotics promise to bring a robust and changing future for the hospitality industry

References

Barrows, C. and Powers, T. (2011), *Introduction to Management in the Hospitality Industry*, John Wiley & Sons, Hoboken, NJ.

Becker, E. (2013), *Overbooked*, Simon & Schuster, New York, NY.

Bender, B., Partlow, C., and Roth, M. (2008), "An examination of strategic drivers impacting U.S. multinational lodging corporations", *Journal of International Hospitality and Tourism Administration*, Vol.9, No.3, pp.219–243, doi: 10.1080/15256480802095862.

Bernstein, C. and Paul, R. (1994), *Winning the Chain Restaurant Game*, John Wiley & Sons, New York, NY.

Blitz, R. and Blas, J. (2014), "Africa is new battleground for global hotel industry", *Financial Times*, available at: https://www.ft.com/content/274c27d6-58e7-11e3-a7cb-00144feabdc0 (accessed 7 August 2019).

Bourget, K. (2012), "Scandinavia remains elusive to global chains", *HotelNewsNow*, available at: http://www.hotelnewsnow.com/Articles/15641/Scandinavia-remains-elusive-to-global-chains (accessed 12 January 2019).

Bradach, J. (1998), *Franchise Organizations*, Harvard Business School Press, Boston, MA.

BrewDog. (2019), "BrewDog history", *BrewDog.com*, available at: https://www.brewdog.com/about/history (accessed 12 January 2019).

Brookes, M. and Roper A. (2010), "The impact of entry modes on the organisational design of international hotel chains", *The Service Industries Journal*, Vol.30, No.9, pp.1499–1512, doi: 10.1080/02642060802626857.

Brotherton, B. (2003), *The International Hospitality Industry: Structure Characteristics and Issues*, Butterworth-Heinemann, Oxford, UK.

Chathoth, P. and Chon, K.S. (2009), "Rai Bahadur Mohan Singh Oberoi: Father of the Indian hotel industry", in Shea, L. and Roberts, C. (Eds.), *Pioneers of the Hospitality Industry: Lessons from Leaders, Innovators and Visionaries*, International CHRIE, Richmond, VA, pp. 99–107.

Chen, L. and Fang, F. (2008), "Economy hotel development trends in Mainland China", *HVS.com*, available at: http://www.hvs.com/article/3119-Economy-Hotel-Development-Trends-in-Mainland-China (accessed 1 January 2019).

China National Tourism Administration. (2009), *The Yearbook of China Tourism Statistics*, China Tourism Publishing House, Beijing.

Cunill, O.M. (2006), *The Growth Strategies of Hotel Chains*, Haworth Hospitality Press, Binghamton, NY.

deRoos, J. (2010), "Hotel management contracts past and present", *Cornell Hospitality Quarterly*, Vol.51, No.1, pp.68–80, doi: 10.1177/1938965509354865.

Dev, C. (2012), *Hospitality Branding*, Cornell University Press, Ithaca, NY.

Enz, C. (2010), *Hospitality Strategic Management*, John Wiley & Sons, Hoboken, NJ.

Franchise Times. (2018), "Franchise Times Top 200", *Franchisetimes.com*, available at: http://www.franchise-times.com/Top200 (accessed 5 December 2018).

Fried, S. (2010), *Appetite for America: How Visionary Businessman Fred Harvey Built a Railroad Hospitality Empire That Civilized the Wild West*, Bantam, New York, NY.

Gee, C. (2008), *International Hotels: Development and Management*, Educational Institute of the American Hotel and Lodging Association, East Lansing, MI.

Geller, L. (1998), "The demands of globalization on the lodging industry", *Hospitality Review*, Vol.16, No.1, pp.1–6, doi: 10.1177/1096348010370855.

Go, F. and Pine, R. (1995), *Globalization Strategy in the Hotel Industry*, Routledge, London, UK.

Higley, J. (2015, May 1), "Opportunity knocks for brands in Latin America", *HotelNewsNow.com*, available at: http://www.hotelnewsnow.com/Article/15783/Opportunity-knocks-for-brands-in-Latin-America (accessed 10 January 2019).

Hotels. (2019), "Hotels 325 2019", *Hotels*, available at: http://cdn.coverstand.com/18556/602570/a8b471b-11fbebe541238139974131341504fcb25.pdf (accessed 7 August 2019).

Hung, K. (2013), "Chinese hotels in the eyes of Chinese hoteliers: the most critical issues", *Asia Pacific Journal of Tourism Research*, Vol.18, No.4, pp.354–368, doi: 10.1080/10941665.2012.658415.

Jackson, L.A. (2012), "Towards an understanding of lodging asset management and its components", *FIU Hospitality Review*, Vol.30, No.1, pp.101–119.

Jackson, L. and Naipaul, S. (2009), "Isadore sharp & four seasons hotels and resorts: Redefining luxury and building a sustained brand", in Shea, L. and Roberts, C. (Eds.), *Pioneers of the Hospitality Industry: Lessons from Leaders, Innovators and Visionaries*, International CHRIE, Richmond, VA, pp.85–97.

Jakle, J., Sculle, K., and Rogers, J. (1996), *The Motel in America*, The Johns Hopkins University Press, Baltimore, MD.

Kim, K. and Olsen, M. (1999), "Determinants of successful acquisition processes in the US lodging industry", *International Journal of Hospitality Management*, Vol.18, No.3, pp.285–307, doi: 10.1016/S0278-4319(99)00028-6 10.1016/S0278-4319(99)00028-6.

Lattin, G., Lattin, T., and Lattin, J. (2013), *The Lodging and Foodservice Industry*, American Hotel & Lodging Association Educational Institute, Lansing, MI.

Lodging. (2018), "Get to Know Top Hotel Franchises", *Lodging Magazine*, available at: https://lodgingmagazine.com/2018-franchise-guide/ (accessed 5 December 2018).

Margolies, J. (1995), *Home Away from Home: Motels in America*, Bulfinch Press, Boston, MA.

Mariani, J. (1991), *America Eats Out*, William Morrow and Company, Inc., New York, NY.

Maritz, J. (2012), KFC's African Adventure, *How We Made It in Africa*, available at: https://www.howwemadeitinafrica.com/kfc%e2%80%99s-african-adventure/15151/ (accessed 7 August 2019).

MASH. (2019), "The history about MASH", *Mashsteak.dk.com*, available at: https://www.mashsteak.dk/history/ (accessed 12 January 2019).

McDonald's. (2019), "Our history, McDonald's", *Mcdonalds.com*, available at: http://www.mcdonalds.com/us/en/our_story/our_history.html (accessed 4 January 2019).

Miller, B. (2009), "Howard Deering Johnson: The man under the orange roof", in Shea, L. and Roberts, C. (Eds.), *Pioneers of the Hospitality Industry: Lessons from Leaders, Innovators and Visionaries*, International CHRIE, Richmond, VA, pp. 51–59.

Mikkeller. (2019), *Mikkeller Brewery*, available at: http://mikkeller.dk/brewery/2019 (accessed 12 January 2019).

Mutegi, M. (2017), "KFC Waiyaki way store raises national branch count to 15", *Business Daily*, available at: https://www.businessdailyafrica.com/corporate/companies/KFC-Waiyaki-Way-store-raises-national-branch-count-to-15/4003102-4151068-wo6l5u/index.html (accessed 10 January 2019).

Parsa, H.G., Self, J., Sydnor-Busso, S., and Yoon, H.J. (2011), "Why restaurants fail? Part II – The impact of affiliation, location, and size on restaurant failures: Results from a survival analysis", *Journal of Foodservice Business Research*, Vol.14, No.4, pp.360–379, doi: 10.1080/15378020.2011.625824.

Pillsbury, R. (1990), *From Boarding House to Bistro: The American Restaurant, Then and Now*, Unwin Hyman, Inc., Boston, MA.

Powell, L. (2018), "What European luxury hotels can learn from their midscale cousins", *Skift*, available at: https://skift.com/2018/10/09/what-european-luxury-hotels-can-learn-from-their-midscale-cousins/ (accessed 11 October 2018).

Rodriguez, A.R. (2002), "Determining factors in entry choice for international expansion: The case of the Spanish hotel industry", *Tourism Management*, Vol.23, No.6, pp. 597–607, doi: 10.1016/S0261-5177(02)00024-9.

Rogerson, J.M. (2011), "The limited service hotel in South Africa: The growth of the city lodge", *Urban Forum*, Vol.22, No.4, pp.343–361, doi: 10.1007/s12132-011-9130-0.

Sampson, H. (2018, September 28), "Marriott CEO to unhappy loyalty members: 'hang with us' ", *Skift.com*, available at: https://skift.com/2018/09/28/marriott-ceo-to-unhappy-loyalty-members-hang-with-us/ (accessed 15 October 2018).

Sigalos, M. and Turner, A. (2018), "Why this local brand is beating McDonald's in the Philippines", *CNBC.com*, available at: https://www.cnbc.com/2018/11/20/jollibee-mcdonalds-philippines-smashburger-burger-king.html (accessed 7 August 2019).

Singh, A.J., Kline, R.D., Ma, Q., and Beals, P. (2012), "Evolution of hotel asset management: The historical context and current profile of the profession", *Cornell Hospitality Quarterly*, Vol.53, No.4, pp.326–338.

Slattery, P. (2012), *The Economic Ascent of the Hotel Business*, Goodfellow Publishers, Oxford, UK.

Smith, A. (2011), *Eating History: Turning Points in the Making of American Cuisine*, Columbia University Press, New York, NY.

Statistica. (2019), "Distribution of independent and chain restaurant foodservice sales", *Statistica.com*, available at: https://www.statista.com/statistics/491986/foodservice-sales-of-chain-and-independent-restaurants-worldwide/ (accessed 5 January 2019).

STR. (2016), "Hotel industry analytic foundations", *Smith Travel Research*, The SHARE Center at Smith Travel Research, Hendersonville, TN.

Stringam, B. and Partlow, C. (2016), *A Profile of the Hospitality Industry*, Business Expert Press, New York, NY.

Sturman, M., Corgel, J., and Verma, R. (Eds.) (2011), *The Cornell School of Hotel Administration on Hospitality: Cutting Edge Thinking and Practice*, John Wiley & Sons, Hoboken, NJ.

Sullivan, M. (2013), "The soft sell: With soft branding independents can act like a chain when it makes good business sense", *Lodging*, Vol 38 No.12, pp.32–33.

Summers, B. (2007), *Hospitality Goes Global*, Cornell Hotel Society, Ithaca, NY.

Timothy, D. and Teye, V. (2009), *Tourism and the Lodging Sector*, Butterworth-Heinemann, Burlington, MA.

Tomiyama, A. (2015), "Southeast Asia's burgeoning restaurant and coffee chains", *Asianikkei.com*, available at: https://asia.nikkei.com/Business/Southeast-Asia-s-burgeoning-restaurant-and-coffee-chains (accessed 10 January 2019).

Turkel, S. (2009), *Great American Hoteliers: Pioneers of the Hotel Industry*, Authorhouse, Bloomington, IN.

Vallen, J. and Vallen G. (2018), *Check-in, Check-out*, Pearson, Upper Saddle River, NJ.

Vermillion, L., Cimini, M., and Hayward, P. (2009), *A Century of Hospitality*, American Hotel and Lodging Association, Washington, DC.

Walker, J.R. (2016), *Introduction to Hospitality Management*, Pearson, Upper Saddle River, NJ.

Watkins, E. (2013), "Accor reorganization reverses asset strategy", *Hotel News Now*, available at: http://www.hotelnewsnow.com/articles/21087/Accor-reorganization-reverses-asset-strategy (accessed 10 January 2019).

Xiao, Q., O'Neill, J.W., and Wang, H. (2008), "International hotel development", *International Journal of Hospitality Management*, Vol.27, pp.325–336, doi: 10.1016/j.ijhm.2007.10.006.

Zhang, H.Q., Pine, R., and Lam, T. (2005), *Tourism and Hotel Development in China*, The Haworth Hospitality Press, New York, NY.

PART II

Culture and International Hospitality Management

5

CUSTOMER EXPERIENCE IN HOSPITALITY AND TOURISM

A Cross-Cultural Perspective

Raija Seppälä-Esser

From Consuming to Experiencing

Throughout the past decades, societies have undergone changes in their value systems. Individualism and hedonism have superseded conformity and restraint in people's lives. In today's advanced economies individuals can more easily satisfy their lower order or 'basic needs' as described by Maslow (1970) and, therefore, the 'higher-order needs' such as self-esteem and self-fulfillment have moved to the fore. People strive for pleasure, enjoyment, and well-being, as well as happiness and positive experiences (Mutz and Kämpfer, 2013; Schulze, 2005). Growing disposable income and flexibility in organizing one's leisure time are framework conditions facilitating these pursuits (Kroeber-Riehl and Gröppel-Klein, 2013). Even in their role as consumers, people are not merely interested in the features and the quality of an offering but expect to gain emotional value and experience self-fulfillment (Bolton et al., 2014; Pine and Gilmore, 1999; Schmitt, 1999).

As a consequence of the rising experience orientation of contemporary societies with more sophisticated and demanding consumers as well as advances in technology and increasing competitive pressures, the economy must adapt to the demands of this transformation (Pine and Gilmore, 1999; Räikkönen and Grénman, 2017). The positioning of products and services based on their experiential value has, therefore, become essential (Kroeber-Riehl and Gröppel-Klein, 2013) and the experience quality of companies' offerings will determine their economic success (Sotiriadis and Sarmaniotis, 2016). Increasing experience-orientation of consumers has also shifted the emphasis of the hospitality and tourism industry in this respect, leading to experiences becoming a fundamental element of the product offer (Voss, 2004; Voss and Zomerdijk, 2007). In a global tourism market place, this development brings a challenge to actors in the hospitality and tourism industry to cater for the needs of culturally diverse customers and impress them with attractive, meaningful and memorable experiences (Lee and Prebensen, 2018; Wang et al., 2015).

The growing demand within international tourism, along with increasing experience orientation of societies, presents the management of hospitality companies with the challenge of reacting aptly to the needs of customers from different cultural backgrounds. Because culture shapes people's values and behavior as well as the way they perceive the world and interact with others, cross-cultural understanding gains importance. Culture influences customers' experiences along the entire customer journey, whereas the most moments-of-truth – contacts between an employee and a customer – in the hospitality setting occur during the service encounter. The awareness of culture's influence on the feelings and behavior of customers and service employees has hence become essential in the contemporary tourism market.

Evoking Experiences in Hospitality and Tourism

Creating Customer Value through Experiences

In the global marketplace, where new markets for both in- and outbound tourism are emerging and competition on the global level is fierce, tourism products increasingly resemble each other. In more prosperous countries, leisure travel has become a commodity and part of the life-style (Scheurer, 2003; Voss and Zomerdijk, 2007). Although 'to experience something' has always been one of the core travel motives, tourism products were long regarded to just be an entrance to experiences. Thereby, the experience itself was not something that could be consumed (Jensen et al. 2015; Stamboulis and Skayannis, 2003). Moreover, in the service management literature, experience has historically not been considered as a distinct construct (Verhoef et al., 2009). However, to cut through the noise in today's marketplace, hospitality and tourism businesses should regard an innovative design of experiences as their key competence and create value for customers by providing experiences that are perceived as enjoyable and meaningful. This kind of value creation facilitates the much-needed differentiation from the competition as well as a strong position in a competitive marketplace (Bolton et al., 2014; Boswijk et al., 2007; Kroeber-Riehl and Gröppel-Klein, 2013; Pine and Gilmore, 2011; Verhoef et al., 2009).

In the 'experience economy,' adapting to the diverse needs of consumers is crucial. Traditional marketing, where the focus is largely on the functional or physical attributes of an offering, proves to be less effective in creating value to customers in the present-day societies (Özlem, 2016). Emotions play a major role in our everyday lives where our decisions and actions as consumers are influenced by our emotions (Kahneman, 2011; Zaltman et al., 2015). People in experience-oriented societies pursue happiness and, therefore, search for stimuli, which give rise to positive emotions (Schulze, 2005).

According to Holbrook and Hirschman (1982), consumption behavior encompasses both utilitarian and hedonic components. The *utilitarian component* includes information processing (searching, weighing, evaluating) before the purchase. At a later stage, it comprises the criteria for evaluating the purchase decision and its value in practical terms or, rather, how well the envisioned purpose was fulfilled. The *hedonic* component or the experiential value of a product or a service emerges mainly during consumption, but also before and after customer's direct interaction with an offering (Chen et al., 2018; Holbrook and Hirschman, 1982). Customers determine this value individually and phenomenologically, with the perceived experiential value being contextual and meaning-laden (Vargo and Lusch, 2008). During direct interactions with customers, companies have the opportunity to co-create value by providing resources and processes with potential value and thereby influence customers' future buying and consumption behavior (Grönroos and Voima, 2013). Prahalad and Ramaswamy (2004, p. 5) argue that these *"co-creation experiences are the basis of value"* and to enable these, companies must innovate *"experience environments."* Co-creation of value does not occur only during service encounters and between customers and firms but also involves other customer-related actors affecting the individual's experience either positively or negatively (Carù and Cova, 2015; Grönroos and Voima, 2013; Kandampully et al., 2018). Evoked emotions, sensory experiences as well as fulfillment of higher-order motives are factors determining whether a consumer will purchase or re-purchase a product or a service (Holbrook and Hirschman, 1982; Jensen et al., 2015). By offering individual products with high emotional value, businesses can better satisfy their customers, increase their loyalty and, hence, become more profitable (Bruhn, 2015; Maklan and Klaus, 2011; Pine and Gilmore, 2011).

The Role of Emotions in the Customer Experience

Experience is a response to stimuli in the mind of an experiencing person. It is therefore essential for tourism service providers to learn to recognize which stimuli might evoke a positive emotional experience (Wirtz et al., 2003). In order to understand and implement the experiential perspective, a systematic analysis is essential (Holbrook and Hirschman, 1982).

Lemon and Verhoef (2016, p. 71) define customer experience as *"a multidimensional construct focusing on a customer's cognitive, emotional, behavioral, sensorial, and social responses to a firm's offerings during the customer's entire purchase journey."* A customer's response may result both from direct or indirect contact with a company (Meyer and Schwager, 2007). According to Helkkula (2011), the customer's experience in the service context can be examined from various perspectives: as a phenomenon, as a process, and as an outcome. The focus of the *phenomenological* characterization is on the subjective, internal, and event-specific service experience. This concept has often been used in connection with the hedonic consumption behavior (Carù et al., 2016). The emphasis of the *process-based* characterization of the service experience lies on the structural elements and different stages or phases of the process as well as on the resulting change (Helkkula, 2011). From the tourists' perspective, these are processes that occur before, during, and after tourist's interaction with tourism environments (Jensen et al., 2015). The *outcomes* of the service experience are measured using various variables (e.g., value, satisfaction, quality, repurchase intention) on an aggregated level (Carù et al., 2016; Helkkula, 2011). These concepts of service experience are complementary and not mutually exclusive. The phenomenological approach is appropriate for analyzing individuals' experiences, but could also provide improvement opportunities for the service experience process and its outcomes (Helkkula, 2011).

When examining the *phenomenological experience* of consumers, insights into the experience as a psychological phenomenon seem appropriate. In emotion psychology, a broad agreement on the main three components of emotion exists. *Physiological arousal* denotes the neurophysiological immediate reaction of a person caused by an internal or external stimulus (Scherer, 2000). The facial expression, change in the voice and the language, as well as gestures, are signs of *expression behavior* related to social communication (Adolphs and Damasio, 2000). The subjective *experiential component* of an emotion can be defined as "feeling" or "sentiment." Motivational factors and cognitive processes may be further added to the scope of emotion components (Scherer, 2000). Beatty (2013) maintains, however, that not all emotions are expressed and followed by action. He names regret, boredom, love, and remorse as examples of such emotions. Beatty argues further that emotions do not always emerge immediately. For instance, pride, shame, contempt, fear, and anger are emotions that sometimes unfold over time.

In the marketplace of experiences, the environmental psychology perspective focuses on interactions of the experiencing subject with its environment (Kroeber-Riehl and Gröppel-Klein, 2013). Although the meaning and value of experiences occur as an internal and personal process, they are influenced by external factors as well (Jensen et al., 2015). The stimuli a person elicits from his environment, combined with his personality traits, have a significant effect on his emotional reactions and the subsequent behavior. People tend to approach environments which evoke positive emotions and avoid environments with negatively perceived cues (Mehrabian and Russell, 1974; Russell and Mehrabian, 1978). Scheurer (2003) describes an environment for tourism experiences as an 'experience-setting' comprising all the stimuli in the physical and social environment of the customer, which potentially influence his emotions. Thus, the surrounding culture influences a person's perception of stimuli from these environments (Kroeber-Riehl and Gröppel-Klein, 2013). People from different cultures may interpret events and environments differently, which results in different emotions. The experience-setting is further influenced by personal resources (motivation, interest, involvement, knowledge, skills) of experiencing individuals as well as by the information offered (Prebensen et al., 2018). Alongside the environment, which we experience first-hand physically or materially, another reality, an environment created by media, has emerged. The media environment has a growing influence on consumers' behavior (Figure 5.1).

The *process-based* examination includes a longitudinal view of the service experience (Helkkula, 2011). A positive encounter at a pre-consumption stage may boost the emotional experience later in the process (Chen et al., 2018). Kahneman (2011) suggests that our long-term memory ("remembering self") plays a pivotal role in our future decisions. Only stimuli that are being regarded as relevant are passed to long-term memory. According to Kahneman, what remains in memory after a series of experiences is the most impressive experience ("peak experience") and the closing event ("end experience"). Beatty (2013) suggests that it would be essential to focus on the potential long-lasting duration of emotions in order to understand their actual role in our lives. A narrow focus on hedonic experiences, i.e., feeling good during an experience, overlooks the benefits tourists gain beyond time spent on traveling (Knobloch et al., 2017). Eudaimonic effects of tourist consumption contribute to an individual's well-being and quality of life (Dolnicar et al., 2012; Knobloch et al., 2017) and may show delayed effects when results are achieved. Even negative emotions or unpleasant experiences (e.g., fear, nervousness, unexpected problems) may, at the end, lead to positive, meaningful experiences (Knobloch et al., 2017). Huta and Ryan (2010, p. 735) argue that *"hedonia and eudaimonia occupy both overlapping and distinct niches within a complete picture of well-being, and their combination may be associated with the greatest well-being."* Thus hospitality and tourism companies should plan their marketing communication and product offer in a manner where they evoke memorable and meaningful experiences among their customers (Chen et al., 2018; Kim et al., 2011; Özlem, 2016). The memories should not fade or blur over time and

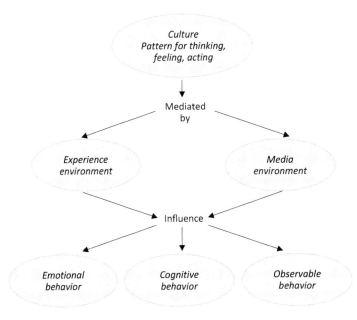

Figure 5.1   Relationships between culture and behavior (based on Kroeber-Riehl and Gröppel-Klein, 2013).

should neither be reconstructed nor replaced by negative false memories (Zaltman et al., 2015) by the "remembering self."

In consideration of the nature and emergence of individual experiences, it seems a challenging task to evoke delighting, or even satisfactory, customer experiences in hospitality and tourism. Schulze (2005) argues that it is, in fact, not possible to produce experiences; it is only possible to provide optimal circumstances which enable experiences to emerge. Moreover, Vargo and Lusch (2008) maintain that companies cannot deliver value; they can only offer value propositions for customers.

Challenges of Cross-Cultural Customer Experiences in the Hospitality Industry

Culture's Influence on Emotions

Culture provides guidelines for thinking, feeling, and behaving in specific situations (Kroeber-Riehl and Gröppel-Klein, 2013). It creates norms of behavior, which help to maintain social order and maximize the function and effectiveness of groups (Matsumoto et al., 2008). It is also linked to tourists' motivations, emotions, and behavior (de Mooij and Hofstede, 2011; Kroeber-Riehl and Gröppel-Klein, 2013; Matsumoto et al., 2008; Reisinger and Turner, 2004). Culture influences the value customers' perceive in the tourism and hospitality products. Therefore, analysis and understanding of customers' diverse needs and behaviors are crucial. In service situations, a service provider's own culture also shapes its encounter with customers from other cultures (Barker and Härtel, 2004) and, hence, the ability to meet expectations and emotional needs.

Emotions are culture-bound and affected by interactions with other persons in the social environment (Adolphs and Damasio, 2000; de Mooij and Hofstede, 2011; Lim, 2016; Reisinger and Turner, 2004). Cross-cultural emotion research has largely focused on cultures that can be labeled either as *individualistic* or *collectivistic* oriented. In the Western individualistic cultures, social relationships are primarily based on the interests and goals of individuals who are independent and whose own thoughts, feelings, and actions are emphasized (Lim, 2016; Markus and Kitayama, 2010; Woodside et al., 2011). Eastern cultures, in contrast, are commonly described as collectivistic, resulting in the 'self' being an interdependent part of the society. People in this cultural context sense themselves as members of a network of social relationships (Lim, 2016; Markus and Kitayama, 2010). They are assumed to adjust to the group and to attune to the emotions of others as well as to cooperate and show conformity to other group members, thereby obtaining in-group harmony (de Mooij and Hofstede, 2011; Lim, 2016; Meng, 2010; Park et al., 2018; Tsai, 2017). It is important to note, however, as Markus and Kitayama (2010) point out, that cultures and also individuals differ in how pronounced these two cultural patterns prevail. Cross-cultural research has exposed cultural differences in how emotions are displayed (de Mooij and Hofstede, 2011; Kroeber-Riehl and Gröppel-Klein, 2013; Lim, 2016; Matsumoto, 2016; Matsumoto and Takeuchi, 1998) and how expressions of emotions are recognized and judged (Wang et al., 2006; Yuki et al., 2006). Moreover, culture has been found out to influence the appropriateness of emotions and feelings and the value and meaning rendered to these (Ellsworth, 1994; Reisinger and Turner, 2004). It has also been discovered that differences exist between people from different cultures regarding their preferred and sought after affective state (Lim, 2016; Tsai, 2017).

Intercultural communication refers to both verbal (language) and nonverbal behavior (e.g., facial expressions, eye contact, voice, gestures, interpersonal space, and silence) of people of different cultures interacting with each other (Matsumoto and Takeuchi, 1998). The signals interactants perceive during communication episodes and what meaning these signals are being rendered to is culturally determined (Beamer, 1992; Matsumoto and Takeuchi, 1998; Reisinger and Turner, 2004). Reisinger and Turner (2004, p. 6) therefore argue that "*culture is the foundation of interaction.*" People interact with others and communicate their emotions primarily through their facial expressions and interpret the emotional states of others by perceiving facial and other interpersonal cues (Reisinger and Turner, 2004; Yuki et al., 2006). Facial expressions are assessed differently in different cultures. Because in-group harmony in collectivistic cultures is vital and has to be maintained, the cultural context implicates the way people should express their emotions (Lim, 2016; Matsumoto, 2016). Therefore, emotional expressions are often controlled and masked (Matsumoto, 2016), especially if they are negative (de Mooij and Hofstede, 2011). Wang et al. (2006) found out that Chinese people have difficulty recognizing negative emotions (e.g., fear and disgust) as accurately as positive emotions. The authors assume this to be due to the test persons' cultural context, where positive emotions are displayed, but negative emotions are often suppressed. By contrast, individualistic cultures are associated with higher expressivity. In both individualistic and collectivistic cultures, emotions are displayed more toward in-groups than toward out-groups (Matsumoto et al., 2008). Yuki et al. (2006) studied how Japanese and Americans interpret emotions expressed through eyes and mouth. Japanese weigh the eyes more than the mouth, whereas Americans pay more attention to the person's mouth while decoding emotions. It is also noteworthy, that in many East Asian cultures avoiding eye contact is more appropriate than to make direct eye contact, which can be perceived as intimidating and disrespectful. In contrast, in most Western countries maintaining direct eye contact is a crucial part of social interaction (Park et al., 2018).

Culture determines expectations and perceptions of service provision, thereby establishing the level of customer's satisfaction with the service (Barker and Härtel, 2004; Reisinger and Turner, 2004). Based on Russell's (1980) representation of affective states of individuals (also called feelings,

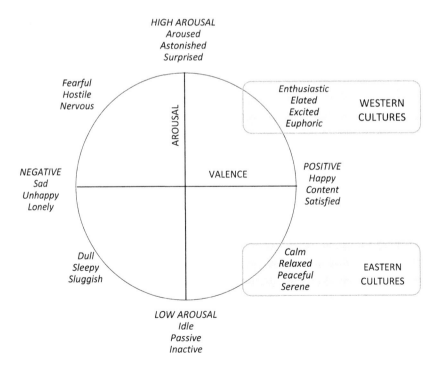

Figure 5.2 Affect valuation and cultural variation.
Adapted from Tsai (2017), Tsai et al. (2006), and Russell (1980).

moods, or emotions) as a circle in a two-dimensional bipolar space, feelings can be located in a pleasure-displeasure (valence) and activation-deactivation (arousal) dimension (Figure 5.2). Whereas people from individualistic, Western cultures prefer positive high arousal emotions (enthusiastic, excited, elated, delighted, happy), people from collectivistic, eastern cultures value and desire more low arousal experiences (calm, peaceful, relaxed, serene, pleased) (Lim, 2016; Tsai, 2017; Tsai et al., 2006).

An unfamiliar cultural background creates uncertainty among interactants, making conflict and misunderstandings unavoidable (Matsumoto and Takeuchi, 1998; Sharma et al., 2009). On the other hand, the familiarity of the culture reduces uncertainty and negative perceptions and, hence, facilitates communication (Beamer, 1992; Reisinger and Turner, 2004; Sharma et al., 2009; Wang et al., 2015). Therefore, service providers are likely more attracted to customers from their own cultural background (Härtel and Fujimoto, 2000). Interactions with service providers often constitute the customers' source for evaluating the level of satisfaction. Customers from diverse cultural backgrounds may sense discomfort due to different behavioral norms (Sharma et al., 2009) and may be dissatisfied when perceiving interactions with service employees unjust and discriminating (Barker and Härtel, 2004). However, people from different cultures have different ways to express their dissatisfaction. Because maintaining harmony is a higher-order need in collectivistic cultures, consumers from these cultures are less likely to voice their dissatisfaction and complain directly to the provider. Instead, they tend to practice negative word-of-mouth in their in-group and silently end the customer relationship with the company (de Mooij and Hofstede, 2011). Matsumoto and Takeuchi (1998) argue that controlling emotions is inevitable for enabling critical thinking about cultural differences and allowing an appropriate reaction/behavior.

Delighting Culturally Diverse Customers

In the hospitality industry, the experience is in the very core of the offer (Räikkönen and Grénman, 2017). Customers do not buy service delivery and quality, but instead, they buy experiences and memories (Hemmington, 2007). Their positive response to the service encounter is the basis for satisfaction (Sotiriadis and Sarmaniotis, 2016). Even the best physical product may not be able to compensate for a potential dissatisfaction (Reisinger and Turner, 2004). Customer experience is holistic, comprising of customer's cognitive, affective, emotional, social, and physical responses. It is also holistic in a sense that it includes all the phases of the customer journey from the search to purchase, consumption and the post-consumption phase, as well as all the interactions customers have with the company during the customer journey (Bolton et al., 2014; Verhoef et al., 2009). The focus in the following will be primarily on the stage of the consumption experience in the service environment of a hospitality company as most "peak-experiences" are likely to happen at this stage. Hotel businesses constitute servicescapes, which are physical environments, where services are produced and consumed and which influence customers' and employees' feelings and behavior (Bitner, 1992). If servicescape is observed within the framework of experiential consumption and from the multi-stakeholder perspective – including customers, employees as well as other stakeholders – it evolves into *experiencescape* (Pizam and Tasci, 2019). Pizam and Tasci (2019, pp. 26 and 34) define experiencescape as

> *the sensory, functional, social, natural, and cultural stimuli in a product or service environment, surmounted with a culture of hospitality, all of which accrue to an experience for consumers, employees, and other stakeholders and result in positive or negative cognitive, affective, and behavioral reactions toward products, services, brands, and firms.*

Hotel businesses constitute such experiencescapes where people interact and experience service.

Sukhu et al. (2019) suggest that customers' emotional response and satisfaction in hospitality companies are influenced by four elements: social elements, room elements, ambiance elements, and public elements. Social elements encompass service encounters, where the performance and hospitality of service employees influence customers' emotional responses. The room elements, amenities provided for customers in the hotel room, have a strong influence on the customer experience, whereby a higher quality appears to lead to emotions that are even more positive. Ambiance elements refer to tangible and intangible elements, such as the design of the space and multi-sensory integration. Public spaces and facilities evoke, especially in upscale hotels, positive emotions and facilitate customer satisfaction (Sukhu et al., 2019). Torres et al. (2014) identified similar elements comprising of the employees' performance, room and public facilities to be the key drivers for customer delight in a hotel experience. Several authors include the customer-to-customer interaction as a social element in the experience setting as it can have significant influence on the customer experience (Boswijk et al., 2007; Kandampully et al., 2018; Khan et al., 2015; Snel, 2011; Verhoef et al., 2009). Hemmington (2007) considers safety and security to be an additional key dimension of a hotel customer's experience. In a hotel setting, the value perceived by customers is affected by their experience, which again is determined by the physical and human environment dimensions (Sotiriadis and Sarmaniotis, 2016).

Designing Physical Experience Setting

The physical experience setting of hospitality companies, room and public elements, is a source of emotions which guides guest behavior and build anticipation. At the same time, it is the space where customers and service employees meet (Voss and Zomerdijk, 2007). The setting should be functional, aesthetic, and facilitate co-creation (Prebensen et al., 2018). At best, it constitutes a contrast to and escape from customer's everyday mundane life and lets him experience something new (Ariffin and Maghzi, 2012; Jensen et al., 2015; Tarssanen and Kylänen, 2007). The design of public spaces should create a pleasant and welcoming atmosphere and contribute to the feeling of safety and security. By assisting customers in finding their way (e.g., with multilingual signage and information material), service providers aid to avoid the feeling of insecurity and the arousal of negative emotions (Müller and Scheurer, 2004; Pizam and Tasci, 2019). Service environments, such as hotels and restaurants, provide stimuli for several senses (Hulten, 2017) and with a skillful application of ambiance elements in the *experiencescape* customers' sensory experiences are stimulated. Physiological perception of the environment with human senses evokes emotions and has the power to intensify the experience (Gelter, 2007; Tarssanen and Kylänen, 2007) which again generates customer-value (Hulten, 2011). Sensory perceptions in relation to visual, sound, smell, and taste perceptions are culturally different, whereby touch perceptions are universal. Regarding visual stimuli, people from different cultural backgrounds differ in how they perceive objects and places as well as in their color preferences. Auditory stimuli have an impact on perceptions of credibility and trust, positive feelings, purchasing, and the time spent. Music and emotions are linked regardless of cultural context, but the choice of music (genres and songs) is culturally dependent (Hulten, 2017). Scents are commonly used in the hotel business, where they have proved to have a positive impact on guests and result in more creativity and problem-solving (Hulten, 2017; Hulten et al., 2009). Hulten et al. (2009) mention, however, that scents are preferred in spaces which customers occupy only temporarily. It should be considered that scents follow the trends and fashions of different cultures and, hence, preferences differ between customers

(Hulten et al., 2009). When applied, however, they have a strong and long lasting effect. Cultural differences regarding multi-sensory perception are not well known and more research is needed (Hulten, 2017).

Managing the Service Encounter

Service encounter in a service setting indicates a face-to-face interaction between a customer and a provider (Solomon et al., 1985). Service experiences emerge in service encounters, which create customers' cognitive, emotional, and behavioral responses (Barker and Härtel, 2004; Chen et al., 2018; Edvardsson, 2005; Hemmington, 2007). These interactions result in a mental mark or a memory and significantly influence customers' quality perceptions (Edvardsson, 2005). For high-contact services, such as in the hospitality industry, understanding how to design the service to meet the needs of major cultural groups would be highly beneficial (Mattila, 1999). In addition, appropriate and well-trained employees can empathize with a guest and provide personalized and individualized service that leads to an enjoyable experience (Bolton et al., 2014). Bolton et al. (2014) suggest that small details in service interactions can have a vital and enhancing effect on the customer's evaluation of the service experience, especially when the customer's personal, social, and cultural aspects are considered and appreciated.

Cultural factors prompt differences in customers' expectations, attitudes towards and interaction with service employees, and evaluation of service performance (Mattila, 1999; Reisinger and Turner, 2004). *True hospitality*, according to Ariffin and Maghzi (2012), means that service providers allow their guests to act as they wish while not expecting them to reciprocate. This, however, is complicated by the fact that service providers tend to be more attracted to customers matching their own culture (Barker and Härtel, 2004). Cultural familiarity facilitates both verbal and nonverbal communication in intercultural settings, whereas cultural distance promotes misunderstandings (Reisinger and Turner, 2004; Sharma et al., 2009; Wang et al., 2015).

Because nonverbal signals have greater impact for expressing attitudes and emotions than verbal messages (Herring, 1990), it is not only necessary to understand the verbal language but also decipher nonverbal cues to provide a delightful service experience. Culturally learned decoding rules for communication have a profound impact on how people interpret the actions of others as they are closely linked to emotions and value judgments (Matsumoto and Takeuchi, 1998). The study of Barker and Härtel (2004) suggests that culturally diverse customers may experience feelings of 'embarrassment' and 'shame' and feeling 'small' and 'inferior' when receiving service which they perceive as discriminatory, especially when this happens in front of their peers and families. Cultural differences often result in discomfort felt by the service employees as well (Sharma et al., 2009). Although bad service experience could be a cause for a complaint, many guests from collectivistic cultures would refrain from doing so in favor of preserving harmony and avoiding loss of face (de Mooij and Hofstede, 2011). A good service recovery and complaint handling are recognized to significantly increase customer satisfaction and loyalty, which in turn can be a source for eudaimonia.

In order to overcome the challenges in cross-cultural service encounters, *emotion regulation* (Matsumoto and Takeuchi, 1998) and *communication accommodation* strategies (Wang et al., 2015) are proposed. Matsumoto (2016) maintains that the arousal of negative emotions due to unavoidable cultural differences is a critical event defining the success of an encounter. To master the challenges that may arise in an encounter of people from different cultures, Matsumoto and Takeuchi (1998, p. 2) suggest that "*emotion regulation is a gatekeeper ability that allows people to engage in successful conflict resolution and leading to effective, long-term intercultural communication.*" They argue that only individuals, who can regulate negative feelings and do not allow them to overcome their subsequent reactions and emotions, are able to engage in critical thinking and consider the possible causes of the differences. In addition, being open and flexible to new ways of thinking is required. By recognizing the diverse cultural backgrounds of tourists, hospitality companies are learning ways and means to develop and promote their services and facilities (Lee and Prebensen, 2018). To enhance the cross-cultural customer experience, hospitality firms can implement strategies to accommodate communications either by aligning the cultural background of the service provider and the customer or facilitating communication with the client's native language (Wang et al., 2015). The study by Wang et al. (2015) shows that these strategies result in customers' positive emotional responses such as increasing pleasure and the feeling of being in control. Moreover, they increase the perceived symbolic value, such as self-enhancement and group membership. In addition, the impact of communications accommodation on perceived symbolic value is reinforced when service employees express a higher intercultural orientation of accommodation practices (Wang et al., 2015). Zaltman et al. (2015) argue that hospitality managers must ensure that both company's communications and the actual service experience of customers stimulate the anticipated emotional response.

Conclusion

The global tourism industry experiences constant growth. The World Tourism Organization (UNWTO) forecasts an increase in international tourism for years to come (World Tourism Organization, 2011). Every year around 43 million additional international tourists enter the tourism market. Destinations in Asia and Pacific are expected to experience remarkable growth while tourism to Europe continues to grow on a somewhat lower level but on top of a large base. Similarly, other world regions are becoming increasingly important markets for international tourism as projected by the UNWTO (World Tourism Organization, 2011). Globalized tourism markets mean an inevitable get-together of tourism service providers and customers from different cultures and inherent challenges thereof. International tourists travel with an individual set of implicit and explicit expectations keen to have them fulfilled. They want to return home with great new experiences that will be reminisced for a long time. In the optimal case, these travel experiences contribute to tourists' long-term happiness and well-being. In order for this to happen, the tourism and hospitality industry faces the challenge to fulfill the needs of individuals from different cultures with different motives, perceptions, and behaviors. Designing the physical and social environment in the hospitality business so that it evokes positive emotions, lives up to every customer's expectations, shows real hospitality, and adjusts the behavior in the service encounter to accommodate individual customer's needs is the way forward for hospitality companies to enable relevant, memorable, and meaningful customer experiences.

References

Adolphs, R. and Damasio, A.R. (2000), "Neurobiology of emotion at a systems level", in Borod, J.C. (Ed.), *The Neuropsychology of Emotion*, Oxford University Press, New York, NY, pp.194–213.

Ariffin, A.A.M. and Maghzi, A. (2012), "A preliminary study on customer expectations of hotel hospitality: Influences of personal and hotel factors", *International Journal of Hospitality Management*, Vol.31, No.1, pp.191–198. doi: 10.1016/j.ijhm.2011.04.012.

Barker, S. and Härtel, C.E.J. (2004), "Intercultural service encounters: An exploratory study of customer experiences", *Cross Cultural Management: An International Journal*, Vol.11, No.1, pp.3–14. doi: 10.1108/13527600410797710.

Beamer, L. (1992), "Learning intercultural communication competence", *The Journal of Business Communication*, Vol.29, No.3, pp.285–303. doi: 10.1177/002194369202900306.

Beatty, A. (2013), "Current emotion research in anthropology: Reporting the field", *Emotion Review*, Vol.5, No.4, pp.414–422. doi: 10.1177/1754073913490045.

Bitner, M.J. (1992), "Servicescapes: The impact of physical surroundings on customers and employees", *Journal of Marketing*, Vol.56, No.2, pp.57–71. doi: 10.2307/1252042.

Bolton, R.N., Gustafsson, A., McColl-Kennedy, J., Sirianni, N.J., and Tse, D.K. (2014), "Small details that make big differences: A radical approach to consumption experience as a firm's differentiating strategy", *Journal of Service Management*, Vol.25, No.2, pp.253–274. doi: 10.1108/JOSM-01-2014-0034.

Boswijk, A., Thijssen, T., and Peelen, E. (2007), "A new perspective on the experience economy – Meaningful experiences", in Kylänen, M. (Ed.), *Articles on Experiences 3*, pp.76–99, University of Lapland, Rovaniemi.

Bruhn, M. (2015), *Relationship Marketing – Das Management von Kundenbeziehungen*, Franz Vahlen, Munich.

Carù, A., Colm, L., and Cova, B. (2016), "Innovating services through experiences: An investigation of servicescape's pivotal role", in Toivonen, M. (Ed.), *Service Innovation: Novel Ways of Creating Value in Actor Systems*, Springer Japan, Tokyo, pp.149–170.

Carù, A. and Cova, B. (2015), "Co-creating the collective service experience", *Journal of Service Management*, Vol.26, No.2, pp.276–294. doi: 10.1108/JOSM-07-2014-0170.

Chen, J.S., Prebensen, N.K., and Uysal, M. (2018), "Dynamic drivers of tourist experiences", in Prebensen, N.K., Chen, J.S., and Uysal, M. (Eds.), *Creating Experience Value in Tourism*, CABI, Oxfordshire/Boston, pp.11–20.

de Mooij, M. and Hofstede, G. (2011), "Cross-cultural consumer behavior: A review of research findings", *Journal of International Consumer Marketing*, Vol.23, pp.181–192. doi: 10.1080/08961530.2011.578057.

Dolnicar, S., Yanamandram, V., and Cliff, K. (2012), "The contributions of vacations to quality of life", *Annals of Tourism Research*, Vol.39, No.1, pp.59–83. doi: 10.1016/j.annals.2011.04.015.

Edvardsson, B. (2005), "Service quality: Beyond cognitive assessment", *Managing Service Quality: An International Journal*, Vol.15, No.2, pp.127–131. doi: 10.1108/09604520510585316.

Ellsworth, P. (1994), "Sense, culture, and sensibility", in Kitayama, S. and Markus, H.R. (Eds.), *Emotion and Culture: Empirical Studies of Mutual Influence*, American Psychological Association, Washington, DC, pp.23–50.

Gelter, H. (2007), "Towards an understanding of experience production", in Kylänen, M. (Ed.), *Articles on Experiences 4*, University of Lapland, Rovaniemi, pp.28–50.

Grönroos, C. and Voima, P. (2013), "Critical service logic: Making sense of value creation and co-creation", *Journal of the Academy of Marketing Science*, Vol.2, No.41, pp.133–150. doi: 10.1007/s11747-012-0308-3.

Härtel, C.E.J. and Fujimoto, Y. (2000), "Diversity is not a problem to be managed by organizations but openness to perceived dissimilarity is", *Journal of Australian and New Zealand Academy of Management*, Vol.6, No.1, pp.14–27. doi: 10.1017/S1833367200005484.

Helkkula, A. (2011), "Characterising the concept of service experience", *Journal of Service Management*, Vol.22, No.3, pp.367–389. doi: 10.1108/09564231111136872.

Hemmington, N. (2007), "From service to experience: Understanding and defining the hospitality business", *The Service Industries Journal*, Vol.27, No.6, pp.747–755. doi: 10.1080/02642060701453221.

Herring, R.D. (1990), "Nonverbal communication: A necessary component of cross-cultural counseling", *Journal of Multicultural Counseling & Development*, Vol.18, No.4, pp.172–179. doi: 10.1002/j.2161-1912.1990.tb00448.x.

Holbrook, M.B. and Hirschman, E.C. (1982, September), "The experiential aspects of consumption: Consumer fantasies, feelings, and fun", *Journal of Consumer Research*, Vol.9, pp.132–140. doi: 10.1086/208906.

Hulten, B. (2011), "Sensory marketing: The multi-sensory brand-experience concept", *European Business Review*, Vol.23, No.3, pp.256–273. doi: 10.1108/09555341111130245.

Hulten, B. (2017), "Branding by the five senses: A sensory branding framework", *Journal of Brand Strategy*, Vol.6, No.3, pp.1–12.

Hulten, B., Broweus, N., and van Dijk, M. (2009), *Sensory Marketing*, Palgrave Macmillan, Basingstoke/New York, NY.

Huta, V. and Ryan, R.M. (2010), "Pursuing pleasure or virtue: The differential and overlapping well-being benefits of hedonic and eudaimonic motives", *Journal of Happiness Studies*, Vol.11, No.6, pp.735–762. doi: 10.1007/s10902-009-9171-4.

Jensen, Ø., Lindberg, F., and Østergaard, P. (2015), "How can consumer research contribute to increased understanding of tourist experiences?", *Scandinavian Journal of Hospitality and Tourism*, Vol.15, No. supl.1, pp.9–27. doi: 10.1080/15022250.2015.1065591.

Kahneman, D. (2011), *Thinking, Fast and Slow*, Penguin, Random House, UK.

Kandampully, J., Zhang, T.C., and Jaakkola, E. (2018), "Customer experience management in hospitality: A literature synthesis, new understanding, and research agenda", *International Journal of Contemporary Hospitality Management*, Vol.30, No.1, pp.21–56. doi: 10.1108/IJCHM-10-2015-0549.

Khan, I., Garg, R.J., and Rahman, Z. (2015), "Customer service experience in hotel operations: An empirical analysis", *Procedia – Social and Behavioral Sciences*, Vol.189, pp.266–274. doi: 10.1016/j.sbspro.2015.03.222.

Kim, J.-H., Ritchie, J.R.B., and McGormick, B. (2011), "Development of a scale to measure memorable tourism eperiences", *Journal of Travel Research*, Vol.51, No.1, pp.12–25. doi: 10.1177/0047287510385467.

Knobloch, U., Robertson, K., and Aitken, R. (2017), "Experience, emotion, and eudaimonia: A consideration of tourist experiences and well-being", *Journal of Travel Research*, Vol.56, No.5, pp.651–662. doi: 10.1177/0047287516650937.

Kroeber-Riehl, W. and Gröppel-Klein, A. (2013), *Konsumentenverhalten*, Franz Vahlen, München.

Lee, Y.-S. and Prebensen, N.K. (2018), "Value creation and co creation in tourist experiences: An East Asian cultural knowledge framework approach", in Prebensen, N.K., Chen, J.S., and Uysal, M. (Eds.), *Creating Experience Value in Tourism*, pp.215–227, CABI, Oxfordshire, UK and Boston, MA.

Lemon, K.N. and Verhoef, P.C. (2016), "Understanding customer experience throughout the customer journey", *Journal of Marketing*, Vol.80, No. AMA/MSI Special Issue, pp.69–76. doi: 10.1509/jm.15.0420.

Lim, N. (2016), "Cultural differences in emotion: Differences in emotional arousal level between the East and the West", *Integrative Medicine Research*, No.5, pp.105–109. doi: 10.1016/j.imr.2016.03.004.

Maklan, S. and Klaus, P. (2011), "Customer experience: Are we measuring the right things", *International Journal of Market Research*, Vol.53, No.6, pp.771–792. doi: 10.2501/IJMR-53-6-771-792.

Markus, H.R. and Kitayama, S. (2010), "Cultures and selves: A cycle of mutual constitution", *Perspectives on Psychological Science*, Vol.5, No.4, pp.420–430. doi: 10.1177/1745691610375557.

Maslow, A. (1970), *Motivation and Personality*, Harper & Flow, New York, NY.

Matsumoto, D. (2016), "Are cultural differences in emotion regulation mediated by personality traits?", *Journal of Cross-Cultural Psychology*, Vol.37, No.4, pp.421–437. doi: 10.1177/0022022106288478.

Matsumoto, D. and Takeuchi, S. (1998), "Emotions and intercultural communication", in *Intercultural Communication Research*, Kanda University of International Studies, Intercultural Communication Institute, pp.1–32, Chiba, Japan.

Matsumoto, D., Yoo, S.H., and Fontaine, J. (2008), "Mapping expressive differences around the world – The relationship between emotional display rules and individualism versus collectivism", *Journal of Cross-Cultural Psychology*, Vol.39, No.1, pp.55–74. doi: 10.1177/0022022107311854.

Mattila, A.S. (1999), "The role of culture and purchase motivation in service encounter evaluations", *Journal of Services Marketing*, Vol.13, No.4/5, pp.376. doi: 10.1108/08876049910282655.

Mehrabian, A. and Russell, J.A. (1974), *An Approach to Environmental Psychology*, MIT Press, Cambridge, MA.

Meng, F. (2010), "Individualism/collectivism and group travel behavior: A cross-cultural perspective", *International Journal of Culture, Tourism and Hospitality Research*, Vol.4, No.4, pp.340–351. doi: 10.1108/17506181011081514.

Meyer, C. and Schwager, A. (2007), "Understanding customer experience", *Harvard Business Review*, Vol.85, No.2, pp.116–126.

Müller, H. and Scheurer, R. (2004), "Angebots-Inszenierung in Tourismus-Destinationen", in Bieger, T., Laesser, C., and Beritelli, P. (Eds.), *Jahrbuch 2003/2004 Schweizerische Tourismuswirtschaft*, IDT-HSG Institut für öffentliche Dienstleistungen und Tourismus der Universität St. Gallen, Bern, pp.71–92.

Mutz, M. and Kämpfer, S. (2013), "Emotionen und Lebenszufriedenheit in der Erlebnisgesellschaft", *Kölner Zeitschrift für Soziologie und Sozialpsychologie*, Vol.65, No.2, pp.253–276. doi: 10.1007/s11577-013-0204-y.

Özlem, G. (2016), "Experience-based service design", in Sotiriadis, M. and Gursoy, D. (Eds.), *The Handbook of Managing and Marketing Tourism Experiences*, Emerson Group Publishing Limited, Bingley, pp.3–20.

Park, G., Lewis, R.S., Wang, Y.C., Cho, H.J., and Goto, S.G. (2018), "Are you mad at me? Social anxiety and early visual processing of anger and gaze among Asian American biculturals", Vol.6, No.2, pp.151–170. doi: 10.1007/s40167-018-0067-1.

Pine, B.J. and Gilmore, J.H. (1999), *The Experience Economy: Work Is Theatre & Every Business a Stage*, Harvard Business School Press, Boston, MA.

Pine, B.J. and Gilmore, J.H. (2011), *The Experience Economy*, Harvard Business Press, Boston, MA.

Pizam, A. and Tasci, A.D.A. (2019), "Experienscape: Expanding the concept of servicescape with a multi-stakeholder and multi-disciplinary approach ", *International Journal of Hospitality Management*, Vol.76, No. pp.25–37. doi: 10.1016/j.ijhm.2018.06.010.

Prahalad, C.K. and Ramaswamy, V. (2004), "Co-creating unique value with customers", *Strategy and Leadership*, Vol.32, No.3, pp.4–9. doi:10.1108/10878570410699249.

Prebensen, N.K., Chen, J.S., and Uysal, M.S. (2018), "Co-creation of tourist experience: Scope, definition and structure", in Prebensen, N.K., Chen, J.S., and Uysal, M. (Eds.), *Creating Experience Value in Tourism*, CABI, Oxfordshire/Boston, pp.1–10.

Räikkönen, J. and Grénman, M. (2017), "The Experience Economy Logic in the Wellness Tourism Industry", in Correia, A., Kozak, M., Gnoth, J., and Fyall, A. (Eds.), *Co-creation and Well-being in Tourism*, Springer, Cham, pp.3–18.

Reisinger, Y. and Turner, L.W. (2004), *Cross-Cultural Behaviour in Tourism: Concepts and Analysis*, Elsevier Butterworth Heinemann, Oxford, UK.

Russell, J.A. (1980), "A circumplex model of affect", *Journal of Personality and Social Psychology*, Vol.39, No.6, pp.1161–1178. doi: 10.1037/h0077714.

Russell, J.A. and Mehrabian, A. (1978), "Approach–avoidance and affiliation as functions of the emotion-eliciting quality of an environment", *Environment and Behavior*, Vol.10, No.3, pp.355–387. doi: 10.1177/0013916578103005.

Scherer, K.R. (2000), "Psychological models of emotion", in Borod, J.C. (Ed.), *The Neuropsychology of Emotion*, pp.137–162, Oxford University Press, New York, NY.

Scheurer, R. (2003), *Erlebnis-Setting: Touristische Angebotsgestaltung in der Erlebnisökonomie*, FIF, Bern.

Schmitt, B.H. (1999), *Experiential Marketing: How to Get Customers to Sense, Feel, Think, Act, and Relate to Your Company and Brands*, The Free Press, New York, NY.

Schulze, G. (2005), *Die Erlebnisgesellschaft – Kultursoziologie der Gegenwart*, Campus Verlag, Frankfurt and New York.

Sharma, P., Tam, J.L.M., and Kim, N. (2009), "Demystifying intercultural service encounters: Toward a comprehensive conceptual framework", *Journal of Service Research*, Vol.12, No.2, pp.227–242. doi: 10.1177/1094670509338312.

Snel, J.M.C. (2011), *For the Love of Experience: Changing the Experience Economy Discourse*, University of Amsterdam, Amsterdam.

Solomon, M.R., Surprenant, C., Czepiel, J.A., and Gutman, E.G. (1985), "A role theory perspective on dyadic interactions: The service encounter", *Journal of Marketing*, Vol.49, No. Winter 1985, pp.99–111. doi: 10.2307/1251180.

Sotiriadis, M. and Sarmaniotis, C. (2016), "Collaborating to provide attractive hotel guests' experiences", in Sotiriadis, M. and Gursoy, D. (Eds.), *The Handbook of Managing and Marketing Tourism Experiences*, Emerson Group Publishing Limited, Bingley, UK, pp.175–194.

Stamboulis, Y. and Skayannis, P. (2003), "Innovation strategies and technology for experience-based tourism", *Tourism Management*, Vol.24, No.1, pp.35–43. doi: 10.1016/S0261-5177(02)00047-X.

Sukhu, A., Choi, H., Bujisic, M., and Bilgihan, A. (2019, January), "Satisfaction and positive emotions: A comparison of the influence of hotel guests' beliefs and attitudes on their satisfaction and emotions", *International Journal of Hospitality Management*, Vol.77, pp.51–63. doi: 10.1016/j.ijhm.2018.06.013.

Tarssanen, S. and Kylänen, M. (2007), "A theoretical model for producing experiences – A touristic perspective", in Kylänen, M. (Ed.), *Articles on Experiences 2*, University of Lapland, Rovaniemi, pp.134–150.

Torres, E.N., Fu, X., and Lehto, X. (2014), "Examining key drivers of customer delight in a hotel experience: A cross-cultural perspective", *International Journal of Hospitality Management*, Vol.36, No. pp.255–262. doi: 10.1016/j.ijhm.2013.09.007.

Tsai, J.L. (2017), "Ideal affect – Cultural couses and behavioural consequences", *Perspectives of Psychological Science*, Vol.2, No.3, pp.242–259. doi: 10.1111/j.1745-6916.2007.00043.x.

Tsai, J.L., Knutson, B., and Fung, H.H. (2006), "Cultural variation in affect valuation", *Journal of Personality and Social Psychology*, Vol.90, No.2, pp.288–307. doi:10.1037/0022-3514.90.2.288.

Vargo, S.L. and Lusch, R.F. (2008), "Service-dominant logic: Continuing the evolution", *Journal of Academy of Marketing Science*, Vol.36, No.1, pp.1–10. doi: 10.1007/s11747-007-0069-6.

Verhoef, P.C., Lemon, K.N., Parasuraman, A., Roggeveen, A., Tsiros, M., and Schlesinger, L.A. (2009), "Customer experience creation – Determinants, dynamics and management strategies", *Journal of Retailing*, Vol.85, No.1, pp.31–41. doi: 10.1016/j.jretai.2008.11.001.

Voss, C. (2004), *Trends in the Experience and Service Eco nomy – The Experience Profit Cycle*, London Business School, London, UK.

Voss, C. and Zomerdijk, L. (2007), "Innovation in experiential services – An empirical view", in DTI (Ed.), *Innovation in Services*, DTI, London, UK, pp.97–134.

Wang, C.-Y., Miao, L., and Mattila, A.S. (2015), "Customer responses to intercultural communication accommodation strategies in hospitality service encounters", *International Journal of Hospitality Management*, Vol.51, No. pp.96–104. doi: 10.1016/j.ijhm.2015.09.001.

Wang, K., Lee, R.H.T., Fu, Y.M.J., and Yang, R. (2006), "Perception of six basic emotional facial expressions by the Chinese", *Journal of Cross-Cultural Psychology*, Vol.37, No.6, pp.623–629. doi: 10.1177/0022022106290481.

Wirtz, D., Kruger, J., Scollon, C.N., and Diener, E. (2003), "What to Do on Spring Break? The Role of Predicted, On-Line, and Remembered Experience in Future Choice", in Psychological Science, Vol. 14, No. 5, pp. 520–524. doi.org/10.1111/1467-9280.03455

Woodside, A.G., Hsu, S.-Y., and Marshall, R. (2011), "General theory of cultures' consequences on international tourism behavior", *Journal of Business Research*, Vol.64, No.8, pp.785–799. doi: 10.1016/j.jbusres.2010.10.008.

World Tourism Organization. (2011), "Tourism towards 2030/global overview", in *Tourism Towards 2030/Global Overview*, World Tourism Organization, Madrid, Spain..

Yuki, M., Maddux, W.W., and Masuda, T. (2006), "Are the windows to the soul the same in the East and West? Cultural differences in using the eyes and mouth as cues to recognize emotions in Japan and the United States", *Journal of Experimental Social Psychology*, Vol.43, No.2, pp.303–311. doi: 10.1016/j.jesp.2006.02.004.

Zaltman, C., Olson, J. and Forr, J. (2015), "Toward a new marketing science for hospitality managers", *Cornell Hospitality Quarterly*, Vol.56, No.4, pp.337–344. doi: 10.1177/1938965515599841.

6

COUNTRY CULTURE VS. ORGANIZATIONAL CULTURE

Steffen Raub and Stefano Borzillo

Introduction

Culture has been defined as the "collective programming of the mind that distinguishes the members of one group or category of people from others" (Hofstede, 2011, p. 3). In general terms, culture is a collective phenomenon that refers to commonalities in the values, preferences, or behaviors of a group of people. However, culture can be observed, studied, and measured at different levels of aggregation, including countries, ethnic groups, organizations, occupations, or even generational groups. In this chapter, we will take a closer look at the international hospitality industry through the lenses of both country culture and organizational culture. The main thrust of this chapter is to demonstrate that cultural values imply numerous challenges but also offer multiple opportunities for international hospitality organizations.

At the national level, cultural values have an important influence on customer behavior. As a result, hospitality firms need to adapt the way they do business, including the nature of their products and services as well as their communication strategies, to the specific cultural requirements of the host context. In addition, cultural values also determine preferences of employees and, therefore, act as boundary conditions for the effective implementation of managerial practices inside the hospitality organization.

At the organizational level, organizational culture and organizational climate are important levers for organizational effectiveness. Cultures and climates serve as the "glue" that holds organizational members together and facilitates their coordinated activities. Cultures and climates also guide the attention of organizational members to preferred outcomes and desired behaviors that will support organizational effectiveness.

This chapter begins with a presentation of different frameworks for analyzing country-level cultural values. We then review research that outlines how country cultural values are related to idiosyncrasies in consumer behavior and employee behavior and what these challenges mean for effective management practices in hospitality firms. From the country level, we proceed to the organizational level, where we outline the basics of two important frameworks for organizational culture: Schein's (1985) framework and the competing values framework (Cameron and Quinn, 1999), together with a discussion of their implications for hospitality. We also review research on service climate and initiative climate. The chapter concludes with a discussion of the implications of organizational culture and climates for the effectiveness of hospitality firms.

Country Culture

One of the foundational models for understanding systematic differences in country cultures was developed by Dutch researcher Geert Hofstede. His research was based on a large-scale employee survey conducted by industrial giant IBM in a large number of subsidiaries in different countries. In the original version of his model, Hofstede (1980) suggested four fundamental cultural dimensions: power distance, individualism/collectivism, masculinity/femininity, and uncertainty avoidance. Additional research (Hofstede, 1991; Minkov, 2007; Hofstede and Minkov, 2010) led to an expanded version of the original model which included a fifth dimension (long-term/short-term orientation) and even a sixth dimension (indulgence).

Power distance refers to the extent to which a cultural group accepts that power is unequally distributed among its members. Whereas a high power distance culture is characterized by general acceptance of clear hierarchies in which every member has a rightful place, in low power distance cultures such distinctions are much less common and less readily accepted. In highly individualistic cultures, members look predominantly after themselves and a lot of emphasis is placed on self-actualization. Conversely, collectivistic cultures are generally more "we-conscious," placing emphasis on loyalty to the group, subordination of individual to collective needs, and interdependence with other members of the society in which the individual needs to "know his or her place."

Masculine cultures differ from feminine cultures in that in a culture characterized by high levels of masculinity the primary emphasis is on achievement and (economic) success – sometimes also characterized as "quantity of life" – whereas in cultures characterized by high levels of femininity, the primary emphasis is on caring for other members of society and on "quality of life." Uncertainty avoidance characterizes the extent to which individuals feel uneasy about ambiguity and lack of certainty. In high uncertainty avoidance cultures, members place emphasis on creating formal rules, rituals, and habits that reduce uncertainty and there is a general desire to "know the truth." In low certainty avoidance cultures, individuals are generally more tolerant to the unknown, the ambiguous, and the uncertain as well as greater openness to innovation and change.

Long-term orientation in a country culture is related to valuing perseverance and preparation for a future in a society that is constantly in flux. In short-term orientation, the focus is more on the pursuit of happiness in the here and now. Last but not least, cultures characterized by high indulgence focus on giving freedom to one's impulses, gratifying fundamental human desires and enjoying life, whereas cultures characterized by high restraint favor a focus on duty, accompanied by control over human desires. Hofstede's model has been a dominant force in research on country culture. However, Hofstede explicitly acknowledges the possibility that it does not provide a comprehensive picture of all possible country-level values. Several authors have suggested alternative models of country culture.

The ambitious "project GLOBE" has extended Hofstede's framework of country culture. In a long-term study in over 60 countries, the team of investigators focused on nine different cultural dimensions (House et al., 2001). Uncertainty avoidance, power distance, and collectivism (which is split up in two different types in the GLOBE logic), as well as future orientation, refer directly to Hofstede's model. Hofstede's masculinity is represented by the separate dimensions of gender egalitarianism and assertiveness. The model is completed with the dimensions of performance orientation (the extent to which improvement and excellence are rewarded) and humane orientation (the extent to which a culture encourages fairness and altruistic behavior). The latter dimensions are anchored in the work of McClelland (1985) as well as Kluckhohn and Strodtbeck (1961).

Last but not least, Schwartz (1992, 1994, 1999) has suggested another influential model of country culture that includes seven different value types. Conservativism emphasizes maintenance of status quo, a traditional societal order, security, conformity, and tradition. Intellectual and affective autonomy emphasize individuals as autonomous entities with their particular interest and desires. Hierarchy is about emphasizing the legitimacy of hierarchical roles and allocation of resources based on hierarchical relationships. Mastery refers to self-directed activity with the goal of modifying one's surroundings and "getting ahead." Egalitarian commitment is about promoting the welfare of others, social justice, responsibility, and loyalty. Finally, harmony emphasizes social harmony as well as being in harmony with nature.

Implications of Country Culture for the International Hospitality Industry

Despite the parallel existence and complementarity of the different models of country culture that were outlined in the preceding section, research on the consequences of country culture for organizations has relied heavily on the Hofstede model. Below we will summarize research that highlights the impact of country culture on consumer behavior, employee behavior as well as the fit between management practices and cultural values.

Impact of Cultural Values on Consumer Behavior

Country cultural differences have important consequences for consumer behavior. Consumers from different cultural backgrounds differ with regard to what they attribute to and how they process information about products, services, and brands (de Mooij and Hofstede, 2011). This has important consequences for various domains of consumer behavior, many of which are highly relevant to the international hospitality industry.

For instance, low uncertainty avoidance is related to higher spending on sports services and more active engagement in sports as a leisure activity (de Mooij, 2004). This could suggest a need for a more diverse fitness and sports offering for guests from low uncertainty avoidance backgrounds. The cultural dimension of masculinity is positively correlated with ownership of "status goods" like luxury watches and jewelry but negatively correlated with heavy gaming behavior on the Internet (de Mooij, 2010). This may suggest that for hotels with a dominant proportion of guests from high masculinity cultures, product and service offerings that allow for the demonstration of social status may be particularly important. Conversely, for guest segments from low masculinity backgrounds, the "fun" and "gaming" aspect of properties may be particularly important. Low uncertainty avoidance and high individualism have also been related to the adoption of innovative products (Tellis et al., 2003; Yeniyurt and Townsend, 2003). This suggests that innovative hotel concepts may find larger numbers of innovators and early adopters and may ultimately be more successful with customer segments from low uncertainty avoidance and high individualism backgrounds.

Another very interesting finding is that cultural values are related to complaining behavior and also have an impact on guests' propensity to engage in word of mouth (or eWOM) behaviors (Wen et al., 2018). For instance, in high collectivism cultures (which are dominant in many Asian countries), consumers are much less likely to express dissatisfaction with a product or service via a formal complaint (Chun-Tung Lowe and Corkindale, 1998). However, they do engage in negative word of mouth (de Mooij and Hofstede, 2011) and service failure recovery as well as regaining their trust may be particularly difficult (Watkins and Liu, 1996). For hospitality companies who operate in high collectivism cultures, these findings imply a dual challenge. On the one hand, they need to be careful in the interpretation of formal complaint data as these may not reflect true guest attitudes. On the other hand, they need to pay particular attention to social media channels as word of mouth may be disproportionally important for guest attitudes towards their brands and properties.

Country cultural values may also have a bearing on the branding and advertising practices of international hospitality firms. The purpose of advertising differs between individualistic and collectivistic cultures, with the former putting a stronger emphasis on persuading the customer while the latter focus more on building and strengthening relationships and trust between the brand and the consumer (de Mooij and Hofstede, 2010). The effectiveness of advertising content may also vary across cultures (Albers, 1994; Zandpour et al., 1994). For instance, the effectiveness of advertising focusing on benefits for groups and families may be more effective in high collectivism cultures, whereas in high individualism cultures advertising is more likely to appeal to individual benefits of a product or service (Han and Shavitt, 1994). In a more general way, advertising tends to be effective when its content reflects the dominant values of a particular culture. Researchers supports this by showing, among other things, that when the content of a corporation's or a brand's communication strategies is adapted to local values, buyers have more positive dispositions towards the content and display a higher propensity to buy (Singh et al., 2006). This could, for instance, be the case when the content was created by advertising specialists or web designers that are well familiar with this culture (Faiola and Matei, 2005).

Impact of Cultural Values on Employee Behavior and Management Practices

While organizational culture plays a very important role for customer behavior in general and, more specifically, for guests' attitudes and perceptions towards the products, services, and communications activities of international hospitality firms, its impact on employee behaviors should not be underestimated. Employees in different national cultures, who espouse different cultural values, show characteristic differences in their behaviors and their reactions to leadership and managerial initiatives in their organizations. As a result, leadership effectiveness and the success of new managerial initiatives also depend on their fit with the cultural context.

In a large-scale, four-country study, Robert et al. (2000) provide empirical evidence for the notion of culture-practice fit. They observed that in the low power distance, countries in their sample empowering management practices were generally positively associated with employee's job satisfaction, whereas in the high power distance culture of India, this relationship was inverted. Essentially, a management practice that had positive outcomes in a low power distance context proved to be inadequate in a high power distance context.

A number of studies conducted in the realm of hospitality and tourism research point in a similar direction. For instance, Ayoun and Moreo (2008) suggested that managers from cultures that differed with regard to their level of power distance also differed in the extent to which they made use of participative leadership techniques, showed openness to strategic change, insisted on formal strategic control, and displayed a people-focused orientation when setting strategic goals. Testa (2009) found that cultural congruence was related to perceived leader-member exchange relationships (LMX) and the display of organizational citizenship behaviors (OCBs). Hope (2004) suggested that high power distance values acted as a barrier to best practice transfer with regard to the adoption of teamwork and empowerment techniques. Last but not least, in a large-scale study, Raub and Robert (2010, 2013) found that cultural values related to power moderated the relationship between empowering leadership (Arnold et al., 2000), psychological empowerment, and challenging extra-role behaviors. For individuals with low power values, empowerment was more strongly related to challenging extra-role behaviors than for individuals with high power values.

In addition to the question of fit between cultural values and management practices, research also suggests that cultural values may have a potentially far-reaching impact on the choice of new managerial initiatives and strategic decisions of hospitality and tourism firms. For instance, in the context of sustainability and CSR initiatives, Kornilaki and Font (2019) suggest that cultural values influence the intentions and behaviors towards sustainability at the level of owner-managers of small tourism firms. In a more detailed study, Kang et al. (2016) provide evidence for the relationship of different cultural values according to the Hofstede model and the implementation of CSR initiatives. Specifically, they found that uncertainty avoidance and power distance were positively related to CSR scores, whereas individualism and masculinity showed negative effects on CSR scores. Last but not least, research also provides evidence for the impact of cultural values on the adoption of new management practices and on strategic business decisions. In a study of marketing managers, Ghanem et al. (2017) found that cultural values had an impact on the adoption of e-tourism. Finally, Calza et al. (2018) found evidence that cultural values influence the strategic decisions of European rural entrepreneurs to diversify into the tourism sector.

Implications of Country Culture for International Hospitality Organizations

As shown in the previous section, a substantial body of research suggests that taking country culture into account is of vital importance for organizational success in international hospitality organizations. From the viewpoint of consumer or guest behavior, this involves generating a better understanding of how cultural values drive particular needs and expectations with regard to hospitality products and services and how guests from different cultural backgrounds deal with service delivery failures. It also requires a better adaptation of organizational communication efforts that should be tailored to local cultural expectations if they are to elicit favorable reactions from current and potential guests.

From the viewpoint of employee behaviors and managerial practices, it is important to understand the extent to which cultural values can drive strategic choices, adoption of new management techniques and initiatives, as well as individual leadership styles. In general terms, for managerial practices to be able to overcome barriers to adoption and to become effective they need to be adapted, i.e., they have to "fit," dominant cultural values of the organization's managers and employees.

Organizational Culture

Whereas country cultural values are acquired by individuals from their earliest age and are therefore deeply rooted in (often unconscious) values, the socialization process in organizations is typically shorter and shallower. Organizational values tend to be more visible, more easily interpretable and anchored and can be inferred from managerial practices that characterize the organization's functioning. Several models for the description and analysis of organizational culture have been suggested.

At the most fundamental conceptual level, Schein (1985) describes organizational culture as being constituted by three interrelated layers. The so-called "artifacts" are to be found at the most superficial level of organizational culture. These include all the visible and tangible elements of an organization that represent and reflect deeper underlying values. Examples include architecture and design, building layouts, documents, employee dress codes, but also preferred language as well as corporate rituals. One level below the artifacts lie the organization's values. Values express the "socially validated" experience of group members which serve as guidelines or rules for behavior in an inherently uncertain and uncontrollable organizational environment. When values are only "espoused," i.e., they lack social validation, they may only be reflective of what organization members will say as opposed to what they will do. At the most basic level of organizational culture one finds the so-called "basic assumption." These are taken-for-granted shared assumptions of the group that are neither debated nor confronted and, therefore, extremely difficult to change.

Whereas Schein's model of organizational culture provides a conceptual overview of different layers of culture – differing in the degree to which they are observable and modifiable – the model does not provide any insights with regard to the specific content of organizational values. Among the different approaches at making the value level of organizational culture more transparent and measurable, the competing values framework developed by Camron and Quinn (1999) stands out. Cameron and Quinn (1999) argue that organizational cultures can be assessed within a framework that is defined by two major axes. The first one contrasts a focus on flexibility and discretion with the opposing focus on stability and control. A second, perpendicular axis contrasts an external focus via differentiation with the opposing internal focus via integration. The two axes form a 2×2 framework with four distinct quadrants representing four different archetypes of organizational culture.

The "clan" culture – representing a focus on internal integration combined with flexibility and discretion – is described as a friendly workplace with highly committed employees that are held together by loyalty. The organization is participative and consensus-oriented and defines success in terms of sensitivity to customers and employees. The "adhocracy" culture – defined as the intersection of a focus on external differentiation combined with flexibility and discretion – carries the features of a dynamic, entrepreneurial organization with a strong emphasis on individual initiative, experimentation, and innovation. Success in this culture is defined as the ability to generate unique new products and services. The "market" culture – a combination of a focus on external differentiation combined with stability and control – epitomizes the results-oriented organization with a strong emphasis on competition driven by demanding leaders. Success is defined by winning market share and penetration. Last but not least, the "hierarchy" culture – at the intersection of a focus on internal integration combined with stability and control – represents a highly structure workplace with heavy emphasis placed on rules, policies, and procedures. Success is defined in terms of the smooth running of the organization, leading to dependable production of goods and services and low cost (Cameron and Quinn, 1999).

Organizational Climates

Closely related to the notion of organizational culture is the concept of organizational climate. Organizational climate refers to the shared perceptions of employees regarding "the kinds of behaviors that get rewarded, supported, and expected in a setting" (Schneider, 1990, p. 384). Similar to organizational culture, which serves as an organizational "glue" and facilitates the coordination of employees' activities, organizational climate guides employee behaviors towards a particular outcome that is desirable from an organizational viewpoint. Researchers have suggested that organizational climates should generally be regarded as having a specific focus or referent, i.e., as a climate "for something" (Schneider, 1975; Schneider et al., 1998). Researchers have suggested a broad range of climate constructs, including, among others, safety climate (Hofmann and Stetzer, 1996), innovation climate (Anderson and West, 1998; Scott and Bruce, 1994), justice climate (Naumann and Bennett, 2000; Liao and Rupp, 2005), and implementation climate (Klein et al., 2001).

In this chapter, we will review research on two particular types of climate that have a particular relevance for the hospitality industry, namely "service climate" and "initiative climate." The service climate construct (Schneider et al., 1980) encompasses "employee perceptions of the practices, procedures, and behaviors that get rewarded, supported, and expected with regard to customer service and customer service quality" (Schneider et al., 1998, p. 151). In an organization where service climate is present, employees understand that employees, organizational processes, and organizational structures are focused on attaining high service quality (Schneider and White, 2004). Research suggests that service climate enhances service employees' engagement in role-prescribed service behaviors (e.g., Liao and Chuang, 2004; Schneider, 1990).

However, role-prescribed service behaviors are only one side of the coin when it comes to guest satisfaction in the hospitality industry. Especially in upmarket segments, exceptional service also encompasses the spontaneous display of service behaviors that contributes to a "wow" effect. Several organizational climate researchers have made efforts to tap into organizational climates with a specific referent for proactivity and initiative-taking. Starting from the extensive research on personal initiative by Frese and associates, Baer and Frese (2003; see also Fay et al., 2004) suggested the construct of proactivity climate. In a similar vein, Raub and Liao (2012) developed a new climate construct with an explicit focus on initiative. Their starting point was Frese's personal initiative construct which encompasses a self-starting, change-oriented, long-term oriented approach, combined with persistence in the face of obstacles (Frese and Fay, 2001; Frese et al., 1996). Self-starting behavior suggests that employees pursue a course of action without specific input from their supervisors (Frese and Fay, 2001; Griffin et al., 2007). Change orientation means that employees try to find solutions to problems in an independent way (Frese et al., 1996; Grant and Ashford, 2008). The long-term oriented facet includes addressing future problems or opportunities and doing something about them in a proactive fashion. Finally, personal initiative also involves persistence in the face of obstacles that may arise as employees attempt to address critical issues (Frese and Fay, 2001). Initiative climate, therefore, encompasses a shared perception by service employees that the organization and its leaders expect, encourage, and reward service behaviors in conformity with the characteristics outlined above.

Using Organizational Culture and Climate to Enhance Organizational Effectiveness in International Hospitality Organizations

Organizational culture can contribute to the effectiveness of international hospitality organizations in a variety of ways. Cultural values can contribute to positive employee attitudes and behaviors. More generally, organizational culture can serve as a critical link between the organization's strategy and leadership and desirable organizational outcomes or performance. Last but not least, organizational culture also has the potential to facilitate the implementation of desirable organizational practices as well as to boost organizational innovation and performance.

Various studies highlighted relationships between organizational culture and critical attitudes and behaviors of hospitality employees. In an investigation from the Thai hospitality industry, organizational culture was negatively related to employee stress and positively related to job satisfaction and retention (Churintr, 2010). Renault de Moraes et al. (2016) found that shared cultural values contributed to higher levels of trust among employees. This result was echoed in a study by Ozturk et al. (2014) which suggested that organizational values related to the "clan," "adhocracy," and "market" organizational cultures were negatively related to turnover intentions of hotel employees in Turkey. Finally, organizational culture was positively related to job satisfaction in a sample from the Indonesian hospitality industry (Pawirosumarto et al., 2017).

Investigating the relationship between culture and organizational performance, Kyriakidou and Gore (2005) suggested that specific cultural values contribute to higher performance in hospitality SMEs. Among these are cooperation in setting missions and strategies, teamwork, and organizational learning. Similar results suggesting a relationship between culture and performance were found in a range of studies across very diverse geographic regions. For instance, in a study conducted in the Polish hospitality industry, Tadeuisak (2018) found that organizational culture mediated the relationship between leadership style and organizational effectiveness. A tourism industry study by Wu and Lin (2013) suggested that culture partially mediated the relationship between business strategy and organizational performance.

In a similar vein, a study in the Chinese hospitality market (Qin et al., 2015) suggested that the core values of happiness and caring facilitated joined efforts of managers and employees to reach important strategic goals. In a study by Asree et al. (2010), leadership competence and organizational culture were found to contribute jointly to organizational responsiveness in the hospitality industry, which in turn was positively related to organizational performance as measured by revenue. Last but not least, organizational cultural values were shown to be positively associated with customer service delight (Kao et al., 2016).

Organizational culture has also been studied with regard to its facilitating role in the implementation of organizational practices. Empirical evidence suggests that cultural values related to a learning culture facilitated the transfer and use of knowledge from education and training as well as problem-solving and innovation on the job (Nicely and Palakurthi, 2018). In a series of several studies, Rahimi found that culture facilitates the implementation of customer relationship management (CRM) in hospitality firms (Rahimi, 2014, 2017a, 2017b).

Last but not least, organizational culture also seems to contribute to the ability of hospitality firms to engage in innovation. Two separate studies used the Cameron and Quinn framework in their empirical investigation. In a study by Del Rosario and René (2017), the values associated with the "adhocracy" culture were found to predict ecological innovation. In a study in the hospitality industry in Turkey, Ergün and Tasgit (2013) concluded that hotels with the features of the "adhocracy" and "market" cultures scored higher on innovation performance compared to those with "clan" or "hierarchy" cultures. Also, in a study by Gürlek and Tuna (2018), a "green" organizational culture was found to contribute to "green innovation" in hospitality.

In a similar vein, organizational climates can serve as an important tool for enhancing guest satisfaction and organizational performance in the international hospitality industry. Hotel companies that manage to consistently create a service climate in their properties will reap benefits in the form of better service delivery and greater customer service satisfaction (Schneider et al., 1998). In the presence of an initiative climate, service employees will feel empowered and encouraged to take initiative and serve guests with a proactive approach. As a result, they will implement more extra-role service behaviors, which will lead to additional benefits in terms of guest service satisfaction.

Because organizational climates reflect shared employee perceptions that it is beneficial to engage in particular types of behavior, leadership plays a key role creating climates that support desirable behaviors (Hong et al., 2013; Schneider, 1990). When leaders role model customer service orientation, their subordinates are more likely to engage in similar behaviors. Moreover, when leaders notice desirable customer service behaviors in their subordinates and reward them appropriately, this will reinforce the organizational climate.

Research also suggests that organizational service climates and initiative climates can be enhanced by appropriate HRM systems (Hong et al., 2016). Through appropriate recruitment and selection practices, hospitality organizations can target and retain employees who are prepared to deliver outstanding service (Schneider et al., 2000). Through training and development practices specific skills that promote in-role and extra-role customer service across a range of different situations can be strengthened (Fay and Sonnentag, 2010). Last but not least, appropriate performance appraisal and reward mechanism can underscore the importance of customer service and increase employees' motivation to deliver outstanding customer service (Schuler and Jackson, 1987).

Conclusion

In summary, the research reviewed in this chapter suggests that culture is an important variable to take into account for organizations in the international hospitality environment. Different levels of culture, in particular country culture vs. organizational culture need to be clearly distinguished. Country culture can be framed as both a challenge and an opportunity for hospitality organizations. Differences in customer values require conscious adaptation of corporate strategies, products, communications, and managerial practices. A mindless application of a one-size-fits-all approach is likely to be unproductive. However, for hospitality organizations that manage to think globally but adapt locally, tapping into cultural differences can also be a source of competitive advantage. Organizational culture and climate should be seen primarily in their function as an "organizational glue" that can help maintain coordinated activity and consistency in behaviors and outcomes. When harnessed appropriately, organizational cultures and climates can support the implementation of organizational strategies and contribute to organizational performance, in particular with regard to customer service outcomes and guest satisfaction.

References

Albers, N.D. (1994), "Relating Hofstede's dimensions of culture to international variations in print advertisements: A comparison of appeals", Dissertation presented to the Faculty of the College of Business Administration University of Houston.

Anderson, N.R. and West, M.A. (1998), "Measuring climate for work group innovation: development and validation of the team climate inventory", *Journal of Organizational Behavior: The International Journal of Industrial, Occupational and Organizational Psychology and Behavior*, Vol.19, No.3, pp.235–258.

Arnold, J.A., Arad, S., Rhoades, J.A., and Drasgow, F. (2000), "The empowering leadership questionnaire: The construction and validation of a new scale for measuring leader behaviors", *Journal of Organizational Behavior*, Vol.21, No.3, pp.249–269.

Asree, S., Zain, M., and Rizal Razalli, M. (2010), "Influence of leadership competency and organizational culture on responsiveness and performance of firms", *International Journal of Contemporary Hospitality Management*, Vol.22, No.4, pp.500–516.

Ayoun, B. and Moreo, P.J. (2008), "Does national culture affect hotel managers' approach to business strategy?", *International Journal of Contemporary Hospitality Management*, Vol.20, No.1, pp.7–18.

Baer, M. and Frese, M. (2003). "Innovation is not enough: Climates for initiative and psychological safety, process innovations, and firm performance", *Journal of Organizational Behavior: The International Journal of Industrial, Occupational and Organizational Psychology and Behavior*, Vol.24, No.1, pp.45–68.

Calza, F., Go, F.M., Parmentola, A., and Trunfio, M. (2018), "European rural entrepreneur and tourism-based diversification: Does national culture matter?", *International Journal of Tourism Research*, Vol.20, pp.671–683.

Cameron, K.S. and Quinn, R.E. (1999), *Diagnosing and Changing Organizational Culture, Based on the Competing Values Framework*, Reading, Addison-Wesley, MA.

Chun-Tung Lowe, A. and Corkindale, D.R. (1998), "Differences in "cultural values" and their effects on responses to marketing stimuli: A cross-cultural study between Australians and Chinese from the People's Republic of China", *European Journal of Marketing*, Vol.32, No.9/10, pp.843–867.

Churintr, P. (2010), "Perceived organisational culture, stress, and job satisfaction affecting on hotel employee retention: A comparison study between management and operational employees", *Employment Relations Record*, Vol.10, No.2, p.64.

De Mooij, M. (2004), *Consumer Behavior and Culture*, Sage, Thousand Oaks, CA.

De Mooij, M. (2010), *Consumer Behavior and Culture: Consequences for Global Marketing and Advertising*, Sage, Thousand Oaks, CA.

De Mooij, M. and Hofstede, G. (2010), "The Hofstede model: Applications to global branding and advertising strategy and research", *International Journal of Advertising*, Vol.29, No.1, pp.85–110.

De Mooij, M. and Hofstede, G. (2011), "Cross-cultural consumer behavior: A review of research findings", *Journal of International Consumer Marketing*, Vol.23, No.3–4, pp.181–192.

De Moraes, L.F.R., de Souza Sant'Anna, A., Diniz, D.M., and de Oliveira, F.B. (2016), "Portuguese and Brazilian national cultures, organizational culture and trust: An analysis of impacts", *Tourism & Management Studies*, Vol.12, No.1, pp.188–195.

Del Rosario, R.S.M. and René, D.P. (2017), "Eco-innovation and organizational culture in the hotel industry", *International Journal of Hospitality Management*, Vol.65, pp.71–80.

Ergün, E. and Tasgıt, Y.E. (2013), "Cultures of adhocracy, clan, hierarchy and market and innovation performance: A case of hotels in Turkey", *Journal of Travel & Tourism Research*, Vol.13, pp. 1–12.

Faiola, A. and Matei, S.A. (2005), "Cultural cognitive style and web design: Beyond a behavioral inquiry into computer-mediated communication", *Journal of Computer-Mediated Communication*, Vol.11, No.1, pp.375–394.

Fay, D., Lührmann, H., and Kohl, C. (2004), "Proactive climate in a post-reorganization setting: When staff compensate managers' weakness", *European Journal of Work and Organizational Psychology*, Vol.13, No.2, pp.241–267.

Fay, D. and Sonnentag, S. (2010), "A look back to move ahead: New directions for research on proactive performance and other discretionary work behaviours", *Applied Psychology*, Vol.59, pp.1–20.

Frese, M. and Fay, D. (2001), "4. Personal initiative: An active performance concept for work in the 21st century", *Research in Organizational Behavior*, Vol.23, pp.133–187.

Frese, M., Kring, W., Soose, A., and Zempel, J. (1996), "Personal initiative at work: Differences between East and West Germany", *Academy of Management Journal*, Vol.39, No.1, pp.37–63.

Ghanem, M.M., Mansour, S.O., and Adel, H. (2017), "The impact of national culture on the adoption of e-tourism in Egyptian tourism companies", *Turizam: Međunarodni znanstveno-stručni časopis*, Vol.65, No.2, pp.234–246.

Grant, A.M. and Ashford, S.J. (2008), "The dynamics of proactivity at work", *Research in Organizational Behavior*, Vol.28, pp.3–34.

Griffin, M.A., Neal, A., and Parker, S.K. (2007), "A new model of work role performance: Positive behavior in uncertain and interdependent contexts", *Academy of Management Journal*, Vol.50, No.2, pp.327–347.

Gürlek, M. and Tuna, M. (2018), "Reinforcing competitive advantage through green organizational culture and green innovation", *The Service Industries Journal*, Vol.38, No.7–8, pp.467–491.

Han, S.P. and Shavitt, S. (1994), "Persuasion and culture: Advertising appeals in individualistic and collectivistic societies", *Journal of Experimental Social Psychology*, Vol.30, No.4, pp.326–350.

Hofmann, D.A. and Stetzer, A. (1996), "A cross-level investigation of factors influencing unsafe behaviors and accidents", *Personnel Psychology*, Vol.49, No.2, pp.307–339.

Hofstede, G. (1980), *Culture's Consequences: International Differences in Work-Related Values*, Sage, Beverly Hills, CA.

Hofstede, G. (1991), *Cultures and Organizations: Software of the Mind*, McGraw-Hill, London, UK.

Hofstede, G. (2011), "Dimensionalizing cultures: The Hofstede model in context", *Online Readings in Psychology and Culture*, Vol.2, No.1, pp.1–26. https://doi.org/10.9707/2307-0919.1014.

Hofstede, G. and Minkov, M. (2010), "Long-versus short-term orientation: New perspectives", *Asia Pacific Business Review*, Vol.16, No.4, pp.493–504.

Hong, Y., Liao, H., Hu, J., and Jiang, K. (2013), "Missing link in the service profit chain: A meta-analytic review of the antecedents, consequences, and moderators of service climate", *Journal of Applied Psychology*, Vol.98, pp.237–267.

Hong, Y., Liao, H., Raub, S., and Han, J.H. (2016), "What it takes to get proactive: An integrative multilevel model of the antecedents of personal initiative", *Journal of Applied Psychology*, Vol.101, No.5, pp.687–701.

Hope, C.A. (2004), "The impact of national culture on the transfer of "best practice operations management" in hotels in St. Lucia", *Tourism Management*, Vol.25, No.1, pp.45–59.

House, R., Javidan, M., and Dorfman, P. (2001), "Project GLOBE: An Introduction", *Applied Psychology: An International Review*, Vol.50, No.4, pp.489–505.

Kang, K.H., Lee, S., and Yoo, C. (2016), "The effect of national culture on corporate social responsibility in the hospitality industry", *International Journal of Contemporary Hospitality Management*, Vol.28, No.8, pp.1728–1758.

Kao, C.Y., Tsaur, S.H., and Wu, T.C.E. (2016), "Organizational culture on customer delight in the hospitality industry", *International Journal of Hospitality Management*, Vol.56, pp.98–108.

Klein, K.J., Conn, A.B., and Sorra, J.S. (2001), "Implementing computerized technology: An organizational analysis", *Journal of Applied Psychology*, Vol.86, No.5, p.811.

Kluckhohn, F.R. and Strodtbeck, F.L. (1961), *Variations in Value Orientations*, HarperCollins, New York, NY.

Kornilaki, M. and Font, X. (2019), "Normative influences: How socio-cultural and industrial norms influence the adoption of sustainability practices. A grounded theory of Cretan, small tourism firms", *Journal of Environmental Management*, Vol.230, pp.183–189.

Kyriakidou, O. and Gore, J. (2005), "Learning by example: Benchmarking organizational culture in hospitality, tourism and leisure SMEs", *Benchmarking: An International Journal*, Vol.12, No.3, pp.192–206.

Liao, H. and Chuang, A. (2004), "A multilevel investigation of factors influencing employee service performance and customer outcomes", *Academy of Management Journal*, Vol.47, No.1, pp.41–58.

Liao, H. and Rupp, D. E. (2005), "The impact of justice climate and justice orientation on work outcomes: A cross-level multifoci framework", *Journal of Applied Psychology*, Vol.90, No.2, p.242.

McClelland, D.C. (1985), *Human Motivation*. Scott, Foresman, Glenview, IL.

Minkov, M. (2007), *What Makes us Different and Similar: A New Interpretation of the World Values Survey and Other Cross-Cultural Data*, Klasika i Stil, Sofia, Bulgaria.

Naumann, S.E. and Bennett, N. (2000), "A case for procedural justice climate: Development and test of a multilevel model", *Academy of Management Journal*, Vol.43, No.5, pp.881–889.

Nicely, A. and Palakurthi, R. (2018), "Organizational culture requirements for high levels of knowledge usage from learning activities among hotel managers", *International Journal of Hospitality & Tourism Administration*, Vol.19, No.1, pp.1–25.

Ozturk, A.B., Hancer, M., and Wang, Y.C. (2014), "Interpersonal trust, organizational culture, and turnover intention in hotels: A cross-level perspective", *Tourism Analysis*, Vol.19, No.2, pp.139–150.

Pawirosumarto, S., Sarjana, P.K., and Gunawan, R. (2017), "The effect of work environment, leadership style, and organizational culture towards job satisfaction and its implication towards employee performance in Parador Hotels and Resorts, Indonesia", *International Journal of Law and Management*, Vol.59, No.6, pp.1337–1358.

Qin, Y., Li, B., and Yu, L. (2015), "Corporate culture and company performance: A case study of home inns in China", *Asia Pacific Journal of Tourism Research*, Vol.20, No.9, pp.1021–1040.

Rahimi, R. (2014), "Organisational culture perspective and implementing customer relationship management (CRM) in hotel industry: Case of a chain hotel in the UK", *European Journal of Tourism Research*, Vol.8, p.162.

Rahimi, R. (2017a), "Customer relationship management (people, process and technology) and organisational culture in hotels: Which traits matter?", *International Journal of Contemporary Hospitality Management*, Vol.29, No.5, pp.1380–1402.

Rahimi, R. (2017b), "Organizational culture and customer relationship management: A simple linear regression analysis", *Journal of Hospitality Marketing & Management*, Vol.26, No.4, pp.443–449.

Raub, S. and Liao, H. (2012), "Doing the right thing without being told: Joint effects of initiative climate and general self-efficacy on employee proactive customer service performance", *Journal of Applied Psychology*, Vol.97, No.3, p.651.

Raub, S. and Robert, C. (2010), "Differential effects of empowering leadership on in-role and extra-role employee behaviors: Exploring the role of psychological empowerment and power values", *Human Relations*, Vol.63, No.11, pp.1743–1770.

Raub, S.P. and Robert, C. (2013), Empowerment, organizational commitment, and voice behavior in the hospitality industry: Evidence from a multinational sample, *Cornell Hospitality Quarterly*, Vol.54, No.2, pp.136–148.

Robert, C., Probst, T.M., Martocchio, J.J., Drasgow, F., and Lawler, J.J. (2000), "Empowerment and continuous improvement in the United States, Mexico, Poland, and India: Predicting fit on the basis of the dimensions of power distance and individualism", *Journal of Applied Psychology*, Vol.85, No.5, p.643.

Schein, E.H. (1985), *Organizational Culture and Leadership*, Jossey-Bass, San Francisco, CA.

Schneider, B. (1975), "Organizational climates: An essay", *Personnel Psychology*, Vol.28, No.4, pp.447–479.

Schneider, B. (1990), "The climate for service: An application of the climate construct", in B. Schneider (Ed.), *Organizational Climate and Culture*, Jossey-Bass, San Francisco, CA, pp. 383–412.

Schneider, B., Parkington, J.J., and Buxton, V.M. (1980), "Employee and customer perceptions of service in banks", *Administrative Science Quarterly*, Vol.25, No.2, pp.252–267.

Schneider, B., Smith, D.B., and Goldstein, H.W. (2000), "Attraction–selection–attrition: Toward a person–environment psychology of organizations", in W.B. Walsh, K.H. Craik and R.H. Price (Eds.), *Person–Environment Psychology: New Directions and Perspectives*, 2nd ed., Erlbaum, Mahwah, NJ, pp. 61–85.

Schneider, B. and White, S.S. (2004), *Service Quality: Research Perspectives*, Vol. 107, Sage, Thousand Oaks, CA.

Schneider, B., White, S.S., and Paul, M.C. (1998), "Linking service climate and customer perceptions of service quality: Tests of a causal model", *Journal of Applied Psychology*, Vol.83, No.2, pp.150–163.

Schuler, R.S. and Jackson, S.E. (1987), "Linking competitive strategies with human resource management practices", *The Academy of Management Executive*, Vol.1, pp.207–219.

Schwartz, S.H. (1992), "Universals in the content and structure of values: Theoretical advances and empirical tests in 20 countries", *In Advances in Experimental Social Psychology*, Vol.25, pp.1–65.

Schwartz, S.H. (1994), "Beyond individualism/collectivism: New cultural dimensions of values", in Kim, U., Triandis, H.C., Kâğitçibaşi, Ç., Choi, S.C., and Yoon, G. (Eds.), *Cross-Cultural Research and Methodology Series, Vol. 18. Individualism and Collectivism: Theory, Method, and Applications*, Sage Publications, Thousand Oaks, CA, pp. 85–119.

Schwartz, S.H. (1999), "A theory of cultural values and some implications for work", *Applied Psychology: An International Review*, Vol.48, No.1, pp.23–47.

Scott, S.G. and Bruce, R.A. (1994), "Determinants of innovative behavior: A path model of individual innovation in the workplace", *Academy of Management Journal*, Vol.37, No.3, pp.580–607.

Singh, N., Fassott, G., Chao, M.C., and Hoffmann, J.A. (2006), "Understanding international web site usage: A cross-national study of German, Brazilian, and Taiwanese online consumers", *International Marketing Review*, Vol.23, No.1, pp.83–97.

Tadeuisak, E. (2018), "Organisational culture as a mediator on the relationship between leadership style and organisational effectiveness: Polish hotel industry", *Journal of Organisational Studies and Innovation*, Vol.5, No.2, pp.14–25.

Tellis, G.J., Stremersch, S. and Yin, E. (2003), "The international takeoff of new products: The role of economics, culture, and country innovativeness", *Marketing Science*, Vol.22, No.2, pp.188–208.

Testa, M.R. (2009), "National culture, leadership and citizenship: Implications for cross-cultural management", *International Journal of Hospitality Management*, Vol.28, No.1, pp.78–85.

Watkins, H.S. and Liu, R. (1996), "Collectivism, individualism and in-group membership: Implications for consumer complaining behaviors in multicultural contexts", *Journal of International Consumer Marketing*, Vol.8, No.3–4, pp.69–96.

Wen, J., Hu, Y., and Kim, H.J. (2018), "Impact of individual cultural values on hotel guests' positive emotions and positive eWOM intention: Extending the cognitive appraisal framework", *International Journal of Contemporary Hospitality Management*, Vol.30, No.3, pp.1769–1787.

Wu, Y.H. and Lin, M.M. (2013), "The relationships among business strategies, organisational performance and organisational culture in the tourism industry", *South African Journal of Economic and Management Sciences*, Vol.16, No.5, pp.1–8.

Yeniyurt, S. and Townsend, J.D. (2003), "Does culture explain acceptance of new products in a country? An empirical investigation", *International Marketing Review*, Vol.20, No.4, pp.377–396.

Zandpour, F., Campos, V., Catalano, J., Chang, C., Cho, Y.D., Jiang, S.F., and Hoobyar, R. (1994), "Global reach and local touch: Achieving cultural fitness in TV advertising", *Journal of Advertising Research*, Vol.34, No.5, pp.35–64.

7

INTERCULTURAL COMPETENCIES AND CULTURAL STANDARDS IN INTERNATIONAL HOSPITALITY

Ulrich Bauer

Cultural Standards and Intercultural Competencies

The first part of this chapter gives some theoretical background on interculturality. International hospitality is characterized by many factors, one of them being the fact that most people working in this field travel a lot and travel a lot abroad. This leads to countless individual experiences, of which many are told and retold as anecdotes. However, as the name says, this is only anecdotal knowledge. Anecdotal knowledge is knowledge based on own experiences, which comes with emotions, with authenticity and often with the personal satisfaction to have overcome a difficult situation. It will often liberally be generalized and, with the gut feeling of conviction be used as a tool to convince oneself, stating, "I really know!" The fact that one seems to master those experiences somehow can quickly make one feel qualified to talk seriously about this subject. The essential difference between (individual) anecdotal knowledge and systematic knowledge, however, is that systematic knowledge is the documented, structured, and analyzed essence of many people. It relates to models and theory, to systematic and documented observation, to controlled reduction of complexity, and hence to the capacity to formulate hypotheses and predictions which in turn can be verified repeatedly. Only this systematic type of scientific knowledge is used in this chapter. It might frustrate some long-time cherished anecdotal obviousnesses of a few readers. Sorry for this.

Introduction to the Topic

It lies in the very nature of the international hospitality business that one deals – in contrast to many other branches of business – not only with a person-related service but usually with a person-related service with strangers. What, if this other – the customer – does not share basic cultural, moral, hygienic, or other assumptions, internalized behavioral codes, and unconscious attributions of meaning of the service provider? What, if the same service provider needs to adjust to customers from very different cultures all the time? That is what makes this topic specific: international hospitality is a person-related service industry with the specific feature that strangeness is usually a constituent key-element in the creation and provision of the service. Often enough, cultural strangeness that requires intercultural competencies is even designed for the customer in order to create and provide a specific, culturally surprising experience. One of the specifics of our topic is, among other things, the distinction between the deliberately created and artificially simplified cultural strangeness and the unwanted and far more complex real strangeness. There is also a difference between the cultural strangeness between service providers and customers on the one hand – this is highly formalized – and the strangeness amongst employees, amongst guests, or between employees, guests, and the environment. If there is a claimed corporate culture, or if the designed experience of strangeness on its part is staged by culturally foreign staff, then the situation becomes even more complex and interesting to analyze.

Dealing systematically with this topic in international hospitality means dealing with cultural standards and intercultural competencies in a quite specific environment. This very short chapter is divided into two parts: first, it presents some theoretical approaches as to how intercultural competencies can be defined in the context of hospitality and why the concept of cultural standards is appropriate for that field. After that, we show in which fields of action the topic intercultural competencies and cultural standards are relevant for international hospitality. As this chapter has the character of a short introduction, the individual topics can only be touched briefly. Nevertheless, it should become clear quickly that the popular superficial "patent solutions" that are offered all too often, in many cases, do not meet the complexity of the challenge in the least.

Enculturation

The term enculturation describes the acquisition of our individual cultural standards at the place and from the people where we grow up. It refers to the first learning of culture, and it means at the same time conquering the world as a toddler and a child. It is the people closest and dearest to us, parents, siblings, close relatives, teachers, friends, neighbors, who teach us how to behave, what to expect, right and wrong. Most of these lessons are not even told explicitly, but are presented and set as examples by our role models and later copied without criticism or questions, even without knowing. We are not even aware of most of these rules and regulations, values, judgments, and habits. However, we might become aware of some of our own assumptions, the very moment when they result in being frustrated. Many concepts and curricula of "Intercultural Competencies" do not go further than showing a few selected routines and rules of a given culture, a sort of monkey training or a behaviorist approach at best. However, it is not just about routines of behavior, but first of all, about the question of what we perceive and how we evaluate and judge the other. Already that depends on our values, internalized assumptions, and therefrom resulting expectations. These, in turn, depend not only on the cultural surrounding of our upbringing but also on the political, legal, and economic system in which we were enculturated (Deardorff 2009).

What Methods and Models Are Useful to Talk about a Particular Culture?

If one wants to develop practical recommendations for encounters with culturally alien people, one has to concentrate on what can be observed most frequently amongst them. This holds especially true of phenomena that stand out from a specific (own) cultural perspective (Chladenius 1742). One speaks therefore of a specific profile of foreignness (Krusche, 1983) if a certain culture is considered from the viewpoint of a certain other culture. Polish guests in a German beer garden for example will hardly notice that on a warm morning in early summer beer is drunk there in public. For them, a beer garden under the open sky is nothing special. On the other hand, guests from the USA would find the consumption of alcohol in the open air very remarkable. A profile of foreignness will, however, usually also include specific hetero-stereotypes, perhaps also a corresponding exoticism. Should this expectation include Bavarians drinking beer in public, guests from the USA would be "reassured," as it were, because the incredible they had already heard of, seems to be true.

Research on intercultural communication is hence about finding common features in perception and behavior of people belonging to a cultural group (Kotthoff 2009; Thomas 2010). Certainly, everyone is a unique person and can feel attached to none, one, two or more cultures, but in the first step, intercultural communication is explicitly not about exploring all of the distinct possibilities of being different, which exist obviously. It is about common traits. Only in a second step, the individual handling of culturally critical or unusual situations is then addressed (and researched). The vast majority of members of a culture – in our case we equate this with a national culture – have surprisingly similar patterns of perception, judgment, routines, and action. Ever since research in intercultural communication has increasingly focused on the practical needs of working together, occupationally similar groups are being investigated (Roth 2014; Meyer 2014). This also applies to international hospitality: the majority of people who interact in this context come from clearly defined groups with specific training and social background: managers, employees, service personnel, et cetera. The comparison between two groups of hotel managers from different countries will therefore highlight, more than anything else, the cultural differences between them. Of course, it is possible and useful to observe also smaller groups as bearers of cultural peculiarities, but the equalizing power of nation-states over common laws, school systems, and media, also allows the inhabitants of such a nation-state to be defined as an observable group.

How can a situation of intercultural encounter be described? Let us systematically go through different options in order to evaluate them. One can differentiate between (I) observations about the conditions under which people live and (II) statements about the so-being of humans. Regarding the (I) conditions under which people live, one can distinguish four approaches: the anecdotal, second the historical, third an analysis of the mémoire collective (Halbwachs, 1939), and fourth the analysis of economic and sociological (also legal) conditions of life. Most common is the anecdotal approach, as every traveller will report what he has seen with utter conviction. Also very common are historical approaches to other cultures. They fill countless pages of travel guides on paper and in the net, but a deeper knowledge of the epoch when China was founded 2,000 years ago will not contribute anything to the understanding of the current Chinese culture. Almost everything that is older than three generations has little or no explanatory value for the practical dealing with people from a different culture today. What shapes our individual memory is to be found rather in recent history. Today's research suggests to limit the historical depth of this memory to about three generations: what our parents and grandparents experienced, be it hunger or inflation, war or certain ideals of education: that is handed down in the family and shapes the picture of what we keep for "normal." The concept of the "mémoire collective" was developed as early as the 1930s. It is a useful and well-structured tool that can replace the vague notion of "mentality," and it refers precisely to that web of values and action routines which we experience with us and others, and for which one can lay out no other explanation than that it is the "so-being" of the people with whom one deals. Part of that collective memory is the respective individual memory that is composed of those values and routines that were handed down to us by your parents and grandparents. If these values and routines are criticized, then the guarantors who conveyed these values to us are also criticized. That is why it is so hard to overcome one's own culture, and a few workshops are not enough to relativize the teachings of one's own parents so easily.

The fourth and most verifiable area is the description of the living conditions in a culture, especially the legal, economic, and social conditions, but also the socially and institutionally represented morality, which determines the life of a person in a given culture as well as the educational system that transports those values. Information on these aspects of living conditions are readily available and they show the environment to which people in a given culture react, and in which they accommodate their lives.

Regarding (II) statements about the so-being of humans, the task is much more complicated. Most common are certainly the statements that origin at the regular's table. These statements need not be discussed here.

A second approach, which is by itself very systematic, unfortunately, does not explain anything either: it is the attempt from the 1960s to understand the so-being of people via questionnaires according to their feelings, preferences, and sensitivities. However, the feelings and desires queried here are described and expressed differently in each culture – if they are expressed so openly at all, so that the individual answers of such questionnaires are not comparable. A larger number of questionnaires does not make the situation any better, as more incomparable answers are still not comparable. Then, aggregating unreliable statements makes the result mathematically impressive, but worthless in content. This approach claims to be able to make highly abstract statements based on a few questions and even to be able to condense these into so-called cultural dimensions. The concept of cultural dimensions which itself was developed by Edward T. Hall in the 1950s (Rogers et al., 2002) can be useful, but it must be fed differently than with Hofstede's unscientific questionnaire or similar tools (Bakerville 2003).

The third way to make statements is the anthropological approach to the topic, which is certainly the oldest of all scientific approaches. Despite its historical merits, this path is no longer important. For this, one must search for models and methods in social psychology or sociology (Thomas 1985; 2018a).

Cultural Standards

The fourth and most important approach to the description of people from a specific culture comes from social psychology (Thomas, 1985). It is a dynamic model and can be defined as "all kinds of perception, thinking, value and action that are considered by the majority of members of a particular culture to be for themselves as well as for others as normal, self-evident, typical and binding." Purpose of this model is to translate individually observable and measurable behavioral routines into social categories so that a core area of usual behavior and (still tolerated) peripheral areas can be described. These categories are then called "cultural standards (Thomas 2018b)." The essential difference between these cultural standards from social psychology on the one hand and on the other hand the cultural dimensions based on statistics used in popular science guidebooks and training is that cultural standards are scientifically based on the observation and documentation of behavior. On the other hand, so-called cultural dimensions are created from questionnaires about feelings and sensitivities of people that cannot be scientifically ascertained at all. Social psychologists observe and document, then evaluate and extract behaviors, which are considered usual and normal in a given culture. In contrast, cultural dimensions are created by asking people how they feel about certain situations. The difference between the two survey methods in terms of objectivity is fundamental.

By far not every difficult situation between people from different cultures is necessarily culturally motivated. Often it is more about linguistic problems such as false friends, grammatical (often syntactic) questions, or sociolinguistic peculiarities. How can one guarantee a sound conceptual foundation for intercultural communication then? By combining linguistic expertise with the sociological theory of the *mémoire collective* and with the *hermeneutic* approaches (Gadamer, 1960) and anthropology, one gains a historically well-grounded approach and an explanation of how a culture has evolved in recent times. This insight has then to be associated with actual and verifiable data of the living conditions: legal, economic, and social conditions, institutionally represented morality, and the educational system that transports those values. This environment sets the framework within which people behave; it frames the ways of perception, thinking, values, and action that are considered by the majority of members of a particular culture to be for themselves as well as for others as "normal." This knowledge is contingent and constantly changing as the situations of encounter and the constellations of intercultural relationships change. Let us have a look at the schematic representation of the eight major approaches to culture-specific behavior. The five in the center are useful and should be combined. The others are common, but they may be dismissed (Figure 7.1).

Intercultural Competencies

Unfortunately, there is not the one and only shortlist of intercultural knowledge, skills, and competencies, we dream of. Rather, a considerable number of elements have to be considered for the

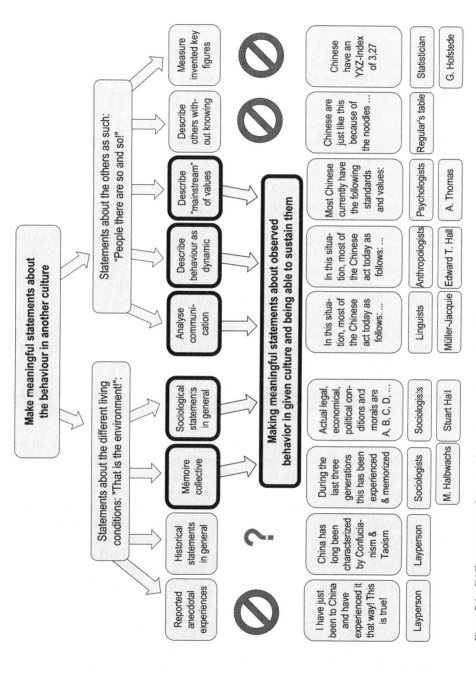

Figure 7.1 Different approaches to make statements about other cultures.

improvement of communication in intercultural encounters. Typically, these encounters bring about unpredictable situations, uncertainty, misunderstandings, critical interactions, and ambiguity or even complete lack of understanding of the other and the situation. Precisely from these difficult situations derive the required competencies for successful intercultural communication: the patient, empathic, and constructive coping with of such encounters is a central element of it.

Most schematic representations break these competencies down into three groups: *cognitive* elements (knowledge), *affective* elements (abilities), and *conative* elements (wanting and doing). If one thinks of somebody who has passed his theoretical exam in order to drive, this person would have achieved the first step, mastering the cognitive side, i.e., knowing in theory that there is an accelerator, an indicator, a brake. This does not make this person a driver yet. The second step would then be the ability to drive, which requires practice. One may know people who not only know the required theory, but also are able to drive, but who do not want to drive. This leads us to the third step, which is the conative or behavioral level: you not only know and are able to drive, but you also are willing to drive. We would suggest a fourth level of competencies, which we call the reflexive dimension. How will the new places you can reach now affect and change you? How best to describe these four levels of competencies? The basic level: Most people assume that the skills needed to manage successfully intercultural situations consist mainly in the acquisition of specific routines. Primarily, one thinks of business protocol, greetings, and culture-specific dos and don'ts. Such clues are a good start, but nothing else. To avoid the violation of taboos, to know a few speech routines and greeting formulas and to have some basic knowledge about the culture of the other in order to show interest, is always good and can help to avoid conflicts or mitigate them at least.

The second level of such competencies for intercultural situations consists of dealing with one's own communicative and emotional abilities and their continuous improvement. This not only requires a critical analysis of one's own language and communication in general, but also a reflection on the quality the globally spoken auxiliary language (often erroneously referred to as "English") which linguists call "internationalish," and which is extremely fault-tolerant. The inaccuracy of "internationalish" is constantly leading to misunderstandings in the management, which are usually noticed too late or sometimes not at all. For Western managers, e.g., to recognize when people from other cultures mean "no" when they say something that does not sound like a clear "no" in Western ears often results in a big problem. One speaks here of different degrees of contextualization of communication (Hall, 1959). In tourism, historically earlier than anywhere else content-less speech formulas have prevailed, where for example everything is done "with pleasure," although each party must be pretty clear that this is often not the case. Dealing with abilities such as bearing ambiguities, reflecting upon role-distance and developing respect towards others completes this second area.

The third level of these competencies refers more deeply to questions of interculturality. It is the question whether one really wants do deal and work with others. The main issue here is to be ready to relativize one's own culture, to distance oneself from one's own culture, and to strike a delicate balance between the rejection of some aspects of other cultures – this may well be justified – and the attitude of cultural relativism or even exoticism. On this level, competencies are attitudes rather than skills (level two) or knowledge (level one). It is helpful to respectfully treat people from other cultures, even if one does not understand their actions and reasons, and even less appreciate them. The insight that others act entangled within their own web of values and routines does not justify their actions and opinions per se. However, it makes the situation and the other's actions hopefully a little more understandable. Encounters with foreigners that have not been reflected upon do not lead – as the so-called *contact hypothesis* wrongly assumes – to an improvement in intercultural competencies, but rather harden the prejudices in most cases. Hence, the fourth level refers to the fact that thoughtful, reflected people in contact with other cultures may also observe how they change themselves. The relativization of one's own Childhood after experiences abroad cannot be undone and will change people, in the best of cases (Figure 7.2).

Cognitive Dimension - to know -	Affective Dimension - to be able -	Conative Dimension - to want -	Reflexive Dimension - to reflect -
Knowledge of one's own and the respective foreign culture and language	Ambiguity tolerance and frustration tolerance De-escalate conflicts	Will to communicate; want to understand.	Reflection upon one's own identity and its continuous changes
Understanding of action contexts in cultures (foreign & own)	Ability to manage stress and reduce complexity	Fundamental willingness to learn and suspend spontaneous attributions	Reflection of one's own ethics and their reach
Knowledge about language and communication as well as cultural differences	Self-confidence and self-efficacy	Willingness to approach the unknown	Reflection of one's own experience and one's own fears
Understanding the special features of intercultural communication	Cultural (and inter-cultural) learning and flexibility	Fundamental respect and patience for others	Reflection of the own ideas of power, law and morals
Knowledge about models and theory of intercultural communication	Role distance or self distance and empathy	Want to succeed together with the other	Reflection of how far one's own concepts reach
Knowledge about and ability of meta-communication	Fundamental accept-ance of others, respect for others	Wanting to overcome one's owns culture's boundaries	Reflection of the growing distance to one's own culture

Figure 7.2 Overview of the four groups of intercultural competencies.
Source: ©Dr. Ulrich Bauer 2019.

Culture and Intercultural Competencies in the International Hospitality

In the second part of this chapter, we focus on international hospitality. This part is divided into a section on intercultural encounters as a product and another one on intercultural encounters as a service. First, the focus is on the customers. The aim is here to look at how (foreign) culture is converted into a product, how it is handled and manipulated, and what impact culture may have on the customer.

In the second part on intercultural relations as a service, the employees and their collaboration and coexistence will be at the center.

Intercultural Encounters as a Product – The Contact with the Customers

In the international hospitality business, intercultural communication is not just a topic for dealing with spoken or written communication between employees or between co-workers and customers. When cultures are commodified in the context of hospitality offerings, they are communicated as a product. Typically, e.g., in a hotel of a country A, the local culture is used as an element of the marketing strategy. In Austria, service personnel will wear a dirndl dress, even if they would not wear it privately at any price in the world. Reduced to pure theatre scenery, sociologists speak of the so-called "staged authenticity" (Urry and Larsen, 2011). This stage set is not really about intercultural communication, but often enough, it is presented as such by marketing. The client wants to believe in meeting another culture, even though in reality it has been "prepared" just for him. In order to achieve this, however, the culture to be sold must first be purposefully simplified and brutally impoverished. Everything that constitutes genuine intercultural communication that is ambiguities, surprises, annoyances, and insecurity should disappear. If we assume that Greece was the country to represent culturally, one can certainly not present Hippocrates for geometry, Isokrátēs for rhetoric, and Aischýlos for literature. On the contrary, intentional impoverishment must focus on more marketable products, in other words, gyros, tzatziki, and ouzo for Greece. One labels the intentional impoverishment and reduction of culture to aspects that are immediately recognized and that can be transformed into products instantly, with the term *paupercultural*.

Globalization also means an ongoing loss of traditional local culture that is being replaced by new forms, by hybrid forms, or simply disappears. Some people experience this loss of tradition as threatening. Hence, the commodification of local or regional culture as stereotypical or even as prototypical is not only created to the foreign guests but increasingly for the guests from their own region, too. In that process, supposedly old patterns of one's own origin are re-activated as demarcation markers, possibly reinvented (Hobsbawm and Ranger, 2012), or at least used more intensively. This dynamic effort, which is contrariwise to transculturality, is labeled with the term *catacultural*.

Commodified Foreign Culture – Expectations and Fantasies as Part of the Product

While the commodification of culture at first only means a purposeful impoverishment, which has to eliminate all surprise and dynamics in order to turn culture into a plannable product, the commodification of *foreign* cultures goes much further. Creating high hopes for intercultural encounters is often part of marketing in international hospitality. Here, the hospitality industry supplies images and hopes for encounters, whose intercultural character should underline the (only-pretended) authenticity of the place, the people, or the product. At the same time, the customer can clandestinely expect that true intercultural encounters will never take place, or will only take place to a controllable extent and accompanied by a guide (DMO, hotel staff, et cetera). Otherwise, he might experience anxiety, fear, and frustration. That is exactly what you want to spare a paying customer obviously. So the best of all are intercultural situations that are not really any. The hotel offers a sheltered space for artificial encounters following a pre-scripted screenplay, often with hired actors. Especially in mass tourism, similar to the globally used "internationalish" instead of English, an "international hotel culture" has developed which obeys rather functional necessities than anything else. At least larger hotels have thus joined the ranks of a globalized transcultural world of things. The transcultural world of things and products such as pictograms, Coca-Cola, Ikea, jeans or fast food, airports, et cetera can essentially be dealt with by applying instrumental reason. International hospitality has thus created a deceitful mixture of transcultural phenomena that require no knowledge beyond instrumental reason, and on the other hand, staged "intercultural" encounters that are none.

When dealing with situations of an arranged mock strangeness, one can speak of a structural asymmetry. The tourist always has a return ticket and thus the guaranteed return to a culturally familiar environment in his pocket, whereas the provider of whatever service has to endure this situation. Particularly catchy examples often come with a mutual speechlessness. The Pakistani, who plays the role of a "local Arab" in the UAE on the "traditional market," is hardly recognized as a Pakistani by the tourist. Many staged intercultural encounters that are produced in the hotel and the destination are thus a kind of silent film with extremely reduced action routines, which perhaps find their complex climax in the payment of a souvenir. These faked encounters are often sufficient to create a sense of achievement that one has "negotiated a price with a local."

Reified Culture – The Hotel as a Learning Environment

Nowadays, billions of people are learning more about the world of industrial hospitality. Although this world is not physically accessible to them, it is increasingly mediated and reified in the media. Five billion out of 7.7 billion people on earth have somehow access to Internet and electronic media, but only a very small percentage of them have the means to travel using professional hospitality infrastructure. Most are not actors in modern hospitality, but they are spectators. Be it films or commercials, photos shared on social media, or YouTube clips: images from the world of hospitality are much more widespread than many realize. Just as other Western concepts and habits such as formal suits, soft drinks, or globalized mainstream-pop have spread around the globe and often locally been adapted and transformed, also in hospitality semiotic content is being spread globally. Particular deviations that individual companies are so terribly proud of, are surprisingly insignificant from this external perspective. Global hospitality thus forms part of the globalization of images and has created an own functional culture, similar to shopping malls and airports.

Irritating Culture – Unexperienced Guests – Unexpected Behavior

Due to travel options becoming rapidly cheaper, more and more customers frequent a modern hotel industry, which come from culturally very distant parts of the world. The wealthier guests are, the more the industry is willing to meet their wishes. In the suite of a wealthy Arab female guest, a female electrician might repair the lamps, as men may not be allowed on the entire floor. However, the hospitality industry's willingness to meet specific culturally based wishes is likely to diminish quickly with lower solvency of its customers.

In situations that become critical due to lack of experience and cultural differences, one should distinguish two fundamentally different settings. On the one hand, there are those that occur within the hotel and to which the service provider should react. These include cases such as that of the Indian tourists, who run the hot shower in Swiss hotels during the whole night in order to get hot, moist air. Similar but the other way around are those German hotels that still serve mainly cheese and milk-products to Chinese tourists.

That would be the classical case for intercultural training. Management as well as the employees can be well prepared for such situations if one is ready to buy two or three days of training. The service provider can be very responsive to clients who have culturally different ideas to the service provider's ones. This might be the very topic that readers of this chapter consider most essential. However, it would be more appropriate to write a separate chapter on this topic, which would have to intersect the most likely situations of encounter. For specific training, a profile of strangeness should be created, which places the culture of the service provider and the culture(s) of the guests in perspective. There should not be a single human resources department that does not know, summon, and encourage such trainings. Obviously, these trainings should go far beyond the usual dos and don'ts and a few simplistic recipes. Unfortunately, the more a training simplifies the complexity of intercultural encounters, the better it is frequently evaluated. Courses that are less stressful and less challenging one's own values and routines are simply more popular. Sadly, they also are worse, and many of them are completely useless. As trainers of intercultural communication need to sell their seminars, they often prefer to focus on offers that are better received by staff than courses that would make the team more successful. This frequently leads to the idea of an oversimplified black and white painting, a Manichean approach, or say: pointless training.

Culture Beyond Control – The Surrounding of a Hotel or a Resort

The other case, where situations that are critical due to inexperience and cultural differences, is beyond the direct control of the hospitality industry. The controllable encounter with culture in the hospitality industry often ends at the hotel door, the latest a few steps away. Here the local vicinity affects and influences the hotel culturally, just as the hotel affects and influences its environment. In any case, the local and perhaps regional environment and the hotel or resort interact mutually in terms of culture. Where, for example, basic standards of working conditions are not met, the hospitality industry can create a culture of poverty and despair in their environment. The sharing industry with AirBnB and Uber creates just about exactly such conditions around established hotels. Locals learn that hospitality brings misery, disguised in a "culture of sharing."

Is there any consideration for handling a situation where the culture of the environment can differ significantly from the culture of the hotel and once again from the culture of the guests? Are such questions asked in the planning or operation of hospitality facilities? Is the staff frequently and sufficiently sensitized? Can you achieve service excellence by ignoring the cultural peculiarities of the environment? As with quality management and other key tasks, here too, only when top management adopts this topic will the facilities achieve the best possible results. It would be a little too easy to say: what happens in front of my door does not concern me. The service provider can very well influence some of these encounters and does so over and over again. Employees who are away from the facilities during their free time can be required to behave in a specific way. How do you deal with the intercultural encounters between the local population and the guests? Only those few providers of hospitality services that have sustainability and cultural sensitivity as core brand values will wonder whether and how their facility has a cultural impact on the environment, and whether perhaps they could inform and prepare their guests as well as the local population. Not because they are necessarily nice guys, but because it is their specific value proposition.

Intercultural Encounters as a Service – Contacts Among Staff

Point of Departure – Possible Situations of Encounter

In the previous section of this chapter, we put the focus on the customers. In this second section on intercultural relations as a service, the employees and their professional collaboration and co-existence should be at the center. From the very early beginnings of tourism, welcoming others meant usually welcoming people who came from other places and probably spoke other languages. Today, the agreed-upon definition as to who is a tourist, implies that he is not in his usual surrounding, hence among people who do not or only partially share his enculturation.

Imagine a larger hotel in Dubai. It belongs, say, to a French chain, has a Swiss manager and a mixed mid-management from Germany, Egypt, and India. Local suppliers include Indians, Pakistani, and Kenyans. The local Dubaian administration is mainly staffed with Egyptians and some Jordanians. Interns from Italy are currently working in the hotel. Malaysians occupy the front desk and most touch-points with the customers. Arab guests come primarily from Saudi Arabia, but also from Oman. Larger groups of guests are from China, Japan, and Germany here. The prostitutes frequenting the house mostly come from Eastern Europe. Overall, guests from 86 countries are staying in this hotel within a year. That is our point of departure.

For almost every person in this setting, we can differentiate quite a few different cultural perspectives in which the persons involved here move. In many encounters, two or more settings overlap partially. First, each person has an own enculturation. One could call his own standards as (the one) auto-cultural standards, as different from the standards of all those who do not share one's own enculturation: their's would be (a number of different) hetero-cultural standards. Much more important, in each individual encounter, there is a specific act of active perception towards a specific alien culture for practically all actors in all situations here. Our relations to others stem from this active act of perception and therefore depend always on two actors: the one who perceives and the one who is perceived. Obviously, the number of culturally different contacts multiplies these acts of perception, which are each different from the next. For the Swiss manager of the hotel, for example, the local Arab culture may be alien, but also the culture of his Malay staff. His perspective on this alien cultures changes not only according to the specific encounter but also according to the specific profile of foreignness that he has in mind for the respective alien culture, he deals with – his personal stereotypes and prejudices. For each person, there are as many perspectives towards alien cultures – always from one's own cultural perspective – as there are culturally different encounters.

I Have Been There – I Know! and it Doesn't Matter Anyway!

Individual anecdotal knowledge will often happily be generalized and, with the gut feeling of conviction be used as a persuasive tool, stating "I really know!" Given these many personal experiences with foreign cultures, there is a growing need to differentiate between whether the behavior and superficial routines of the two sides do not match in an intercultural communication situation, or whether the difficulties stem from deeper lying values and beliefs. An iceberg model usually illustrates this, where the visible and perceptible acts and deeds lie above the surface of the water, while deep underwater the values of early childhood, the assumed normalities, fears, moral, and truths are hidden. The further you go up in this model, the faster and easier elements may change. In the West, we have more and more freedom to design our own lives because the increasing liberty and mobility gradually reduce the regulating and braking effect of our enculturation. A growing individualization of our lifestyles is particularly noticeable among the younger employees in hospitality, who are highly mobile and thus seemingly escape the social control of their enculturation. As the modern Western world brings with it now a hitherto unimaginable pluralization of lifestyles and unprecedented freedom of choice for such designs, employees in the hospitality industry often feel free to try out new ways. This also holds true for encounters with other cultures. One hundred and fifty years ago, life was slow, gradually changing, and even 30 years ago, for example, in Germany, only one telephone company, a dozen television programs, two major religious communities, and news from the newspaper formed the setting in which life evolved. Today one can – and has to – choose one's profession freely, one's faith, one's gender, one's lifestyle, one's community, one's professional peer group, one's social media profile, and one's therapist. This infinite freedom of choices has trivialized most of these selection processes and rendered us indolent and indifferent as people who have to make a choice.

This leads to a feeling of being overwhelmed with possible choices and at the same time to resignation and indifference, which also makes it easier to deal with other cultures, at least on the surface. Not because you understood anything, or because your own culture was reflected upon, but simply because it always seems less important anyway. Indifference and resignation do not lead to solutions however, and potential intercultural conflicts do not become less, only because a few young employees don't care.

Can Communication and Culture be Judged and Measured?

In the real business world, there are plenty of phenomena that can be measured only indirectly, for example by an index. Interesting enough, some indices, which are scientifically quite daring, such as the "Balanced Score Card" are fully accepted in management, whereas others of the same complexity are not, or at least, much less so. Anything that is not physically real can only be measured by operationalizing a systematic set of observations, delimiting the range of underlying assumptions. In order to operationalize abstract concepts, such as "cultural characteristics" or "successful intercultural communication" one needs to recur already with the questions that are supposed to produce raw data on equally abstract concepts, such as satisfaction, respect, personal life, happiness, notions of time, sense of cleanliness, et cetera. Obviously, in every culture each and any of these merely abstract concepts is filled with a different reality, a different set of values and, even more important, a different feeling regarding the degree of openness when it comes to answering questions so intimate.

Aggregating these highly theoretical constructs means than increasing the uncertainty exponentially. Breaking these extremely questionable results finally down to one number seems as serious as the answer to the ultimate question of life, the universe, and everything, which is in a famous novel "42" (Adams, 1979).

The operationalization of the measurement of customer satisfaction is considerably easier with tangible goods than with intangible services. Simple, because real, indicators could be the amount of the tip or the number of new bookings. The measurement of intercultural competencies and their impact on the customers is possible, but particularly difficult, because there are two very different methodical issues to deal with. First, the question of which statements can be used to measure these specific abilities and which ones one would want to measure. For example, while it is customary in some cultures for women to have little to do in public life, in any Western culture one may want to know how the female manager at the front desk worked for international guests – whether they came from a culture with less equality or not.

Second, because it is very difficult to judge which cultural background allows what kind of answers. Guests from different cultures may have very different forms of feedback. A bad meal is referred to by a German as "bad," while a guest from the USA may say it is "actually good, but next time I will choose something different." A Japanese guest will most likely say that even the worst food was "excellent." While it is relatively careless to call too hard a bed simply "too hard," judging staff or management in questionnaires or guest interviews makes people feel much more uncomfortable, according to their culture.

Surveys that do not consider such aspects have not even understood the cultural limitations of response. "Trash in – trash out" is what researchers call that. However, it is possible to obtain reliable feedback on culture-specific weightings and on indirect questions. It is one of the specific challenges in intercultural communication that malaise, injuries, and anger are often not expressed, as long as it is not really serious occurrences. The guest may angrily register the culturally inappropriate behavior of an employee and waives a complaint, while at the same time classifying this employee as incompetent. What then perhaps remains in the feedback is the unclear statement that there are "incompetent employees." From this, no strategy can be derived. It would be better, therefore, to continuously work on expanding the intercultural competencies of all employees from the director to the last person at a touchpoint.

Preparing Staff for Real and for Fake Intercultural Communication

There are a large number of offers for seminars, trainings, and qualifications in the field of intercultural communication. Depending on which academic tradition they stem from, they may address very different questions. The quality of the offers is extremely heterogeneous. Many very dedicated trainers offer good introductions to the topic. Care should be taken that the courses are tailored to the contact situation in hospitality or at least in the service industry. Many courses are focused on specific countries, which is usually not helpful for international hospitality. Better are courses that make reference to the concrete issues of the facility in which they are offered. Of course, there are also black sheep. Not a few do not go beyond the bold and extremely simplified representation of "the other," and again other providers try to breathe something "scientific" into their work with pointless numbers from quantitative models (cultural dimensions).

Above all, it is important to take the concrete challenges in situ as a starting point and work together with useful methods and cultural standards. One can work on current cases, which were experienced by present employees themselves. As they describe and explain this to their colleagues, they often gain more clarity about the situation. Supported by application-based models and simplified theories, all employees can better understand what matters. It is also important that the focus is on the respective own culture of the employees concerned. The critical elucidation about one's own values, assumptions, and normalities is always the first step in understanding a critical situation. This approach also has the highest potential for transfer, as understanding better one's own expectations and their sources helps communicate with anyone else, regardless of their respective culture. Fifty percent of any intercultural problem is always oneself.

A proven method for dealing with difficult situations is the so-called critical incident method. Working with this method, one assumes that one's own experiences and routines could be a hindrance if one is confronted with very different world-views and intercultural challenges. After the description of the difficult situation one tries to put together ideas, what the origins of the conflict could be. This might be the language, religion, the concrete situation, or many other reasons. In a good training, participants would then look for a number of possible ways out of the problem, and weigh their options according to effort and possible success. Joint discussions of such challenges – if done in-house – also motivate finding a common solution that can be very different for each participant depending on their own perspective on the culture in speech.

References

Adams, D. (1979), *The Hitchhiker's Guide to the Galaxy*, Macmillan, London, UK.

Bakerville, R.F. (2003), "Hofstede never studied culture", *Pergamon. Accounting, Organizations and Society*, Vol.28, pp.1–14.

Chladenius, J.M. (1742), *Einleitung zur richtigen Auslegung vernünftiger Reden und Schriften*, n.p., Leipzig.

Deardorff, D. (Ed.) (2009), *The Sage Handbook of Intercultural Competence*, Sage, Los Angeles, CA.

Gadamer, H.G. (1960), *Truth and Method*, Bloomsbury, London, UK.

Halbwachs, M. (1939), *La mémoire collective*, Presses Universitaires de France, Paris.

Hall, E.T. (1959), *The Silent Language*, Doubleday, New York, NY.

Hobsbawm, E. and Ranger, T. (Ed.) (2012), *The Invention of Tradition*, Cambridge University Press, Cambridge, UK.

Kotthoff, H. (Ed.) (2009), *Handbook of Intercultural Communication*, Mouton de Gruyter, Berlin; New York, NY.

Krusche, D. (1983), "Fremdheitsprofile. Das Eigene als Fremdes. Zur Sprach- und Literaturdidaktik im Fache Deutsch als Fremdsprache", *Neue Sammlung*, Vol.23, pp.27–41.

Meyer, E. (2014), *The Culture Map: Decoding How People Think, Lead, and Get Things Done Across Cultures*, PublicAffairs, New York, NY.

Rogers, E., et al. (2002), "Edward T. Hall and the history of intercultural communication", *Keio Communication Review*, Vol. 24, No.3, pp.3-26..

Roth, J. (Ed.) (2014), *Culture Communication Skills. Handbook for Adult Education* [Xpert culture communication skills] = Interkulturelle Kompetenz, EduMedia, Stuttgart.

Thomas, A. (1985), "Stand und Entwicklung der psychologischen Austauschforschung in ihrem Beitrag für die internationale Zusammenarbeit", in *Zentrum für Interdisziplinäre Forschung* (ZiF), Universität Bielefeld, Göttingen.

Thomas, A. (Ed.) (2018a), "Orientation in cultural and ethnic diversity. The concept of cultural Standards", in *Cultural and Ethnic Diversity*, Hogrefe, Göttingen, pp.25–38.

Thomas, A. (Ed.) (2018b), "The contribution of psychology to the development of intercultural competences", in *Cultural and Ethnic Diversity*, Hogrefe, Göttingen, pp.39–52.

Thomas, A. and Kinast, E.-A. (Eds.) (2010), *Handbook of Intercultural Communication and Cooperation: Basics and Areas of Application*, Vandenhoek & Rupprecht, Göttingen.

Urry, J. and Larsen, J. (2011), *The Tourist Gaze 3.0*, Sage, London, UK.

8

INTERNATIONAL HOSPITALITY DEVELOPMENT

Training to Enhance the Understanding of 'The Art of Hospitality' Business Model

Robert J. Harrington, Yimo Liu, Rhonda Hammond,
Anders P.F. Herdenstam, and Byron Marlowe

Introduction

The notion and understanding of international hospitality management as a specific business model and, thus, representing a specific field of study has received much debate (Lashley, 2017). The general field of management seems to focus on various models and frameworks to explain organizational behavior; this approach applied to international hospitality management usually focuses on theories, typologies, and taxonomies of management models applied to this social science using the scientific method.

While a more general study of hospitality seems to fall into three domains (cultural/social, private/domestic, or commercial/industrial) (Lashley, 2017), the field of international hospitality management is generally viewed as a more applied business approach in terms of both research and skills needed to understand the business and execute a quality product, service, or experience. Historically, dining room service skills, culinary skills, and guest service skills are all based on more craft or aesthetic approaches using a master-apprentice method to transfer technical skills and hospitality tacit knowledge.

While the notion of tacit knowledge has been described as a core area to create competitive advantage (limiting the ability of others to copy or imitate) (Harrington, 2004), pedagogical methods have generally focused on principles, theory, and research rather than reflective practice and action research. The notion of the meaning of "what hospitality is" and "what it is not" is held as tacit knowledge in practicing professionals rather than articulated in international hospitality management texts, lectures, or examinations. This weakness raises the question of how an international hospitality business model can best be conveyed and understood by students or practitioners.

This chapter addresses these questions in two steps. First, it describes a model and key components associated with international perspectives of what is the "art of hospitality." Second, it provides analysis of an adapted approach to training students and practitioners in understanding and articulating what this means and how analogies, metaphors, and examples can be used to express this understanding as part of a professional hospitality culture.

Background and Framework

The definition of hospitality takes many forms but in general relates to "encounters between strangers, friends and relatives," – in other words, individuals that are not consistent members of a domicile (Schreurs, 2017, p. 171). Others define hospitality based on 'the business of furnishing food or lodging or both to paying visitors who are typically called guests' (Heffernan, 2014, p. 11).

Schreurs (2017) suggested that 'speech acts' performed in hospitality encounters reveal important implications related to 'standard hospitable language usage' (p. 171) and how hospitality experiences are perceived. She concludes that although standard hospitality language is difficult to define, hospitality situations and language are intertwined conveying messages of requests, greetings, and invitations that vary by meaning and linguistic forms.

The consumption of the hospitality experience has been described as containing a varied set of practices, processes, and outcomes with an opportunity to leverage and define its unique and independent nature within the service field (Ottenbacher et al., 2009). While the study of hospitality can be assessed from a sociological, literary, practical, or business perspective, hospitality studies in a variety of sectors appear to agree that the "interest in hospitableness as a means of delivering customer experiences that enhance satisfaction and loyalty" (Lashley, 2017, p. 2) is desired.

While the commercial hospitality industry is not a new phenomenon nor is the academic study of international hospitality management, the lack of consensus in the academic literature and how it can provide superior value for consumers is an important gap that needs addressing for students and practitioners. This chapter proposes that a better understanding of these concepts by those studying to be professionals in the industry is likely to provide several benefits. These benefits include (1) greater empathy and understanding of consumer needs and values in a hospitality context, (2) higher self-worth in understanding the importance of hospitality in stakeholders quality of life, and (3) how the concept of hospitality and an internationally derived hospitality business model can be articulated to future leaders in the field.

Our approach to furthering an understanding and international application of hospitality management was based on two main steps. First, the creation of 'the art of hospitality management' model used a qualitative and iterative process for feedback and clarification of key constructs. This process included geographically disbursed one-on-one interviews with professionals and academics with expertise, feedback from presentations, and panel discussions in the USA, Sweden, France, and Germany. The authors defined an acronym for 'the art of hospitality' as TAOH (i.e., the Chinese term Tao with an H on for hospitality), signifying a 'way,' 'path,' or 'principle.' The resulting model (see Figure 8.1) emerged from this process that included core aspects described as (1) the art of thinking small, (2) the art of innovation and creativity, (3) the art of tacit knowledge, (4) the art of the experience, (5) the art of exceeding expectations, and (6) instilling a hospitality heart.

The connection of these six aspects to the international hospitality management concept and research is discussed in the next chapter section. A second process was used to assess how the concepts of the model (TAOH) that are associated with the current international hospitality business model can best be communicated to students and industry professionals to enhance appreciation for this modern hospitality management mindset.

The Art of Thinking Small

The concept of 'the art of thinking small' was an idea that emerged out of two areas related to hospitality. First, this concept is derived from very traditional hospitality notions and comments when defining key components during the interview process such as the *golden rule, attentive, caring industry*, and *attention to detail*. Second, this descriptor ties in with theory emerging from the literature in service-dominant logic and memory-dominant logic with a core concept of co-creation (Harrington et al., 2018). This personalized service experience is not passive but instead is (at least in part) co-created among hospitality producers and consumers in an iterative process of practices and staff employee involvement. This joint, collaborative process is thought to co-create superior

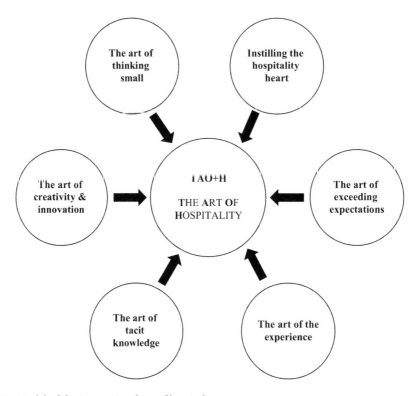

Figure 8.1 Model of the international art of hospitality.

hospitality experiences through the simultaneous input of staff members and customers (Chathoth et al., 2016). Further, this component tied to TAOH relies on on-going communication and involvement to ensure the hospitality value received is not restricted to just the best available choice (i.e., a limited menu item selection, or choice of a hard or soft pillow). Instead, value creation is received throughout the hospitality process and is based on personalized attention to the guests' needs at that moment. This TAOH factor also builds on the Golubovskaya et al. (2017) finding of what they called "employee-customer contact moments."

The Art of Creativity and Innovation

Not surprisingly, the importance of creative thinking and innovation emerged as a second key component of international hospitality and crossed geographic boundaries. This relates to the traditional business concept of continuous improvement (i.e., incremental innovation) through new-to-the-world hospitality concepts or services. This was both expressed during interviews with comments such as "the need to use creativity and flexibility to solve problems," "technology is driving dynamic changes in hospitality" as well as the authors' empirical research that crossed national boundaries (e.g., United States, Canada, Germany, Spain, France, Hong Kong) and sectors (e.g., restaurants, hotels, casinos, hospitality, IT).

Some of the outcomes derived from earlier international studies in hospitality innovation support the value and necessity of creativity and innovation management to become or maintain status as a high-performing firm (Ottenbacher and Harrington, 2009, 2008). Additionally, studies indicated (1) innovative hospitality organizations demonstrate stronger market performance, financial performance, and employee/customer relationship enhancement; (2) successful hospitality innovations demand a balancing act between encouraging open-ended, free-flowing creativity with management of the process; and (3) a variety of best practices are key to success and within the control of hospitality leadership (Harrington and Ottenbacher, 2013; Ottenbacher and Harrington, 2010).

The Art of Tacit Knowledge

The notion of tacit knowledge as a component for creating competitive advantage has been established in the resource-based view (RBV) and is tied to one of the four criteria for competitive advantage – the bundle of resources/capabilities must be rare, valued, non-substitutable, and not easily imitated. Tacit knowledge has been tied to the non-imitable factor of competitive advantage (Harrington, 2004).

Tacit knowledge has been defined as a learn-by-doing approach or a "do not know what we know" type of knowledge (Henderson, 2013). This concept is closely tied to traditional craft and master-apprentice situations (Herdenstam et al., 2018), which has been a traditional method of training and passing on knowledge in many areas of hospitality (culinary arts, mixology, service). Therefore, the art of tacit knowledge was included as an integral component of hospitality because (1) it serves as an instrumental method to pass along knowledge within the field, and (2) it creates casual ambiguity for competitors wanting to copy the art of hospitality business model. Thus, tacit know-how is achieved through experience, creating complexity in the number, and heterogeneity of routines and experiences in the international hospitality organizational environment. This greater complexity leads to difficulty in grasping a clear understanding of all inter-dependent relationships. This process limits imitation by rivals and increases complexity safeguards for hospitality firm information from being expropriated by rivals (Harrington, 2004).

While the question of the value of practice associated with tacit knowledge is not a new one, several other fields have established value in technical proficiency, tacit knowledge, or aesthetic methods in the pedagogical process including engineering, technology, and graduate education. The recognition of the value of experience-based knowledge and the difficulty of articulating this type of knowledge in traditional educational settings has been due to a tendency to discount its value and ignore the master-apprentice dimension of learning (Herdenstam et al., 2018; Ratkić, 2009).

The Art of the Experience

Not surprisingly, the concept of experience was expressed by professionals as a key component of international hospitality. The germinal experience economy concept elucidated by Pine and Gilmore (1999) described the nature of the experience economy and resulting four Es (education, escapism, esthetics, and entertainment) that lead to consumer experiential value. The concept of experiences in hospitality and tourism has received substantial study (Harrington et al., 2018) and modern concepts relate to consideration of all sensory aspects of the customer experience. Comments expressed in this area included "excellent customer relations at all levels of a person's experience," "helping others enjoy an experience," and "giving the customer a unique experience."

The Art of Exceeding Expectations

The relationship between a priori expectations and whether or not these expectations have been met, exceeded, or fall below expectations have a long history in hospitality and the study of services in the business literature (Pizam and Milman, 1993). So, it is not surprising that this concept emerged as an important international aspect of hospitality management. Therefore, a common recommendation is to 'under promise and over deliver' to facilitate exceeding expectations and create wow factors for guests.

While this relationship with unanticipated outcomes has been supported in some empirical studies and not supported in others, hospitality professionals generally supported the notion of exceeding expectations as a core principle for international hospitality management success. Thus, comments such as "creating unanticipated experiences," "going above and beyond," and "delighting the guest" relate to exceeding guest expectations. Early research by Golubovskaya et al. (2017) also established exceeding expectations as a factor using their sample in Australia.

Instilling the Hospitality Heart

The concept of the "hospitality heart" was a term from an executive who was interviewed by a major international lodging firm. The hospitality heart concept reflects instilling a belief in the importance of serving guests as a professional approach to what is reflected in the concept of hospitality that includes social, practical, and business perspectives. The concept overlaps with creating a firm and employee culture with interest in "hospitableness" as a means for delivering superior hospitality experiences (e.g., Lashley, 2017).

This factor crosses the boundaries of personality and organizational culture suggested in earlier research (Golubovskaya et al., 2017). Therefore, this concept also relates to a socialization process to instill an understanding of what is the hospitality heart and its relation to a firm's organizational culture and an individual's professional hospitality culture.

Summary

The art of hospitality model was developed based on a synthesis of literature and feedback from professionals engaged in international hospitality management. The resulting factors of the art of thinking small, creativity and innovation, tacit knowledge, experience, exceeding expectations, and hospitality heart provides some key concepts that can be used to articulate a mindset and coach staff and other mentees. While we are not arguing that other factors and concepts could also be included, these six factors emerged from the authors' investigation of the key elements of international hospitality from business, social, and practice perspectives.

After this framework was developed, the authors used a dialogue method to determine the effect when training students and practitioners in understanding and to articulate what TAOH means and how the use of analogies, metaphors, and examples can assist in expressing this understanding as part of a hospitality professional culture. The need for this process has been established in the early study of frontline employees; these employees demonstrated a lack in the ability to articulate the meaning of hospitality and differentiation from other service management and service process paradigms (Golubovskaya et al., 2017). The dialogue method builds on the idea of Schön (1991) suggesting the need for reflection that is separated from action particularly when learning demands experts to describe what they are doing (tacit skills) when reflecting on professional action. This has been described as 'reflection on reflection-in-action' (Schön, 1991).

TAOH – Analogies, Metaphors, and Examples

A variety of adjectives have been used to describe the term hospitality: "genuine, authentic, commercial, private, academic, social, reciprocal, redistributive, altruistic, contemporary, good and humanitarian" (Gehrels, 2017: 247). These adjectives create a broad range of terms and context

Table 8.1 The art of hospitality (TAOH) components and dialogue method outline

TAOH component	Brief description	Inspirational videos (TED talk)
The art of thinking small	Individualized, co-created services	The paradox of choice by Barry Schwartz
The art of creativity & innovation	Managing the process; innovative solutions/value creation	How AirBnB designs for trust, Joe Gebbia
The art of tacit knowledge	Learn-by-doing; knowledge that is difficult to transfer or copy	What we think we know, Jonathon Drori; Reading – tacit knowledge – making it explicit, London School of Economics
The art of the experience	Understanding the multi-sensory aspects of hospitality; the four Es; value-in-experience, memorable experiences	The riddle of experience vs. memory, Daniel Kahneman; Reading – the cat in the hat, Dr. Suess
The art of exceeding expectations	Wow or excitement factors; creating engagement and emotional arousal	The surprising science of happiness, Dan Gilbert
Instilling the hospitality heart	Professional culture; balancing connectedness with escape/otherness	Are you a giver or a taker?, Adam Grant
Overall meaning of TAOH	Synthesizing key reflections, interesting impulses, or examples/analogies/ metaphors that describe meaningful elements of hospitality	Students create written group document of idea protocols and overall group reflections

for international hospitality. Gehrels (2017) proposes wine serves as a metaphor for "liquid hospitality" due to its similar connections and facilitative nature of virtue, sophistication, and the good life as that proposed in the social domain of hospitality.

Table 8.1 provides an outline of the six TAOH components that were presented, analyzed, and discussed as part of this training process. The table includes the name of the six hospitality components, a brief description of each, and the inspirational TED Talk videos used to stimulate impulse texts along with readings for two of the components. The following section provides an outline of the dialogue process with the hopes of facilitating better understanding, examples, analogies, and metaphors for what defines "hospitality" and in a more meaningful way for articulation to others.

The Analogical Perspective

The impact of the metaphor in communication has also been argued for in neurocognitive studies when investigating how conceptual thoughts and language work in the human brain in real life situations (Lakoff, 2014). Because the basis of understanding a metaphor, as well as analogies, is analogical thinking, these neurocognitive studies reveal the importance of this approach when communicating the wholeness of sensory experience. It also shows the potential need for analogical training in order to handle sensory communication in different contexts. In a study on sommelier training, Herdenstam (2011) showed that analogical tools such as metaphors, analogies, and practical examples were essential for the sommelier when communicating complex sensory sensations.

When performing analogical training or adapting an analogical perspective, the main question becomes – what does the experience awaken in you? This concept in learning has been described as the flow experience; this is experienced in a flow rather than the more traditional analytical perspective. In cognitive science, this concept has been investigated by studying the effect of implicit skill-based knowledge. It is proposed that "flow" is a necessary prerequisite state that enables temporary suppression of the analytical and meta-conscious capacities, comparable with writing and free-jazz improvisation (Dietrich, 2004). The analogical approach is well represented in the literature when it comes to describing complex emotional sensations (Herdenstam et al., 2018).

Dialogue Seminar Method

The dialogue seminar method was originally developed at The Royal Institute of Technology, Sweden (KTH) to investigate experience-based knowledge and concept building in groups of professionals in different fields (Goranzon and Hammarén, 2006). The general idea is that language develops by defining how words and concepts are used in different contexts. The thoughts behind this approach are the philosophical idea formulated by Wittgenstein (1968) and have been widely used in other research contexts in order to facilitate reflection and verbalization of complex experiences and tacit knowledge within different professions, e.g., engineers, mathematician, meteorologists, musicians, actors, and nuclear power workers (Ratkić, 2006, 2009). The common methodological element in these studies has been the reading of classic texts from the history of science and philosophy.

The scientific perspective is a prerequisite in analytical thinking when investigating complex attributes. Analogical thinking is necessary when trying to grasp the wholeness and tacit dimensions of complex experiences because no single analytical attribute can hold the same communicative content. Metaphors, analogies, and examples (both narrative and practical) are the tools that signify this skill when approaching the practical level (Herdenstam et al., 2009). Thus, the analogical mode of reasoning in a practice appears relevant for facilitating an understanding of international hospitality as a competitive business model in its context. The study aimed to investigate practical analogical training – involving reflection, verbalization, and exploring concepts, as a training method for understanding and articulating the art of hospitality.

Methods

Data was collected over one semester with two student groups enrolled in a junior-level hospitality leadership class. While the actual process was more extensive, a brief outline of the process is provided below.

Step 1: Students were given a handout of the upcoming assignments and provided definitions for adjectives, analogies, metaphors, and examples for hospitality. They were asked to individually complete a "What is the art of hospitality (TAOH)?" questionnaire prior to the training exercises.

Step 2: Students were given an overview of key elements of TAOH, formed groups of five people, were instructed on roles as moderator, definitions of impulse text, idea protocol, and inspirational readings/videos. Given the short timeframe and to test the impact, TED Talk videos that related to key aspects of TAOH were selected and assigned as inspirational items to facilitate individual impulse texts, group discussion, and idea protocols. During this process, students watched assigned videos, created individual impulse texts, interacted in groups to reach consensus, and served as rotating group moderators to draft idea protocols based on interesting and key reflections by the group.

Step 3: The final group step was to synthesize the idea protocols and present a group presentation on their perception of TAOH. Additionally, students individually completed a post-process questionnaire addressing "What is TAOH?"

The data created two levels of analysis: groups and individual. It was primarily qualitative in nature. The first step was to investigate student terminology and their initial thoughts or examples of hospitality. At the group level, idea protocols provided an ability to assess similarities and differences across assigned groups for each of the six components shown in Figure 8.1. Finally, final group presentations and post-process individual responses provided the ability to assess changes and the impact of the dialogue seminar approach to learning outcomes associated with understanding and internalizing the meaning of the international hospitality business model.

Student Groups and Protocol

The students selected for the study were 36 students in total majoring in hospitality management from a university in the North Western USA. In order to investigate analogical training, the experiment was performed during regular class time. One common methodological element in the original setting using the dialogue seminar method was the reading of classic texts; in this case, given the timeframe, TED talks and related readings were provided to awaken understanding from within. Another element was the introduction of a group reflective dialogue while working with impulse texts written by the participants. The essence of the impulse text writing was reflection involving analogies, metaphors, and examples expressing personal experiences, skill, and tacit knowledge (i.e., dimensions of practical knowledge is not possible to articulate in a word and must be *shown*).

The methodological approach was modified using inspirational videos rather than classical readings; these videos were selected by the researchers to articulate unique thoughts on components key to the international hospitality business model. This method was used to stimulate verbalization, reflection, and the use of analogies and examples. By so doing, this facilitated the study of participants' ability to progress into analogical thinking. On a practical level, the students were first divided into groups. In each group, one moderator was selected for each session/key hospitality component discussion. His or her job was to manage the dialogue in the sense of creating a creative and democratic dialogue atmosphere. This process required that moderators took an active part in the seminar and were responsible for facilitating the dialogue; grasping interesting reflections, exploring complex concepts, and making sure the group stayed on track with the task at hand. A second person in each group was selected to be the responsible protocol keeper. This person was required to keep track of interesting reflections and examples that emerge through the dialogue. The nature of the seminar exercise went through individual reflection, then later moving towards a collective group reflection. In so doing, each individual in the group first tried to assess the inspirational video and its potential connection to understanding the characteristics of hospitality.

After that, a dialogue was initiated where each person read his or her notes and reflections while the other members of the group were obliged to make a comment or reflect upon each other's experience. One of the important roles of the moderator was being able to grasp examples where different concepts and meanings emerge during the dialogue. When this occurred, the members of the group were instructed to show examples and illustrate their meanings. This meant they could illustrate different meanings and experiences by putting them in a certain context by showing practical examples. This pragmatic approach was similar to the original method (Göranzon et al., 2005) but modified to fit the context and learning objectives as suggested in earlier studies (Herdenstam, 2011; Herdenstam et al., 2018).

Student group members were then asked to view the assigned video and create an individual impulse text (spontaneous reactions) to its content and how or if the ideas related to that sessions' TAOH key component or overall. This methodological setup corresponded to the original dialogue seminar concept with the idea of finding similarities and recognitions in experiences emerging through the dialogue, while exploring crucial concepts.

Results and Discussion

After the classroom sessions, content analyses on the pre and post-training questionnaires and protocols were performed to analyze discriminating attributes and concepts. Content analysis is a widely used qualitative research technique and has a long history dating back to the 18th century (Rosengren, 1983). The approach in this study used a combination of conventional and summative content analysis involving both codings of categories derived from questionnaires, protocols and counting of keywords (Hsieh and Shannon, 2005). This method allowed an analysis of how the study's dialogue seminar and related analogical activities affected hospitality concepts and terminology. Table 8.2 provides frequencies (as a percentage) for the resulting 16 categories that emerged. Eight of the 16 categories varied in frequency between the pre-training questionnaire and the post-training questionnaire.

The top five categories prior to training were above and beyond, customer service, friendly and caring, hospitality businesses, and quality. The top five categories after training were above and beyond, customer relations, customer service, friendly and caring, and new experiences. In addition, these responses placed more emphasis on customer relations, hospitality heart, innovative hospitality, new experiences, and uniqueness. Pre-training examples, metaphors, and analogies had more emphasis on customer service, hospitality business types, memorable experiences, and quality. While customer service was still a frequent attribute, the importance of creating a relationship with customers was much higher post-training. Pre-training students frequently mentioned types of hospitality businesses that make up the hospitality industry rather than thinking about hospitality as an international business model.

While memorable experiences were less frequent as a percentage of responses post-training, it still represented an important component. A similar relationship was shown with "quality" when comparing pre- and post-training responses. In the post-training feedback, new experiences, unique experiences, and innovative hospitality became more frequent examples of quality predictors.

Table 8.2 Frequency of responses pre and post dialogue training*

Key coded terms	Pre-training frequency (%)	Post-training frequency (%)
Above + beyond	8.18	8.76
Customer relations	7.81	**12.44**
Customer service	**17.47**	12.90
Details+ responsible	2.23	1.38
Friendly + caring	13.75	14.29
Guests	3.72	4.61
Hospitality businesses	**9.67**	2.76
Hospitality heart	5.20	**6.45**
Image	2.23	1.84
Innovative	2.97	**5.53**
Leadership-followership	4.09	4.61
Memorable experience	**7.81**	5.53
New experiences	0.00	**8.29**
Profession culture	4.09	3.23
Quality	**9.67**	5.07
Unique	1.12	**2.30**
Total	100	100

*Significant at p < .05

Conclusions

This chapter asks the following questions: What is international hospitality business? Is it a business model? Does it have key factors that are shared across geographic locations?

How might this be communicated to current and future professionals in the industry? While earlier studies have wrestled with whether hospitality represents cultural/social aspects, domestic approaches or commercial aspects (Lashley, 2017), our synthesis suggests an international concept of hospitality integrates all of these aspects as part of an international hospitality business model or logic.

While the authors do not propose that the six factors in the TAOH framework are all-inclusive, these factors emerged as important for integrating into a socialization process, firm culture, and business logic mindset. And, our synthesis of international input and the literature indicates these elements are not restricted to geographic boundaries.

An important contribution of this chapter is to ask and express – how to plan training programs using dialogue methods to enhance understanding of TAOH and communicate it to staff. This understanding by industry professionals is likely to increase empathy and understanding of consumer needs and values, create higher self-worth in understanding the importance of hospitality in stakeholders quality of life, and enhance understanding of how the concept of hospitality as an internationally derived business model can be articulated to peers and subordinates by leaders in the field.

References

Chathoth, P.K., UngsonG.R., Harrington, R.J., and Chan, S.W. (2016), "Co-creation and higher order customer engagement in hospitality and tourism services: A critical review", *International Journal of Contemporary Hospitality Management*, Vol.28, No.2, pp.222–245.

Dietrich, A. (2004), "Neurocognitive mechanisms underlying the experience of flow", *Consciousness and Cognition*, Vol.13, No.4, pp.746–761.

Gehrels, S. (2017), "Liquid hospitality: Wine as the metaphor", in Lashley, C. (Ed.), *The Routledge Handbook of Hospitality Studies*, Routledge, New York, NY, pp.247–259.

Golubovskaya, M., Robinson, R.N.S., and Solnet, D. (2017), "The meaning of hospitality: Do employees understand?, *International Journal of Contemporary Hospitality Management*, Vol.29, No.5, pp.1282–1304.

Göranzon, B. and Hammarén, M. (2006), "The methodology of the dialogue seminar", in Göranzon, B., Ennals, R., and Hammarén, M. (Eds.), *Dialogue, Skill and Tacit Knowledge*, John Wiley & Sons Ltd., London, UK, pp.57–65.

Göranzon, B., Hammarén, M., and Ratkic, A. (2005), "Training in analogical thinking: The dialogue seminar method in basic education, further education and graduate studies 2005–2007", in Göranzon, B., Ennals, R., and Hammarén, M. (Eds.), *Dialogue, Skill and Tacit Knowledge*, John Wiley & Sons Ltd., London, UK.

Harrington, R.J. (2004), "Part I: The culinary innovation process, a barrier to imitation", *Journal of Foodservice Business Research*, Vol.7, No.3, pp.35–57.

Harrington, R.J., Hammond, R.K., Ottenbacher, M.C., and Chathoth, P.K. (2018), "From goods-service logic to a memory-dominant logic: Business logic evolution and application in hospitality", *International Journal of Hospitality Management*, Vol.76, pp.252–260.

Harrington, R.J. and Ottenbacher, M.C. (2013), "Managing the culinary innovation process: The case of new product development", *Journal of Culinary Science & Technology*, Vol.11, No.1, pp.4–18.

Heffernan, J.A.W. (2014), *Hospitality and Treachery in Western Literature*, Yale University Press, New Haven, CT, p.11.

Henderson, P. (2013), *You Can Kill an Idea, You Can't Kill an Opportunity*, John Wiley & Sons, Hoboken, NJ.

Herdenstam, A. (2011), "The working palate: The double grip of the wine taster, from analysis to experience", *Den arbetande gommen: Vinprovarens dubbla grepp, från analys till upplevelse*, KTH Royal Institute of Technology, Stockholm, Sweden.

Herdenstam, A., Hammarén, M., Ahlström, R., and Wiktorsson, P.-A. (2009), "The professional language of wine: Perception, training and dialogue. *Journal of Wine Research*, Vol.20, No.1, pp.53–84.

Herdenstam, A., Nilsen, A., Ostrom, A., and Harrington, R.J. (2018), "Sommelier training – Dialogue seminars and repertory grid method in combination as a pedagogical tool", *Journal of Gastronomy and Food Science*, Vol.13, pp.78–89.

Hsieh, H.-F. and Shannon, S. E. (2005), "Three approaches to qualitative content analysis", *Qualitative Health Research*, Vol.15, No.9, pp.1277–1288.

Lakoff, G. (2014), "Mapping the brain's metaphor circuitry: Metaphorical thought in everyday reason", *Frontiers in Human Neuroscience*, Vol.8, p.958.

Lashley, C. (2017), *The Routledge Handbook of Hospitality Studies*, Routledge, New York, NY.

Ottenbacher, M.C. and Harrington, R.J. (2010). "A study of innovative versus incremental new service developments: Different strategies for achieving success", *Journal of Services Marketing*, Vol.24, No.1, pp.3–15.

Ottenbacher, M.C. and Harrington, R.J. (2009), "North American Indian gaming innovations", *Hospitality Review*, Vol.11, No.1, pp.11–18.

Ottenbacher, M.C. and Harrington, R.J. (2008), "U.S. and German culinary innovation processes: Differences in involvement and other factors", *Journal of Foodservice Business Research*, Vol.11, No.4, pp.412–438.

Ottenbacher, M.C., Harrington, R.J., and Parsa, H.G. (2009), "Defining the hospitality discipline: A discussion of pedagogical and research implications", *Journal of Hospitality & Tourism Research*, Vol.33, No.2, pp.263–283.

Pine, B.J. and Gilmore, J.H. (1999), *The Experience Economy*, Harvard Business Review Press, Boston, MA.

Pizam, A. and Milman, A. (1993), "Predicting satisfaction among first-time visitors to a destination using the expectancy disconfirmation theory", *International Journal of Hospitality Management*, Vol.12, No.2, pp.197–209.

Ratkić, A. (2006), "The dialogue seminar as a foundation for research on skill," in Göranzon, B., Ennals, R., and Hammarèn, M. (Eds.), *Dialogue, Skill and Tacit Knowledge*, John Wiley & Sons Ltd., London, UK, pp.46–56.

Ratkić, A. (2009), "Dialogue seminars as a tool for post graduate education," *AI & Society*, Vol.23, No.1, pp.99–109.

Rosengren, K.E. (1983), "Advances in content analysis," *American Political Science Review*, Vol.77, No.4, p.1147.

Schön, D.A. (1991), *The Reflective Turn: Case Studies in and on Educational Practice*, Teachers College Press, New York, NY.

Schreurs, L. (2017), "Observing hospitality speech patterns," in Lashley, C. (Ed.), *The Routledge Handbook of Hospitality Studies*, Routledge, New York, NY, pp.169–179.

Wittgenstein, L. (1968). *Philosophical Investigations*, 3rd ed., Macmillan, New York, NY.

9

ORGANIZATION, CULTURE, AND LEADERSHIP

Steffen Raub and Stefano Borzillo

Introduction

Like most organizations, international hospitality firms face the challenge of adaptation and survival in a competitive market environment. Global hospitality firms face unique challenges. Being part of the service sector, they have to adapt to the local needs and preferences of guests in the various markets in which they operate. At the same time they have to ensure the smooth functioning of the internal working mechanisms in a complex organizational system. This situation reflects the fundamental purpose of organizational design: maintaining internal consistency, while at the same time, responding to environmental demands (Mintzberg, 1993).

In this chapter, we will outline the foundations of and relationships between organizational design, organizational culture, and leadership as they apply to service industry organizations. Organizational structure and organizational culture are the main pillars of organizational design. Organizational structure involves choices with regard to the division of labor and the hierarchy of authority in organizational units. Organizational culture concerns the systems of goals and values that guide the behaviors of employees at all levels of the organization. Organizational structure, culture, and leadership jointly influence the service behaviors that employees display in hospitality organizations. In turn, these service behaviors will have an impact on relevant service outcomes, such as guest satisfaction.

Structure, culture, and leadership will be analyzed in this chapter from two different angles that are relevant to global hospitality firms. The internal perspective focuses on the need to maintain operational efficiency. The external perspective involves ensuring consistently high levels of service quality and guest satisfaction. We will begin this chapter with a look at an integrative model of structure, culture, and leadership in hospitality. We then discuss structure, culture, and leadership in three independent sections.

An Integrative Model of Structure, Culture, and Leadership in Hospitality Firms

Figure 9.1 outlines our view of the relationships between the core topics of this chapter. The left-hand side of the framework illustrates that structure, culture and climate(s), and leadership jointly set the stage for service employees. The unique mix of hierarchies, roles, and procedures at the structural level, the values and encouraged behaviors at the culture and climate level, and the direct instructions, encouragements, and role modeling displayed by leaders ultimately

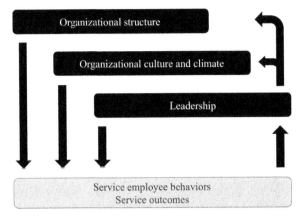

Figure 9.1 An integrative model of structure, culture and leadership in hospitality.

influence service employees' behaviors. These behaviors then translate into desirable (or undesirable) service outcomes at the guest level.

The right-hand side of the framework illustrates that these processes also operate in the opposite direction. Service employees are at the receiving end of guest behaviors (be they encouraging or abusive). They can challenge instructions received from their leaders and actively contribute to building productive leader-member relationships. Ultimately, leaders who receive this feedback can also play a decisive role in creating, challenging, and adapting cultural values, organizational climates, and structural features of the hospitality organization.

Organizational Structure

In this section of the chapter, we will provide a basic definition of organizational structure. We will outline main challenges for organizational structure and different frameworks for analyzing and describing organizational structures. We conclude with implications of organizational structure for firms in the international hospitality industry.

Basic Definition and Function

What most people associate spontaneously with the term "organizational structure" is the notion of an organizational chart that illustrates individual positions, departments, and divisions in an overall organizational setting. Despite its shortcomings (Mintzberg and Van der Heyden, 1999) an organization chart may be a useful way of representing an organization structure. However, it does not explain the basic reason for why organizational structures exist. As a matter of fact, all organizations face a common dilemma. On the one hand, they rely on division of labor which results in the emergence of specialized roles and functions. Organizational theorists refer to this as "differentiation." The productivity and efficiency benefits of differentiated organizations have been documented ever since Adam Smith's seminal work on the wealth of nations (Smith, 1776) and the more recent contributions of Taylor (1911). On the other hand, increasing differentiation means that the contributions of increasingly specialized employees need to be aligned in such a way that they effectively contribute to achieving the organization's objectives. This is what organizational theorists call "integration," and it encompasses the use of effective coordination mechanisms to make sure that individual efforts result in organizational performance.

Coordinating individual employees implies control over their activities. The main idea that comes to mind is that of the hierarchical relationship between superior and subordinate in which the former exerts control over the latter. This is reflected in some traditional definitions of organizational structure, for instance, the one by Jones (1997, p. 11) which defines it as "the formal system of task and authority relationships that control how people coordinate their actions and use resources to achieve organizational goals." However, direct supervision is only one possible coordinating mechanism. Alternative solutions to the challenge of coordination exist in the shape of informal coordination via direct communication between employees, or in the more formal coordination through depersonalized procedures and routines.

The fundamental challenge of balancing differentiation and integration is at the heart of organizational structure. This led the seminal organizational theorist Henry Mintzberg to define organizational structure as "the sum total of the ways in which its labor is divided in distinct tasks and then its coordination is achieved among these tasks" (Mintzberg, 1993, p. 2). According to Mintzberg, the main coordinating mechanisms that can be used in organizations involve direct supervision (i.e., hierarchical control), mutual adjustment (i.e., decentralized informal coordination), and standardization (i.e., procedures and routines).

"Mechanistic" vs. "Organic" Organizational Structures

While there is an abundance of frameworks for classifying different types of organizational structures, the distinction between "mechanistic" and "organic" structures proposed by Burns and Stalker (1966) continues to be popular. Mechanistic and organic organizational structures differ fundamentally in their choice of differentiation and integration. A mechanistic organizational structure is characterized by a high level of individual specialization. The coordination relies mainly on a clear hierarchy of authority combined with extensive use of rules and standard operating procedures. Mechanistic organizations are typically very centralized and at the informal level, they put a lot of emphasis on status and turf-protection.

Conversely, organic organizational structures rely on a much lower level of specialization and favor a "collective" or "joint" type of specialization in which individuals have less clearly defined roles and carry out a broader spectrum of tasks. Coordination in an organic organizational structure relies predominantly on mutual adjustment, i.e., the direct informal exchange between employees in task forces and teams. The organic structure is typically rather decentralized and the informal organization is characterized by a strong emphasis on expertise rather than status.

The optimal choice of an organizational structure can not be considered without regard for the environmental challenges an organization is facing (Child, 1972). The advantages and disadvantages of mechanistic and organic structures stand in stark contrast to each other. Mechanistic organizations excel in stable and predictable environments, where the focus is on reliable delivery of outputs, cost control, and economic efficiency. Conversely, they are ill-equipped to deal with major disruptive changes in the organizational environment. Organic organizations, on the other hand, are well positioned in rapidly changing environments where flexible adaptation and innovation are required. However, they are inherently more resource-intensive and tend to be less economically efficient.

Different features of mechanistic and organic structures can be combined as conditions and requirements may vary quite considerably from one organizational unit to another. With regard to the hospitality industry, the F&B sector may serve as a case in point. In a kitchen environment, where the focus is on highly reliable reproduction of high-quality outputs and centralized control via the chef is a necessity, many elements of a mechanistic structure may be beneficial. However, on the F&B service side, where customers participate in the co-production of the service, organic elements may be predominant.

Relational Bureaucracy

In analogy to the distinction between mechanistic and organic structures, organizational researchers have compared the benefits of "relational" vs. "bureaucratic" forms of organization (Follett, 1949; Weber, 1984/1920). Similar to the organic organization, the relational organization relies strongly on information processing in informal personal relationships. A possible drawback of the relational form is that it may give rise to the abuse of personal power and favoritism and it may have limited replicability and scalability. The bureaucratic form is characterized by high degrees of specialization and a strong reliance on formal rules and procedures. While it neutralizes some of the weakness of the relational form, it is itself vulnerable to sub-goal optimization at the expense of the overall organizational purpose and it is not well suited to delivering individualized, caring, and speedy responses to outside stakeholders

Based on a wealth of empirical investigation in service industry environments, Gittell and her colleagues (e.g., Gittell and Douglass, 2012) have proposed the "relational bureaucracy" as a hybrid organizational structure capable of "combining the best of both worlds" for service sector organizations. The relational bureaucracy "uses formal structures to embed reciprocal relationships into the roles of customers, workers, and managers" (Gittell and Douglass, 2012, p. 714). In other words, it favors the relational coordination among employees – which relies on shared goals, shared knowledge, and mutual respect – while at the same time making relational coordination scalable, replicable, and sustainable by embedding them in formal work roles and structures.

Implications of Organizational Structure for International Hospitality

Research on organizational design and organizational structure in the international hospitality industry recognizes that rather than being an end in itself, organizational structures need to be designed in such a way that they support organizational strategy (Schaffer, 1986) and contribute to desirable outcomes such as service quality and guest satisfaction (Parasuraman et al., 1988). This view is supported by contingency theory perspectives (Shamir, 1978), which suggest that organizational structures need to be adapted to the organization's competitive environment.

Various studies underpin the role of organizational structure as either a mediator or a moderator of the relationship between organizational strategy and organizational success. For instance, in a study among U.S. hotel owners, Tavitiyaman et al. (2012) show that a competitive HR strategy was related to hotel's behavioral performance, and a competitive IT strategy predicted their financial performance. In both cases, organizational structure was found to have a moderating effect. For hotels with a mechanistic structure, the relationship between a competitive HR strategy and behavioral performance was stronger than for those with an organic structure. Conversely, when it came to IT strategy, hotels with an organic structure displayed greater behavioral performance compared to those with a mechanistic structure.

Several studies have investigated the specific benefits of decentralized organizational structures. For instance, in a series of case studies in the hotel sector in Zimbabwe, Hales and Tamangani (1996) highlighted the benefits of decentralized structures in terms of greater autonomy, more responsibility and more attentiveness to unit performance for unit managers. In a similar vein, Altinay and Altinay (2004) suggested that decentralized structures had beneficial consequences for the entrepreneurial orientation and expansion success of hospitality companies.

Research has also investigated the role of organizational structure in supporting specific managerial initiatives and practices. For instance, in a large-scale study of 3-star, 4-star, and 5-star hotels, Pertusa-Ortega et al. (2018) found that organizational design supported the implementation of environmental management practices. In particular, their study highlighted the importance of structural features such as specialization, complex linking mechanisms via cross-functional working groups, formalization, informal social relations, and decentralization. In a similar vein, López-Gamero et al. (2016) found that a similar set of structural choices supported environmental proactivity and the implementation of environmental practices in hotels.

Organizational structures also play an essential role for an organization's ability to attract, select, and retain employees and organizational design needs to be adapted to the requirements of the targeted employee population (Blum, 1996). In research focused on the specific requirements of generation Y employees, Chacko et al. (2012) advocated the need for a radically new type of organizational structure that meets the needs of this particular employee generation. Labeled the "seamless hotel organization" (Chacko, 1998), they promote a circular, flat, and dynamic design, which includes the abolishment of traditional departments. In this seamless structure, employees are divided into only two job categories (guest service and internal service) depending on whether or not they are in direct contact with guests. Whether such a radical design will ever see the light of day remains to be seen.

Finally, there is rich evidence from a variety of different service sectors regarding the benefits of the type of "relational coordination" that would be prevalent in an organizational structure that is aligned with the hybrid "relational bureaucracy." In the healthcare setting, for instance, relational coordination was found to predict customer satisfaction and intent to recommend (Gittell, 2002) as well as increased perceived quality of care and reduced length of stay (Gittell et al., 2010). Interestingly, the relationship with customer satisfaction and intent to recommend was at least partly mediated by customer/service provider relationships. This finding has interesting implications for the hospitality industry. When service providers in a hospitality setting have high levels of relational coordination with other service providers, this will enable them to appear better informed and more competent towards the guest, which in turn promotes greater confidence and satisfaction at the guest level. Other research has highlighted similar benefits of relational coordination in service industries like air transportation (Gittell, 2003).

Organizational Culture and Climate

Organizational culture has been defined as a set of shared values and norms that has an impact on the interactions between organization members as well as on their interactions with outside stakeholders (Smircich, 1983). From an organizational viewpoint, it has also been described as a "glue" that holds organization members together. This metaphor refers to the function of organizational culture as a coordinating mechanism. In the previous section, we outlined how formal organizational structure can contribute to the coordination of activities of individual members of the organization. Organizational culture fulfills a similar purpose at the informal level. When organization members align their behaviors with a shared set of values and norms, this can contribute to coordinated action.

Different theoretical frameworks of organizational culture and climate have been explored in detail in another chapter in this volume (see chapter "Country Culture vs. Organizational Culture"). Therefore, our overview of these frameworks will be relatively concise. Fundamentally, organizational culture has been described as a construct that can be understood at different levels of depth (Schein, 1985). The surface level is characterized by so-called "artifacts" which constitute the visible and tangible traces of organizational culture, including, design, layout, furniture, dress codes, documents, etc. Below the artifacts one finds the level of organizational values, which can either be socially validated by the members of the organization or be limited to so-called "espoused" values to which only lip-service is paid. At the deepest level, organizational culture encompasses taken-for-granted "basic assumptions."

Building on Schein's fundamental description of organizational values, various authors have attempted to fill this essential level of organizational culture with life by linking it to specific content and thereby making it easier to describe and to assess. One of the predominant frameworks in this area is the so-called "competing values" framework developed by Cameron and Quinn (1999). The authors suggest that organizational cultures can be assessed on two major dimensions. The first focuses on flexibility and discretion vs. stability and control. The second concerns an external focus via differentiation vs. an internal focus via integration. The two dimensions form a 2×2 framework representing four different archetypes of organizational culture.

The "clan" culture – internal integration combined with flexibility and discretion – is a friendly workplace with highly committed employees that are held together by loyalty and a participative and consensus-oriented management style. The "adhocracy" culture – external differentiation combined with flexibility and discretion – characterizes a dynamic, entrepreneurial organization with a strong emphasis on individual initiative, experimentation, and innovation with the goal of creating unique new products and services. The "market" culture – external differentiation combined with stability and control – represents a results-oriented organization with a strong emphasis on competition, where success is measured in terms of market share. Last but not least, the "hierarchy" culture – internal integration combined with stability and control – is equivalent to a highly structured workplace with emphasis placed on rules, policies, and procedures, which ultimately lead to a "well-oiled," dependable and reliable organization (Cameron and Quinn, 1999).

A discussion of organizational culture would not be complete without a quick look at the related concept of organizational climate. Again, we refer the reader to the more detailed discussion of this concept in the companion chapter in this volume (see chapter "Country Culture vs. Organizational Culture"). Organizational climate has been defined as encompassing the shared perceptions of employees regarding the work behaviors that are encouraged, supported, and rewarded in a particular organizational setting (Schneider, 1990). The study of organizational climates requires a specific focus on a desirable outcome. In this context, we will focus on two types of climate with particular relevance for the hospitality industry: "service climate" and "initiative climate." Service climate (Schneider et al., 1980) focuses on "employee perceptions of the practices, procedures, and behaviors that get rewarded, supported, and expected with regard to customer service and customer service quality" (Schneider et al., 1998, p. 151). The "proactivity climate" (Baer and Frese, 2003; Fay et al., 2004) and the "initiative climate" (Raub and Liao, 2012) constructs focus on expectations and rewards for "proactive" types of service behaviors which contribute to customer delight in a hospitality setting. Initiative climate, therefore, encompasses a shared perception by service employees that the organization and its leaders expect, encourage, and reward service behaviors that are self-starting, change-oriented, with long-term oriented approach, and persistent in the face of obstacles (Frese and Fay, 2001).

Implications of Organizational Culture for International Hospitality

In addition to their general function as a coordinating mechanism, organizational culture can have beneficial effects for international hospitality organizations at a variety of different levels. Some studies point to a general relationship between organizational culture and performance. For instance, the results of a study of medium-sized hospitality organizations conducted by Kyriakidou and Gore (2005) suggests that best-performing units shared a certain number of "supporting" cultural values, including a focus on building the future together, the cooperative setting of strategies, as well as an emphasis on teamwork and learning.

There are several studies that highlight the relationship between culture and more specific desirable outcomes such as service quality or innovation and creativity. For instance, a study conducted in the People's Republic of China by Hon and Leung (2011) suggests that three different types of culture, which they term innovative culture, traditional culture, and cooperative culture act as moderators for the relationship between individual motivation and creativity. And a study by Davidson (2003) suggests that organizational culture has beneficial effects on service quality in hotels. Culture has other beneficial effects at the employee level. For instance, Moncarz et al. (2009) suggest that organizational culture contributes to employee retention. In an industry that is plagued by chronically high turnover levels this is definitely a desirable outcome. Also, a study of Jamaican hotels by Nicely and Palakurthi (2018) concludes that a learning culture is related to higher levels of knowledge usage in hospitality organizations.

Last but not least, culture also supports the implementation of specific managerial strategies. For instance, in a study in the hospitality industry in the United Kingdom, Rahimi and Gunlu (2016) found that culture facilitated the implementation of customer relationship management (CRM). In the context of research on environmental and sustainability issues, Scholz and Voracek (2016) found support for the hypothesis that culture supports "green" management initiatives. In a similar vein, Gürlek and Tuna (2018) found support for the idea that a "green" organizational culture has a positive effect on "green" innovation and also on the competitive advantage of hospitality firms.

Research on organizational climate in the service sector also points towards the beneficial effects of service climate and initiative climate for international hospitality firms. When a service climate is present, employees understand that employees, organizational processes, and organizational structures are focused on attaining high service quality (Schneider and White, 2004). Empirical evidence suggests that when hotel companies manage to create a consistent service climate in their properties this will enhance service employees' engagement in role-prescribed service behaviors (e.g., Liao and Chuang, 2004; Schneider, 1990) and, as a result, organizations will reap benefits in the form of better service delivery and higher customer service satisfaction (Hong et al., 2013; Schneider et al., 1998). Similarly, in the presence of an initiative climate, service employees will feel empowered and encouraged to take the initiative and serve guests with a proactive approach. As a result, they will implement more extra-role service behaviors, which will lead to additional benefits in terms of guest service satisfaction. In the end, this translates into greater guest satisfaction (Raub and Liao, 2012).

Leadership

There are almost as many definitions of leadership as there are authors on the topic. A very comprehensive definition (Yukl, 2002, p. 7) suggest that "(l)eadership is the process of influencing others to understand and agree about what needs to be done and how it can be done effectively, and the process of facilitating individual and collective efforts to accomplish the shared objectives." In their efforts to facilitate individual and collective efforts, leaders will necessarily bring about organizational change that modifies the structure and culture of organizations (Kotter, 1990). In this sense, leadership can be regarded as a key lever of organizational design. Leaders have a significant influence on key features of organizational structures as well as on the core values of an organization.

Conversely, leadership also encompasses individual influence attempts through direct interaction between leaders and followers. Searching for answers to the question of what distinguishes effective from less effective leaders, researchers have come up with a variety of labels and descriptions for different leadership behaviors or "styles." Before we review the hospitality-related literature on the outcomes of these leadership approaches, we will briefly describe and define four dominant approaches: transformational leadership, empowering leadership, servant leadership, and ethical leadership.

Transformational leadership has been juxtaposed to transactional leadership approaches (Bass, 1985). Whereas transactional leadership is essentially based on an (economic) exchange process in which leaders provide benefits for followers in return for their contributions and performance, transformational leadership relies on a different set of behaviors. Transformational leaders highlight the importance and the meaning of individual and collective work outcomes, incite followers to overcome their self-interest in the interest of collective action and activate "higher-order needs" in their followers. *Empowering leadership* focuses on a range of leader behaviors that focus on creating work conditions which increase followers' perceptions of self-efficacy and control (e.g., through participative decision making), and removing work conditions that foster a sense of powerlessness (e.g., bureaucratic structures, excessive rules, and procedures). Leadership behaviors that are productive in a work environment of empowered teams include leading by example, coaching, participative decision making, informing and showing concern for/interacting with team members (Arnold et al., 2000).

Servant leadership encompasses leadership behaviors that place the fulfillment of followers' needs above their own objectives (Greenleaf, 1970, 1977; Liden et al., 2014). Servant leaders are humble and dedicated to helping their followers realize their full potential. More specifically, it involves seven dimensions, including emotional healing, creating value for the community, conceptual skills, empowering, helping subordinates grow and succeed, putting subordinates first, and behaving ethically (Liden et al., 2008). Last but not least, *ethical leadership*, which shares some intellectual ground with the servant leadership construct but remains relatively difficult to define, focuses on leaders' personal ethics as well as their ability to engage in ethically correct decisions and courses of action in the pursuit of their activities (Yukl, 2002).

Implications of Leadership for International Hospitality

Researchers in hospitality management and general management have generated a very comprehensive body of research on the outcomes of various leadership styles and behaviors in the context of international hospitality organizations. With regard to the attitudinal consequences of leadership, there is evidence that negative or *destructive forms of leadership* will lead to negative consequences for hospitality employees. For instance, Tromp and Blomme (2014) found that autocratic leadership styles contributed significantly to negative work-home interference (also called work-family conflict). In a study in hotels in Sweden, Poland, and Italy, Nyberg et al. (2011) found evidence that autocratic and malevolent leadership styles are both negatively related to the psychological well-being of employees.

Conversely, positive forms of leadership can generate favorable attitudinal outcomes with hospitality employees. The impact of *transformational leadership* is particularly evident in this context. For instance, in a study in the German hospitality industry, Rothfelder et al. (2012) found that transformational leadership predicted employee job satisfaction much more than transactional and non-leadership behaviors. A study in Turkey, conducted by Kara et al. (2018) suggests that both transformational and transactional leadership styles are significant predictors of quality of work life. Based on a U.S. sample, Gill et al. (2006) found that the degree of perceived burnout and perceived stress was negatively related to transformational leadership. Finally, a study by Ariyabuddhiphongs and Kahn (2017) in the restaurant industry in Thailand suggests that transformational leadership negatively predict turnover intention and that trust and job performance mediate this relationship.

In addition to its benefits for work attitudes, *transformational leadership* has been shown to predict a host of desirable behavioral outcomes. For instance, a study by Barling et al. (2002) highlights consequences that are particularly relevant for the restaurant industry. In a sample of Canadian restaurants, safety-specific transformational leadership predicted occupational injuries through the effects of perceived safety climate, safety consciousness, and safety-related events (Barling et al., 2002). Several studies have demonstrated the beneficial effects of transformational leadership for the display of organizational citizenship behaviors by hospitality employees. An influential study by Detert and Burris (2007) found that transformational leadership and GM openness jointly predicted voice behavior in a sample of U.S. restaurant employees. Two independent studies by Buil et al. (2019) in the Spanish hospitality industry and by Liang et al. (2017) in the Taiwanese hospitality context suggest that transformation leadership predicts organizational citizenship behaviors. Both studies identified employee identification and work engagement as mediators of this relationship. In a similar vein, a study in Spain by Quintana et al. (2015) and another study conducted in Cyprus by Özduran and Tanova (2017) suggest similar beneficial consequences for "idealized influence" behaviors and an "incremental mindset" in leaders which predict organizational citizenship behaviors as well as perceived work performance and job satisfaction. Last but not least, the results from a study with a mixed U.S. and Chinese sample conducted by Luo et al. (2019) suggest that transformational leadership is also positively related to service recovery performance in a hospitality environment. This relationship was mediated by employees' engagement in deep acting emotional labor strategies.

Enhanced service performance has also been shown to be related to a different leadership approach, namely *empowering leadership*. In a sample from Taiwan, Wu and Chen (2015) demonstrated that empowering leadership was positively related to psychological contract fulfillment and knowledge exchange, which in turn were positively related to service performance. Clark et al. (2009) showed that managers who were committed to service quality and employed an empowering leadership style could create a transformational climate which conveyed commitment to quality service to their frontline employees.

A large number of studies from diverse geographical settings have highlighted attitudinal and behavioral consequences of *servant leadership* in hospitality contexts. An important study conducted by Liden et al. (2014) in the U.S. restaurant industry suggests that servant leaders create a serving culture, which was positively related to restaurant performance, employee job performance, creativity, and customer service behaviors, and negatively related to turnover intentions. Three independent studies demonstrated that servant leadership predicts service employees' citizenship behaviors. Zou et al. (2015) and Wu et al. (2013) found that this relationship was mediated by leader-member exchange (LMX), whereas Bavik et al. (2017) suggested employee job crafting as an additional mediator.

At the attitudinal level, a study conducted in China by Ling et al. (2017) shows that servant leadership increases employees' positive work attitudes (i.e., organizational commitment and work engagement), which ultimately influence work performance. Independent studies conducted by Zhao et al. (2016) in China and by Jang and Kandampully (2018) in the U.S. restaurant industry suggest that servant leadership is also negatively related to turnover intentions. Both studies highlight the importance of organizational identification and organizational commitment as mediators of this relationship. Last but not least, Huertas-Valdivia et al. (2019) demonstrated based on a sample from Spain that empowering and servant leadership jointly predicted the job engagement of hospitality employees.

With regard to creativity and innovation in hospitality, different studies found support for a range of leadership styles and behaviors as predictors of these outcomes. *Transformational leadership* was identified as a predictor of employee creative self-efficacy and creativity in a study by Wang et al. (2014) conducted in Taiwan. It also emerged as a predictor of innovation in a study in Serbia, by Vuković et al. (2018) and it was shown to predict innovative service behavior in Norwegian hospitality employees (Slåtten and Mehmetoglu, 2015). More specifically, "green" transformational leadership was shown to promote "green" creativity in a sample of Indian hospitality employees (Mittal and Dhar, 2016) and top management values and leadership predicted environmental commitment in a sample of U.S. restaurants (Jang et al., 2017).

Similar results were found for *empowering leadership*, which predicted team creativity via team self-concordance and team creative efficacy in a survey in China (Hon and Chan, 2013) as well as innovative employee service behaviors in Indonesia (Wihuda et al., 2017). Finally, *ethical leadership* promoted innovative service behavior of Indian hotel employees mediated through leader-member exchanges (Dhar, 2016) and in a U.S. study, Kim and Brymer (2011) found that ethical leadership also had positive consequences for middle managers' job satisfaction and their affective organizational commitment.

We conclude this review with a look at research that has investigated the relationship between leadership and organizational performance in the hospitality industry. In a study in Malaysia, Asree et al. (2010) found that leadership competency and organizational culture had a positive relationship with organizational responsiveness which, in turn, predicted hotel revenue. Tran (2017) found that transformational leadership CEO tenure was associated with return on equity (ROE) and return on assets (ROA) in a large sample of major hospitality corporations. Last but not least, a study set in the context of the Australian hospitality industry found that transformational leadership style was positively associated with non-financial performance, which, in turn, was positively associated with financial performance of hotel departments (Patiar and Mia, 2009). Another study from Australia suggested that transformational leadership predicted hotel departments' non-financial as well as social and environmental performance dimensions directly and indirectly through organizational commitment (Patiar and Wang, 2016).

Conclusion

As we have outlined in this chapter, organizational structure, culture, and leadership are tightly interwoven concepts. They influence each other, and they jointly determine important service employee behaviors which, in turn, will have a bearing on international hospitality firms' competitiveness and performance. A detailed understanding of the various facets of these three concepts and of the influence process that link them to relevant outcomes for international hospitality firms is essential for every manager in this industry.

References

Altinay, L. and Altinay, M. (2004), "The influence of organisational structure on entrepreneurial orientation and expansion performance", *International Journal of Contemporary Hospitality Management*, Vol.16, No.6, pp.334–344.

Ariyabuddhiphongs, V. and Kahn, S.I. (2017), "Transformational leadership and turnover intention: The mediating effects of trust and job performance on café employees in Thailand", *Journal of Human Resources in Hospitality & Tourism*, Vol.16, No.2, pp.215–233.

Arnold, J.A., Arad, S., Rhoades, J.A., and Drasgow, F. (2000), "The empowering leadership questionnaire: The construction and validation of a new scale for measuring leader behaviors", *Journal of Organizational Behavior*, Vol.21, pp.249–269.

Asree, S., Zain, M., and Razalli, M.R. (2010), "Influence of leadership competency and organizational culture on responsiveness and performance of firms", *International Journal of Contemporary Hospitality Management*, Vol.22, No.4, pp.500–516.

Baer, M. and Frese, M. (2003), "Innovation is not enough: Climates for initiative and psychological safety, process innovations, and firm performance", *Journal of Organizational Behavior: The International Journal of Industrial, Occupational and Organizational Psychology and Behavior*, Vol.24, No.1, pp.45–68.

Barling, J., Loughlin, C., and Kelloway, E.K. (2002), "Development and test a model linking safety-specific transformational leadership and occupational safety", *Journal of Applied Psychology*, Vol.87, No.3, pp.488–496.

Bass, B.M. (1985), *Leadership and Performance Beyond Expectations*, Free Press, New York, NY.

Bavik, A., Bavik, Y.L., and Tang, P.M. (2017), "Servant leadership, employee job crafting, and citizenship behaviors: A cross-level investigation", *Cornell Hospitality Quarterly*, Vol.58, No.4, pp.364–373.

Blum, S. (1996), "Organizational trend analysis: Preparing for change", *International Jonurnal of Contemporary Hospitality Management*, Vol.8, No.7, pp.20–32.

Buil, I., Martínez, E., and Matute, J. (2019), "Transformational leadership and employee performance: The role of identification, engagement and proactive personality", *International Journal of Hospitality Management*, Vol.77, pp.64–75.

Burns, T. and Stalker, G.M. (1966), *The Management of Innovation*, 2nd ed., Tavistock Publications, London, UK.

Cameron, K.S. and Quinn, R.E. (1999). *Diagnosing and Changing Organizational Culture*, Reading, Addison-Wesley, MA.

Chacko, E.H. (1998), "Designing a seamless hotel organization", *International Journal of Contemporary Hospitality Management*, Vol.10, No.4, pp.133–140.

Chacko, H.E., Williams, K., and Schaffer, J. (2012), "A conceptual framework for attracting generation Y to the hotel industry using a seamless hotel organizational structure", *Journal of Human Resources in Hospitality & Tourism*, Vol.11, No.2, pp.106–122.

Child, J. (1972), "Organizational structure, environment, and performance: The role of strategic choice", *Sociology*, Vol.6, pp.1–22.

Clark, R.A., Hartline, M.D., and Jones, K.C. (2009), "The effects of leadership style on hotel employees' commitment to service quality", *Cornell Hospitality Quarterly*, Vol.50, No.2, pp.209–231.

Davidson, M.C.G. (2003), "Does organizational climate add to service quality in hotels?", *International Journal of Contemporary Hospitality Management*, Vol.15, No.4, pp.206.

Detert, J.R. and Burris, E.R. (2007), "Leadership behavior and employee voice: Is the door really open?", *Academy of Management Journal*, Vol.50, No.4, pp.869–884.

Dhar, R.L. (2016), "Ethical leadership and its impact on service innovative behavior: The role of LMX and job autonomy", *Tourism Management*, Vol.57, pp.139–148.

Fay, D., Lührmann, H., and Kohl, C. (2004), "Proactive climate in a post-reorganization setting: When staff compensate managers' weakness", *European Journal of Work and Organizational Psychology*, Vol.13, No.2, pp.241–267.

Follett, M.P. (1949), *Freedom and Co-ordination: Lectures in Business Organization by Mary Parker Follett*, Management Publications Trust, London, UK.

Frese, M. and Fay, D. (2001), "4. Personal initiative: An active performance concept for work in the 21st century", *Research in Organizational Behavior*, Vol.23, pp.133–187.

Gill, A.S., Flaschner, A.B., and Shachar, M. (2006), "Mitigating stress and burnout by implementing transformational-leadership", *International Journal of Contemporary Hospitality Management*, Vol.18, No.6, pp.469–481.

Gittell, J.H. (2002), "Coordinating mechanisms in care provider groups: Relational coordination as a mediator and input uncertainty as a moderator of performance effects", *Management Science*, Vol.48, No.11, pp.1408–1426.

Gittell, J.H. (2003). *The Southwest Airlines Way: Using the Power of Relationships to Achieve High Performance*, McGraw-Hill, New York, NY.

Gittell, J.H. and Douglass, A. (2012), "Relational bureaucracy: Structuring reciprocal relationships into roles", *Academy of Management Review*, Vol.37, pp.709–733.

Gittell, J.H., Seidner, R., and Wimbush, J. (2010), "A relational model of how high-performance work systems work", *Organization Science*, Vol.21, No.2, pp.490–506.

Greenleaf, R.K. (1970). *The Servant as Leader*, Center for Applied Studies, Cambridge, MA.

Greenleaf, R.K. (1977), *Servant Leadership: A Journey into the Nature of Legitimate Power and Greatness*, Paulist Press, New York, NY.

Gürlek, M. and Tuna, M. (2018), "Reinforcing competitive advantage through green organizational culture and green innovation", *Service Industries Journal*, Vol.38, No.7/8, pp.461–491.

Hales, C. and Tamangani, Z. (1996), "An investigation of the relationship between organizational structure, managerial role expectations and managers' work activities", *Journal of Management Studies*, Vol.33, No.6, pp.731–756.

Hon, A.H.Y. and Chan, W.W.H. (2013), "Team creative performance: The roles of empowering leadership, creative-related motivation, and task interdependence", *Cornell Hospitality Quarterly*, Vol.54, No.2, pp.199–210.

Hon, A.H.Y. and Leung, A.S.M. (2011), "Employee creativity and motivation in the Chinese context: The moderating role of organizational culture", *Cornell Hospitality Quarterly*, Vol.52, No.2, pp.125–134.

Hong, Y., Liao, H., Hu, J., and Jiang, K. (2013), "Missing link in the service profit chain: A meta-analytic review of the antecedents, consequences, and moderators of service climate", *Journal of Applied Psychology*, Vol.98, No.2, pp.237–267.

Huertas-Valdivia, I., Gallego-Burín, A.R., and Lloréns-Montes, F.J. (2019), "Effects of different leadership styles on hospitality workers", *Tourism Management*, Vol.71, pp.402–420.

Jang, J. and Kandampully, J. (2018), "Reducing employee turnover intention through servant leadership in the restaurant context: A mediation study of affective organizational commitment", *International Journal of Hospitality & Tourism Administration*, Vol.19, No.2, pp.125–141.

Jang, Y.J., Zheng, T., and Bosselman, R. (2017), "Top managers' environmental values, leadership, and stakeholder engagement in promoting environmental sustainability in the restaurant industry", *International Journal of Hospitality Management*, Vol.63, pp.101–111.

Jones, G.R. (1997), *Organizational Theory: Text and Cases*, Pearson, Upper Saddle River, NJ.

Kara, D., Kim, H. (Lina), Lee, G., and Uysal, M. (2018), "The moderating effects of gender and income between leadership and quality of work life (QWL)", *International Journal of Contemporary Hospitality Management*, Vol.30, No.3, pp.1419–1435.

Kim, W.G. and Brymer, R.A. (2011), "The effects of ethical leadership on manager job satisfaction, commitment, behavioral outcomes, and firm performance", *International Journal of Hospitality Management*, Vol.30, No.4, pp.1020–1026.

Kotter, J. (1990), *Leading Change*, Harvard Business School Press, Boston, MA.

Kyriakidou, O. and Gore, J. (2005), "Learning by example: Benchmarking organizational culture in hospitality, tourism and leisure SMEs", *Benchmarking: An International Journal*, Vol.12, No.3, pp.192–206.

Liang, T.L., Chang, H.F., Ko, M.H., and Lin, C.W. (2017), "Transformational leadership and employee voices in the hospitality industry", *International Journal of Contemporary Hospitality Management*, Vol.29, No.1, pp.374–392.

Liao, H. and Chuang, A. (2004), "A multilevel investigation of factors influencing employee service performance and customer outcomes", *Academy of Management Journal*, Vol.47, No.1, pp.41–58.

Liden, R.C., Wayne, S.J., Liao, C.W., and Meuser, J.D. (2014), "Servant leadership and serving culture: influence on individual and unit performance", *Academy of Management Journal*, Vol.57, No.5, pp.1434–1452.

Liden, R.C., Wayne, S.J., Zhao, H., and Henderson, D. (2008), "Servant leadership: Development of a multidimensional measure and multi-level assessment", *Leadership Quarterly*, Vol.19, pp.161–177.

Ling, Q., Liu, F., and Wu, X. (2017), "Servant versus authentic leadership: Assessing effectiveness in China's hospitality industry", *Cornell Hospitality Quarterly*, Vol.58, No.1, pp.53–68.

López-Gamero, M.D., Pertusa-Ortega, E.M., Molina-Azorín, J.F., Tarí-Guilló, J.J., and Pereira-Moliner, J. (2016), "Organizational antecedents and competitive consequences of environmental proactivity in the hotel industry", *Journal of Sustainable Tourism*, Vol.24, No.7, pp.949–970.

Luo, A., Guchait, P., Lee, L., and Madera, J.M. (2019), "Transformational leadership and service recovery performance: The mediating effect of emotional labor and the influence of culture", *International Journal of Hospitality Management*, Vol.77, pp.31–39.

Mintzberg, H. (1993), *Structure in Fives: Designing Effective Organizations*, Prentice Hall, Englewood Cliffs, NJ.

Mintzberg, H. and Van der Heyden, L. (1999), "Organigraphs: Drawing how companies really work", *Harvard Business Review*, Vol.77, No.5, pp.87–94.

Mittal, S. and Dhar, R.L. (2016), "Effect of green transformational leadership on green creativity: A study of tourist hotels", *Tourism Management*, Vol.57, pp.118–127.

Moncarz, E., Zhao, J., and Kay, C. (2009), "An exploratory study of US lodging properties' organizational practices on employee turnover and retention", *International Journal of Contemporary Hospitality Management*, Vol.21, No.4, pp.437–458.

Nicely, A. and Palakurthi, R. (2018), "Organizational culture requirements for high levels of knowledge usage from learning activities among hotel managers", *International Journal of Hospitality & Tourism Administration*, Vol.19, No.1, pp.1–25.

Nyberg, A., Holmberg, I., Bernin, P., and Alderling, M. (2011), "Destructive managerial leadership and psychological well-being among employees in Swedish, Polish, and Italian hotels, *Work*, Vol.39, No.3, pp.267–281.

Özduran, A. and Tanova, C. (2017), "Manager mindsets and employee organizational citizenship behaviours", *International Journal of Contemporary Hospitality Management*, Vol.29, No.1, pp.589–606.

Parasuraman, A., Zeithaml, V.A., and Berry, L.L. (1988), "Servqual: A multiple-item scale for measuring consumer perc", *Journal of retailing*, Vol.64, No.1, p.12.

Patiar, A. and Mia, L. (2009), "Transformational leadership style, market competition and departmental performance: Evidence from luxury hotels in Australia", *International Journal of Hospitality Management*, Vol.28, No.2, pp.254–262.

Patiar, A. and Wang, Y. (2016), "The effects of transformational leadership and organizational commitment on hotel departmental performance", *International Journal of Contemporary Hospitality Management*, Vol.28, No.3, pp.586–608.

Pertusa-Ortega, E.M., López-Gamero, M.D., Pereira-Moliner, J., Tarí, J.J., and Molina-Azorín, J.F. (2018), "Antecedents of environmental management: The influence of organizational design and its mediating role between quality management and environmental management", *Organization & Environment*, Vol.31, No.4, pp.425–443.

Quintana, T., Park, S., and Cabrera, Y. (2015), "Assessing the effects of leadership styles on employees' outcomes in international luxury hotels", *Journal of Business Ethics*, Vol.129, No.2, pp.469–489.

Rahimi, R. and Gunlu, E. (2016), "Implementing customer relationship management (CRM) in hotel industry from organizational culture perspective", *International Journal of Contemporary Hospitality Management*, Vol.28, No.1, pp.89–112.

Raub, S. and Liao, H. (2012), "Doing the right thing without being told: Joint effects of initiative climate and general self-efficacy on employee proactive customer service performance", *Journal of Applied Psychology*, Vol.97, pp.651–667.

Rothfelder, K., Ottenbacher, M.C., and Harrington, R. J. (2012), "The impact of transformational, transactional and non-leadership styles on employee job satisfaction in the German hospitality industry", *Tourism & Hospitality Research*, Vol.12, No.4, pp.201–214.

Schaffer, J. D. (1986), "Structure and strategy: Two sides of success", *Cornell Hotel & Restaurant Administration Quarterly*, Vol.26, No.4, pp.76.

Schein, E.H. (1985), *Organisational Culture and Leadership: A Dynamic View*, Jossey-Bass, San Francisco, CA.

Schneider, B. (1990), *Organizational Climate and Culture*, Jossey-Bass, San Francisco, CA.

Schneider, B., Parkington, J.J., and Buxton, V.M. (1980), "Employee and customer perceptions of service in banks", *Administrative Science Quarterly*, pp.252–267.

Schneider, B. and White, S.S. (2004), *Service Quality: Research Perspectives*, Vol. 107, Sage, Thousand Oaks, CA.

Schneider, B., White, S.S., and Paul, M.C. (1998), "Linking service climate and customer perceptions of service quality: Test of a causal model", *Journal of Applied Psychology*, Vol.83, pp.150–163.

Scholz, P. and Voracek, J. (2016), "Organizational culture and green management: innovative way ahead in hotel industry", *Measuring Business Excellence*, Vol.20, No.1, pp.41–52.

Shamir, B. (1978), "Between bureaucracy and hospitality – some organizational characteristics of hotels", *Journal of Management Studies*, Vol.15, No.3, pp.285–307.

Slåtten, T. and Mehmetoglu, M. (2015), "The effects of transformational leadership and perceived creativity on innovation behavior in the hospitality industry", *Journal of Human Resources in Hospitality & Tourism*, Vol.14, No.2, pp.195–219.

Smircich, L. (1983), "Concepts of culture and organizational analysis", *Administrative Science Quarterly*, Vol.28, No.3, pp.339–358.

Smith, A. (1776), *An Inquiry into the Nature and Causes of the Wealth of Nations: Volume One*, printed for W. Strahan and T. Cadell, London, UK.

Tavitiyaman, P., Zhang, H.Q., and Qu, H. (2012), "The effect of competitive strategies and organizational structure on hotel performance", *International Journal of Contemporary Hospitality Management*, Vol.24, No.1, pp.140–159.

Taylor, F.W. (1911), *The Principles of Scientific Management*, The Norton Library, New York, NY.

Tran, X. (2017), "Effects of leadership styles on hotel financial performance", *Tourism & Hospitality Management*, Vol.23, No.2, pp.163–183.

Tromp, M.D. and Blomme, J.R. (2014), "Leadership style and negative work-home interference in the hospitality industry", *International Journal of Contemporary Hospitality Management*, Vol.26, No.1, pp.85–106.

Vuković, A.J., Damnjanović, J., Papić-Blagojević, N., Jošanov-Vrgović, I., and Gagić, S. (2018), "Impact of leadership on innovation: Evidence from the hotel industry", *Management: Journal of Sustainable Business & Management Solutions in Emerging Economies*, Vol.23, No.3, pp.57–66.

Wang, C.-J., Tsai, H.-T., and Tsai, M.-T. (2014), "Linking transformational leadership and employee creativity in the hospitality industry: The influences of creative role identity, creative self-efficacy, and job complexity", *Tourism Management*, Vol.40, pp.79–89.

Weber, M. (1984), *Bureaucracy*, in Fischer, F. and Sirianni, C. (Eds.), *Critical Studies in Organization and Bureaucracy*, Temple University Press, Philadelphia, PA, pp.24–39.

Wihuda, F., Kurniawan, A.A., Kusumah, A.I., and Adawiyah, W.R. (2017), "Linking empowering leadership to employee service innovative behavior: A study from the hotel industry", *Tourism*, Vol.65, No.3, pp.294–313.

Wu, C.M. and Chen, T.J. (2015), "Psychological contract fulfillment in the hotel workplace: Empowering leadership, knowledge exchange, and service performance", *International Journal of Hospitality Management*, Vol.48, pp.27–38.

Wu, L.Z., Tse, E.C.Y., Fu, P., Kwan, H.K., and Liu, J. (2013), "The impact of servant leadership on hotel employees' "servant behavior.", *Cornell Hospitality Quarterly*, Vol.54, No.4, pp.383–395.

Yukl, G. (2002), *Leadership in Organizations*, Prentice Hall, Upper Saddle River, NJ.

Zhao, C., Liu, Y., and Gao, Z. (2016), "An identification perspective of servant leadership's effects", *Journal of Managerial Psychology*, Vol.31, No.5, pp.898–913.

Zou, W.-C., Tian, Q., and Liu, J. (2015), "Servant leadership, social exchange relationships, and follower's helping behavior: Positive reciprocity belief matters", *International Journal of Hospitality Management*, Vol.51, pp.147–156.

PART III

Hospitality Paradigms and Business Models

10

HOSPITALITY IN ASIA
The Dawn of a New Paradigm

Kaye Chon and Markus Schuckert

Introduction: The Cradle and Traits of Modern Hospitality

The 21st century has already witnessed an explosion in the number of visitors coming to Asia and traveling within Asia, and even greater numbers of tourists are expected to visit the region in the coming decades. But why has this tourism shift toward Asia occurred? To study this phenomenon, it is worthwhile to examine the history of hospitality and tourism education in terms of stages or "waves" in the tourism industry and also in terms of the shift in paradigms across continents. According to the Oxford English dictionary, a paradigm is a worldview underlying the theories and methodology of a particular scientific subject or, more simply, a philosophical or theoretical framework of any kind. Historical developments in this industry have taken a long time, with progress made in academic research having resulted in three different paradigms that emerged in different regions of the world. Each successive paradigm did not replace what had come before because the industry has evolved from the existing paradigm as new, additional knowledge has been accumulated. The main drivers of each paradigm had been – to paraphrase John of Salisbury – *standing on the shoulders of giants*, meaning that they had been able to advance further because of the vital contributions that preceded them. Tourism and hospitality are not modern phenomena, however; these concepts have existed as long as humankind has walked the earth. Our earliest ancestors traveled because they needed to hunt for their food. Thus, they followed the herds and moved to different places where they knew they could find prey, leaving their homes to bring food back to feed their families. As civilization developed, merchants and traders traveled for business, including Marco Polo, who arrived in China, then known as Cathay, as a merchant to explore what items he could buy or sell.

The European Paradigm

International tourism in Europe can be segmented in different stages, and the middle of the 19th century marks the beginning of the modern era of tourism and hospitality in that region. Prior to around 1840, people traveled by foot, on horseback, or using early transportation such as carriages, sailing vessels, and simple boats (Freyer, 2015). Until that time, tourism had been a purpose-driven, sometimes forced form of mobility. Nomadic peoples sustained their lives by moving from place to place. Explorers traveled with their entourage to discover new regions, and generals traveled with their armies to conquer others. Pilgrims traveled for worship, merchants to buy and sell goods, and teachers and students for the purpose of learning. The popular phenomenon of the Grand Tour for aristocratic young men in Europe serves as a synonym for early tourism by the elites, the nobles, the educated, and the merchants (Towner, 1985). Hospitality at that time was a social concept across several cultures and developed as social virtue and natural host-guest relationships based often on social or religious norms (O'Connor, 2005; Kirillova, Gilmetdinova and Lehto, 2014). The time between the mid-1800s and the start of World War I in 1914 is often considered the beginning of modern tourism and hospitality. The literature refers to the year 1841, when Thomas Cook offered a packaged day trip from Leicester to Loughborough by rail. Based on the industrial boom and technological revolution in Europe, a new middle class was able to enjoy traveling by train for recreation and regeneration on expanding rail networks or even abroad on comfortable and fast steamships (Cresswell, 2006). The hospitality formula evolved from small inns, maisons meublée, and guesthouses to hotels, witnessed by the opening of what came to be known as grand hotels, for example, in England (Grand Hotel Covent Garden, 1774), Germany (Breidenbacher Hof, Dusseldorf, 1812), Switzerland (Baur au Lac, Zurich, 1844), and Austria (Grand Hotel Wien, 1870).

Based on this first wave of tourism throughout Europe, continental hotel hospitality evolved to accommodate a wealthy clientele, demanding the development of a new, professional way of running hospitality businesses and, thereby, forming the European paradigm (Chon, 2019). The spearhead of a new hospitality education program was the Lausanne Hotel School, a hospitality veteran-aided Swiss institution founded in 1893 (Johnson, 1998). At this pioneering school, future generations of hospitality associates were trained through apprenticeships based on the development of practical skills through a formula that set the pace for emerging management education in tourism and hospitality (Oktadiana and Chon, 2017). The market for traditional accommodation in Europe is still structured and impacted by its legacy. In several domestic markets or markets beyond large cities and metropolitan areas, small- and medium-sized individual hotels are the norm. On one hand, this makes the sector very much entrepreneurial-driven, involving families in operations as lifestyle entrepreneurs who choose the location and a certain lifestyle over traditional entrepreneurial styles. On the other hand, new business formulas and franchises, as well as larger hotel chains, can hardly be found beyond certain areas, and the degree of innovation is limited to single entrepreneurs, thin financial margins, and scarce available capital.

The North American Paradigm

Tourism and hospitality transitioned into a developmental stage when the middle class broadened and the wealthier segment of the working class was able to participate in travel. The means of transportation, including car, train, bus, ship, and early aircraft, allowed more individual tourism for recreation and leisure as well as business. However, the two World Wars brought tourism to a standstill throughout Europe. Following World War II, North America took the lead in tourism, due largely to favorable economic conditions and development of automobiles as well as interstate highways and turnpikes after World War II. These included massive infrastructure networks, comprising predominantly interstate highway systems that were developed, enabling individuals and families to travel long distances by car or to fly from state to state, thus creating a highly mobile society. These very different conditions led to the emergence of the North American paradigm in hospitality. In contrast to the individually owned, designed, and operated small hotels in Europe, which emphasized dependable quality, individual service, luxury, and immaculate precision, the North American hospitality formula was facing different requirements. Of the four hotel-chain giants (Hilton, Marriott, Ramada, and Holiday Inn) of the early days, Holiday Inn pushed hotel operations and management to new heights (Lee, 1985). Based on his own miserable vacation experiences, Kemmons Wilson founded the Holiday Inn chain in 1952. Until the 1950s, roadside hotels were individually owned and operated, and therefore, quality and price were unpredictable. With the emergence of Holiday Inns across the country, hotel stays became predictable for travelers. The large, new properties offered well-equipped hotel rooms with standardized quality, so guests knew what to expect before they made their reservations and checked in. In addition, Wilson contributed to the development of the industry with Holiday Inns' innovative and advanced marketing, its reservation network known as Holidex, and the concept of franchising and a centralized sourcing and purchasing network (Jackson and Jung, 2017). With the continued growth of the interstate highway system, Holiday Inn expanded its branded, modern, and standardized hotel chains right along with the network of roads. Thus, it is clear that the North American paradigm modernized the existing hospitality industry and made it scalable in terms of units, reliable in terms of service delivery, and standardized in terms of operations and management (Chon, 2013). With brands and companies such as Holiday Inn Hotels & Express, the Hilton Hotel Corporation with Hampton and Hilton Inns, Doubletree and Embassy Suites, Marriott International with Marriott Hotels, Courtyard or Fairfield Inn, the Hyatt Hotel Corporation with its hotels and resorts as well as the former Starwood hotels and resorts worldwide with Sheraton, Westin, and Four Points, the industry set the pace into the 21st century (Piccoli et al., 2003). An additional factor driving the North American paradigm was the emergence and influence of hotel schools in the United States (Chon, 2019). Founded in 1922, the Cornell Hotel School was the first institution of its kind in the United States, and it was instrumental in getting hospitality and tourism education recognized as a legitimate area of study and research at the university level (Oskam et al. 2017). Over time, the Cornell Hotel School developed to become the Cornell School of Hotel Administration and gained a reputation as a prestigious institution that turned hospitality management into a serious academic discipline (Chon, 2014; Kay and Russette, 2000). Cornell was able to cater to the growing North American hospitality industry by providing it with professional talent, and it played a significant role in the development of the hospitality management curriculum as it is known today. Following the lead of the Holiday Inn chain, McDonald's, and others, franchising was expanding in the hospitality and restaurant industry, and companies understood that their future management needed to have not only hospitality know-how but a business administration tool kit that included expertise in human resource management, finance and accounting, marketing and sales, and strategic management in order to manage businesses effectively and on a much larger scale (Chon, 2019; Chon and Maier, 2010).

Implications and Further Research the Asian Paradigm

It can be said that Asia – compared to Europe and North America – came to the party late; the region was still finding its direction in a post-colonial and post-war modern era. Thailand was a first tourism hot spot and popular destination for recreation among U.S. servicemen in the Vietnam War in the 1960s (Suntikul, 2013; Winter, 2009; Winter et al., 2008). Soon they started visiting other Asian countries and city-states including Singapore and Hong Kong. The awareness of Asia as a tourism destination was further fuelled in developed Western markets by films like *Man with the Golden Gun* or *The Beach* (Connell, 2012; Kim and Reijnders, 2018; Law et al., 2007).

Today, Asia is the world's largest continent by land mass and population and has the world's two most populated countries, China and India, with 1.4 billion people each. In total, Asia comprises approximately 60% of the global population of 4.5 billion people. In the past, most Asians did not enjoy the same level of economic mobility as Europeans and Americans, and they were not able to afford the luxury of traveling by air and staying in hotels for vacation (Chon, 2019). With the rising growth and success of the "dragon and the tiger states" of dynamic Asian economies and the region's rapid industrial development and entrepreneurial culture, a rising share of the Asian population now has the necessary disposable income to allow them to travel abroad to desired and famous destinations that were once only dreamed about (Cochrane, 2008; Winter, 2009).

South Korea can be seen as a dramatic example for economic change in the region, which has been incredibly rapid for the "Asian dragons." Once one of the poorest countries in the world, it is now one of the wealthiest global economies, with world-spanning brands, and pop-culture celebrities that have become household names internationally, bringing huge revenue and prosperity to the country (Chon, 2019). However, domestic or intra-Asian tourism has had the greatest impact on Asian tourism and hospitality, according to UNWTO (2018). In 2018, over 600 million people entered Asian countries as visitors compared to 28 million tourists in 1980. This sharp increase in arrival numbers in a relatively brief span of time indicates the shift in the center of gravity from the West to the East (Chon, 2019; Lew et al., 2003; Tolkach et al., 2016). Nowadays, visitors from Europe and North America represent only a small segment of tourists; Asians traveling within the region account for 80% of the travel volume. With its powerful and thriving economy, China is the growth engine for trade and tourism in Asia (Lew, 2000; Singh, 2009). It is the largest contributor to traveler numbers and will continue to be, with over 130 million tourists increasing toward the largest market share of the world's top destinations by 2020.

The demands of modern trade and tourism pushed Asian governments to invest into tourism infrastructures such as high-speed rail links, airports, highways, and cruise terminals that connect China, Asia, and the world. Regarding its hospitality infrastructure, nearly half of all hotel rooms under construction worldwide were in China in the first decade of the new millennium (STR, 2014). A similar boom is taking place in the Asia-Pacific region, where nearly 1.6 million hotel rooms have been built, whereas China's development translates into 60% of all hotel rooms in the pipeline in Asia according to STR. In such a highly competitive market, hotel companies are pushed to sign lease and management contracts for ten years; by contrast, in the past, a famous brand usually secured a 20-year contract. However, to gain a foothold in the crowded market, major companies agree to 10 years or even less (Chon, 2019). Chon writes:

> *In a few decades, the region has experienced a huge rise in the number of visitors, and that has given Asian tourism and hospitality operators the chance to put their own unique stamp on management in the sector.*

Asian countries have their own culture, history, religion, and practices that are unique to the region; that is why Asian hospitality sectors could never fully embrace the methodologies of the European or American paradigms (Wan and Chon, 2010). To do so would have meant a loss of their true identity as people who put hospitality at the heart of whatever they do (Chon, 2019, pp. 3–4).

Asia's tourism and hospitality sector has been greatly supported by service innovations and a unique entrepreneurial spirit that is an integral part of the Asian culture. As symbols of Asian hospitality, many Asian hotel brands from the East to the West have established themselves by expanding beyond their own borders to open and operate hotels worldwide, including, for instance, the Shangri-La Group, Mandarin Oriental Hotel Group, and Hong Kong and Shanghai Hotels (The Peninsula) from Hong Kong; the Banyan Tree Resorts and Dusit Thani Group from Thailand; or the Oberoi Hotel Group and Indian Hotels Company Limited (Taj), to name a few.

Turning to the skies, the same development can be witnessed in the aviation sector. Asian airlines and airports are leading related consumer rankings consistently and are positioned to become the best in the world. Carriers such as Cathay Pacific, Singapore Airlines, Korean Air, and other Asian airlines are regularly awarded for their high service standards and product performance, including airports in Singapore, Hong Kong, and Seoul. Of course, new industry trends and business models do not stop short of the Asian market. Prominent low-cost carriers such as the AirAsia Group, which was founded in 1993, enable ordinary citizens to travel overseas – once a privilege of the wealthy jet-set only – with economical prices so that, as AirAsia's motto states, "Now Everyone Can Fly." These airlines pride themselves on being highly ranked for reliability and for hospitality service that incorporates the caring Asian values the region is renowned for (Sucher et al., 2013).

Its Asian-ness has distinguished Asia from the rest of the world, and the assumption can be made that Asia's time has come (Wan and Chon, 2010). If the European paradigm was about apprenticeship and being mentored by a master, and the North American paradigm was largely about managing multiple units of hospitality businesses, particularly in multicultural business environments, and therefore providing the necessary skills and knowledge needed for rapid expansion domestically and internationally, the Asian paradigm represents the balance between Europe's practical side of acquiring necessary skills and the processual-analytical side of the United States.

But what makes the Asian paradigm truly different from the other two is the Asian culture and its integration into service performance and management, whether it is the warm smile from a bellman willing to go the extra mile at a hotel in Thailand or the deep bow of a waitress at a Japanese restaurant when customers enter. Comparable to the European and American paradigms, which were developed based on their respective sociocultural and economic circumstances and key factors, the paradigm shift to the "center of gravity" in Asia has come about through what is called the *Asian Wave* (Chon, 2019, p. 4).

What Are the Pillars of the Asian Paradigm in Hospitality?

There might be various academic definitions of hospitality, which differentiate the social phenomenon in detail, for example, by Chon and Maier (2010, p. 33), where hospitality is *the behavior that is defined by amenities and features material comfort, convenience, and smoothness in social interactions.* However, the phenomenon of hospitality is much older than that and can be found in Buddhism, Christianity, Hinduism, and Islam, where it is, in general, related to being a good person and treating well others who are in need. From a secular perspective, pineapples, for instance, have been a symbol of hospitality dating back to America's colonial past, when seamen returning from South and Central America placed a pineapple on the top of their fence posts outside their New England homes.

Turning to Asia, the Japanese language borrowed the term *hospitality* from English. However, in Japanese, the existing and equivalent term for hospitality is much more precise and closer to a modern understanding of what hospitality is; literally, *omotenashi* means "to provide good service and to make guests happy," a claim that can be found in a wide array of mission statements of modern hospitality enterprises. In the Chinese language system, the term *kuan dai* comes close but does not have the same exact meaning as the term hospitality. However, the Chinese language is very detailed in its use of four different terms to describe the traditional term "hotel." Based on natural embedded values, hospitality can be seen as a cultural domain, where its development is a process leading to a culture of how persons in need are treated or how service is provided to make guests happy.

This leads to the following induction regarding what hospitality in Asia is and what the Asian paradigm constitutes (see Figure 10.1).

Confucianism

Confucianism is a moral system traced to Confucius, who lived in China around 500 BC and taught his philosophy of morality, ethics, and the ideals of society. This system was spread and further developed by generations of followers over 2,500 years, and Confucian beliefs and values now stretch all across East Asia and Southeast Asia as the dominant philosophy of people and societies in countries and regions such as Mainland China, Japan, South Korea, Singapore, Thailand, Taiwan, and Hong Kong. The key to understanding Confucianism is aligned with understanding

Figure 10.1   Conceptualization of an Asian paradigm in hospitality.

the five key pillars of this philosophy, as there are five constant virtues of humanity: *ren, li, yi, zhi,* and *xin,* as well as the values of *filiality,* the *doctrine of mean,* and etiquette, which is named as *five relationships.*

Ren can be characterized as a virtue of consistently being kind and showing concern for others, which allows everyone to live in harmony based on respect for all life and all living things. This virtue is the cornerstone for building a caring society that emphasizes empathy and compassion. This resonates in Asian hospitality with its personal care and attention towards guests. *Li* stands for "ritual" and, in a wider interpretation, for courtesy, etiquette, or accepted social standards. In combination with the earlier *ren,* this means to continue a ritual of caring about people and the etiquette of doing things persistently and consistently. International travelers coming to Asia recognize this, for example, with the etiquette of handing over business cards or room keys with both hands or a slight bowing of the upper body when greeting or being greeted. Most foreign travelers probably recognize these from Thailand or Japan, countries that have blended traditional rituals and formulas into their hospitality and service concepts. *Yi, zhi,* and *xin* have to do with the self-cultivation of persons, a concept that is deeply rooted in Confucianism. In a Western context, it can be compared with the concept behind the word "gentleman," referring to a male who understands what is morally fitting, fair, and righteous. *Zhi* is knowledge or, in this context, wisdom, and has to do with what is righteous and appropriate, nurturing the *yi* to be a good judge, a wise person, and a cultivated person. *Xin* stands for trustworthiness or, related to the Chinese characters constituting this term, person who speaks truthfully. These three virtues play a role in the high standards of the hospitality industry today and can be linked to concepts such as service standards, service proposal and delivery, and quality. In this context, a famous motto of a renowned hotel brings this *à point* by claiming "Ladies and Gentlemen serving Ladies and Gentlemen."

Finley (xiao) is an important Confucian value in the East Asian context, as it means, in a very narrow sense, respect for the father; however, a wider meaning is respect and obedience to one's parents. This is interwoven with the *five relationships* that basically involve the etiquette for showing respect in the way that children behave toward their parents, younger siblings toward older ones, married partners toward each other, friends toward each other, and finally employees toward their superiors. This includes the concept of *giving face* in the understanding of offering attention, honor, and respect. This sounds similar to being hospitable to others and offering hospitality; that is, guests are treated with respect and are always considered to be right.

The latter culminates in the so-called *Doctrine of the Mean,* which translates fundamentally as a balance between extremes and the value of moderation in all things. It is also described as the path of duty that one must never leave if one is a gentleman or gentlewoman (Chon, 2019). The meaning as it is transferred to the hospitality industry is various and implicit. It calls for consistent duty and professionalism while serving guests, treating guests fairly and equitably regarding service and quality, and maintaining the proper attitude by being self-aware and learning from one's mistakes.

Leadership and Management

There is no doubt that, based on the latter and the Asian paradigm in hospitality, there is a need for Asian leaders in this sector (Chen and Chon, 2016). The appointment of Ms. Rainy Chan as general manager of the Peninsula Hong Kong is a symbol for a new era and a time of trailblazing. The Peninsula Hotel is an institution as well as a symbol, and with its location at the front of Victoria Harbor on the Kowloon side, it literally stands for Hong Kong's hotel industry. Looking into this appointment, it becomes clear that the desirable qualities of future leaders include the following (Chon, 2019, p. 31):

- *Excellent industry and management know-how;*
- *Communication and language skills;*
- *Networking skills;*
- *Technological savvy;*
- *Internationalism and a global perspective;*
- *Personal and professional grooming skills; and*
- *Career commitment.*

Innovation

Innovation is an important factor and a necessity for every industry. Constant innovation leads to the sustainability of firms while new, disruptive innovations have the ability to change the landscape of an industry, shifting competition and market segments. A famous example from the hospitality sector is Starbucks. In a nutshell, the development of Starbucks and the so-called Starbucks Effect (Vishwanath and Harding, 2000) shows how an ordinary coffee business can be redefined by innovation and business leadership, transforming not only this business but an entire industry. For the Asian hospitality industry, Banyan Tree Hotels and Resorts came up with a truly innovative and unique type of hotel resort in 1994 (Shen, 2015). Banyan Tree started with a completely new concept of a resort with a limited number of bedrooms and a private swimming pool attached to each individual unit. Furthermore, every resort embraces a unique, distinct style that creates a link with the local culture, heritage, and customs of its hosting location, in effect, building "a sense of place." Banyan Tree was set for becoming a global brand because the founders recognized a need and a gap in the market, subsequently creating a concept that was new to the industry and corresponded with customers' needs (Chon, 2012). The School of Hotel and Tourism Management at Hong Kong Polytechnic University, with its Hotel Icon, is a recent example of the Asian innovative spirit (Chon, 2014). The hotel operation is closely interwoven with a famous hospitality school. From a guest perspective, the hotel offers upscale, five-star boutique hotel service (Tse, 2012, 2013). From an educator and student perspective, this purpose-built teaching hotel integrates excellent teaching facilities to optimize students' understanding and knowledge all along their academic journey, from a theory-based on top research to hands-on and real-world experience in the school's own five-star establishment (Chon, 2014).

Organizational Culture, Passion, and Drive

For understanding the Asian paradigm of hospitality, two additional cornerstones are important to mention. The first is about creating an independent, different organizational culture that reflects and resembles Asian values. Second and related to the organizational culture, striving for innovation and leadership can be successful only if leaders demonstrate passion and drive.

An *organizational culture* based on Asian values emerged from the idea of controlling an organization with the concept of supporting the employees in fulfilling customers' needs, where customers are understood as external customers (hotel guests) and internal customers (a.k.a. employees). By changing the organizational culture from control to support changes the environment, making the workplace fun; SHTM and Hotel Icon are vivid examples of practicing these values. This upgrading and valuing of employees and other stakeholders leads, ultimately, to a newly created and vibrant corporate culture, and in the context of SHTM, a group of professors and students unlike any other (Chon, 2019, p. 63).

Passion and drive are the fuel that nurtures an organizational culture, the enterprise as well as the individual. From an individual perspective, the right attitude is as important as proper self-development and self-cultivation, which aligns with the earlier described Confucian virtues. To transform this into a successful formula on a personal and professional level, the following steps seem important (Chon, 2019, p.76):

1 Define your purpose (mission),
2 Set goals,
3 Have passion,
4 Apply creativity,
5 Act with humility and integrity, and
6 Demonstrate leadership.

Conclusion and Outlook

Hospitality in Asia can be regarded as a new paradigm that is emerging based on two contemporary developments. First, with the rise of the Asian continent as an economic powerhouse, the demand for hospitality services is strongly increasing and, thereby, opens up a wide range of business opportunities in the hospitality sector as well as the need for hospitality location. Second, modern hospitality emerged with European characteristics. Later, and with its growth in North and South America, the way hospitality was conducted had to be changed and adjusted to the new environment of a much larger market and a globalizing world economy. However, in Asian countries, hospitality was to be reinvented and built on a different foundation reflecting the values and principles of Asian societies with their legacy of Confucianism. Subsequently, a new Asian hospitality paradigm is based on Confucian values that reflect on innovation, leadership, organizational culture, and a passion for how to pursue hospitality.

This opens wide the door not only for a range of new hospitality businesses and service formulas but also for the need for new thinking and execution of hospitality training and education. The present trends are witness to how Asian hospitality companies are expanding from East to West as well as how Asian hospitality schools are successfully emerging in the region in an Asian wave that has turned the Asian paradigm theory into reality, further reinforcing that the real framework is here to stay.

References

Chen, A.L. and Chon, K.S. (2016), "Transferability of Asian paradigm in hospitality management to non-Asian countries", in Kozak, M. and Kozak, N. (Eds.), *Tourism and Hospitality Management*, Vol.12, Emerald, Bigley, UK, pp.143–157.
Chon, K.S. (2013), *Tourism in Southeast Asia: A New Direction*, The Haworth Hospitality Press, Oxford, UK.
Chon, K.S. (2014), *The Practice of Graduate Research in Hospitality and Tourism*, Routledge, Abingdon, UK.
Chon, K.S. (2019), *Hospitality in Asia: A New Paradigm*, Routledge, Abington, UK.
Chon, K.S. and Maier, T. (2010), *Welcome to Hospitality: An Introduction*, Delmar, Singapore.
Cochrane, J. (Ed.) (2008), *Asian Tourism: Growth and Change*, Elsevier, Oxford, UK.

Connell, J. (2012), "Film tourism–Evolution, progress and prospects", *Tourism Management*, Vol.33, No.5, pp.1007–1029.

Cresswell, T. (2006), *On the Move: Mobility in the Modern Western World*, Routledge, Abingdon, UK.

Freyer, W. (2015), *Tourismus: Einführung in die Fremdenverkehrsökonomie*, 11th ed., DeGruyter Oldenbourg, München and Berlin.

Jackson, L.A. and Jung, H. (2017), "The lodging franchise relational model: A model of trust, commitment, and resource exchanges", *The Journal of Hospitality Financial Management*, Vol.25, No.1, pp.56–73.

Johnson, C. (1998), "Lausanne: Updating after a century of service", *Cornell Hotel and Restaurant Administration Quarterly*, Vol.39, No.1, pp.74–79.

Kay, C. and Russette, J. (2000), "Hospitality-management competencies: Identifying managers' essential skills", *Cornell Hotel and Restaurant Administration Quarterly*, Vol.41, No.2, pp.52–63.

Kim, S. and Reijnders, S. (2018), *Film Tourism in Asia*, Springer, Singapore.

Kirillova, K., Gilmetdinova, A., and Lehto, X. (2014), "Interpretation of hospitality across religions", *International Journal of Hospitality Management*, Vol.43, pp.23–34.

Law, L., Bunnell, T. and Ong, C.E. (2007), "The Beach, the gaze and film tourism", *Tourist Studies*, Vol.7, No.2, pp.141–164.

Lee, D.R. (1985), "How they started: The growth of four hotel giants", *Cornell Hotel and Restaurant Administration Quarterly*, Vol.26, No.1, pp.22–32.

Lew, A.A. (2000), "China: A growth engine for Asian tourism", in Hall, C.M. and Page, S. (Eds.), *Tourism in South and South East Asia: Issues and Cases*, Butterworth- Heinemann, Oxford, pp.268–285.

Lew, A.A., Yu, L., Ap, J., and Zhang, G. (2003), *Tourism in China*, Routledge, Abingdon, UK.

O'Connor, D. (2005), "Towards a new interpretation of 'hospitality' ", *International Journal of Contemporary Hospitality Management*, Vol.17, No.3, pp.267–271.

Oktadiana, H. and Chon, K.S. (2017), "Vocational versus academic debate on undergraduate education in hospitality and tourism: The case of Indonesia", *Journal of Hospitality & Tourism Education*, Vol.29, No.1, pp.13–24.

Oskam, J.A., Dekker, D.M., and Wiegerink, K. (2017), *Innovation in Hospitality Education: Anticipating the Educational Needs of a Changing Profession*, Vol.14, Springer, Cham, CH.

Piccoli, G., O'Connor, P., Capaccioli, C., and Alvarez, R. (2003), "Customer relationship management – A driver for change in the structure of the US lodging industry", *Cornell Hotel and Restaurant Administration Quarterly*, Vol.44, No.4, pp.61–73.

Shen, H. (2015), "Critical success factors for leading hotel brands in Asia: A case study of Banyan Tree", *International Journal of Marketing Studies*, Vol.7, No.3, pp.19–26.

Singh, S. (2009), *Domestic Tourism in Asia: Diversity and Divergence*, Earthscan, London, UK.

STR Global (2014), *China Hotel Performance Survey 2014*, Hendersonville, London, Singapore.

Sucher, W., Pusiran, A.K., Dhevabanchachai, N.T., and Chon, K.S. (2013), "The influences of Asian cultural values in the Asian hospitality services", paper presented at the 11th APacCHRIE Conference, 21–24 May, Macau S.A.R, P.R. China, pp.21–24.

Suntikul, W. (2013), "Thai tourism and the legacy of the Vietnam War", in Suntikul, W. and Butler, R. (Eds.), *Tourism and War*, Routledge, Abingdon, pp.92–105.

Tolkach, D., Chon, K.S., and Xiao, H. (2016), "Asia Pacific tourism trends: Is the future ours to see?", *Asia Pacific Journal of Tourism Research*, Vol.21, No.10, pp.1071–1084.

Towner, J. (1985), "The grand tour: A key phase in the history of tourism", *Annals of Tourism Research*, Vol.12, No.3, pp.297–333.

Tse, T.S. (2012), "The experience of creating a teaching hotel: A case study of Hotel Icon in Hong Kong", *Journal of Hospitality & Tourism Education*, Vol.24, No.1, pp.17–25.

Tse, T.S. (2013), "The marketing role of the internet in launching a hotel: The case of Hotel ICON", *Journal of Hospitality Marketing & Management*, Vol.22, No.8, pp.895–908.

UNWTO. (2018), *UNWTO Tourism Highlights 2018 Edition*, UNWTO, Madrid.

Vishwanath, V. and Harding, D. (2000), "The Starbucks effect", *Harvard Business Review*, Vol.78, No.2, pp.17–18.

Wan, S. and Chon, K.S. (2010), "ASIANESS": An emerging concept in hospitality management", paper presented at 8th APacCHRIE Conference, 12–14 August, Phuket, Thailand, pp.175–186.

Winter, T. (2009), "Asian tourism and the retreat of Anglo-western centrism in tourism theory", *Current Issues in Tourism*, Vol.12, No.1, pp.21–31.

Winter, T., Teo, P., and Chang, T.C. (2008), *Asia on Tour: Exploring the Rise of Asian Tourism*, Routledge, Abingdon, UK.

11

DIGITAL TRANSFORMATION

The Blurring of Organizational Boundaries in Hotel Distribution

Peter O'Connor

Introduction

The hotel industry is steeped in tradition, with roles sharply defined and companies highly resistant to change. Such inflexibility is problematic in today's hyper-competitive business environment, where the adoption of digital technology is revolutionizing not just business models but the entire structure of industries themselves (Weill and Woerner, 2015). In contrast to the rigid attitudes of hoteliers, profiting from such digital transformation requires a fundamental change in mindset away from 'what we have always done' towards 'what do we really need to do and how best can we use digital to help us do it' (van Zeebroeck and Bughin, 2017). And these effects can be clearly seen within the hotel distribution arena.

Hotel rooms are the ultimate perishable product, as if unsold, they cannot be stored and sold on a subsequent night, making effective and efficient distribution a key success factor for hotels (O'Connor, 1999). Gaining access to superior distribution has traditionally been a key driver of hotel chain membership (Lam et al., 2015). As well as profiting from the marketing power of the brand itself, hotels got cost-effective access to technology, distribution channel connectivity as well as sales and marketing expertise (Kim et al., 2012). For example, hotels that signed up with a hotel are typically distributed through the travel agent-oriented Global Distribution Systems, as well as through the chain's call centers, websites, mobile, and social presences. In return, the hotel property pays percentage fees for the use of the brand's trademarks and operating procedures and, depending on the distribution channel used, a transaction fee on each reservation (O'Connor and Piccoli, 2003). Thanks largely to this distribution advantage, chain hotels typically outperformed their peers, driving a global movement towards branding (Claver-Cortés et al., 2007).

However, today these benefits are largely being eroded because of developments in the digital space. In particular, the transparency and connectivity enabled by the Web have radically redefined how hotel rooms are being bought and sold. For example, while accessing corporate customers through GDS and travel agents was once key, a powerful set of new, alternative, online channels have developed over the past two decades, most of which can be used without the costs and constraints of joining a chain (Carroll and Siguaw, 2003). For example, challengers known as online travel agencies (OTAs) now deliver large proportions of business to hotels, both branded and independent (Lee et al., 2013). Properties can also leverage web-direct channels, using online- and social media–marketing to reach out to their target audiences (Kang et al., 2007).

In effect, one of the major effects of the increase in the use of digital by travellers is that being a member of a brand is no longer important for capturing client bookings.

In addition, advances in technology are also enabling alternative solutions that allow hotels to access similar benefits to chain membership without the associated constraints and expense. For example, third party Central Reservation Systems can provide comparable (or in some cases identical) facilities on a pay-per-reservation, rather than a percentage of overall revenue, basis. Similarly, several state-of-the-art booking engines are now available to power direct websites. And both technology companies and so-called soft brands have significantly expanded the port-folio of services they provided and now represent a viable alternative to traditional hotel brands. In effect the net effect of this digital transformation is that the incumbent hotel chains are being disrupted. At a time when costs are increasing due to heightened competition, the once sure ben-efits of chain membership are gradually being eroded as their supposed benefits are cherry-picked away by smaller, nimbler, technology-based companies providing superior service for a lower price (Teixeira, 2019).

This chapter first examines how digital transformation has revolutionized hotel distribution from a hotel perspective. The traditional role of chains in hotel success is first examined. The ef-fect of the digital revolution on both the chains themselves and the macro-level hotel distribution environment is then assessed. The reaction of the incumbents to this challenge to their business model is then assessed, and likely future developments evaluated.

The Traditional Approach

Although independent properties remain in the majority when the hotel sector is considered from a global perspective, chain membership has been growing consistently as hotel properties find it increasingly difficult to compete in an increasingly competitive business environment (Ling et al., 2014). The war to capture scarce customer bookings has intensified, with hotels now needing to compete not just with nearby hotels but with an increasingly powerful range of intermediaries, all fighting to facilitate the reservation transaction, as well as new players (e.g., Airbnb, HomeAway) proposing a growing range of alternative accommodation types. Participating in this battle for the customer alone has become increasingly difficult, leading many to consider acquiring allies by joining one of the major branded hotel chains (Carvell et al., 2016).

From the hotelier's perspective, there are several reasons why they might sign up with a brand (O'Connor, 2016). These include:

Profit from Brand Equity: By flying the flag of a well-known hotel brand, hotels send a powerful signal to potential customers to help them better understand the product likely to be encoun-tered if they stay in the property in question. This helps to mitigate the risk of purchasing an unseen and unexperienced product, thus, in theory at least, making the property more at-tractive to potential customers (Bilgihan and Bujisic, 2014). Because of this brand advantage, chain properties typically outperform their independent colleagues in terms of occupancy (O'Neill and Carlbäck, 2011), with numerous industry studies (see for example KPMG, 2002) reporting high-single-digit uplifts in EBITDA for branded properties compared to indepen-dent operators.

Access to Distribution: As highlighted above, effective distribution has become a key issue in hotel success, making access to world-class distribution a key motivator for joining a chain (O'Con-nor, 2016). Thanks to their scale, chains can more easily develop and maintain sophisticated distribution-focused systems, both technological and otherwise, to help member properties to be both visible and booked in the electronic and online marketplaces. Examples include Central Reservations Systems, which facilitate onward distribution to travel agent–focused Global Distribution Systems (GDS) as well as online, consumer-focused, channels such as Online Travel Agents (OTAs) (Gazzoli et al., 2013). Hotel chains also typically maintain extensive sales teams that negotiate corporate contracts with companies to attract business travellers (Christodoulidou et al., 2013), as well as invest considerable resources in driving business to their own online direct web presences (Díaz and Koutra, 2013). Given the challenges and costs associated with trying to navigate the complex distribution environment for themselves, gaining access to such facilities by joining a chain is often the least complicated option available to those wishing to improve their distribution performance.

Access to Technology: Closely linked to the issue of distribution is technology. In addition to sophisticated systems that facilitate distribution, most chains also provide (or mandate) other portfolios of integrated technology-based systems to help manage the hotel property more efficiently (Lee and Kim, 2004). Examples of such technology may include local systems such as property management systems, which improve operational efficiency, as well as access to chain-wide systems such as revenue management systems (RMS) or customer relationship management (CRM) systems, which gain synergies from being part of a larger whole. In addition, if these systems are not proprietary (as is increasingly becoming the case – see for example Choice Hotels International or InterContinental Hotel Group), then chain members typically benefit from preferred access to, pricing and service levels with nominated third-party technology suppliers.

Access to Expertise: Driving distribution effectively has become a highly specialist task, requiring knowledge of sales, marketing, pricing, merchandising, content management, search, technology trends, consumer behavior and much more (Thakran and Verma, 2013). To be able to profit fully from the power of online channels, managers now need specialist support to help make the right commercial decisions and put in place the systems and technologies to support effective distribution (Ert and Fleischer, 2016). Thanks to economies of scale, being part of a chain makes it easier and more cost-effective to access such expertise, with dedicated personnel typically employed at the corporate level to help manage and support member actions (Law and Jogaratnam, 2013).

Loyalty Program: Facilitated access to the X million customers in a brand's loyalty program is an oft-touted benefit of chain membership (Gan et al., 2008). Chains are quick to quote both the size of their database as well as the percentage of business that comes from loyalty club members, claiming that the latter stay more often and spend more than 'normal' guests (Fernández-Sabiote and Román, 2012). Such benefits, at least in part, help explain recent efforts by chains to drive loyalty club membership through their so-called 'book direct' campaigns (Kalibri Labs, 2018). By promising discounts in return for membership, and facilitating instant sign-up, brands have managed to grow significantly their loyalty club membership. For example, Hilton claims to have increased membership in their Hilton Honors program by 16% in the year to Q3 2018, with members now accounting for 60% of global occupancy (Phocuswire, 2019). Similarly, Hyatt's loyalty program membership increased by nearly 50% in 2018, driven primarily by an instant discount of up to 10% for booking directly (Travelweekly, 2019).

Access to Finance: Most hotel developments involve at least some level of debt financing, and lenders such as banks have traditionally been reassured by the presence of a major brand (Enz et al., 2014). As discussed above, this supposedly increased performance and thus reduces risk, making investors more willing to finance the project, or at least finance it at an acceptable cost.

As can be seen from the above discussion, most of the motivations for joining a hotel chain have traditionally directly or indirectly been related to distribution-related issues and consistently being able to fill perishable hotel rooms. While the chains themselves tend to stress the intrinsic value of their brands, in practice property owners place much more value on the physical aspects, most notably the chain's CRS, its agency agreements, and its loyalty schemes than the more intangible, and supposedly more valuable, brand promise (KPMG, 2002). The challenge for hotel chains today is that as a result of the recent technological revolution hotel properties can now gain access to similar and in some cases superior, facilities and benefits in cheaper and more cost-effective manners.

Digital Disruption

Advances in information technology have had a dramatic effect on travel over the past three decades (Ham et al., 2005). In particular the widespread adoption of the developing Web as a consumer information medium in the late 1990s presented independent hotel properties with an alternative way to compete without becoming a chain member. In theory at least, being on the web offered such properties the possibility to be visible in front of, and bookable by, potential customers who were increasingly using the developing medium to search for and book travel components for themselves (Hahn et al., 2017). Initially at least this led to speculative claims about disintermediation and the supposed death of travel intermediaries (Cantoni and Danowski, 2015). However, in reality, having an effective web presence requires not just specialized expertise but the implementation of technical systems such as booking engines, as well as a commitment to spending scarce marketing funds on gaining online visibility and driving web traffic (Herrero and San Martín, 2012). In most cases, these challenges were beyond the capabilities of independent hotel properties already struggling to manage day-to-day hotel operations (Toh et al., 2011).

In a classic manifestation of the Innovator's Dilemma (Christensen, 1997), at first, the fledgling market offered by the developing Web medium was not thought to be significant enough to merit sufficient interest from either the hotel chains or the existing travel intermediaries. This oversight allowed a series of tech-orientated, pure-play challengers to gain a foothold in the rapidly developing market, establishing themselves in the mind of the consumer as the place to search for and book travel (Murphy and Chen, 2016).

Free from historical constraints and pre-existing business relationships, these fledgling companies (which subsequently evolved into what we today call the OTAs) successfully leveraged their agility to introduce innovative new business practices that challenged the status-quo and radically disrupted the marketplace (Chang et al., 2019). For example, unlike hotel chains who only distributed their own hotel property members, these new players increased customer value by not just consolidating available rooms from multiple suppliers, but also broadened their product offering by distributing complementary products such as air and car rental (Lee et al., 2013). Furthermore, in contrast to the chains who charge a percentage of a hotel property's overall room revenue in return for their services, OTAs instead charged only for business delivered (Ling et al., 2014). This changes the rules of the game as to the cost basis for working with third parties for distribution purposes, as well as the metrics that hotel chains need to use to justify their value to hotel owners. In effect, they have decoupled important elements of the distribution process, stealing market share by focusing on what is important for the customer, in this case, both the end consumer and the hotel owner (Teixeira, 2019).

As online booking became increasingly mainstream, the subsequent rapid growth stage of these challengers' product lifecycle, coupled with the continued reluctance of incumbent companies to properly engage with the developing online market, reinforced the market power of these new companies (Kim et al., 2009). As a result, OTAs have now grown to the point where they control approximately 60% of online hotel reservations (Phocuswright, 2018) and pose a significant threat to the business model of hotel chains in particular. To be successful, the latter must convince hotel owners that branding their property is the best option for ensuring long-term profitability. Thus 'controlled' distribution – the percentage of overall bookings that flow through the chain's CRS – is a critical and highly visible metric and one which is severely threatened by the growth of OTAs and similar channels as a distribution method (Stangl et al., 2016). With OTAs driving increasingly significant proportions of online business to properties, both branded and independent, owners are increasingly questioning the value of having a brand (O'Connor, 2016).

In parallel, many of the other benefits of being a chain member are also been eroded. In particular, the supposed value of the brands themselves is increasingly being questioned for several reasons. While previously chains maintained a small number of iconic brands that could be easily understood by the customer, today both the number and variety of brands have exploded. At last count, Marriott owned 30 brands, Accor has 33, Wyndham has 18, Hilton has 14, IHG has 13, Choice has 11, and Hyatt has 10. As a result, it is highly questionable as to whether the customer perceives, and values, any significant difference between these brands.

Furthermore, brands are struggling to maintain standards and deliver a consistent experience to customers, again threatening brand equity. The increased use of franchises has accentuated this challenge as control over capital and operational budgets now rests with owners, who can be difficult to convince to make the necessary investments to maintain brand standards. Lastly, overall consumers are paying less attention to brand signals and more to social indicators such as peer reviews or satisfaction scores, again bringing into question the continued value of paying the substantial costs of flying the brand flag.

In addition, while gaining cost-effective access to distribution channels was once a key motivator for chain membership, an increasing number of third-party technology companies have developed to facilitate hotel distribution. Both third party CRS providers such as Sabre Hospitality's Synxis and Travelclick, as well as channel management companies such as Site-Minder and FastBooking, now enable access to both the GDS and online channels without the costs and constraints of chain membership. Similarly, technological advancements such as they move towards the Cloud and the development of APIs mean that many of the difficulties associated with, and costs of running, state-of-the-art technology-based systems have been significantly reduced. A wide variety of technology-based systems (often the same ones used by the major chains) are now available on the marketplace, often on a subscription basis, with integration between systems made easier by initiatives such as HTNG (Hotel Technology Next Generation) or the technology platform approaches of companies such as SnapShot and Book-ingSuite (Phocuswire, 2018).

Increasingly, other players within the distribution ecosystem are also making technology-based systems available to their users. For example, Booking.com provides independent properties using their system with a consumer-facing website with a state-of-the-art bookings engine and has also experimented with forwardly integrating revenue management type systems for use by hotel properties. Similarly, Expedia provides users with strong market intelligence data that can be used to inform their pricing and distribution decisions. Such companies are also broadening their customer proposition to provide access to marketing and distribution expertise and thus encourage broader and more intensive usage of their products/systems. As a result, independent properties can access these benefits in a cost-effective manner, again challenging the need for chain membership (Law et al., 2012).

Lastly, the supposed power of hotel loyalty programs is also gradually being undermined. Although loyalty programs bring some concrete benefits, the reality underperforms the promises made by chains. Most travellers, particularly the high desirable frequent business traveller, are typically members of multiple hotel loyalty programs, making such schemes less pertinent in the hotel selection decision. In addition, the recent 'book direct campaigns' have compromised what was once an important strategic asset by compromising the integrity of hotel chain loyalty databases. While as discussed above these campaigns have successfully swelled chains' loyalty membership figures, such members are in reality opportunistic rather than loyal in even the broadest sense, which will ultimately have a detrimental effect on program effectiveness.

At the same time, owners are also becoming more attentive to the exploding cost of loyalty programs. These are typically funded by loyalty fees paid on every booking, but overall costs increase when points are subsequently redeemed at their properties, displacing regular customers. Furthermore, the discounts given in the recent Book Direct campaigns have also been financed by properties through lower average room rates, even though most of the benefits gained flowed directly to the brands themselves through higher controlled distribution figures and increased loyalty club memberships. The effectiveness of these discounts has also been questionable, with a recent BDRC study (2019) claiming that, although direct bookings initially increased, the balance of OTA and direct bookings has ultimately remained unchanged, leaving hotels with increased costs but no incremental revenue.

Meanwhile, the hotel chains themselves are facing an increasingly competitive business environment. In addition to their benefits being eroded, new, potentially powerful, alternatives to traditional brands are developing, with peer-to-peer network Airbnb now offering distribution services to independent hotel properties, e-commerce giants such as Taoboa in China and Amazon in the U.S. experimenting with travel distribution, and search engine Google.com becoming more focused on enabling travel distribution. New forms of chain are also developing, such as India's Oyo Hotels and Homes, a $5 billion travel start-up backed by SoftBank's Vision Fund and Sequoia Capital. Rather than requiring owners to refurbish their property to conform to brand standards, Oyo uses its own capital to renovate and equip rooms within a property, which it subsequently provides with technology, expertise, and distribution services. Targeting the profitable economy sector, the concept has the potential to be very attractive to small hotel owners currently not well served by franchise brands from the major chains. And from Oyo's perspective, it secures access to, and control of, quality valuable room supply which it can then optimize in terms of revenue potential.

The Incumbents' Reaction

While individually small in scope, each new threat eats away at the traditional competitive advantage of hotel chains, causing more owners to question the continued value of maintaining a hotel brand. Thus, with their business model under threat, chains are begrudgingly being forced to evolve their customer proposition to adapt to this new reality.

One way in which the global brands have reacted to this strategic threat is by launching what have become known as 'soft' brands or 'collections' – in effect lighter versions of their franchise agreements where independent properties can benefit from the distribution, technology, and expertise of a chain without the fees and quality constraints of being a full member. Examples include Marriott's Autograph Collection, Hilton's Curio Collection, MGallery by Sofitel and Hyatt's Unbound Collection, amongst others. Hotel chain proponents' argument is that certain hotels are inherently unique, and rather than forcing them to conform to the constraints of existing brands, they should be allowed to create their own unique identity while at the same time being able to benefit from the benefits of chain membership. From the owner's perspective, this brings the best of both worlds. The property benefits from the best aspects of chain membership while at the same time maintaining control over both strategy and operations and pays a significantly reduced cost. And for the chain using such an approach allows the significant cost of running its central distribution, technology, loyalty, and expertise assets to be spread over a larger number of properties / transactions than might otherwise be possible.

However, widespread adoption of this soft-brand approach would ultimately severely threaten the market value of hotel brands. If the majority of hotel chain members were to move towards a soft brand approach, then hotel chains as we know them would cease to exist. The global players in effect would evolve into something more akin to what we currently know as OTAs, which as has been discussed are already snapping at hotel chains' heels in terms of service provision to hotel owners. Such a development would force hotel chains to reconsider their core business model, and, for example, explore scenarios where they might only charge fees on bookings driven through controlled channels rather than overall room revenue. A great example is Accorhotels, with its now discontinued Marketplace product, where it experimented with distributing independent properties on its branded online presences in return for a commission, in effect turning itself into an OTA from both the customer's and the property's perspectives (Phillips et al., 2017).

Another approach is to try to diversify their revenue sources. Hotel chains have traditionally been financed by a series of royalty and reservation fees, supplemented by contributions to support sales, marketing, and loyalty efforts (Russell and Kim, 2017). With owners increasingly questioning both the legitimacy and level of these fees, hotel chains are increasingly been forced to look elsewhere to grow revenues. Some, for example, Accorhotels (through FastBooking) and Choice Hotels, sell mission-critical software services to competitors in an attempt to more effectively monetize their assets and expertise. Others (for example IHG) are partnering with technology companies (in this case Amadeus) to leverage their expertise to develop portfolios of technological services that can both be leveraged by the company itself and sold to competitors.

Disruption has not been limited to just the hotel chains. The growth of digital has also prompted radical changes in the structure, methods of operation, and profitability of tour operators (Berne et al., 2012). Traditionally vertically integrated, controlling not just supply through their ownership or contracting with hotels, airlines, and other travel suppliers but also demand through their networks of owned and franchised retail travel agencies, these mega-travel companies have been forced by market pressure to evolve, increasingly adopting tactics adopted from their OTA competitors (Buhalis, 2008). In an effort to stem the hemorrhage of bookings towards alternative channels, most have disinvested physical assets and are copying the more flexible business practices of the OTAs in an effort to survive in an increasingly electronic marketplace (Guo and He, 2012). Most are also attempting to drive increasing amounts of business through online channels, further complicating efforts by suppliers to drive business directly (Berne et al., 2012).

And increasingly new concepts, enabled by the increasing digitization of the travel ecosystem, are even beginning to challenge the challengers. For example, leisure-focused OTA Booking. com, faced with more demand than it could comfortably supply, has been forced to adopt innovative solutions to compete effectively. For example, through its BookingSuite product, the company helps hotels to more effectively distribute themselves directly, in effect competing with itself but also critically securing access to essential room supply. And OTAs are significantly broadening their definition of accommodation, in particular acquiring or partnering with vacation rental sites such as HomeAway or OneFineStay to augment their existing customer proposition. Lastly, technology suppliers have also expanded their portfolio of services, in many cases providing consulting, online marketing, and other services alongside their historical connectivity, thus in effect moving them into the same space as chains and marketing groups. As such, they represent another alternative for owners questioning whether to become chain members, further increasing the competitive pressure on traditional hotel chains.

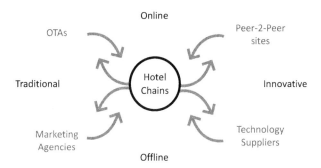

Figure 11.1   The Changing Dynamics of Hotel Distribution

Conclusion

As they adapt to the digital world, hotels are waking up to the fact that business today is less about limitations and strict definitions and more about providing effective solutions to their customer. As a result, the hotel distribution space is mutating, with the traditional value chain collapsing and the boundaries between industry players becoming much less well defined, forever changing the nature of the relationship between suppliers, intermediaries, and consumers. Disintermediation and reintermediation have become the name of the game as participants up and down the travel distribution chain struggle to establish and maintain their role in the new hotel distribution dynamic. As we move towards the digital economy, differentiation between hotel chains, soft brands, technology suppliers, and online distribution players is rapidly and irreversibly being eroded. As can be seen from Figure 11.1, thanks to the digital revolution hotel chains are becoming more like OTAs, who in turn are providing hotel chain-like services and benefits. New players are challenging the incumbents, who are being forced to evolve their business models or risk dying out. And the pace of change is constantly accelerating. If current developments are analyzed, increasingly it looks like the future of hotel distribution will most closely resemble what we currently know as an Online Travel Agent – a two-sided platform providing multi-brand choice as well as a one-stop shopping for customers seeking travel accommodation. Given the competitive dynamics of the current hotel distribution landscape, this conclusion that the future of hotel chains looks likely to be their much-despised OTA model can only be described as ironic!

References

Berne, C., Garcia-Gonzalez, M., and Mugica, J. (2012), "How ICT shifts the power balance of tourism distribution channels", *Tourism Management*, Vol.33, No.1, pp.205–214. doi: 10.1016/j.tourman.2011.02.004.

BDRC. (2019), *Hotel Guest Survey Reveals Surprising Trends on OTAs and Direct Booking,* available at: https://www.hospitalitynet.org/news/4089678.html (accessed 22 December 2018).

Bilgihan, A. and Bujisic, M. (2014). The effect of website features in online relationship marketing: A case of online hotel booking. *Electronic Commerce Research and Applications*. 14 (4), 222–232. doi:10.1016/j.elerap.2014.09.001

Buhalis, D. (2008), "Relationships in the distribution channel of tourism: Conflicts between hoteliers and tour operators in the Mediterranean region", *International Journal of Hospitality & Tourism Administration*, Vol.1, No.1, pp.113–139. doi: 10.1300/J149v01n01_07.

Cantoni, L. and Danowski, J. (2015), *Communication and Technology*, de Gruyter, Zürich, Switzerland.

Carroll, B. and Siguaw, J. (2003), "The evolution of electronic distribution: Effects on hotels and intermediaries", *Cornell Hotel and Restaurant Administration Quarterly*, Vol.44, No.4, pp.38–50. doi: 10.1177/0010880403444004.

Carvell, S.A., Canina, L., and Sturman, M.C. (2016), "A comparison of the performance of brand-affiliated and unaffiliated hotel properties", *Cornell Hospitality Quarterly*, Vol.57, No.2, pp.193–201. doi: 10.1177/1938965516631014.

Chang, Y.W., Hsu, P.-Y., and Lan, Y.C. (2019), "Cooperation and competition between online travel agencies and hotels", *Tourism Management*, Vol.71, pp.187–196. doi: 10.1016/j.tourman.2018.08.026.

Christensen, C. (1997), *The Innovator's Dilemma: When New Technologies Cause Great Firms to Fail*, Harvard Business School Press, Boston, MA.

Christodoulidou, N., Connolly, D. J. and Brewer, P. (2013). An examination of the transactional relationship between online travel agencies, travel meta sites, and suppliers. *International Journal of Contemporary Hospitality Management*. 22(7): 1048–1062.

Claver-Cortés, E., Molina-Azorín, J.F., and Pereira-Moliner, J. (2007), "The impact of strategic behaviours on hotel performance", *International Journal of Contemporary Hospitality Management*, Vol.19, No.1, pp.6–20. doi: 10.1108/09596110710724125.

Díaz, E. and Koutra, C. (2013), "Evaluation of the persuasive features of hotel chains websites: A latent class segmentation analysis", *International Journal of Hospitality Management*, Vol.34, pp.338–347. doi: 10.1016/j. ijhm.2012.11.009.

Enz, C., Peiró-Signes, Á., and Segarra-Oña, M. (2014), "How fast do new hotels ramp up performance?", *Cornell Hospitality Quarterly*, Vol.55, No.2, pp.141–151. doi: 10.1177/1938965513506518.

Ert, E. and Fleischer, A. (2016), "Mere position effect in booking hotels online", *Journal of Travel Research*, Vol.55, No.3, pp.311–321. doi: 10.1177/0047287514559035.

Fernández-Sabiote, E. and Román, S. (2012), "Adding clicks to bricks: A study of the con-sequences on customer loyalty in a service context", *Electronic Commerce Research and Applications*, Vol.11, No.1, pp.36–48. doi: 10.1016/j.elerap.2011.07.007.

Gan, L., Sim, C.J., Tan, H.L., and Tan, J. (2008), "Online relationship marketing by Singapore hotel websites", *Journal of Travel & Tourism Marketing*, Vol.20, No.3–4, pp.1–19. doi: 10.1300/j073v20n03_01.

Gazzoli, G., Kim, W.G., and Palakurthi, R. (2013), "Online distribution strategies and competition: Are the global hotel companies getting it right?", *International Journal of Contemporary Hospitality Management*, Vol.20, No.4, pp.375–387. doi: 10.1108/09596110810873499.

Guo, X. and He, L. (2012), "Tourism supply-chain coordination: The cooperation between tourism hotel and tour operator", *Tourism Economics*, Vol.18, No.6, pp.1361–1376. doi: 10.5367/te.2012.0179.

Hahn, S.E., Sparks, B., Wilkins, H., and Jin, X. (2017), "E-service quality management of a hotel website: A scale and implications for management", *Journal of Hospitality Marketing & Management*, Vol.26, No.3, pp.694–716. doi: 10.1080/19368623.2017.1309612.

Ham, S., Kim, W.G., and Jeong, S. (2005), "Effect of information technology on performance in up-scale hotels", *International Journal of Hospitality Management*, Vol.24, No.2, pp.281–294. doi: 10.1016/j. ijhm.2004.06.010.

Herrero, Á. and San Martín, H. (2012), "Developing and testing a global model to explain the adoption of websites by users in rural tourism accommodations", *International Journal of Hospitality Management*, Vol.31, No.4, pp.1178–1186. doi: 10.1016/j.ijhm.2012.02.005.

Kalibri Labs. (2018), *2018 Book Direct Campaigns 2.0: The Costs and Benefits of Loyalty in 2018*, Kalibri Labs, New York, NY.

Kang, B., Brewer, K.P., and Baloglu, S. (2007), "Profitability and survivability of hotel distribution channels: An industry perspective", *Journal of Travel & Tourism Marketing*, Vol.22, No.1, p.37. doi: 10.1300/ j073v22n01_03.

Kim, H., Ham, S., and Moon, H. (2012), "The impact of hotel property size in determining the importance of electronic distribution channels", *Journal of Hospitality and Tourism Technology*, Vol.3, No.3, pp.226–237. doi: 10.1108/17579881211264503.

Kim, J., Bojanic, D.C., and Warnick, R.B. (2009), "Price bundling and travel product pricing practices used by online channels of distribution", *Journal of Travel Research*, Vol.47, No.4, pp.403–412. doi: 10.1177/0047287508328658.

KPMG. (2002), *The Performance of Management Agreements and Franchise Contracts in the European Marketplace*, KPMG, London, UK.

Lam, C., Ho, G.K.S., and Law, R. (2015), "How can Asian hotel companies remain internationally competitive?", *International Journal of Contemporary Hospitality Management*, Vol.27, No.5, pp.827–852. doi: 10.1108/ijchm-05-2013-0226.

Law, R., Leung, D., Au, N., and Lee, H.A. (2012), "Progress and development of information technology in the hospitality industry: Evidence from the Cornell hospitality quarterly", *Cornell Hospitality Quarterly*, Vol.54, No.1, pp.10–24. doi: 10.1177/1938965512453199.

Law, R. and Jogaratnam, G. (2013), "A study of hotel information technology applications", *International Journal of Contemporary Hospitality Management*, Vol.17, No.2, pp.170–180. doi: 10.1108/09596110510582369.

Lee, H., Guillet, B.D., and Law, R. (2013), "An examination of the relationship between online travel agents and hotels: A case study of choice hotels international and Expedia.com", *Cornell Hospitality Quarterly*, Vol.54, No.1, p.95. doi: 10.1177/1938965512454218.

Lee, S. W. and Kim, D. J. (2004). Driving factors and barriers of information and communication technology for e-business in SMEs: A case study in Korea. *Proceedings of the IADIS* International Conference on e-Society, Ávila, Spain. 163–171.

Ling, L., Guo, X., and Yang, C. (2014), "Opening the online marketplace: An examination of hotel pricing and travel agency on-line distribution of rooms", *Tourism Management*, Vol.45, pp.234–243. doi: 10.1016/j.tourman.2014.05.003.

Murphy, H.C. and Chen, M.-M. (2016), "Online information sources used in hotel bookings: Examining relevance and recall", *Journal of Travel Research*, Vol.55, No.4), pp.523–536. doi: 10.1177/0047287514559033.

O'Connor, P. (1999), *Electronic Distribution Technology in the Tourism and Hospitality Industries*, CABI, New York, NY.

O'Connor, P. (2016), "Distribution channel management", in Magnini, V., Ivanova, M., and Stanislav, I. (Eds.), *Handbook of Hotel Chain Management*, Routledge, London and New York, pp.251–261. doi: 10.4324/9781315445526-17.

O'Connor, P. and Piccoli, G. (2003), "Marketing hotels using global distribution systems": Revisited", *Cornell Hotel and Restaurant Administration Quarterly*, Vol.44, No.5, pp.105–114. doi: 10.1177/001088040304400515.

O'Neill, J. and Carlbäck, M. (2011), "Do brands matter? A comparison of branded and independent hotels' performance during a full economic cycle", *International Journal of Hospitality Management*, Vol.30, No.3, pp.515–521. doi: 10.1016/j.ijhm.2010.08.003.

Phillips, P., Barnes, S., Zigan, K., and Schegg, R. (2017), "Understanding the impact of online reviews on hotel performance: An empirical analysis", *Journal of Travel Research*, Vol.56. No.2, pp.235–249. doi: 10.1177/0047287516636481.

Phocuswire. (2018), *Booking.com Tests Marketplace Offering Third Party Technology*, available at: https://www.phocuswire.com/booking-bookingsuite-marketplace (accessed 21 March 2019).

Phocuswire. (2019), *Fragmentation Continues to Shape the Competitive Landscape for Hoteliers*, available at: https://www.phocuswire.com/Fragmentation-competitive-landscape-hoteliers/ (accessed 1 February 2019).

PhoCusWright. (2018), *PhoCusWright's U.S. Online Travel Overview*, 8th ed., available at: http://www.phocuswright.com (accessed 22 December 2018).

Russell, K. and Kim, B (2017), *2016/17 United States Hotel Franchise Fee Guide*, Hotel Valuation Services (HVS), New York, NY.

Stangl, B., Inversini, A., and Schegg, R. (2016), "Hotels' dependency on online intermediaries and their chosen distribution channel portfolios: Three country insights", *International Journal of Hospitality Management*, Vol.52, pp.87–96. doi: 10.1016/j.ijhm.2015.09.015.

Teixeira, T. (2019), *Unlocking the Customer Value Chain: How Decoupling Drives Consumer Disruption*, Harvard University Press, Boston, UK.

Thakran, K. and Verma, R. (2013), "The emergence of hybrid online distribution channels in travel, tourism and hospitality", *Cornell Hospitality Quarterly*, Vol.54, No.3, pp.240–247. doi: 10.1177/1938965513492107.

Toh, R.S., Raven, P., and DeKay, F. (2011), "Selling rooms: Hotels vs. third-party websites". *Cornell Hospitality Quarterly*, Vol.52, No.2, pp.81–189. doi: 10.1177/1938965511400409.

Travelweekly. (2019), "Hotels' direct bookings making up ground on OTAs," available at: https://www.travelweekly.com/Travel-News/Hotel-News/Hotels-direct-bookings-making-up-ground-on-OTAs/ (accessed 17 March 2019).

Van Zeebroeck, N. and Bughin, J. (2017), "The best response to digital disruption", *MIT Sloan Management Review*, Vol.58, No.4, pp.82–86.

Weill, P. and Woerner, S.L. (2015), "Thriving in an increasingly digital ecosystem", *MIT Sloan Management Review*, Vol.56, No.4, pp.27–34.

12

THE FUTURE OF CSR IN THE HOSPITALITY INDUSTRY

Next Stop, Global Responsibility?

Henri Kuokkanen

Introduction

The hospitality industry has regularly been considered a laggard in corporate social responsibility (CSR). Part of this image links with the early days of environmental responsibility in hotels, and the poor reputation largely hangs on towels. According to Font and Lynes (2018), the common suggestion to reuse towels during a hotel stay in the name of environmental sustainability may have been the catalyst for the term 'greenwashing.' Despite this dubious honor, the practice is still common in the industry, and it still prompts guest skepticism over hotel CSR initiatives. The industry is, after all, a culprit of wasteful use of natural resources, and it is generally weak in CSR implementation (Font et al., 2012).

During the past decade, hotels have attempted to catch up with the times, and CSR research particular to the industry has snowballed (Serra-Cantallops et al., 2018). For example, AccorHotels has developed a series of CSR initiatives and publicly communicated the group's commitment to ethical business behavior (AccorHotels, 2016). Both Marriott and Intercontinental Hotel Group were quick to partially replicate EU's ban on single-use plastics not only in Europe but worldwide (IHG, 2018; Marriott International, 2018). The hotel industry, known for difficult working conditions and poor remuneration (Zientara et al., 2015), has also used CSR practices to motivate and attract employees and to improve customer perception of its practices. However, the world around the traditional hotelier is changing rapidly, and the prominent rise of luxury hospitality has introduced a fresh set of challenges. The new topics include, for example, how luxury and sustainable development can be combined (Achabou and Dekhili, 2013), and how such combination will impact consumer perceptions and expectations of the service (Janssen et al., 2013; Kapferer and Michaut, 2015). Therefore, the industry must explore new approaches to CSR.

Based on contemporary phenomena in the approach companies take toward their responsibilities within the society, this chapter suggests that an emerging role of responsibility could create a CSR revolution in the international hospitality business. Companies whose primary goal and raison d'être is responsibility have already existed for some time in other fields of business. For example, 7th Generation, a manufacturer of biodegradable cleaning products could be classified as such a company. Within the hospitality sector, the Good Hotel builds on a social business model that reinvests profits in local community development (Good Hotel, 2018). However, the two companies founded by entrepreneur Elon Musk – Tesla and Space-X – represent a new breed of for-profit, multi-billion dollar business with responsible objectives at the core of each company. The explicitly expressed goal of each company is to protect humanity from disaster and extinction, be it via cleaner energy or the possibility to colonize other planets (The Falcon, 2018) while pursuing profitable business. More importantly, both companies have credibly challenged incumbents in industries with high barriers to entry and attracted significant investor interest and market valuation: Their large scale makes them distinct from earlier examples of companies that hail from an ethical basis.

Since the early days of CSR, the potential existence of a link between corporate social and financial performances has been a topic of ongoing study, and consensus mostly supports a mildly positive relationship between the two variables (Orlitzky et al., 2003; Peloza, 2009). However, many caveats to this exist (Barnett and Salomon, 2012; Surroca et al., 2010), and there is no clear explanation on how social performance contributes in financial terms (Peloza, 2009). In the hospitality industry, the results have followed these general patterns: CSR initiatives can improve financial performance and improve customer satisfaction, but limitations to these findings exist (Benavides-Velasco et al., 2014; Gao and Mattila, 2014; Parsa et al., 2015). Better business practice is desirable, but CSR cannot be acclaimed a significant competitive advantage based on existing knowledge. However, consumers are willing to support responsible companies, and surveys suggest a preference for products from companies that behave ethically and sustainably (Accenture, UN Global Compact and Havas Media, 2014; Nielsen, 2014, 2015). This inconsistency raises two questions. First, why does the bottom line of responsible companies not reflect these preferences? The second question is even more important: What kind of an approach would allow unfolding the elusive business case for CSR in the hospitality industry? Mainstream CSR practice still reflects the TBL-based reporting and focus on CSR initiatives per stakeholder, as guided by the widely applied Global Reporting Initiative (GRI) guidelines (GRI, 2016). However, the rise of the new type of a responsible company, such as Tesla, coincides with like developments in consumer views; sustainability is an increasingly important purchase criterion particularly for the millennial consumer (Nielsen, 2019). This chapter proceeds to explore the examples from non-hospitality CSR and applies them to the hospitality industry. The aim is to provide a future CSR agenda that responds to the changing CSR landscape and allows the industry to reach ethical leadership.

Tesla and Space-X as Harbingers of a New Era

While in entirely different types of business (consumer goods vs. a true niche market of space transportation), Tesla and Space-X are united by their core focus beyond immediate sales of products and services. Tesla's mission is to provide solutions for sustainable forms of energy to support the survival of the planet. The change of the company name from Tesla Motors to Tesla reflects the ever-increasing importance of solar power and batteries to the company over the earlier, vehicle-centered focus (Musk, 2006; The Falcon, 2018). Similarly, while Space-X competes in transporting cargo and, in the future, human passengers to orbit the planet, Mr. Musk declares his fundamental reason for starting Space-X to be survival of the human race through providing a means to colonize neighboring planets (The Falcon, 2018). While undoubtedly also targeted to attract public attention, these messages differ significantly from common corporate goals usually aimed at shareholder wealth maximization. In both cases, a deeper goal to support humanity is included.

Tesla and Space-X are not the first businesses to highlight CSR. For example, companies such as Patagonia, Ben, and Jerry's and The Body Shop have been hailed as examples of responsible and ethical business (Visser, 2011), and Banyan Tree promotes sustainable luxury hospitality. A crucial aspect separates these four from the two companies focused on in this chapter: the mission of the business. Even with responsibility built into the culture of the four companies, their mission is still to bring pleasure to consumers, be it via apparel, ice cream, health products, or a luxurious holiday setting. Tesla, on the other hand, offers electric vehicles and aims to maximize the pleasure of driving them, but its core mission is to make the internal combustion engine obsolete and to protect the environment through cleaner energy (The Falcon, 2018). The two approaches are mirror images of responsibility; one represents selling consumer goods and services that are produced in a responsible manner, while the other sells responsibility that is produced in a consumable manner.

Companies with responsibility as the mission of the business are not entirely new. Manufacturers of renewable energy equipment or LED light bulbs could be classified in such a manner. Similarly, 7th Generation, a manufacturer of biodegradable cleaning products, aims to convert the act of consumption into a sustainable event. However, the unique aspect of Tesla and Space-X is the size of each company. With 60 billion and 21 billion USD, respectively (The Falcon, 2018), both companies are known worldwide and considered market leaders.

Moreover, Tesla has broken into a market dominated by several traditional car manufactures, an act considered unimaginable until now, while Space-X has become a key player in a business characterized by high costs of market entry and little competition. Reversing the prevailing logic of CSR and making responsibility the company mission has plausibly contributed to these achievements, highlighting the business potential the approach possesses. Therefore, these two companies form the practical reference for exploring a new concept of CSR. As summarized by Baker (2017), the Musk approach has transformed responsibility from a distraction to a solution for societal problems.

Responsibility as the Core of a Company

The new approach to CSR this chapter proposes builds on the notion of CSR as the corporate mission that can be profitable in its own right. This proposal reflects particularly the case of Tesla as a publicly listed company. Investors are confident in Tesla's future profitability, as evidenced by its high stock market valuation with little profit earned so far. The valuation of Space-X suggests a similar story of investor confidence, although its financials are not public. Therefore, it seems plausible to propose a relationship between 'core CSR' as demonstrated by Tesla, and financial profitability; this could be considered as an economic stance of the novel CSR approach. The stance removes the need to develop a separate business case for CSR and repositions CSR from a manner of conducting business to become the core business. Selling this responsible core, be it in the form of environmentally friendly products (Tesla) or technological development toward a goal beneficial to humanity (Space-X) is profitable in its own right under the new approach. It also coincides with the broad purpose of business to serve humanity, as laid out by Donaldson and Walsh (2015).

CSR as the corporate mission includes a second channel through which responsibility can improve profitability. A company with a responsible core goal is inclined to fulfill the legal and ethical expectations of its stakeholders; should this not be the case, responsibility would not genuinely be the core of the company. Fulfilling these expectations can be described as the moral stance of the new CSR approach. The moral stance, thus, incorporates integrated social contracts theory (ISCT, Donaldson and Dunfee, 1994) in the approach. Three observations support this argument. First, CSR as the core of a company allows stakeholders "to make an adequate assessment of the intentions and capabilities of a prospective partner" (van Oosterhout et al., 2006, p. 530). Second, the model allows the inclusion of a moral substance in stakeholder management as required in ISCT, as the economic stance of the model fulfills the expectation for a business case and instrumental pressure is thus reduced. Finally, the norms for regulating the relationship between a company and its stakeholders arise from the core of such a company, or "the argumentative structure of the contract model itself" (van Oosterhout et al., 2006, p. 524), fulfilling the criteria to avoid the contractualist fallacy linked with ISCT. Good stakeholder relations, in turn, increase profitability in multiple ways; earlier findings support several such indirect benefits of CSR. These include increased employee satisfaction and commitment (Glavas, 2016), reduction in the risk of scandals or costly arguments (Petersen and Vredenburg, 2009) and improved supplier cooperation (Mason and Simmons, 2014; Zhang et al., 2014).

Tesla demonstrates new engagement with competitors as stakeholders by providing open access to its technology (Carroll and Buchholtz, 2018). This highly unusual move in for-profit business emphasizes that the core of the company is not its technology but its mission and that this responsible mission has arguably assumed the usual role of technology as the source of profits. Jones et al. (2018) investigated how the implementation of instrumental stakeholder theory could result in a sustainable competitive advantage. In their view, "a communal sharing relational ethics strategy – characterized by an intention to rely on relational contracts, joint wealth creation, high levels of mutual trust and cooperation, and communal sharing of property" (Jones et al., 2018, p. 371) can lead to such an advantage. The sharing of intellectual property with competitors supports the image of Tesla as a visionary in stakeholder management that aims at such a sustainable competitive advantage.

The ethical stance does not automatically result in fulfilling the expectations of all stakeholders every time, and contradicting goals among the various parties will contribute to this. In particular, the Tesla case reveals examples of stakeholder dissatisfaction and controversy. For example, when Mr. Musk decided to combine Tesla with Solar City, a struggling solar panel manufacturer also under his ownership, concerns of wasting Tesla shareholders' money in saving the solar panel company were voiced (The Falcon, 2018). The announcement of Tesla's delisting from the stock exchange through a private buy-out, canceled after a week, led to investor lawsuits (Stempel and Singh, 2018), and eventually forced Mr. Musk to step down as the chairman of the board (Letting go, 2018). These examples suggest a fascinating antagonism when comparing Tesla with the traditional business approach: shareholders have usually received the most attention among stakeholders, but they appear to express the loudest dissatisfaction in Tesla's case.

Agle et al. (2008) identified the main difference between shareholder and stakeholder approaches to business to be the mission of the company. This observation can help in connecting the proposed new approach with existing CSR models. A business that maximizes shareholder value aims at profits, and should it follow Carroll's (1991) thesis, it may employ CSR to achieve this goal. On the other hand, a company that follows the stakeholder approach believes that profits will follow as a result of "a very simple idea about how people create value for each other" (Agle et al., 2008, p. 166) and by balancing the needs of stakeholders (Freeman and Elms, 2018). From a theoretical perspective, the new approach incorporates the key aspects of Carroll's CSR pyramid, stakeholder theory, and ISCT by connecting legal and ethical behavior to address stakeholder expectations. Profitability becomes the specific outcome of selling a fundamentally responsible core; this aims to address the critique presented by Freeman and Liedtka (1991) over Carroll's alleged acceptance of profit maximization as the sole corporate goal.

Similarly, philanthropy as a separate responsibility item could disappear, as the corporate mission combined with ethical business practice can replace explicit spending on charity. While historically a key component of CSR (Carroll, 2016), the benefits of such spending are contested (Su and Sauerwald, 2018). The approach can also further the integration of normative and instrumental approaches to responsibility, as requested by Agle et al. (2008). Once the core of a company builds on a mission to benefit the society, achieved by selling goods or services that simultaneously produce a profit, the significance of the normative-instrumental divide diminishes. While a company with a traditional approach to CSR is expected to embed existing aspects of responsibility in its core operations, the new breed of responsible companies embeds their operations in responsibility.

A New Role for CSR in the Hospitality Industry

The new approach to CSR presented above could be shrugged off as merely one more attempt to consolidate the CSR domain and emphasize the role of responsibility in business. Tesla and Space-X could fail as businesses. However, this time it could be different and have lasting effects on companies and the nexus between business and society. Major companies are including aims outside the traditional profit maximization in their corporate goals. Danone's CEO Emmanuel Faber has stressed that instead of a traditional profit motive, the company focuses on delivering healthy food while creating value for all stakeholders (Choosing Plan B, 2018). Danone has further registered parts of the company as B-Corporations that emphasize transparency and responsibility to give profit and cause equal weights (B Lab, 2018). While still shy of transforming the raison d'être of the company to benefit humanity, this is a significant effort to level the playing field between the well-off and the have-nothing. Such an example from an established multinational corporation highlights the need for fresh thinking also in the hospitality industry. The large, international hotel companies are particularly well-positioned for leading a change toward a new type of responsibility.

Currently, CSR initiatives in the hospitality industry range from the earlier-mentioned (and sometimes contested) environmental activities to charitable donations, and further to initiatives linked with improving the livelihoods of the local communities where properties operate (Bohdanowicz and Zientara, 2008; de Grosbois, 2012; Levy and Park, 2011). While local community support connects well with the hotel business, it is an unlikely candidate for a fundamental mission of the hospitality business. After all, such a mission would require significant financial investment outside company operations and, even then, not represent the business itself. Instead, a possible solution lies within the name of the industry. The word 'hospitality' is derived from its adjective form 'hospitable'; Merriam-Webster (2018, para 4) defines 'hospitable' as "promising or suggesting generous and friendly welcome," "offering a pleasant or sustaining environment" and further "readily receptive: open." The best-practice examples and companies in the industry reflect these definitions toward customers, but the focus should be extended beyond customer interaction.

The world is arguably undergoing a period where generosity and openness are on the decline. Events such as Brexit, largely motivated by a desire to limit free movement of people granted within the EU, and the rise of Trumpian politics in the United States and elsewhere that emphasize border control and the dominance of domestic goals over international cooperation, support this argument. During this period, an industry, whose essence is to be welcoming and to offer a pleasant environment, could expand these principles beyond the immediate walls of the hotels and become a global champion of ethical behavior. For an international hotel chain, adopting such a stance of morality toward others could transform CSR into the essence of the business, following the example set particularly by Tesla. Such adoption does not equal hotels becoming political actors (Scherer et al., 2014); the extended core of hospitality should not be directed against any single nation or political movement. Instead, the message should rely on the core definition of being hospitable toward others as the ethically right thing to do, linking it with non-political CSR. The connection between hospitality, a service industry striving toward a more hospitable world, and the call of Donaldson and Walsh (2015) for business to serve the society, would also be remarkable.

A fundamental mission that sets an example of encountering the world in a hospitable manner and caters for respectful and inclusive relationships would also address some of the issues linked with connecting CSR and luxury hospitality. Luxury hospitality business often creates a stark contrast with its surroundings, particularly in the developing world. Instead of working to justify the contradiction through various CSR initiatives, treating everyone humanely and respectfully could elevate local community relationships into a powerful competitive advantage for the industry. Such an advantage could result from attracting the consumer of the future, who searches for offers that extend goodness to the world (Nielsen, 2019). Such a path could activate both the economic and moral stances of the new CSR approach and meet the expectations of the future hotel guest.

This chapter presents the hospitality industry with an exploratory challenge to investigate the potential for adopting the proposed CSR approach. A crucial first step is to define representations of 'hospitable' that are both feasible and fitting to the stakeholder network of the industry. Merely developing a slogan (e.g., 'for a more hospitable world') would threaten a repeat of the towel reuse example described early in this chapter. Therefore, academics and practitioners must jointly set out to seek a definition for the term and develop initiatives that manifest the message in the real world. Local communities, employees, and the natural environment, previously demonstrated significant to the success of the industry, form a set of stakeholders fitting for the initial application. However, communication, with supportive evidence that connects individual initiatives with a comprehensive framework of amicable and inclusive operations, is crucial. The approach must be carefully adapted to fit the hospitality context to avoid the mistakes of the past.

Conclusion

The ethical implications of adopting a 'hospitable approach' toward others as the core of the hospitality industry and the embodiment of its CSR are compelling. However, why should important actors in the industry choose to shift their strategies so fundamentally? The answer lies in the potential power of the new approach. Relying on responsibility and profit simultaneously, a new entrant to the market could fundamentally change the dynamics of the business. The success of Tesla in penetrating the automobile industry serves as early evidence of this potential: earlier, the industry would have been considered extremely challenging, if not impossible, to enter. The hotel industry shares this same notion, but it cannot merely rely on unsurmountable barriers to entry. Incumbents must carefully evaluate the opportunities that adopting a new CSR approach could generate for them. Alternatively, they must weigh the risk of facing existing or new competitors that embrace the new model. A decade ago, when Tesla was founded, few people believed in its potential to shape the industry. Currently, even with the success of the company still highly uncertain, the founders of Tesla have been proven right, as most traditional car manufacturers now develop their electric vehicles. Pivotal moments in business can cause dominant actors to dwindle when facing new competition, and a transformation of CSR could create such a moment also in the hospitality industry.

References

Accenture, UN Global Compact and Havas Media. (2014), *The Consumer Study: From Marketing to Mattering*, UN Global Compact Reports, United Nations, New York, NY, pp.1–15.

AccorHotels. (2016, April 14), *AccorHotels Takes Its Corporate Responsibility to the Next Level with Bold New CSR Commitments Looking*, available at: https://press.accorhotels.group/accorhotels-takes-its-corporate-responsibility-to-the-next-level-with-bold-new-csr-commitments-looking/ (accessed 28 December, 2018).

Achabou, M.A. and Dekhili, S. (2013), "Luxury and sustainable development: Is there a match?", *Journal of Business Research*, Vol.66, No.10, pp.1896–1903. http://doi.org/10.1016/j.jbusres.2013.02.011.

Agle, B.R., Donaldson, T., Freeman, R.E., Jensen, M.C., Mitchell, R.K., and Wood, D.J. (2008), "Dialogue: Toward superior stakeholder theory", *Business Ethics Quarterly*, Vol.18, No.2, pp.153–190. http://doi.org/10.5840/beq200818214.

B Lab. (2018), *About B Corps*, available at: https://bcorporation.net/about-b-corps (accessed 28 September, 2018).

Baker, M. (2017, March 23), "The corporate social responsibility of Elon Musk [Blog post]", available at: http://mallenbaker.net/article/clear-reflection/the-corporate-social-responsibility-of-elon-musk (accessed 16 March, 2018).

Barnett, M.L. and Salomon, R.M. (2012), "Does it pay to be really good? Addressing the shape of the relationship between social and financial performance", *Strategic Management Journal*, Vol.33, No.11, pp.1304–1320. http://doi.org/10.1002/smj.1980.

Benavides-Velasco, C.A., Quintana-García, C., and Marchante-Lara, M. (2014), "Total quality management, corporate social responsibility and performance in the hotel industry", *International Journal of Hospitality Management*, Vol.41, pp.77–87. http://doi.org/10.1016/j.ijhm.2014.05.003.

Bohdanowicz, P. and Zientara, P. (2008), "Corporate social responsibility in hospitality: Issues and implications. A case study of Scandic", *Scandinavian Journal of Hospitality and Tourism*, Vol.8, No.4, pp.271–293. http://doi.org/10.1080/15022250802504814.

Carroll, A.B. (1991), "The pyramid of corporate social responsibility: Toward the moral management of organizational stakeholders", *Business Horizons*, Vol.34, No.3, pp.39–48. http://doi.org/10.1016/0007-6813(91)90005-G.

Carroll, A.B. (2016), "Carroll's pyramid of CSR: Taking another look", *International Journal of Corporate Social Responsibility*, Vol.1, No.3, pp.1–8. http://doi.org/10.1186/s40991-016-0004-6.

Carroll, A.B. and Buchholtz, A.K. (2018), *Business and Society: Ethics, Sustainability, and Stakeholder Management*, 10th ed., Cengage Learning, Boston, UK.

Choosing Plan B. (2018, August 9), Choosing plan B: Danone rethinks the idea of the firm. *The Economist*, available at: http://www.economist.com/ (accessed 13 September, 2018).

de Grosbois, D. (2012), "Corporate social responsibility reporting by the global hotel industry: Commitment, initiatives and performance", *International Journal of Hospitality Management*, Vol.31, No.3, pp.896–905. http://doi.org/10.1016/j.ijhm.2011.10.008.

Donaldson, T. and Dunfee, T.W. (1994), "Toward a unified conception of business ethics: Integrative social contracts theory", *Academy of Management Review*, Vol.19, No.2, pp.252–284. http://doi.org/10.5465/amr.1994.9410210749.

Donaldson, T. and Walsh, J.P. (2015), "Toward a theory of business", *Research in Organizational Behavior*, Vol.35, pp.181–207. http://doi.org/10.1016/j.riob.2015.10.002.

Font, X. and Lynes, J. (2018), "Corporate social responsibility in tourism and hospitality", *Journal of Sustainable Tourism*, Vol. 26, No.7, pp.1027–1042. http://doi.org/10.1080/09669582.2018.1488856.

Font, X., Walmsley, A., Cogotti, S., McCombes, L., and Häusler, N. (2012), "Corporate social responsibility: The disclosure–performance gap", *Tourism Management*, Vol.33, No.6, pp.1544–1553. http://doi.org/10.1016/j.tourman.2012.02.012.

Freeman, R.E. and Elms, H. (2018, January 4), "The social responsibility of business is to create value for stakeholders", *MIT Sloan Management Review*, available at: https://sloanreview.mit.edu/article/the-social-responsibility-of-business-is-to-create-value-for-stakeholders/ (accessed 31 August, 2018).

Freeman, R.E. and Liedtka, J. (1991), "Corporate social responsibility: A critical approach", *Business Horizons*, Vol.34, No.4, pp.92–98. http://doi.org/10.1016/0007-6813(91)90012-K.

Gao, Y. and Mattila, A.S. (2014), "Improving consumer satisfaction in green hotels: The roles of perceived warmth, perceived competence, and CSR motive", *International Journal of Hospitality Management*, Vol.42, pp.20–31. http://doi.org/10.1016/j.ijhm.2014.06.003.

Glavas, A. (2016, February), "Corporate social responsibility and organizational psychology: An integrative review", *Frontiers in Psychology*, Vol.7, pp.1–14. http://doi.org/10.3389/fpsyg.2016.00144.

Good Hotel. (2018), *The Concept*, available at: https://www.goodhotellondon.com/ (accessed 28 December, 2018).

GRI. (2016), *GRI Standards*, available at: https://www.globalreporting.org/standards/gri-standards-download-center/ (accessed 11 May, 2017).

IHG. (2018, October 11), *IHG to Remove Plastic Straws from Hotels Worldwide*, available at: https://www.ihgplc.com/news-and-media/news-releases/2018/ihg-to-remove-plastic-straws-from-hotels-worldwide (accessed 28 December, 2018).

Janssen, C., Lindgreen, A., and Drive, C. (2013), "The catch -22 of responsible luxury: Effects of luxury product characteristics on consumers' perceptions of fit with corporate social responsibility", *Journal of Business Ethics*, Vol.119, No.1, pp.45–57. http://doi.org/10.1007/s10551-013-1621-6.

Jones, T.M., Harrison, J.S., and Felps, W. (2018), "How applying instrumental stakeholder theory can provide sustainable competitive advantage", *Academy of Management Review*, Vol.43 No.3, pp.371–391. http://doi.org/10.5465/amr.2016.0111.

Kapferer, J.N. and Michaut, A. (2015), "Luxury and sustainability: A common future? The match depends on how consumers define luxury", *Luxury Research Journal*, Vol.1, No.1, pp.3. http://doi.org/10.1504/LRJ.2015.069828.

Letting go. (2018, October 4), "Letting go of the wheel: Elon Musk's grip on Tesla loosens", *The Economist*, available at: http://www.economist.com/ (accessed 18 October, 2018).

Levy, S.E. and Park, S.-Y. (2011), "An analysis of CSR activities in the lodging industry", *Journal of Hospitality and Tourism Management*, Vol.18, No.1, pp.147–154. http://doi.org/10.1375/jhtm.18.1.147.

Marriott International. (2018), "Marriott International to remove plastic straws worldwide by July 2019", available at: http://news.marriott.com/2018/07/marriott-international-to-remove-plastic-straws-worldwide-by-july-2019/ (accessed 28 December, 2018).

Mason, C. and Simmons, J. (2014), "Embedding corporate social responsibility in corporate governance: A stakeholder systems approach", *Journal of Business Ethics*, Vol.119, No.1, pp.77–86. http://doi.org/10.1007/s10551-012-1615-9.

Merriam-Webster. (2018), *Definition of Hospitable*, available at: https://www.merriam-webster.com/dictionary/hospitable (accessed 28 December, 2018).

Musk, E. (2006, August 2), "The secret Tesla motors master plan (just between you and me)" [Blog post], available at: https://www.tesla.com/blog/secret-tesla-motors-master-plan-just-between-you-and-me (accessed 14 March, 2018).

Nielsen. (2014), *Doing Well by Doing Good*, available at: https://www.nielsen.com/us/en/insights/report/2014/doing-well-by-doing-good/ (accessed 14 December, 2014).

Nielsen. (2015), *The Sustainability Imperative*, available at: https://www.nielsen.com/eu/en/insights/report/2015/the-sustainability-imperative/ (accessed 29 December, 2017)

Nielsen. (2019), *Was 2018 the Year of the Influential Sustainable Consumer?*, available at: https://www.nielsen.com/us/en/insights/article/2018/was-2018-the-year-of-the-influential-sustainable-consumer/ (accessed 28 December, 2018).

Orlitzky, M., Schmidt, F.L., and Rynes, S.L. (2003), Corporate social and financial performance: A meta-analysis. *Organization Studies*, Vol.24, No.3, pp.403–441. http://doi.org/10.1177/0170840603024003910.

Parsa, H.G., Lord, K.R., Putrevu, S., and Kreeger, J. (2015), "Corporate social and environmental responsibility in services: Will consumers pay for it?", *Journal of Retailing and Consumer Services*, Vol.22, pp.250–260. http://doi.org/10.1016/j.jretconser.2014.08.006.

Peloza, J. (2009), "The challenge of measuring financial impacts from investments in corporate social performance", *Journal of Management*, Vol.35, No.6, pp.1518–1541. http://doi.org/10.1177/0149206309335188.

Petersen, H.L. and Vredenburg, H. (2009), "Morals or economics? Institutional investor preferences for corporate social responsibility", *Journal of Business Ethics*, Vol.90, No.1, pp.1–14. http://doi.org/10.1007/s10551-009-0030-3.

Scherer, A.G., Palazzo, G., and Matten, D. (2014), "The business firm as a political actor: A new theory of the firm for a globalized world", *Business & Society*, Vol.53, No.2, pp.143–156. http://doi.org/10.1177/0007650313511778.

Serra-Cantallops, A., Peña-Miranda, D.D., Ramón-Cardona, J., and Martorell-Cunill, O. (2018), "Progress in research on CSR and the hotel industry (2006–2015)", *Cornell Hospitality Quarterly*, Vol.59 No.1, pp.15–38. http://doi.org/10.1177/1938965517719267.

Stempel, J. and Singh, S. (2018, September 6), *Tesla, Musk Sought to "Burn" Citron, Other Short-Sellers: Lawsuit*, available at: https://www.reuters.com/article/us-tesla-lawsuit/shortseller-citron-files-lawsuit-against-tesla-musk-idUSKCN1LM2OX (accessed 18 October, 2018).

Su, W. and Sauerwald, S. (2018), "Does corporate philanthropy increase firm value? The moderating role of corporate governance", *Business & Society*, Vol.57, No.4, pp.599–635. http://doi.org/10.1177/0007650315613961.

Surroca, J., Tribo, J.A., and Waddock, S. (2010), "Corporate responsibility and financial performance: The role of intangible resources", *Strategic Management Journal*, Vol.31, pp.463–490. http://doi.org/10.1002/smj.820.

The Falcon. (2018, February 10), "The Falcon heavy's creator is trying to change more worlds than one – How Elon Musk does it", *The Economist*, available at: http://www.economist.com/ (accessed 9 March, 2018).

van Oosterhout, J.H., Heugens, P.P.M.A.R., and Kaptein, M. (2006), "The internal morality of contracting: The contractualist advancing endeavor in business ethics", *The Academy of Management Review*, Vol.31, No.3, pp.521–539. http://doi.org/10.5465/AMR.2006.21318915.

Visser, W. (2011), *The Age of Responsibility: CSR 2.0 and the New DNA of Business*, Wiley, London, England, UK.

Zhang, M., Ma, L., Su, J., and Zhang, W. (2014), "Do suppliers applaud corporate social performance?", *Journal of Business Ethics*, Vol.121, pp 4. http://doi.org/10.1007/s10551-013-1735-x.

Zientara, P., Kujawski, L., and Bohdanowicz-Godfrey, P. (2015), "Corporate social responsibility and employee attitudes: Evidence from a study of Polish hotel employees", *Journal of Sustainable Tourism*, Vol.23, No.6, pp.859–880. http://doi.org/10.1080/09669582.2015.1019511.

13

SUSTAINABILITY WITHOUT LIMITS

Strategic and Operational Innovations in the Hospitality Industry

Willy Legrand, Elena Cavagnaro, Robert Schønrock Nielsen, and Nicolas Dubrocard

Introduction

A section of the hospitality industry seems to be fully aware of the urgency in acting to mitigate climate change impacts while also catering to their customers' needs and mindset (Legrand and Schønrock Nielsen, 2016). Several innovative players in the hotel industry have inspired others to explore the limits of what is possible, including testing limits of current technologies related to sustainability including the implementation of current technologies related to sustainability (e.g., installation of first-, second-, and third-generation solar cells in the form of organic or polymer photovoltaic cells) (Legrand et al., 2016). Beyond reducing carbon dioxide emissions or mitigating food waste production, the next trend among the most innovative hotels is to become power-houses for what we label as '*production of sustainability*' to the surrounding society.

This chapter is structured in three sections: (1) Climate Change Metanarrative and the Hospitality Industry; (2) Innovation, Disruption, and Sustainability; and (3) Investing and Implementing Strategic and Operational Innovations.

Literature Review

Sustainability as the Grand Narrative in a Postmodern Society

The 1987 report titled *Our Common Future*, better known as Brundtland report, is considered a reference work on how sustainable development can be understood as a social phenomenon. The report's key statement is that present generations must not deprive future generations' opportunities for social and economic progress (WCED, 1987). Now more than 30 years down the road, the Brundtland report de facto made the concept of 'sustainability' an international metanarrative. In a postmodern society, this is rather quite novel. Indeed, the French philosopher Jean-Francois Lyotard (1924–1998) claimed, along with several philosophers including Pierre Bourdieu (1930–2002), Jacques Derrida (1930–2004), Gilles Deleuze (1925–1995), and Michael Foucault (1926–1984), that we live in a so-called postmodern society where there no longer exists a 'common value-based decision making' or 'grand narratives' that unite us (Loytard, 1984). In a compact form, the argument among the postmodern thinkers (which includes Bauman) is that modern society's ideas about rationality, scientific breakthroughs, and economic progress are replaced by a darker perspective, where a society after modernity is without long-term stability and cohesion (Bauman, 2015). Bauman argues that the order in modernity is replaced by contingency, uncertainty, and ambivalence in the postmodern society (Bauman, 2002, 2015). However, climate change, scarcity of resources, and society's greater demands for ethics, in particular, business ethics, crystalized in the common understanding of 'sustainability' provides a new 'grand narrative' in a postmodern world. And so, sustainability as a global, social, and value-laden phenomenon seems to break with the argument that the grand narratives are dissolved in postmodern society. Sustainability conflicts with the statement that people are "*incredulous towards metanarratives*" (Loytard, 1984). Such conflictual situation is important to the extent in which our societies have reached what researchers call the 'Great Acceleration' whereby the sum of all human activities is the principal change agent of the earth system (Steffen et al., 2015). And while Holocene, a geological era started after the last major ice age, is "*characterized by a soft and spotty human impact on Earth*" (Certini and Scalenghe, 2015, p. 246), it is proposed that this new era of Great Acceleration, where significant human impacts on the planet are recorded, be called the *Anthropocene* (Certini and Scalenghe, 2015). As Steffen et al. report, "*hitherto human activities were insignificant compared with the biophysical Earth System, and the two could operate independently. However, it is now impossible to view one as separate from the other*" (p. 14). When Steffen et al. ask "*will the next 50 years bring the Great Decoupling or the Great Collapse?*" (p. 14), it is argued that *sustainability* should (and must?) be the grand narrative to ensure some kind of planet stewardship required in light of the many challenges now and ahead. In some ways, the Paris Agreement, under the United Nations leadership, provides proof of a global movement and hints of metanarrative (for lack of *stewardship*). It is the first time in history that such an agreement "brings all nations into a common cause to undertake ambitious efforts to combat climate change and adapt to its effects" (UNFCCC, 2019). The Agreement, a result of COP21 (Conference of the Parties) negotiations in 2015, was adopted by 195 countries and the EU (ratified by 185 countries as of early 2019). As a reminder, the Paris Agreement provides a global framework towards "*holding the increase in the global average temperature to well below 2°C above preindustrial levels and pursuing efforts to limit the temperature increase to 1.5°C*" (UNFCCC, 2015, p. 2). The agreement can be summarized with a basic equation: *mitigation + adaptation + support*. Mitigation refers to "*efforts to reduce or prevent emission of greenhouse gases*" (Ilegbune, 2016, p. 211). Mitigation translates into "*using new technologies and renewable energies, making older equipment more energy efficient, or changing management practices or consumer behavior*" (Ilegbune, 2016, p. 211). Adaptation is the actions taken to help communities and ecosystems cope with changing climate conditions. Support is to channel finance, technologies and building capacity where needed, here US$100 billion from 2020 onwards has been secured to help climate financing in developing countries (UNFCCC, 2015).

As a summary, our generation has entered a new era where the sum of human impacts is now changing the earth's natural balance. While there is discussion about the role of metanarratives in postmodern societies, it is argued that *sustainability* fills that gap either out of virtue or most probably out of necessity. The Paris Agreement is a global effort in charting a course of action to mitigate and adapt in the face of climate uncertainty and risks. Great hopes are set on the ability of societies, communities, and businesses to innovate.

Innovation, Disruption, and Sustainability

Innovation is a popular phenomenon. According to Schumpeter, innovation can be a new product on the market which contains a new development that customers are not familiar with.

Innovation could also involve a new method of production or the opening of a new market. Finally, innovation can take a new form of organization which supports a company's desire for profit maximization and increased market shares (Schumpeter [1934], in Baumol, 1990, p. 896). The core of the innovation process is the invention of new combinations. This can translate into the introduction of new products as well as the improvements of existing products which leads to new developments (Schumpeter [1934] 1990). The combination of a product or service ingeniously designed elicits "creative destructions" where innovation results in the demise of whatever existed before. Thus, the benefits lie with the entrepreneurial company that is able to develop the right innovative and radical combinatorics (Schumpeter 1934). Schumpeter's idea about creative destructions is comparable to Clayton Christensen's concept of disruptive innovation as both refer to fundamental changes in the market (Christensen, 1997, 2016). Christensen adds Schumpeter's insights on innovation by exploring the unintended effects of technology. If innovations in the form of new technological solutions are devised without taking in consideration customers' needs, the company fails rather rapidly (Christensen, 1997, 2016; Christensen et al., 2016). The creation of innovative solutions in the area of sustainability must be considered as an important method with which society can contain some of the negative effects of climate changes. Innovations that respectively reduce carbon dioxide emissions and generate the invention of environmental solutions that reduce waste in water consumption will help to support a process toward a more sustainable world with a better ecological balance than is the case today. Additionally, innovations, whether in form of product, experience, or sustainability have become essential factors of success in gaining a competitive advantage in the hospitality industry.

In an industry where competition is fierce due partly to the oversupply in some markets combined with the general fragmentation of the hotel sector with multiple branded and non-branded businesses, hospitality companies closely observe the moves of competitors and industry leaders. As reported by Legrand et al.,

> *a competitive advantage cannot be gained by only one single improvement; rather it requires a company to constantly question its strategic position. Gaining and maintaining competitive advantage, either through differentiation- or cost advantage (Porter, 2004), is also a strong motivator for many hospitality companies embarking on sustainable business initiatives.*
>
> *(2016, p. 18)*

For the sake of common understanding, sustainable hospitality is defined as "*hospitality operations managing resources considering the economic, social and environmental costs and benefits in order to meet the needs of present generations while protecting and enhancing opportunities for future generations*" (Legrand et al., 2016, p. 26).

Radical Innovations

Whereas incremental innovations build on familiar technologies or concepts, radical innovations are the opposite. These are game changers that move or revolutionize markets and competitors, thereby driving customer satisfaction to new levels (Christensen et al., 2016). Radical innovation is a kind of quantum leap. However, technical innovation alone is not a sufficient prerequisite to avoid future ecological damage and climatic collapse. Sustainability must be incorporated as a form of social architecture in society. Sustainability requires ethical considerations, and in this context, politicians, consumers, enterprises, suppliers, researchers, intellectuals, and opinion-formers all play a decisive role in relation to changing global society toward a more sustainable direction.

Hospitality Industry Growth and Climate Challenge

The global demand for travel combined with the relatively easy access to money has fueled growth. In the past five years, the global hotel industry has grown by 2.3% to reach revenues of over €1.28 trillion in 2018 (IBISWorld, 2018; Statista, 2018). Revenue is forecasted to grow at a rate of 6.4% and reach €1.75 trillion by 2023 (Statista, 2018). The UNWTO predicts 1.8 billion international tourist arrivals by 2030 (UNWTO, 2017). Investments in the hotel industry are high as an attempt to meet that demand but also secure money in real estate projects. The global hotel construction pipeline (hotels currently being built, or in the planning or pre-planning stages) is currently peaking at over 12,800 hotels (HotelManagement, 2018). Of those 12,800 hotels in the pipeline, almost 6,000 are currently under construction, which results in roughly 15 new hotel opening a day (HotelManagement, 2018). Considering the current and future growth (at the continuing pace, more than 80,000 hotels will join the current supply by 2050) and for the hotel industry to keep the pace set in global commitments such as the Paris Agreement on Climate Change, the *"global hotel industry will need to reduce its greenhouse gas (GHG) emissions per room per year by 66% from 2010 levels by 2030, and 90% by 2050"* (ITP, 2017, p. 3). The authors of the Hotel Decarbonization Report, released in 2017, also mentioned that *"this is above and beyond what most hotel companies have set for carbon targets this far"* (ITP, 2017, p. 3), and thus *"hotel companies will need to set science-based carbon reduction targets"* (ITP, 2017, p. 3). UNWTO Secretary-General Pololikashvili acknowledged the fact that growth of our industry is a double-edged sword whereby *"...this growth reminds us of the need to increase our capacity to develop and manage tourism in a sustainable way, building smart destinations and making the most of technology and innovations"* (UNWTO, 2018). Decisions made today will impact those who take the industry reigns tomorrow.

Impact of Hotel Facilities

Buildings *"consume 40% of the annual energy consumption, 20% of the annual water usage, and generate up to 30% of all energy-related greenhouse gas (GHG) emissions"* (UN DTIE, 2013, p. 1). As discussed previously, the hotel industry is a significant owner and operator of buildings globally and with the continuous investment in new properties, certainly an important real estate player. Hotels are *"among the largest consumers of energy of all commercial buildings in terms of kilowatt-hours per square meter (kWh/m²)"* (Legrand et al., 2016, p. 51). Hotel infrastructures and installations, providing guests with complex and multi-faceted comfort and exclusive amenities, require energy – much of it in the form of electricity. On a global basis, the energy used in hotels is predominantly fossil fuel-based. Typically, a significant amount of the energy used is wasted, leaving ample room for innovative measures of energy efficiency and conservation. Factors such as type and size of hotels, service level, hotel category, size and number of rooms, location, and customer profiles all play a critical role in the overall energy consumption and thus substantial variances are noticed across the industry. However, various studies point out that hotel energy use is in the range of 200–600 kWh/m²/year (Energy Star Portfolio Manager Data Trends, 2015; Hotel Energy Solutions, 2011), keeping in mind the many factors listed above, in particular, the geographical location of hotels. Typically, about half the energy is used for thermal comfort, hence for space conditioning purposes (ventilating, heating, and cooling).

Purpose of Inquiry and Leading Questions

For this chapter and considering the growth of the hotel sector globally as well as the challenges posed by the science-based target presented previously, four key questions are asked:

1   *What type of hotel facilities are we currently building?*
2   *What type of hotel facilities are we planning to build in the next decade?*

And considering that once built, a hotel facility will not undergo major renovations and upgrades of some of the key components related to energy usage such as HVAC (heating, ventilation, and air conditioning) as well as insulation (windows, roofs, walls, etc.) within the first 10–20 years of the building, the third question is:

3   *Are those facilities being built and planned a liability to this and future generations considering the enormous task of regulating greenhouse gas emissions as per the Hotel Decarbonization Report?*

Finally, taking into consideration the short discussion on innovation, the fourth question is:

4   *What is the role played by radical innovations in regard to climate change impact mitigation and the hotel industry?*

The answer to these questions may on one hand give us theoretical insights on the linkages between innovations and sustainability in hospitality, and provide us with a more practical and entrepreneurial approach to identifying future sustainability innovations in the hospitality industry on the other hand. However, this is a preliminary study on complex issues. Conclusions are based on abductive reasoning. As such, this chapter is a foundation of a larger study which is based on the gathering of qualitative and quantitative data to either support or reject the results presented here based on literature review, previous studies, and observations.

Theoretical Framework

Unsustainable Production, Sustainable Production, and Production of Sustainability

Hotel operations that increase environmental, social, and economic capital beyond the expected through or supported by the development and implementation of new innovative radical solutions based on tackling urgent problems with a unique value proposition (Lindic and Marques, 2011) are what we define as *power-houses of sustainability*. Figure 13.1 illustrates the theoretical underpinning of the idea of *sustainability without limits*. The y-axis represents the condition of a chosen system. Systems can be represented by the state of the biodiversity or the climate but also by the physical environment or the community in which a hotel operates. Owners and managers of those operations are faced with multiple decisions, from long-term strategic choices to daily managerial and operational problem resolutions.

Unsustainable Production: Making Wrong Decisions

Should decisions be made based on unilateral procedures rather than taking into consideration the three pillars of sustainability being the economic, environmental, and social pillars, the results of those decisions may lead the business to an undesired future. A future where both the business and society or system condition are worse off. This situation is what we labeled as *unsustainable production* (see Figure 13.1). The constant pressure on all systems (biodiversity loss, climate risks, social inequity, etc.) resulting from a widespread, wide-scale system of unsustainable production inevitably leads to an uncertain, chaotic future.

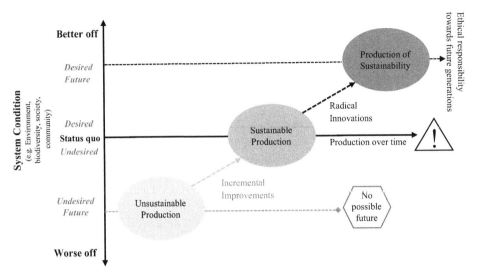

Figure 13.1 Radical innovation and production framework.

Sustainable Production: Aiming for Incremental Improvements

Due to multiple factors, from governmental and legislative pressure to consumer demands and non-governmental organization scrutiny, businesses, across a large spectrum of industry types, have incorporated (to some extent) sustainability within the organization. From Corporate Social Responsibility strategy to integrating the Sustainable Development Goals (SDGs), from climate initiatives towards zero carbon emissions to intense community involvement, incremental improvements make it possible for business to eventually attain a state of *sustainable production*. Sustainable production is what we also label as the *desired status quo*. Businesses that wish to go beyond *sustainable production* are rare, mostly due to the fact that reaching *sustainable production* is considered an enormous task by most businesses in the first place. Additionally, there is an inherent limit to the concept of sustainable production due to the sheer size of the industry growth as discussed previously, much of it which is not considered sustainable in any case. As such, over time, the impact of the aggregated growth and current supply is greater and not compensated by those few players reaching the *sustainable production* stage.

Production of Sustainability: Radical Innovations for a Desirable Future

Some entrepreneurs have managed to build and operate hotels that even *produce sustainability* instead of only repairing, recycling, offsetting, or limiting the impact of hospitality buildings and operations. In this sense, we can make a distinction between (1) *sustainable production* and (2) *production of sustainability* (see Figure 13.1). As stated above, (1) *sustainable production* happens when the output takes place in an ecological balance with the input used to the production. On the other hand, (2) *production of sustainability* takes place when the ecological, social, or climate systems are in better condition because the company is present in society. *Sustainable production* created by an increasing number of hotels around the world might be the result of several incremental improvements while the *production of sustainability* is a radical innovation with a lot of added value to the environmental, social, and economic pillars. The *production of sustainability* is in fact what we consider to be *sustainability without limits*.

Evidence of Sustainability without Limits

We investigate the field combining industry development observations and case study analysis. A purposive sampling approach is adopted whereby participants are recruited from *The Explorer Hotel Group* with hotels located in southern Germany and Austria, *Boutiquehotel Stadthalle* in Austria, the *Hotel Verde* in South Africa, *Soneva* in the Maldives and Thailand as well as *The Romantik Hotel Muottas Muragl* in Switzerland. Those five businesses, each in the hands of private owners and operators, have been identified as candidates providing evidence of 'sustainability without limits.' Each is described in further detail here and linked to Figure 13.1, Radical Innovation and Production Framework.

Sustainable Production Case 1: The Explorer Hotel Group

The Explorer Hotel Group, with hotels located in southern Germany and Austria, is one of the first hotel groups, with eight hotels and another 32 properties planned until 2027 (Leveringhaus, 2019) using passive-housing techniques in the building and operation of all its facilities. The result is a carbon neutral operation or near-carbon neutral also known as a Nearly Zero Energy Hotel (neZEH). The cutting edge in terms of energy efficiency in the field of ultra-low energy techniques and buildings is known as Passive Housing (*Passivhaus* in German). Key to Passive Housing is the maximum space heating requirements of 15 kilowatt-hours per square meter per year (kWh/m²/year) for *total energy use for all purposes* of 120 kWh/m²/year (Passivhaus, 2016; Passive House Institute, 2015). Since 2015, the standard for '*total energy use for all-purpose*' has been updated to "the total energy to be used for all domestic applications (heating, hot water and domestic electricity) [and] must not exceed 60 kWh per square meter of treated floor area per year for Passive House Classic" (Passivhaus, 2016). The additional energy needed is known as "Renewable Primary Energy Demand (PER)." The term 'Classic' refers to the traditional Passive House. Two additional categories have been introduced being the *Passive House Plus* and the *Passive House Premium*. A *Passive House Plus* produces additional energy (e.g., via photovoltaic panels) so as to achieve energy neutrality whereby the building produces about as much energy as the residents require and consume (Passivhaus, 2016). The *Passive House Premium* are buildings that produce far more energy than required and thus achieve a plus-energy status. Such buildings have an energy production standard of 120 kWh/m²/year. It is worth mentioning that in the case of *Passive House Premium*, the "*renewable energy generation plants which are not spatially connected to the building may also be taken into account (except for biomass use, waste-to-energy plants, and geothermal energy)*" (Passive House Institute, 2016, p. 6). A Passive House "*works similar to a thermos with very efficient thermal insulation of the building, with a ventilation system that allows for heat exchanger and recovery (to pre-heat outside air coming in the building)*" (Legrand and Schønrock Nielsen, 2017, p. 73). Additionally, Passive Housing puts a "*special emphasis on both the material used (thermal mass of material) and the orientation and lighting needs of the building (to maximise the use of the natural resources in terms of heat and light)*" (Legrand and Schønrock Nielsen, 2017, p. 73). Considering, that half of the current hotel average of 200–600 kWh/m²/year is energy used for space conditioning (so anywhere between 100 and 300 kWh/m²/year), there is room ahead for greater energy efficiency (Energy Star Portfolio Manager Data Trends, 2015; Hotel Energy Solutions, 2011). The Passivhaus Institut located in Germany also offers certification.

The owners of the Explorer Hotel Group have implemented the Passive Housing techniques and made the hotels an example of cutting edge energy efficiency. Catering to an active tourist and focusing on the beautiful outdoors, the chain is Europe's first certified passive energy hotel group (properties are certified *Passivhaus*) and 100% carbon neutral (Legrand and Schønrock Nielsen, 2017). The hotel has an overall 70% reduction in energy demand and reading an 85% reduction in energy required for heating considering the mountainous location of all hotels (Explorer Hotels, n.d.). One of the most interesting aspects of the case study is the expansion strategy which shows that Passive Housing techniques combined with a clear concept and well-thought-out environmental strategy payout. According to Figure 13.1, the Explorer Hotel Group belongs to the category of sustainable production due to the carbon neutrality of their operations. It can be argued that the growth in terms of new hotel properties, requiring raw material and resulting in a considerable amount of embodied energy, should be compensated. This compensation could be achieved if the building would be a *producer of sustainability* (see Figure 13.1) for example if the hotel is a net producer of energy, or plus-energy property and supplying the electricity grid for others to use.

Sustainable Production Case 2: Boutiquehotel Stadthalle

While the Explorer Hotel Group builds and operates hotel properties located in a rural, mountainous region which can be advantageous to harvest sunlight for the photovoltaic panels, for example, the Boutiquehotel Stadthalle is located in an urban center, the city of Vienna in Austria. Via a set of conscious practices, the 79-room boutique property has achieved the status of zero-energy balance, a first for an urban hotel. A series of remodeling and modernization of its main property with the addition of photovoltaic panels and the addition of 38 new rooms and suites in an adjacent building following passive housing techniques, the hotel now produces as much energy as is needed to operate (Leifer, 2017). Interesting features also include a roof-top lavender garden and a vertical garden on the façade.

Additionally, the most recent round of refurbishment of the seven rooms in the main building included many features using upcycling as the main driver for design. As examples, umbrellas became lampshades, empty bottles were turned into chandeliers, books were transformed into bedside tables, cutlery was repurposed as clothes hangers, tennis rackets turned into mirrors, and wood pallets used for shelving (Leifer, 2017). The hotel strives to achieve zero-waste status. Similar to the Hotel Explorer Group, the Boutiquehotel Stadthalle is a prime example of *sustainable production* (see Figure 13.1) due to the carbon neutrality of their operations and the overall effort on upcycling.

Sustainable Production Case 3: Hotel Verde in South Africa

The third case, Hotel Verde, is based in Cape Town, South Africa. The region, Sub-Saharan Africa, is at the forefront of climate change threats which already present itself in the form of severe resource scarcity, in particular water (Flynn, 2018; Welch, 2018). This 145-room airport hotel is 100% carbon neutral (Farrell, 2017). A series of interventions were necessary to achieve this status including the implementation of *"3 vertical axis wind turbines, 220 photovoltaic panels, an intelligent building management system, geothermal technology, regenerative drive elevators, a greywater recycling and rainwater capture system, responsible procurement, waste management and biodiversity management"* (Farrell, 2017, p. 30). Similar to the Explorer Hotel Group and the Boutiquehotel Stadthalle, Hotel Verde implemented a series of passive design features to optimize the overall building efficiency. The passive design features include natural ventilation, improved insulation, night cooling as well as natural lighting. In 2016, Hotel Verde became *"the first hotel in the world to be certified LEED Platinum (Leadership in Energy and Environmental Design) for both New Construction and Operations and Maintenance from the United States Green Building Council"* (Farrell, 2017, p. 31). Hotel Verde is also categorized as sustainable production within Figure 13.1, Radical Innovation and Production Framework. It achieves 100% carbon neutrality by offsetting scope 1 and 2 emissions by purchasing certified carbon credits. Scope 1 emissions are *"direct emissions from owned or controlled sources"*

(WRI and WBCSD, n.d.) such as natural gas, refrigerants, or gasoline usage. Scope 2 is *"indirect emissions from the generation of purchased energy"* (WRI and WBCSD, n.d.) such as electricity sourced from the public grid. Those purchased carbon credits then benefit socially responsible environmental projects in the Lake Kariba area in Zimbabwe which include reforestation, sustainable farming, and job creation (Farrell, 2017).

Sustainable Production Case 4: Soneva in the Maldives and Thailand

The fourth case is of particular interest as it is located in atolls of the Maldives. Storlazzi et al. (2018) in an article published in *Science Advances* argue that many of those atoll islands will become uninhabitable by mid-21st century due to the constant and frequent damages to the infrastructures from repeated annual flooding. When establishing the Soneva Fushi, the very first Soneva resort, it was a priority to have the highest sustainability standards in place from the start. This included material used for the construction, such as wood, and interior design. Considering the impacts linked to the use of energy and the challenges posed by decarbonization, the Soneva Fushi has put in place a 700 kWp (kilowatt peak) solar photovoltaic (solar PV) panels system which partly covers the electricity needs throughout daytime (Shivdasani, 2019). Kilowatt 'peak' is the amount of power generated when panels are working at full capacity for one hour. Soneva Fushi is planning to install a further 2 MWp (megawatt peak) solar PV along with 3 MW (Megawatt) of batteries for energy storage for both Soneva Fushi and another Soneva Resort, the Soneva Jani (Shivdasani, 2019). The expansion of PV and additionally storage capacity will result in complete reliance on renewable energy during the day (Shivdasani, 2019). The resort also implemented a mandatory 2% environmental levy to the guests' bills as a way to offset the travel emissions. The funds are then invested in carbon mitigation projects such as *"planting half a million trees in Thailand, funding a wind turbine in India and providing over 240,000 people with energy efficient cookstoves in Darfur and Myanmar"* (Shivdasani, 2019, p. 37). The result is carbon neutrality for both direct and indirect operations at the resort, which includes guest flights to and from the Maldives. The Soneva Fushi resort is another example of *sustainable production* (see Figure 13.1).

Production of Sustainability Case: Romantik Hotel Muottas Muragl, Switzerland

The fifth, and final, case is an example of a hotel that fits within the *production of sustainability* concept as shown in Figure 13.1. The Romantik Hotel Muottas Muragl, located in Samedan, Switzerland was the first plus-energy hotel in the Swiss Alps. As such, the property produces more energy per year than required for its operation (Sloan et al., 2013). Following major renovation and construction with an increase of 50% in heated floor space, the hotel was able to reduce its energy required by two-thirds following the renovation (Sloan et al., 2013) from 436,600 kWh/year to 157,400 kWh/year (Muottas Muralg, 2019). A combination of a photovoltaic system, solar water system and geothermal plant allows for carbon neutral operations. A total of 56 m² tubular collectors placed on the windows provide the necessary energy required for hot water (Muottas Muralg, 2019). Sixteen earth probes supply the building with geothermal energy and the photovoltaic system placed along the railway track generates the required electrical energy (Muottas Muralg, 2019). In the event of excess solar energy, it *"is stored in the thermal loop field in the ground and drawn on when required by means of a heat pump"* (Sloan et al., 2013, p. 55). Finally, waste heat is recovered from cooling systems, engine room and exhaust air provides an additional source of energy (Muottas Muralg, 2019). The overall focus is thus on plus-energy buildings. As stated above, *"these are concepts that generate more renewable energy for heating, hot water production and air replenishment than they need themselves*" (Muottas Muralg, n.d., p. 6). The *production of sustainability* as demonstrated by the Romantik Hotel Muottas Muragl is in fact what we consider to be a hotel fitting our understanding of a *sustainability without limits*.

Concluding Remarks

Sustainability without limits is our attempt at a theoretical concept that can explain how innovations implemented by hoteliers are key in addressing solutions to urgent challenges linked to climate change. The cases presented are different in many aspects from the type and location of the property but all share one particular commonality: the strong desire to be part of a solution. This, according to our framework, is achieved at various levels. Four of the five hotels presented are categorized as '*sustainable production*' whereby one common goal is carbon neutrality. The fifth property is categorized as '*production of sustainability*.' Production of sustainability is one more step in the framework whereby the hotel manages to produce sustainability, in this case being additional energy, which can be used by others within the electricity grid system. Considering the global growth of the hospitality industry, projects which are *producing* rather than '*using*' resources should be attractive to many parties. The investors are wanting to differentiate in their investment portfolio; the operators wishing to have highly efficient (and low cost) buildings; and supported by governments in their claims (hopes!) to meet climate targets.

Limitations and Future Research

This conceptual chapter suffers from the scarcity of literature on some of the concepts explored. It is however an open door to future research on the subject of radical innovations in the hospitality industry, linked to climate change mitigation, with the goal to help industry innovators to become 'producers of sustainability.' In particular, the use of case study analysis of practices (what works, what does not) in the 'production of sustainability' in hospitality would be beneficial to give confidence to newcomers in hospitality and yet kick-start more radical sustainable innovations in this industry.

References

Bauman, Z. ([1992] 2015), *Intimations of Postmodernity*, Routledge, London, UK.

Bauman, Z. (2002), *Society Under Siege*, Polity Press, Cambridge, MA.

Certini, G. and Scalenghe, R. (2015), "Holocene as anthropocene", *Science*, Vol.349, No.6245 [online], available at: doi: 10.1126/science.349.6245.246-a (accessed 18 February 2019).

Christensen, C.M. ([1997] 2016), *The Innovators Dilemma. When New Technologies Cause Great Firms to Fail*, Harvard Business Review, Boston, US.

Christensen, C.M., Hall, T., Dillon, K., and Duncan, D.S. (2016), *Competition Against Luck. The Story of Innovation and Customer Choise*, HarperCollins, New York, NY.

Energy Star Portfolio Manager Data Trends. (2015) *Energy Use in Hotels* [Online], available at: https://www.energystar.gov/sites/default/files/tools/DataTrends_Hotel_20150129.pdf (accessed 18 February 2019).

Explorer Hotels. (n.d.) *What Exactly Is a Passive Hotel?* [Online], available at: https://www.explorer-hotels.com/en/sustainable/ (accessed 18 February 2019).

Farrell, S. (2017), "Challenges and opportunities in sustainable hotel development in sub-Saharan Africa: A case study of Hotel Verde, Africa's greenest hotel", in Legrand, W. (Ed.), *The Hotel Yearbook Special Edition – Sustainable Hospitality 2018*, Wade and Company SA, Maastricht, The Netherlands, pp.30–31.

Flynn, J. (2018), *How Cape Town Defeated Day Zero – For Now* [Online], available at: https://pulitzercenter.org/reporting/how-cape-town-defeated-day-zero-now (accessed 18 February 2019).

Hotel Energy Solutions. (2011) *Analysis on Energy Use by European Hotels: Online Survey and Desk Research* [Online], available at: https://hes.unwto.org/sites/all/files/docpdf/analysisonenergyusebyeuropeanhotelsonlinesurveyanddeskresearch2382011-1.pdf (accessed 19 February 2019).

HotelManagement. (2018) *These Two Countries Have 61% of the World's Hotel Pipeline* [Online], available at: https://www.hotelmanagement.net/own/these-two-countries-have-61-world-s-hotel-pipeline (accessed 17 February 2019).

IBISWorld. (2018), *Global Hotels and Resorts Industry: Industry Market Research Report* [Online], available at: https://www.ibisworld.com/industry-trends/global-industry-reports/hotels-restaurants/hotels-resorts.html (accessed 17 February 2019).

Ilegbune, T. (2016), "The land use act, Nigerian urban and regional planning act, and climate change in Nigeria?" in Utuama, A.A. (Ed.), *Critical Issues in Nigerian Property Law*, Malthouse Press, Lagos, Nigeria.

ITP. (2017), *Hotel Global Decarbonization Report* [Online], available at: https://www.tourismpartnership.org/blog/itp-carbon-report-provides-hotel-sectors-goal-mitigate-climate-change/ (accessed 18 February 2019).

Legrand, W. and Schønrock Nielsen, R. (2016), "The construction of climate-conscious identity through innovation in the hospitality industry", in *EuroCHRIE Congress*, 26–28 October 2016, Budapest, Hungary.

Legrand, W. and Schønrock Nielsen, R. (2017), "Climate-conscious identity and climate-adaptive innovations in hospitality", in Chen, J.S. (Ed.), *Advances in Hospitality and Leisure*, Vol.13, Emerald Publishing Limited, pp.63–78 [online], available at: https://doi.org/10.1108/S1745-354220170000013006 (accessed 18 February 2019).

Legrand, W., Sloan, P., and Chen, J.S. (2016), *Sustainability in the Hospitality Industry: Principles of Sustainable Operations*, 3rd ed., Routledge, London, UK.

Leifer, M. (2017), "Vienna's Boutiquehotel Stadthalle: 'Be the change you want to see in the world' " in Legrand, W. (Ed.), *The Hotel Yearbook Special Edition – Sustainable Hospitality 2018*, Wade and Company SA, Maastricht, The Netherlands, pp.56–57.

Leveringhaus, K. (2019), "Explorer hotels: A discovery voyage and best practice in passive housing' in Legrand, W. (ed.), *The Hotel Yearbook Special Edition – Sustainable Hospitality 2020*, WIWIH AG, Maastricht, The Netherlands, pp.28–31.

Loytard, J.F. (1984), "The postmodern condition: A report on knowledge", *Theory and History of Literature*, Manchester University Press, Manchester, UK.

Lindic, J. and Marques, C. (2011), "Value proposition as a catalyst for customer focused innovation", *Management Decision*, Vol.49, No.10 [Online], available at https://doi.org/10.1108/00251741111183834 (accessed 18 February 2019).

Muottas Muralg. (2019), *Erstes Plusenergie-Hotel der Alpen* [Online], available at: https://www.mountains.ch/de/hotels/romantikhotel-muottas/ueber-uns/plusenergie-hotel (accessed 20 March 2019).

Muottas Muralg. (n.d.), *Plus-Energy Hotel in the Engadin Sunlight* [Online], available at: http://www.clean-energy.ch/fileadmin/user_upload_cleanenergy/user_upload/pdf/Muottas_Muragl_e_Flyer_Plusenergie.pdf (accessed 20 March, 2019).

Passivhaus. (2016), *Der Passivhausstandard* [Online], available at: https://www.passivhaus.de/passivhaus/ (accessed 20 March 2019).

Passive House Institute. (2015), *Passive House Requirements* [Online], available at: https://passivehouse.com/02_informations/02_passive-house-requirements/02_passive-house-requirements.htm (accessed 20 March, 2019).

Passive House Institute. (2016), *Criteria for the Passive House, EnerPHit and PHI Low Energy Building Standard* [Online], available at: https://passiv.de/downloads/03_building_criteria_en.pdf (accessed 20 March 2019).

Porter, M. (2004), *Competitive Advantage: Creating and Sustaining Superior Performance*, Free Press., New York, NY.

Schumpeter, J.A. (1934), "The theory of economic development", *Journal of Political Economy*, Vol.8, No.5 [in Baumol, W.J. (1990), *Entrepreneurship: Productive, Unproductive, and Destructive*, The University of Chicago].

Shivdasani, S. (2019), "Decarbonization of the global hotel industry", in Legrand, W. (Ed.), *The Hotel Yearbook Special Edition – Sustainable Hospitality 2020*, WIWIH AG, Maastricht, The Netherlands, pp.36–37.

Sloan, P., Legrand, W., and Chen, J.S. (2013), *Sustainability in the Hospitality Industry: Principles of Sustainable Operations*, 2nd ed., Routledge, Oxford, UK.

Statista. (2018), *Hotels Global* [Online], available at: https://www.statista.com/outlook/267/100/hotels/worldwide?currency=eur#market-revenue (accessed 17 February 2019).

Steffen, W, Broadgate, W, Deutsch, L., Gaffney, O., and Ludwig, C. (2015), "The trajectory of the Anthropocene: The great acceleration", *The Anthropocene Review* [online], available at https://doi.org/10.1177/2053019614564785 (accessed 17 February 2019).

Storlazzi, C.D., Gingerich, S.B., van Dongeren, A., Cheriton, O.M., Swrzenski, P.W., Quataert, E., Voss, C.I., Field, D.W., Annalai, H., Piniak, G.A., and McCall, R. (2018), "Most atolls will be uninhabitable by the mid-21st century because of sea-level rise exacerbating wave-driven flooding", *Science Advances*, Vol. 4, No. 4 [online], available at DOI: 10.1126/sciadv.aap9741 (accessed 17 February 2019).

UNEP DTIE. (2013), *Cities and Buildings* [Online], available at: http://energies2050.org/wp-content/uploads/2013/09/2013-06-UNEP-Cities-and-buildings-activities_16-pages-GB.pdf (Accessed 19 February 2019).

UNFCCC. (2015) *Adoption of the Paris Agreement* [Online], available at: https://unfccc.int/resource/docs/2015/cop21/eng/l09r01.pdf (accessed 17 February 2019).

UNFCCC. (2019) *What Is the Paris Agreement?* [Online], available at: https://unfccc.int/process-and-meetings/the-paris-agreement/what-is-the-paris-agreement (accessed 17 February 2019).

UNWTO. (2017) *UNWTO Tourism Highlights, 2017 Edition* [Online], available at: https://www.e-unwto.org/doi/pdf/10.18111/9789284419029 (accessed 17 February 2019).

UNWTO. (2018) *International Tourism Exceeds Expectations in the First Months of 2018* [Online], available at: http://media.unwto.org/press-release/2018-06-25/international-tourism-exceeds-expectations-first-months-2018 (accessed 17 February 2019).

WCED. (1987) *Report of the World Commission on Environment and Development: Our Common Future* [Online], available at: http://www.un-documents.net/our-common-future.pdf (accessed 17 February 2019).

Welch, C. (2018) *Why Cape Town Is Running Out of Water, and Who's Next* [Online], available at: https://news.nationalgeographic.com/2018/02/cape-town-running-out-of-water-drought-taps-shutoff other-cities/ (accessed 19 February 2019).

WRI and WBCSD. (n.d.) *FAQ Greenhouse Gas Protocol* [Online], available at: https://ghgprotocol.org/sites/default/files/standards_supporting/FAQ.pdf (accessed 20 March 2019).

14

HOTEL ASSET MANAGEMENT

A Professional Approach and
International Perspective

Florian Aubke and Theodor Kubak

Introduction

'Asset Management – Here to Stay' is what Deborah Feldman put forward in her early academic publications on hotel asset management in 1995. Since then, the hotel industry at large experienced fundamental structural changes, which fueled the evolution of hotel asset management (HAM). Most notably, the emergence of silent investors with a thirst for hotels commercial real estate which in turn entrusted the operation of the properties to independent operators (Denton, 2009). Some 14 years later, the hotel industry has largely turned into an investment marketplace and playground for owners and operators. As an investment, hotels are "income-producing assets, which are bought, developed, operated and disposed at the appropriate time" (Jackson, 2013, p. 92). The achievement of investment goals is, therefore, dependent on the effective operational and strategic property management. Increasingly, owners seek specialized expertise for maximizing the long-term value of the real estate investment. In the financial services industry, asset management is the process of managing investments for clients (Singh et al., 2012). Consequently, hotel asset management has evolved from a niche service to an organized profession of high strategic relevance.

This chapter intends to provide the reader with a fundamental understanding of the genesis and evolution of the HAM profession, its principles, and practices. It can serve as a reference for introductory units in hotel asset management but also as a starting point for developing research agendas in this field. First, the state-of-art of the asset management profession is discussed, including international developments. An exemplary asset management process is outlined based on the Temple Bar Hotel project in Dublin, Ireland. The chapter concludes with an outlook for the HAM profession.

The Genesis of the Hotel Asset Management Profession

Stephen Rushmore succinctly described the asset management function as follows:

> *In general terms, hotel asset management is the service of assisting hotel owners in realizing their investment goals. Asset managers act as owner's agent or representative to ensure that a hotel is acquired for a reasonable price; is then operated properly during the period of ownership; and ultimately is disposed of at an appropriate time and price.*
>
> *(Rushmore, 1994, p. 20)*

As changes in the hotel industry happen gradually, no definite date or event marks the genesis of hotel asset management. However, authors agree that the key factor, which triggered the evolution of the HAM profession, is the aftermath of the 1980s US-American development bubble and the simultaneous economic downturn (Singh et al., 2012). In this environment, many hotel properties came in distress, and banks found themselves as involuntary owners of hotel real estate. Institutional investors also discovered hotels as an asset class worthy of investment. Institutional investors, Real-Estate Investment Trusts (REITs) and investment funds increasingly became owners of hotel real estate, yet were in dire need of operational expertise to guarantee the desired returns. In consequence, hotel management companies shifted their business model from owner-operated businesses to hotel operating companies, which manage the hotel property on behalf of the owner. The relationship between owner and operator is regulated in a management contract, an operating mode that is nowadays found in all major markets (de Roos, 2012).

The lack of operating expertise on the side of the owners was overcome by hiring operating companies that managed the hotel on behalf of the owner, in return for a fee. While this freed the owner from the burden of operation, it created the need to control the activities of the operators and to monitor the performance. Both owners and management companies could now focus on their core skills, but former hotel management agreements typically granted management companies extensive decision-making authority (Beals and Denton, 1995), leaving the owners with limited control over their investment. According to Eyster (1997), owners were increasingly dissatisfied with the goal misalignment of the two parties and demanded greater influence on the decisions that affected their investment.

In order to overcome this dilemma, owners employed asset managers to ensure that their properties are managed viably. Management contracts regulate the agent-principle relationship of owners and operators, whereas operators manage the property (as agent) on behalf of the owner (as principle). Although the distribution of power shifted with the evolution of hotel management contracts (de Roos, 2010; Eyster, 1993) the operators still generate the greatest proportion of their income through fees and reimbursable charges based on top-line revenues. Seldom operators are incentivized to make decisions, which are in the owner's best interest (Turner and Guilding, 2010). Consequently, the owner's investment goals, which involves bottom-line cash flows and debt services, are typically not one of the operator's primary concerns. Owner's, therefore, have a strong interest in closely monitoring operators' activities and decisions in managing the property, at least because owners carry most of the financial risk of the operation. In recent years, owners managed to strengthen their position in hotel management agreements through performance clauses and guarantees (Beals and Denton, 2005; de Roos, 2010), yet they still often struggle to get a strong hold on operating issues. Whilst it is now relatively common for the owner to have a vote in appointing the General Manager, the operator has a strong interest in defending their non-disturbance clause in management contracts, leaving them with relative freedom for operational decisions. The scope of influence and reciprocal attempts to gain advantage out of the partnership has long been a matter of dispute.

The owner-operator relationship (and thus the emergence of the hotel asset management function) can be best explained through agency theory (Eisenhardt, 1989). In this view, owners are principles who contract a management company as agents to operate the hotel property on their behalf. The challenge in this relationship is that each party has a set of own goals, which may be in conflict. This poses a challenge primarily for the owner as their investment is at stake. Owners, therefore, attempt to mitigate the agency problem by negotiating hotel management contracts that provide them with extensive rights of control and then hire or employ asset managers to perform these duties. The asset manager thus enters the owner-operator relationship as an additional agent to overseeing the long-term value of the property. Accordingly, hotel asset managers are hired by hotel owners in order to "make recommendations about the operating performance, physical plant, market position, and management" of a hotel (Brener, 1991, p. 21). Whilst hotel asset managers are more likely to be hired in the case of a hotel management agreement (Hodari et al., 2018), advising owners on the optimal operating mode and selection of operators fall under the responsibility of the hotel asset manager.

Besides a few seminal articles describing the genesis and evolution of hotel asset management (Beals, 1996; Brener, 1991; Singh et al., 2012), the literature is scarce. Feldman (1995) reports on a series of qualitative interviews with members of the Hospitality Asset Managers Association (HAMA) and provides a first comprehensive record of the roles and tasks of hotel asset managers. In 2012, Singh et al. undertook an empirical study also with members of HAMA. The authors assert that with the evolution of the hotel industry, the roles of hotel asset managers changed accordingly. What used to be a control function set forth by the owner, driven by management contracts that often favored operators, is today more of an intermediary between the operating and investment discipline. As such, hotel asset managers are expected to align the goals of owners and operators and as such, somewhat equalize the power relationship of the two. The perceived misalignment of the owner and operator goals formed the basis for the investigations by Hodari et al. (2017, 2018).

In 1991, a group of six hotel asset managers, all facing similar issues, held their first organized meeting back and initiated the HAMA. The founding members of what was to become the Hotel Asset Manager Association early established a loose platform to exchange information and to enhance the value of their respective hotels. The group soon realized that the united front to the much larger and well organized larger branded hotel companies had an effect and started to organize themselves in a non-profit association, scheduling regular meetings and structuring a platform for ongoing exchange for a broader group of likeminded hotel owners and hotel asset managers. The membership has grown steadily since to its current 200 count in the USA. In 2013 through 2015 chapters in Europe, Middle East Africa, Asia Pacific, China, and Japan all established a presence to support investors and hotel owners.

Today Hotel Asset Managers are required to conduct and bring together a wide range of disciplines that ultimately, very much like an orchestra, when harmoniously acting together and, subject to the investors' objectives, focusing on different levers, can produce outstanding results. One of these best in class examples are described herein. The Temple Bar Hotel in Dublin was the worthy recipient of the HAMA Europe Asset Management Achievement Award of 2017. Since 2015, HAMA Europe with the help of a distinguished international panel of judges representing asset managers, architects, owners and investors, debt providers, developers, and media on an annual basis has been recognizing these concerted efforts.

Internationally, the HAM profession has developed at different speeds, largely due to local intricacies such as preferred operating forms, the role of institutional investors, and the maturity of the hotel real estate market. Arguably, the North American Hotel Investment and Asset Management space has the longest tradition. Due to the institutional character in many parts of Europe, Hotel Asset Management has found its way into the set-up of professional investors and service providers alike as of 2010. Table 14.1 lists the top 25 global Hotel Asset Management Companies.

The capital source varies between private owners that hold just a few assets to REITs and Fund structure that hold multiple properties. With the *Asset Light Strategy* by the brands that manifested itself at the turn of the century many brands either divested and sold the actual building or split the company into a property company ("PropCo") and an operational company ("OpCo"). As a result, many of the brands are now employing their own Hotel Asset Management personnel or have set up an entire Hotel Asset Management Group to control the OpCo on behalf of the PropCo.

Whereas the USA is a homogeneous contract landscape that is dominated by Franchise and Management Agreements, Europe – also due to its multiple jurisdictions and its history – is very fragmented. In some countries such as Austria, Germany, and Scandinavia, long-term lease agreements have a strong presence whereas in other countries such as the UK, Spain, most parts of

Table 14.1 Top 25 Global hotel asset management companies

Asset management company	Properties	Rooms
Hilton AssetMgt	92	32,609
Park Hotel & Resorts REIT	51	29,917
BRE Hotels & Resorts LLC	159	29,470
CHMWarnick	57	26,608
Event Hotelgruppe AssetMgt	77	13,962
WHI	45	12,122
Rockbridge Capital, LLC	59	11,590
Japan Hotel REIT Advisors	42	11,092
Pyman Hospitality Properties	7	10,110
Hamilton Hotel Partners Assetm	54	9,832
Millennium & Copthorne Hotels	42	9,695
Colliers International Group Inc.	49	8,043
The Chartres Lodging Group	10	7,803
Garfield Traub Development	17	7,732
Capital Hotel Management	13	7,639
Axios	34	7,496
Hoshino Resort Asset Management Co., Ltd.	55	6,748
Michels and Taylor	39	6,201
Omni Hotels & Resorts	12	5,289
hotelAVE	16	4,745
M&L Hospitality	12	3,653
SilverBirch Hotels & Resorts	10	3,460
Woodbine Development Corp	5	2,943
SAMHI Hotels Private Limited	18	2,795
Island Hospitality Management	19	2,599

Source: STR Global.
Note: As of April 2019.

the Middle East and Africa, Asia Pacific, and China there is a clear preference for Management Agreement Structures. The exceptions have Japan and Singapore that could be regarded as mature markets; lease agreements within the hospitality sector have been preferred by some. With markets maturing, brands are generally feeling more comfortable in also granting franchise and license agreement to White Label Operators and Investors/Operators alike. Contrary to Management Agreements, with a long-term Lease Agreement the commercial risk is almost entirely shifted from the owner to the tenant. In such a case, the focus of the asset manager is still very much to protect and enhance the value. Contrary to the Asset Manager of a managed property who actively proposes measures to enhance and improve the operation, the involvement of the asset manager under a lease agreement is one which is best described with an auditor who monitors and flags any situation that might pose a threat to the asset value. Such threats could be lack of investment into the property to keep up the standards, low rent coverage, use of rent guarantees, and similar.

The Hotel Asset Management Process

The hotel asset manager's overarching task is to ensure the long-term value appreciation of the investment. In contrast to other forms of real-estate such as housing and office space, hotels generate revenue through the short-term utilization of the asset, rather than long-term leases. Hotel rooms are sold daily, other revenue-generating facilities such as food and beverage outlets and leisure facilities accommodate guests on a use basis, too. Given this specificity of hotel real estate, an effective asset utilization is paramount for reaching the investment goals. One, the asset manager will have to ensure that the property generates returns on capital employed in excess of the cost of capital. Second, properties are typically valued based on expected future cash flows (Rushmore, 2001). Thus superior operating and financial performance is elementary for achieving the long-term investment goals. As outlined before, the hotel asset manager acts as an intermediary between owners and operators, with the aim to align the business interests of both parties. The primary interest of the operator lies in the generation of fees and reimbursable charges, most of which are based on revenues achieved. The owner is concerned with net cash flows and, consequentially, long-term value appreciation of the asset. In the delicate act of balancing both interests, one shall not forget that the asset manager carries fiduciary responsibility to the ownership. In this role, asset managers advise the owner along the entire investment cycle. Boettger (2009) proposes four phases of the HAM process:

1   Determining ownership objectives
2   Acquiring and absorbing the asset
3   Unlocking value and monitoring operating performance
4   Disposing of the asset

Hotel owners come in many forms, and their philosophies regarding capital investment, investment horizon, and risk tolerance can differ significantly. Typically, future hotel owners seek the expertise of asset managers prior to asset acquisition. Only then, asset managers are able to match investment opportunities with the needs and requirements of investors.

The value creation through hotel asset management requires the interplay of a number of elements (see Figure 14.1). While all elements can form the basis of HAM activities, the needs of the investor determine the scope and time invested in each component of the asset management process.

Value creation is the key objective of hotel asset management. In turn, successful HAM assignments are evaluated based on the values they created. Since 2016, HAMA Europe has recognized outstanding achievements of repositioning and value add activities within the hospitality industry on an annual basis. Figure 14.2 demonstrates the values added across all entries for the HAMA Europe Asset Management Achievement Award for the years 2017–2019. The numbers provided are a good indication that effective asset management has a strong potential for value enhancement and value protection of the asset.

In 2018, the following asset management activities were recognized by HAMA Europe (Kubak, 2018):

•   The *Overall Asset Management Achievement Award* was presented to The Global Holdings: The Pulitzer Amsterdam project focused on the renovation of the famous Pulitzer Amsterdam hotel including the renovation of the 25 independent 17th and 18th century canal houses, launch of new F&B outlets as well as the launch of the Pulitzer brand positioned as a unique independent hotel creating an authentic Amsterdam experience. Billy Skelli-Cohen, Managing Director of Global Holdings, said:

> *With the renovation and re-positioning of the new Pulitzer Amsterdam we achieved something unique in the world. We took all that was great already about this property and added the right elements to make it even better. We injected new life into historic buildings with a fantastic design, giving longevity for the next decades to come.*

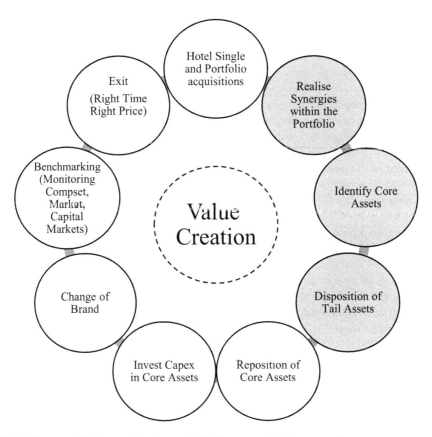

Figure 14.1 Elements of value creation through HAM processes (author created).
Note: Shaded fields are relevant for portfolio management.

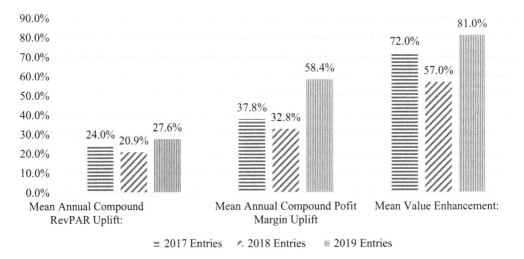

Figure 14.2 Asset management initiatives maximize value KPIs across applicable entries.

- The *Value Add Strategy* was presented to Art Invest Real Estate Management: The Le Méridien Frankfurt was focused on the complete restructuring of a 300-guest room hotel in a prime location in Frankfurt. By effectively combining its real estate construction know-how with its expertise in the hotel business Art-Invest overcame legal risks arising from the acquisition out of insolvency by restructuring the operational framework together with Munich Hotel Partners as well as technical risks with regard to the building condition. Due to the owner's insolvency and existing over-rent, the property suffered from a significant maintenance backlog. About €12.0 million were invested in the refurbishment and modernization including the renovation of the guest rooms and bathrooms as well as the refurbishment including a complete restructuring of all public areas to improve operating efficiency. After completion of the business plan, the asset was sold to First Sponsor Group from Singapore at the end of 2017. Dr. Peter Ebertz, Managing Partner and Head of Hotels at Art-Invest, said:

> *The Le Méridien is a prime example for the successful implementation of a value add strategy by restructuring the operational model and by repositioning an old hotel through an extensive refurbishment program. In line with Art-Invest's "Manage-to-Core" approach, we spotted the asset in a difficult owner situation, identified its potential and developed a strategy for value creation. After successful implementation of the defined strategy, the property sold just 2.5 years after acquisition. With passion for hotel real estate and faith in the future of the hotel we created a hotel that not only meets the requirements of today's traveler, but also the demands of international investors.*

Asset Management Case – Temple Bar Hotel

After the broad introduction to the evolution and principles of Hotel Asset Management, the following section is dedicated to the HAM activities and processes. The classic HAM processes, as outlined above, are exemplified on a redevelopment project of 'Temple Bar Hotel' (TBH) in Dublin, Ireland under the management and supervision of Pyramid Hotel Ltd.[1]

Hotel Asset Managers facilitate the management of income-producing assets, thus overseeing the product life cycle from acquisition to management and eventually, the disposal of the hotel property at an appropriate time. During this time, the asset manager acts as an advisor to the owner of the property whilst ensuring the investment goals of the owner are met.

In 2015, Pyramid Hotel Group (PHG), together with a major equity partner, acquired the 3-star independent hotel located at the edge of the Temple Bar district in Dublin, Ireland for €27.25 million (€206k per key). Upon acquisition, the property had 132 keys, three F&B outlets as well as one meeting room. The investment thesis meant the acquisition, renovation, and repositioning of the asset as a 4-star property. In December 2016, the virtual asset sold for €55.1 million (€405k per key). During a 21-month investment cycle, asset value was increased by €27.85 million or 102.2%. The project generated returns of 88.4%. For PHG, this was the first assignment of its kind in Europe.

Acquiring and Absorbing the Asset

Prior to the acquisition of the asset in early 2015, PHG was actively involved in sourcing the asset, monitoring the underwriting process, and conducting a comprehensive Due Diligence on the asset and the investment opportunity. During this phase, highest and best use analyses were conducted to find opportunities to unlock the value of the property. The key actions and initiatives were as follows.

Determining the Ownership Objectives

For the joint venture, it was intended to leverage a revitalized product in a unique location to strengthen existing leisure demand and replace low yielding segments with previously neglected corporate business. The investor, a global private equity fund with a strong affinity for real estate, is specialized in acquiring underperforming assets and initiating a turn-around process. Thus, unlike other institutional investors, a short holding period was sought with superior return opportunities. PHG acted as a minority equity holder and contributes its hotel management and project management expertise to the joint venture. Although PHG entered the joint venture to manage the property in the long term, the initial focus was on advising the major equity partner on the acquisition of the property and on guiding the turn-around process. In essence, the interests of the joint venture partners were aligned.

Unlocking Value and Monitoring Operating Performance

In terms of operations, the goal was the implementation of PHG's quality-, project-, and cost-management practices as well as considering alternative uses of existing Food & Beverage facilities. Over the 21-month holding period, the joint venture has undertaken a number of key initiatives to improve both, the physical asset as well the operating efficiency.

Changes to the Physical Asset

Upon acquisition, the key count of the property was 132 keys. After detailed assessment of the current space utilization, it was decided to convert three admin offices to guestrooms. Additionally, one shared bedroom (containing eight beds) was converted into two keys. These changes increased the key by net 4–136.

The original product was considered a low 3-star facility with significant deferred maintenance and a lack of cleanliness. An initial deep clean of the asset was conducted, followed by a re-integration of the housekeeping function in order to maintain superior cleanliness levels. A comprehensive renovation in the scope of €6.2 million (€46k per key) was undertaken including bringing all Fire, Life and Safety systems up to code. As a result, the property can now be considered a 4-star equivalent with an improved look and feel for guests and employees. During the renovation, PHG applied aggressive project management, thus minimizing renovation displacement and still achieved above-market RevPAR growth.

The original property included a large basement venue, named Alchemy Nightclub. The venue had been in operation for over seven years and had undergone a renovation for over €2 million only a year before the joint venture acquired the Temple Bar Hotel. During the due diligence process, it was ascertained that the current facility was unlikely to provide the necessary returns in due time, primarily because the nightclub business in Dublin has migrated from the Temple Bar district to other parts of the city. Consequently, PHG developed a unique-to-market social sports and games bar after realizing that there are plenty of spaces in Dublin to get a beer, but few places support social and active gatherings. The new 'Busker's – On The Ball' required a €400k renovation, and now provides pool, ping-pong, foosball, and shuffleboard tables plus a video wall for sport event broadcasting. In the first five months of operations, the new venue generated in excess of €550k in total revenue, which was €300k above the 2016 budget. A pizza-based new food concept, utilizing a former cloakroom for the pizza oven, was introduced to drive F&B revenue while not pushing the existing kitchen beyond its capacity.

Changes to Revenue Management and Operations

Upon acquisition, the employee count was at 106 full-time equivalents (FTEs) with an annual payroll of €2.62 million. Through PHG's operational experience, the employee count was reduced by 33 FTEs (−31%), resulting in a payroll reduction by €167k (−6.4%). Notably, this was achieved whilst elevating service levels to 4-star expectations and bringing the entire housekeeping back in-house. All staff reductions were achieved through attrition. At the original Temple Bar Hotel, F&B accounted for half the overall revenue. Therefore PHG put a strong focus on this part of the business. By improving the food quality and menu, applying light refurbishment to revitalize space and an optimized seating scheme the total food revenue could be increased by 35% from €651k pre-acquisition to €877k year-end 2016. Breakfast pricing was increased considerably from €6 to €19.95 to reflect the overall improvement of facility levels of the property and pricing levels of competitors. The price increase was introduced in phases and did not result in noticeable capture loss. PHG aggressively leveraged local relationships with suppliers and utilized creative stock subsidy deals to optimize terms. As a result, F&B Cost of Goods Sold went down 1.9% for Food (from 28.1%) and 6.1% for Beverage (from 29.4%).

As far as rooms are concerned, the previous management placed heavy reliance on FIT & Tour business, accounting for 28% of all room nights at the below-market contracted rate of €84. In 2015, PHG optimized the remaining segments whilst enduring the legacy FIT & Tour Business until these contracts expired. As a result, the hotel experienced a 21.3% RevPAR growth, nearly matching market growth. Post-renovation in 2016, strategic pursuit of the corporate segment was implemented. This resulted in RevPAR growth of 26.4%, well above market growth. Channel management was optimized by implementing sophisticated geo-marketing and direct booking incentives. In 2016, direct bookings were up 26% year-on-year with corresponding revenues up 81.4%. The multi-pronged efforts in optimizing segmentation and channel management, improving the physical asset as well as establishing 4-star service levels produced a 53.3% RevPAR increase (from €73.35 to €112.48) and a 4.5 point increase in RevPAR Index (from 79.4 to 83.9). Within 21 months of the new management, Trip Advisor ranking improved by 57 places.

Value creation for Owners

During the 21 month of asset-managing the property, all activities which have been detailed above resulted in both, operational and financial performance increases. Next, it is worth detailing the top-line as well as bottom-line results as the objective of the joint venture was to achieve significant property value appreciation during the holding period. Table 14.2 shows that Pyramid Ltd. managed to improve the top-line performance also in relative terms compared to the comp set significantly.

Three important findings can be read from the data above: First, the RevPAR growth in 2015 nearly matched the one of the comp set (21.3% vs. 22.9%), despite recent takeover of an under-capitalized 3-star product and a high proportion of FIT & Tour Series legacy contracts, locking in 28% of the inventory at €84 (well below market rates). Second, in 2016 the Temple Bar Hotel beat the Comp Set RevPAR growth by 6.1 points despite extensive renovations that have taken place during the year. Third, The RevPAR index improved from 79.4% in 2014 to 83.9% in 2016 (or 95.3% when normalized for displaced room nights).

One commonly applied hotel property valuation method is based on future expected cash flows. Therefore, to show the achievements of the joint venture in terms of the bottom-line performance, Table 14.3 provides relevant revenue performance data.

Table 14.2 RevPAR penetration vs. comp set

Temple bar hotel				
	YE2014	YE2015	E2016	2017 B
	Prior management		.enovation	
Occ %	83.3%	84.2%	72.5%	83.5%
ADR (€)	88.05	105.64	155.13	170.13
RevPAR (€)	73.35	88.95	112.47	142.06
Occ growth		1.1%	−13.9%	15.2%
ADR growth		20.0%	46.8%	9.7%
RevPAR growth		21.3%	26.4%	26.3%
Comp set				
	YE 2014	YE2015	YE2016	2017 B
Occ %	84.5%	86.0%	84.8%	84.9%
ADR (€)	109.27	131.99	158.01	172.39
RevPAR (€)	92.33	113.51	133.99	146.33
Occ growth		1.8%	0.2%	0.1%
ADR growth		20.8%	20.1%	9.1%
RevPAR growth		22.9%	20.3%	9.2%
Occupancy Index	98.6%	97.9%	85.5%	98.4%
ADR index	80.6%	80.0%	98.2%	98.7%
RevPAR index	79.4%	78.4%	83.9%	97.1%

As one can read from the performance figures above, over the 21-month holding period, the partnership improved the hotel profit by €1.48 million or 103%.

The classic asset management process ends with the *disposition of the asset* (Boettger, 2009). In this particular case, the joint venture sold the virtual asset for €55.1 million to a foreign investor and Pyramid Hotel Group. PHG continues to operate the hotel until today. In terms of value creation – which is the core aim of the hotel asset management process – the Temple Bar Hotel project was an exceptionally successful endeavor. Over the 21-month holding period, the joint venture increased the asset value by €27.85 million, or 102.2%. The project generated returns for the joint venture of 88.4%.

Future Outlook for the Hotel Asset Management Profession

The hotel asset management profession has seen significant growth since its first advances in the early 1990s, and all indications are that the development continues. For large parts of the industry, the business model has shifted from providing hospitality services in the traditional sense to one where hotel performance is a mean towards achieving real estate investment goals. Today, hotel real estate is an established and sought-after asset class for institutional investors and as such has become a fixed component in many portfolios. The asset-light strategy of hotel companies is likely to continue, particularly in light of international expansions. Hotel

Table 14.3 Financial performance 2014–2016 plus budgeted 2017

| | PRIOR MANAGER | | | | PYRAMID MANAGEMENT | | | |
	YE 2014	% Δ	YE 2015	% Δ	YE 2016 Reno (Feb–June)	% Δ	2017 (Budget) New ownership	% Δ
Occupancy	85.5%	n/a	84.2%	−1.5	72.5%	−13.8	83.5%	15.1
ADR	86.85	n/a	105.64	21.6	155.13	46.8	170.13	9.7
RevPAR	74.26	n/a	88.95	19.8	112.53	26.5	142.02	26.2
Revenue	€	% Δ	€	% Δ	€	% Δ	€	% Δ
Rooms revenue	3,533,411	n/a	4,287,663	21.3	5,529,261	29.0	7,050,360	27.5
F&B revenue	4,264,943	n/a	4,138,117	−3.0	3,825,259	−7.6	4,394,958	14.9
Other dept. revenue	29,896	n/a	37,231	28.8	59,308	59.3	92,024	55.2
Total revenue	**7,827,250**	**n/a**	**8,463,001**	**8.1**	**9,413,828**	**11.2**	**11,537,342**	**22.6**
Operating profit								
Rooms profit	2,477,762	n/a	3,160,268	27.5	5,392,762	70.6	5,425,521	0.6
F&B profit	1,337,984	n/a	1,530,503	14.4	1,493,530	−2.4	1,819,613	21.8
Other dept. profit	15,295	n/a	27,053	76.9	45,944	69.8	61,353	33.5
Total operating profit	**3,831,041**	**n/a**	**4,717,824**	**23.1**	**5,705,236**	**20.9**	**7,306,487**	**28,1**
Total undistributed expenses	**1,460,100**	**n/a**	**1,613,457**	**10.5**	**1,717,194**	**6.4**	**1,786,065**	**4.0**
GOP	2,370,941	n/a	3,104,367	30.9	3,988,042	28.5	5,520,422	38.4
Cumulative GOP gain			733,426		1,617,101		3,149,481	
€ and %			30.9		68.s		132.8	
Total fixed expenses	**700,246**	**n/a**	**920,100**	**31.4**	**790,872**	**−14.0**	**892,676**	**12.9**
Net operating income	1,435,878	n/a	1,930,376	34.4	2,914,755	51.0	4,281,626	46.9
Cumulative NOI gain			494,499		1,478,878		2,845,749	
€ and %			34.4		103.0		198.2	

companies grow at speeds beyond what is feasible within organic growth patterns, and new hotel companies appear on the market at a speed that would only suggest the support of in-stitutional investors. The contractual relationship between owners and operators is becoming increasingly complex, creating the need for specialized expertise that hotel asset managers can offer. Then, as some of the examples provided in this chapter suggest, showcases exist that verify the potential for value creation with hotel real estate.

At the same time, the wider hotel industry faces a set of challenges that had not been seen in a decade and are likely to show effects over the next few years:

- Owners and operators question, whether the market had reached peaked cycle, fearing lower investment returns in case of an economic downturn.
- Economical and geopolitical instability even within the borders of Europe, had made predictions ever so more uncertain.
- Further disruption of the market place on various fronts. New distribution channels, besides the already established online travel agents, raise questions about the control over room inventory. New and currently unregulated accommodation platforms provide alternative housing for the consumer.
- Technological advancement and with it high degrees of uncertainty, opportunities, and threats have a profound financial impact in the short- and medium-term.

It seems fair to argue that the challenges will endure, and others will emerge. The degrees of uncertainty will remain indicative of the hotel investment landscape for many years to come. All stakeholders are therefore called upon to prepare themselves for the unknown, stay ahead of the curve, and allocate time and energy to innovative solutions. Conservation of the status quo, as positive as it may seem at current, is unlikely to be sufficient for staying ahead of the game.

Due to their function of advisors and bridge-builders of key stakeholders, hotel asset managers appear to have a bright future, despite – or even because of – the challenges ahead. HAM positions are found in all parts of the industry, with owners, operators, and consultants. Unfortunately, the demand oftentimes exceeds the supply. Singh et al. (2012) showed that only a small percentage of asset managers in their sample underwent task-specific formal education; the vast majority learned their trade on-the-job. Today, a number of reputable Universities and other higher education institutions have incorporated HAM in their curricula. Short-cycle professional development courses are available, oftentimes online. HAMA itself offers to its members a well-regarded designation, the 'Certified Hotel Asset Manager' (CHAM). The CHAM has been developed in close collaboration with the advisory board of HAMA in order to set standards of excellence for the profession. The certification serves as proof that designees hold advanced knowledge of the profession. However, the CHAM is an executive certification, with high access barriers and a comparatively small number of designees. With the anticipated growth of the HAM profession, there will also be an emerging need for relevant education on all levels. It should be in the interest of the hotel real estate industry to push for an educational agenda and connect with institutions in order to voice their needs. Only career pathways that consider the needs of various stakeholders can be the foundation for the required, sustainable growth of the profession.

Note

1 The case and related information presented in this chapter are published with kind permission of the Pyramid Hotel Group. Pyramid manages and leases selected, full service and independent hotels and resorts throughout the continental United States, Hawaii, the Caribbean, Ireland, and the United Kingdom. The Principals and Senior Executives of Pyramid Hotel Group have worked together for more than 30 years. Founded in 1999, Pyramid Hotel Group has quickly grown to be one of the leading hotel and resort management companies in the United States. Pyramid has formed partnerships with some of the largest and most prominent real estate investors in the United States, Asia, Caribbean, Germany, Ireland, and United Kingdom (www.pyramidhotelgroup.com).

References

Beals, P. (1996), "Hotel asset management: A valued function with a problematic future", *Real Estate Review*, Vol.25, No.4, pp.42–46.

Beals, P. and Denton, G. (1995), "The current balance of power in North American hotel management contracts", *Journal of Retail & Leisure Property*, Vol.4, No.2, pp.129–146. doi: 10.1057/palgrave.rlp.5090204.

Boettger, J.C. (2009), "The asset management cycle and the development of the asset management plan", in Denton, G., Raleigh, L.E. and Singh, A.J. (Eds.), *Hotel Asset Management Principles & Practices*, 2nd ed., AHLEI, Lansing, MI, pp.51–72.

Brener, S. (1991), "Fielding distressed calls", *Lodging Hospitality*, Vol.47, No.4, p. 21.

Denton, G. (2009), "The historical context of the hotel industry and hotel asset management", in Denton, G., Raleigh L.E., and Singh, A.J. (Eds.), *Hotel Asset Management Principles & Practices*, 2nd ed., AHLEI, Lansing, MI, pp.3–27.

De Roos, J. (2010), "Hotel management contracts: Past and present", *Cornell Hospitality Quarterly*, Vol.51, No.1, pp.68–80; doi: 10.1177/1938965509354865.

De Roos, J. (2012), "Current management contract themes", in Raleigh, L. and Roginsky, R.J. (Eds.), *Hotel Investments: Issues and Perspectives*, 5th ed., AHLEI, Lansing, MI, pp.233–237.

Eisenhardt, K.M. (1989), "Agency theory: An assessment and review", *Academy of Management Review*, Vol.14, No.1, pp.57–74. doi: 10.5465/amr.1989.4279003.

Eyster, J.J. (1993), "The revolution in domestic management contracts", *Cornell Hotel and Restaurant Administration Quarterly*, Vol.34, No.1, pp.16–26. doi: 10.1016/0010-8804(93)90026-F.

Eyster, J.J. (1997), "Hotel management contracts in the U.S.: Twelve areas of concern", *Cornell Hotel and Restaurant Administration Quarterly*, Vol.38, No.3, pp.21–34. doi: 10.1177/001088049703800313.

Feldman, D.S. (1995), "Asset management: Here to stay", *Cornell Hotel and Restaurant Administration Quarterly*, Vol.32, No.5, pp.36–51. doi: 10.1177/001088049503600522.

Hodari, D., Turner, M.J., and Sturman, M.C. (2017), "How hotel owner-operator goal congruency and GM autonomy influence hotel performance", *International Journal of Hospitality Management*, Vol.61, pp.119–128. doi: 10.1016/j.ijhm.2016.11.008.

Hodari, D., Turnert, M.J., Sturman, M.C., and Nath, D. (2018), "The role of hotel owners across different management and agency structures", *International Journal of Hospitality and Tourism Administration*, Vol.21, No.1, pp.92–113, doi: 10.1080/15256480.2018.1429342.

Jackson, L.A. (2013), "Towards an understanding of lodging asset management and its components", *Hospitality Review*, Vol.30, No.6, pp.91–110.

Kubak, T. (2018), "2019 HAMA Europe Asset Management Achievement Award presented to Starwood Capital Group at 2019 IHIF". Retrieved from: http://hama-europe.org/asset-management-achievement-award/past-winners/ (accessed 07 October 2019).

Rushmore, S. (1994), "Who needs an asset manager?", *Lodging Hospitality*, Vol.50, No.1, p.20.

Rushmore, S. (2001), *Hotel Investment Handbook 2002*, The West Group, New York, NY.

Singh, A.J., Kline, R.D., Ma, Q., and Beals, P. (2012), "Evolution of hotel asset management: The historical context and current profile of the profession", *Cornell Hospitality Quarterly*, Vol.53, No.4, pp.326–338. doi: 10.1177/1938965512458351.

Turner, M.J. and Guilding, C. (2010), "Hotel management contracts and deficiencies in owner-operator capital expenditure goal congruency", *Journal of Hospitality & Tourism Research*, Vol.34, No.4, pp.478–511. doi: 10.1177/1096348010370855.

15

GLOBALIZATION AND THE LODGING-SHARED ECONOMY

Jeffery C. Kreeger

Introduction

The Lodging-Shared Economy (LSE) can be defined as a dwelling or a portion of a dwelling that is rented to short-term travelers through a third party such as Airbnb or Vacation Rental by Owner (VRBO). One of the most unique attributes the LSE has compared to traditional lodging (e.g., hotel) is that these companies do not own a single room they rent. Some of the advantages of LSE include a less expensive room, staying at someone's home (with all of the amenities of home), and the possibility of having a more authentic experience through contact with the host. LSEs began with property owners/renters who rent their entire property or merely a portion of it for short periods to generate additional income.

The LSE has blossomed into a profitable industry where an entrepreneurial host purchases multiple rental properties for the express purpose of renting them out as LSEs for profit. Potential guests select a property from an LSE Internet website that meets their needs, then reserve and pay for their stay using the company's website. The mediating organization acts as a broker as it connects an LSE renter with a guest. In addition, a comprehensive search engine called *HomeToGo* searches for all options for a given city by searching the top rental websites including Airbnb, VRBO, HomeAway, Booking.com, TripAdvisor, Trivago, Expedia, Kayak, Hotwire, Travelocity, as well as hotel offerings and other accommodation rental sites. This website also arranges the obtained information according to price.

Airbnb became a company in 2008 and within four years had 141,000 guests renting an Airbnb room on New Year's Eve of 2012 – this number of rented rooms represents almost 50% more rooms than the Las Vegas strip contains (Geron, 2013). According to Airbnb's website, they have over 5 million listings in 191 countries in over 81,000 cities. Although Airbnb boasts of the largest number of listings, Airbnb was not the pioneer into this LSE environment. Airbnb was preceded by HomeAway, which began in 2005 – three years prior to Airbnb's birth – and is the parent company to VRBO. According to the HomeAway website, it has over 2 million listings in 190 countries. This chapter will focus on Airbnb and HomeAway because they command the majority of guests worldwide.

Lodging-Shared Economy

How the LSE works

The LSE essentially works much like a hotel stay with a few exceptions. A guest finds a property they desire at a price they are willing to pay and then reserves one or more nights as desired.

All financial transactions are completed online through a specific website (e.g., Airbnb.com). Each LSE host has the freedom to set his own rules and policies for his property such as check-in/check-out times and access to the property using a lockbox on the front door or a combination to the front door combination lock if the host is not going to be at the property. Other policies could include removing shoes in the house, access to garage, access to the refrigerator, use of a TV, and number of guests. Many guests seeking an authentic experience cite host participation as their main reason for choosing an LSE option versus a hotel; however, in some instances, guests may not ever make physical contact with the host depending on the type of arrangement (see LSE Options below). Often, LSE guests enjoy the personalized attention from their hosts and feel more like locals receiving inside information about a particular destination. Barnes and Mattsson (2016) interviewed 25 experts who identified technologies such as the Internet and Smartphones as the greatest enablers of the LSE. They discovered that a low price (lower than a hotel room) was the leading reason guests frequent an LSE property. One other reason guests choose an LSE – in the case of a shared or private room – is the desire to be social with the host(s) and experience their surroundings like a resident.

LSE Options

There are several types of LSE options from sleeping on someone's couch to renting a whole property. Airbnb specifies a 'shared room' as a couch-type experience where guests sleep in a common area such as a living room and typically does not include a locked personal room/area. A 'private room' includes sleeping quarters that can be locked although common areas of the house are shared such as a kitchen and living room. A third option would be to rent the 'entire property' (e.g., house, condo, apartment). This option can be very economical for groups traveling together or families seeking a home away from home. These options not only provide various price points for guests, but they also allow hosts to participate by sharing a part or all of their homes.

A poll that was taken in the USA and Europe in three consecutive years: 2015, 2016, and 2017, indicated that the general population is becoming more familiar with Airbnb accommodations. In 2015, 59% of those polled had never heard of Airbnb, but in 2017 that percentage dropped to less than half of that number to 28%. However, while the general population is becoming more familiar with Airbnb, guests seem to have more concerns over privacy [36% in 2017 up from 19% in 2015] and safety [13% in 2017 up from 7% in 2015] (Conrad, 2018).

Personal safety has been a concern for lodging guests for a long time. For example, as far back as 1960, Alfred Hitchcock's classic suspense thriller movie *Psycho* featured Norman Bates using low-tech means (a hole in the wall) to spy on his guests; however, today there are many high-tech options that perform the same function and yet are not as obvious. Covert surveillance cameras and 'Nanny cams' are available that look like an electrical outlet, picture, or clock radio. Dozens of movies including '*Speed*' and '*Blade Runner*' feature spycams. More recently, the movies '*13 Cameras*' and '*14 Cameras*' featured a landlord who installed spycams around his rental property so he could spy on his tenants. Hopefully, this type of activity doesn't occur at LSE properties, but with stealthier cameras, recording guests is a very viable possibility and therefore is justifiably a concern for guests. Additionally, Hollywood keeps this potential privacy threat in the forefront of each viewer's mind; however, Airbnb claimed that while this type of thing happens occasionally, they maintain a zero-tolerance for such activity and not only exclude such hosts from further participation, but also fully cooperate with the police to bring such individuals to justice (Brown, 2017).

Although in the United States VRBO focuses mostly on leisure travelers, Airbnb has recently focused on attracting business guests by implementing stricter criteria that mandate certain requirements for business travelers including: whole property rentals (e.g., whole house, apartment, or condominium), high speed Internet, desk working stations that accommodate notebook computers and USB charging stations. As of August 2018, almost 700,000 companies were using Airbnb to book their employees' travel (Airbnb, 2018, August 6). During 2018, the number of companies in Germany who have rented rooms from Airbnb increased by roughly 250%, which represents over 40,000 German companies who have booked with Airbnb for business. Further, over one-fourth of those companies (almost 11,000 companies) have at least one employee who coordinates with Airbnb directly to book rooms for employees traveling on business as well as for corporate meetings and team building retreats (Airbnb, 2018, December 10). As mentioned before, the savings on renting a house that accommodates many people can be much more economical than individual hotel rooms and can be a better environment for corporate meetings and building comradery.

Airbnb is well on its way to weakening hotels' stronghold of business guests and establishing itself as a viable alternative for business travelers. Perhaps it is most difficult to convince business travelers to stay at an LSE if they are employed by a non-Airbnb-supporting company. Because business travelers are spending 'other people's money' (paid by a company), they are more likely to choose the nicest available accommodations within their corporate travel guidelines. Presumably, self-employed business guests may be more willing to purchase a less expensive LSE room because they are typically more cognizant of maximizing profits by lowering their travel costs as they are directly linked to their wallet. Therefore, it is a big 'win' for LSE companies when businesses require employees to use an LSE as the preferred choice of accommodations.

Additional travel advantages Airbnb capitalizes on are experiences that can be paired with LSE accommodations (see Experiences and Attractions section below). Airbnb spends significant resources in research trying to determine global differences among countries regarding emerging trends and consumer preferences by country or region. In fact, Airbnb's Press Room found that "while main Airbnb business travel hubs like London, Paris, New York, and Sydney remain prominent destinations, we're seeing the highest growth of trips to locations in regions like Latin America and Africa this year over last" (Airbnb, 2018, December 6). An increasingly popular trend with business travelers is their desire to experience the culture of the locale which they visit for business. Some of the most popular local experiences worldwide include the following as listed in Table 15.1.

AirDNA (https//optimizemyairbnb.com), which is an acronym for <u>Air</u>bnb <u>D</u>ata and <u>A</u>nalytics, is a company that helps Airbnb hosts optimize the revenue they receive from their listings. For a small fee, Airbnb hosts can receive assistance with many tools and customized reports to make their property rentals more profitable including revenue management data and information to assess how their rates compare to other competing properties. Because many LSE hosts typically are not familiar with revenue management practices (Kreeger and Smith, 2017), companies like AirDNA further assist hosts in successfully renting their properties by implementing property specific Revenue Management strategies. The AirDNA functions like a 'life coach' for LSE hosts as it moves them up the learning curve for increasing revenue. Without these applications, the average

Table 15.1 Airbnb travelers' favorite (top) global experiences

Experience	*Location*
Paris' best kept secrets	Paris, France
Lakehouse Jazz & Funk	San Francisco, CA, USA
Lisbon's best flavors – Local gastronomy tour	Lisbon, Portugal
Show me the city walking tour	Toronto, Canada
Hike Runyon Canyon	Los Angeles, CA, USA
With a Rescue Dog	

★ Data from Airbnb (2018, December 6).

LSE host would not have the knowledge or expertise to make money renting their properties and would only gain these skills through experience. VRBO also offers suggestions on their website for hosts to be better hosts and to gain more revenue but it may not be as extensive as AirDNA service to LSE hosts.

Differences between a Hotel and an LSE

There are definite differences between a hotel and an LSE property. Here is a list of differences between a stay at an LSE (specifically one of three Airbnb 'types') and a hotel. These differences may not be comprehensive and may not apply for LSE properties outside the USA and it is meant merely as a guideline. Typically, in LSE properties, privacy and safety go hand in hand with the accommodation type. The most private and safe accommodation is one where locks are involved.

The shared room scenario offers little, if any, privacy as the guest is typically sleeping on the host's couch in a shared room like a living room. Access to a bathroom is also a consideration. Most shared and private room scenarios involve accessing a bathroom through a common area (a hallway) and may or may not be a shared bathroom; therefore, one may need to carry individual toiletries to and from the bathroom instead of leaving them on the counter as many choose to do while staying in a hotel or whole house arrangement.

Another difference is anonymity and reciprocity associated with each accommodation type. In the case of a hotel room, there is no need to speak to anyone. Likewise, when renting a whole house, there is also no possibility of bumping into the host during the stay; however, with a shared or private room, there is the chance a guest will encounter the host or other guests as they enter and exit the property. Therefore, they may feel obligated to talk with those they encounter.

Many guests who choose a shared or private LSE type like having contact with the host and state this contact with the host is the greatest benefit to them as they experience a given city/ location as 'a local.' Griffiths and Gilly (2015) discuss the popularity of public spaces and how Millennials in particular like such spaces where they can be a member of the community. While this is perhaps one of the best benefits to the LSE guest, it also can be a deterrent to loyal hotel and whole house guests who want to be left alone.

Several hotel brands were designed specifically to target Millennials' preferences. Two brands include *Marriott's Aloft* and *Home2 Suites* by Hilton, both of which feature public spaces for this very purpose of encouraging community. Recently a guest stayed at a Home2 Suites by Hilton property and for the first time, spent time in the lobby doing work because he felt so *at home*. That is something he had never done before in any other hotel, which underscores how a property's design can affect how a guest 'consumes' an accommodation experience. Further, during this same stay, the guest unpacked his clothes onto the shelves – another thing he had never done before. He just felt very much at home!

Cleanliness and Comfort Standards

Most higher scale hotel brands have specific cleanliness standards documented in their franchise manuals and pride themselves in providing cleanliness standards which meet or exceed these specifications. LSE properties have no such standards and therefore can be inconsistent from one property to another. Further, if a guest shows up to an LSE property that does not meet their cleanliness expectations (or is unacceptable for any reason), s/he has little recourse such as requesting another room because most LSE properties usually have only one option.

Climate control is another differing factor. With a shared or private room, the guest is typically not able to control the temperature for their particular room and that could be an issue for some travelers. This comparison is not meant to suggest one accommodation type is better than another but instead to highlight differences associated with each type of accommodation choice. Ultimately, the choice is made based on what type of experience the guest wants.

Traveler Preferences: Which Type of Accommodations Are Preferred?

Many guests who frequent LSE properties enjoy feeling like a local, but as Table 15.2 demonstrated, there can be a substantial difference between staying at an LSE property versus a hotel stay. Additionally, a guest's accommodation preference may differ based on the nature of the trip. For example, is this a trip where a guest's time is already scheduled such as a conference or is it an exploration, pleasure sight-seeing trip? As a 'mind candy' exercise, choose an upcoming or dream trip and proceed through Table 15.2 and mark those differences that are most

Table 15.2 Differences between hotel and Airbnb stays

Attribute	Hotel		Airbnb		
	Hotel room	Hotel suite	Shared room	Private room	Whole house
Privacy	Yes	Yes	No	Some	Yes
Safety	Lock on door	Lock on door	Limited	Lock on bedroom door	Lock on door
Personal property protection	Safe available	Safe available	None	Some – but typically no safe	Some – but typically no safe
Anonymity (freedom to come and go)	Yes	Yes	No	No	Yes
Reciprocity – obligation to chat with host	No	No	Yes – some	Yes – some	No
Cleanliness standards	Established by brand	Established by brand	Inconsistent	Inconsistent	Inconsistent
Recourse (choose another room)	Usually	Usually	Limited	Limited	Limited
Property location	Typically near desired locations	Typically near desired locations	Typically residential neighborhoods	Typically residential neighborhoods	Residential or near desired locations
Personal contact with host	Limited	Limited	Varies, but typically yes	Varies, but typically yes	Limited
Access to a kitchen	No	Yes	Yes	Yes	Yes
Access to a bathroom and shower	Private	Private	Shared – down the hall	Shared – down the hall	Private
Climate control	Have control	Have control	Typically no	Typically no	Have control
Hosts pay hotel taxes	Yes	Yes	(a) No for most cities	(b) No for most cities	(c) No for most cities
Legal to rent rooms	Yes	Yes	(d) Not legal in all cities	(e) Not legal in all cities	(f) Not legal in all cities
Sustainable	Depends	Depends	Yes	Depends	Depends

Note: The assessments of these categories are not clear cut and represent the opinion of the author of this chapter.

interesting. Is interaction with locals important or is it more important to explore attractions as a typical tourist? Is the goal for the trip to be with people or to be left alone? Is it desirable to do one's own cooking or eat out for each meal? How one answers these questions will determine which accommodation type will best meet the needs for the particular travel purpose. Some guests will alter their accommodation choices while others will always choose their favorite accommodation type.

International Focus

Worldwide, Airbnb rented the greatest number of whole house rentals in 2017 in the following cities: London, 10,239; Paris 3,724; New York, 3,229; Moscow, 1,878 (Shatford, 2015). As expected, the top four cities for private rooms and shared rooms are also in those same cities. Differences among various regions are explored and they reflect various rental options that are most popular in each region and emphasize the need to customize marketing and delivery based on customs and traditions of each country. The following section on China emphasizes that a 'one size fits all' approach is not always effective.

China

Uber, the *shared economy* 'taxi service' failed to establish itself in China for a number of reasons including not being able to navigate the regulatory waters, of which there are different regulations in varying parts of China. Airbnb is trying to learn from Uber's mistakes. Airbnb invested $5 million to market to the Chinese market (Ting, 2018). Airbnb has also played a substantial role in attracting other companies into the International LSE market, which tried to emulate Airbnb's business model – three of which were Chinese companies (Ting, 2018).

China has been a challenging market for Airbnb to claim a fair market share. According to Andre (2016), those from the Chinese culture typically do not feel comfortable sharing accommodations with people they don't know. Additionally, as of 2017, the entire country of China only had 30,000 listings (out of 3 million worldwide) and was implementing a name change to try to assist with their image (Huang, 2017). Unfortunately, the new name Airbnb chose to use – Aibiying – was difficult to pronounce in Mandarin and could easily have been a descriptive brand name for a sex pill like Viagra. Instead of translating 'Welcome each other with love' as intended, the meaning seemed to translate as 'loving' for many Chinese and fell short of its intended meaning. It was mocked by some of the Chinese bloggers, who indicated that a 'Chinese-language consultant' was critically needed in order to find a suitable name (Huang, 2017).

Beyond the name, issue is the home field advantage. China-based companies Tujia and Xiaozhu have imitated the overall idea behind Airbnb but have tailored their versions to the wants and desires of the Chinese people (Andre, 2016). Airbnb has a distinct disadvantage of being an 'outsider' but if they can stay the course, the potential for success is a very real possibility assuming regulations do not prevent the California-based company from reaping profits from a country with the largest population in the world.

Tujia partnered with HomeAway (Vacation Rentals by Owner [VRBO] is 'part of the HomeAway family') and is one of Airbnb's greatest competitors in China and has over 650,000 listings on its site. To cater to specific Chinese cultural preferences, Tujia is run more like a resort and not like individuals renting out their own property. Therefore, cleanliness is more consistent. Tujia uses property management staff to clean their properties and this includes 24/7 service availability of staff. Tujia's also offers butler services, bicycles, and car rentals at some properties. Tujia is essentially like Airbnb, but with a team of people who act as housekeepers and engineers for the properties. Also, Tujia addresses Chinese customers' dislike of staying with people they don't know and therefore, Tujia's strategy is based on renting whole houses or apartments or condominiums. In pursuing this type of listing practices, Tujia's customers were able to accommodate large numbers of guests. It takes advantage of Chinese travelers traveling with a large number of family members and friends.

Xiaozhu was launched in 2012 and most closely imitated the Airbnb business model by encouraging hosts to be hospitable and personable in making guests feel like they are at home or the home of a close relative. This is very similar to Airbnb's marketing push to live like a local while staying at LSE (CIW Team, 2017). However, in April 2018, Xiaozhu introduced a full-service version of their product that does not include any human interaction (Reuters, 2018). As of October 2018, Xiaozhu had over 500,000 listings and is taking advantage of Internet technology to unlock doors based on a facial recognition application.

Israel

China is not the only country where Airbnb is under fire. In November of 2018, Airbnb withdrew all listings in the West Bank area of Israel. The Human Rights Watch organization delivered a 65-page report that details the origin of the land on which Airbnb listings (properties) were built and they requested Airbnb to quit contributing "to making settlements sustainable economically and [allowing hosts to] benefit from the serious rights abuses and entrenched discriminatory practices stemming from the settlements" (Human Rights Watch, 2018, p. 1). On the other side of the debate are Israelis who believe that there is no abuse taking place. The history of the West Bank is complex and beliefs of what is correct are passionately held by each side. The purpose of addressing this topic has nothing to do with these strongly held beliefs on either side. Instead, this issue underscores how a company can make a decision that is not popular with all factions of a given population. Presumably, Airbnb spent a substantial amount of time and research on their decision to withdraw from the West Bank. Time will be the judge of whether their decision was the best decision for their company.

Spain

Gutiérrez, García-Palomares, Romanillos, and Salas-Olmedo (2017) analyzed hotel and Airbnb locations in Barcelona, Spain and not surprisingly found Airbnb locations were more evenly spread out across the city than were hotels – plus, hotels, by definition, have many rooms located on the same property. Also, not surprising was their finding that Airbnb locations were located much further away from the city's center. These locations can be an advantage for guests, who typically like to get as close as they can to the attractions they plan to visit. Almost 40 years prior to Airbnb's creation, Arbel and Pizam (1977) posited that there was a demand for mid-sized hotels located in the 'urban periphery' to allow travelers to stay closer to the attractions they sought. It appears that the demand they identified is being supplied by the LSE. However, not all parties applaud LSE participation in neighborhoods. O'Sullivan (2014) describes Barcelona residents protesting LSE guests in their neighborhoods as being drunk and disorderly, which is prohibited in Covenants of homeowner's associations (HOAs).

Japan

Many travelers to Japan comment about how clean the country is and are told the cleanliness is a function of everyone doing what they are supposed to do (e.g., residents pick up after themselves). Other LSE differences for Japan were few until June of 2018, when the Japanese government issued a law that those who want to be an LSE provider must own their property (not renters) and must register their property with the government – and that a property cannot be rented for more than 180 days in a given calendar year (Delilah, 2018). This regulation was the result of years of complaints from neighbors of LSE providers but caught many LSE providers by surprise.

Airbnb ran into forced cancellations in Japan due to regulations which required hosts to register their homes with the government as properties that engaged in short-term rentals. This deadline was June 15, 2018 – during the peak of their tourism season – and while most hosts completed the registration process, many others did not finalize the process in time and as a result, Airbnb was forced by the Japanese government to remove all listings that were not successfully registered two weeks prior to the June 15 deadline. This regulation resulted in a decrease of 80% of Japan listings from 62,000 to 13,800 – this resulted in more than a $10 million added expense for Airbnb as they attempted to contain ill feelings from guests who had their accommodations canceled at the last minute (Rodriguez, 2018). LSE guests have been advised to verify their future Japanese LSE property is owned and registered – an inconvenient request for travelers. This was not the first time Airbnb had to retract listings: in 2016 Airbnb removed 2,233 listings "in anticipation of its mayor signing into law a regulation that would make it illegal in NYC for an LSE provider to list more than one residence" (Newcomer, 2016).

In response to this regulation and increased legislation, a Japan association for accommodations rentals was formed in 2019 including nine of the largest LSE companies (Hamdi, 2018). Other companies in other countries have also formed similar vacation rental associations to cooperate with and influence governments with how they regulate LSE providers. The countries with such associations include: "Vacation Rental Management Association in the U.S., Short Term Accommodation Association in the UK, UNPLV in France and Fevitur in Spain" (Hamdi, 2018, p. 1).

India

The number of Airbnb listings in India as of 2014 was 5,000 – less than 1% of worldwide Airbnb guests (Sharma, 2014), but the 2019 goal of Airbnb's CEO Brian Chesky is to have 50,000 hosts in India. According to the VRBO website, VRBO had 4,026 listings in 2019. Fifty percent of India's population is under the age of 25, whose top traveling desires are: value, amenities, and local experience. Further, 40% of Indian Airbnb travelers booked a *private room* in order to maximize the local experience from the local site. The company, WanderTrails, a competitor in the LSE market, capitalized on this as they focus on India's love affair with experiencing a given location and all it has to offer. WanderTrails especially strives to offer local cuisine, adventures, and activities that are unique from those that most tourists explore.

Some religions frown upon unmarried couples sleeping together in the same room/bed: Hinduism is one such religion and is honored by about 80% of India's population. This religion scorns this practice of unmarried couples sleeping together not only for social mores. Culturally, many hosts have been reluctant to house couples who are not married – they required proof of marriage before they would allow the couple to stay with them, which offended many potential guests (Eadric, 2015). Culturally Indians do not condone co-habitation by unmarried individuals especially in LSEs based on the fear that it may lead to disguised prostitution. In such instances, the hosts risk the ire of their neighbors and local government official for cultural and legal reasons.

Cultural Differences

Brochado et al. (2017) found in their study that guests from the United States, India, and Portugal valued the same types of things from their Airbnb stay. These three countries were chosen because of their varied scores of individualities as specified in Lonner et al.'s (1980) work – the

United States had the highest score for individuality (it scored 91 on a scale of 0–100); India scored more moderately with a value of 48; and Portugal scored the lowest with a value of 27. One would expect there to be vastly different values from each of the countries based on these very different individuality scores, but Brochado et al. (2017) found little difference in what guests value from each country. They concluded that there is a convergence for Airbnb guests that supersedes individuality.

Another example of the need to be respectful of other cultures includes modesty in those accommodation types where there is interaction with a host or other guests. For example, it would be disrespectful for a female guest staying with a Muslim host to walk through the house in a sports bra or other clothing that reveals more skin than is customary by the locals. Obeying cultural mores not only prevents offending hosts but can also prevent personal harm. For example, there are many pointers that direct how a female should dress in a Muslim country in order to avoid harassment or assault. Another cultural blunder would be to cook a non-Kosher meal of pork chops with clam chowder on their Sabbath day while staying with a Jewish host – this would be very offensive to Jewish hosts, who might charge guests for the cost of returning their kitchen to its original Kosher condition.

Experiences and Attractions

In 2006, Airbnb launched 'Airbnb Experiences,' which offers unique, personalized tours of local places and activities that are not directly associated with LSE hosts, but is a natural extension of a trip for a guest who wants to participate in unique experiences. These experiences include a tour of Robben Island Prison, west of Cape Town, South Africa, where Nelson Mandela was held for 27 years guided by one of Mr. Manella's jailers or taking a rainforest water slide tour in Puerto Rico (Airbnb Experiences, n.d.). The list of possible experiences is lengthy and has a wide variety of activities. Airbnb's goal is to allow guests to feel like they are locals wherever they sleep. Other top experiences include learning how to make dough and filling for soup dumplings in Shanghai, China; taking a surfing class in Sydney, Australia; Touring the Louvre museum in Paris, France with a comedian; tapas and cava in Barcelona, Spain; and hiking to the Hollywood sign in Los Angeles (Airbnb Experiences, n.d.). Airbnb's promotional commercial released in 2017 pleaded that guests, "Don't go to Paris. Don't tour Paris," and "Please don't 'do' Paris. Live in Paris." ("Airbnb Opening Video," 2017).

Experiences and Immersions (Trips) enhance an LSE experience and Airbnb makes a distinction between *experiences* and *immersions*. They insist that "Trips is the catchall term the company uses to describe the tours and activities it offers: Experiences refer to shorter activities that are only for one day, while Immersions refer to longer, multi-day tours" (Ting, 2017, p. 1). There were 800 experiences listed in 2017 and of those, over 90% are positively listed as five out of five stars.

Legal Challenges

As mentioned above, in the Japan section, governmental policies can have a substantial impact on LSE rentals. This emphasizes the importance of LSE companies to work with jurisdictions cooperatively. Airbnb has done that with New York City, NY and San Francisco, CA, where they pay appropriate taxes as mandated by each municipality (Cusumano, 2014).

Not all parties are supportive of this LSE movement. Many neighbors of LSE providers are not fans of their neighborhood having additional traffic and a steady stream of visiting strangers. The Victorian Australia Supreme Court gave a ruling in Swan v Uecker which brought into question whether tenants (at least in this building) can sub-lease their properties on Airbnb (Greenberger, 2016). The significance of this decision was not to identify an illegal condition but instead highlights the contractual facets of the issues involved in listing a property as an LSE property. Many LSE properties violate laws prohibiting subletting properties or rooms. Additionally, many LSEs do not pay a bed tax or hospitality tax, like many hotels are required to pay.

Both VRBO and Airbnb have disclaimers that hosts are responsible for ensuring short-term renting of their properties is legal and permitted by all applicable authorities including HOA covenants and leases; however, Airbnb has detailed resources by country and in many cases city that give additional information about different laws or requirements. The Airbnb (2017) website offers advice for 'Responsible Hosting' divided into regions of Asia-Pacific, Europe, and North America. Each of these three options has further detailed countries such as the contents of Asia-Pacific includes laws and requirements for Australia, French Polynesia, India, Japan, New Zealand, and Singapore.

Items covered for each country are safety; neighbor considerations; permissions needed; general regulations; and insurance. As with most documents reviewed by lawyers, there are disclaimers that encourage hosts to use the website information as a starting point and not as legal advice. As one can imagine, there are many possible laws, rules, and regulations that can apply to any given property such as a "hotel/transient occupancy tax, sales, and other turnover taxes such as Value Added Tax (VAT) or Goods and Services Tax (GST), or income tax" (Airbnb, 2017). Some properties are prohibited from subletting and others may have a limit of days that the host can rent to a short-term tenant. Therefore, the host must verify there are no permits or registrations needed in order to sublet their property. Additionally, the host must check to see if their property is part of a neighborhood that is rent controlled or stabilized housing.

LSE Gentrification

Traditionally, gentrification occurs when a neighborhood is updated and 'cleaned up' and as a result of the improved appearance, housing and rent amounts increase such that residents are forced out of the neighborhood. Wachsmuth and Weisler (2018) mention how the popularity of LSE is raising housing prices and forcing long-term residents out of the housing they have enjoyed for years and in some cases, decades. Many LSE hosts have found they can make good money by purchasing properties to use as a rental property. These actions elevate housing prices and contribute to this gentrification effect which displaces local residents from their homes.

Disruptive Innovation

Guttentag (2015) describes disruptive innovation as "how products that lack in traditionally favoured attributes but offer alternative benefits can, over time, transform a market and capture mainstream consumers" (p. 1192). As recently as ten years ago, the thought of staying with a host in their house while they were there did not have much appeal to most travelers. Today, however, it is not only favorable for millions of guests each year but is actually a preferred mode of accommodation for those guests who want to experience travel that is more 'authentic.' This search for authenticity and the desire to get to know 'the innkeeper' is contrary to the U.S. customs of not even knowing one's neighbors, but it is flourishing, nonetheless.

While using an LSE may not appeal to every traveler, it is nonetheless having an impact on hotels and resorts. The Airbnb website claims they are not competing with hotels but instead they claim they attract additional travelers who otherwise would not travel. However, Zervas et al. (2017) found in their study a direct correlation between the introduction of Airbnb properties and a decrease in hotel ADR – "each additional 10% increase in the size of the Airbnb market resulted in a 0.35% decrease in hotel room revenue" (Zervas et al., 2017, p. 4). Granted, one-third of a percent decrease is not a huge loss of revenue, but as Airbnb hosts increase in number, the losses could become more substantial. Many who have considered their hotel immune to the LSE movement may want to keep watch for LSE competition to disrupt their hotel's loyal guest base.

While some of the LSE hosts use the money received from LSE guests for vacations or other discretionary products or services, other LSE hosts earn a substantial percentage of their income from their LSE property revenue. Many of these hosts need to operate multiple properties in order to generate enough revenue on which to live solely based on LSE revenue. Fabo, Hudáčková, and Nogacz (2017) found a large discrepancy among various countries regarding how easy it was to make a living through renting properties through Airbnb. They found that in Mozambique, one could make up to double the amount of revenue (201.23%) that one would need to live off of LSE income from a whole house. Alternatively, they found that listing a property in Finland only provided 13.03% of a living wage. However, most of their findings were more modest than the Mozambique example indicating that most LSE hosts do not rely totally on LSE revenue for their livelihood.

Conclusion

LSE companies have only emerged recently, but they have penetrated the travel market as they have become a competitor to hotels and resorts, similar to how Amazon and other online retailers have greatly impacted many brick-and-mortar retail stores. The future of the LSE is dependent on cooperation among LSE companies and government entities as well as with hotels and resorts. The LSE community has claimed they are creating new demand and are not in competition; however, as their popularity grows, this claim is being disproved. Additionally, as economic downturns occur, hotels and resorts may be less benevolent in their strategies toward LSEs which may be encroaching on their business by enlisting the aid of governing bodies to ensure LSEs are paying their fair share of taxes and specifically hotel or hospitality taxes.

Perhaps the future prosperity of LSE companies depends on forming associations and alliances to work with government agencies in a win-win fashion. Anti-LSE regulation is perhaps the greatest threat to future LSE success. Additionally, LSE success relies on continually monitoring the likes and dislikes of each culture in which they operate. Airbnb discovered in China that one size does not fit all but instead that each country – and even some parts of a given country – may need unique marketing methods that cater to local wants and needs. In order for LSE companies to thrive globally, they will need not only to navigate and cooperate with government entities but, of equal importance, they will need to fully understand their guests in each country/region and ensure their marketing plan caters to each guest population specifically and uniquely.

References

Airbnb. (2017), "I rent out my home in London. What short-term rental laws apply?", available at: https://www.airbnb.com.au/help/article/1340/i-rent-out-my-home-in-london–what-short-term-rental-laws-apply (accessed 18 December 2018).

Airbnb. (2018, August 6), "Companies booking airbnb for business travel more than double with nearly 700,000 using Airbnb for work", available at: https://press.airbnb.com/airbnb-for-work-700000/ (accessed 1 October 2018).

Airbnb. (2018, December 6), "Work beyond the conference room: Airbnb's business travel trends for 2019", available at: https://press.airbnb.com/airbnb-business-travel-trends-for-2019/ Accessed 28 October 2018.

Airbnb. (2018, December 10), "Airbnb for work sees nearly 250 percent growth in Germany," *Airbnb Press Room*, available at: https://press.airbnb.com/Airbnb-for-work-sees-nearly-250-percent-growth-in-germany/ (accessed 15 November 2018).

Airbnb Experiences. (n.d.), available at: https://www.airbnb.com/s/experiences?refinement_paths%5B%5D= %2Fexperiences (accessed 28 September 2018).

"Airbnb opening video". (2017), available at: http://www.airbnb.com (accessed 28 February 2018).

Andre, T. (2016, 14 April), "Airbnb in China and its competition", *Daxueconsulting Blog*, available at: http:// daxueconsulting.com/airbnb-in-china-and-its-competition/ (accessed 13 March 2018).

Arbel, A. and Pizam, A., (1977), "Some determinants of urban hotel location: The tourists' inclinations", *Journal of Travel Research*, Vol.15, No.3, pp.18–22. https://doi.org/10.1177/004728757701500305.

Barnes, S.J. and Mattsson, J. (2016), "Understanding current and future issues in collaborative consumption: A four-stage Delphi study", *Technological Forecasting and Social Change*, Vol.104, pp.200–211. https://doi. org/10.1016/j.techfore.2016.01.006.

Brochado, A., Troilo, M., and Shah, A. (2017), "Airbnb customer experience: Evidence of convergence across three countries", *Annals of Tourism Research*, Vol.63, No.C, pp.210–212. https://doi.org/10.1016/j. annals.2017.01.001.

Brown, J. (2017, October 11), "Airbnb guests discover hidden camera, host charged for 'video voyeurism'", *GISMODO Online Journal*, 11 Oct, available at: https://gizmodo.com/airbnb-guests-discover-hidden-camera-host-charged-for-1819359508.

CIW Team. (2017, March 4), "An overview of China's "Airbnb": Xiaozhu, Tujia, Zhubaijia", *China Internet Watch*, available at: https://www.chinainternetwatch.com/ 14626/chinas-airbnbs/.

Cusumano, M.A. (2014), "How traditional firms must compete in the sharing economy", *Communications of the ACM*, Vol.58, No.1, pp.32–34. doi:10.1145/2688487.

Delilah. (2018), "Thinking of staying in an Airbnb in Japan? What you need to know.", *Travel Blog*, 30 January, available at: https://www.fleurdelilah.com/renting-an-airbnb-in-japan/.

Eadric, J. (2015, November 27), "Is Airnbn legal in India?", *Quora*, available at: https://www.quora.com/ Is-Airbnb-illegal-in-India.

Fabo, B., Hudáčková, S., and Nogacz, A. (2017), "Can Airbnb provide livable incomes to property owners?: An analysis on national, regional and city district level", *SSRN Electronic Journal*. WP 168.

Geron, T. (2013, February 11), The share economy, *Forbes*, Vol.191, No.2, pp.58–66.

Greenberger, N. (2016, June 29), "Airbnb gets tested in the Victorian Supreme Court", *LegalVision*, available at: https://legalvision.com.au/airbnb-gets-tested-in-the-victorian-supreme-court/.

Griffiths, M. and Gilly, M. (2015), "Sharing space: Extending Belk's (2010) 'Sharing' ", *Journal of Research for Consumers*, Vol.22, pp.1–24, available at: https://ssrn.com/abstract=2630651.

Gutiérrez, J., García-Palomares, J.C., Romanillos, G., and Salas-Olmedo, M.H. (2017), "The eruption of Airbnb in tourist cities: Comparing spatial patterns of hotels and peer-to-peer accommodation in Barcelona", *Tourism Management*, Vol.62, pp.278–291. https://doi.org/10.1016/j.tourman.2017.05.003.

Guttentag, D. (2015), "Airbnb: disruptive innovation and the rise of an informal tourism accommodation sector", *Current Issues in Tourism*, Vol.18, No.12, pp.1192–1217. https://doi.org/10.1080/13683500.2013. 827159.

Hamdi, R. (2018, December 12), "Airbnb, HomeAway and others form international vacation rental group in Japan", *Skift*, available at: https://skift.com/2018/12/12/airbnb-homeaway-and-others-form-international-vacation-rental-group-in-japan/.

Huang, Z. (2017, 22 March), "China's consumers hate Airbnb's new Chinese name so much that they are brainstorming a new one", *Quartz*, available at: https://qz.com/939253/chinas-consumers-hate-airbnbs-new-chinese-name-so-much-that-they-are-brainstorming-a-new-one/.

Human Rights Watch. (2018, November 20), "Bed and breakfast on stolen land: Tourist rental listings in West Bank settlements", *Reliefweb*, available at: https://reliefweb.int/report/occupied-palestinian-territory/ bed-and-breakfast-stolen-land-tourist-rental-listings-west.

Kreeger, J.C. and Smith, S. (2017), "Amateur innkeeper's utilization of minimum length stay restrictions", *International Journal of Contemporary Hospitality Management*, Vol.29, No.9, pp.2483–2496. https://doi. org/10.1108/IJCHM-09-2016-0502.

Lonner, W.J., Berry, J.W., and Hofstede, G.H. (1980), "Culture's consequences: International differences in work-related values", *University of Illinois at Urbana-Champaign's Academy for Entrepreneurial Leadership Historical Research Reference in Entrepreneurship*, University of Illinois at Urbana, Champaign: IL.

Newcomer, E. (2016, July 7), "Wooing governor Cuomo, Airbnb boots 2,233 New York city listings", *Bloomberg Technology*, available at: http://www.bloomberg.com/news/articles/2016-07-07/wooing-governor-cuomo-airbnb-boots-2-233-new-york-city-listings.

O'Sullivan, F. (2014), "Barcelona organizes against 'binge tourism' – and eyes a street protester for mayor", in *CityLab*, The Atlantic, New York, available at: https://www.citylab.com/equity/2014/08/ barcelona-organizes-againstbinge-tourismand-eyes-a-street-protester-for-mayor/379239/.

Reuters. (2018, October 9), "China Airbnb rival Xiaozhu.com raises nearly $300 million from Jack Ma fund", *Reuters Technology News*, available at: https://www.reuters.com/article/us-xiaozhu-fundraising-idUSKCN1MK085.

Rodriguez, M. (2018, June 8), "Airbnb forced to cancel thousands of listings in Japan", *Fortune*, available at: http://fortune.com/2018/06/08/airbnb-cancels-japan-listings/.

Sharma, S. (2014, May 26), "What is happening at Airbnb India?", available at: https://yourstory.com/2014/05/airbnb-india/.

Shatford, S. (2015, September 18), "The biggest Airbnb cities in the world", available at: https://www.airdna.co/blog/biggest_airbnb_cities_in_the_world.

Ting, D. (2018), "Airbnb China names new president", *Skift*, available at: https://skift.com/2018/07/10/airbnb-china-names-new-president/.

Ting, D. (2017), "This is what Airbnb trips hosts really think of Airbnb's newest product", *Skift*, available at: https://skift.com/2017/03/27/this-is-what-airbnb-trips-hosts-really-think-of-airbnbs-newest-product/.

Wachsmuth, D. and Weisler, A. (2018), "Airbnb and the rent gap: Gentrification through the sharing economy", *Environment and Planning A: Economy and Space*, Vol.50, No.6, pp.1147–1170. https://doi.org/10.1177%2F0308518X18778038.

Zervas, G., Proserpio, D., and Byers, J.W. (2017), "The rise of the sharing economy: Estimating the impact of Airbnb on the hotel industry", *Journal of Marketing Research*, Vol.54, No.5, pp.687–705. https://doi.org/10.1509/jmr.15.0204.

16

INTEGRATED RESORT AND CASINO TOURISM

A Global Hospitality Trend but a Sure Win?

Glenn McCartney

Introduction – Casinos as Part of Tourism-Oriented Projects

Representing some of the largest hospitality structures being developed in an increasing number of tourism destinations in terms of both physical spaces, capital investment and diverse leisure product and service offerings are 'Las Vegas-style' or integrated resorts (IRs). With the rarest of exceptions, IRs have casinos which will be a significant revenue source for the IR, and with the mix of non-gaming products. These non-gaming elements will include accommodation, retail, events, shows, entertainment, meeting space, spas, theme park, dining, and nightlife – all add to the overall attractiveness of these mega casino resort complexes which are visited by multiple travel segments with varying motives. While locations such as Las Vegas, Macao, and Singapore have become well recognized with iconic IR imagery, many other locations in the past decade have introduced IRs or have debated the option of having IRs as part of stimulating the economy and tourism industry.

IRs are intrinsically linked to the gambling industry with the need to initially successfully introduce gambling as a legal product into the destination. Unlike many other forms of special interest tourism, the decision to legalize or liberalization casino gambling can often be a highly contentious and political one. Seen as a panacea to growing tourism deficits, growing unemployment or a tourism economy stagnating or in decline, the introduction of casinos to stimulate and rejuvenate the destination has seen considerable global momentum and acceptance as part of tourism development and destination product offering in the past few decades. Casinos can also link to the *latent human motive* or desire to gamble, which can be packaged within a travel experience and stimulate travel to locations where it is legally permitted, especially if prohibited at home (Zagorsek and Jaklic, 2009). As destinations jostle for competitive advantage, the introduction of casinos normally within a resort or integrated resort (IR) setting are seen as offering more choice to visitors, or with some cases becoming increasingly aware of leakage (whereby locals travel overseas to gamble and spend) and the competitive advantage offered by neighbors who have a casino resort. The commercial success of an IR means that multiple other revenues and taxes can be secured by authorities from food and beverage, retail, entertainment, accommodation, including those who supply the casino resort. Casinos can adopt two key strategic roles in tourism development (Zagorsek and Jaklic, 2009). The property can become the main purpose for the visit operating in rural, cross-border, or remote locations. The casino can also be a secondary reason for a visit to the tourism destination. The casino adds appeal, consumer value, and competitive advantage to the destination with those visiting to do other leisure and business activities beyond gambling, but also by the gambler who may appreciate the broader offerings within and external to the casino.

Casinos and the introduction of IRs as a platform for tourism development or rejuvenation have become the mantra. Prime Minister Shinzo Abe of Japan has specified that the recent casino legislation through which IRs can be introduced, be specifically tourism-oriented. Although casino gambling is prohibited throughout the country and a casino legalization process would be required, with the hosting of the Olympics in 2016, Brazil is looking to continue building on its tourism industry with IR development being floated as a possibility. Island destinations with tourism as a priority sector also see IR or casino resort development as important to maintain their tourism appeal and ongoing competitiveness. Cyprus awarded the first ever casino resort license to Melco (who have IRs in Macao and Manila) in 2017 with a 15-year exclusivity period with the contract valid for 30 years. The IR is estimated to cost over €500 million including land and construction costs (GGRAsia, 2017). The length of the casino license period highlights the important consideration by investors and operators to make back an adequate return on investment (ROI) on what is significant IR construction and operating costs. Tenerife is undergoing a casino rejuvenation process and inviting private companies to tender for the island's three publicly owned casinos. As well as the Tenerife government receiving revenues from the sale of the casinos starting at €24.9 million, the tender submission must include at least €4.5 million towards a tourism investment project (Casino Review, 2019). Jamaica has committed to having its first IR open by 2020 emphasizing that having a casino was not a requirement in Jamaica, an already popular tourist destination, but that the IR could offer enhanced tourism potential by providing greater experiences across non-gaming products such as shopping, entertainment, and music (Jamaica Observer, 2019). A key consideration for these destinations has been the move away from the standalone gambling parlor which essentially, as will be highlighted in this chapter, does little in terms of enriching the location's tourism environment.

The introduction of casino tourism and IRs as this chapter will show is highly political and controversial and are often seen as a last tourism product to consider. Some countries prohibit casinos (e.g., Brazil), others leave it to state or local governments to decide (e.g., USA), while some countries adopt legislation that can place casinos within special zones (e.g., Cagayan Special Economic Zone and Freeport, Philippines). While considerable revenues can be provided to government coffers by commercial gaming, the embedding of a casino within a destination does not inevitably enhance or progress tourism. Eadington and Christiansen (2009) in their analysis of casino resort development in European locations as part of tourism, state that the casino facilities attract visitors mostly wishing to gamble as there are limited activities beyond this. 'As a consequence, European gaming markets resemble Atlantic City far more than they do Las Vegas; they are day-trip markets, with little or no long-distance tourist destination customers' (Eadington and Christiansen, 2009, p. 7).

Eadington and Christiansen (2009) further question whether or not these European locations will become tourism-oriented when a significant number of attractions are added to the casino complex. The question of the capability of using casino resorts to transform the tourism destination is a crucial one. It will only transpire with deliberate and appropriate legislation and regulation in place to guide and the opening of IRs that can position and compete with appealing products and services to attract spending consumers. Atlantic City went through a phrase of IR and casino expansion and multiple property openings but faced with rising casino regional competition, experienced tourism destination decline with casino property bankruptcies and closures. This also negatively impacted the local community and neighborhood landscape as many were made unemployed as visitation and tourism spending declined. New IR properties are re-emerging in Atlantic City. The Hard Rock opened in mid-2018 by renovating the former Trump Taj Mahal resort at the cost of US$500 million. The Ocean Resort opened on the site of the previous Revel casino (Parry, 2018). The need to maintain a close observation on IR product relevance and possible risks to IRs are important and ongoing issues from the Atlantic City case.

The 'Las Vegas' IR Model

Las Vegas is often the global reference to achieving tourism development through casino introduction and expansion. In 2017, the USA commercial casino industry generated over US$40 billion in gross gaming revenues (GGR)[1] with direct taxes from 460 commercial casino locations (defined as land-based casinos, riverboat casinos, racetrack, or racinos and jai alai frontons) contributing more than US$9 billion in direct casino tax. It directly employed 361,000 staff who earned over US$17 billion. In what is intense competition across the USA as commercial casino gambling expands with more properties such as the opening of New York's first IR in 2017, the Las Vegas Strip held the status of having the largest commercial casino market (American Gaming Association, 2018). Showing the diversity of the tourism economy, accommodation, dining, entertainment, retail, and nightlife have become the main revenue centers for IRs along the Las Vegas Strip. In 1998, casino and non-gaming revenues on the Las Vegas Strip were balanced at US$3.72 billion and US$3.68 billion respectively. While casino revenue also increased, a slow progression and much greater spending in the past 20 years on non-gaming, on shows, events, restaurants, retail, and accommodation meant that by 2017 casino revenues were US$6.04 billion and non-gaming was US$11.8 billion, being a 34%/66% split (UNLV, 2019). The transformation and appeal of the Las Vegas brand and position as an entertainment city able to host large conventions and exhibitions with leading restaurants, events, entertainment, and nightlife has attracted a wide mix of leisure and business tourism segments.

In terms of GGR, Las Vegas was surpassed by Macao in 2006. In 2012, Macao a 30 km[2] isthmus and Special Administrative Region within China with a population of around 650,000 had overtaken all of the commercial casinos of the USA in terms of GGR (McCartney, 2015). The city reached US$45.09 billion in gaming revenues in 2013 (Table 16.1), with a significant decline in gaming revenues after 2014, dropping from US$43.94 billion to US$27.90 by 2016, due to a corruption crackdown in China. The extraordinary revenues have been generated by cross border visitation from China. In 2017, nearly 70% of Macao's 32.6 million visitors were from Mainland China. The case is a notable one in terms of tourism development and a gradual dependency on gaming revenues rather than a diverse mix of tourism and hospitality products. In 2017, non-gaming gross revenues were US$4.1, around 12% of total revenue (GGRAsia, 2018a). In 2004 the first smaller casino properties opened after the liberalization of the Macao casino market, thereby signaling the ending of the previous casino monopoly. While the Macao authorities have seen greater contributions from the casino industry, they have become increasingly reliant on casino tax revenues with 61.2% of government revenues being from gaming tax in 2005 to 84.6% in 2017 (Table 16.1).

Table 16.1 Macao's casino revenues, casino contributions, and visitation

Revenues	2005	2012	2013	2014	2015	2016	2017
Casino revenues★	5.76	38.02	45.09	43.94	28.89	27.90	33.22
Total government revenue★	3.53	16.19	19.44	20.23	14.51	12.80	14.76
Tax revenue from gaming sector★	2.16 (61.2%)	14.17 (87.5%)	16.80 (86.4%)	17.09 (84.5%)	11.20 (77.2%)	10.55 (82.4%)	12.48 (84.6%)
Total visitation#	18.71	28.082	29.324	31.526	30.714	30.950	32.611
Mainland China visitation#	10.46 (55.9%)	16.902 (60.2%)	18.632 (63.5%)	21.252 (67.4%)	20.410 (66.4%)	20.454 (66.1%)	22.196 (68.1%)

Note: ★ In US$ billions; #in millions.
Sources: Macao Statistics and Census Service (2019) and Macao Gaming and Inspection Department (2019).

While Macao has become a wealthy city and has often been referred to as the 'Las Vegas of Asia,' the city has not replicated Las Vegas in terms of tourism diversification. Some of the largest integrated resorts have been developed in the once Portuguese enclave showing the extraordinary economic impact that casino tourism can have on a destination. Macao was ranked number 1 globally in 2017 on visitor exports contribution to exports and the spending of visitors to Macao on leisure (94.3%) (World Travel and Tourism Council, 2018).

The Integrated Resort and Destination Resort

The IR will have multiple products all hosted under one roof including casino, retail, accommodation, restaurants and bars, sports betting lounges, nightclub, spa and fitness facilities, convention center, arena, and theme park. Various iconic and built features will be made within the IR, to attract as a backdrop for photo-taking and viral marketing. The IR is a highly attractive tourism product to entice long-haul visitation for leisure or business purposes. The convention facilities can host meetings, conventions, and exhibitions, while various leisure outlets provide a variety of experiences to different visitor segments. Local residents can also benefit from the addition of more restaurants, entertainment, as well as children play centers and shopping choices. Sands China, which holds one of the six casino concessions in Macao is the world's largest IR in terms of product offerings. With approximately 13,000 rooms across 7 branded hotels the IR has 3 theatres with 1,800, 1,200, and 1,700 seats respectively, including 850 retail outlets from luxury to mid-market, as well as a 15,000-seat Arena and 'Cotai Expo' with around 1.2 million square feet of exhibition space (Sands China Ltd, 2019). Along with a fleet of complimentary coaches and limos, the IR has its own 14 custom-built Cotai Water Jet catamarans each with a capacity of 400, operating from Hong Kong to Macao (Cotai Water Jet, 2019). The opening of the Parisian in 2016 at Sands China with a half-scale replica of the Eiffel Tower created around 30,000 employed across the IR (The Parisian Macao, 2016), showing the impact of the IR on employment opportunities.

As fabricated and themed environments, IRs are constantly charged with providing the most up-to-date products and services and innovations for its consumers. Shorter life-cycles in terms of consumer interest and relevance on themes and entertainment means that IRs need to constantly review, replace, and reinvest in offerings. Capital investment will depend on land, labor, and construction costs (McCartney and Mihara, 2018). Artificial, adapted, and virtual worlds all have been created within the IR with themes such as ancient Rome, Venetian canals, cowboy towns, and medieval villages. Elements of the real, nature, and culture are adapted and accepted by an expanding number of visitors (Gosar, 2009). Being attuned to industry trends and innovations, virtual and augmented reality are increasingly integrated within IR products and services such as entertainment and events. Major entertainment and movie companies have partnered with IRs such as Universal Studios (Resorts World, Singapore), Fox Studios (Resorts World Genting, Malaysia), Lionsgate (Jeju Shinwa World, South Korea), and DreamWorks (City of Dreams, Philippines). The entertainment company importantly gets access to new and growing audiences through these IR partnerships.

Given the multiple products and services within the IR environment, this presents immense marketing power to package with many derivations presenting the ability to target numerous travel segments based on various demographic attributes, lifestyle choices, travel motives, and spending ability. The capability to host a food court with various themed food outlets or acclaimed high-end restaurants, or have high street and deluxe retail all within the same IR means the complex can promote on price point or to consumers with different tastes. More reasons can be presented to the IR guest to stay longer such as a show or menu promotion at a particular restaurant. The IR will have numerous co-branding partnerships with internationally or domestically known hospitality brands presenting the IR with greater brand presence and appeal.

With the substantial financial and resource commitment required by IRs to enter a jurisdiction, these companies will look for various governance indicators. These will include stable government; history of gambling; consumer market access (domestic and foreign); labor cost, access, and availability (local and foreign); length of casino license contract; taxation policy and incentives (gaming and non-gaming); authority oversight and physical infrastructure. These various gambling, labor, and tourism policies in place or predicted could inhibit or assist the IR to make profits. While the local authorities are tasked to ensure that the casino and tourism industry has an adequate and sustainable tourism master plan and long-term view, oversight, and leadership from the government sector, the IR must not view these as too restrictive or simply be deterred to bid for a license or invest in the location. The issue of who does what is important.

The growth of IRs or casino complexes capable of being a significant catalyst for economic and tourism development, as shown in Las Vegas and Macao, is largely spearheaded and lead by global multi-national entertainment corporations with experience and the capital in developing IRs. Many emerged and garnered their experience from Las Vegas such as Sands, Wynn, Caesars, and MGM, although others are Asian companies such as Genting, Galaxy, and Melco. In smaller regions and developing countries, where the returns may be less but still significant, smaller casino companies operate. While all these corporations now seek out new locations, the destination must ultimately determine the rationale behind IR and casino introduction or liberalization and the operator(s) best suited to achieve this.

The Cost-Benefit Analysis of Casino Tourism

While there is a growing acceptance of casino gaming as a leisure and recreational activity a number of issues need to be considered within a robust analysis and evaluation framework on the benefits to the tourism destination through casino introduction or expansions, and beyond anti-casino or pro-casino sentiment and rhetoric. Casino gambling prohibition can be emotionally charged based on little economic or social assessment, but rather influenced by various religious, moral, or social outrage. There is a level of stigma and controversy behind the mere suggestion of introducing commercial casinos, with a legacy of prohibition and anti-gambling opposition (Eadington, 1999). Hawaii is one of three states in the USA to have no legalized casino gambling (Utah and Tennessee have no casinos) but has considered casino legislation on various occasions to diversify tourism offerings and create greater visitation (Agrusa, 2000). The opposition to casino gambling in Hawaiian is a fairly global reflection on why casinos are not permitted. Most Hawaiians and various anti-gambling coalitions oppose casinos due to the perception on the increase in organized and violent crime, problem and pathological gambling in the community, deterioration of the family unit, bankruptcies, and disproportionately negative impact on the youth and poor (City and County of Honolulu, 2010).

As ultimately casino or IR introduction is to improve the lives of local residents some jurisdictions put the issue of casino or IR introduction to public consultation. While the Taiwanese Government approved the construction of a casino in outlying Kinmen Islands in 2009, this was under the provision that the local residents approved in a referendum, which they overwhelmingly rejected. In Japan, some local authorities wishing to open an IR are conducting neighborhood campaigns to better inform locals more on what exactly an IR is. Gambling in Japan mainly consists of Pachinko parlors which are omnipresent throughout towns and cities in Japan and have limited impact on tourism development. Pachinko is not recognized as gambling within Japan's penal code so there are limited safeguards or responsible gaming programs for those who may have additive behaviors. In 2016 there were estimates that Pachinko in Japan had 9.4 million players with a total wager of US$197 billion. GGR could be considered as 10% of this wager (McCartney and Mihara, 2018). In many locations globally, slot machines (or 'Pokies' as referred to in Australia) are permitted in several locations such as bars and restaurants. Sometimes termed as 'fruit machines' these can be available in amusement arcades accessible for all ages. Any negative impression towards casinos and IR introduction could stem from other forms of gambling and would require careful investigation by authorities.

Casino licenses are often awarded as concessions to the few (or perhaps only 1) by local authorities and more often within a restrictive operating environment. The controversy of IR or casino resort introduction can start with the initial suggestion or tendering process when only a few maybe awarded a license. The debate may include the use of land for commercial gaming, although IRs often get land on more barren regions. These include a desert (Las Vegas); a water location with the need to reclaim (Macao); or abandoned locations such as the former site of Ellinikon International Airport in Athens. A €8 billion Hellinikon IR project is being pitched by authorities in a bid to reposition Athens as a world-class tourist destination to increase longer staying and higher spending visitors.

Wherever the casino resort is built, resources will need to be allocated for the purposes of financial oversight, police and security, legal system, and public utilities. A committee or commission may be formed for the primary objective of casino oversight. Legislation will need to be written related to anti-money laundering (AML), compliance, staff and supplier background checks, casino operations (on table and slot numbers permitted), smoking policy in the casino, age limits, casino advertising and marketing. If it is perceived that the casino growth has created excessive gambling opportunities or possible cannibalization, moratoriums can also be placed on casino expansion as was done in 2018 by the Philippine Amusement and Gaming Corporation (PAGCOR), a government owned and controlled corporation that owns casinos as well as being responsible for licensing the competing casinos in Manila's IRs.

How newly generated tax revenues are used can also stir some debate. Gu et al. (2015) discuss the dual purpose of casino taxation to maintain public morality and at the same time generate tax revenues for government coffers, essentially presenting a dichotomy where on one hand casino gambling is encouraged, while on the other a wish to depress. The tax burden is exported and if used appropriately can offset costs on other sectors such as education, health, and welfare. Informed decisions about tourism development opportunities by introducing IRs and casino resorts are needed. Becoming less detached from urban settings, connected to poor infrastructure and with a heavy tax burden and high expectations from authorities to still generate good revenues may mean the economic benefits from IRs and the casinos within may not materialize.

Merging Tourism and Casino Policies – The Regulated Casino Tourism Market

High expectations, particularly on the issues of revenue and taxes to the government, job creation, and tourism destination rejuvenation, will often be applied and expected from casino resort or IR introduction. Regulations regarding casinos are often nestled within a criminal code or specific casino legislation and will therefore rarely fall under the remit of tourism authorities. These casino policies can impact tourism. Policies can include issues on money laundering, corruption, illegal credit, operator and employee background checks, game integrity, and third-party agent licensing. Some factors will impact tourism macro issues such as the number of licenses allowed, length of casino license and renewal terms (if a renewal is specified), number of casinos and their locations (as a number of casinos might be permitted to operate within a single license). Daily operation regulations can impact visitation such as gambling age, casino smoking policy, operating hours restrictions, and tax rate on winnings. Casino complimentary policy on rewarding high-end net worth gamblers with free accommodation, food, beverage, transportation, events, and entertainment can mean preference and product design at times to satisfy casino players over those of non-gaming visitors. As the IR industry now stretches globally, cross-jurisdictional issues become issues to consider such as the transfer of personal data, money transfers, and that the IR is compliant to the standards set by legislation in another jurisdiction it may have an IR property. Casino tourism policy is a dynamic process constantly amended based on market conditions, license renewal, or retender or the possibility of closing previously overlooked legal loopholes.

As part of tourism destination development and maintaining the overall appeal of the location, regulatory and legislation must lead to job creation and economic and tourism growth outside the resort, where small businesses are able to compete and remain open. A small restaurant outside an IR must still attract sufficient customers and be able to find suitable employees. Inflation connected to rents and goods often occur with the introduction of IRs and again present challenges to small companies operating outside the IR. Illegal hospitality products and services will occur on the IR peripheral, with the challenge on how authorities manage this responsibly, on whether to permit and provide regulatory frameworks and assistance or continue to prohibit thereby requiring additional law enforcement.

Casino Industry Structure – From Monopoly to Open Competition

The market conditions, structure, policy, and oversight of how casinos are placed within a tourism environment will determine the success of both the casino property and the tourism destination. An example of a highly competitive casino and market-driven tourism economy is the state of Nevada where potential casino operators must show they have the ability to meet probity standards and have the legitimate financial backing to obtain a license from the Nevada Gaming Control Board (Eadington, 1999). Under such competitive conditions, there is a greater need to invest in non-gaming product innovations and constant upgrades in areas such as accommodation, entertainment, events, retail, restaurants, and conventions. Even with increasing competition as more casinos opened across America taking casino market share from Nevada, the State and Las Vegas developed new casinos and seen profit increase. Similarly, Macao, with the termination of the casino monopoly and introduction of several new casino companies, achieved the creation of extraordinary revenues (Thompson and Prentice, 2013).

More often casino licenses are restricted to the few. Restrictions are often applied to casinos based on casino floor size and the numbers of table games and slot machines, or allocated to a special zone in the city. With the focus by the operator being on generating revenues and shareholder return, there can be limited incentive to have product diversification beyond the casino. Government direction in terms of providing appropriate casino and tourism policy and legislation to spearhead a diverse tourism economy will be important. Two locations that Genting Entertainment operates in is Malaysia where it has the sole casino license, and in Singapore, where only two casino licenses were awarded. In these locations tourism master plans (TMP) were enacted namely the Genting Integrated Tourism Plan at Resorts World Genting, Master Plan Refresh 2010 at Sentosa where Resorts World Sentosa IR is located, and Marina Bay Masterplan which includes the building of the Marina Bay Sands IR property. Public and pedestrian areas, marine areas, access and transportation links, environmental protection and green areas, skyline, historical conservation, and mixed-use buildings (residential and commercial properties) become part of the plan.

A major issue is the focus of the debate on casino introduction into the landscape. As it is often political, the debate centers around moral and social issues rather on appropriate casino structure, whether monopoly, oligopoly, or open competitive market, that can best generate considerate employment opportunities and tax revenues for the location (Thompson and Prentice, 2013). Globally, several ownership models and location preferences have emerged. The casinos can be government or state-run enterprises (Sweden, Denmark), private ownership (Monaco, UK), or public-private partnerships. The Indian Gaming Regulatory Act (1988), a US federal Law, establishes the regulatory framework for gaming on Indian land. Casino gambling due to legislation banning land-based casinos, may need to operate on water on offshore riverboats or cruise ships. Modern cruise ships are similar to land-based IRs in terms of the gaming and multiple non-gaming facilities on board. Casino resort properties can be in clusters or zones (Las Vegas, Macao, Atlantic City). There can be some level of perception of containment by governments, but such settings can provide considerable visitor appeal, location branding, and economies of scale for the casino properties. A popular tactic globally is to have casino properties close to the border of another jurisdiction with limited, less attractive gambling or no casino gambling thereby attracting gamblers in close proximity to the casino location, being the key reason behind the casino success of Macao.

Domestic Tourism Dilemma

In tourism, it is rare that foreign and domestic travelers would be treated differently in getting permission to visit or use a local attraction or service, especially in excluding local participation. Cultural and heritage sites may differentiate between locals and foreigners by having a two-tier pricing structure, charging foreign visitors more to enter the site. Casinos can be the exception. A major policy consideration with the introduction of casino gambling is on whether to permit and/ or restrict domestic visitation. The main concern is on possible negative social impacts occurring especially problem gambling which will then resonate back to the family. Some governments take a paternalistic view on the matter enacting a ban or levy on casino entry by locals.

A good case to illustrate the debate on permitting domestic visitation to casinos within an IR is South Korea (North Korea also has a few casinos). Sixteen out of the 17 casino hotels and resorts in South Korea are for foreigners only. Kangwon Land, a state-run casino resort enterprise located in a remote former coal mining region is the only casino in the country that permits locals to gamble. This single casino accounted for 56% (US$1.371 billion) of total GGR for South Korea in 2017 (Table 16.2). Measures have been put in place to limit domestic visitor spending at this casino which would run counter to regular international casino operations and profit generating objective. Under a directive from the South Korean government, the Kangwon Land closes from 4 am to 10 am each day and reduced the number of casino tables (GGRAsia, 2018b). Notably, the casino industry in South Korea represents only 30% of gambling revenues with locals gambling on lottery, toto, bullfighting, and sports (motorboat, bicycle, and horse racing). The issue of creating a fair policy on whether to permit domestic visitors to casinos is a contentious one globally. A casino operator will most likely factor this potential revenue source into return on investment

Table 16.2 South Korean Casino revenues generated by domestic and foreigners

	2008		2017	
	Kangwon land	*Foreigner only*	*Kangwon land*	*Foreigner only*
GGR (million)	US$959	US$678	US$1,371	US$1,086
Share of gambling market	16.19%	11.43%	16.49%	13.07%
No. of visitors	2,915,000	1,277,000	3,115,000	2,216,000
National taxes (million)	US$146	US$27	US$232	US$67
Local taxes	US$16	US$5	US$20	US$21
Total taxes	US$161	US$32	US$252	US$87
Tax contribution rate to GGR	16.81%	4.68%	18.37%	8.04%

Source: National Gambling Control Commission (2019).

opportunity and whether to invest. From 2008 to 2017 there has been an increase in visitation and GGR at South Korean casinos showing the appeal of the industry. The national government gets the bulk of total taxes, being 92% (US$232 million) in 2017 from those who visited Kangwon Land, and 77% (US$67) for the other 16 casinos. A major tax debate policy consideration is on how much taxes from the casino industry are reinvested locally to adequately provide for tourism infrastructure needed to continually develop and sustain a diverse tourism economy.

Singapore became one of the first jurisdictions to impose a casino entry levy for locals (US$76). Japan will follow this with a US$56 entry levy which is higher in terms of GDP comparison between the two countries. Japan will also restrict the number of visits per week to three for locals. Research is suggested to investigate if such a charge does deter or curb local visitation or in fact results in the local patron spending longer in the casino (McCartney and Mihara, 2018). The levy becomes an additional tax contribution to government coffers. Visitor identification is required to enter those casinos banning or charging locals to enter. Locals may avoid this government oversight by going to jurisdictions without identification requirements.

Casino Tourism Risk, Uncertainty, and Resilience

There are various reasons why casino properties may close. It could be for the simple cancelation or expiration of a casino license. A key reason although is a failure to achieve commercial success. The competitive landscape can change with the introduction of new casinos with better facilities within the same destination or close neighbor in the region. There could be a level of cannibalization if gambling supply outweighs visitor demand. As fabricated and themed products there is a need to continually upgrade these to remain relevant to visitors. A lack of capital expenditure in new features or rejuvenated gaming and non-gaming offerings will make the casino property susceptible to losing market share.

Although with reference to the Asian casino sector, the casino resilience capability and viability factors highlighted by McCartney (2017a, 2017b) could be applied globally. Five key areas were isolated namely competitive landscape, integrated resort packaging and offering, government and community sentiment, Asian visitor market and growing affluence, and political will and policy. Too much casino and IR competition within the destination or in neighboring jurisdictions can lead to cannibalization, diminishing market share and profits, which occurred in Atlantic City and Reno with casino property closures. Other gambling products may have an indirect impact on casino success and revenues such as online gambling or lotteries and subsequently casino companies may lobby for their exclusion in the tourism location. Sports betting if permitted by local authorities has been included within IRs as an additional attraction attribute. As casino licenses are granted or awarded as an opportunity for normally the few to operate, the casino operators will also review government sentiment towards the industry.

Conclusion

While casinos are present in jurisdictions globally, a standalone gambling parlor or casino with few facilities will have the minimal advantage to the tourism industry. The IR model has therefore become an attractive global hospitality trend with the growth of multinational corporations who operate these across jurisdictions and continue to leverage on this experience to bid for access to new locations. There are locations with just a few IRs (Singapore, Macao, Philippines) or in the process of having a few (Japan, Cyprus) as immense benefits can be achieved by this casino model. Some countries wish to transform their casino gambling industry into Vegas-style complexes seeing the success of these not only as a stimulus to the economy and local employment but as iconic structures to attract visitors willing to spend and stay longer. Co-branding opportunities with leading hospitality and entertainment companies have given IRs and the destination greater global presence and position. IRs can bring significant economic and employment benefits to the destination starting at the construction phase, as the destination ramps up to meet the expectations of an escalation in tourism arrivals.

The market structure that national or local authorities determine for casino introduction or expansion into the tourism landscape will be a crucial consideration for the IR in terms of foreseeing an acceptable return on investment. In a normal tourism business environment, the most efficient enterprise might force others to close and a monopoly or just a few companies might remain to enjoy the possible profits. This cannot be applied to the casino industry that are provided a license through a competitive tender process or emerge as the solitary qualified bidder (Thompson and Prentice, 2013). The casino bid often contains terms requiring the casino to pay an entrance fee as well as a beautification program perhaps along a waterfront or urban redevelopment. Australia's cities have also increased their interest in IR development. At an estimated cost of US$2.5 billion, an IR and waterfront wharf complex is being constructed at Queen's Wharf Brisbane, a private venture between The Star Entertainment Group and Hong Kong-based Chow Tai Fook Enterprises and the Far East Consortium. It is being positioned as a world-class IR, entertainment, and lifestyle destination. The urban regeneration project consists of the public precinct, contemporary architecture mixed with heritage buildings, and a new pedestrian bridge across the river (Queen's Wharf Brisbane, 2019).

IRs must also factor in construction costs as well as operational costs, casino taxation, and other regular fees to community development programs often contained in the license agreement. While some forms of tourism may require government subsidy such as heritage, culture, or some destination events, casinos and the IR industry are at the opposite end of the spectrum having to pay considerably to gain access and operate in the location. IRs are highly capital intensive requiring constant innovation and reinvestment, particularly with non-gaming products such as events and entertainment. The large-scale visitation and facility usage of IRs will require refurbishment perhaps at a greater pace than a non-gaming hotel resort. The IR must have a level of assurance that all these capital investments and expenses will be covered working within the house advantage margins provided by gambling and profits from non-gaming to provide returns to shareholders and operators.

Yet the term gambling still has a level of stigma and barriers created through the perceptions of social costs such as an increase in problem gambling, crime, money laundering, corruption, and a decline in community values. This chapter discussed the need to conduct a thorough cost-benefit assessment of the introduction of a casino property. Government agencies will need to ensure appropriate policies are provided to place IRs within the destination as a conduit for tourism growth and development. Forward-thinking statements such as a tourism master plan can guide the destination. As a relatively new area of growth in global hospitality expansion, even with their immense presence, capital investment, and economic impact to the jurisdiction, IRs remain a largely under-researched hospitality sector. As destination resorts and their ability to shape and direct tourism development, IRs need to be examined within the framework of tourism destination strategy as well. As this chapter outlines, IRs are part of casino tourism and therefore an initial obstacle will be in alleviating the concerns and perceptions towards gambling and the communication of what an IR is.

Note

1 GGR is defined as the amount earned by the casino less the amount paid as winnings to customers. It does not equate to profits as the casino will need to deduct numerous expenses, operating costs, staff salaries, taxes, and fees.

References

Agrusa, J. (2000), "Legalization of gambling in Hawaii and its potential effects on Japanese intention to visit: A philosophical inquiry", *Journal of Travel & Tourism Marketing*, Vol.9, No.1, pp.211–217. doi: 10.1300/J073v09n01_13.

American Gaming Association. (2018), *State of the States 2018*, available at: https://www.americangaming.org/wp-content/uploads/2018/08/AGA-2018-State-of-the-States-Report_FINAL.pdf (accessed 30 January 2019).

Casino Review. (2019, January), "Four operators to take part in Tenerife casino tender", p.10.

City and County of Honolulu. (2010), *HB146. Proposing an Amendment to the Hawaii Constitution to Permit Gambling in the State*, available at: https://www.capitol.hawaii.gov/session2010/testimony/HB146_TESTIMONY_JUD_02-09-10_.pdf (accessed 30 January 2019).

Cotai Water Jet. (2019), *Our ferries*, available at: https://www.cotaiwaterjet.com/our-ferries.html (accessed 30 January 2019).

Eadington, W.R. (1999), "The economics of casino gambling", *Journal of Economic Perspectives*, Vol.13, No.3, pp.173–192. doi: 10.1257/jep.13.3.173.

Eadington, W.R. and Christiansen, E.M. (2009), "Tourism destination resorts, market structures, and tax environments for casino industries: An examination of the global experience of casino resort development", in Eadington, W.R. and Doyle, M.R. (Eds.), *Integrated Resort Casinos. Implications for Economic Growth and Social Impacts*, College of Business, University of Nevada, Reno, pp.3–20.

GGRAsia. (2017), *Melco International Confirms Approval for Cyprus Licence*, available at: http://www.ggrasia.com/melco-international-confirms-approval-for-cyprus-licence/ (accessed 30 January 2019).

GGRAsia. (2018a). *No Meaningful Upping of Macau Non-Gaming on Cards: MS*, available at: http://www.ggrasia.com/no-meaningful-upping-of-macau-non-gaming-on-cards-ms/ (accessed 30 January 2019).

GGRAsia. (2018b), *Kangwon Land Post 30pct Profit Decline in Jan–Mar*, available at: http://www.ggrasia.com/kangwon-land-posts-30pct-profit-decline-in-jan-mar/ (accessed 30 January 2019).

Gosar, A. (2009), "Gaming tourism in the context of modern tourism flows", in Eadington, W.R., and Doyle, M.R. (Eds.), *Integrated Resort Casinos. Implications for Economic Growth and Social Impacts*, College of Business, University of Nevada, Reno, pp.193–205.

Gu, X., Li, G., and Tam, P.S. (2015), "Casino tourism, social cost and tax effects", *International Gambling Studies*, Vol.13, No.2, pp.221–239. doi: 10.1080/14459795.2012.760641.

Jamaica Observer. (2019, December 9), *Jamaica Will Not Be a Casino Destination, Says Barlett*, available at: http://www.jamaicaobserver.com/latestnews/ (accessed 30 January 2019).

Macao Statistics and Census Service. (2019), *2017 Macao in Figures*, available at: https://www.dsec.gov.mo/Statistic.aspx?NodeGuid=ba1a4eab-213a-48a3-8fbb-962d15dc6f87(accessed 30 January 2019).

Macao Gaming and Inspection Department. (2019), *Information*, available at: http://www.dicj.gov.mo/web/en/information/DadosEstat/2005/estat.html#n1 (accessed 30 January 2019).

McCartney, G.J. and Mihara, T. (2018), "Japanese Casino & IR (integrated resort) legislation & framework. An analysis of key social, economic and tourism assertions", *Gaming Law Review & Economics*, Vol.22, No.8, pp.441–451. doi: 10.1089/glr2.2018.22810.

McCartney, G.J. (2017a). "Managing accommodation in integrated resorts", in Wood, R. (Ed.), *Hotel Accommodation Management*, Routledge Hospitality Essentials Series, Routledge, London and New York, pp.94–109.

McCartney, G.J. (2017b), "Betting on Casino tourism resilience: A case study of Casino expansion in Macao and the Asia Region", in Butler, R.W. (Ed.), *Tourism and Resilience*, CAB International, Wallingford, UK, pp.195–205.

National Gambling Control Commission. (2019), *Introduction of Gambling Industry*, http://www.ngcc.go.kr/eng/stats/scale_speculation.do (accessed 30 January 2019).

Parry, W. (2018), *Hard Rock and a View of the 'Ocean' as 2 Atlantic City Casinos Rise Again*, available at: https://www.nbcphiladelphia.com/news/local/New-Atlantic-City-Casinos-Hard- (accessed 30 January 2019).

Queen's Wharf Brisbane. (2019), *Home*, available at: https://queenswharfbrisbane.com.au (accessed 30 January 2019).

Sands China. (2019), *Company Information*, available at: https://www.sandschina.com/the-company/company-information.html (accessed 30 January 2019).

The Parisian Macao. (2016). *Las Vegas Sands and Sands China Celebrate Grand Opening of the Parisian Macao*, available at: https://www.parisianmacao.com/press-club/2016/09/14-sands-celebrate-grand-opening-of-the-parisian-macao.html (accessed 30 January 2019).

Thompson, W.N. and Prentice, C. (2013), "Should casinos exist as monopolies or should casinos be in open markets?" *UNLV Gaming Law Journal*, Vol.4, No.1, pp.32–47.

UNLV. (2019), *Nevada Casinos: Departmental Revenues, 1984–2017*, available at: https://gaming.unlv.edu/reports/NV_departments_historic.pdf (accessed 30 January 2019).

World Travel & Tourism Council. (2018). *Economic Impact 2018 Macau*, World Travel & Tourism Council (WTTC), London, UK.

Zagorsek, H. and Jaklic, M. (2009), "Resort casino development and its linkage to national and international tourism: A Slovenian perspective", in Eadington, W.R. and Doyle, M.R. (Eds.), *Integrated Resort Casinos. Implications for Economic Growth and Social Impacts*, College of Business, University of Nevada, Reno, pp.21–53.

17

NEW TRENDS IN CHINESE OUTBOUND TOURISM

Consequences for the International Hospitality Industry

Wolfgang Georg Arlt

China: A Growing but Changing Source Market

China reported a total of 1.39538 billion inhabitants at of the end of 2018, with 15 million births during that year (NDRC, 2019). The growth of China's population has almost plateaued and is expected to peak in 2030 at 1.45 billion inhabitants. By that time India will have overtaken China as the most populous country in the world with about 1.5 billion inhabitants (Euromonitor, 2018).

Nevertheless, China will continue to be the biggest international tourism source market in the world, a position first achieved in 2012. The steady growth of the Chinese economy in the last three decades has mainly resulted in an increase in the urban upper-middle-class population, which has enough disposable income to afford overseas travel (Arlt and Burns, 2013). Ten percent of the Mainland Chinese population are passport holders and represent this top 10% of the population, with roughly another 10% of the population able to afford to travel to Hong Kong and Macau Special Administrative Regions, for which no passport but a permission is required (Wassler et al., 2018).

As the current proportion of household income devoted to leisure activities in China is low compared to countries in Europe or the USA, and international travel is considered an important status symbol (barring Black Swan incidents), the number of Chinese not only eager but also able to afford international travel will continue to increase (Schuckert et al., 2016). The total number of Chinese passport holders is forecasted to increase to about 20% of the Chinese population – close to 300 million citizens – within the next decade. These numbers are reflected in the number of car owners in China, which stands at around 170 million, and the number of persons with a driver's license, which stands at around 300 million (Arlt, 2013).

Wealth distribution is very uneven in China, with the Gini Coefficient of income reported as 0.46. According to a recent study by United Nations University, the Gini Coefficient would jump to 0.65 if data on the largest incomes were included in Chinese national statistics, putting China well above the threshold of "extreme inequality." Urban citizens earn on average of almost three times as much as citizens in rural areas (Li et al., 2019; Wang and Wing, 2011).

The wealth distribution defined by dollar-per-day spending amounts expressed in Purchasing Power Parity terms is shown in Table 17.1. Only the upper-middle class (annual spending power 7,300–18,250 USD per year) and the upper class (above 18,250 USD) are affluent enough to consider outbound leisure tourism paid by themselves. In comparison, the data for India are also given.

Table 17.1 Wealth distribution in China compared to India 2018

Class segmentation	Spending amount per day in US$	Percentage of population China (%)	India (%)
High	>50	0.8	0.1
Upper-middle	20–50	9.7	0.6
Lower-middle	10–20	29.0	2.6
Low	2–10	59.6	72.2
Poor	<2	0.9	24.5

Source: CSIS (2019).

The Chinese outbound travel market has grown dramatically over the last two decades. The total number of outbound departures from Mainland China increased from 8 million in 1997 to 162 million in 2018 according to COTRI (2019). Trips starting in Mainland China with destinations in the Greater China region (Hong Kong SAR, Macau SAR, and Taiwan) accounted for 79 million, while 83 million trips had destinations around the world. Among the TOP 10 destinations in terms of the total numbers of arrivals, all except the USA were located in Asia.

Many millions of Chinese are still poised to take their first overseas trips, joining group tours and visiting big cities and popular destinations, predominantly in Asia (Chen et al., 2016). Most of these package tour travelers do not live in the first tier cities (Beijing, Shanghai, Guangzhou, and Shenzhen); the number of travelers from first tier cities has now been overtaken by the combined total originating from second and, increasingly, third tier cities. The growth rate for outbound bookings of urban dwellers in first and major second tier cities in China has slowed down, whereas smaller second and third tier cities reported dramatic growth, supported by the steadily increasing number of international direct air connections from the airports in such cities (Chen et al., 2014).

Nevertheless, the tendency to search for new destinations on other continents is increasing, especially among the more experienced travelers (Chen et al., 2016). They are looking forward to experiencing local lifestyles – including eating local food, exploring nature, enjoying outdoor activities, relaxing, and participating in wellness activities. The number of more experienced overseas travelers continues to increase as Chinese travelers take their second, fifth, or tenth trips overseas – and, in the process, become more confident traveling on their own and pursuing more unique and personalized experiences (Kim et al., 2017). These experienced travelers are more likely to travel as FITs in small groups of couples, families, friends, or colleagues, or in "customized tours," which are organized by a tour operator according to the specific demand, interest, and travelling style of the travelers (COTRI, 2018). They might also use, as they are called in China, "free and easy" tours, which only provide the skeleton of the trip with a visa, air tickets, and some hotel reservations. The typical Chinese package group tours, which follow a fixed itinerary and bring together strangers in the same tour group, are mostly used by Chinese travelers with less travel experience and fewer language abilities (Arlt and Feng, 2007; Wong and Kwong, 2004).

The "Second Wave" Chinese travelers, who invest more time, interest, and money into a service or destination than package tourists – who simply rush between famous sights, various photo opportunities, shopping malls, and Chinese restaurants – are accordingly becoming increasingly important for many destinations (Thraenhart et al., 2012; Arlt and Thraenhart, 2011). These "Second Wave" travelers can be characterized as being younger, more independent, and having a taste for more sophisticated adventures and experiences. Many have studied overseas and/or work for an international company in China (Arlt, 2013). While the global tourism industry is still just starting to comprehend the "Second Wave" of Chinese outbound travelers, the "Third Wave" is already on the horizon in the form of the widening age band of Chinese outbound travelers (Arlt, 2011; Liu and McKercher, 2016). International travel is perceived less and less by frequent travelers as being special or dangerous, while more children are joining their parents on trips or are travelling in youth travel groups with their classmates or friends.

These results support the fact that, as China's outbound tourism started to increase more than ten years ago, the first cohorts of teenagers who have been travelling internationally with their parents since childhood are now entering the market (Huang et al., 2015). They are the *linglinghous* (born after 2000), adding to the majority groups of *balinghous* and *jiulinghous* (people born in the 1980s and 1990s, respectively). Similarly, on the other end of the scale, the first age groups of affluent Chinese pensioners are joining the ranks of outbound travelers. Most are "Best Agers" aged 55–65, with only a few being older than 65 years. Unlike the majority of middle-aged affluent travelers who are "money rich but time-poor," these "Silver Travelers" are able to spend time on trips that can last several weeks.

The most visited destinations during the current decade have remained stable, with Hong Kong SAR and Macau SAR having the greatest importance by far, followed by Thailand or South Korea. In recent years Vietnam and Japan have become more popular, whereas Taiwan and Singapore lost ground. In all years, at least 10 out of the 15 top destinations have been located in Asia, with the USA in several years at seventh position, representing the highest entry of a non-Asian destination (COTRI, 2019; Lin et al., 2015).

China, the world's top tourism spender, reported USD 277 billion in international tourism expenditure in 2018, a 5% increase in real terms from a year earlier. This is almost double the amount of the United States, the second-largest tourism spender, spending 7% more to reach only USD 144 billion (UNWTO, 2019).

However, significant changes in spending behavior are continuously taking place, especially among more experienced Chinese travelers (Arlt, 2006). Chinese travelers' ideas of consumption are changing, not least because of the constantly easier access to foreign products in China (Liu and McKercher, 2016). The decrease in per head per trip spending is mainly due to decreases in spending on shopping. More Chinese travelers are increasingly focusing on enjoying high-quality local resources when travelling abroad (Wassler et al., 2017). This includes paying for and taking part in tourism-related activities, dining out to try up-market and local cuisines, inspecting and purchasing real estate, and generally travelling at a slower pace in order to visit places "like a local" (Arlt, 2008). Many travelers are also pursuing a special hobby like golf, photography, sports, and so on at different destinations. Even short-term beach holidays, once considered by most Chinese outbound travelers a waste of precious time, are becoming more important, especially in terms of spending quality time with the family (COTRI, 2019).

Consequences for the International Hospitality Industry

The most important change in the attitude of Chinese travelers towards the preferences of traditional and non-traditional accommodation types and the services provided at the accommodation is that the more experienced Chinese leisure travelers have come to learn what they want and prefer. This is, in general, not a new development and was observed among other source markets earlier (Ryan, 1998, 2010).

In regard to the Chinese outbound tourists, this is true regarding the accommodation type they feel most comfortable in, what services they demand, and how they want to encounter and enjoy the local culture and contacts with the local population. In coming years the current trend will probably result in a market split into three parts of equal size:

First, the traditional package group tours for those proudly holding up their brand-new passport, still looking for a cheap tour and value for money, with little regard towards the quality of the accommodation, which, as a consequence of a packed program and little information about the destination, is mainly used for resting. The brand of accommodation is of secondary nature. The locational of the accommodation is anyway choosing by the tour operator rather than the tourists, mostly on the practical considerations, en-route, where the proximity to the main attraction is as well of secondary importance.

Second, the customized group tours for small groups of friends, family, or colleagues, who know what they want but are too busy to organize the trip themselves. This group is rather interested in staying at a commercial accommodation with a local touch that offers well-developed activities for Chinese guests of different ages, including kids and seniors. Location and branding are of high importance for this customer segment. However, most important the product, configuration of rooms and services are relevant criteria for this customer segment. For the management of traditional accommodation and international hospitality providers is important to understand, that this segment is about to look for accommodation opportunities in the non-traditional sector as known as peer-to-peer rentals. This is mainly based on the suitability and functionality of the accommodation regarding the configuration of rooms and the possibility to accommodate larger families or smaller groups.

Third, the free and independent (FIT) travelers, who are confident and able to experience the perfect trip without the help of tour operators, but are still happy to be offered concierge services. This segment books and troubles like their experienced (Western) counterparts. They are more likely to use booking.com and other travel-related platforms and applications. This segment is definitely taking into consideration to stay at AirB2B and similar short-term non-traditional accommodations with kitchen facilities, washing machines, etc. Beyond the fact, that the segment is seeking the authenticity of those accommodation types, this group is also the most likely one to be interested in eco-friendly or green hotels and resorts, showing their care of to environment as deeper than the ubiquitous "Do not wash the towel" sign. This FIT segment prefers a range of options to customize and personalize their short-term environment and hotel room. FITs as a good source for a story to share with their peers on Chinese social media platforms such as WeChat.

In general, free Wi-Fi is already expected by all these groups. For the immediate future, mobile payment options such as the Chinese Alipay or WeChatpay are becoming an important requirement across accommodation types and hotels. Mobile payment is increasingly popular in China and a source of increased revenue for service providers within and outside the country. Mobile payment has the advantage: the Chinese customers can pay easily in their own currency in foreign countries, without applying for international credit cards all the hassle of foreign money exchange. Considering Chinese guests' reliance on technology and information easily accessible from their mobile device, technology and digitization are getting ever more important, with translated tourism guides and other materials made available in apps and mobile payment options welcomed by the guests. Hotels adapting to that, offering, for example, WeChat Mini Programs in addition to their Chinese website will have a competitive advantage, as all information for Chinese guests can be provided in the same ecosystem the guests are accustomed to using daily back home. In addition, being present in other Chinese travel applications such as Ctrip.com (Trip.com), fliggy.com from Alibaba, or mafengwo.cn, a hybrid between content platform and OTA, needs to be seriously taken into consideration.

Consumer surveys indicate that "safety" is the most important factor in selecting and choosing a destination as well as "being welcomed," which has been named as the second most important criterion for choosing a destination or accommodation. The feeling of "being welcomed" can be enhanced and supported by offering information in Chinese language, showing the Chinese flag among other flags at the entrance, or having selected Chinese food options, beverages or snacks available. Those details are important for all kinds of accommodations. Positive comments and reviews that hotels treat Chinese travelers well is a major factor when determining which hotel to stay in (Chan, 2019).

For luxury hotels, a new development that is gaining ground fast is the collaboration between fashion and hotels. In order to strive for more meaningful, cultural, and engaging experiences, the two sides are beginning to become more intertwined and creative. "Travelling in style is very hot worldwide at the moment, especially for China's young generation. Travelers are spending a good amount of time in their hotel, and the environment is providing great opportunities for retail," said Chinese designer Yang Du in the online magazine Jing Daily (Rapp, 2018). Yang Du, a Dalian (North China) born fashion designer set up a pop-up store at London's South Kensington Gallery in The Exhibitionist Hotel, selling a selection of her playful clothing and accessories to both travelers and Chinese art and design students studying in the UK.

The increase in Chinese guests in hotels around the world has resulted in changes that also benefit other guests. Almost all higher-class hotels now offer disposable slippers, dental kits, and sanitary kits; the infamous water kettle has also become a standard offering, pushing out, in some cases, the supply of ice cubes. How to go the extra mile is shown in a video that is part of the new CTT China Tourism Training Hospitality project, developed by COTRI (China Outbound Tourism Research Institute) together with Hong Kong Polytechnic University, School of Hotel and Tourism Management. Dan Hotels in Israel provide disposable slippers and a water kettle, as well as a special edition package with different Chinese tea leaves that have the Dan Hotels logo and a Chinese description (CTT, 2019) on the packing. Many are making their way to China as inexpensive but effective brand ambassadors.

References

Information is based on COTRI and COTRI ANALYTICS databases if not cited otherwise.

Arlt, W.G. (2006), *China's Outbound Tourism*, Routledge, Abingdon, UK.

Arlt, W.G. (2008), "Feeling welcome: Internet tourism marketing across cultures", in IGI Global (Ed.), *Information Communication Technologies: Concepts, Methodologies, Tools, and Applications*, Shanghai and Beijing, pp.2877–2897.

Arlt, W.G. (2011), "Make hay from the second wave", *China Daily*.

Arlt, W.G. (2013), "The second wave of Chinese outbound tourism", *Tourism Planning & Development*, Vol.10, No.2, pp.126–133.

Arlt, W.G. and Burns, P. (2013), "Chinese outbound tourism", *Tourism Planning & Development*, Vol.10, No.2, pp.123–125.

Arlt, W.G. and Feng, G. (2007), "On the development of tourism organizations responsible for China's tourists to Europe and future tasks", *Tourism Tribune*, Vol.5, pp.40–50.

Arlt, W.G. and Thraenhart, J. (2011), "Social media tourism marketing in China", in Conrady, Roland and Buck, Martin (Eds.), *Trends and Issues in Global Tourism 2011*, Springer, Berlin and Heidelberg, pp.149–154.

Chan, A. (2019), "China outbound tourism trends prediction 2022", available at: https://www.traveldailynews.asia/china-outbound-tourism-trends-prediction-2022 (accessed July 2019).

Chen, Y., Schuckert, M., Song, H., and Chon, K.S. (2014), "Why package tours fall in popularity: Evidence from China's outbound tourism market", in 2014 GMC Global Marketing Conference, Singapore, July 15–18, 2014, pp.496–510.

Chen, Y., Schuckert, M., Song, H., and Chon, K.S. (2016), "Why can package tours hurt tourists? Evidence from China's tourism demand in Hong Kong", *Journal of Travel Research*, Vol.55, No.4, pp.427–439.

COTRI. (2018, Autumn), *COTRI Market Report*, Hamburg.

COTRI. (2019, Spring), *COTRI Market Report*, Hamburg.

CSIS (2019), "How well-off is China's middle class?" China Power Project, Pew Research Center. China Power Team. April 26, 2017. Updated May 29, 2019, available at:https://chinapower.csis.org/china-middle-class/ (accessed 17 August 2019).

CTT (2019, December), *CTT China Tourism Training Hospitality*, COTRI, Hamburg.

Euromonitor. (2018), *India in 2030: The Future Demographic*, Euromonitor, London, UK.

Huang, S., Keating, B.W., Kriz, A., and Heung, V. (2015), "Chinese outbound tourism: An epilogue", *Journal of Travel & Tourism Marketing*, Vol.32, No.1–2, pp.153–159.

Kim, S.S., Schuckert, M., Im, H., and Elliot, S. (2017), "An interregional extension of destination brand equity: From Hong Kong to Europe", *Journal of Vacation Marketing*, Vol.23, No.4, pp.277–294.

Li, Q., Li, S., and Wan, H. (2019), "The missing billionaires: Correcting the data on top incomes in China", *WIDER Research Brief 2019/3*, UNU-WIDER, Helsinki, available at: https://www.wider.unu.edu/publication/missing-billionaires (accessed June 2019).

Lin, V.S., Liu, A., and Song, H. (2015), "Modeling and forecasting Chinese outbound tourism: An econometric approach", *Journal of Travel & Tourism Marketing*, Vol.32, No.1–2, pp.34–49.

Liu, A. and McKercher, B. (2016), "The impact of visa liberalization on tourist behaviors – The case of China outbound market visiting Hong Kong", *Journal of Travel Research*, Vol.55, No.5, pp.603–611.

NDRC (National Development and Reform Commission). (2019), "Report on the implementation of the 2018 plan for national economic and social development and on the 2019 draft plan for national economic and social development", delivered at the Second Session of the thirteenth National People's Congress on March 5, 2019, available at: https://www.wsj.com/public/resources/documents/2019NPC_NDRCReport_EN.pdf?mod=article_inline (accessed June 2019).

Rapp, J. (2018, July 10), "Fashion flirts with hotels to bring Chinese travelers new shopping experiences" *Jing Daily*, available at: https://jingdaily.com/fashion-hotels-chinese-travelers/ (accessed June 2019).

Ryan, C. (1998), "The travel career ladder an appraisal", *Annals of Tourism Research*, Vol.25, No.4, pp.936–957.

Ryan, C. (2010), "Ways of conceptualizing the tourist experience: a review of literature", *Tourism Recreation Research*, Vol.35, No.1, pp.37–46.

Schuckert, M., Wassler, P., and Chon, K.S. (2016), "China travels – Remarks on the development of tourism in China", in Siller, H. and Zehrer, A. (Eds.), *Entrepreneurship und Tourismus: Unternehmerisches Denken und Erfolgskonzepte aus der Praxis*, Linde Verlag, Vienna, pp.219–228.

Thraenhart, J., Chang, K., and Arlt, W.G., (2012), "Essential China travel trends 2012", Beijing, available at: www. chinatraveltrendsbook com/downloads/Essential_China_Travel_Trends_ Dragon_Edition. Pdf, Version 21.01.2014 (accessed June 2019).

UNWTO. (2019), "Exports from international tourism hit USD 1.7 trillion", available at: https://www2.unwto.org/press-release/2019-06-06/exports-international-tourism-hit-usd-17-trillion (accessed June 2019).

Wang, X. and Wing, T.W. (2011), "The size and distribution of hidden household income in China", *Asian Economic Papers*, Vol.10, No.1, pp.1–26.

Wassler, P., Schuckert, M., Chon, K.S., and Song, H. (2017), "Still happy here? How Chinese tourists perceive the service in Hong Kong", in 27th Annual CAUTHE Conference, Vol. 27, 7–10 February 2017, Dunedin, New Zealand.

Wassler, P., Schuckert, M., Hung, K., and Petrick, J.F. (2018), "You're welcome? Hong Kong's attitude towards the individual visit scheme", *International Journal of Tourism Research*, Vol.20, No.5, pp.637–649.

Wong, C.S. and Kwong, W.Y. (2004), "Outbound tourists' selection criteria for choosing all-inclusive package tours", *Tourism Management*, Vol.25, No.5, pp.581–592.

PART IV

Internationalization Strategies and Business Operations

18

THE ROLE OF MERGERS AND ACQUISITIONS AS GROWTH STRATEGIES IN THE INTERNATIONAL HOSPITALITY INDUSTRY

Volkan Genc, Seray Gulertekin Genc, and Engin Aytekin

Introduction

In the 21st century, the tourism industry has become one of the largest industries in the world. As of 2018, international tourist arrivals reached 1.326 billion per year and international tourism revenues equaled US$1.340 billion (UNWTO, 2018). Thus, it has become necessary for hospitality companies in the tourism industry to adapt to make the changes required to maintain market shares and open up new markets in the face of globalization and technological innovations. As part of this process, hospitality businesses have had to develop strategies oriented towards achieving growth, development, and competitiveness depending on market conditions (Ibis and Batman, 2015). Today, one of the most salient growth strategies is the Merger and Acquisition (M&A).

M&As are one of several potential investment projects that businesses can follow, and they play a critical role in the growth of the hospitality industry, allowing businesses to grow faster through natural means. M&As are essential to change issues and need to be evaluated in a multifaceted way. Growth is generally considered to be critical to the health of a business. In general, growing companies attract more customers, higher quality employees, and investors. At the same time, M&As offer businesses assorted advantages through economies of scale such as cost efficiency, increases in market share, sales growth, financial stability, and increases in profitability, benefits, and shareholder value (Hsu and Jang, 2007; Kim et al., 2018).

M&As are widely used by the hospitality industry as a significant growth strategy (Park and Jang, 2011). According to the Thomson One Banker database, only two M&A deals, valued at $248.53 million, were announced in the hospitality industry in 1980. In contrast, the frequency and total value of hospitality M&A deal increased to 265 deals with a value of $17.50 billion in 2016 (Kim et al., 2018). These statistical data show that M&As are increasingly used in the global hospitality industry as an important competition tool. For example, the merger of Marriott International/Starwood Hotels & Resorts Worldwide and the merger of Accor Hotels/Fairmont Hotels & Resorts are among the most prominent international mergers of recent years. Market analysts predict that the best hotel chains take up approximately 33% of traditional hotel rooms globally. Besides, the larger scale of recent M&As and the dominance they have in terms of market share indicate that international M&As will continue to be utilized against the growing threat of alternative accommodation businesses such as Airbnb and OneFineStay. Although M&As are considered to be preferred business growth and renewal tool in the competitive global tourism industry, research has shown that achieving success in M&As is complex and difficult (Gomes et al., 2013). Studies carried out on the impact of M&As' performance demonstrate that, contrary to expectations, they do not necessarily advance the financial performance of businesses (Zollo and Meier, 2008). The weakness of most of these studies is that they measure a short period of time ranging from a few days to a three-year period around the time of the M&A, when the integration process is still in progress (Teerikangas and Thanos, 2018).

On the other hand, the very few studies undertaken from a longer-term perspective (Laamanen and Keil, 2008; Quah and Young, 2005; Teerikangas and Thanos, 2018) suggest that the impact of M&As on the performance of businesses will be negative in the initial years after an agreement is reached and highlight that, in the long run, the outlook is positive (Quah and Young, 2005). In this context, the M&A seems to be complex and dependent on the level of operational, organizational, and socio-cultural integration. It has been noted that it takes an average of five to ten years to be able to report positive performance figures in businesses where acquisition has taken place. These findings reveal the complexity of natural management to the success of M&As.

In this study, M&As will be considered as a growth strategy and will be examined conceptually. The theories related to M&A will be put forward and it will explain why M&As are undertaken by hospitality businesses. Finally, M&As' human aspect will also be revealed.

Growth Strategy

The basic strategies of hospitality businesses include growth, downsizing, stagnation, and mixed strategies. Hospitality businesses of different sizes and management levels use a variety of techniques to implement corporate, competitive, and functional strategies. Some hospitality businesses apply these techniques on their own, without setting up another business, while other businesses apply them depending on or in relation to other businesses. Hospitality businesses that demand growth endeavor to achieve this goal through internal growth or external growth. Internal growth is based on investments within the business itself whereas external growth comes as a result of the purchasing of shares in another business, control of shares or cooperation with another business. External growth has been the preferred method for business managers in recent years, with a significant tendency for concentration in the tourism industry, including the development of industrial and hotel chains (Ulgen and Mirze, 2010).

A growth strategy is a strategy that may allow the realization of expectations in the hospitality industry and increase welfare and is aimed at increasing the profitability and market share of hospitality businesses depending on the market conditions of the goods/services. Therefore, managers endeavor to implement and maintain this basic strategy (Clarke and Chen, 2007).

Growth in businesses can also be distinguished between quantitative and quantitative growth. Digital growth and development refer to a quantitative increase in factors such as returns in sales, product variety, resource size (number of employees, capital size), asset size (increase in investments) and capacity utilization, according to the characteristics of businesses. On the other hand, qualitative growth is related to an increase in the quality of elements in the business (Ulgen and Mirze, 2010). Hospitality businesses undergo M&As in order to grow, maintain their current situation, and compete with rivals.

Merger and Acquisition Concepts

A business merger is described as the *"termination of past and legal entities of two or more independent businesses for coming into operation as a new and independent business, under a new name by putting together all the assets and capabilities*" (Ulgen and Mirze, 2010, p. 349). The merger usually takes place on equal terms. Equal conditions, here, does not mean that shares or partnerships are 50-50 in terms of the distribution of shares. For instance, a very big, rich hospitality business and a small hospitality business with a good location can establish a new independent business with relatively equal conditions, with a share of 90% to 10%. Equality does not occur in terms of shares; equality means relative equality and refers to the rights upon which the businesses agree and accept.

A business acquisition happens when a business acquires the whole (100%) or a majority of the shares of another business, turning it into an affiliation of the acquiring (Ulgen and Mirze, 2010, p. 350). Here, just like in the merger, the identity and legal personality of the acquired and purchased company does not come to an end. Both businesses go on operating exactly as before. The only thing that changes is the ownership of all or a majority of the shares of the hospitality business acquired, and as a consequence, the management of the business passes to the control of the acquirer.

At this point, it is required that all or a majority of the shares of the acquired business must be purchased. Generally, the acquisition takes place unilaterally in line with the wishes and intentions of the purchasing company. In some cases, this one-sided intent may be hostile and destructive. In addition, businesses that have talent in the market but lack financial strength may intend and want to be acquired by a strong business in order to strengthen and continue operating. They may even bring forward suggestions for other businesses to buy the business (Ulgen and Mirze, 2010).

When the history of M&As is examined, it may be seen that M&As happened more frequently during certain periods. In the literature, this is called the M&A Wave. According to the literature, six main M&A waves have been identified especially in the United States (Martynova and Renneboog, 2008). The volume and value of the M&As of each wave have been higher than during the previous waves. The First Wave (1897–1904) mirrored migration and technological changes. Mergers were largely between competitors and were concentrated on metals, transport, and mining industries. The Second Wave (1916–1929) was the result of the economic boom following World War I. The Third Wave (1965–1969) was experienced mainly due to increases in the stocks of merged firms. The Fourth Wave (1981–1989) occurred in the 1980s, following hostile takeovers of many large corporate groups. The Fifth Wave (1992–1999) emerged as a result of the reduction of trade barriers, the development of information technology, and the global trend towards privatization. The Sixth Wave (2003–2008) developed rapidly until the 2008 economic crisis thanks to the low credit possibilities provided by banks. Historically, each merger wave has varied in terms of a particular development (such as the emergence of new technology), sectoral focus (such as railway, oil, or financial services), degree of regulation, and type of operation (such as horizontal) (DePamphilis, 2014).

International growth in the hospitality industry began to increase during the so-called third wave after World War II when hotels such as Hilton, Sheraton, and InterContinental started to invest overseas. Between the 1980s and 1990s, when globalization was a major trend, many hospitality businesses spread across the world to find opportunities to grow (Met, 2005). During this period, M&As were concentrated in the hospitality industry.

It is suggested that certain market conditions trigger or facilitate periodic waves of M&As (Kim and Zheng, 2014). International hospitality businesses have been influenced by industry activities and merger waves, such as the emergence of new technologies, distribution channels, replacement products, or continuous increases in the prices of such products. Such happenings often enable businesses to obtain all or part of other businesses (Park and Jang, 2011). In this process, it is necessary to know the methods of M&A applied by hospitality businesses: vertical, horizontal, and conglomerate.

Merger and Acquisition Methods

Vertical Mergers and Acquisitions

M&As between businesses in the same sector/market and supply chain are called vertical M&As. Vertical mergers or acquisitions may be applied forward or backward. It is claimed that they offer a variety of benefits for hotel businesses.

An M&A with other firms that distribute the products of the business to the consumer market in the supply chain is an example of a prospective vertical M&A (Ulgen and Mirze, 2010). On the other hand, an M&A made with firms that provide the inputs of a business is defined as a backward vertical M&A (Figure 18.1).

Horizontal Mergers and Acquisitions

M&As among competitors in the same sector are called horizontal M&As. Horizontal M&As refer to the expansion of the activities of a firm to other geographical regions or an increase in the range of products and services offered to existing markets. Horizontal M&As generally include the acquisition of another firm in the same sector (an example of external growth) and the expansion of a firm's products into the existing market (e.g., through line extensions) or to another geographical region (e.g., internal growth). They aim to increase the business' market share to a great extent. Therefore, an M&A that may hamper competition in the market is subject to the authorization of the authorities. Therefore, employing an M&A, once-rival businesses may form a monopoly or become a dominant power in the market, which can hamper competition and disrupt the market structure and price mechanism. This kind of structure, which damages the free market economy, is not allowed in modern market economies. However, M&As that do not constrain competition or disrupt the market structure can be undertaken freely (Ulgen and Mirze, 2010).

Conglomerate Mergers and Acquisitions

Conglomerate M&As occur between different sectors and businesses in the market. Firms may wish to access new markets to generate above-average returns, but have little or no information or experience of those markets, or for other reasons. Because it is a dependent diversification strategy,

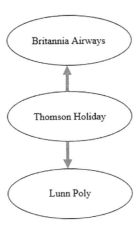

Figure 18.1 Vertical mergers and acquisition example.

businesses in different sectors can merge with mutual desire and agreement, in this form of M&A. It may also arise when one company decides to acquire a firm in a different sector; in this case, the desire to merge is unilateral (Ulgen and Mirze, 2010).

Theories of Mergers and Acquisitions

Distinct reasons have been introduced to explain why merger and acquisition strategies are used. In order to understand this strategy, there is a need to explain some theories that explore this subject. These are Productivity Theory, Monopoly Theory, Raider Theory, Valuation Theory, Empire-Building Theory, Process Theory, Economic Disturbance Theory, and Adaptation Theory (Trautwein, 1990).

- Productivity Theory

  According to productivity theory, M&As are carried out to obtain financial, operational, and managerial synergies. Financial synergies arise as a result of conglomerate mergers in order to minimize investment risk. At the same time, M&As are another source of financial synergy that can lead to business expansion. Thus, they can facilitate access to capital at a low cost. On the other hand, operational synergy is achieved when marketing either production capacities and skills can be used together. As a result of an M&A, managerial synergies are generated through the abilities and skills of the managers who join the business (Cunill, 2006).

- Monopoly Theory

  According to this theory, businesses perform mergers or acquisitions in order to increase their competitiveness. Horizontal mergers may reduce market competition. For that reason, some states try to interfere with such mergers or acquisitions in order to prevent the formation of monopolies. However, firms that engage in vertical mergers can also create situations where competition is restricted. For example, a customer may have problems with the supply of certain goods if the supplier has been taken over by a competitor, or a business may use business resources that operate in a different market to increase its market potential (Cunill, 2006).

- Raider Theory

  This theory refers to when businesses make proposals to purchase and take control of shares in other businesses. In this situation, there has either been no negotiation between the businesses, or no results could be reached as a result of negotiations. Thus, an offer, open to the public, is made for stocks at a fixed price and, thus the purchasing business takes the other under its control. Sometimes in such cases, businesses may have to pay a higher price than would have been produced through friendly negotiations (Cunill, 2006).

- Valuation Theory

  According to this theory, mergers and acquisitions are carried out by managers who have been able to gain more accurate information in the investment market about the real value of the business to be acquired. The opportunism of the manager plays a key role in this theory. This information may include identifying advantages such as the benefits obtained from the acquisition of a business or the financial depredation of a business (Cunill, 2006).

- Empire-Building Theory

  Empire-Building Theory is based on the idea that the managers responsible for formulating and implementing such strategies have only one goal, which is to maximize their field of activity. By including a power-oriented target, this theory argues that when a business attains more market power, the power of the business' administration increases as well (Cunill, 2006).

- Process Theory

  Trautwein (1990) indicates that this theory intends to justify M&As by linking them to the limited logic of decision-making management teams without providing an in-depth examination of alternative facilities.

- Economic Disturbance Theory

  Economic Disturbance Theory supports the idea that M&As influence each other in waves. They are activated by economic disturbances (Mueller, 1989) that change individual behavior patterns and expectations. Industrial economy theories and transaction cost theory constitute a part of – or are related to – this theory.

- Adaptation Theory

  This theory is about changes in businesses and their adaptation to environmental conditions. This theory can be divided into two approaches; resource dependency and transaction cost. In the resource dependency approach, businesses have to use inputs from their environment in order to survive. However, the amount, characteristics, importance, and ease of the acquisition of such inputs are disparate. There are uncertainties and difficulties in the provision of some inputs that are important for the business. Businesses take various steps to ensure the acquisition of inputs that are essential for their survival and arduous to secure. Among these measures are M&As. Transaction cost theory, meanwhile, predicts that businesses will act proactively to secure their future and will ensure that their conformity behaviors and their outputs flow into the environment safely (Ulgen and Mirze, 2010).

Why Mergers and Acquisitions Happen in the Hospitality Industry

There are many reasons why M&As arise. Synergy is at the forefront of these reasons. Synergy is the value gained by an increase in cash flow generated by bringing two businesses together. That is to say, if the market value of two companies is $150 million and $75 million, respectively, and their combined market value is $250 million, the implied value of their synergy is $25 million. There are two main types of synergy: operational and financial. Operational synergy includes economies of scale and economies of scope, which can be vital determinants of the creation of shareholders' assets. Gains obtained by productivity may result from either factors or advanced managerial practices. On the other hand, financial synergy refers to the decrease in the capital costs of a business created through a merger or acquisition. This situation may lead to merged firms having relatively unrelated cash flows, savings in terms of transaction costs, and the better matching of investment opportunities with internally generated funds (DePamphilis, 2014).

Hospitality businesses also perform M&As in order to diversify. The acquisition of business outside the existing business' area is called diversification. Diversification can create a financial synergy that reduces capital costs (DePamphilis, 2014). In addition, the target markets of the hospitality business may attract businesses with its higher growth expectations, including when the businesses are operating in different markets. Many hospitality businesses within a conglomerate may prefer to pursue this option.

Kiymaz (2004) mentions that M&As help hospitality businesses increase their economies of scale, increase and share their market power, reduce financing costs, and increase financial stability through diversification. Hospitality businesses positioned within M&As go through significant increases in short-term sales growth (Park and Jang, 2011) and market valuation (Chatfield et al., 2011). M&As not only increase their competitive advantage, but also bring new skills, capabilities, and productivities, especially to companies intending to grow beyond national borders (Dyer et al., 2004).

Businesses conduct M&As in order to reduce competition and increase profitability, seeking opportunities for investments, or to increase stocks (Glueck, 1980). In addition, a hospitality business may enter into an M&A due to a decrease in access to capital, or if the company is aging. What is more, there is limited power and decreasing operating margin in a managed maintenance contract. Because all of these factors contribute to the inability of the business to compete based on its services and competencies. Businesses often seek a partner that will increase the market share of the unsuccessful business in the partnership. Finally, the effects and advantages of an M&A-based growth strategy for hospitality businesses are described below (Cunill, 2006):

- Having acquired a business, the acquirer will have expanded its geographic coverage and / or will have acquired new brand names. Thus, by this way, the acquirer may achieve its growth targets, gain stronger assets in the hospitality industry, expand its markets or market segments. In addition, it may have the opportunity to increase its competitive advantages, including both strategic complementary work as well as something new gained from the business that has been acquired.
- The more dynamic hotel businesses in the hospitality industry are constantly working to increase their market share in order to obtain economies of scale in areas such as reservation, information technology, marketing, and acquisition. In short, the aim is to secure the resources and capabilities that the firm cannot have or cannot use optimally because it does not have sufficient reach.
- Customers are increasingly expecting hospitality businesses to offer them a quality service that includes worldwide discounts and hotel coverage and meets their expectations.

Although M&As have several advantages, Dickerson et al. (1997) state that M&As cannot ensure that a business' aims, upon entering into an M&A, will be achieved as they are acquiring an already-existing business or company. As a result, M&As can lead to a decline in the performance of a business. In addition, there may be some difficulties in integrating the two companies. One of the major risks relates to cultural differences between merging firms. Previous studies have acknowledged that integration after an M&A is a time-consuming process and that businesses should not expect a synergy immediately after an M&A. Based on a simulation study, Miczka and Größler (2004) claimed that cultural integration is generally completed in the first three years after an M&A. However, a real synergy may take longer. Therefore, based on the idea that M&A integration tends to take time, this study intended to examine the effects of an M&A for up to five years (Park and Jang, 2011).

The Human Aspect of Merger and Acquisition Outcomes

M&As have become increasingly popular as a means of organizational growth and internationalization. When M&As are examined, it is recognized that between 50% and 80% of them are unsuccessful (Gunkel et al., 2015; Kusstatscher and Cooper, 2005; Sinkovics et al., 2011). One of the most essential reasons for this failure is the fact that the owners and managers of the firms involved often concentrate on the financing and economic aspects of this strategic decision, ignoring the human dimension of the issue. M&As are serious issues of change and need to be evaluated in a multifaceted way. In this context, employees are influential actors in the process of change and constitute the dimension most affected by the results of the change. Therefore, it can be argued that an acquisition will not be successful unless the employees involved are ready for and accepting of the change, thus overcoming any humanitarian problems that may arise (Vos, 2006).

Resistance to change is, in a sense, an employee behavior that includes distrust, doubt, and change prevention carried out within the organization. Employees may show resistance to changes within the organization for different reasons. For example, they may resist change because they believe that the change will not be beneficial in the way it is intended to, or fear being fired or losing power and status as a result of the change. The change also brings along with it several new business relationships. During the process of change, in particular, it is quite common for highly qualified personnel to be recruited and employed in positions higher than existing employees. In such cases, employees with a certain level of power and influence under the old system may be resistant to change that will mean a loss of that power and influence (Akoglan Kozak, 2004). Another reason why employees may be resistant relates to the allocation of resources. The individuals or groups that control and distribute resources within the organization may regard the change as a threat to themselves and so may fight back (Ozkalp, 2013). The crucial thing here is to identify the psychology of resistance among employees. Reacting against change is part of human nature as each person has habits and it is not easy to change one's habits or sacrifice one's position (Peker and Ayturk, 2000).

Scott and Jaffe (1988) explained the process of change takes place in four stages including denial, resistance, gradual exploration, and commitment. The first two stages are natural or unnatural reactions among employees due to known or unknown, but still expected events. It is not easy to avoid these stages. Adapting to change is a cognitive and emotional process experienced by employees. Marks and Mirvis (1988) describe this process as merger syndrome. This syndrome, in a way, signals the reactions of employees during the process of change due to factors such as the centralization of decision-making, power games, stress, insecurity, and concern. It is quite common for new managers to be recruited to upper-tier positions in the purchased company during and after the acquisition process. In this situation, existing employees who had power and influence under the old system may go on resisting if they fear that they may lose their power and influence either may mobilize the informal structure within the business to aid their resistance (Akoglan Kozak, 2004).

Studies show that the feelings of employees are not taken into consideration when changes are carried out both in innovations in customer satisfaction (Coch and French, 1948; Klarner et al., 2011; Vos, 2006). Emotions are an essential part of human behavior and affect roles and behaviors in business life (Erkus and Gunlu, 2008). Emotions can either positively or negatively affect life-oriented perspectives as well as the morale and performance of employees, depending on how well they are managed (Kusstatscher and Cooper, 2005; Oreg, 2006).

Emotions reflect one's interpretation of events in the face of change and uncertainty (Klarner et al., 2011). Therefore, an important part of understanding the dynamics of change is understanding the relationship between change and negative emotions. For example, Sinkovics et al. (2011) identified that employees experience negative emotions during the M&A process. For this reason, managers play an important role in the prevention of resistance. In a study by Gunkel et al. (2015), it was revealed that administrative support in the process of mergers and acquisitions positively affects the feelings and active resistance behaviors of employees.

Consequently, when managers do not fathom or do not want to accept employees as part of this process, this may lead to results that are hard to compensate for in the future. Poorly managed change can lead to resistance through an exaggeration of the negative aspects of the change among employees (DiFonzo et al., 1994). Cultural diversity and organizational and cultural mismatch are often regarded as the main causes of poor performance among employees (Cartwright and Schoenberg, 2006). The feelings of employees should not be suppressed in the process of change and the causes of emotions should be properly analyzed. During this period, employees' fears should be sensed and their perceptions of the change should be managed. Huy (1998) stated that it is a far-reaching competence of managers to have empathy during the management of the change process.

Six change strategies proposed in previous studies (Clarke et al., 1996; Kotter and Schlesinger, 1979; Schermerhorn et al., 2002) suggest that there are various ways hotel enterprises can use to manage change. These include training and communication, participation and internalization, facilitation and support, depreciation and agreement, and manipulation and cooptation. Communication, training, participation, internalization, planning, and power emerged as important means used by administrators in Okumus and Hemmington's study (1998). Communication was the paramount factor in the change process with training the second essential and widely accepted aspect, followed by participation and internalization. Many managers consider managing change to be a learning process. Thus, they have suggested that the experience and knowledge gained from this process help them cope with continuous change (Akoglan Kozak, 2004; Burnes and Jackson, 2011; Yeniçeri, 2002). In the following years, research conducted by Erem (2003) on service businesses found that participation can be an effective method of preventing resistance to change among employees. However, if "change plans" prepared by employees are not suitable for the business, change can be time-consuming.

The success of a change is highly dependent on the development of effective communication between managers and subordinates (Keenan, 2002). The research demonstrated that some methods of communication are more effective than others at preventing resistance among employees (Chiang, 2010). Akbaba and Mesci (2007) also emphasized that a lack of communication in hotel businesses will cause resistance. Additionally, Bovey and Hede (2001) stated that the most important reason for the failure of change in service businesses is the resistance factor. If resistance is to be prevented in the process of change, it is required that managers recognize the importance of communication. In another study performed by Ince (2008) in the following years, it was affirmed that resistance among employees in hotel businesses can be prevented by ensuring effective communication. Even though communication is considered a method that is commonly used by businesses (Burnes and Philip, 2011; Pieterse et al., 2012), it is believed to be time-consuming when a particular change concerns a large number of people. For that reason, it can be said in this context that using the communication method alone will not be sufficient for preventing resistance.

Change means that new information and processes can enter the organization constantly. In some cases, as new information and processes are unknown, they may be seen as issues to be feared by some employees. Therefore, being able to overcome this fear, arising from not knowing the new information and processes, depends upon the successful implementation of repeated training in the process of change (Basim et al., 2009).

In a study conducted by Leana and Barry (2000), it was indicated that group structures affect the feelings of employees. A study conducted by Bartunek et al. (2006) focused on the effects of emotional contagion and determined that it is the emotions of individuals within the organization that particularly affect the actions of the group. This is because groups remain intact when their members have common goals and shared beliefs about how these goals can be achieved. If these goals are positive, they may provide support for the formation of the group. If they are negative, however, they may constitute an obstacle to the formation of the group. The satisfaction of group members will be high in business as long as their common desires and requirements are satisfactorily met and an appropriate emotional environment is continued. The more robust and rigid the group structures are in the organization, the more difficult it is to make that group adopt and apply changes. Making fixed-structured groups adopt changes depends on the morale of the group and the attitude of the group leader (Eren, 2012). A study carried out by Cevik and Akoglan Kozak (2010) stated that leadership is important in order to prevent resistance among employees during the process of change in tourism businesses. Because if the leader of the group considers the changes to be appropriate, they may not have any difficulty persuading their colleagues to accept the changes. In this context, it can be argued that the psychological and social situations experienced by employees during M&As should be taken into consideration.

Conclusion

M&As are of great importance for the hospitality industry as strategic competitive instruments that form an important part of a growth strategy. M&As provide a basis for hospitality businesses to expand their market segments, benefit from information technologies, diversify their products and services, and create new brands. When M&As are studied in the context of the hospitality industry, it is observed that failure is common during the first stage. The most important reason for this is the resistance of employees to change. In particular, managers ignore the human side while focusing on the financial aspects of changes. M&As are significant changes and need to be evaluated in a multifaceted way. The key role of managers here is to be aware of the emotions of employees and to be in direct contact with them.

As explicitly stated in this chapter, as a growth strategy, each step of an M&A should be evaluated in detail and a realistic fashion. There is no point in performing an M&A without going over the economic, social, political developments in the world, the wave of M&As, and the situations of competitors and target markets. In addition, unpredictable and costly changes can drive businesses into bankruptcy. Hospitality businesses should keep in mind the future of the hospitality and accommodation industry when considering M&A activities. In this sector, where competition and political uncertainty are intense, each business should implement a viable and traceable strategy that reflects its short- and long-term goals. Consequently, it is expected that hospitality businesses that follow the market, pay attention to social, cultural, and environmental developments and dominant trends, and observe the status of competitors have high growth potential in their sector, with the help of M&As.

References

Akbaba, A. and Mesci, M. (2007), "Otel işletmelerinde toplam kalite yönetimine geçişte sorun yaşanabilecek alanların belirlenmesi: Antalya Belek bölgesinde bir araştırma" (Determination of areas that may cause problems in transition to total quality management in hotel enterprises: A research in Antalya/Belek), *Selçuk Üniversitesi Karaman İ.İ.B.F. Dergisi*, Vol.12, pp.33–50.

Akoglan Kozak, M. (2004), *Değişim Yönetimi Otel İşletme Müdürlerinin Değişim Yönetimi ile İlgili Algılamaları Üzerine Bir Araştırma (A Research on the Change Management of Hotel Management Managers' Perceptions of Change Management)*, Detay Yayıncılık, Ankara.

Bartunek, M.J., Denise, M.R., Jenny, W.R., and Judith, A.D. (2006), "On the receiving end sensemaking, emotion, and assessments of an organizational change initiated by others", *The Journal of Applied Behavioral Science*, Vol.42, No.2, pp.182–206.

Basim, H.N., Yeloglu H.O., Sagsan, M., Sesen, H., and Çetin, F. (Eds.). (2009), *Örgütlerde Değişim ve Öğrenme (Change and Learning in Organizations)*, Siyasal-Yayın Dağıtım, Ankara.

Bovey, H.W. and Hede, A. (2001), "Resistance to organizational change: The role of cognitive and affective processes", *Leadership & Organization Development Journal*, Vol.22, No.8, pp.372–382.

Burnes, B. and Jackson, P. (2011), "Success and failure in organizational change: An exploration of the role of values", *Journal of Change Management*, Vol.11, No.2, pp.133–162.

Cartwright, S. and Schoenberg, R. (2006), "30 years of mergers and acquisitions research", *British Journal of Management*, Vol.15, pp.51–55.

Cevik, S. and Akoglan Kozak, M. (2010), "Değişim yönetiminde dönüşümcü liderlik ve hizmetkar liderlik" (Transformational leadership and servant leadership in change management), in *11. Ulusal Turizm Kongresi Bildiri Kitabı*, 2010, 2–5 Aralik 2010, Kuşadası, Detay Yayıncılık, Kuşadası, Türkiye, pp.80–87.

Chatfield, H.K., Dalbor, M.C., and Ramdeen, C.D. (2011), "Returns of merger and acquisition activities in the restaurant industry", *Journal of Foodservice Business Research*, Vol.14, No.3, pp.189–205.

Chiang, C.F. (2010), "Perceived organizational change in the hotel industry: An implication of change schema", *International Journal of Hospitality Management*, Vol.29, pp.157–167.

Clarke, A. and Chen, W. (2007), *International Hospitality Management, Concepts and Cases*, Elsevier, San Diego, CA.

Clarke, S.J., Chad, D.E., Bateman, J.M., and Rugutt, J.K. (1996), "Faculty receptivity/resistance to change, personal and organizational efficacy, decision deprivation and effectiveness in research I universities, to the Educational Resources (Eric).

Coch, L. and French, J. (1948), "Overcoming resistance to change", *Human Relations*, Vol.1, pp.512–532.

Cunill, O.M. (2006), *The Growth Strategies of Hotel Chains Best Business Practices by Leading Companies*, Routledge, New York, NY.

DePamphilis, D.M. (2014), *Mergers, Acquisitions, and Other Restructuring Activities an Integrated Approach to Process, Tools, Cases, and Solutions*, Elsevier, San Diego, CA.

Dickerson, A.P., Gibson, H.D., and Tsakalotos, E. (1997), "The impact of acquisitions on company performance: Evidence from a large panel of UK firms", *Oxford Economic Papers*, Vol.49, No.3, pp.344–361.

DiFonzo, N., Bordia, P., and Rosnow, R.L. (1994), "Reining in rumors", *Organizational Dynamics*, Vol.23, No.1, pp.47–62.

Dyer, J., Kale, P., and Singh, H. (2004), "When to ally & when to acquire", *Harvard Business Review*, Vol.82, No.7–8, pp.108–115.

Erem, N.G. (2003), Toplam Kalite Yönetiminin Hizmet İşletmelerinde Uygulanması ve Süleyman Demirel Üniversitesi Tıp Fakültesi ve Uygulama Hastanesinde Bir Uygulama (The Application of Total Quality Management at Service Enterprises and a Model Practice at Süleyman Demirel University Faculty of Medicine and Practice Hospital), (Unpublished PhD thesis), Süleyman Demirel Üniversitesi, Isparta, Turkey.

Eren, E. (2012), *Örgütsel Davranış ve Yönetim Psikolojisi (Organizational Behavior and Management Psychology)*, Beta Yayıncılık, İstanbul.

Erkus, A. and Gunlu, E. (2008), "Duygusal zekanın dönüşümcü liderlik üzerine etkileri" (The effects of emotional intelligence on transformational leadership), *Dokuz Eylül Üniversitesi, İşletme Fakültesi Dergisi*, Vol.9, No.2, pp.187–209.

Glueck, W.E. (1980), *Strategic Management and Business Policy*, McGraw-Hill, New York, NY.

Gomes, E., Angwin, D.N., Weber, Y., and Tarba, S.Y. (2013), "Critical success factors through the mergers and acquisitions process: Revealing pre- and post-M&A connections for improved performance", *Thunderbird International Business Review*, Vol.55, No.1, pp.13–35.

Gunkel, M., Schlägel, C., Rosseutscher, T., and Wolff, B. (2015), "The human aspect of cross-border acquisition outcomes: The role of management practices, employee emotions, and national culture", *International Business Review*, Vol.24, pp.394–408.

Hsu, L.T.J. and Jang, S.C.S. (2007), "The postmerger financial performance of hotel companies", *Journal of Hospitality & Tourism Research*, Vol.31, No.4, pp.471–485.

Huy, N.Q. (1998), "Emotional capability, emotional intelligence, and radical change", *Academy of Management Review*, Special Multilevel Issue.

Ibis, S. and Batman, O. (2015), "Konaklama sektörünün küreselleşme süreci" (Globalization process of accommodation industry), in Batman, O. (Ed.), *Uluslararası Otel İşletmeciliği (International Hotel Management)*, DeğişimYayınları, İstanbul, pp.59–88.

Ince, C. (2008), "Toplam kalite yönetimi ve otel işletmelerinde işgören tatminine etkileri" (Total quality management and its effects on employee satisfaction in hotel businesses), *Anatolia: Turizm Araştırmaları Dergisi*, Vol.19, No.1, pp.57–70.

Keenan, J.P. (2002), "Whistleblowing: A study of managerial differences", *Employee Responsibilities and Rights Journal*, Vol.14, No.1, pp.17–32.

Kim, J. and Zheng, T. (2014), "A review of merger and acquisition wave literature: Proposing future research in the restaurant industry", *Hospitality Review*, Vol.31, No.3, pp.93–117.

Kim, J., Zheng, T., and Schrier, T. (2018), "Examining the relationship between the economic environment and restaurant merger and acquisition activities", *International Journal of Contemporary Hospitality Management*, Vol.30, No.2, pp.1054–1071.

Kiymaz, H. (2004), "Cross-border acquisitions of us financial institutions: Impact of macroeconomic factors", *Journal of Banking & Finance*, Vol.28, No.6, pp.1413–1439.

Klarner, P., By, R.T., and Diefenbach, T. (2011), "Employee emotions during organizational change", *Scandinavian Journal of Management*, Vol.27, pp.332–340.

Kotter, J. and Schlesinger, L. (1979), "Choosing strategies for change", *Harvard Business Review*, Vol.57, No.2, pp.106–114.

Kusstatscher, V. and Cooper, C. (2005), *Managing Emotions in Mergers and Acquisitions*, Edward Elgar Publishing Ltd., Cheltenham, UK.

Laamanen, T. and Keil, T. (2008), "The performance of serial acquirers: Toward an acquisition program perspective", *Strategic Management Journal*, Vol.29, No.6, pp.663–672.

Leana, C.R. and Barry, B. (2000), "Stability and change as simultaneous experiences organizational life", *Academy of Management Review*, Vol.25, No.4, pp.753–759.

Marks, M.L. (1988), "The Merger syndrome: The human side of corporate combinations", *Journal of Buyouts & Acquisitions*, Vol.1, pp.18–23.

Martynova, M. and Renneboog, L. (2008), "Spillover of corporate governance standards in cross-border mergers and acquisitions", *Journal of Corporate Finance*, Vol.14, pp.200–223.

Met, Ö. (2005), "Çok uluslu otel zincirlerinin büyüme ve uluslararasılaşma stratejileri" (Growth and internationalisation strategies of multinational hotel chains), *Akdeniz Üniversitesi İktisadi ve İdari Bilimler Fakültesi Dergisi*, Vol.10, pp.111–138.

Miczka, S.F.L. and Größler, A. (2004), "Merger dynamics-a system dynamics analysis of post-merger integration processes", Paper presented at the 22nd International System Dynamics Socienty Conference, July 25–29, Oxford, UK.

Mueller, D.C. (1989), "Mergers: Causes, effects and policies", *International Journal of Industrial Organization*, Vol. 7, No.1, pp.1–10.

Okumus, F. and Hemmington, N. (1998), "Barriers and resistance to change in hotel firms:an investigation at unit level", *International Journal of Contemporary Hospitality Management*, Vol.10, No.7, pp.283–288.

Oreg, S. (2006), "Personality, context, and resistance to organizational change", *European Journal of Work and Organizational Psychology*, Vol.15, No.1, pp.73–101.

Ozkalp, E. (2013), *Sosyolojiye Giriş (Introduction to Sociology)*, Ekin Basın Yayın, Bursa.

Park, K. and Jang, S.C.S. (2011), "Mergers and acquisitions and firm growth: Investigating restaurant firms", *International Journal of Hospitality Management*, Vol. 30, pp.141–149.

Peker, O., and Ayturk, N. (2000), *Etkili Yönetim Becerileri (Effective Management Skills)*, Yargı Yayinevi, Ankara.

Pieterse, H.J., Marjolein, C.J.C., and Thijs, H. (2012), "Professional discourses and resistance to change", *Journal of Organizational Change Management*, Vol.25, No.6, pp.798–818.

Quah, P. and Young, S. (2005), "Post-acquisition management: A phases approach for cross-border M&A", *European Management Journal*, Vol.23, No.1, pp.65–75.

Schermerhorn, R.J., James G.H., and Osborn, R.N. (2002), *Organizational Behavior*, John Wiley & Sons, New York, NY.

Scott, C.D., and Jaffe, D.T. (1988), "Survive and thrive in times of change," *Training & Development Journal*, Vol.42, No.4, pp.25–28.

Sinkovics, R.R., Zagelmeyer, S., and Kusstatscher, V. (2011), "Between merger and syndrome: The intermediary role of emotions in four cross-border M&As", *International Business Review*, Vol.20, No.1, pp. 27–47.

Teerikangas, S. and Thanos, I.C. (2018), "Looking into the 'black box' – unlocking the effect of integration on acquisition performance", *European Management Journal*, Vol.36, pp.366–380.

Trautwein, F. (1990), "Merger motives and merger prescriptions", *Strategic Management Journal*, Vol.11, No.4, pp.283–295.

Ulgen, H. and Mirze, S.K. (2010), *İşletmelerde Stratejik Yönetim (Strategic Management in Business)*, Beta Yayınları, İstanbul.

UNWTO. (2018), *UNWTO Tourism Highlights 2018 Edition*, available at: https://www.e-unwto.org/doi/pdf/10.18111/9789284419876 (accessed 26 December 2018).

Vos, J. (2006), "The role of personality and emotions in employee resistance to change", Unpublished PhD Thesis, Erasmus University, Rotterdam, Holland.

Yeniçeri, Ö. (2002), *Örgütsel Değişmenin Yönetimi (Management of Organizational Change)*, Nobel Yayıncılık, Ankara.

Zollo, M. and Meier, D. (2008), "What is M&A performance?", *Academy of Management Perspectives*, Vol.22, No.3, pp.55–77.

19

HOTEL FIRMS

Who internationalizes and How?
Evidence from the Spanish Hotel Industry

Oriol Anguera-Torrell

Introduction

The economics literature on cross-border business activities has focused on analyzing which firms engage in global activities and how they do so. Firm-level productivity has been proven to be a key factor. Firms operating across borders are, on average, more productive than firms operating only in domestic markets (Helpman et al., 2004; Melitz, 2003). Moreover, firms engaging in foreign direct investment (FDI) are, on average, more productive than those contracting with independent producers or distributors when operating abroad (Antràs and Yeaple, 2014; Kohler and Smolka, 2009; Tomiura, 2007). Much of this evidence has been shown for manufacturing industries. Yet, eating a McDonald's burger in Sri Lanka, drinking a Starbucks coffee in Moscow, or sleeping in a Hilton hotel in Poland are icons of what globalization represents nowadays. The service sector, despite its importance, has been greatly ignored in the studies that relate firm-level productivity with cross-border business activities.

Accordingly, this chapter aims to start filling this gap by empirically documenting how firm-level productivity varies with the different internationalization strategies undertaken by firms in a specific service industry: the hotel industry. Specifically, this study proposes to investigate, using firm-level data from the Spanish hotel industry, if the patterns found for manufacturing firms' globalization decisions extend to hotel firms. To this end, first, a Kolmogorov-Smirnov test is performed to verify if there exists a positive relationship between hotel firm-level productivity and the decision to operate across borders. Second, the estimations of a linear probability model and a multinomial logit one evaluate the extent to which firm-level productivity relates to the different foreign entry modes employed in the hotel industry.

As already mentioned, this study uses data from the Spanish hotel industry, which seems to make an especially relevant case study as Spanish hotels are spread out all around the globe. Moreover, among the 300 largest hotel firms in the world, 9% of them are Spanish (Weinstein, 2018). Likewise, the average outward Spanish FDI in the hotel and restaurant industry more than triples that made by the United States between 2003 and 2012, according to OECD (2019).

Theoretical Overview and Hypotheses

Internationalization of the Hotel Industry

The international expansion strategies of hotel firms have been studied at least since the influential work of Dunning and McQueen (1981, 1982). The literature on the hotel industry has focused on identifying the specific factors associated with the different entry modes used by hotel firms when going international (e.g., Contractor and Kundu, 1998a, 1998b), and less attention has been devoted to studying the factors that directly correlate with the decision to internationalize (Ivanova, 2013). As a consequence, the hotel industry literature discussed in this chapter relates to the factors associated with the different chosen foreign entry modes.

Entry Modes

Choosing the right foreign entry mode is a crucial decision for the international expansion strategies of hotel firms (León-Darder et al., 2011). This decision shapes the level and extent of control that hotel firms are able to exert on their establishments as well as the associated costs. The four entry modes typically used in the hotel industry are (1) ownership and management, (2) lease and management, (3) management contracts, and (4) franchise agreements.

Under the first of these, ownership and management, a hotel firm owns and fully operates a hotel establishment located abroad. That is, a hotel establishment is owned and managed by the same hotel firm whose logo can be seen outside of the hotel building. Under the second option, lease and management, the hotel firm manages the establishment in the same manner as in the previous case. However, the hotel firm rents the physical building from a third party rather than owning it. Under the third alternative, a management contract, the hotel firm agrees to assume responsibility for the operational control of a property that is supplied by a third party. The hotel firm, on behalf of this third party, manages the property by appointing a general manager and imposing its own established methods, procedures, and human resources policies (León-Darder et al., 2011). In return, the third party pays certain fees and royalties to the hotel firm. Finally, under a franchise agreement, a hotel firm licenses a third party to use its brand name and procedures in exchange for certain fees and royalties. That is, the property is supplied and managed by the franchisee, which uses the hotel firm's brand, know-how, and procedures (Pla-Barber et al., 2011).

As a result, when a hotel firm needs to select a foreign entry mode for a particular establishment, it faces a tradeoff between the level of the needed resource commitment and the control it can exert on the establishment (Contractor and Kundu, 1998b; Erramilli and Rao, 1993; Sanchez-Peinado and Pla-Barber, 2006). Thus, hotel firms can expand internationally using equity modes, such as ownership and management or lease and management, which allow a high degree of control over their establishments. Alternatively, they may opt for non-equity modes, such as management contracts and franchise agreements, which allow for expansion with lower fixed costs of entry but also with less control on the establishments (Martorell et al., 2013).

Correlates of Entry Modes

The hotel industry literature has paid special attention to establishing which factors are related to the foreign entry mode of hotel firms. These studies are mainly based on three theories: the transaction cost theory, the organization capabilities perspective, and the agency theory. First, the transaction cost theory argues that firms decide to internalize any transaction for which the implied transactions costs are higher through a market exchange than within the firm (Coase, 1937). If the transaction costs between a hotel firm and a third party are low, then it is predicted that hotel firms prefer to enter foreign markets with non-equity modes (Pla-Barber et al., 2010). Second, the organizational capabilities perspective specifies that the likelihood of choosing a non-equity mode increases with the hotel firm's ability to transfer the needed capabilities to run a hotel establishment to a third party (Erramilli et al., 2002; León-Darder et al., 2011). Finally, the agency theory asserts that the entry mode depends on the ability to monitor the employees of foreign-located hotels (Contractor and Kundu, 1998b).

The combination of these complementary theories predicts that the foreign entry mode hinges on host country-, hotel firm- and hotel establishment-level characteristics. In fact, the empirical evidence shows that the chosen entry modes correlate with host country characteristics, such as the perceived risk level, economic development, attractiveness of the destination, cultural distance from the hotel firm's country of origin, and availability of trustworthy local partners; with hotel firm-level characteristics, such as international experience, firm size, and degree of internationalization; and with hotel establishment-level characteristics, such as size and intangibility of the service offered in a particular establishment (Andreu et al., 2017; Brown et al., 2003; Contractor and Kundu, 1998a, 1998b; Erramilli et al., 2002; León-Darder et al., 2011; Kruesi and Zámborský, 2016; Kruesi et al., 2018; Martorell et al., 2013; Pla-Barber et al., 2011; Quer et al., 2007; Ramón-Rodriguez, 2002).

Firm-Level Productivity

The hotel industry literature, to the best of the author's knowledge, has overlooked the connection between firm-level productivity and the hotel firms' internationalization decisions. Nevertheless, this relationship lies at the heart of the analysis of the economics literature on international trade and multinational firms, which has proven that firm-level productivity is a key factor for analyzing the internationalization patterns of manufacturing firms.

Firms participating in international markets tend to be more productive than those that remain domestic (Bernard and Jensen, 1995, 1999; Helpman et al., 2004). Two competing theories have been proposed to explain this fact. First, a self-selection interpretation argues that only the most productive firms find it profitable to operate across borders. Second, a learning-by-internationalization explanation theorizes that, by participating in international markets, firms learn how to be more productive through the interaction with foreign consumers and competitors (Gattai et al., 2019). In fact, causality can potentially run in both directions and the two theories seem to be complementary.

Regarding the self-selection hypothesis, Melitz (2003) proposed a theoretical model in which firms with different productivity levels need to pay a fixed cost if they want to export. This model predicts that only the most productive firms find it optimal to do so. Nevertheless, this cannot be tested in the hotel industry, because virtually all hotels are exporters. The revenue that hotels generate from foreign tourists' overnight stays and consumption in their establishments must be considered as export and, as a consequence, the decision for a hotel firm to become an exporter is not completely in its hands.

However, Melitz's (2003) model has been extended to also study different internationalization modes beyond exporting. For instance, Helpman et al. (2004) generalized Melitz's (2003) model by incorporating the possibility of engaging in horizontal FDI to serve foreign markets. Their model predicts that firms with low levels of productivity remain domestic, firms with intermediate levels of productivity become exporters, and firms with high levels of productivity engage in horizontal FDI. They provided empirical support for these predictions in the manufacturing industry.

Moreover, the strand of this literature that focuses on multinational firm boundaries studied the role played by firm-level productivity in the decision of producing in another country either through FDI or through arm's-length licensing or subcontracting. This part of the literature builds on the idea of Williamson (1975) that contracts are imperfect.

On the one hand, Antràs and Helpman (2004) proposed a model of vertical FDI, based on Grossman and Hart's (1986) property rights theory, in which firms with different levels of productivity need intermediates to assemble a final good. In their model, firms can source these intermediates from abroad either by vertically integrating or by foreign outsourcing. That is, a firm can become a multinational firm or contract with an independent foreign supplier. In the case of becoming a multinational firm, the firm needs to pay a higher fixed cost than if it were to contract with a supplier. Nevertheless, vertical integration allows the mitigation of the effects of contractual imperfections. Under some conditions, their model predicts that among firms acquiring intermediates abroad, the firms that vertically integrate are more productive than firms doing foreign outsourcing. Several studies provide empirical support for this sorting in manufacturing industries (Antràs and Yeaple, 2014; Békés and Muraközy, 2018; Corcos et al., 2013; Kohler and Smolka, 2009; Tomiura, 2007).

On the other hand, Antràs and Yeaple (2014) proposed a model based on the transaction-cost theory in which they formalize the decision between horizontal FDI and licensing. They argue that horizontal FDI requires a higher fixed cost of entry than licensing but allows avoiding possible contractual frictions, such as rent dissipation issues. Their model predicts that firms engaging in horizontal FDI are more productive than firms choosing to license.

Therefore, the discussed theoretical models of Antràs and Helpman (2004) and Antràs and Yeaple (2014) predict that firms engaging in FDI, either horizontally or vertically, are more productive than firms contracting with third parties. The foreign entry mode chosen by hotel firms can be considered as either a horizontal FDI versus licensing decision or as a vertical FDI versus outsourcing decision. The interpretation of the former is that hotel firms duplicate an activity by opening a new hotel establishment abroad. This establishment can either be owned and managed by the hotel firm (horizontal FDI) or licensed to a third party, who operates it using the hotel firm brand (licensing). The interpretation of the latter is that the hotel production process can be sliced into two stages. Hotel firms' headquarters are the upstream suppliers and provide support and assistance to the establishments, such as hotel operations assistance, marketing support, and purchasing power. In turn, hotel establishments are the downstream producers and are in charge of delivering the service to customers. That is, vertical integration or outsourcing occurs with a downstream producer rather than with a supplier of intermediate inputs, as is generally the case in the manufacturing industry. This downstream producer can be part of the hotel firm (vertical FDI) or can be outsourced to a third party (outsourcing).

Consequently, the literature discussed above has theoretically and empirically shown two main facts for manufacturing firms. First, firms that operate across borders are, on average, more productive than firms that remain domestic. Second, among firms operating across borders, firms engaging in FDI are, on average, more productive than firms contracting with third parties. It seems reasonable that these two results extend to hotel firms. Accordingly, the following two hypotheses are formulated:

Hypothesis 1: Hotel firms that operate across borders are, on average, more productive than hotel firms that remain domestic.

Hypothesis 2: Hotel firms that engage in FDI are, on average, more productive than hotel firms that contract with third parties when going international.

However, the foreign entry mode decision for a hotel firm is not a dichotomous choice between FDI and contracting with third parties. Hotel firms can choose, at least, among the four options considered earlier (franchise contract, management contract, lease and management or ownership and management). At one extreme, the ownership and management mode fully coincides with FDI. At the other, a franchise agreement entails intensely contracting with an independent producer. The other two entry modes fall somewhere on this spectrum when it comes to costs, control, and contracting. In particular, the lease and management mode is close to FDI, and a management contract is in between a lease and management mode and a franchise agreement. Certainly, the fixed costs associated with each entry mode as well as the control that the hotel firm can exert in each mode increase in the following order: franchise agreements, management contracts, lease and management, and ownership and management. Conversely, possible contractual frictions, such as rent dissipation or quality dilution issues, are likely to decrease in this same order.

Hence, considering these observations jointly with the previously discussed predictions of Antràs and Helpman (2004) and Antràs and Yeaple (2014), it seems reasonable to assume a positive connection between hotel firm-level productivity and the different entry modes. Specifically, the following hypothesis is formulated:

Hypothesis 3: The most productive firms are more likely to use ownership and management; the second most productive firms are more likely to engage in lease and management; the second least productive firms are more likely to engage in management contracts; and the least productive firms are more likely to engage in franchise agreements when globalizing.

Data

Two main data sources are combined in this chapter. The first is the 2017 Spanish Hotel Directory designed and administered by Alimarket (2018). This directory includes a representative sample of all hotel properties located in Spain. Moreover, it also contains all hotel properties located outside Spain but marketed under the name of Spanish hotel firms. For each hotel establishment in the sample, there is information on its exact location, number of rooms, category, name of the hotel firm under which the establishment is marketed, and the exact relationship between the establishment and the hotel firm (franchise agreement, management contract, lease and management, or ownership and management). Therefore, this data allows identifying the extent to which each hotel firm operates across borders as well as whether it engages in FDI or contracts with third parties when operating abroad. In this database, some firms form a hotel group and operate several properties under one or several brands. Alternatively, some other firms operate only a single establishment.

The second source of information is the Iberian Balance Sheet Analysis System database (SABI), a panel of more than 2 million firms operating in Spain and Portugal generated by Informa D&B and Bureau Van Dijk (2018). This database gathers annual accounts and balance sheet information at the firm level, and it is used in this chapter to estimate a hotel firm-level productivity measure.

Both sources of information, the Hotel Directory and SABI, include the fiscal identification code of each firm, which allows combining them to create the database for this chapter. The final sample includes 3,291 hotel establishments in Spain. Among these, 92% of them are marketed under the name of one of 1,460 Spanish hotel firms and the remaining 8% are marketed under the name of one of 27 foreign hotel firms.

The final sample also includes 901 hotel establishments outside Spain but marketed under the name of 37 hotel firms. Among these, 135 hotels were in the pipeline when the Hotel Directory was created. The results in the following sections are robust even if they are not included. Columns 2 and 3 of Table 19.1 report the absolute number and the percentage of properties that correspond to each organizational mode of those establishments located outside Spain. Franchise contracts and management contracts are, respectively, the least often chosen and the most often chosen options among Spanish hotel firms when operating internationally, whereas the other two are chosen with approximately the same frequency. It is important to mention that only 35% of Spanish hotel firms in the sample engaged in a single organizational mode for all their properties.

Some additional sources of information which are discussed below are also used to proxy the main country-level characteristics that the hotel industry literature has shown to be related to the different entry modes. The Appendix reports a detailed description of all the variables that are used in this chapter as well as their summary statistics.

Table 19.1 Foreign entry modes

(1)	(2)	(3)
Entry modes	Establishments	Percentage
Franchise agreements	17	1.89
Management contracts	325	36.07
Lease & management	272	30.19
Ownership & management	287	31.85

Empirical Strategies

This section briefly describes the methodology used to obtain a measure of productivity at the hotel firm level, and presents the specific empirical strategy that is employed to test each of the three formulated hypotheses.

Productivity Estimation

Following the empirical literature on multinational firm boundaries, firm-level productivity is derived from an estimation of the firm's total factor productivity (TFP) (Antràs and Yeaple, 2014; Benfratello and Razzolini, 2008; Kohler and Smolka, 2009; Mayer and Ottaviano, 2008).

In particular, the Levinsohn and Petrin (2003) approach is adopted to estimate a firm-level TFP measure. Ten years of data are used, explicitly between 2006 and 2015, which is the last decade for which data is available for the majority of hotel firms in SABI. Information on added value, net capital stock, employment, and spending on materials is employed to estimate a TFP measure per hotel and year. All variables are defined, transformed and used as in Holl (2016), who also used data from SABI to estimate the Levinsohn and Petrin (2003) TFP measure. In order to obtain a better TFP estimate, all firms in SABI whose principal economic activity is the hotel industry are included in the estimation. Once the Levinsohn and Petrin (2003) firm-level TFP estimates are obtained, the average across the years is calculated. Finally, the standardized TFP measure per each firm is computed.

First Hypothesis

It is important to note that the constructed database for this chapter includes Spanish firms operating exclusively inside Spain, Spanish firms operating both inside and outside Spain, and foreign firms operating inside Spain. Correspondingly, the firms in the chapter's database can be classified into three groups: domestic Spanish firms (DSF), internationalized Spanish firms (ISF), and internationalized foreign firms operating in Spain (IFF). This categorization implies that two comparisons can be done to test the first hypothesis. The productivity of DSF can be contrasted to the productivity of ISF and IFF. To this end, a probability density function of firm-level productivity is estimated for each of the three groups of firms. Then, these density functions are used to non-parametrically verify, by means of a Kolmogorov-Smirnov test, if there exists a sorting pattern between domestic and internationalized firms. This test is commonly used in studies analyzing if the productivity distribution function for one group dominates the corresponding distribution function for another group (Benfratello and Razzolini, 2008; Delgado et al., 2002; Kohler and Smolka, 2009). It consists of testing the following two sets of hypotheses:

$$H_0 : F(z) - G(z) = 0 \ \forall z \in \mathbb{R} \text{ vs } H_1 : F(z) - G(z) \neq 0 \text{ for some } z \in \mathbb{R} \tag{19.1}$$

$$H_0 : F(z) - G(z) \leq 0 \ \forall z \in \mathrm{R} \ \text{vs} \ H_1 : F(z) - G(z) > 0 \ \text{for some} \ z \in \mathrm{R}. \tag{19.2}$$

Specifically, the distribution function F(z) stochastically dominates the distribution function G(z) when the null hypothesis of (19.1) can be rejected, and the null hypothesis of (19.2) cannot be rejected. Hence, in the context of this chapter, if the productivity distribution functions of ISF and IFF stochastically dominate the productivity distribution function of DSF, then the first hypothesis can be confirmed.

Second Hypothesis

As explained above, it is common for hotel companies not to use a single foreign entry mode for all their establishments. This can be explained by the fact that the chosen entry mode does not only depend on firm-level characteristics, but also on establishment- and country-specific characteristics. Accordingly, the relationship between a firm's productivity and its tendency to engage in FDI is proposed to be estimated by means of the following linear probability model:

$$FDI_{hcj} = \alpha + \beta \ TFP_j + Z_h'\rho + W_c'\delta + X_j'\gamma + \epsilon_{hcj}, \tag{19.3}$$

where h, c, and j stand for a hotel establishment h in a country c that is marketed under the name of a hotel firm j; FDI_{hcj} is a dummy variable equal to one when a hotel property is either owned and managed or leased and managed by the firm j; TFP_j is the firm-level measure of productivity; X_j are firm-level controls; Z_h are establishment-level controls; W_c are country-level controls; and ϵ_{hcj} is the error term. The definition of the variable FDI_{hcj} implies that leased and managed properties are assumed to also correspond to the case of FDI, as the empirical literature on multinational firm boundaries does not distinguish whether a firm owns or leases a plant. However, the firm is contracting ownership in such a case, and as this chapter's database discriminates properties depending on ownership, the variable FDI_{hcj} is later redefined to a more restrictive case in which is a dummy variable equal to one only when a hotel property is owned and managed.

This linear probability model allows analyzing the relationship between firm-level productivity and FDI while also taking into account other controls at the establishment, firm, and country level that had been proven to be relevant in the previously discussed literature. At the establishment level, the stars and the logarithm of the number of rooms of each hotel are included to measure the intangibility and complexity of the service offered, respectively. At the firm level, the number of workers is introduced to measure the size of each hotel firm, whereas the number of foreign establishments associated to a firm and the number of foreign markets in which a hotel firm operates indicate the level of international experience. The age of each firm is also included to measure overall experience in the hotel industry. At the host country level, the rule of law index from the World Bank's Governance Indicators is considered to proxy the risk level, the logarithm of GDP per capita is an indicator of the economic development, and the logarithm of international tourism receipts is a measure of the touristic attractiveness. Finally, a standard measure of cultural distance between Spain and the host country is also incorporated. Some of the variables have been introduced in logarithms because they are positively skewed. A detailed description of all the variables is reported in the Appendix.

Equation (19.3) is estimated using ordinary least squares with clustered standard errors at the firm level. Moreover, and as a robustness check, Equation (19.3) is also estimated with a more restrictive specification that uses country fixed effects to control for country-specific characteristics instead of the discussed country-level controls. This alternative specification allows taking into account any country-level characteristic that might be related to the chosen entry mode. Therefore, the second hypothesis can be confirmed if the alternative estimates of the coefficient β are positive and statistically significant.

Third Hypothesis

A multinomial logit model is proposed to estimate the third hypothesis. In this regard, for each property h in a country c that is marketed under the name of a hotel firm j, a variable called $mode_{hcj}$ is defined. This variable equals 1, 2, 3, and 4 depending on whether the property is run under a franchise agreement, a management contract, a lease and management mode, or an ownership and management mode, respectively. The log-odds of the multinomial logit are defined as follows:

$$\ln \frac{\text{Prob}\left(mode_{hcj} = m\right)}{\text{Prob}\left(mode_{hcj} = 4\right)} = \alpha_m + \beta_m\ TFP_j + X'_j\gamma + Z'_h\rho + W'_c\delta + \epsilon_{hcj}, \tag{19.4}$$

where the same notation as in Equation (19.3) is used, $m \in \{1,2,3\}$ and the base category is ownership and management. Each estimated β_m shows the estimated change in the relative log odds of choosing the corresponding mode relative to ownership and management when there is an increase in the firm-level TFP. Thus, if the estimated β_ms are statistically significant and such that $\hat{\beta}_1 < \hat{\beta}_2 < \hat{\beta}_3 < 0$, then the third hypothesis can be confirmed.

Results

Productivity and Internationalization

Figure 19.1 shows the estimation of the probability density function of the firms' TFP for the three different groups of firms (DSF, ISF, and IFF). On average, DSF are the least productive, whereas ISF and IFF are the most productive ones.

As discussed in the previous section, this sorting pattern is non-parametrically tested by means of a Kolmogorov-Smirnov test. Table 19.2 displays the results of comparing DSF with ISF and IFF. The first column describes the tested null hypothesis, where $TFPD^i$ stands for the TFP distribution function for firms in group i. In turn, the second and third columns report the p-value for each of the considered comparisons. These results confirm what Figure 19.1 suggests. The underlying productivity distribution of Spanish domestic firms is different from the ones of internationalized

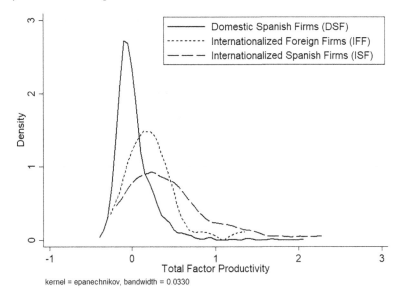

Figure 19.1 Firm-level productivity and internationalization.

Table 19.2 Kolmogorov-Smirnov test

(1)	(2)	(3)
Null hypothesis	$i = \text{ISF}, j = \text{DSF}$ p-value	$i = \text{IFF}, j = \text{DSF}$ p-value
$TFPD^i - TFPD^j = 0$	0.000	0.000
$TFPD^i - TFPD^j \leq 0$	1.000	0.991

Spanish and foreign firms. Indeed, the productivity distributions of the last two stochastically dominate the productivity distribution of the former. Consequently, these results show that hotel firms that operate across borders are more productive than hotels firms that remain domestic. Thus, the first hypothesis of this chapter can be confirmed.

Productivity and FDI

The different estimates of Equation (19.3) are reported in Table 19.3. The first two columns display the estimates corresponding to the original definition of the dependent variable, that is, in these cases, FDI is a dummy variable equal to one when a hotel establishment is either under an ownership and management mode or a lease and management one. Alternatively, the last two columns show the estimates for the more restrictive definition of this variable, that is, in these cases, FDI is a dummy equal to one only when an establishment is under an ownership and management mode. In turn, the first and third columns present the estimates that include the discussed country-level controls, whereas the second and fourth columns correspond to the more restrictive case in which country fixed effects are included instead.

The coefficient on TFP is positive and statistically significant across all four columns. In fact, it is the only coefficient associated to a firm-level control that remains statistically significant across the different specifications. These estimates show a positive relationship between firm-level productivity and the choice of FDI relative to contracting with third parties when operating across borders. Thus, the second hypothesis of this study can be confirmed. Some of the estimates on the coefficients of the other controls are also statistically significant, as previous studies predicted.

Productivity and Entry Modes

Table 19.4 shows the estimated multinomial logit of Equation (19.4). The first row shows the estimated relationship between TFP and the relative log odds of choosing either a franchise agreement, a management contract, or a lease and management mode versus an ownership and management mode, which is the base category. The coefficients of TFP for the first two columns are negative and statistically significant. Moreover, the coefficient of TFP associated with franchise agreements is lower than the coefficient of management contracts. These results provide suggestive evidence of a productivity ranking. On average, the most productive firms are more likely to use ownership and management or lease and management modes; the second least productive firms are more likely to engage in management contracts, and the least productive firms are more likely to engage in franchise contracts when globalizing. Thus, the third hypothesis of this study can be partially confirmed in the sense that firms engaging in ownership and management are, on average, more productive than firms engaging in management contracts which, in turn, are more productive than firms engaging in franchise agreements. However, it cannot be claimed that there

Table 19.3 Linear probability model

	(1)	(2)	(3)	(4)
	FDI	FDI	FDI	FDI
Firm-level productivity				
TFP	0.398**	0.381***	0.294**	0.272*
	(0.163)	(0.137)	(0.139)	(0.135)
Establishment-level controls				
Stars	0.061	0.004	0.050	−0.003
	(0.048)	(0.038)	(0.058)	(0.036)
Ln(Rooms)	0.029	0.025	0.028	0.007
	(0.047)	(0.022)	(0.044)	(0.019)
Firm-level controls				
Workers	0.000	0.000	0.000	0.000**
	(0.000)	(0.000)	(0.000)	(0.000)
Foreign establishments	−0.000	−0.000	−0.002	−0.003**
	(0.001)	(0.001)	(0.001)	(0.001)
Foreign markets	−0.016**	−0.015**	−0.012	−0.004
	(0.007)	(0.006)	(0.008)	(0.007)
Age	−0.003	−0.006	0.003	0.005
	(0.008)	(0.006)	(0.007)	(0.007)
Country-level controls				
Rule of law	0.081		−0.110**	
	(0.066)		(0.051)	
Ln(GDP per capita)	0.177*		0.220**	
	(0.087)		(0.099)	
Ln(Tourism receipts)	−0.018		−0.046**	
	(0.030)		(0.020)	
Cultural Distance	66.329		−31.061	
	(58.759)		(61.263)	
Constant	−0.999		−1.094*	
	(0.673)		(0.589)	
Country fixed effects	No	Yes	No	Yes
Observations	763	874	763	874
R^2	0.317	0.535	0.229	0.452
F	556.277	9.225	54.058	15.811

Note: Coefficients are statistically different from zero at the following levels: $^*p<0.1$, $^{**}p<0.05$, $^{***}p<0.01$. Clustered standard errors at the firm level are in parentheses.

exists a statistically significant difference, with respect to the level of productivity, between firms engaging in ownership and management and firms engaging in lease and management modes.

Final Remarks

Discussion

This chapter documents three main results. First, there exists, on average, a positive relationship between hotel-firm level productivity and the firm's status of operating across borders.

Table 19.4 Multinomial logit

	(1)	(2)	(3)
	Franchise agreements	*Management contracts*	*Lease & management*
Firm-level productivity			
TFP	−16.979***	−2.250**	−0.709
	(1.671)	(0.886)	(1.075)
Hotel-level controls			
Stars	−1.806***	−0.398	−0.114
	(0.368)	(0.351)	(0.370)
Ln(rooms)	−0.394**	0.099	−0.468**
	(0.196)	(0.313)	(0.198)
Firm-level controls			
Workers	0.010***	−0.000	−0.000**
	(0.000)	(0.000)	(0.000)
Foreign establishments	0.457***	0.005	0.011
	(0.026)	(0.007)	(0.008)
Foreign markets	−3.254***	0.094**	0.045
	(0.176)	(0.042)	(0.049)
Age	0.261**	0.007	−0.047
	(0.106)	(0.048)	(0.042)
Country-level controls			
Rule of law	0.262	−0.082	1.021***
	(0.643)	(0.374)	(0.318)
Ln(GDP per capita)	−0.547	−1.464***	−0.929
	(0.765)	(0.524)	(0.867)
Ln(Tourism receipts)	−0.172	0.250	0.363*
	(0.244)	(0.153)	(0.214)
Cultural Distance	−817.693	−147.790	434.681**
	(1153.037)	(443.209)	(205.084)
Constant	0.306	10.670**	2.870
	(8.440)	(4.541)	(5.135)
Observations		763	
Pseudo R^2		0.296	

Note: Coefficients are statistically different from zero at the following levels: *$p<0.1$, **$p<0.05$, ***$p<0.01$. Clustered standard errors at the firm level are in parentheses.

This result is in line with Bernard and Jensen (1995, 1999) and Helpman et al. (2004) who also found this correspondence for manufacturing firms. Second, this chapter also shows that among internationalized hotel firms, the firms that tend to engage in FDI are more productive than the firms that tend to contract with third parties when operating abroad. This result is in agreement with Tomiura (2007), Kohler and Smolka (2009), Corcos et al. (2013), Antràs and Yeaple (2014), and Békés and Muraközy (2018), who also showed this relationship for manufacturing firms. Finally, this chapter also presents evidence of an association between firm-level productivity and the different foreign entry modes typically used in the hotel industry. In particular, it is shown that, on average, the most productive firms are the ones that tend to use ownership and management or lease and management modes; firms with average levels of productivity are the ones that tend to use management contracts, and the least productive firms are the ones that tend to engage in franchise agreements. This result is related to the theoretical predictions of Antràs and Helpman (2004, 2008) and Antràs and Yeaple (2014). Therefore, this study documents that some of the main internationalization patterns found for manufacturing firms extend to the Spanish hotel industry.

Conclusion

The relationships between firm-level productivity and the different internationalization decisions of firms have been overlooked in the hotel industry, to the best of the author's knowledge, while they occupied a central position in the economics literature on cross-border activities. Therefore, the three documented connections in this chapter highlight that firm-level productivity might also be an important factor to consider in the academic literature on the internationalization of hotel firms.

Limitations of This Study

This study has some limitations which should be addressed in future research. First, it mainly takes into consideration Spanish hotel firms, which might behave differently from hotel firms of other nationalities. Hence, more studies are needed to analyze whether the found patterns are robust to other markets. Second, the final database that was used for the estimation is a cross-section and, consequently, it allows only for an estimate of static relationships. Future studies working with panel data might further explain the results of this chapter. Finally, a causal relationship between firm-level productivity and the different internationalization decisions is not estimated. Accordingly, future studies should also try to understand better the mechanisms underlying the relationships between firm-level productivity and the different internationalization decisions.

Acknowledgments

The author is extremely thankful to Giacomo Ponzetto and Nicola Gennaioli for their support, guidance, and advice. He also greatly appreciates the different feedback and contributions from Alessandra Bonfiglioli, Gino Gancia, Jaume Ventura, Gene Ambrocio, Bruno Caprettini, Dmitry Khametshin, and Tom Schmitz for their comments and suggestions. The author is also grateful to José-Antonio Pérez-Aranda and CETT for facilitating the last stage of this study.

Appendix

Table 19A.1 Description and source of variables

(1)	(2)
Variable	*Description and source*
TFP	It equals the firm-level TFP estimate; the higher the numbers, the higher the productivity estimate. Source: Author's elaboration based on Informa D&B and Bureau Van Dijk (2018)
Stars	It equals the stars of a given establishment. Source: Alimarket (2018)
Ln(rooms)	It equals the establishment-level logarithm of number of rooms. Source: Alimarket (2018)
Workers	It equals the firm-level number of workers. Source: Informa D&B and Bureau Van Dijk (2018)
Foreign establishments	It equals the firm-level number of foreign establishments associated to the firm. Source: Alimarket (2018)
Foreign markets	It equals the number of foreign markets in which a firm operates. Source: Alimarket (2018)
Age	It equals the age of each firm in the year 2017. Source: Informa D&B and Bureau Van Dijk (2018)
Rule of law	It equals the country-level average of the Rule of Law index between 2006 and 2015. This index reflects perceptions of the extent to which agents have confidence in and abide by the rules of society, and in particular, the quality of contract enforcement, property rights, the police, and the courts, as well as the likelihood of crime and violence. Higher values indicate better institutional quality. Source: World Bank (2018a)
Ln(GDP per capita)	It equals the country-level logarithm of the average gross domestic product per capita between 2006 and 2015. Source: World Bank (2018b)
Ln(tourism receipts)	It equals the country-level logarithm of the average expenditure by international inbound visitors between 2006 and 2015. Source: World Bank (2018b)
Cultural distance	It equals the country-level cultural distance index proposed by Kogut and Singh (1988) between each country and Spain. This index uses the four cultural dimensions proposed by Hofstede (1980): power distance, uncertainty avoidance, masculinity/femininity and individualism. Source: Author's elaboration based on Hofstede (1980)

Table 19A.2 Summary statistics for the first hypothesis

	N	*Mean*	*St. Dev.*	*Min*	*Max*
TFP	1487	0.040	0.258	−0.363	2.298

Table 19A.3 Summary statistics for the second and third hypotheses

	N	Mean	St. Dev.	Min	Max
FDI	874	0.322	0.467	0	1
TFP	874	1.182	0.481	−0.091	2.298
Stars	874	4.354	0.638	2	6
Ln(rooms)	874	5.200	0.828	2.079	7.231
Workers	874	2340.189	2458.452	8	6197
Foreign establishments	874	165.978	108.341	1	279
Foreign markets	874	26.503	13.441	1	44
Age	874	25.478	9.134	1	40
Rule of law	865	0.301	0.952	−1.702	1.869
Ln(GDP per capita)	795	9.932	0.683	6.852	11.709
Ln(tourism receipts)	865	18.443	1.291	14.483	21.331
Cultural distance	763	0.003	0.001	0.001	.0067

References

Alimarket. (2018), "Directorio de Establecimientos de Hoteles y Apartamentos en España", *Alimarket Database*, available at: https://www.alimarket.es/establecimientos_directorio

Andreu, R., Claver, E., and Quer, D. (2017), "Foreign market entry mode choice of hotel companies: Determining factors", *International Journal of Hospitality Management*, Vol.62, pp.111–119.

Antràs, P. and Helpman, E. (2004), "Global sourcing", *Journal of Political Economy*, Vol.112 No.3, pp.552–580.

Antràs, P. and Helpman, E. (2008), "Contractual frictions and global sourcing", in Helpman, E., Verdier, T., and Marin, D. (Eds.), *The Organization of Firms in a Global Economy*, Harvard University Press, Cambridge, MA, pp.9–54.

Antràs, P. and Yeaple, S.R. (2014), "Multinational firms and the structure of international trade", in Gopinath, G., Helpman, E., and Rogoff, K. (Eds.) *Handbook of International Economics*, Vol.4, Elsevier, New York, NY, pp.55–130.

Békés, G. and Muraközy, B. (2018), "The ladder of internationalization modes: Evidence from European firms", *Review of World Economics*, Vol.154, No.3, pp.455–491.

Benfratello, L. and Razzolini, T. (2008), "Firms' productivity and internationalisation choices: evidence for a large sample of Italian firms", Working paper 236, 30 January, Centro Studi Luca d'Agliano, Milan.

Bernard, A.B. and Jensen, J.B. (1995), "Exporters, jobs, and wages in U.S. manufacturing: 1976–1987", *Brookings Papers on Economic Activity, Microeconomics*, Vol.1995, pp.67–119.

Bernard, A.B. and Jensen, J.B. (1999), "Exceptional exporter performance: Cause, effect, or both?", *Jounral of International Economics*, Vol.47, pp.1–25.

Brown, J.R., Dev, C.S., and Zhou, Z. (2003), "Broadening the foreign market entry mode decision: Separating ownership and control", *Journal of International Business Studies*, Vol.34, No.5, pp.473–488.

Coase, R.H. (1937), "The nature of the firm", *Economica*, Vol.4, No.16, pp.386–405.

Contractor, F.J. and Kundu, S.K. (1998a), "Franchising versus company-run operations: Modal choice in the global hotel sector", *Journal of International Marketing*, Vol.6, No.2, pp.28–53.

Contractor, F.J. and Kundu, S.K. (1998b), "Modal choice in a world of alliances: Analyzing organizational forms in the international hotel sector", *Journal of International Business Studies*, Vol.29, No.2, pp.325–357.

Corcos, G., et al. (2013), "The determinants of intrafirm trade: Evidence from French firms", *Review of Economics and Statistics*, Vol.95, No.3, pp.825–838.

Delgado, M.A., Fariñas, J.C., and Ruano, S. (2002), "Firm productivity and export markets: A non-parametric approach", *Journal of International Economics*, Vol.57, pp.397–422.

Dunning, J.H. and McQueen, M. (1981), "The eclectic theory of international production: A case study of the international hotel industry", *Managerial and Decision Economics*, Vol.2, No.4, pp.197–210.

Dunning, J.H. and McQueen, M. (1982), "Multinational corporations in the international hotel industry", *Annals of Tourism Research*, Vol.9, No.1, pp.69–90.

Erramilli, M.K., Agarwal, S., and Chekitan, S.D. (2002), "Choice between non-equity entry modes: An organizational capability perspective", *Journal of International Business Studies*, Vol.33 No.2, pp.223–242.

Erramilli, M.K. and Rao, C.P. (1993), "Firms' international mode choice: A modified analysis approach", *Journal of Marketing*, Vol.57, No.3, pp.19–38.

Gattai, V., Mechelli, R., and Natale, P. (2019), "ODI from BRIC countries: A conceptual framework", in Gattai, V., Mechelli, R., and Natale, P. (Eds.), *ODI from BRIC Countries*, Palgrave Pivot, Cham, UK, pp.25–38.

Grossman, S.J. and Hart, O.D. (1986), "The costs and benefits of ownership: A theory of vertical and lateral integration", *Journal of Political Economy*, Vol.94, No.4, pp.691–719.

Helpman, E., Melitz, M.J., and Yeaple, S.R. (2004), "Export versus FDI with heterogeneous firms", *The American Economic Review*, Vol.94, No.1, pp.300–316.

Hofstede, G. (1980), *Culture's Consequences: International Differences in Work Related Values*, Sage, London, UK.

Holl, A. (2016), "Highways and productivity in manufacturing firms", *Journal of Urban Economics*, Vol.93, pp.131–151.

Informa D&B and Bureau Van Dijk. (2018), "Sistema de Análisis de Balances Ibéricos (SABI)", *SABI Database*, available at: https://sabi.bvdinfo.com/ip/

Ivanova, M. (2013), "Factors for the internationalization of hotel chains", *Izvestiva*, Vol.1, pp.107–118.

Kogut, B. and Singh, H. (1988), "The effect of national culture on the choice of entry mode", *Journal of International Business Studies*, Vol.19, No.3, pp.411–432.

Kohler, W.K. and Smolka, M. (2009), "Global sourcing decisions and firm productivity: evidence from Spain", Working paper 2903, Ifo Institute – Leibniz Institute for Economic Research at the University of Munich, Munich, December.

Kruesi, M.A., Hemmington, N.R., and Kim, P.B. (2018), "What matters for hotel executives? An examination of major theories in non-equity entry mode research", *International Journal of Hospitality Management*, Vol.70, pp.25–36.

Kruesi, M.A. and Zámborský, P. (2016), "The non-equity mode choices of international hotel organizations in New Zealand", *International Journal of Hospitality and Tourism Administration*, Vol.17, No.3, pp.316–346.

León-Darder, F., Villar-García, C., and Pla-Barber, J. (2011), "Entry mode choice in the internationalisation of the hotel industry: A holistic approach", *The Service Industries Journal*, Vol.31, No.1, pp.107–122.

Levinsohn, J. and Petrin, A. (2003), "Estimating production functions using inputs to control for unobservables", *Review of Economic Studies*, Vol.70, pp.317–341.

Martorell, O., Mulet, C., and Otero, L. (2013), "Choice of market entry mode by Balearic hotel chains in the Caribbean and Gulf of Mexico", *International Journal of Hospitality Management*, Vol.32, pp.217–227.

Mayer, T. and Ottaviano, G.I.P. (2008), "The happy few: The internationalisation of European firms", *Intereconomics*, Vol.43 No.3, pp.135–148.

Melitz, M.J. (2003), "The impact of trade on intra-industry reallocations and aggregate industry productivity", *Econometrica*, Vol.71, No.6, pp.1695–1725.

OECD. (2019), "FDI flows by industry", *OECD Data*, available at: https://data.oecd.org.

Pla-Barber, J., León-Darder, F., and Villar, C. (2011), "The internationalization of soft-services: Entry modes and main determinants in the Spanish hotel industry", *Service Business*, Vol.5, No.2, pp.139–154.

Pla-Barber, J., Sanchez-Peinado, E., and Madhok, A. (2010), "Investment and control decisions in foreign markets: Evidence from service industries", *British Journal of Management*, Vol.21, No.3, pp.736–753.

Quer, D., Claver, E., and Andreu, R. (2007), "Foreign market entry mode in the hotel industry: The impact of country- and firm-specific factors", *International Business Review*, Vol.16, pp.362–376.

Ramón-Rodriguez, A. (2002), "Determining factors in entry choice for international expansion. The case of the Spanish hotel industry", *Tourism Management*, Vol.23, pp.597–607.

Sanchez-Peinado, E. and Pla-Barber, J. (2006), "A multidimensional concept of uncertainty and its influence on the entry mode choice: An empirical analysis in the service sector", *International Business Review*, Vol.15, pp.215–232.

Tomiura, E. (2007), "Foreign outsourcing, exporting, and FDI: A productivity comparison at the firm level", *Journal of International Economics*, Vol.71, No.3, pp.113–127.

Weinstein, J. (2018, July/August), "Hotels 325", *Hotels Magazine*, pp.19–32.

Williamson, O.E. (1975), *Markets and Hierarchies: Analysis and Antitrust Implications*, Free Press, New York, NY.

World Bank. (2018a), "Worldwide Governance Indicators", *WGI Data*, available at: http://www.govindicators.org

World Bank. (2018b), "World Bank Open Data", *World Bank Open Data*, available at: https://data.worldbank.org/

20

BRAND RELEVANCE AND RELEVANCE OF BRANDS IN THE GLOBAL HOTEL INDUSTRY

A Look at Research and Practice

Marco A. Gardini

Introduction

The strategic relevance of branding as a key driver for success in the hospitality industry has been increasingly recognized in the last years and brand expansion has become a major trend in many hospitality markets worldwide (Cai and Hobson, 2004; Carvell et al., 2016; Dev et al., 2002; Forgacs, 2003; Gardini, 2015; Harrington and Ottenbacher 2011; Kayaman and Arasli, 2007; King, 2017; So et al., 2013; Tsai et al., 2015). But not only hotel or restaurant operators seem to agree that branding is an essential component of a company's market success, also hotel investors, banks, consultants, and developers emphasize the value of branding, especially referring to the ability of the brand to facilitate access to capital and the ability to support growth (Dev, 2012; Gerhard and Nadrowski, 2011; Hanson et al., 2009; Olsen et al., 2005; O'Neill and Mattila, 2010). Accordingly, the last decade has seen a massive proliferation of hotel brands worldwide as the international hotel industry, driven by increasing pressure from investors for growth, has created, introduced, and reactivated numerous new brands and sub-brand concepts.

Nevertheless, the relationship between brand strategy and corporate performance appears to be ambivalent in the hotel industry to the present day, as both, academics as well as practitioners, exhibit very divergent opinions and assessments referring to the relevance of hotel brands as buying decision criterion and/or competitive success factor. While in some industries and markets the economic relevance of brands and their influence on consumer decision-making processes is an accepted competition dictum, it also can be observed that in other industries and markets, the ability of brands to influence consumer behavior, to provoke buying preferences and to generate economic value, is not a necessary prerequisite for corporate success (Donnevert, 2009). Against the backdrop of this observation, the role and the relevance of a hotel brand as an economic success factor in the global hotel industry has to be questioned. This chapter reports on a systematic review of the hospitality literature over a 20-year period, to gain an understanding into how brand research has been conducted in the hospitality context, and to explore the level of integration and representation of brand-related topics within the academic field of hospitality.

Branding and Brand Management in the Global Hotel Industry

In the hotel industry, the importance of the hotel brand as a competitive success factor has been highlighted for some time: "*Competitive Strategy in the 1990s will be based on the concept of brand loyalty. For the hotel customer of the 1990s, service quality will increasingly become synonymous with brand image*" (Francese and Renaghan, 1990, p. 60). Nevertheless, the role and the relevance of the hotel brand as an economic success factor remains quite unclear to the present day, as the study and research landscape reflects a certain ambiguity. While on one side there is some evidence showing that brand affiliated hotels outperform unaffiliated hotels on various metrics (i.e., ADR, RevPAR, OCC, NOP/GOP) and hotel brand conversions (rescaling/rebranding) may enhance a property's market value and financial performance, other research has shown the opposite or produced ambiguous empirical results (Carvell et al., 2016; Dev, 2015; Hanson et al., 2009; O'Neill and Carlback, 2011; O'Neill and Mattila, 2010; O'Neill and Xiao, 2006; Prasad and Dev, 2000; Tsai et al., 2015). Furthermore, there are findings stating an increased brand consciousness of the hotel guest (Amadeus, 2007; Back, 2005; Dubé and Reneghan, 2000; Deloitte, 2010; fvw, 2015; Kayaman and Arasli, 2007; O'Neill and Mattila, 2010), whereas other studies reveal that the hotel brand is a subordinated buying criterion for the hotel customer (Fraunhofer, 2014; Koob, 2011; Schneider, 2008; Soller, 2016; VDR, 2018) and consumers do not identify strongly with hotel brands (So et al., 2013). The very heterogeneous data situation, whether stemming from academia or business practice, seems to illustrate a classic chicken and egg dilemma. Hence, the question is being raised whether brands are de facto irrelevant as a competitive success factor and/or buying decision criterion in the hotel industry or if business and leisure customers display a corresponding brand indifference because they are not able to identify meaningful and differentiating hotel brands in the market.

The idea of brand image as the consumer's idea of a product, as being formulated by advertising icon David Ogilvy almost 50 years ago, seems not to have been clearly worked out in the past in large parts of the hotel industry: "*...hoteliers fail to articulate the compelling experience found in their hotel, even though guests can feel and explain that experience. Another concern is that many hotel properties have great authenticity that they fail to use*" (Dev and Withiam, 2012, p. 7). Among other things, this might be due to a restricted understanding of the brand concept according to which the power or strength of a hospitality brand is mainly defined by a name, a logo, a specific design, sales pressure, or intense advertising. The all-too narrow understanding of what a brand really is, or should deliver in the hospitality industry is frequently expressed by focusing on certain performance indicators (e.g., level of service, loyalty programs, reservations systems) or product characteristics (e.g., design and lifestyle hotels/restaurants, location, architecture, amenities), which appear if a brand is only seen as a set of product or service features offering certain functional advantages (Buer and Groß, 2006; Frehse, 2008; Gardini, 2015). Although a brand has certain performance characteristics and product/service features, it basically is designed to offer orientation, identification, and differentiation in addition to functional advantages (Kapferer, 2012; Keller et al., 2008). Hence, the purpose of a hotel brand is to develop meaningful images and associations in order to establish emotional relationships with designated target groups, way beyond mere product characteristics or features (Aaker and Joachimsthaler, 2012; Berry, 2000; Fournier, 1998), a phenomenon being described as brand relevance (Aaker, 2012). This implies, as Bailey and Ball suggest (2006), that having a brand-name alone is not a guarantee of success within the hotel industry.

Although the hotel industry has many brands which are relatively well known, still too many of them are being perceived as inconsistent in what they provide to consumers and as such they not only suffer from poor perception of positioning, image, product and service quality but very often they are being perceived as interchangeable (Bailey and Ball, 2006; Daun and Klinger, 2006; Dev and Withiam, 2012; Frehse, 2008). Various studies in the global hospitality industry indicate that travellers and hotel guests in many cases experience difficulties in specifying any particular associations while comparing different hotel brands and that the hotel guest, unless an experienced traveller, is probably unable to differentiate between the levels of service offered from one sub-brand to another (Frehse, 2008; Gerhard and Nadrowski, 2011; Olsen et al., 2005; Zehle, 2011). Particularly, global hotel chains like Best Western, Marriott, NH Hotels, Steigenberger, Hilton, Accor, Wyndham, Choice, or Intercontinental with their different company sub-brands – the list could be continued at will – often fail to deliver a differentiating brand promise as they stay mainly vague in their brand message and do not dispose of a clear brand positioning strategy (Dev and Withiam, 2012; Gardini, 2015; So et al., 2013). Beyond that, many industry executives and academics believe that a strong hotel brand needs multiple units as being requested in the brand definition of the German International Hotel Association (IHA, 2019) or as O'Neill and Mattila recently suggested as a question for future research: "*How small can a brand be in terms of the number of hotels units and still be a brand?*" (O'Neill and Mattila, 2010, p. 33). This quote reflects the inconsistencies and confusion amongst practitioners and academics about what the concept of the hotel brand or hotel branding really is and denies that a consequent brand management approach may also be a feasible strategy for independent or unaffiliated hotels, what is obviously underlined by various examples from the hotel practice (i.e., hotels such as the Bayerischer Hof, Munich; Beverly Hills Hotel, Los Angeles; Waldorf Astoria, New York/Berlin; Claridge's, London; Atlantis, Bahamas/Dubai). Apart from a lack of a consistent understanding of the concept of the brand amongst many industry executives and academics, another misconception in terms of brand success is to be found in the belief that strong brands need huge media budgets. It should not be concealed that this might be helpful in the course of developing and establishing competitive brands, but the problem of limited brand awareness and brand differentiation in the hotel industry is not merely a question of limited financial resources. Some of the world's best-known brands like Starbucks, Tupperware, Body Shop, Häagen Daz, Weight Watchers, Aldi, and others have shown that the competitiveness of a brand is not only a question of massive advertising and communication pressure as these brands were entirely established and positioned beyond mass media in the past (Joachimsthaler and Aaker, 1997). Ultimately, the hotel industry's brand strategies often display weaknesses in terms of creating a relevant value proposition and communicating the essence of this value to its customers (Daun and Klinger, 2006).

These industry brand practices and the lack of differentiation of many hotel brands contradicts the intended function of branding, a situation seen from a customer perspective makes a significant contribution to unease and to confuse hotel guests (Kim et al., 2008; Olsen et al., 2005; So and King, 2010). The current development of the global proliferation of new brands reflects the conviction of many hotel companies that they have to occupy niches and business segments before their competitors do so (Katz and Withiam, 2012; Lynn, 2007). However, many hotel firms and executives still focus on product development rather than brand development, seeing branding merely as a way of introducing new hotels products into the market, while missing to exploit the full potential of branding as a competitive and customer-driven strategy (Gardini, 2015; Olsen et al., 2005; Zhang et al., 2008). Furthermore, the rapid growth and the launches of new hotel brands is often driven more by opportunistic rather than strategic reasons, as the use of brand names is often mainly being offered by hotels firms to entice hotel owners and investors to sign franchise agreements or management contracts (Gerhard and Nadrowski, 2011; Olsen et al., 2005), rather than investing into long-term brand strategies aiming to create and build a unique brand experience for a designated target group. This customer confusion is often being reinforced by regular changes of operator ownership, rebranding or rescaling strategies, or numerous takeovers, mergers and acquisitions in the industry during the restructuring of many international hotel markets.

It appears, that in the future developing positive and meaningful value propositions and brand associations should be more important tasks of hotel brand management, as in the affiliated and chain hotel industry worldwide there are too many hotel brands without concrete message, without specific profile, without a differentiating character (Bailey and Ball, 2006; Daun and Klinger, 2006; Dev and Withiam, 2012; Frehse, 2008; Gardini, 2015; Olsen et al., 2005). Hence, an appropriate brand strategy in the hospitality industry necessitates a different and consistent management approach and it is for this reason that is being suggested that brand management and brand performance within the hospitality industry can be improved through more effective brand differentiation strategies (Bailey and Ball, 2006; Dev and Withiam, 2011). It is therefore a core objective of a systematic brand management approach in the hospitality industry to achieve as far as possible congruence between the envisaged identity and the image of a brand as being perceived by the relevant target group(s) of a company (Burmann et al., 2009; De Chernatony, 1999; Esch 2016). In an industry, in which historically seen successful companies have always been living from their good reputation, it is all the more remarkable that practitioners from the industry only hesitantly realize "…*the importance of brand management as a critical skill…*" (Dev and Withiam, 2011, p. 7) and a major driver for superior market performance. With this background in mind, our review will seek to understand the focus of the body of hospitality brand research, addressing specifically the contributions of hotel-related brand research in order to gain a better understanding of the role of brands in the global hotel industry context.

Methodology

The systematic literature review approach was chosen because it is an established scientific tool designed to assist in appraising, summarizing, and communicating the results and implications of large and complex data sets (Briner and Denyer, 2012; Denyer and Tranfield, 2009). To offer a comprehensive overview of recent hospitality research related to branding and brand management in the hotel industry, the study approach followed a four-step screening process of identifying, selecting, and critically appraising relevant research on the topic, as being suggested for a systematic literature review by different authors (Tranfield et al., 2003; Webster and Watson, 2002) and applied in a variety of different research settings in the hospitality industry (Dev et al., 2010; Kandampully et al., 2018; Kusluvan et al., 2010; Law et al., 2012; Ottenbacher and Harrington, 2011). The study adopted a content analysis approach looking at the number, the percentage, and the topics of brand-related articles published in four leading hospitality journals from 1996 through 2018. The basic objective of this process was to determine the popularity of branding and brand management as an academic field in hospitality and the most frequently studied topic areas related to branding or brand management in the hotel industry. A summary of this methodology is provided in Figure 20.1.

The first step in the research process was to determine which journals to include in the analysis. Choice criteria for journal selection include, besides scientific relevance, focus, and accessibility, also the research scope which has to allow a manageable and practicable scheme for the researcher. For the identification of relevant and top tier hospitality journals, a ranking-based approach is being pursued as suggested by different authors (Kandampully et al., 2014; Ottenbacher and Harrington, 2011). From this process, this study selected four journals to be included in the analysis based on three main criteria such as highest mean ranking across the most recent ranking studies (Gursoy and Sandstrom, 2014; Law and van der Veen, 2009; McKercher et al., 2006; Pechlaner et al., 2004), primary focus of the journal on management-related issues in hospitality, and manageable number of publications to assess:

1 Cornell Hospitality Quarterly
2 International Journal of Hospitality Management
3 International Journal of Contemporary Hospitality Management
4 Journal of Hospitality and Tourism Research

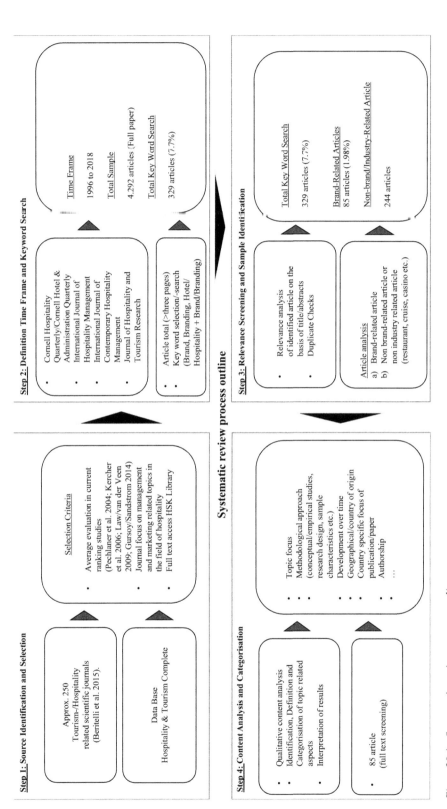

Figure 20.1 Systematic review process outline.

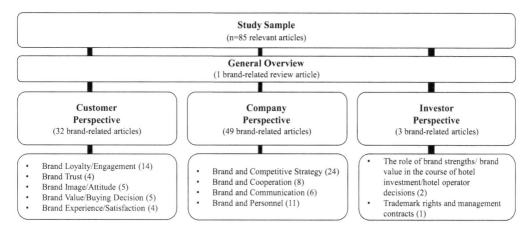

Figure 20.2 Main perspectives and key topic areas in branding and brand management research in the hotel industry.

Although ranking approaches are not without criticism (van Fleet et al., 2000), these particular specialist journals will provide an appropriate sample of the integration of branding research into the mainstream hospitality academic literature over the period 1996–2018. The timeframe was deemed appropriate for two reasons: (1) it provided for a sufficiently wide reference period to be able to observe research patterns and topics over time and (2) it corresponds to the period where the proliferation of hotel brands gained momentum and reached a certain maturity.

Another important step to control the sample in terms of data quality and quantity is – apart from source identification and determination of the timeframe – the definition of relevant keywords. In this study the level of substantive relevance was established by selecting articles containing at least one primary keyword in their title or abstract, which were as follows: BRAND(S), BRANDING, HOTEL/HOSPITALITY BRAND(S)/ BRANDING including their linguistic extensions such as BRAND MANAGEMENT, BRAND IMAGE, BRAND LOYALTY, BRAND STRATEGY, and so on. From a total pool of 4,292 articles published in the 4 journals during the reference period, a subset of 329 papers with the keywords brand or branding in the title or abstract was identified for initial consideration. To ensure further research relevance this preliminary list was specified, eliminating articles that did not proof to be explicitly brand-specific in their focus or which aimed at other hospitality industries such as restaurant, cruise, or casino. After all the filters had been applied the final sample collected for analysis totaled 85 articles.

The fourth and final step of the research process contains the identification, definition, and categorization of brand-specific research patterns and topics on the basis of qualitative content analysis (Charmaz, 2006; Schreier, 2014). To classify the chapters, three main research domains could be identified: namely (1) a customer perspective, (2) a company perspective, and (3) an investor perspective. The classification process was guided by theory using a deductive approach leading to a category system, which enabled the researcher to assign the works with relevant brand-specific content and topics to the main categories. The corresponding subcategories evolved inductively, during the process of the in-depth content analysis of the material included in the final sample (see Figure 20.2).

Key Findings

Table 20.1 indicates that the final sample population includes 85 articles with hotel brand-related content, representing almost 2% of the total pool of the articles found in the four

Table 20.1 Quantitative data framework of literature analysis during reference period (1996–2018)

Journal name	Total articles	Total articles after keyword search	Hotel brand-related article	Percentage hotel brand-related article (%)
Cornell Hospitality Quarterly★	966	100	23	2.38
a International Journal of Hospitality Management	1,490	89	27	1.81
b International Journal of Contemporary Hospitality Management	1,420	92	22	1.54
Journal of Hospitality & Tourism Research	476	48	14	2.94
Total/overall percentage	4,292	329	85	1.98

Note: ★ Published as Cornell Hotel and Administration Quarterly (1960–2008).

journals over 22 years, with an average of approximately 3 to 4 articles per year. To give a sense of the chronological progression of branding and brand management in hospitality research, a ten-year comparison of the sample implies that research on branding and brand management in the hotel industry did not begin until the mid-to-late 2000s. The number of brand-related articles increased significantly in the second period of the study (2008–2018) compared to the years 1996–2008, accounting for almost three-quarters of the entire sample. At first glance, this indicates an increase in interest in branding and brand management as a new and growing field in hospitality research. However, compared with other systematic literature reviews in hospitality research, it has to be acknowledged that branding and brand management in the hotel industry still receives only limited attention as a research topic. To illustrate a reference value, Ottenbacher and Harrington found in their review on strategic management in hospitality, strategy to be a popular research area in the academic field of hospitality, extracting 225 articles from the same 4 scientific journals which are also relevant in this study, representing 27% of the total journal articles in a five-year research period (Ottenbacher and Harrington, 2011). In two recent systematic literature reviews in hospitality, one on service research the other on customer experience management, Kandampully et al. found a relevant sample of 10% in the case of service research (Kandampully et al., 2014) and a sample of 16% in the case of customer experience management (Kandampully et al., 2018). The notion of inadequate representation of hotel branding as a research topic within the hospitality research agenda is also being supported by Yoo et al. (2011) in their study on hospitality marketing research, where branding only ranked no. 8 amongst 17 marketing research subjects identified, accounting for approx. 4% of the investigated marketing-focused articles (while including other hospitality industries such as airlines, restaurants, casinos beyond the hotel industry, etc.).

As indicated, 85 papers could be identified during the screening process, making original contributions to the development of an enhanced knowledge on branding and brand management in the hotel industry. Within the three categories, the corporate perspective was the most researched field with 49 contributions, followed by the customer perspective with 32 and the investor perspective with 3. One article was a literature review. The top three fields of research across the categories were Brand Strategy (*n* = 24), Brand Loyalty/Engagement (*n* = 14), and Internal Branding (*n* = 11).

Main Category 1: Company Perspective

The intensified brand activities and the increased brand consciousness in the hotel industry in the past years have shown that the industry is getting more and more sensitive in terms of creating a relevant value proposition and communicating the essence of this brand value to their customers. In consequence, the market share of brands in the hospitality industry will continue to grow in the future and thus also the necessity of a systematic, consequent, and competitive brand management approach (Dev and Withiam, 2012; Gardini, 2015; Zhang et al., 2008). Accordingly, the majority of the articles from the sample examine the topics of branding and brand management from the strategic perspective of the company. Competitive considerations are dominating the research scope such as brand positioning, brand equity, brand cooperation, and brand internationalization and in recent times, the issue of internal or employer branding. Especially the function and the role of the brand as a value driver in terms of its ability to build brand equity and enhance financial performance is a central point of discussion in the current research landscape. The focus lies on the financial implications of changes in operator ownership, rebranding or rescaling strategies, the impacts on brand equity in the course of takeovers, mergers and acquisitions, or the economic effects of brand affiliation or franchise system changes. However, the strategic question of what makes up for a strong and successful hotel brand or what are the prerequisites and challenges of promising brand differentiation strategies in the hotel industry is hardly being discussed.

Moreover, this point seems to be taken as a given in the current hospitality literature despite of the fact that that travellers and hotel guests are often hardly able to specify any particular associations that differentiate one hotel brand from the other (Olsen et al., 2005) and accordingly do not identify strongly with hotel brands (So et al., 2013). Other strategic or organizational questions of the brand value management system in the hotel industry (i.e., stakeholder management), the impact of digitalization on hotel branding, the possibilities and limitations of brand management in the light of small- and medium-sized companies, individual/independent hotel operators or family-owned hotels, have received little to none attention in this sample. Also, studies related to the role of brands within the operational marketing context or studies analyzing branding and brand management seen from a leadership perspective (i.e., brand co-creation, brand culture, brand alliances, brand architecture) could only be identified in isolated cases.

Main Category 2: Customer Perspective

There is a broad consensus amongst academics and practitioners about the relevance, the role, and the function of brands in terms of winning and keeping customer share and customer's trade. The characteristics and functionality of a brand therefore is, to develop a unique and meaningful brand identity and brand personality which should be a synthesis of physical, rational, aesthetic, and emotional product or service attributes, in order to unfold its orientation, identification, and differentiation potential in the designated target market (Aaker and Joachimsthaler, 2012; Keller, 1993; Murphy, 1998). Against the backdrop of this definition of the essence of brands, from a hospitality research perspective one question is paramount: *"Are brands really relevant for customers in the hotel industry and/or what kind of role do hotel brands play in consumer decision making processes related to hotel choice?"* At present, only rudimentary approaches are discernible in the academic field of hospitality to assess the influence and the impact of brands on hotel guests, aiming to understand the relationship between brand relevance, consumer benefits, and corporate success (Cai and Hobson, 2004; Dubé and Reneghan, 2000; So et al., 2013). In the present sample, the question of the relevance of hotel brands from a hotel guest perspective was widely not at the core of research interest and could only be identified in single cases as a research question. Major research interest could be identified in the area of branding and customer loyalty/engagement, mainly addressing the impact and the relationships between customer loyalty programs and the respective hotel brands. Studies about the differentiation capability of hotel brands in their specific competitive environment, the perception and assessment of hotel brand value/strength/image from a customer point of view, or the relative importance of brands compared to other hotel choice criteria, could only be spotted in isolated cases within the scope of the present sample. The few studies which could be identified in this respect investigated brand attitudes and brand perceptions of hotel customers referring to the ability of a hotel brand to establish trust, create value, or communicate a specific image. Especially, the relevance and influence of brands during the decision-making process of different target groups (end consumer, business to business consumer, leisure/business traveler, individual/group traveler) is largely not examined, as only one study could be identified in the present sample addressing this topic. Furthermore, studies on classical psychographic target figures of branding and brand management such as brand awareness, brand image, brand knowledge, brand attitude, brand satisfaction, brand commitment, brand citizenship, etc. are widely missing in the hospitality literature. Finally, the external and internal effects of hotel brand conversions (rebranding/rescaling) on customer and employee behavior have to be considered an underexposed area in hospitality research.

Main Category 3: Investor Perspective

Hotel investors are considered to be the key driver of the actual developments and changes in the brand landscape of the international hotel industry. In the last couple of years hotel transaction volumes have set new records worldwide (JLL 2020, 2017) and the added value of a brand is very often a major criterion in the course of the valuation of a lease, managed, or franchised hotel property (Dev et al., 2002; Oak and Dalbor, 2010; O'Neill and Xiao, 2006). Thus, hotel properties have evolved to be an attractive investment option for a broad range of different types of investors. However, as the current literature review reveals, hospitality research didn't catch up with the increasing interest in hotel property investments of different market actors and participants, as the perspective of the hotel investor in relation to the role and the relevance of brands against the backdrop of investment decisions, the choice of hotel operators and/ or operating models, has hardly been explored. Is the strength of a hotel brand relevant for a hotel owner or hotel operator concerning their role and position as a potential partner of hotel investors? Which characteristic makes a hotel brand attractive for hotel investors and which impact does the strength of a brand have in comparison to other criteria referring to the choice of an operator or the operating model? The great heterogeneity amongst the different types of hotel investors and their specific objectives and individual interests could probably lead to very diverse assessments about the relevance of a brand as an investment criterion when it comes down to decisions about a hotel property, an operator or an operating model. At present, the hospitality literature is offering very limited insights about the motivation, the process, and the criteria of investment decisions of hotel investors and thus the question of the role and the significance of brands within the context of hotel property investments is awaiting further research. Furthermore, the consideration of the particular stakeholder situation in the hotel industry, with shareholders, investors, and operators being linked through contractual agreements (i.e., franchise, management, lease, equity), framing the institutional and structural background of a hotel brand value system and the operational framework of hotel brands, being incorporated and influenced by managers, employees, customers, competitors, etc. is widely missing in the current hospitality literature.

Conclusions and Implications

The economic impact of branding and brand management in the hotel industry presents itself as a widely ambivalent and diffuse phenomenon. The role and the relevance of brands in the hotel industry is obviously debatable, starting with the core question if the comprehension of the essence of branding in the hotel industry is comparable to concepts of branding in other industries, such as consumer goods, automotive, fashion, service or other, or, if we have to diagnose an all-too narrow understanding or misconception of what a brand really is or should deliver in order to be relevant for a sufficient number of hotel customers. There appears to be some inconsistency and confusion amongst practitioners and academics about the difference between a hotel product and a hotel brand and the perception of what the concept of the hotel brand or hotel branding really is or should be and whether the topic of brand relevance might be over- or underrated in the hotel industry.

The research findings reveal some interesting points of discussion. First, the topic of hotel branding and hotel brand management seems to receive limited attention in the hospitality research literature, as well as referring to its strategic relevance as known from other industries, as compared to other kinds of research areas in the hotel industry. Hence, the answer to the question to what extent brand equity components such as brand awareness, brand image, brand knowledge, brand loyalty, and perceived brand quality contribute to the economic success in the hotel industry remains currently without reply and warrants further research. Second, further research is needed to determine whether brands are really relevant in decision-making processes of hotel guests related to hotel choice and if so, whether the relevance of those brands is rooted in their ability to fulfill guest expectations and needs and/or their differentiation potential within the competitive set. Third, as hotel investors are considered to be the key driver of the ongoing proliferation of brands, emphasizing their ability to facilitate access to capital and to support growth, a broader stakeholder perspective is considered essential in future research on hotel branding in order to understand the relevance of brands within the context of hotel property investments and owner/operator relationships.

Overall, the analysis illustrates that we have to ascertain knowledge gaps with regard to the role of brands as value drivers for hotel companies, customers, and investors as the current research efforts deliver only modest contributions. Specifically, our understanding of the different objectives, responsibilities, interdependencies, interactions, and relationships of those key stakeholders surrounding the discourse of brand building and brand management processes has to be considered very limited, as the present chapter couldn't identify particular research efforts in this direction. Accordingly, an intensified theoretical discussion is being reminded (King, 2017), as a holistic understanding of hotel branding is being considered essential for future corporate success (Dev and Whitiam, 2012). Although the analysis of the brand literature related to company, consumer, and investor provides a good initial focus, we shouldn't limit our future research efforts to those three key stakeholders, rather than broadening our research perspective in terms of the identification of further relevant actors, forces, and relationships within the context of hotel branding and brand co-creation.

Limitations

Although there have been prior reviews in the hospitality and hotel marketing domain (e.g., Dev et al., 2010; Hwang and Seo, 2016; Oh et al., 2004; Yoo et al., 2011), as well as some work centered around predicting future service (e.g., Grove et al., 2003; Kandampully et al., 2014; Ostrom et al., 2010) and hospitality research priorities (e.g., Law et al., 2012; Ottenbacher et al., 2009; Solnet et al., 2010), only isolated contributions related to a holistic understanding of hotel brand management and hotel brand theory can been identified in the hospitality literature (King, 2017). The present systematic literature review fills a void in this respect; however, like any other study, this research is not free from limitations. The systematic literature review as a research approach has many methodological constraints, as discussed by many scholars (Law and Chon, 2007; Saur-Amaral et al., 2013; Zhao and Ritchie, 2007). The inherent limitation of literature reviews is that they depend on the quality of the search process, and the quality of the search process depends amongst other things predominantly on the professional background of the researcher, prior research experiences, the specific methodology applied, potential biases of the researcher (conceptual/interpretational), etc. To address these constraints the study mirrored similar approaches of systematic literature reviews in the field of hospitality such as Ottenbacher and Harrington (2011) and Kandampully et al. (2014), applying a virtually identical methodological frame of reference. To keep the amount of articles manageable, the study focused on four of the top hospitality journals, for the 1996–2018 time period. While this approach provided a manageable method of defining and categorizing branding in hospitality, future research might expand this assessment process over a longer time period and include additional journals.

Finally, it has to be said that the scope of this chapter was to provide a general overview of the role of brands and branding in the global hotel industry and its representation and focus in hospitality research. Hence, the content analysis in this study followed a purely quantitative approach, based on identifying categories and counting the numbers of selected journal articles grouped into different categories for descriptive analysis, rather than attempting to analyze the data and the findings in detail such as research methodology approach, categorization by author or institution, country of origin, sampling sizes, etc. As this study did not aim to capture the influence, the importance or the quality of the publications, it is for this reason that the quantitative approach of the content analysis was deemed to be most appropriate (Zhao and Ritchie, 2007). At this point, the general findings of the present case provide some clear implications and directions for future research, which may lead to an advanced understanding of the future role of brands and branding in the global hotel industry. Future research in this stream, however, needs to refine the methodology used in this study while aiming to enrich our knowledge on branding and brand strategies in the hotel industry and supporting hotel chains, affiliations, or independent properties in their endeavor to become or to stay relevant for their selected target group(s) with their brand strategy and their brands.

References

Aaker, D.A. (2012), "Win the brand relevance battle and then build competitor barriers", *California Management Review*, Vol.54, No.2, pp.43–57.

Aaker, D.A. and Joachimsthaler, E. (2012), *Brand Leadership*, Simon and Schuster, New York, NY.

Amadeus. (2007), *Die Zukunft der Hotellerie*, Amadeus, München.

Back, K.J. (2005), "The effects of image congruence on customers' brand loyalty in the upper middle-class hotel industry", *Journal of Hospitality & Tourism Research*, Vol.29, No.4, pp.448–467.

Bailey, R. and Ball, S. (2006), "An exploration of the meanings of hotel brand equity", *The Service Industries Journal*, Vol.26, No.1, pp.15–38.

Beritelli, P., Bieger, T., Laesser, C., and Wittmer, A. (2015), "Challenging 'common knowledge' in tourism – A partial polemic", in Pechlaner, H. and Smeral, E. (Eds.), *Tourism and Leisure – Current Issues and Perspectives of Development*, Springer, Wiesbaden, pp.23–38.

Berry, L.L. (2000), "Cultivating service brand equity", *Journal of the Academy of Marketing Science*, Vol.28, No.1, pp.128–137.

Briner, R.B. and Denyer, D. (2012), "Systematic review and evidence synthesis as a practice and scholarship tool", in Rousseau, D.M. (Ed.), *Handbook of Evidence-Based Management: Companies, Classrooms and Research*, University Press, New York, NY, pp.112–129.

Buer, C. and Groß, A. (2006), "Markenführung in der Hotellerie", in Deichsel, A. and Meyer, H. (Eds.), *Jahrbuch der Markentechnik 2006/2007*, Deutscher Fachverlag, Frankfurt/Main, pp.171–202.

Burmann, C., Jost-Benz, M., and Riley, N. (2009), "Towards an identity-based brand equity model", *Journal of Business Research*, Vol.62, No.3, pp.390–397.

Cai, L.A. and Hobson, J.S.P. (2004), "Making hotel brands work in a competitive environment", *Journal of Vacation Marketing*, Vol.10, No.3, pp.197–208.

Carvell, S.A., Canina, L., and Sturman, M.C. (2016), "A comparison of the performance of brand-affiliated and unaffiliated hotel properties", *Cornell Hospitality Quarterly*, Vol.57, No.2, pp.193–201.

Charmaz, K. (2006), *Constructing Grounded Theory: A Practical Guide Through Qualitative Analysis*, Sage Publications, London, UK.

Daun, W. and Klinger, R. (2006), "How premium hotel brands struggle to communicate their value proposition", *International Journal of Contemporary Hospitality Management*, Vol.18, No.3, pp.246–252.

De Chernatony, L. (1999), "Brand management through narrowing the gap between brand identity and brand reputation", *Journal of Marketing Management*, Vol.15, No.1–3, pp.157–179.

Deloitte (2010), *Hospitality 2015 – Game Changers or Spectators*, Deloitte, München.

Denyer, D. and Tranfield, D. (2009), "Producing a systematic review", in Buchanan, D.A. and Bryman, A. (Eds.), *The Sage Handbook of Organizational Research Methods*, Sage Publications, Thousand Oaks, CA, pp.671–689.

Dev, C.S. (2012), *Hospitality Branding*, Cornell University, Ithaca.

Dev, C.S. (2015), "Hotel brand conversions: What works and what doesn't", *Cornell Hospitality Report*, Vol.15, No.21, pp.3–11.

Dev, C.S., Buschman, J.D., and Bowen, J.T. (2010), "Hospitality marketing: A retrospective analysis (1960–2010) and predictions (2010–2020)", *Cornell Hospitality Quarterly*, Vol.51, No.4, pp.459–469.

Dev, C.S., Erramilli, M.K., and Agarwal, S. (2002), "Brands across borders: Determining factors in choosing franchising or management contracts for entering international markets", *Cornell Hotel & Restaurant Administration Quarterly*, Vol.43, No.6, pp.91–104.

Dev, C.S. and Withiam, G. (2011), "Fresh thinking about the box", *Cornell Hospitality Roundtable Proceedings*, Vol.3, No.6, pp.6–16.

Dev, C.S. and Withiam, G. (2012), "Branding hospitality – Challenges, opportunities and best practices", *Cornell Hospitality Roundtable Proceedings*, Vol.4, No.5, pp.6–16.

Donnevert, T. (2009), *Markenrelevanz: Messung, Konsequenzen und Determinanten*, Springer/Gabler, Berlin.

Dubé, L. and Reneghan, L.M. (2000), "Creating visible customer value – How customers view best-practice champions", *Cornell Hotel and Administration Quarterly*, Vol.41, No.1, pp.62–72.

Esch, F. R. (2016), *Identität: Das Rückgrat starker Marken*. Campus, Frankfurt.

Forgacs, G. (2003), "Brand asset equilibrium in hotel management", *International Journal of Contemporary Hospitality Management*, Vol.15, No.6, pp.340–342.

Fournier, S. (1998), "Consumers and their brands: Developing relationship theory in consumer research", *Journal of consumer research*, Vol.24, No.4, pp.343–373.

Francese, P.A. and Renaghan, L.M. (1990), "Data-base marketing: Building customer profiles", *Cornell Hotel and Administration Quarterly*, Vol.31, No.2, pp.60–63.

Fraunhofer (2014), *Futurehotel Gastbefragung*, Fraunhofer-Institut für Arbeitswirtschaft und Organisation - IAO Stuttgart.

Frehse, J. (2008), "Das vernachlässigte Versprechen – Die Markenpolitik internationaler Hotelketten im Spiegel aktueller Erkenntnisse des Dienstleistungsmarketings", *Der Markt*, Vol.47, No.1, pp.4–15.

fvw. (2015), *fvw Studie: Hotel- und Clubmarken*, fvw medien, Juni, Hamburg.

Gardini, M.A. (2015), "The challenge of branding and brand management: Perspectives from the hospitality industry", in Pechlaner, H. and Smeral, E. (Eds.), *Tourism and Leisure: Current Issues and Perspectives of Development*, Springer, Wiesbaden, pp.247–268.

Gerhard, S. and Nadrowski, M. (2011), "Zur Relevanz der Marke aus Kunden- und Investorensicht", in Gardini, M.A. (Ed.), *Mit der Marke zum Erfolg: Markenmanagement in Hotellerie und Gastronomie*, Stuttgart, Matthaes, pp.12–67.

Grove, S., Fisk, R.P., and John, J. (2003), "The future of services marketing: Forecasts from ten service experts", *Journal of Services Marketing*, Vol.17, No.2, pp.107–121.

Gursoy, D. and Sandstrom, J.K. (2014), "An updated ranking of hospitality and tourism journals", *Journal of Hospitality & Tourism Research*, Vol.40, No.1, pp.3–18.

Hanson, B., Mattila, A.S., O'Neill, J.W., and Kim, Y. (2009), "Hotel rebranding and rescaling: Effects on financial performance", *Cornell Hotel and Restaurant Administration Quarterly*, Vol.50, No.3, pp.360–370.

Harrington, R.J. and Ottenbacher, M.C. (2011), "Markenwert aus Sicht der Gastronomie", in Gardini, M.A.(Ed.), *Mit der Marke zum Erfolg: Markenmanagement in Hotellerie und Gastronomie*, Matthaes Verlag. Stuttgart, pp.129–142.

Hwang, J. and Seo, S., (2016), "A critical review of research on customer experience management: Theoretical, methodological and cultural perspectives", *International Journal of Contemporary Hospitality Management*, Vol.28, No.10, pp.2218–2246.

International Hotel Association, IHA. (2019), *Hotelmarkt Deutschland*, IHA Service GmbH, Berlin.

JLL (2017), "Hotels schneiden sich immer größere Stücke vom Investmentkuchen ab", Jones Lang LaSalle,. *Press Release 10th of January 2017*, available at: http://www.jll.de/germany/de-de/Documents/jll_germany_hotelinvestment_2016_1.pdf (accessed 20.5.2017).

JLL (2020), *Hotel Investment Outlook 2020*, available at: https://www.jll.de/en/trends-and-insights/research/hotel-investment-outlook-2020 (accessed 20.2.2020).

Joachimsthaler, E. and Aaker, D.A. (1997), "Building brands without mass media", *Harvard Business Review*, Vol.71, No.1, pp. 64–73.

Kandampully, J., Keating, W.B., Beomchol, K., Mattila, A.S., and Solnet, D. (2014), "Service research in the hospitality literature: Insights from a systematic review", *Cornell Hospitality Quarterly*, Vol.55, No.3, pp.287–299.

Kandampully, J., Zhang, T.C., and Jaakkola, E. (2018), "Customer experience management in hospitality: A literature synthesis, new understanding and research agenda", *International Journal of Contemporary Hospitality Management*, Vol.30, No.1, pp.21–56.

Kapferer, J.N. (2012), *The New Strategic Brand Management: Advanced Insights and Strategic Thinking*, 5th ed., Kogan, London, UK.

Katz, J.H. and Witham, G. (2012, May), "The international hospitality industry: Overcoming the barriers to growth", *Cornell Hospitality Proceedings*, Vol. 4, No.3, pp.4–13.

Kayaman, R. and Arasli, H. (2007), "Customer based brand equity: Evidence from the hotel industry", *Managing Service Quality*, Vol.17, No.1, pp.92–109.

Keller, K.L. (1993), "Conceptualizing, measuring, and managing customer-based brand equity", *Journal of Marketing*, Vol.57, No.1, pp.1–22.

Keller, K.L., Apéria, T., and Georgson, M. (2008), *Strategic Brand Management: A European Perspective*, Pearson Education, New York, NY.

Kim, W.G., Jin-Sun, B., and Kim, H.J. (2008), "Multidimensional customer-based brand equity and its consequences in mid-priced hotels", *Journal of Hospitality Management and Tourism Research*, Vol.32, No.2, pp.235–254.

King, C. (2017), "Brand management – Standing out from the Crowd – A review and research agenda for hospitality management", *International Journal of Contemporary Hospitality Management*, Vol.29, No.1, pp.114–140.

Koob, C. (2011), "Markenpositionierung in der Hotellerie: Konsequenzen der Studie 'Hotellerie der Zukunft' ", in Gardini, M.A. (Ed.), *Mit der Marke zum Erfolg: Markenmanagement in Hotellerie und Gastronomie*, Matthaes, Stuttgart, pp.102–113.

Kusluvan, S., Kusluvan, Z., Ilhan, I., and Buyruk, L. (2010), "The human dimension: A review of human resources management issues in the tourism and hospitality industry", *Cornell Hospitality Quarterly*, Vol.51, No.2, pp.171–214.

Law, R. and Chon, K.S. (2007), "Evaluating research performance in tourism and hospitality: the perspective of university program heads", *Tourism Management*, Vol.28, No.5, pp.1203–1211.

Law, R., Leung, D., and Cheung, C. (2012), "A systematic review, analysis, and evaluation of research articles in the Cornell Hospitality Quarterly", *Cornell Hospitality Quarterly*, Vol.53, No.4, pp.365–381.

Law, R. and van der Veen, R. (2009), "The popularity of prestigious hospitality journals: A GoogleScholar approach", *International Journal of Contemporary Hospitality Management*, Vol.20, No.2, pp.13–125.

Lynn, M. (2007), "Brand segmentation in the hotel and cruise industry: Fact or fiction?", *Cornell Hospitality Report*, Vol.7, No.1, pp.4–15.

McKercher, B., Law, R., and Lam, T. (2006), "Rating tourism and hospitality journals", *Tourism Management*, Vol.27, No.6, pp.1235–1252.

Murphy, J.M. (1998), "What is branding?", in Murphy, J.M. and Hart, S. (Eds.), *Brands – The New Wealth Creators*, Interbrand, New York, NY, pp.1–12.

O'Neill, J.W. and Mattila, A.S. (2010), "Hotel brand strategy", *Cornell Hospitality Quarterly*, Vol.51, No.1, pp.27–34.

O'Neill, J.W. and Carlback, M. (2011), "Do brands matter? A comparison of branded and independent hotels' performance during a full economic cycle", *International Journal of Hospitality Management*, Vol.30, No.3, pp.515–521.

O'Neill, J.W. and Xiao, Q. (2006), "The role of brand affiliation in hotel market value", *Cornell Hotel and Administration Quarterly*, Vol.47, No.13, pp.210–223.

Oak, S. and Dalbor, M.C. (2010), "Do institutional investors favor firms with greater brand equity? An empirical investigation of investments in US lodging firms", *International Journal of Contemporary Hospitality Management*, Vol.22, No.1, pp.24–40.

Oh, H., Kim, B.Y., and Shin, J.H. (2004), "Hospitality and tourism marketing: Recent developments in research and future directions", *International Journal of Hospitality Management*, Vol.23, No.5, pp.425–447.

Olsen, M.D., Chung, Y., Graf, N., Lee, K., and Madanoglu, M. (2005), "Branding: Myth and reality in the hotel industry", *Journal of Retail & Leisure Property*, Vol.4, No.2, pp.146–162.

Ostrom, A.L., Bitner, M.J., Brown, S.W., Burkhard, K.A., Goul, M., Smith-Daniels, V., Demirkan, H., and Rabinovich. E. (2010), "Moving forward and making a difference: Research priorities for the science of service", *Journal of Service Research*, Vol.13, No.1, pp.4–36.

Ottenbacher, M.C. and Harrington R.J. (2011), "Strategic management: An analysis of its representation and focus in hospitality research", *International Journal of Contemporary Hospitality Management*, Vol.23, No.4, pp.439–462.

Ottenbacher, M.C., Harrington, R.J., and Parsa, H. (2009), "Defining the hospitality discipline: A discussion of pedagogical and research implications", *Journal of Hospitality & Tourism Research*, Vol.33. No.3, pp.263–283.

Pechlaner, H., Zehrer, A., Matzler, K., and Abfalter, A. (2004), "A ranking of international tourism and hospitality journals", *Journal of Travel Research*, Vol.42, No.5, pp.328–332.

Prasad, K. and Dev, C. (2000), "Managing hotel brand equity: A customer centric framework for assessing performance", *Cornell Hotel and Administration Quarterly*, Vol.41, No.3, pp.22–31.

Saur-Amaral, I., Ferreira, P., and Conde, R. (2013), "Linking past and future research in tourism management through the lens of marketing and consumption: a systematic literature review", *Tourism & Management Studies*, Vol.9, No.1, pp.35–40.

Schneider, J. (2008), *Geschäftsreisende 2008: Strukturen – Einstellungen – Verhalten*, IUBH, Bad Honnef.

Schreier, M. (2014), "Qualitative content analysis", in Flick, U. (Ed.), *The SAGE Handbook of Qualitative Data Analysis*, Sage, London, UK, pp.170–183.

So, K.K.F. and King, C. (2010), "'When experience matters': Building and measuring hotel brand equity, the customers' perspective", *International Journal of Contemporary Hospitality Management*, Vol.22, No.5, pp.589–608.

So, K.K.F., King, C., Sparks, B.A., and Wang, Y. (2013), "The influence of customer brand identification on hotel brand evaluation and loyalty development", *International Journal of Hospitality Management*, Vol.34, No.3, pp.31–41.

Soller, J. (2016), *Das heutige Buchungsverhalten von Hotelgästen und deren Auswirkungen auf die Hotelmarke und Hotelfinanzierung*, Institut für Tourismus Berlin e.V., Berlin.

Solnet, D.J., Paulsen, N., and Cooper, C. (2010), "Decline and turnaround: A literature review and proposed research agenda for the hotel sector", *Current Issues in Tourism*, Vol.13, No.2, pp.139–159.

Tranfield, D., Denyer, D., and Smart, P. (2003), "Towards a methodology for developing evidence-informed management knowledge by means of systematic review", *British Journal of Management,* Vol.14, No.3, pp.207–222.

Tsai, Y.L., Dev, C.S., and Chintagunta, P. (2015), "What's in a brand name? Assessing the impact of rebranding in the hospitality industry", *Journal of Marketing Research*, Vol.52, No.6, pp.865–878.

Van Fleet, D.D., McWilliams, A., and Siegel, D.S. (2000), "A theoretical and empirical analysis of journal rankings: The case of formal lists", *Journal of Management*, Vol.26, No.5, pp.839–861.

VDR. (2018), *Geschäftsreiseanalyse 2018*, Verband Deutsches Reisemanagement e.V, Frankfurt/Main.

Webster, J. and Watson, R.T. (2002), "Analyzing the past to prepare for the future: Writing a literature review", *MIS Quarterly*, Vol.26, No.2, pp.xiii–xxiii.

Yoo, M., Lee, S., and Bai, B. (2011), "Hospitality marketing research from 2000–2009 – Topics, methods, and trends", *International Journal of Contemporary Hospitality Management*, Vol.23, No.4, pp.517–532.

Zehle, F. (2011), "Markenführung und Hotel Business Positioning am Beispiel von Marriott International", in Gardini, M.A. (Ed.), *Mit der Marke zum Erfolg – Markenmanagement in Hotellerie und Gastronomie*, Matthaes, Stuttgart, pp.189–209.

Zhang, J., Cai, L.A., and Kavanaugh, R.R. (2008), "Dimensions in building brand experience for economy hotels – A case of emerging market", *Journal of China Tourism Research*, Vol.4, No.1, pp.61–77.

Zhao, W. and Ritchie, J.R. (2007), "An investigation of academic leadership in tourism research: 1985–2004", *Tourism Management,* Vol.28, No.2, pp.476–490.

21

BRAND IDENTITY AND POSITIONING IN SELECTED INDIAN CHAIN HOTEL COMPANIES

Saurabh Kumar Dixit and Abijith Abraham

Background

The hospitality industry is known as the provider of personalized services that deliver a unique customer experience. Hotels sell offerings comprising of a mixture of intangible service components and tangible goods components (Tajeddini, 2010). The intangible service components make the hotel services a challenging business to manage (Kuada and Hinson, 2014). The individual consumer is motivated not only by rational decisions but also by emotions and experiences (Dixit, 2017). In today's modern and digital world, consumer behavior may be the central theme to understand the key facets of our changing lifestyles (Dixit, 2016). The need for the marketer to be flexible and adaptable to the changing world around them has never been so robust (Dixit et al., 2019). The hospitality industry is considered as highly fragmented, where the largest hotel chains employ over 100,000 employees in their over 6,000 hotels and they are growing (International Labour Organization, 2010).

In recent years, the global hotel industry has without doubt accepted the importance of branding as a significant constituent of its marketing strategy (Dev et al., 2009), particularly given the extensive hotel brand segmentation. Beginning with Quality International (now Choice Hotels International) in 1981, most hotel companies have developed diverse brands to serve multiple market segments (Jiang, et al., 2002). Forty-one percent of the global branded hotel market is under the accounts of five leading branded hotel companies along with over 72% of the global development pipeline (Intercontinental Hotel Group, 2019).

Brands create unique experiences in the mind of the consumer that serve as the primary basis for the brand preference (Brakus et al., 2009). Schmitt (1999) proposed that customers of the 21st century are rational as well as emotional decision makers, and the emotions can be created through unique brand experiences. Fournier (1998) proposed that the customer and the brand carry a two-way relationship, and the values are co-created. Customers are seen as equal partners in the value creation of the product and services through their emotions and experiences (Prahalad and Venkat, 2004). The customer and the brand relationship can be rationally or emotionally based (Brakus et al., 2009). The exceptional growth of hotel branding is based on the concept that brands provide added value to both guests and hotel companies, in large part because they nurture brand loyalty (O'Neill and Xiao, 2006). The value of a brand primarily resides in the minds of customers and is based chiefly on customers' brand awareness, their perceptions of its quality, and their brand loyalty (Olsen and Zhao, 2008).

The direct contribution of travel and tourism industry in India is 6.8% of the total GDP, and it is expected to grow by 7.2% (Government of India, 2019). The revenue generation from the industry was $7.6 trillion and it supported a total of 292 million jobs across the world, equivalent to 1 in 10 jobs in the world economy (WTTC, 2017). In response to the growing competition of developing a unique brand identity in the market, organizations have amplified efforts to strengthen their brands by adopting experiential techniques that cater unique and personalized experiences to the customer (Smilansky, 2009).

The current rate of investment in the Indian hotel sector seems to point towards the business opportunities available in the sector. Almost all the International brands have pitched camp in the Indian hotel sector. With the entry of these international players and more high-rated star hotels, competition in the Indian hotel sector has become more intense. Therefore, branding is the biggest challenge in the hospitality industry. The branding strategy, for a hotel company, starts off with a clear comprehension of the business, including who and what is being satisfied, as well as how needs of customer are being satisfied. This chapter aims to analyze branding strategies adopted by the Indian hotel chain companies.

Significance of the Study

Hospitality and tourism studies are the emerging disciplines where the body of knowledge is evolving with the advancements in the society, culture, and human behavior (Dixit, 2018). When it comes to a hotel, branding has been established as an important component in their marketing strategies. Hence, over the years, there have been many researchers giving their verdicts on the effects of branding on guest loyalty (O'Neill and Mattila, 2010). According to a report by HVS and The World Travel and Tourism Council, the travel industry in India is expected to reach 1,747 million travelers by 2021, which will require 1,88,500 additional hotel rooms. Mid-market hotels will be the driving force because they usually have more rooms per hotel than a 5-star or a luxury hotel and they, according to the reports, could be built faster and more cost-effectively in multiple micro-markets as well as in most tier I, II, and III cities. Media reports further suggest that International hotel chains are increasing their presence in the country, and it is forecasted to account for around 47% share in the Hospitality sector of India by 2020 and 50% by 2022 (HVS Anarock, 2019). The International hotel chains, by increasing their presence in India, pose a huge competition and big challenge for Indian chain hotels to sustain in the vibrant domestic market. Thus, there is a need for India chain hotels to differentiate their brand identity and product positioning strategies from those of competitors. Branded hotels in India are facing challenges like stiff competition, reluctance to increase room rates, dipping consumer loyalties, and unavailability of profitable locations. Competition among branded hotels in India is also becoming stiffer because "differentiation is harder to achieve" (Deloitte, 2010).

Establishing and successfully overseeing strong brands is considered to be one crucial factor which determines the extent of triumph in hotel industry. The hotel-stay decisions taken by the consumers are more often based on how they perceive a specific hotel's brand name. Brand portfolio is an important concept as far as investors are concerned; it helps in improving the future returns while at the same time minimizing the foreseeable risks (Markowitz, 1952) (Wang and Chung, 2015). However, before diversifying its portfolio, the hotel management must ensure whether the quality of service at each hotel is up to the customer expectations. If at all the perceived service quality shoots short of the customer expectations, the brand may face repercussions from its expansion strategy and further hamper the growth of the umbrella brand.

The present chapter highlights the issues of hospitality branding by presenting the cases of two successful hotel chains of India, i.e., Oberoi Hotels & Resorts (East India Hotels Ltd.) and The Indian Hotels Company Limited (IHCL) popularly known as Taj Group of Hotels. The chapter further provides brief evidence relating to branding strategies opted in the selected Indian hotel chains. It concludes by highlighting the corporate strategies that lead to establishing brand identity and positioning amongst the brands.

Branding in Indian Hotels

Branding is popularly used as a marketing technique by most hotel chains that have multiple product lines. Marketing of such products can be challenging to manage and at times, even confusing for the guests. Prasad and Dev (2000) demonstrated that branding would be a quick way for hotel chains to identify and differentiate themselves in the minds of the customers. Luxury, premium, 5-star and up-market are the common terms thrown around the marketers in order to differentiate their respective hotel brands. According to Kim and Kim(2005), in the hospitality industry, customers often base their purchase decisions on their perceptions of a company's brand (e.g., Marriott, Hilton, Hyatt, McDonald's, Burger King, Wendy's, Chili's, Applebee's, and TGI Friday's). That is, hotel guests usually consider hotel brand associations rather than the brand association of product items. A hospitality company must formulate its basic strategic brand principles in view of two central themes, which are *brand architecture* and *brand portfolio*.

Brand architecture is associated with the way in which a product is signed by a brand, and whether it does the same independently of another brand (Douglas et al., 2001; Rao et al., 2004). A brand has four facets: name, symbol, object, and concept. As many firms have a plethora of products, this calls for some thought to be given about the system of names and symbols (brand names, logos, and colors) to be given to the individual products. This system is referred to as *brand architecture* (Kapferer, 2000a). A direct quote from the works of Aaker and Joachimsthaler (2000) goes, "*Brand architecture is an organizing structure of the brand portfolio that specifies brand roles and the nature of relationships between brands.*" Olins (1989) and Laforet and Saunders (1999), for example, differentiate three levels of brand architecture, which are monolithic brands:

1   *corporate branding (one name for all products);*
2   *endorsed brands / mixed branding (two brands associated with one product); and*
3   *branded products / house of brands (each product has its own brand).*

(Olins, 1989)

As defined by Riezebos (2003), a brand portfolio is a set of brands owned by one company. According to Dawar (2004), the brands needed to be considered as a part of the team rather than as individual superstars. While Kapferer (2000b) asks us the question of how many brands needed to be offered within the same product category? The issue of brand portfolio optimization is strategic in nature and the options considered will in no doubt have a deep and lasting impact on the outcome. Also, the strategy that is ultimately pursued will either facilitate or impede the concept of having a sustainable competitive advantage.

A brand is not only an identity but also a promise to the hotel customers that the hotel will bring in the quality of care and desired services (Speak, 1996). Hospitality branding demands planning and dedication to deliver with superior standards of consistency across product and services (Mangini, 2002). The brand strategists should focus on addressing issues like building trust between customer and brand and administering the senses and experiences of customers toward hospitality organizations (Mangini, 2002). From a corporate strategy viewpoint, well-run hotel brands have a tendency to enhance their market share (O'Neill and Mattila, 2004), despite the fact different parent companies have different modus operandi on how to manage their brand identity. The hospitality industry has been experiencing an ongoing proliferation of hotel brands that overwhelmed both consumers and hotel investors (O'Neill and Mattila, 2010); (Wang and Chung,

2015). Currently, the seven largest worldwide hotel corporate groups hold almost 90 different brands, and the number will be even higher if we count the local-based ones.

Brand Portfolio of Indian Hotels Company Limited (IHCL): Founded by Jamsetji Tata in 1868, the Tata group is a global enterprise, comprising over 100 independently operating companies. The group operates in all six continents with a mission to improve the quality of life of the communities it serves globally. Based on 'Leadership with Trust,' the Tata brand has overseen creation a long-term stakeholder value. The Tata brand stands as a lasting promise behind its businesses, many of these businesses are industry leaders in their respective fields. IHCL is kept in high honor for being one of the first of those timeless and tireless initiatives.

The Indian Hotels Company Limited is South Asia's largest hospitality-focused enterprise with Indian origins, relentlessly redefining opportunities in the best interest of all its stakeholders. With businesses ranging from iconic luxury to upscale and budget stopovers as well as in-flight catering, IHCL's pioneering leadership is backed by a rich 115-year legacy. IHCL's emerging initiatives in urban leisure, service retail, and concept travel are a part of its evolution, one that is continuously recrafted for future generations. The Indian Hotels Company Limited (IHCL) encompassing all hotels of the Tata group, covers its vivid brands (Figure 21.1) i.e., Taj, SeleQtions, Vivanta, The Gateway, Ginger, Ama Plantation Trails, and TajSATS. The philosophy behind the multi-brand

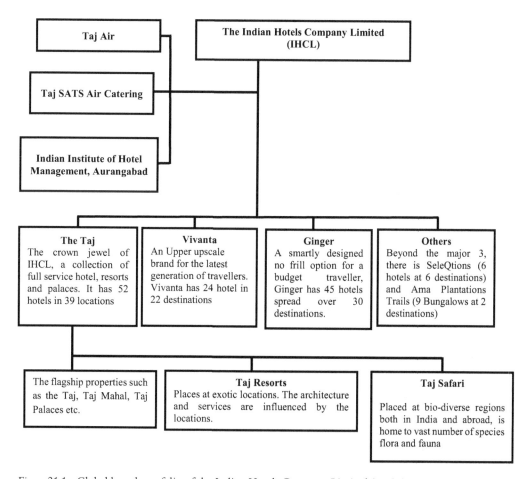

Figure 21.1   Global brand portfolio of the Indian Hotels Company Limited (IHCL).

Source: Adapted by the authors from https://www.theindianhotels.com/our-brands/

portfolio strategy of IHCL was that one brand does not fit all (Bhandari, 2010). The IHCL brands are present in New York, Boston, San Francisco in the USA, London (UK), Dubai (UAE), Cape Town (South Africa), Lusaka (Zambia), Colombo and Bentota (Sri Lanka), Thimphu (Bhutan), and the Maldives.

The Taj brand represents the luxury full-service branch of IHCL; it includes hotels, resorts, palaces, and safaris. The brand has its properties spread over 52 locations, the more famous of the Indian properties being the Taj Mahal Palace Hotel (Mumbai), Ram Bagh Palace (Jaipur), Umaid Bhavan Palace Hotel (Jodhpur), etc. (Taj Hotels, 2019). Vivanta is a brand that was added to the portfolio in the year 2010. It is being marketed as an upper upper-scale segment above Ginger and Gateway brands (Bhandari, 2010). Surveys conducted by STR and Gallup found that Vivanta had the highest RevPAR and customer engagement amongst its fellow market competitors (Landor, 2013).

This multi-brand portfolio strategy was initiated by the company to ensure that the market share of 25–30% was protected from the threats of its contemporary market competitors such as the Marriot group. The global brands, such as Taj or Marriot, use the multi-brand strategy to ensure the unwavering loyalty of their customers and, they achieve the same mainly through their strategically priced options of hospitality at every price point – in this case, the sub-brands – thereby forcing other hotel chains to offer competitive prices for their services (Landor, 2013).

To further understand the multi-brand portfolio strategy, let us consider the brand 'Vivanta,' which is targeted at the young traveler – one who looks to catch a break from his or her work. Such a customer is expected to favor a more relaxed service rather than a full-formalized service (Bhandari, 2010). Hence the brand is normally priced 15–20% cheaper than the Taj property in a city, competing with the likes of Hyatt, Westin, and Sheraton (Bhandari, 2010). The 'Gateway' brand (now merged with Vivanta) on the other hand was targeted at the young traveler who is determined to work round the clock after he or she has got the first taste for success. The gateway hotels rarely have anything more than one specialty restaurant and a 24-hour diner. Also, the rooms at a Gateway property are marketed by keeping the prices competitively lower than a Vivanta property in the same city. 'Ginger' is a sub-brand that is marketed as the no-frill option for a budget traveler. These hotels are normally placed near a railway station or bus stands as an option of budget accommodation for the travelers (Bhandari, 2010). Hence, Taj has formed its web of hospitality brands to ensure that its presence is felt in every price segment in the domestic market and it has remained a fierce competitor against the other global brands competing for the same market.

The case of IHCL stands as testimony on how market segmentation facilitates in achieving a competitive advantage, retain market share when under threat from the fellow competitors as well as posing as a threat themselves to the global competitors entering the domestic market. Thus, segmentation not only helps in improving sales but also helps in investing strategically in those segments that are used frequently by travelers while ignoring the others (Sufi, 2018). The strategy of using four different brands under the same umbrella brand (IHCL) ensures that the customer sticks to the brands as he or she moves forward through life (Bhandari, 2010). Furthermore, IHCL plans to expand its sub-brands into the global scenario by competing in the international markets (Bhandari, 2010).

Brand Portfolio of the Oberoi Group of Hotels: The Oberoi Group, founded in 1934, operates 31 hotels, Nile Cruisers, and a Motor Vessel in the backwaters of Kerala. The Group has presence in six countries (India, Egypt, Indonesia, Mauritius, Saudi Arabia, and UAE) under the luxury 'Oberoi' and 5-star 'Trident' brand. The Group is also associated with inflight catering, travel and tour services, airport restaurants, corporate air charters, project management, and car rentals (The Oberoi Group, 2019).

The common tendency in the international hospitality industry is to have separate brands for each segment in which a hotel group operates. In the context of the fact that The Oberoi Group product portfolio (Figure 21.2) offered distinct sets of products to distinct sets of customers, the

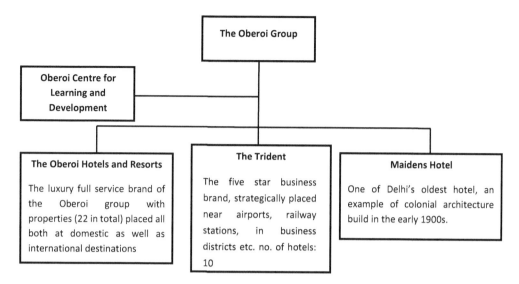

Figure 21.2 Global brand portfolio of the Oberoi group of hotels.
Source: Adapted by authors from https://www.eihltd.com/ and other external sources.

establishment of separate brands for different product categories seemed to be the most effective choice (Bharwani, 2011).

As far as the Oberoi group is concerned, their business strategies were centered on exceeding the average room rate (ARR), revenue per available room (RevPAR), and the average occupancy by insisting on the highest degree of service and quality and thereby, reinforcing the visibility of 'The Oberoi' and 'the Trident' brands (Bharwani, 2011). This strategy further illustrated its fundamental ability to position the business hotels segment to the needs and requirement of the target market and, to ensure the continued loyalty as well as repeat customers (Bharwani, 2011). Multiple brand portfolio strategy has also been used by the East India Hotels Ltd. (EIH Ltd.) (the parent company of Oberoi group), as a marketing tool. The brand, 'Oberoi Hotels' cater to the luxury-business segment of the EIH. Their target customers being both domestic as well as international. Being full-service luxury as well as business hotels, they are placed at prime locations in order to provide the convenience of access to the various business districts (Bharwani, 2011). The brand 'Trident Hotels,' is found to be of preference among both businesses as well as leisure traveler, in both international and domestic market segments. The brand had a strategic alliance with Hilton International Co. from 2004 till 2008. During this period, it was under the 'Trident Hilton' brand (Bharwani, 2011). The high-end luxury brand of EIH, The Oberoi Vilas properties is considered by many to be one of the best luxury leisure brands in the world. These properties are located in the predominantly tourist destinations such as Jaipur, Udaipur, Ranthambore, Agra, etc. and also a luxury backwater cruiser 'the Oberoi Vrinda' (Oberoi, 2019) in Kerala (Bharwani, 2011).

Hotel Brand Identity and Positioning

The branded hotel sector comprises of a collection of around 50 hotel companies, each actively competing to find mind share with hotel owners and developers, who are further looking to either convert or build a new property (HVS Anarock, 2019). As per this report over 170 new hotel brand signings took place from 2016 to 2017, whereas in 2018, the industry added 201 hotels with the total room inventory crossing 19,000. The number of new hotel brand signings was an industry record and signals the strong growth in the investor sentiment (HVS Anarock, 2019). Having said so, the quantum of rooms signed by all mainstream hotel operators dwarfs in comparison to the aggressive growth marked by the outlier companies such as Oyo, who alone in 2018 signed more than 120,000 rooms, a whopping over 700% higher than all the others put together (HVS Anarock, 2019). In 2018, Goa witnessed the largest brand signing of rooms, eclipsing Bengaluru by a mere margin of 192 rooms. It was heartening to witness Goa rank at the top of the list, as the strong increase in supply will prove to be beneficial for the destination (HVS Anarock, 2019).

Hotels with a strong brand create values for both the customer as well as the firm (Fung So, et al., 2013). Previous studies conducted has shown the importance of brand value and how the brand identity improve the chances of having a higher net income in tough market conditions (Fung So et al., 2013; O'Neill and Carlback, 2011). A brand needs to be easily identifiable and hence, the hotel brands try to create brand equity through brand awareness and brand image. The awareness part of the brand comes from the ability of an individual to recall or recognize a particular brand from various cues (Cai and Hobson, 2004). As an example of such a strategy, a case can be made of IHCL introducing the brands such as Gateway and Vivanta in early 2000 and late 2009 respectively (Roy and Mohapatra, 2014). Similarly, EIH ltd., re-imagined their brand by adding the suffix 'Vilas' to the names of the resort properties under the Oberoi resorts all over the country.

The presence of a multi-brand portfolio strategy may suggest an advantage for a company but, if the customer gets often confused and is unable to differentiate values of one brand from another, the situation will most likely turn out to of disadvantageous in nature. Keeping in mind this reason, IHCL went on to create the 'Tajness' to find an order to the chaos to their multi-brand portfolio (The Economic Times, 2017). But, all of these changes would have been a success only if the guest was able to resonate with these brands on an emotional level (Cai and Hobson, 2004). Studies have shown that customers tend to pay the premium rates for the brands they associate with high quality (O'Neill and Mattila, 2006, 2010).

A research was conducted on how components of image cognition affect overall image of green hotels. The aforementioned study was able to reveal the positive effects of cognitive image components on their hotels' overall image. It revealed that a brand and an image, if and when developed scientifically, will act as an important factor in determining the customer's intentions. It will act as a factor in determining the customer's intentions to revisit the hotels, their willingness to pay the premium, and even suggest the brand to others (Lee, et al., 2010). Oberoi Hotels and Resorts have taken a recent step towards further differentiating themselves from rest of the pack by unveiling a brand new logo and newly revamped website in the hope to rediscover themselves as a brand (Fortune India, 2019).

Using Branding as Sustainable Differentiating Strategy

In the modern ruthless market, differentiation is key to survival. The brands need to stand out from the mix of its competitors. Hotel chains have adopted different strategies, but only a handful have escaped from the short-lived fate of such strategies (Cai and Hobson, 2004). The strategies vary from:

1   *Cost reduction*
2   *Modifications to the existing fixtures and operational procedures; and*
3   *Using pricing of the service as a variable by applying discounts, and promotional packages.*

Another method to ensure sustainability is through the long-term plan of market segmentation. But all these strategies will be fruitful up to the point of imitation by competitors (Cai and Hobson, 2004). Branding is a proven long-term strategy that can create emotional bonds to ensure long-term loyalty of the customers (Cai and Hobson, 2004). A brand portfolio can be a tool to manage the complex scenarios emerging with regard to the accumulation of brand, and it could be used to overcome the obstacles faced through the competition in the market, creating a lasting presence and sustainable competitive advantage (Chailan, 2008). Adhering to the aforementioned steps, the hotel chain will be able to align itself to the consumer demands, resulting in profitable business.

The Roadmap Ahead

IHCL is now in a battle with the entry of international brands eying the Indian market. The business environment will only get tougher for the brand as it competes against the international brands for a market consisting of the ever-rising middle class along with ample amount of disposable income (Sharma and Kochher, 2018). Taj, being heavily depended on the revenue generation through its luxury brand, will need to compete with heavyweights of the industry such Marriott-Starwood alliance, Accor-Fairmont alliance – seemingly forming alliances to tackle the global market. The properties of the Vivanta brand are forced to charge a rate that is much lower than what they used to charge earlier due to heightened competition. The experts at the Oberoi group were found to accuse supply exceeding the demand in many cities, with both groups even cautioning their respective shareholders about the intensifying competition (Baggonkar, 2013). But, in 2018, both IHCL and Oberoi groups were found to take up an asset-light model. This approach is supposed to let the groups manage hotels that are not owned by them, gradually moving away from their previous approach of owning the real estate. This model will allow the groups to continue strategic investments in assets of their choice, while at the same time diversifying the brand portfolio (Chaturvedi, 2018). Studies suggest that the midscale hotel segment is going to be the one that will grow the most, thanks to the number of customers from the middle class income group having developed an affinity towards full-service hotels. Moreover, the mainstream brands such as Taj and the Oberois are now being challenged, and will continue to be so, by the relative newcomers such as Oyo, Treebo, Fabhotels, etc. (HVS Anarock, 2019).

Conclusion

Indian Travel and tourism industry, with its huge growth potential, is expected to have international brands account for 50% of share in the Tourism and Hospitality sector of the country by the year 2022 (IBEF, 2019). The overall growth and the successive investment and expansion of domestic and foreign hotel chains have become the validation for the competitive advantage of having a strong brand identity and effective product positioning in the market. The intensifying competition of developing a unique brand identity in the market is further pushing the hotel chains to strengthen their strategies by developing new techniques in order to cater to the unique, and personal, experiential needs of the customer. This chapter observes the reasons that lead certain hospitality companies to develop a brand portfolio and the role of a brand portfolio in creating a lasting and sustainable competitive advantage. Therefore, the chapter identifies that in order to have long-term sustainable business operations, a cohesive branding approach is to be adopted by the hotel chains.

It is noteworthy that brand loyalty had a significantly positive effect on the performance of luxury hotels. A luxury hotel guest who repeatedly tends to stay at the same brand hotel and who attaches great importance to hotel brands in his or her choice is said to be brand loyal (Odin et al., 2001). The likelihood of a loyal customer switching to a competitor, merely because of price, is considerably less, and the frequency of purchase is much lesser in case of the comparable non-loyal customers (Bowen and Shoemaker, 1998).

References

Aaker, D. and Joachimsthaler, E. (2000), *Brand Leadership*, The Free Press, New York, NY.

Arendt, S. and Brettel, M. (2010), "Understanding the influence of corporate social responsibility on corporate identity, image and firm performance", *Management Decision*, Vol.48, No.10, pp.1469–1493, available at: http://doi.org/10.1108/00251741011090289.

Baggonkar, S. (2013), "Taj, Oberoi under pressure from foreign hotel chains", available at: https://www.business-standard.com/article/companies/taj-oberoi-under-pressure-from-foreign-hotel-chains-112071700074_1.html (accessed 25 March 2019).

Balmer, J. (2001), "Corporate identity, corporate branding and corporate marketing: Seeing through the fog", *European Journal of Marketing*, Vol.35, pp.249–291. doi: 10.1108/03090560110694763.

Bhandari, B. (2010), "Indian hotels' four-brand strategy for success", available at: http://business.rediff.com/special/2010/oct/11/spec-indian-hotels-four-brand-strategy-for-success.htm (accessed 15 March 2019).

Bharwani, S. (2011), "The Oberoi resorts: Luxury redefined", *Emerald Emerging Markets Case Studies*, Vol.1, No.3, pp.1–22, available at: http://doi.org/10.1108/20450621111166130.

Bowen, J.T. and Shoemaker, S. (1998), "Loyalty: A strategic commitment", *Cornell Hotel and Restaurant Quarterly*, Vol.39, No.1, pp.12–25, available at: http://doi.org/10.1177/001088049803900104.

Brakus, J., Schmitt, B., and Zatantonello, L. (2009), "Brand experience: What is it? How is it measured? Does it affect loyalty?", *Journal of Marketing*, Vol.73, No.1, pp.52–68, available at: http://doi.org/10.1509/jmkg.73.3.052.

Cai, A.L. and Hobson, J.S.P. (2004), "Making hotel brands work in a competitive environment" *Journal Of Vacation Marketing*, Vol.10, No.3, pp.197–208, available at: http://doi.org/10.1177/135676670401000301.

Chailan, C. (2008), "Brands portfolios and competitive advantage: An empirical study" *Journal of Product & Brand Management*, Vol.17, No.4, pp.254–264, available at: http://doi.org/10.1108/10610420810887608.

Chaturvedi, A. (2018), "Taj, Oberoi, other Indian hotel chains take to asset-light model for growth", available at: https://economictimes.indiatimes.com/industry/services/hotels-/-restaurants/taj-oberoi-other-indian-hotel-chains-take-to-asset-light-model-for-growth/articleshow/64487500.cms (accessed 30 March 2019).

Dawar, N. (2004), "What are brands good for?", *MIT Sloan Management Review*, Vol.46, No.1, pp.31–37.

Deloitte. (2010), *Hospitality 2015: Game Changers or Spectators?*, Deloitte, New York, NY.

Dev, C., Zhou, K.Z., Brown, J., and Agarwal, S. (2009), "Customer orientation or competitor orientation: Which marketing strategy has a higher payoff for hotel brands?", *Cornell Hospitality Quarterly*, Vol.50, No.1, pp.19–28, available at: http://doi.org/10.1177/1938965508320575.

Dixit, S.K. (2016), "eWOM marketing in hospitality industry", in Singh, A. and Duhan, P.(Eds.), *Managing Public Relations and Brand Image Through Social Media*, IGI Global, Hershey, PA, pp.266–280, available at: http://doi.org/10.4018/978-1-5225-0332-3.

Dixit, S.K. (2018), "The Routledge handbook of hospitality studies", *Hospitality & Society*, Vol.8, No.1, pp.99–102, available at: http://doi.org/10.1386/hosp.8.1.97_5.

Dixit, S.K. (2017), "Introduction", in Dixit, S.K. (Ed.), *The Routledge Handbook of Consumer Behaviour in Hospitality and Tourism*, Routledge, London, UK, pp.1–3.

Dixit, S.K., Lee, K.-H., and Loo, P.T. (2019), "Consumer behavior in hospitality and tourism", *Journal of Global Scholars of Marketing Science*, Vol.29, No.2, pp.151–161, available at: http://doi.org/10.1080/21639159.2019.1577159.

Douglas, S., Craig, C., and Nijssen, E. (2001), "Integrating branding strategy across markets: Building international brand architecture", *Journal of International Marketing*, Vol.9, No.2, pp.97–114, available at: http://doi.org/10.1509/jimk.9.2.97.19882.

Fortune India (2019), "Oberoi hotels unveils new logo", available at: https://www.fortuneindia.com/enterprise/the-oberoi-group-unveils-new-logo/103070 (accessed 30 March 2019).

Fournier, S. (1998), "Consumers and their brands: Developing relationship theory in consumer research", *Journal of Consumer Research*, Vol.24, No.4, pp.343–373, available at: http://doi.org/10.1086/209515.

Fung So, K.K., Ceridwyn, K., Sparks, B.A., and Wang, Y. (2013), "The influence of customer brand identification on hotel brand evaluation and loyalty development", *International Journal of Hospitality Management*, Vol.34, pp.31–41, available at: http://doi.org/10.1016/j.ijhm.2013.02.002.

Government of India (2019), "Annual reports", available at: http://tourism.gov.in/annual-reports (accessed 1 April 2019).

Kim, H. and Kim, W. (2005), "The relationship between brand equity and firms' performance in luxury hotels and chain restaurants", *Tourism Management*, Vol.26, No.4, pp.549–560, available at: http://doi.org/10.1016/j.tourman.2004.03.010.

HVS Anarock (2019), *India Hospitality Industry Review 2018*, HVS Anarock Hotel Advisory Services Pvt. Ltd., Gurugram.

IBEF (2019), "Tourism & hospitality industry in India: Market size, govt initiatives, investments", available at: https://www.ibef.org/industry/tourism-hospitality-india.aspx (accessed 01 April 2019).

Intercontinental Hotel Group (2019), "Annual report 2013", available at: www.ihgplc.com/files/reports/ar2013/ (accessed 24 February 2019).

International Labour Organization (ILO) (2010), "Developments and challenges in the hospitality and tourism sector", available at: www.ilo.org/wcmsp5/groups/public/@ed_norm/@relconf/documents/ meetingdocument/wcms_166938.pdf (accessed 20 March 2019).

Jiang, W., Dev, C., and Rao, V. (2002), "Brand extension and customer loyalty: Evidence from the lodging industry", *Cornell Hotel and Restaurant Administration Quarterly*, Vol.43, No.4, pp.5–16, available at: http://doi.org/10.1016/s0010-8804(02)80037-4.

Kapferer, J.N. (2000a), *Strategic Brand Management, First South Asian Edition*, Kogan Page, New Delhi.

Kapferer, J.N. (2000b), *Re-Marques*, Les Editions D'Organisation, Paris.

Kuada, J and Hinson, R (2014), *Service Marketing in Ghana: A Customer Relationship Management Approach*, Adonis & Abbey Publishers, London, UK.

Laforet, S and Saunders, J. (1999), "Managing brand portfolios: Why leaders do what they do", *Journal of Advertising Research*, Vol.39, No.1, pp.51–66.

Landor (2013), "Taj Group: Three new brands for a changing India", available at: https://landor.com/work/taj-group (accessed 23 February 2019).

Lee, J.S., Hsu, L.T., Han, H., and Kim, Y. (2010), "Understanding how consumers view green hotels: How a hotel's green image can influence behavioural intentions", *Journal of Sustainable Tourism*, Vol.18, No.7, pp.901–914, available at: http://doi.org/10.1080/09669581003777747.

Mangini, K. (2002), "Branding 101. It's time for healthcare to embrace this marketing mainstay.", *Marketing Health Services*, Vol.22, No.3, pp.3–20.

Markowitz, H. (1952), "Portfolio selection", *Journal of Finance*, Vol.7, No.1, pp.77–91, available at: http://doi.org/10.2307/2975974.

Martínez, P., Pérez, A., and del Bosque, I.R. (2014), "Exploring the role of CSR in the organizational identity of hospitality companies: A case from the Spanish tourism industry", *Journal of Business Ethics*, Vol.124, No.1, pp.47–66, available at: http://doi.org/10.1007/s10551-013-1857-1.

O'Neill, J.W. and Carlback, M. (2011), "Do brands matter? A comparison of branded and independent hotels' performance during a full economic cycle", *International Journal of Hospitality Management*, Vol.30, pp.515–521, available at: http://doi.org/10.1016/j.ijhm.2010.08.003.

O'Neill, J.W. and Mattila, A.S. (2004), "Hotel branding strategy: Its relationship to guest satisfaction and room revenue", *Journal of Hospitality & Tourism Research*, Vol.28, No.2, pp.156–165, available at: http://doi.org/10.1177/1096348004264081.

O'Neill, J.W. and Mattila, A.S. (2006), "Strategic hotel development and positioning: The effect of revenue drivers on profitability", *Cornell Hotel and Restaurant Administration Quarterly*, Vol.47, No.2, pp.146–154, available at: http://doi.org/10.1177/0010880405281519.

O'Neill, J.W. and Mattila, A.S. (2010), "Hotel brand strategy", *Cornell Hospitality Quarterly*, Vol.51, No.1, pp.27–34, available at: http://doi.org/10.1177/1938965509352286.

O'Neill, J.W. and Xiao, Q. (2006), "The role of brand affiliation in hotel market value", *Cornell Hotel and Restaurant Administration*, Vol.47, No.3, pp.210–223, available at: http://doi.org/10.1177/0010880406289070.

Oberoi (2019), "The Oberoi vrinda Luxury Kerala Cruiser", available at: https://www.oberoihotels.com/kerala-backwaters/overview (accessed 26 March 2019).

Odin, Y., Odin, N., and Valette-Florence, P. (2001), "Conceptual and operational aspects of brand loyalty: An empirical investigation", *Journal of Business Research*, Vol.53, No.2, pp.75–84, available at: http://doi.org/10.1016/s0148-2963(99)00076-4.

Olins, W. (1989), *Corporate Identity: Making Business Strategy Visible Through Design*, Thames and Hudson, London, UK.

Olsen, M. and Zhao, J. (2008), *Handbook of Hospitality Strategic Management*, Butterworth-Heinemann, Amsterdam.

Prahalad, C. and Venkat, R. (2004), "Co-creation experiences: The next practice in value creation", *Journal of Interactive Marketing*, Vol.18, No.3, pp.5–14, available at: http://doi.org/10.1002/dir.20015.

Prasad, K. and Dev, C.S. (2000), "Managing hotel brand equity: A customer-centric framework for assessing performance", *Cornell Hotel and Restaurant Administration Quarterly*, Vol.41, No.3, pp.22–31, available at: http://doi.org/10.1177/001088040004100314.

Rao, V., Manoj, K., and Dahlhoff, D. (2004), "How is manifest branding strategy related to the intangible value of a corporation", *Journal of Marketing*, Vol.68, No.4, pp.126–141, available at: http://doi.org/10.1509/jmkg.68.4.126.42735.

Riezebos, R. (2003), *Brand Management: A Theoretical and Practical Approach*, Prentice-Hall, Harlow, UK.

Roy, S. and Mohapatra, S. (2014), "IHCL's menu of hotels: Competing for the Indian hotelscape", *The CASE Journal*, Vol.10, No.2, pp.171–184, available at: http://doi.org/10.1108/tcj-02-2014-0017.

Schmitt, B. (1999), "Experiential marketing", *Journal of Marketing Management*, Vol.15, No.1–3, pp.53–67, available at: http://doi.org/10.1362/026725799784870496.

Sharma, A. and Kochher, P. (2018), "Taj hotels, palaces and resorts: The road ahead", *Emerald Emerging Markets Case Studies*, Vol.8, No.3, pp.1–21, available at: http://doi.org/10.1108/eemcs-01-2018-0001.

Smilansky, S. (2009), *Experiential Marketing: A Practical Guide to Interactive Brand Experiences*, Kogan Page Publishers, London, UK.

Speak, K. (1996), "The challenge of healthcare branding", *Journal of Healthcare Marketing*, Vol.16, No.1, pp.40–42, PubMed PMID: 10184734.

Sufi, T. (2018), A case study on market segmentation, positioning and classification of multi-brand hotel chains, in *Emerging Dynamics of Indian Tourism and Hospitality*, COPAL Publishing, Ghaziabad, pp.87–97.

Taj Hotels (2019), "Our company", available at: https://www.tajhotels.com/en-in/about-taj-group/who-we-are/our-company/ (accessed 25 March 2019).

Tajeddini, K. (2010), "Effect of customer orientation and entrepreneurial orientation on innovativeness: Evidence from the hotel industry in Switzerland", *Tourism Management*, Vol.31, No.2, pp.221–231, available at: http://doi.org/10.1016/j.tourman.2009.02.013.

The Economic Times. (2017), "IHCL brings all its hotels under single brand", available at: https://economictimes.indiatimes.com/industry/services/hotels-/-restaurants/ihcl-brings-all-its-hotels-under-single-brand/articleshow/57066275.cms (accessed 29 March 2019).

The Oberoi Group. (2019), "About us: Oberoi hotels and resorts", available at: https://www.oberoihotels.com/About-Us (accessed 23 March 2019).

Wang, Y.-C. and Chung, Y. (2015), "Hotel brand portfolio strategy", *International Journal of Contemporary Hospitality Management*, Vol.27, No.4, pp.561–584, available at: http://doi.org/10.1108/ijchm-01-2014-0031.

WTTC. (2017), *Travel and Tourism Economic Impact 2017 World*, World Travel and Tourism Council, London, UK, pp.1–2.

22

THE DEVELOPMENT OF HOTEL MANAGEMENT CONTRACTS IN CHINA

Lianping Ren

Hotel Industry in China – Development and Structure

The tourism industry in China has been developing at a steadily fast pace in the past four decades. The size of the tourism industry in China now takes a significant part in contributing to both GDP and employment. According to the statistics released by the Ministry of Culture and Tourism, PRC (2019), in 2018, there were 5.539 billion domestic trips (up by 10.8%), 291 million inbound trips (up by 7.8%), and 148.72 million outbound trips (up by 14.7%). The fast development is due largely to the fine economic development, increased disposable income, development in key infrastructures such as the high-speed railway system, and favorable government support and policies (The Fung Group, 2017).

Responding to the fast growth of the number of travelers, the hotel sector in China has also been developing fast. There is no official statistics so far reflecting the real picture on how many hotels there are in China, but according to a recent estimation based on the distribution of hotels on online travel agencies, the total number of hotels in China has reached 250,000 up till the end of 2018, with an estimated 30–35 million rooms (Anon, 2019a). Considering its short development history – hotel sector in China started to develop only after the Reform and Opening Policy in the late 1970s, with only 137 hotels (15,539 rooms) to start with (Zhang et al., 2005) – the speed of growth has been tremendous. Apart from these numbers, there are signs that the hotel sector in China has grown stronger, with quite a few mega hotel companies playing a significant role in the hotel market. According to the most recent Hotel 325 Report (2018), among the top 20 hotel groups worldwide, based on number of rooms, by the end of 2017, 6 were from China, including Shanghai Jin Jiang International Hotel Group Co. (6,794 hotels, 680,111 rooms), the BTG Homeinns Hotels (Group) Co. (3,172 hotels, 384,743 rooms), China Lodging Group (3,746 hotels, 379,675 rooms), GreenTree Hospitality Group (2,289 hotels, 190,807 room), Dossen International Group (1,087 hotels, 105,951 rooms), and Qingdao Sunmei Group Co. (1,697 hotels, 91,706 rooms).

The hotel statistics released by Inntie (2018) in "2018 China Lodging Industry Development Report" probably reflect a better picture of the hotel industry structure in China. According to the report, the overall size of the lodging industry in China by the end of 2017 was 457,834 hotels, with 16,770,394 rooms. These statistics have taken all lodging facilities into account, including hotels (those with 15 rooms or above – 317,476 hotels, with 15,480,813 rooms) and other lodging facilities (those with less than 15 rooms, 140,358 units, with 1,289,581 rooms). Among the hotels, the budget category (or hotels at/below 2-star level) accounts for the majority – 87.3%, while the luxury category (or hotels at/above 5-star level) takes the smallest percentage – 1.4%, the rest are the midscale (3-star equivalent) – 7.5%, and the upscale (4-star equivalent) – 3.9%, respectively. Majority of the hotels are clustered in gateway cities such as Beijing, Shanghai, and Guangzhou, and megacities such as Chongqing, Xi'an, Chengdu, Shenzhen, Wuhan, Hangzhou, and Nanjing. The three gateway cities have over 440,000 rooms respectively. The megacities such as Chongqing and Chengdu have over 350,000 rooms respectively.

At the early stage of development (in the 1980s), state ownership occupied a majority of the hotels in China. According to statistics, over 74 % of the hotels belonged to the category of state-owned enterprise by the end of 1989, out of a total of 1,788 hotels nation-wide (Yu, 1992), and the rest of the hotels involved little international collaboration. The high percentage of state owner-ship of the hotels in this stage well reflected the planned economy that China was going through (Yu, 1992). Over the years, there is a substantive decrease in the state-ownership in hotels. By the end of 2017, only 23.38% of the hotels in the nation-wide star-rating system belonged to the state-owned enterprises, while only 3.14% of the hotels in this system belonged to the category of "collective ownership," and less than 4% of the hotels were foreign or Hong Kong/Macao/Taiwan invested hotels.

However, there is a large percentage of hotels (69.56%) belonging to the "others" category, in terms of ownership (Ministry of Culture and Tourism, PRC, 2018), reflecting the change and increased complexity of ownership. In terms of hotel performance, the average ADR (average daily rate) of the star-rated hotels in 2017 was 343.43 yuan (roughly 6.7 yuan = 1 US dollar), and the average occupancy was 54.80%, and average RevPAR (revenue per available room) 188.20 yuan (Ministry of Culture and Tourism, PRC, 2018). However, the statistics from the star-rating system have limitations; because for various reasons, many hotels now opt not to take the stars anymore, and the number of hotels included in the star rating systems is estimated to be only about 10% of the total hotels in the country (Inntie, 2018).

The Adoption of the Management Contract and the International Hotel Operators in China

At the early stage, due to the fast increasing demand from tourism arrivals, China was in serious shortage of both hotels and hotel management expertise and therefore started to encourage for-eign investment and involvement in hotel development (Yu, 1992; Xiao et al., 2008). At the turn of the century, China's entry into the World Trade Organization (WTO) in 2001 marked the opening of China's hotel market to the international hotel companies (Yu and Gu, 2005). Most international hotel operators found their way into this lucrative market, via different collaboration and business modes. Among them, the management contract has been one of the most popular business modes. The reform of the hotel industry in China, especially the ownership structure, further laid the foundation for collaboration between international hotel operators and Chinese hotel owners (Yu and Gu, 2005).

Eyster and deRoos (2009, p. 5) define management contract as *"...a written agreement between the operator of a full-service hotel or select-service hotel by which the owner employs the operator to assume full responsibility for operating and managing the property."* In this collaboration, the owner makes the investment in property building and development, while the operator has the opportunity to ex-pand to the other markets with low risk. This business format fitted the Chinese hotel sector well, especially at the turn of the century. On the one hand, the demand for quality hotel was high; on the other hand, domestic hotels, especially the upscale ones, could not meet the international hotel standard. Naturally, upscale and luxury hotels in China opt for international hotel operators more than domestic hotel managing companies because international operators have better experience and expertise in hotel operation and management. The establishment of Jianguo Hotel in Beijing in 1982, a joint venture managed by the Peninsular Group, marked the beginning of the collaboration between the Chinese owners (government departments at the beginning) and international hotel operators via the business format of hotel management agreement (or management contract) (Wang and Sun, 2009). Since then, major international hotel operators started to enter the Chinese market. Most operators had well established themselves in this vast market at the turn of the century. The widespread preference for international hotel operators was due to a few factors.

First, the preference has been demand-driven. The hotel industry in China started to develop at a considerably later stage compared to the Western countries. The reform and opening policy in the end of 1970s had marked not only the start of hotel development but also economic development throughout the country. The demand for quality hotels far surpassed the supply, and because most public attention was on the primary and secondary industry development, very little amount of people had good knowledge and expertise in hotel management. Therefore, borrowing expertise from international hotel operators became highly necessary. In addition, there has been a steady increase in tourism arrivals from overseas. This high demand for good quality hotels has not only necessitated the presence of international hotel brands, but also attracted investment interest from the Western countries (Gu et al., 2012).

Second, the branding effect, along with the strong network support from the international hotel operators, can benefit the Chinese hotels considerably. Wang and Sun (2009) made comparisons among hotels operated by international operators, domestic operators, and owners, and found that the hotels managed by international operators perform significantly better than those managed by domestic hotel operators or by the owners themselves, in terms of average daily rate (ADR), RevPAR, and income before fixed charges (IBFC). Although the management fee charged by the international operators is usually higher, the profit that the international hotel operators bring is much higher, and therefore hotel owners preferred international operators more.

Third, having been admiring the reputation of the international hotel brands, the Chinese real estate owners and property owners entrust the international hotel operators for managing their high-end properties, so as to achieve steady return and cash flow (Wang and Sun, 2009), as well as a value adding effect for the commercial complex or properties (Tourism Monitoring Department and China Tourism Academy (TMD and CTA), 2011). From the turn of the century, the ownership of hotels in China and the investment mode gradually changed. Private investment or corporate investment has seen considerable increase. Business modes such as real estate project plus hotel, tourism integrated complex, and city urban commercial complex become popular (TMD and CTA, 2011). Having a reputable hotel brand adds value to these projects.

Therefore, currently, the upscale and luxury hotels in China are still dominated by international hotel operators such as IHG, Marriott, Accor, Hilton, and Hyatt. According to a recent ranking of hotel management companies in China in terms of scale, the following international hotel operators have strong performance in the Chinese markets (the numbers are based on statistics by the end of 2017) (Table 22.1).

Major international hotel operators favor franchising over management contracts for the hotels in their home countries or developed regions. However, for the hotel markets in the developing regions, or regions with greater cultural distance and uncertainties, the operators tend to adopt more management contracts, especially so with the upscale and luxury hotels. Taking Hilton for example, by the end of 2018, Hilton has 19 Conrad Hotels and Resorts (5,853 rooms) in the Asia Pacific, 17 of them are managed (5,035 rooms), one franchised (654 rooms), and one owned/leased (164 rooms). The company has 106 Hilton Hotels and Resorts (39,710 rooms) in Asia Pacific. Among them, 92 hotels (33,447 rooms) are managed, only 7 franchised (2,826 rooms), and 7 owned/leased (3,437 rooms) (Hilton, 2019). Similarly, according to the Hotels Portfolio of Accor by December 2018, the company has a total of 713 hotels (159,382 rooms) in Asia Pacific Region, with China as the main player in this region, under the arrangement of management contracts,

Table 22.1 Top 60 hotel management companies in China (Anon, 2019b)

Ranking	Hotel group	Number of hotels	Number of rooms
5	Wyndham hotels and resorts	1,400	138,787
7	InterContinental Hotel Group (IHG)	323	99,161
9	Marriott International	268	88,553
11	Accor Hotels	231	49,868
13	Hilton Hotels and Resorts	123	38,153
21	Shangri-La Hotels and Resorts	49	21,447
24	Hyatt Hotels Corporation	57	18,633
47	Manhattan Hotel Group Singapore	47	7,518

while 329 hotels (46,208 rooms) under the arrangement of franchising, and a small amount of hotels under fixed lease or variable lease modes (Accor, 2019). Both of the above two companies have China as their main market in the Asia Pacific, and management contract has been their preferred business model, especially for the upscale and luxury brands.

The Growth of Domestic Hotel Companies

The Chinese domestic hotel operating companies, however, have been developing and growing fast in the past few decades. Some of the well-known companies, such as Jinjiang and Jinling, have the international operators run the hotels which the domestic hotel companies own (Wang and Sun, 2009) so that their management team can learn the hotel operation and management from the world-leading operators. In the 1980s, because Jianguo Hotel adopted the management contract model, the whole country started a vast wave of "learning from Jianguo." The China National Tourism Administration (CNTA) even started an initiation of promoting the Jianguo mode, which was approved by the central government (TMD and CTA, 2011). As time goes by, these companies have gradually developed hotel management expertise, management system and procedures, as well as a vast human resource system. In addition, the domestic hotel companies have advantages such as having no cultural conflicts and being competitive in providing local food and beverage service, which add value to the management profile. In fact, recent years have seen a growing number of domestic hotel management companies, and the increased popularity with the hotel owners. Some hotel companies, such as Jinjiang, have grown much stronger and competitive, that they have even started to manage hotels abroad.

In addition, the domestic hotel management companies have more advantages in developing into the second-, third-, and fourth-tier cities (Wang and Sun, 2009). For one thing, the ADR in those cities is much lower than the hotels in the gateway cities and first-tier cities, and thus it is difficult to break even if international hotel operators are involved. For another, these cities have less international exposure and are less adaptive to international hotel operating practices, making it difficult for international hotel operators to win the market. For example, Ren et al. (2017) described the case of Howard Johnson Hotels developed in cities such as Ningbo, a second-tier coastal city not far from Shanghai, and discussed how Howard Johnson Hotels had to adopt the localization strategies in service to cater for the local market. In addition, Howard Johnson adopts a more flexible collaborating mode with the Chinese local owners in their management contract practice such as adopting a shorter management term, so as to better cater for the needs of the owners in the second and third-tier cities (Ren et al., 2017).

Another competitive advantage of the domestic hotel management companies lies in the lower scale hotel markets, such as the budget hotel sector. Budget hotel, by the term, is a business that requires faster development and simpler operation, lower investment but fast return, and is thus seldom the focus of the international hotel operators in China. The Jin Jiang International Hotel Group developed the first budget hotel in Shanghai in 1997 (Li, 2009). The company soon became an expert in developing and managing budget hotels, and its budget hotel brand – Jin Jiang Inn – has been one of the most well-established budget hotel brands in the Chinese market. A few other Chinese domestic companies, such as Home Inns, followed and established themselves well in the market, and even expanded to the entire country within ten years time (Zhang et al., 2013). Some international hotel operators have also been attempting to introduce their budget hotel brands into the Chinese market. For example, Ibis from Accor, Hampton from Hilton, and Holiday Inn Express from the InterContinental Hotel Group (IHG), and Super 8 have so far entered the Chinese market. But they are not comparable to the domestic hotel companies such as China Lodge, Jin Jiang International Hotel Group, and Home Inns, in terms of scale and development speed. In fact, by the end of 2018, the Chinese hotel companies have taken up the majority of the market share if all hotel segments are taken into account. Table 22.2 shows that the major Chinese hotel companies (Jinjiang International Hotel Group, the BTG Home Inns Hotel Group, China Lodge, HNA, GME Hotel Group) occupy almost 60% of hotels in the entire country.

Major Issues in HMC and the Future Development Trends – The International Operators

The past 40 years have seen tremendous development in hotel industry as well as major changes in practices. Many upscale and luxury hotels managed by the international hotel operators have come to the end of the contract terms. Some will be renewed, but some will not. The market demand is developing toward a more diversified structure. And the development of Chinese domestic hotel companies is increasingly changing the industry structure and posing a challenge for the international hotel operators. The following is a discussion on the main issues of HMC and the key trends of the development of hotel management contracts in China.

First, the number of management contracts continues to grow, although the growth rate has slowed down compared to franchising. Despite the fact that, there is a proliferation of hotel management companies in China, and the supply has surpassed the demand, the increasing trend remains (Anon, 2018), which has resulted in increased competition among the hotel operators. As a result, the HMC terms are gradually evolving toward a more balanced state, which is rather different from 20 years ago when the international hotel operators can almost dictate the terms. For example, there is a significant decrease in management fee and the incentive management fee (Anon, 2018). The operators are trying to make their proposals more attractive by offering terms that did not use to be considered, such as including Performance Tests, Performance Guarantees, and Key Money in some projects (JLL and McKenzie, 2018). The initial contract terms are shorter compared to those signed ten years ago.

Table 22.2 Top 5 Chinese domestic hotel groups and their market share (CHA and Inntie, 2018)

Ranking	Hotel group	Headquarters	Number of hotels	Number of rooms	Percentage in total hotel market (%)
1	Jin Jiang International Hotel Group	Shanghai	6,794	680,000	20.95
2	BTG Home Inns Hotel Group	Beijing	3,712	384,743	11.86
3	China Lodge	Shanghai	3,746	379,675	11.70
4	HNA	Beijing	1,349	218,660	6.7
5	GME (GreenTree) Hotel Group	Shanghai	2,289	190,807	5.88

Second, instead of focusing on the upscale and luxury segment, international hotel operators have now shifted their attention to the midscale market (Horwath, 2018). By the end of 2017, there had been 450 contracts signed by international midscale and above brands, and this was a 36% increase compared to that in 2016 (Horwath, 2018). CHA and Inntie (2018) have also noticed the growth of the midscale hotel segment in China in the recent few years. Brands such as DoubleTree (Hilton) and Courtyard (Marriot) have gained fast development. This is probably due to consumption upgrade and the continuous increase in domestic tourism. According to an estimation, the number of Chinese middle class is expected to increase from 174 million families in 2012 to 271 million families by 2022 (CHA and Innite, 2018). The growth of the middle class in China will greatly push up the demand for midscale hotel products.

Third, it is noted that the proportion of franchise contracts increased substantively in recent years (Horwath, 2018). There are a few causes. One of them is due to the increased popularity of the midscale hotels and the fact that there has been a big increase in domestic expertise in hotel management. In addition, it is also noted that small- to medium-sized hotels are preferred by investors, who are now more rational and are paying more attention to the market demand (Horwath, 2018), and smaller-sized hotels opt for a franchise more often. The other major cause is that there has been a significant increase in Chinese domestic expertise, making franchise contracts more feasible. For example, IHG, one of the first international hotel operators entering the Chinese market (with Lidu Hotel in Beijing as the start, 1984), used to stick to management contract only in this market, but the company started to release its franchise contract in 2016 for the first time in China, with selected brands such as Holiday Inn Express (Anon, 2018). In fact, the collaborative initiative between Hilton and the Plateno Hotel Group in 2014, and the collaboration between Accor and China Lodge starting from the same year, and the collaboration between Marriot and Dossen in 2016 have been laying the foundation for more franchising contracts to be signed.

Fourth, having noticed a saturation of luxury and upscale hotels in the first-tier cities in China, the international hotel operators and hotel developers have shifted their attention to the second-, third-, and even fourth-tier cities for hotel development (Horwath, 2018). Cities such as Changsha and Guiyang have attracted much attention and investment, listing them among the Top 10 cities in terms of number of contracts signed (Horwath, 2018). Some hotel operators such as Howard Johnson has been mainly targeting at the second- or third-tier cities since it entered the Chinese market (Ren et al., 2017).

Fifth, as the Chinese owners and hotel developers gain more hotel expertise, they are more involved in hotel operation, which invariably leads to some conflicts with the international hotel operators. The international hotel operators usually charge a higher management fee and have stricter restrictions and conditions on the local Chinese owners. However, as the Chinese owners have increased bargaining power, they become more demanding about the hotel performance. The other cause of the conflict is derived from cultural difference. Conventionally, the international hotel operators assign an expatriate General Manager (usually non-Chinese) to take care of the hotel operation. The General Manager assigned usually becomes the central communication point between the operator and the local Chinese owner. However, cultural difference often makes the communication less smooth. Therefore, in recent years, there has been a major change in the assignment of the General Manager (GM) position. Either the operator appoints a Chinese native to take up the GM position, or the local Chinese owner recommends a GM to the operator for their appointment.

Chinese Domestic Hotel Companies and Their Developing Trend

Chinese domestic hotel companies are getting stronger and start to manage hotels internationally. The Chinese companies have been pursuing expansion into foreign markets via a few ways such as merger and acquisition, strategic investment, management export, and even self-construction (Ministry of Commerce PRC, 2017), and there is an increasing trend. The Jin Jiang International Hotel Group was the first Chinese hotel company to adopt international expansion strategies. In 2010, the company acquired the Interstate Hotels and Resorts (a third-party hotel management firm based in the USA) jointly with Thayer Lodging Group (Gross et al., 2017), and later acquired the Louvre Hotel Group, and since then there has been a decision to increase its share in Accor. For example, the HNA Hospitality Group acquired Carlson Hotel Group, and also 25% of the shareholdings of the Hilton Group (Ministry of Commerce PRC, 2017). In addition, the trend of Chinese domestic hotel companies managing hotels in overseas countries is also a result of the increase in Chinese outbound tourism. Hotels managed by Chinese home brands have a competitive advantage in attracting Chinese tourists as they can better cater to the accommodation habit and taste bud of the Chinese tourists.

In addition, recent years have seen emergence and increase of the Chinese domestic hotel brands. These brands are either managed by Chinese domestic hotel companies or even developed by local Chinese owners (CHA and Inntie, 2018). Although there is still a noticeable gap between the operating standard and expertise of hotel management between the Chinese domestic hotel companies and their international counterparts, the progress is encouraging. Factors such as huge market demand, increased management expertise, a revolution in technology, and the mindset change among the younger generation, have contributed to the fast development of the Chinese hotel companies (CHA and Inntie, 2018).

Summary

The above account of the development of the hotel management contract practices in China well reflects the evolution of the hotel industry and the changing market demand in the past 40 years. The hotel industry in China started its development relatively later than those in the Western countries, but the fast development in both economy and tourism industry in China has urged a fast development in the hotel industry, which has benefited from the HMC practices tremendously. The international hotel operators used to dominate the upscale and luxury market, although they are gradually losing their competitive advantages, especially when there is an increasing demand in midscale hotel products. The growth of domestic hotel companies has intensified the competition in HMC practice. As a result, some companies have started to offer franchise contracts in selected brands, instead of offering entrusted management contracts only.

References

Accor. (2019), *Accor Hotels Portfolio as of December 2018*, available at: https://www.accorhotels.com (accessed 12 January 2019).

Anon. (2018), *Development Route Change of the Upscale Hotels in China*, available at: http://finance.sina.com. cn/roll/2018-07-02/doc-ihespqry2476303.shtml (accessed 1 February 2019).

Anon. (2019a), *2019 China Hotel Statistics and Analysis*, available at: http://k.sina.com.cn/article_6831240063_1972c737f00100hpgv.html?cre=tianyiandmod=pcpager_newsandloc=20andr=9andrfunc=100andtj=noneandtr=9 (accessed 26 February 2019).

Anon. (2019b), *Top 60 Hotel Companies in China in 2017*, available at: https://www.jointwisdom.cn/newslist/123.html (accessed 1 March 2019).

China Hospitality Association (CHA) and Inntie. (2018), *China Hotel Chain Development and Investment Report 2018*, available at: http://www.chinahotel.org.cn/ (accessed 2 February 2019).

Eyster, J. and deRoos, J. (2009), *The Negotiation and Administration of Hotel Management Contracts*. 4th ed., Pearson Custom Publishing, London.

Gross, M.J., Huang, S., and Ding, Y. (2017), "Chinese hotel firm internationalization: Jin Jiang's joint venture acquisition", *International Journal of Contemporary Hospitality Management*, Vol.29, No.11, pp.2730–2750.

Gu, H., Ryan, C., and Yu, L. (2012), "The changing structure of the Chinese hotel industry: 1980–2012", *Tourism Management Perspectives*, Vol.4, pp.56–63.

Hilton. (2019), *Hilton Reports Fourth Quarter and Full Year Results; Exceeds Net Income, Adjusted EBITDA and Net Unit Growth Expectations*, available at: https://www3.hilton.com/en/index.html (accessed 16 January 2019).

Horwath. (2018), *Market Report: China: Hotels Deals Signing*, available at: https://www.horwathhtl.com (accessed 26 February 2019).

Inntie. (2018), *2018 China Lodging Industry Development Report*, available at: https://www.inntie.com (accessed 15 March 2019).

JLL and McKenzie. (2018), *Trends and Insights in Hotel Management Contracts (Asia Pacific) 2018*, available at: https://www.bakermckenzie.com/en/insight/publications/2018/10/hicap-master-class (accessed 15 January 2019).

Li, Z. (2008), Success Road for Chinese Budget Hotels, Shanghai Communication University Press, Shanghai.

Ministry of Commerce. (2017), *China Lodging Industry Development Report 2017*, available at: http://images mofcom.gov.cn/fms/201803/20180312100415642.pdf (accessed 16 March 2019).

Ministry of Culture and Tourism, PRC. (2018), *Communique on Star-Rating Hotel Statistics in China in 2017*, available at: http://zwgk.mct.gov.cn/auto255/201809/t20180930_835204.html?keywords= (accessed 2 April 2019).

Ministry of Culture and Tourism, PRC (2019). Basic Information of the Tourism Market in 2018. from http://zwgk.mct.gov.cn/auto255/201902/t20190212_837271.html?keywords (accessed 3 May 2019).

Ren, L., Chen, P.J., Zhao, J., and Wang, P. (2017), "The reverse model of repositioning: A case study of the Howard Johnson hotel chain in China", *Journal of Global Scholars of Marketing Science*, Vol.27, No.4, pp.227–242.

The Fung Group (2017). A glance at the domestic tourism market in China. Retrieved from https://www.fbicgroup.com/sites/default/files/CCS_Chi_series03.pdf (accessed 3 May 2019)

Tourism Monitoring Department and China Tourism Academy (TMD and CTA). (2011), *Development Report of China's Hotel Industry – Hotel Groups*, China Tourism Publishing, Beijing, China.

Wang, L. and Sun, T. (2009), *Hotel Management Contract: From Negotiation to Implementation*, Tourism Education Publishing, Beijing, China.

Xiao, Q., O'Neill, J.W., and Wang, H. (2008), "International hotel development: A study of potential franchisees in China", *International Journal of Hospitality Management*, Vol.27, No.3, pp.325–336.

Yu, L. (1992), "Hotel development and structures in China", *International Journal of Hospitality Management*, Vol.11, No.2, pp.99–110.

Yu, L. and Gu, H. (2005), "Hotel reform in China – A SWOT analysis", *Cornell Hotel and Restaurant Administration Quarterly*, Vol.46, No.2, pp.153–169.

Zhang, H.Q., Pine, R.J., and Lam, T. (2005), *Tourism and Hotel Development in China: From Political to Economic Success*, Haworth Hospitality Press, New York, NY.

Zhang, H.Q., Ren, L., Shen, H., and Xiao, Q. (2013), "What contributes to the success of Home Inns in China?", *International Journal of Hospitality Management*, Vol.33, pp.425–434.

23

INTERNATIONAL HUMAN RESOURCE MANAGEMENT IN THE HOSPITALITY INDUSTRY

Yoy Bergs and Xander Lub

Introduction

Macro-level changes in the business environment have created an increasingly unstable and un-predictable, and increasingly global, marketplace (Ottenbacher and Gnoth, 2005). Therefore, businesses have become more internationally oriented and more complex in the way they are organized. This has had an impact on what is required of Human Resource (HR) professionals within organizations. Human Resource Management (HRM) can be defined as the

> policies, practices, and systems that influence employees' behavior, attitudes, and performance.
>
> *(Noe et al., 2006, p. 5)*

Employees constitute the essence of hospitality organizations: the better the people in a company are able to translate strategic business goals into operational performance, the higher the service quality, customer satisfaction and, therefore, the competitive advantage (Kusluvan et al., 2010; Noe et al., 2006). Consequently, it is of utmost importance that the company attracts and retains skilled, committed, engaged, and motivated employees to achieve sustained competitive advantage in a globalized world. Organizations therefore adopt a more, international, strategic approach to HRM. More specifically, the HRM department needs to support global strategic planning processes by creating a pattern of planned human resource practices that are aligned to certain employee attitudes and behaviors (Wright and Snell, 1991). In the case of global strategic orientations, even more, emphasis is placed on international strategies, effective global talent management, compliance with international laws and regulations, and cross-cultural orientations.

As explained above, International Human Resource Management (I-HRM) is a crucial topic to address for hospitality organizations. However, how is I-HRM different from 'normal' HRM? I-HRM is defined by Poole as:

> ...the **worldwide** management of people in the multinational enterprise.
>
> *(Poole, 1990, p. 1)*

A more recent definition is from Sparrow and Braun (2008) who explain it as:

> ... the ways in which the HRM function contributes to the process of globalization within multinational firms.
>
> *(p. 96)*

According to Björkman and Stahl (2006), I-HRM encompasses

> all issues related to the management of people in an international context [including] human resource issues facing MNCs in different parts of their organizations [and] comparative analyses of HRM in different countries.
>
> *(p. 1)*

To sum up, International Human Resources Management is concerned with:

1   Issues that are cross-national in nature and are executed in locations other than the home country headquarters.
2   The relationships between different HR activities of the organization, as well as the external environment in which the organization operates.
3   Comparative HRM studies that look at differences in specific HRM activities between diverse countries.

Consequently, I-HRM is a practice that is key to implement in Multi-National Corporations (MNCs). Such a corporation has been defined as:

> an enterprise that operates in several countries but is managed from one home country. In practice, once an enterprise derives more than one-quarter of its revenues from outside its home country, it is considered an MNC.
>
> *(Brewster et al., 2016, p. 4)*

It is the international organizational structure of such an MNC that provides the context for the international HR issues faced by the organization, which include, for example, the enhancement of global strategic planning, alignment of HR practices with the company strategy, executing change initiatives on a global scale, establishing global company cultures, and recruiting A-level global leaders (Deresky, 2017).

HR in the International Hospitality Industry: An Outside-Inside Approach

Over the past decades, we have witnessed a transformation of the HRM function. The HR department is now seen as a core business function that has become integrated into all organizational processes of companies, rather than having a sole focus on *personnel management*. Multinational hotel chains have penetrated foreign markets and are therefore located in different countries. As strategies are set at the home country headquarters, but HR practices will vary from country to country, HRM needs to become a business partner in the top management team, and needs to contribute to business strategy development, as well as function as the linking pin to local operational processes.

However, this was not always the case, and the role of HRM has shifted dramatically in recent years. According to Ulrich and Dulebohn (2015), this HR transformation is characterized by four waves.

1   The administrative wave of HR
2   HR practices wave
3   HR strategy wave
4   HR and context

The first wave is labeled as '*the administrative wave of HR.*' This wave is characterized by an HR department that solely performs administrative maintenance functions (Vosburgh, 2007).

Administrative tasks are mainly focused on delivering standard HR services, such as the delivery of payroll checks and the assurance of complying with employment and tax law legislations.

The second wave is labeled '*the HR practices wave.*' This wave constitutes the design, development, and implementation of innovative human resource practices that are aligned with organizational needs. Such practices include, for example, new ways of recruitment, training, and career development. HR aims for fair, ethical, and equitable employment processes and practices and functions therefore as a third-party advocate, or ombudsman (Ulrich, 1996). These employment processes are characterized by an open-system decision model that includes all elements that are entailed in employing employees from organizational entrance to exit (Zedeck and Cascio, 1984).

The third wave is the '*HR strategy wave,*' which is a change that has had an upsurge over the past 30 years (Wright et al., 2015). In fact, companies have come to realize the importance of HR and the necessity to align HR more closely with their business strategy to achieve company objectives and to add value to the business strategy. More specifically, it is the alignment of specific bundles of HR practices with the corporate strategy, as well as the effect these practices have on internal and external performance indicators (e.g., on employee turnover, service quality, and financial performance) (Becker and Huselid, 1998).

The '*HR strategy wave*' undoubtedly highlights the importance of supporting the underlying business strategy of an organization, yet it still represents an inside-outside perspective. More specifically, this approach aims to align the organization's human capital and certain internal HR practices and it does not directly integrate the external business environment changes and developments. Therefore, this view overlooks a crucial aspect of what we see as the future of HR development, particularly in the contexts of MNCs: it is the external dynamic and international environment and stakeholders that influence what HR needs to do inside the organization.

This missing aspect is represented in the fourth wave of HR: '*HR and context.*' This is the wave that, according to Ulrich and Dulebohn (2015), is characterized by an *outside-inside approach* and focuses on a movement from HR practices that are connected to the business strategy to a stronger and more direct connection of HR to the broader business context in which the corporation operates. This movement is particularly important for multinational companies (MNCs) that have to respond to a quickly changing environment by anticipating on changes in external business conditions (e.g., the global trends) to ensure that increased value can be delivered to all relevant stakeholders; the company, the customers, their families, their community, and for HR itself.

The above highlights that adding value for international hospitality organizations does not solely mean that the HR department needs to serve its employees by implementing HR practices that are focused on the development of employee behaviors that are in line with the company's strategy (Boswell, 2006). Rather, HR can only add value in the future by aligning their HR practices and policies with external, macro- and meso-level trends. Different contextual trends and developments in the business context create an increasingly complex business environment for organizations to attract, motivate, and retain top talented people (Beechler and Woodward, 2009).

Figure 23.1 shows the so-called outside-inside approach that can be used for investigating international HR practices (Brewster, 1995). This view can be used to review the factors both exogenous and endogenous that together create challenges that affect the MNC's I-HRM strategy. Exogenous, such as technological developments, an ongoing process of individualization in the Western world and beyond, globalization processes, demographic developments, and environmental challenges all affect the nature of HR (see Table 23.1). Additionally, specific contextual, local laws and regulations, and diverse cultural norms create certain region and industry-specific challenges and can make it rather difficult for firms to implement global generic I-HRM practices (endogenous factors). Such endogenous forces are the internal challenges of the organization and include, amongst others, the strategic position of the company, the international orientation, organizational structure, and workforce capability (Schuler et al., 1993). The challenge lies in

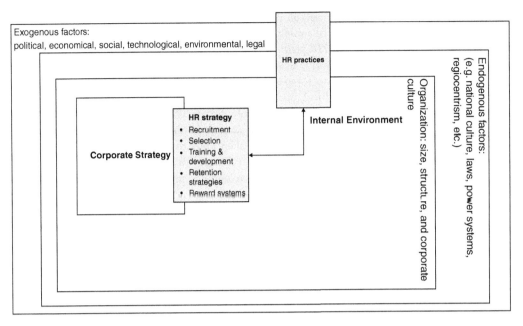

Figure 23.1 An outside-inside approach for investigating international HR practices. Adapted from Brewster (1995).

the attraction of a regional workforce by means of appropriate regional talent strategies, and the retainment of talent in specific regions (Tarique and Schuler, 2010).

In order to translate the main reasoning behind the outside-inside approach (the *Why* part) to more concrete steps that can be taken by the I-HRM department (the *How* part), Wright et al. (2003) suggest taking the following steps:

1   The organization needs to have formal mechanisms in place for tracking developments in the external environment of the organization, and HR strategies need to be aligned with identified key trends and developments.
2   HR needs to take an evidence-based approach that identifies the business- and people's key performance indicators that determine the success of the company. In turn, these indicators need to be constantly monitored and communicated to the internal HR community.
3   A deep understanding of the organizational processes and people in the organization needs to be developed. Only then HR processes and systems can be considered accordingly.
4   The combination of external drivers and internal business metrics will form a solid foundation for the development of an HR strategy that aims to drive performance.
5   A formal process needs to be developed that enforces the creation of HR bundles and strategies together with the line managers of the organization. A key point to consider is the fact that an HR strategy is a non-linear process, an over-time task that needs to be implemented, executed, and tracked rather than a formal document or a one-time event. One should consider the relevance of a flexible and adaptive HR system that is able to respond to both global, as well as specific contextual changes (Figure 23.1).

Based on the reference points that have been established earlier in this chapter, the remaining paragraphs will focus on concurrent topics and key practices that are relevant to the I-HRM department of hospitality organizations. It reviews various key practices that need to be discussed by HR professionals in light of internationalization processes. We will explore multiple previous studies, theories, and models related to Global Talent Management, International Mobility and the Management of Expatriates, and finally Cross-Cultural Training. In other words, it reviews a range of topics HR managers need to take into account when creating an HR strategy that aligns with the MNC's international strategy.

Global Talent Management

Globalization is a key driver of organizational expansion in international markets. Because of new strategic alliances, cross-border mergers and culturally distant markets, staffing issues tend to be more complex (Collings et al., 2007). Ever since the dawn of modern business, companies have aimed to attract and retain the best staff they could (Morgan, 2017). There is no panacea for directly finding the perfect person for the available position, and especially in a changing international landscape it gets more challenging to find, and retain, the best talent in the world. Despite the economic slowdown, the majority of MNCs aim to attract top talent and keep investing in learning and development programs for their employees (Guthridge et al., 2008). MNCs realize that employees with global experience and expertise are key to the global success of the organization (Deresky, 2017). In the end, it is only the top 20% of 'A-players' of workers that can raise an organization's operational productivity, profit, and sales revenue (Axelrod et al., 2001). Multinational organizations need to recruit, select, develop, and retain 'talented' workers that are located anywhere in the world and that have the competences and commitment that are required for functioning in the organization. In other words, they need to create a well-selected global talent pool.

Instead of looking at a talented person as an employee with 'natural' aptitude or skills, the holistic view on talent considers it as the aggregation of competence, commitment, and contribution (Ulrich, 2006). The person that is hired needs to have the knowledge, skills, and attitudes, or so-called KSAs, that are required to work in an international environment. Such KSAs include, for example, cross-cultural communication skills, design thinking, resilience, emotional intelligence, creativity, and problem-solving. Furthermore, he or she needs to be committed, have perseverance, and put their energy and focus on the company's success. Finally, the person needs to find meaning and purpose in the job that is offered, so that he/she protects personal resources (e.g., time, energy) and can sustain personal psychological well-being over time (van der Klink et al., 2016). Key accountabilities of the I-HRM department therefore include overseeing structured processes for the selection of candidates suitable for a job in an international environment. Failure of expatriate assignments are costly (which we elaborate upon in one of the following paragraphs) and selection procedures that contribute uniquely to the success of future international assignments are therefore specifically relevant. Selection procedures such as assessment centers, where candidates have to participate in a number of job-related activities might be expensive, but they often do predict success of training and performance on the job and, therefore, perhaps on expatriate assignments. The I-HRM department can, for example, ask candidates in simulations to engage in an international business deal or have a performance review with an expatriate employee.

Alternative Work Arrangements in the War for Talent

In the so-called 'War for Talent' (Beechler and Woodward, 2009), it is not only the organization but also the applicants who decide whether they want the job in the hospitality organization. MNCs need to profile themselves to leave a good impression with the applicants so that top candidates do not withdraw, join competing organizations, or even talk negatively about the organization. Additionally, as non-linear, discontinuous or so-called 'boundaryless' careers become more common in the 'gig-economy,' the smart and talented individuals that companies aim to attract might even decide to work in an online freelance marketplace (Morgan, 2017). Specifically, in the expatriate literature it has been indicated that there is a shift from the long-term, gold-lined expatriate employment contracts to shorter (i.e., three-month) deployments and more local hires (De Ruiter et al., 2016). In other words, the War for Talent trend does not solely seem to indicate that MNCs are competing against each other on a global scale. Perhaps more importantly there is the need for a change in traditional employment and business models to attract valuable A-players.

Morgan (2017) critically mentions that in order to attract and retain the right talent and to create an optimal employee experience, one needs to realize that the world is going to be dominated by freelancers and short-term employees. Rather than fighting against such changes, it is better to go along with them and offer employees alternative work arrangement in order to survive in the freelance economy (Katz and Krueger, 2016).

A number of international companies are already taking steps to break out of the old business model and see this as the only way to win the talent war. These steps could serve as interesting starting points for further discussion in the I-HRM department of multinational hospitality organizations (Morgan, 2017):

1   In designing a selection system, HR managers sometimes decide for shorter expatriate employment contracts (i.e., three-months) or more local hires for short-term projects that are selected from the freelance economy. *Example:* Cisco often works with hand-picked freelance one-off project teams to develop innovations for their next hardware technologies.
2   Employment systems are starting to be redesigned by changing global staffing policies, compensation schemes, and promotion opportunities so that a potential talent pool in the organization is created. *Example*: Nokia Corp. changed its compensation scheme by creating a more regionally based practice, rather than a traditional Finnish one. In this way, they became a superior global competitor for talent (Fernandez-Araoz, 2007).
3   Because of demographic changes, some companies purposefully decide to attract and retain baby boomers because 'boomers' have more tacit knowledge, experience, and are not aiming for boundaryless careers. Most probably they will remain in the workplace until their sixties and seventies. *Example*: IBM and P&G seek to hire older workers that can work on projects and at the same time share their expertise with younger workers.
4   There is an increase in focus on diversity management which is believed to have an impact on organizational success (Table 23.1). Organizations aim to create a diverse employee base which forms their talent pool. Team diversity allows for more out-of-the-box innovation, as well as more empathy with a diverse customer base (Hunt et al., 2015). *Example*: Ernst and Young and IBM both assess the managers in during performance reviews on how well they stimulate the career development of women and minorities.
5   MNCs invest in the implementation of learning practices that aim to retain the most valuable employees. This is mainly done by offering opportunities in Life Long Learning (LLL) which helps employees to grow and develop. *Example:* In line with the global trend of individualization, Deloitte engages in 'mass career customization' and focuses on personalized career paths for their employees that are facilitated by interactive exercises and online resources.
6   International organizations aim to develop partnerships with top universities to build a well-educated next generation workforce. Educational communities and tailored curricula are put in place that helps students to plan their career paths. *Example*: Nyenrode Business University in the Netherlands offers part-time bachelor and master's degrees in accountancy which are designed for starters in accountancy that combine a study with a job.

The hospitality industry is a proper context to experiment with alternative work arrangements in a range from online intermediaries to offline intermediaries (Katz and Krueger, 2016). Online intermediaries include capital platforms, such as Deliveroo, or labor platforms, such as Airbnb.

Table 23.1 Contextual trends and developments in the business context

Environmental factor	Current trends and developments
Political	Changes in political environments are characterized by a rise of populistic leaders and identity politics. Their popularity has given rise to trends and developments such as involuntary migration (refugee crisis), income and wealth disparity, and a decline in trust in local and regional governments. Other developments in the political landscape include the lower migration and immigration barriers, resulting in employees relocating abroad (Tung and Lazarova, 2007). Moreover, the support of governmental policies resulted in more talent flow across different countries (Carr et al., 2005).
Economical	Even though the global GDP has been growing, productivity growth slowed and has not recovered since the economic crisis in 2008 (IMF, 2017). Moreover, the global public department has nearly doubled since the 2008 crisis up to \$60.99 trillion (Economist, 2018). The GDP of the G7 countries is predicted to drop from \$34.1 trillion in 2015 to \$18.8 trillion in 2050 and a rise of the GDP of the E7 countries is expected from \$69.3 trillion in 2015 to \$138.2 trillion in 2050 (PwC, 2016).
Societal	The global population is estimated to reach to over 11 billion people in 2050 and the current global life expectancy of 71.9 years will rise to 82.6 years in 2100 (UN-DESA, 2013). The working population of the developed countries is ageing, the baby boom cohort will start retiring in the coming decade and fewer young people will enter the labor market due to lower birth rates in the past few decades. Yet, the older people will remain in the workforce longer than in the past. A shift in age distribution will affect the labor pool supply (Hotopp, 2005).
	Moreover, an increasingly international environment leads to the management of a diverse group of employees. There are increasing levels of ethic, cultural, generational, and gender diverse individuals working for different organizations (Beechler and Woodward, 2009). Lastly, changing education and income levels will affect both employee and consumer behavior. Personal lifestyles of people are changing that is characterized by an on-going process of individualization and focus on well-being (Mintel, 2018).
Technological	An explosive growth in the global economy of digitization, automation, robotics, and artificial intelligence are driving a digital transformation that calls for a shift in a mixture of skills, tasks, and activities. Rapid developments in technology have decreased the costs for communication as well as international commuting (Bryan and Fraser, 1999).
Environmental	Many complicated and interrelated environmental problems we face today will threaten the future of our planet and the quality of lives of the inhabitants. This results in a need for MNCs that play a key role in the realization of true sustainable development of our society.

Offline intermediaries include contracted-out workers, such as possible in food and beverage arrangements, on-call/temporary workers, such as flying in expatriates.

International Mobility and the Management of Expatriates

Within the newly emergent global markets, the earlier mentioned 'War for Talent' is fierce; MNCs compete for top-level candidates that they can send out on foreign assignments. In recent years, not only a number of MNCs have increased, but global relocation of workers continues to increase as well (Littrell and Salas, 2005). In order for MNCs to staff such foreign assignments, they can decide on the following possibilities:

1   The relocation of an employee and his/her family to the target country (expatriates).
2   The development of staff in the local country for managerial positions (so-called 'impatriates').
3   Short-term transits of employees for specific assignments (so-called 'flexpatriates') (Mayerhofer et al., 2004; McCaughey and Bruning, 2005).

Organizations that aim to fill international management positions often decide to go for option 1 and migrate expatriate employees. These are the employees that "are assigned to a country other than their own" (Deresky, 2017, p. 342). Besides the employee that flows to another country as initiated by the organization, there are also the self-initiated expatriates who deliberately cross international borders to pursue an international career (Thorn and Inkson, 2013).

Even though we see a continuous rise in expatriate deployments and overseas assignments, the importance of formal processes and policies regarding foreign assignments is still underestimated. The Brookfield Global Relocation Trends Survey (Brookfield Global Mobility Trends, 2014) indicated that only 22% of the HR departments in organizations have implemented formal career management processes in foreign countries. Additionally, only 19% of those companies had international assignment candidate pools in place. Such underestimated importance often results in incidents of expatriate failure, low job satisfaction and, in turn, the loss of valuable employees to other companies (Stahl et al., 2002). It has been estimated that 10–50% of expatriates return early, and the problems associated with relocation and training cost the MNCs between $250,000 and $1 million (Eschbach et al., 2001). Therefore, more emphasis needs to be placed on the right HR policies and procedures. Organizations tend to overlook the necessary skills and competences of cross-cultural awareness and interpersonal skills that are key for moving to a foreign country.

Moreover, because of an increase in dual-earner couples, an international relocation not only impacts the career of the expatriate employee, it also impacts his or her partner's career (Rushing and Kleiner, 2003). Other causes of expatriate failure mentioned by Deresky (2017) include:

1   A selection of a candidate based on criteria that are set by the headquarters, rather than the assignment needs.
2   Insufficient preparation, training, and orientation of the candidate and their family prior to the assignment.
3   Minimal organizational support coming from the headquarters.
4   Difficulties in adapting to local countries and working cultures.
5   Difficulties in adapting to new cultures experienced by the spouse and children.
6   Insufficient reward systems, compensation schemes, and financial support.
7   Poorly implemented career development and support programs.

In order to minimize expatriate failure, tasks of the I-HRM department inherently involve supporting the expatriates with their new work tasks, cultural adjustment, and their learning and growth possibilities. Consequently, the following processes of the HR cycle need to be specifically taken into consideration:

The *selection criteria* of expatriates should not be based on prior domestic performance (Black et al., 1999) but rather on characteristics such as passion for success, risk-taking, assertiveness (Ruben and Ruben, 1989), cultural sensitivity, and local language ability (Mol et al., 2005). Personality characteristics that have been found to be good predictors for performance include emotional stability, extraversion, openness, agreeableness (Shaffer et al., 2006) and lack of ethnocentrism (Caligiuri and Di Santo, 2001). In designing a selection system, HR managers have to consider such characteristics and determine what instruments to include to measure them.

In order to help expatriates to *adjust*, scholars have found three types of adjustment to focus on. The most prominent theory is the one from Black, Mendenhall and Oddou (1991) who argue that expatriates need to be supported in work adjustment (such as new job roles, responsibilities, and work contexts), interaction adjustment (integrating to new cultures regarding norms and modes of interaction) as well as general adjustment (the adjustment of the full living situation in a host country together with their families). Expatriate *effectiveness* therefore often depends on the ease of managing tasks and relationships in the host country. The paragraph cross-cultural management will elaborate on this topic.

An Alternative Agenda for the Management of Expatriates

Global Talent Management has been high on the agenda of MNCs for a while now, but it is the I-HRM department that is not always able to keep up the pace with putting policies in place for the management of expatriates (Brewster et al., 2004). The I-HRM department often neglects the considerable (economic) disadvantages and the problems that arise with sending employees to foreign countries (Scullion and Brewster, 2001). Organizations might therefore also dive into possibilities of alternative forms of international assignments (Collings et al., 2007). When taking an outside-inside approach, external factors such as the scarce supply of international employees and dual-career families tend to aggravate difficulties in the relocation of whole families to target countries. On the other hand, external factors such as international markets, global economic growth, and the integration of industrialized countries emphasize the need of employees to go on international assignments (Mayerhofer et al., 2004).

International recruitment and selection should therefore not solely focus on long-term (three to five years) international assignments but rather look at opportunities of short-term alternatives that are stimulating the well-being of employees, as well as balance trade-offs in dual-career couples (Meyskens et al., 2009). Because of the macro-level challenges, as well as individual-level require-ments there is no one-size-fits-all approach and it is therefore argued that specific HR policies and procedures need to be developed that are aligned with different demands and requirements (Dowling and Welch, 2004). Table 23.2 demonstrates a range of emerging alternatives that might be taken into consideration for international hospitality organizations (Collings et al., 2007).

In order for I-HRM departments to manage their expatriates in the most optimal way, we have elaborated on taking different routes for certain international assignments. There is no generic solution and MNCs need to consider which of the alternatives, whether it is a traditional expatriate assignment or one of the alternative forms, meets the assignment's requirements. To sum up, it is suggested for I-HRM departments to develop a portfolio with a range of possibilities that can be implemented when there is a demand for international assignments. Supporting HR bundles and practices of recruitment and selection, training, reward systems, and occupational health and safety policies need to be in place to ensure effective implementation of a specific form of international assignment. Furthermore, there needs to be a constant follow-up system in place to evaluate the outcomes of the implemented solution. The next paragraph will go more into detail on cross-cultural management which aims to improve the success rates of expatriates on foreign assignments.

Cross-Cultural Management

When companies expand from a single domestic context to operating on a global scale, a natural consequence is that organizations have to make a shift from managing from a local domestic con-text to managing 'across cultures.' Cross-cultural management refers to:

> accommodating differences in cultural practices when managing outside one's home country and it often takes a comparative perspective.
>
> *(Bird and Mendenhall, 2016, p. 115)*

Table 23.2 An alternative agenda for the management of expatriates

Alternative form of international assignment	Operational issues
Short-term international assignment	This is a company-specific temporal international assignment that is longer than a business-trip, but shorter than a full-working year. A key characteristic is that the family of the employee often remains in the home country. A short-term International Assignment can be used in an MNC for: (1) problem solving issues/skill transfer- opportunities such as with a short project; (2) control purposes and; (3) managerial development (Tahvanainen et al., 2005).
Frequent flyer assignments	Frequent Flyer Assignments entails a job description in which one of the essential components is to frequently go on a business travel. This, in turn, would mean that neither the family nor the employee himself needs to move to a different country. The worker is able to have face-to-face interactions with certain stakeholders, but is not bound to move to that particular location. Frequent Flyer Assignments can be used for (1) developing markets and/or volatile countries to which the person does not want to move; (2) countries that can be reached by a short flight (one to three hours) and for; (3) irregular and specific tasks. One should, however, not underestimate the health and well-being issues related to frequent business travels such as the experience of jet-lags and work-family conflict (Nicholas and McDowall, 2012).
Commuter and rotational assignments	Commuter assignments require the worker to commute from their home country to a foreign country on a weekly/every other week basis (Collings et al., 2007). For a rotational assignment the worker commutes from their home country to another country for a longer period of time, which is followed by a time-off period back at the home base (Welch and Worm, 2006).
Global virtual teams	As a result of technological developments, companies are more and more able to use technological mediated applications (e.g., the Internet but even more so in the future Virtual Reality) to coordinate work by means of global virtual teams. Virtual assignments are particularly useful for (1) routine activities; (2) conference calls and; (3) enhancement of skills by means of e-learning (which will be elaborated upon in the following chapter).

Source: Adapted from Collings et al. (2007).

Research shows that cross-cultural groups often perform better in the long run, because of a mix of knowledge, experiences, and backgrounds (van Knippenberg et al., 2004). However, satisfaction levels in cross-cultural groups in comparison to homogeneous groups tend to be lower as they experience more conflicts in the team. Moreover, besides the increasingly diverse team compositions also the earlier mentioned experienced difficulties by expatriates lead to the fact that cross-cultural communication cannot be ignored. Expatriates need to be facilitated in adjusting to the host culture, as well as employees of the host culture need to be supported in adjusting to the expatriates.

The focus of the I-HRM department should therefore be on the development of intercultural competences of their employees. Intercultural competence relates to being able to communicate one's own cultural identity in a culturally diverse environment (Chen and Starosta, 2000). The ability of employees to communicate and interact with offshore teams is key for adding value to the corporate global strategy. Rather than executing 'cross-cultural' training that focuses on handshakes and dining etiquette, more emphasis needs to be placed on deeper core value differences that might affect team dynamics or business relationships. Skills that therefore need to be developed include, amongst others, cognitive flexibility, behavioral flexibility, tolerance of ambiguity, and cross-cultural empathy (Bird and Mendenhall, 2016).

Cross-Cultural Training Development and Implementation

A cross-cultural training (CCT) program for the management of expatriates can be divided into seven different categories: attribution training, cultural awareness training, cognitive-behavior modification training, interaction training, language training, didactic training, and experiential learning (Littrell and Salas, 2005). Table 23.3 includes a short summary of each of those training and how they can be implemented in the international hospitality industry.

Table 23.3 Cross-cultural training strategies

Cross-cultural training strategy	Implementation of the intervention in the international hospitality industry
Attribution training	Attribution techniques can be used to develop skills and competences that are needed to understand the behavior of people in the host country in a similar way as the inhabitants of the host country. This would, in turn, help to reduce a degree of ethnocentrism in the expatriate and increase his/her intercultural awareness.
Cultural awareness training	The focus of cultural awareness training is to make the individual more aware of his/her own country, in order to better be able to empathize with the host countries' culture. The expatriate will be taught about their own values and cultural aspects, so that differences with the host country will be better appreciated.
Cognitive-behavior modification training	This training aims the expatriate to develop new habitual behaviors that are specifically rewarded by the host culture. Rather than solely avoiding inappropriate behaviors, the individual needs to develop new behaviors that fit the host culture.
Interaction training	Interaction training is also known as "overlap-training." In this case the expatriate learns from the expatriate he/she is replacing. The incumbent expatriate will give hands-on training about his/her experience in the host country to the incoming expatriate and introduce the employee to business practice, work tasks, and daily life rituals.
Language training	In case the employee is not familiar with the host countries' language, it is important to get introduced to the new language in order to be able to have some "small talk" as well as understand some of the work-related information pieces that pass by on a daily basis.
Didactic training	Didactic training interventions focus on the giving of information on working conditions, living conditions, and cultural differences. It involves all standard information of both the work, as well as living situation in the host country.
Experiential training	Experiential training emphasizes that the expatriate will learn by experience. This means that he/she will be confronted with situations / critical incidents that are common in the host country so that necessary skills are developed to deal with those situations. Interventions could include, for example, look-see visits, role-plays, intercultural workshops and (virtual) simulations. Especially with recent developments in VR more experiential possibilities arise.

Source: Adapted from Littrell and Salas (2005).

Table 23.4 Guidelines for the implementation of cross-cultural trainings in three distinct phases: design, delivery, and evaluation

Design	Delivery	Evaluation
Guideline 1: Cross-cultural training should be customized to match the expatriate's needs. A needs assessment should be conducted to identify the individual's requirements.	**Guideline 8:** Training delivery should correspond to a dynamic adjustment process. Rather than having a sole focus on pre-departure training and post-arrival training, one should offer training interventions structured in such a way that it follows the adjustment process of the individual employee. Each employee might be receptive during a different stage of the expatriate assignment and the cross-cultural training should cater for such flexibility.	**Guideline 11:** The MNC needs to establish success criteria for the cross-cultural training program. Indications of failure include, amongst others, early return to the home country, insufficient transfer of managerial practices, difficulties in adjustment, loss of opportunities, decreased productivity, turnover rates, and broken business relationships.
Guideline 2: Cross-cultural training should not stand alone. As mentioned in the paragraph on expatriate management, solely training is not enough. Relocation specialists should assist the expatriate and his/her family in relocation procedures.	**Guideline 9:** The difficulties surrounding repatriation should be addressed. The success of the cross-cultural training program can be assessed by evaluating the experiences of a returning expatriate. Also when returning, the expatriate needs to be offered position choices, family repatriation support, and acknowledgement.	**Guideline 12:** Organizations must evaluate whether the acquired skills and competences from the cross-cultural training have been transferred to the job. This means that the earlier established KSAs are actually applied by the expatriate.
Guideline 3: Training rigor should be tailored to the cultural toughness of the destination country. Because some countries might be more difficult to adapt to, the rigor of the training – e.g., mental involvement and effort –should be tailored to the toughness of the host country.	**Guideline 10:** Multiple media strategies should be used to deliver the cross-cultural training. With the rise of new technologies, more tools are available to deliver time and place independent trainings.	**Guideline 13:** Organizations must assess whether the investment in cross-cultural trainings yield positive organizational outcomes. The IHRM department can investigate whether the training indeed resulted in increased performance and adjustment of the expatriate employee. Moreover, a return-on-investment analysis can be conducted to analyze the impact and identify the problems encountered with the training.

Design	Delivery	Evaluation
Guideline 4: MNCs should develop a global mind-set. Because corporate trainings are embedded in the full organization, a global mind-set needs to be created for the entire company by, for example, multicultural trainings. An international mind-set of employees will benefit both the employees of the host country, as well as the expatriates.		
Guideline 5: Organizations must use a skill-based approach when designing cross-cultural trainings. Rather than solely creating awareness, the training program needs to actually build skills and competencies that are required. Necessary KSAs need to be identified and methods and practical applications needed for training need to be developed.		
Guideline 6: MNCs should apply and use strategies based on the science of training in designing the cross cultural training program. Four key training elements need to be integrated, namely: tools, competencies, methods, and instructional strategies.		
Guideline 7: Scenario-based training should be implemented. (Virtual) real-world environments need to be developed which help the employee to experience real-life cues and situations. Issues such as the experience of a "cultural shock" can be practiced with and directly given feedback on.		

Source: Adapted from Littrell and Salas (2005).

Even though different studies claim that CCTs are critical in the preparation of expatriates for overseas assignments (e.g., Morris and Robie, 2001), there is no guarantee for full expatriate success (Littrell and Salas, 2005). Because deficiencies still exist and I-HRM departments experience difficulties in what to focus on, Littrell and Salas (2005) developed a detailed synthesis on what organizations can, and perhaps should, do to enhance the success of the cross-cultural training program and, in turn, the expatriates probability of success on the assignment (Table 23.4). The guidelines can be used by the I-HRM department for developing, demystifying, and monitoring theory-based CCT interventions. The guidelines describe the process of CCT development in three categories: (1) Design, (2) Delivery, and (3) Evaluation.

Conclusion

When a more international perspective to HR is taken, one needs to be concerned with HR policies, practices, and systems that are aligned with the internationalization process and the global strategy of the organization. In order to do so, the I-HRM function needs to take an outside-inside perspective. The HR practices need to anticipate on exogenous and endogenous challenges and make careful decisions regarding aspects such as recruitment and selection, training and development, and reward systems. In this way, increased value is delivered to all relevant stakeholders (e.g., the company, the customers, their families, and the community). This chapter has presented some complex challenges that are currently encountered by the HR department working in an international environment, including global talent management, international mobility and the management of expatriates, and cross-cultural management. MNCs need to be aware of such challenges and emphasize on the importance of investing in their human capital for the implementation of a global strategy.

References

Axelrod, E.L., Handfield-Jones, H., and Welsh, T. A. (2001), "War for talent, part two", *The McKinsey Quarterly*, Spring 2001, p.9.

Becker, B.E., and Huselid, M.A. (1998), "Human resources strategies, complementarities, and firm performance", *SUNY Buffalo*, Unpublished manuscript.

Beechler, S. and Woodward, I.C. (2009), "The global "war for talent", *Journal of International Management*, Vol.15, No.3, pp.273–285. https://doi.org/10.1016/j.intman.2009.01.002.

Bird, A. and Mendenhall, M.E. (2016), "From cross-cultural management to global leadership: Evolution and adaptation", *Journal of World Business*, Vol.51, No.1, pp.115–126. https://doi.org/10.1016/j.jwb.2015.10.005.

Björkman, I. and Stahl, G.K. (2006), "International human resource management research: An introduction to the field", in Stahl, G.K. and Björkman, I. (Eds.), *Handbook of Research in International Human Resource Management*, Edward Elgar, London, UK, pp.1–11.

Black, J.S., Gregersen, H.B., Mendenhall, M.E., and Stroh, L.K. (1999), *Globalizing People Through International Assignments*, Addison-Wesley Longman, New York, NY.

Black, J.S., Mendenhall, M., and Oddou, G. (1991), "Toward a comprehensive model of international adjustment: An integration of multiple theoretical perspectives ", *Academy of Management Review*, Vol.16, No.2, pp.291–317. https://doi.org/10.5465/amr.1991.4278938.

Boswell, W. (2006), "Aligning employees with the organization's strategic objectives: Out of 'line of sight', out of mind", *The International Journal of Human Resource Management*, Vol.17, No. 9, pp.1489–1511. https://doi.org/10.1080/09585190600878071.

Brewster, C. (1995), "Towards a 'European' model of human resource management", *Journal of International Business Studies*, Vol.26, No.1, pp.1–21. https://doi.org/10.1057/palgrave.jibs.8490163.

Brewster, C., Mayrhofer, W., and Morley, M. (2004), *Human Resource Management in Europe: Evidence of Convergence?*, Elsevier, London, UK.

Brewster, C., Vernon, G., Sparrow, P., and Houldsworth, E. (2016), *International Human Resource Management*. CIPD – Kogan Page Publishers, London, UK.

Brookfield Global Mobility Trends. (2014), *Global Mobility Trends Survey*, Brookfield Global Relocation Services, Woodridge, IL.

Bryan, L. and Fraser, J. (1999), "Getting to global", *The McKinsey Quarterly*, Vol.4, pp.68–81.

Caligiuri, P. and di Santo, V.D. (2001), "Global competence: What is it, and can it be developed through global assignments?", *Human Resource Planning*, Vol.24, p.3.

Carr, S.C., Inkson, K., and Thorn, K. (2005), "From global careers to talent flow: Reinterpreting 'brain drain' ", *Journal of World Business*, Vol.40, No.4, pp.386–398. https://doi.org/10.1016/j.jwb.2005.08.006.

Chen, G.M. and Starosta, W. (2000), "The development and validation of the intercultural sensitivity scale", *Human Communication*, Vol.3, No.2, pp.1–15.

Collings, D.G., Scullion, H., and Morley, M.J. (2007), "Changing patterns of global staffing in the multi-national enterprise: Challenges to the conventional expatriate assignment and emerging alternatives", *Journal of World Business*, Vol.42, No.2, pp.198–213. https://doi.org/10.1016/j.jwb.2007.02.005.

Deresky, H. (2017), *International Management: Managing Across Borders and Cultures*, Pearson Education Limited, Harlow, pp.372–403.

Dowling, P. and Welch, D. (2004), *International Human Resource Management: Managing People in a Global Context*, Thomson Learning, London, UK.

Eschbach, D.M., Parker, G.E., and Stoeberl, P. A. (2001), "American repatriate employees' retrospective assessments of the effects of cross-cultural training on their adaptation to international assignments", *International Journal of Human Resource Management*, Vol.12, No.2, pp.270–287. https://doi.org/10.1080/09585190010014647.

The Economist. (2018), "The next recession", available at: http://www.economist.com/ (accessed 27 December 2018).

Fernandez-Araoz, C. (2007), *Great People Decisions*, John Wiley and Sons, Inc, Hoboken, NJ, pp.105–108.

Guthridge, M., Komm, A.B., and Lawson, E. (2008), "Making talent a strategic priority", *McKinsey Quarterly*, Vol.1, p.48.

Hotopp, U. (2005), "The employment rate of older workers", *Labour Market Trends*, Vol.113, No.2, pp.73–88.

Hunt, V., Layton, D., and Prince, S. (2015), "Diversity matters", *McKinsey and Company, London and Atlanta*, available at: https://www.mckinsey.com/business-functions/organization/our-insights/why-diversity-matters (accessed 11 January 2018).

International Monetary Fund (IMF). (2017), *Seeking Sustainable Growth: Short-Term Recovery, Long-Term Challenges*, available at: https://www.imf.org/en/Publications/WEO/Issues/2017/09/19/world- economic-outlook-october-2017 (accessed 28 December 2018).

Katz, L.F. and Krueger, A.B. (2016), *The Rise and Nature of Alternative Work Arrangements in the United States, 1995–2015*, National Bureau of Economic Research, Washington, DC.

van Knippenberg, D., De Dreu, C.K.W., and Homan, A.C. (2004), "Work group diversity and group performance: An integrative model and research agenda", *Journal of Applied Psychology*, Vol.89, No.6, pp.1008–1022. http://dx.doi.org/10.1037/0021-9010.89.6.1008.

Kusluvan, S., Kusluvan, Z., Ilhan, I., and Buyruk, L. (2010), "The human dimension: A review of human resources management issues in the tourism and hospitality industry", *Cornell Hospitality Quarterly*, Vol.51, No.2, pp.171–214. https://doi.org/10.1177/1938965510362871.

Littrell, L.N. and Salas, E. (2005), "A review of cross-cultural training: Best practices, guidelines, and research needs", *Human Resource Development Review*, Vol.4, No.3, pp.305–334. https://doi.org/10.1177/1534484305278348.

Mayerhofer, H., Hartmann, L., Michelitsch-Riedl, G., and Kollinger, I. (2004), "Flexpatriate assignments: A neglected issue in global staffing", *The International Journal of Human Resource Management*, Vol.15, No.8, pp.1371–1389. https://doi.org/10.1080/0958519042000257986.

McCaughey, D. and Bruning, N.S. (2005), "Enhancing opportunities for expatriate job satisfaction: HR strategies for foreign assignment success. *Human Resource Planning*, Vol.28, No.4, pp.21–30.

Meyskens, M., von Glinow, M.A., Werther, Jr, W.B., and Clarke, L. (2009), "The paradox of international talent: Alternative forms of international assignments", *The International Journal of Human Resource Management*, Vol.20, No.6, pp.1439–1450. https://doi.org/10.1080/09585190902909988.

Mintel. (2018), *Global Consumer Trends 2019*, available at: http://www.mintel.com/global-consumer-trends/ (accessed 27 December 2018).

Mol, S.T., Born, M.P., Willemsen, M.E., and Van Der Molen, H.T. (2005), "Predicting expatriate job performance for selection purposes: A quantitative review", *Journal of Cross-Cultural Psychology*, Vol.36, No.5, pp.590–620. https://doi.org/10.1177/0022022105278544.

Morgan, J. (2017), *The Employee Experience Advantage: How to Win the War for Talent by Giving Employees the Workspaces They Want, the Tools They Need, and a Culture They Can Celebrate*, John Wiley and Sons, Hoboken, NJ.

Morris, M.A. and Robie, C. (2001), "A meta-analysis of the effects of cross-cultural training on expatriate performance and adjustment", *International Journal of Training and Development*, Vol.5, No.2, pp.112–125. https://doi.org/10.1111/1468-2419.00126.

Nicholas, H. and McDowall, A. (2012). "When work keeps us apart: A thematic analysis of the experience of business travelers", *Community, Work & Family*, Vol.15, No.3, pp.335–355.

Noe, R., Hollenbeck, J., Gerhart, B. and Wright, P., (2006), *Human Resources Management: Gaining a Competitive Advantage, Tenth Global Edition*, Cengage Learning, Boston, MA.

Ottenbacher, M. and Gnoth, J. (2005), "How to develop successful hospitality innovation", *Cornell Hotel and Restaurant Administration Quarterly*, Vol.46, No.2, pp.205–222. https://doi.org/10.1177/0010880404271097.

Poole, M. (1990), "Human resource management in an international perspective", *International Journal of Human Resource Management*, Vol.1, No.1, pp.1–15. https://doi.org/10.1080/09585199000000037.

PwC. (2017), *The Long View: How Will the Global Economic Order Change by 2015?*, available at: http://www.pwc.co.uk/ (accessed 27 December 2018).

Ruben, D.H. and Ruben, M.J. (1989), "Why assertiveness training programs fail", *Small Group Behavior*, Vol. 20, No.3, pp.367–380. https://doi.org/10.1177/104649648902000307.

De Ruiter, M., Lub, X., Jansma, E., and Blomme, R.J. (2016), "Psychological contract fulfillment and expatriate intrinsic career success: The mediating role of identification with the multinational corporation", *International Journal of Human Resource Management*, Vol.29, No.8, pp.1426–1453. https://doi.org/10.1080/09585192.2016.1244099.

Rushing, K. and Kleiner, B.H. (2003), "New developments in executive relocation practices", *Management Research News*, Vol.26, No.2, pp.12–19. https://doi.org/10.1108/01409170310783745.

Schuler, R.S., Dowling, P.J., and De Cieri, H. (1993), "An integrative framework of strategic international human resource management", *Journal of Management*, Vol.19, No.2, pp.419–459. https://doi.org/10.1016/0149-2063(93)90059-V.

Scullion, H. and Brewster, C. (2001), "The management of expatriates: Messages from Europe?", *Journal of World Business*, Vol.36, No.4, pp.346–365. https://doi.org/10.1016/S1090-9516(01)000608.

Shaffer, M.A., Harrison, D.A., Gregersen, H., Black, J.S., and Ferzandi, L.A. (2006), "You can take it with you: Individual differences and expatriate effectiveness", *Journal of Applied Psychology*, Vol.91, No.1, pp.109–125. http://dx.doi.org/10.1037/0021-9010.91.1.109.

Sparrow, P.R. and Braun, W. (2008), "HR sourcing and shoring: Strategies, drivers, success factors and implications for HR", in Dickmann, M., and Brewster, C., and Sparrow, P.R. (Eds.), *International Human Resource Management: A European Perspective*, Routledge, London, UK, pp.39–66.

Stahl, G.K., Miller, E.L., and Tung, R.L. (2002), "Toward the boundaryless career: A closer look at the expatriate career concept and the perceived implications of an international assignment", *Journal of World Business*, Vol.37, No.3, pp.216–227. https://doi.org/10.1016/S1090-9516(02)00080-9.

Tahvanainen, M., Welch, D., and Worm, V. (2005), "Implications of short-term international assignments", *European Management Journal*, Vol.23, No.6, pp.663–673. https://doi.org/10.1016/j.emj.2005.10.011.

Tarique, I. and Schuler, R.S. (2010), "Global talent management: Literature review, integrative framework, and suggestions for further research", *Journal of world business*, Vol.45, No.2, pp.122–133. https://doi.org/10.1016/j.jwb.2009.09.019.

Thorn, K. and Inkson, K. (2013), "Self-initiated expatriation and talent flow", in Andersen, M., Al Ariss, A., and Walther, M. (Eds.), *Self-Initiated Expatriation: Individual, Organizational and National Perspectives*, Routledge, London, UK, pp.75–89.

Tung, R. and Lazarova, M., (2007), "The human resource challenge to outward foreign direct investment aspirations from emerging countries: The case of China", *International Journal of Human Resource Management*, Vol.18, No.5, pp.868–889. https://doi.org/10.1080/09585190701249198.

Ulrich, D. (1996), *Human Resource Champions*, Harvard Business School Press, Boston, MA.

Ulrich, D. (2006), " 'The talent trifecta', development and learning on organizations", *An International Journal*, Vol.22, No.2, pp.32–33. https://doi.org/10.1108/dlo.2008.08122bad.003.

Ulrich, D. and Dulebohn, J.H. (2015), "Are we there yet? What's next for HR?", *Human Resource Management Review*, Vol.25, No.2, pp.188–204. https://doi.org/10.1016/j.hrmr.2015.01.004.

United Nations, Department of Economic and Social Affairs, Population Division. (2013), *World Population Prospects: The 2012 Revision. Key Findings and Advance Tables*, United Nations Department of Economic and Social Affairs, New York.

Van der Klink, J.J., Bültmann, U., Burdorf, A., Schaufeli, W.B., Zijlstra, F.R., Abma, F.I., ... & Van der Wilt, G.J. (2016), Sustainable employability—definition, conceptualization, and implications: A perspective based on the capability approach. *Scandinavian Journal of Work, Environment & Health*, Vol. 42, No. 1 (January 2016) pp.71–79.

Vosburgh, R.M. (2007), "The evolution of HR: Developing HR as an internal consulting organization", *People and Strategy*, Vol.30, No.3, pp.11–23.

Welch, D.E. and Worm, V. (2006) "International business travellers: A challenge for I-HRM", in Stahl, G.K. and Björkman, I. (Eds.), *Handbook of Research in International Human Resource Management*, Edward Elgar, Cheltenham, pp.283–533.

Wright, P.M., Guest, D., and Paauwe, J. (2003), "Current approaches to HR strategies: Inside-out vs. outside-in", *Human Resource Planning*, Vol.27, No.4, pp.36–47.

Wright, P.M., Guest, D., and Paauwe, J. (2015), "Off the mark: Response to Kaufman's evolution of strategic HRM", *Human Resource Management*, Vol.54, No.3, pp.409–415. https://doi.org/10.1002/hrm.21723.

Wright, P.M., and Snell, S. A. (1991), "Toward an integrative view of strategic human resource management", *Human Resource management Review*, Vol.1, No.3, pp.203–225. https://doi.org/10.1016/1053-4822(91)90015-5.

Zedeck, S. and Cascio, W.F. (1984), "Psychological issues in personnel decisions", *Annual Review of Psychology*, Vol.35, No.1, pp.461–518. https://doi.org/10.1146/annurev.ps.35.020184.002333.

24

INNOVATION MANAGEMENT IN THE INTERNATIONAL HOTEL INDUSTRY

Ige Pirnar

Introduction

Severe competition in the global hospitality industry gives a special importance to innovation practices as they contribute greatly to the differential marketing advantages and performance efficiency efforts of the international hotels. Innovation is an effective differential tool for the competitive hospitality industry due to the adaptability for flexible management systems, dynamic structure, rapidly changing customer preference and trends. With the entrepreneurs from many age groups, hospitality industry is a fruitful industry for creative innovative application areas resulting in profitable and sustainable outcomes.

Innovation Management in International Hospitality Industry

The etymology of the word innovation is derived originally from the Latin verb "*innovare*," and the Latin noun "*innovatus*" or "*innovatio*" stands for renewing or alteration or "*make changes in something established*" (English and Ehrich, 2015; Peters and Pikkemaat, 2006, p. 2). Joseph Schumpeter defined innovation from a manufacturing perspective (1935) as the "pushing force of economic development by the introduction of new technical methods, products, sources of supply, and forms of industrial organization" which is about "to produce other things or the same things by a different method, means to combine these materials and forces differently." Schumpeter (2000) states that entrepreneurs with the help of financial intensives invest in innovation by applying new methods and using new technologies, invent new resources and when their innovations are successful, imitators of the innovation follow in the industry leading to circular movements of the economic development. Drucker (1998) stated that innovation is an entrepreneurial tool for producing a different product or service. Drucker, also (1998) emphasized that innovation is essential as a discipline as it provides company's a unique opportunity for differentiation and competitive advantage by focusing and serving on changing needs of society. The Organization for Economic Co-Operation and Development's (OECD) document "The Measurement of Scientific and Technological Activities, Proposed Guidelines for Collecting and Interpreting Technological Innovation Data" (also known as the Oslo Manual) has a globally accepted definition. The Oslo Manual defines innovation as: "*the implementation of a new or significantly improved product (good or service), or process, a new marketing method, or a new organizational method in business practices, workplace organization or external relations*" (Turker, 2012, p. 148). Nowadays, innovation is considered "*as the key strategic dimension for the firms to drive long-term growth and profitability*" that is "*necessary for the survival of the organization*" (Rajapathirana and Hui, 2018, p. 53).

Service industry innovation studies followed the manufacturing industry studies where *"service innovation was first studied by Richard Barras in 1986"* (Nagy, 2012, p. 365) and tourism and hospitality industry–related studies started at 1997 by Anne-Mette Hjalager (Hjalager, 1997).

Hospitality is a highly competitive global industry which is very dynamic because trends and changes in the markets and tastes of customers are getting increasingly faster (García-Villaverde et al., 2017). Within such a competitive industry with a low entrance barrier, keeping up with ongoing dynamic changes in customer tastes and trends in customer preferences and service offerings for long-term profits and sustainability becomes more vital to hotels (Presenza et al., 2019). Hence, innovation becomes essential for hotels competing in the international hospitality industry and hotel of any size needs to continually innovate for differential advantage to survive (Carvalho and Costa, 2011).

Hotels need innovation to sustain in the long run through competitive advantage like successful marketing and effective management operations, new hotel product offerings, various cost reduction methods, and higher quality services applications (Martin-Rios and Ciobanu, 2019; Nieves et al., 2014). Because heterogeneous hospitality services are highly perishable and services innovations are easy to imitate, *"innovation differs between the service and manufacturing sectors and within the service sector"* (Martínez-Ros and Orfila-Sintes, 2009, p. 633). Innovation in hospitality has its principles, specifics, and application characteristics.

The characteristics of international hospitality innovation may be stated as development of a new or better hospitality product, service, or process which is consistent, holistic, and has a cumulative structure. The principles of international hospitality innovations may be stated as being customer focused, process focused, and continuous improvement (Nagy, 2012; Nieves et al., 2014). The common outcomes of international hospitality innovations like the customer satisfaction and exceeding their expectations, being process focused on achieving for improvement and adaptation of the better hospitality services and continuous improvement for keeping up with the trends in the industry are all essentially vital for sustainability in international hospitality industry (Nagy, 2012; Tajeddini and Trueman, 2012). Thus, it is important to research and understand hospitality industry customers' needs and expectations first, because when international hospitality *"manager understands customers' preferences, the challenge then becomes prioritizing those preferences which add the greatest value to the hotel's existing service offering"* (Martin-Rios et al., 2018, p.197).

Sources, Advantages, and Challenges of Innovation Management in International Hospitality Industry

Innovation is an essential term for business survival and sustainability in international hospitality industry. Innovation results from two main sources as being internal and external (Drucker, 1994). Internal sources are unexpected formations resulting from the internal hospitality organization and may even arise from internal conflicts occurring from the changes in the marketplace whereas external sources may be the environment, the WEB, media and social media, industry fairs, conventions, hospitality industry–related academic literature, industry trade journals, and educational events (Varis and Littunen, 2010). Some authors divide the source as managerial and non-managerial (Gyurácz-Németh et al., 2013). Regardless of the source, application of international hospitality innovations has many positive impacts on the performance and productivity of the international hotels (Gray et al., 2000).

From international independent accommodation facilities to global chain hotels, all the international establishments serving in the hospitality industry require innovation applications for long-term financial profitability and customer and brand loyalty. In addition, innovation helps them in overcoming the competition through differentiation, overcoming the obstacles in the market, and achieving sustainable marketing success in the global market (Nagy, 2012; Tajeddini and Trueman, 2012). Reduction of managerial costs, energy and labor savings, improved hotel image, better positioning, new service development, and increase in the sales and market share are the advantages of innovation in the hospitality industry. Increase in the service quality and market share, increase in customer value, to be able to find the creative and differential customer need, increase in work-place life quality, and increase in revenues are also among the benefits provided by hospitality innovation applications (Hon and Lui, 2016; Pirnar et al., 2012). Some other advantages of innovative applications provide to international hotels are better supplier relationships, less waste, better sanitation, faster service and flexibility, higher quality services, finding new markets and segments to serve, decreasing the new service development and process costs, and reducing the time period for new service development (Kaynak and Maden, 2012; Rodgers, 2007). To conclude, there are many advantages of innovative international hospitality applications (Ottenbacher, 2007) which may be grouped under different subcategories for simplification as: financial, organizational, marketing and customer related, performance, IT and technology, and organization-related benefits as Figure 24.1 indicates.

Applied research on the topic indicates that "if employees and managers are innovative and open to new ideas in meeting field customer needs they are more likely to enhance company performance in the hotel industry. This sentence highlights the need for a customer-driven approach to innovation in organizations because continuous innovation has an impact upon financial measures and is critical for long-term profitability" (Tajeddini and Trueman, 2012, p. 1127).

Innovations in the hospitality industry have drawbacks and challenges, as well. Some of these challenges are due to intangible nature of services and simultaneous consumption and production process, because measurement, comparison, and standardization is relatively harder and more complex for services when compared to manufacturing industries (Gomezelj, 2016; Orfila-Sintes and Mattsson, 2009). In addition, the lack of strategic human resources and qualified staff is another challenge because application of sophisticated technology like Internet of Things, network technology, or sustainable hospitality management involving waste management (collection of reusable items, etc.) requires sophisticated management systems and qualified staff with know-how skills (Bandyopadhyay, 2016; Martin-Rios et al., 2018). Furthermore, high failure rate of adaptation, high involvement risks, requirements for a long time involvement, adaptation and improvement costs, new service development costs, lack of resources, resistance to change, reluctance to share the know-how, reluctance to work in teams and insufficient access to essential technology

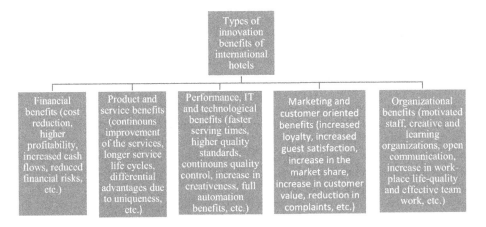

Figure 24.1 Types of innovation benefits of international hotels.

Source: Based on: Rodgers (2007); Ottenbacher (2007); Pirnar et al. (2012); Nagy (2012); Tajeddini and Trueman (2012); Hon and Lui (2016).

are some other challenges that international hotels face (Gyurácz-Németh et al., 2013; Hu et al., 2009; López-Fernández et al., 2011; Victorino et al., 2005).

Hospitality Innovation Process and Innovation Motivators

Hospitality innovation is a process starting with an idea and ending as an end result of a new or adapted service or technology to be implemented as a practice. Innovation process consists of sequential activities and procedures, where the first step is the identification of the innovation objective or the problem, followed by the search and evaluation of the best idea for optimization of the goal or opportunity. The third step of the process consists the planning of the most promising business model for innovation. Finally, development and design steps are followed by implementation and feedback (Konovalova and Jatuliavičienė, 2015).

In today's highly competitive global hospitality world, innovation is essential for profitability and sustainability, but some of the hotels operating in the industry are static and conservative. These conservative international hotels prefer to keep up with the standard procedures and processes. Unless they are severely challenged or forced to change, they prefer stability and need to be motivated for innovation (Sipe and Testa, 2009). These innovation derived motivations may be grouped under two categories as push factors and the pull factors. Push factors are related to technology and new ways of doing things and adapting procedures, whereas pull factors consist of innovations resulting from consumer demands and trends (Hjalager, 2002). It is important to remember that the hospitality industry is a service industry, where guests and hotel staff interact with each other and consumption and production is simultaneous; therefore, innovations should tend to be customer-friendly for better results (Pechlaner et al., 2006). This reality emphasized the importance of pull factors of motivation.

Innovation Types in International Hospitality Industry

Classification and grouping of hospitality innovation types are quite complex as there exists various heterogeneous innovation activities and various groupings in the literature (Konovalova and Jatuliavičienė, 2015; Nicolau and Santa-María, 2013; Sipe and Testa, 2009). It is understood that, in addition to derived motivational forces, international hospitality innovation types may be grouped under many categories. Figure 24.2 shows the most common categorization bases for innovation types. For simplification, the figure groups innovation types under four headings as: fieldwork of hospitality innovation application and the innovation areas, relation to hospitality technology, adaptation levels of innovation and the place, and scale of the hospitality innovation application.

The first distinction of the hospitality innovation takes place in the fieldwork of innovation application and the innovation areas, where subgroups consist of product or service innovations, process innovations, networking and organizational innovations, and marketing innovations.

- Product and service innovations: are related to bringing a new or improved product or service to the market (Sipe and Testa, 2009). There are many examples of product or service innovations in the international hospitality industry from totally new products like hotels fully made of ice (called Ice hotels) to sustainable eco-friendly hotels with organic restaurants and sustainable hotels operating underwater. Other related examples consist of themed hotels, fully automated hotels with none or minimum staff (Pirnar et al., 2012), and hotels using altered services with little modifications like providing a personal tablet to guests during their visiting period.
- Processes innovation: is related to generating brand new or partly improved service process ways, methods, equipment, technology, and/or software for producing and delivering the hotel services (Rajapathirana and Hui, 2018). The system-wide leadership development

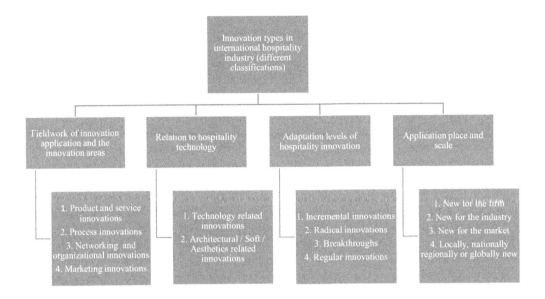

Figure 24.2 Innovation types in international hospitality industry (different classifications).
Source: Based on: Sipe and Testa (2009); Ottenbacher (2007); Stoneman (2010); Pirnar et al. (2012); Nicolau and Santa-María (2013); Konovalova and Jatuliavičienė (2015); Dzhandzhugazova et al. (2016); Rajapathirana and Hui (2018).

program of an international hotel chain or finding new suppliers resulting in better business may be an example of administrative innovation (Sipe and Testa, 2009). Benchmarking of hospitality services, total quality management applications, or faster and safer food preparation, or room cleaning methods, are some other examples of innovative process practices in the hospitality industry (Rodgers, 2007). In hospitality industry, the classical distinction between product and process innovation is more complicated because production and consumption process is simultaneous and one innovation in one field usually leads to innovation in another (De la Peña et al., 2016).

- Marketing innovations: are related to the application of improvement or changes in marketing techniques applicable and marketing related product, pricing, distribution, and promotion strategies of the hospitality firms (Stoneman, 2010). Some of the examples are appealing to new segmentation bases, marketing synergy, effective marketing communication, appealing to new markets, developing new sales markets, and integrating with new supply markets. Furthermore, implementing co-branding practices, using sensory marketing, applying brand loyalty packages, targeting niche markets, using guerrilla marketing techniques for promotion, CRM applications, customization of services as tailor-made services for guests like flexible check-in/check-out times, personalized room décor or mood lightning are also among popular hospitality marketing innovations (Dzhandzhugazova et al., 2016; Victorino et al., 2005).
- Organizational innovations: are about applying new or improved approaches to managing or organizing the working process (Dzhandzhugazova et al., 2016). In other words, they relate to finding a new way to organize the business. Better organizational methods, improved operational hospitality practices, developing organizational procedures, organizing through learning, encouraging collaboration and team work, reorganization or restructuring the hotel are some examples of international hospitality organizational innovations (Hon and Lui, 2016; Nicolau and Santa-María, 2013).

The second distinction shows hotel's technology orientation. Some of the international hospitality innovations may be technology oriented, whereas the others may be related to aesthetics, architectural and design aspects of the hotels, which are not related to technology. A hotel is made of a blend of tangible and intangible products and services, as well as positive images and unique experiences it creates; therefore, for successful innovation management, both hard technological innovations and soft aesthetics–related innovations are essential. As Buhalis and Leung confirms, *"automated hotel operations with collaborative international and external marketing strategy can co-create a holistic and coherent experience to hotel guest"* (2018, p. 44).

- Technological or hard innovations are innovations in hospitality, focusing on functional areas, R&D, and technology usage in hotels. They are usually associated with the implementation of information and communication technologies (ICT), digital applications, networking (Jacob et al., 2003) e-innovations, three-D printing, artificial intelligence (AI), in the hotel appliances and hotel facilities. Hotels optimizing big data and cloud technologies, AI, CRM and other ICT tools are called smart hotels which utilize technological hospitality innovations (Buhalis and Leung, 2018). With the help of these technological applications, smart hotels improve their operations' productivity, maximize hotel turnover and profit, develop organizational performance and co-create marketing experiences for their guests (Leung, 2019). Sensor networks, electronic room door locks, voice recognition system, online check-in and check-out systems, e-reservations, all social media marketing, video library, digital reservation books, in-room tablets and personal computers, virtual and augmented reality applications, computer modem connections, robot usage for routine housekeeping, room services and F&B services are among the popular technological hospitality innovations.
- Soft innovations are associated with aesthetic improvements that add value to offered products and services (Stoneman, 2010). They appeal to "sensual notes of hospitality like i.e., sight, hearing, smell, taste, touch, intuition and impression" (Dzhandzhugazova et al., 2016). There are two types of soft innovation. One is about the improvements and adaptations related to products and services in the creative industries, whereas the other is about the aesthetic improvements and adaptations of services which are naturally functional (Stoneman, 2010). Music, décor, color, lighting, and scent are related to some of the soft aspects of innovation applications in international hospitality industry. Many chain hotels use the same scent and similar design and color combinations in all their affiliated member hotels to provide brand identity and create brand awareness through customers' senses. The various soft innovation aspects appealing to consumer's senses create much of the dynamics and the uniqueness that make a hotel memorable, which leads to loyalty, repeat visits, and positive word of mouth advertising. Furthermore, architectural designs and related soft innovations may be a distinguishing competitive advantage for hotels in the international industry. Dogan et al. (2013, p. 703) indicate that *"innovations in architectural (exterior and interior) design are required to obtain a strategic advantage for hotels in the competition"* and *"that originality in exterior design has an influence on buying decisions of hotel customers."*
- Another non-technological type of innovation is social innovation, which is about the *"new ideas and solutions with the purpose of addressing the social and cultural challenges which the society faces"* (Dzhandzhugazova et al., 2016, p. 10391).

The third distinction for hospitality innovation classification lies in the intensity and continuity of the hospitality innovation. These are stated as incremental innovations, radical innovations, breakthrough innovations, and regular innovations which are briefly described below.

- Incremental innovations involve additional improvements to already existing characteristics of the hotel service. They may be through modification, simplification, or refinement adaptations of present methods or current technology. Incremental innovations are less costly and have more predictable results than radical innovations (Martínez-Ros and Orfila-Sintes, 2009). Using yield management systems requiring integrated information systems for room pricing is an example for incremental hospitality innovation.
- Radical innovations involve adoptions of new attributes or developments of totally new services for a new target market (Pechlaner et al., 2006). The implications of radical innovations are more costly, riskier, and more unpredictable when compared with incremental innovations.
- Breakthroughs are also called as disruptive innovations as they are about inventing totally new services or methods. They are very rare and significantly unique as they come as a surprise to the industry. Their outcomes are usually unpredictable, and their impacts on the industry are tremendous.
- Regular innovations *"conserve existing collaborative structures and competences but the impact over time can be radical"* (Pechlaner et al., 2006, p. 35). Promoting new investments that raise productivity may lead to such innovations.

Forth distinction takes place at the place or scale dissemination of the innovation. Hence, the innovation may be new for the hotel, new for the hospitality industry, new for the whole market or new as a scale of distribution area as locally, nationally, regionally, or globally. The globally new innovation may be characterized as a totally unique invention which may start up a global hospitality trend within the industry.

Levels of Hospitality Innovations

Regardless of the type of innovation, there is another distinguishing innovation characteristic related to innovation adaptation level of an international hotel. It is called the degree of innovativeness indicating the hospitality firms' orientation towards innovative applications and the level of innovation's complexity (Sipe and Testa, 2009). The related model called, "The Seven Levels of Change Model was developed by Rolf Smith, a retired Air Force colonel and founder of the first Air Force Innovation." The model takes into consideration the difficulty level of the innovations where Level 1 stands for the easiest and simplest innovation, where it gets more complex and difficult with each next step, as Level 7 being the last step indicates the most complex almost impossible innovation achievement. The contents indicating the complexity levels of Smith's Change Model are as follows (Sipe and Testa, 2009):

- Level 1 innovativeness stands for effectiveness. This step is the easiest, the simplest, and is about doing the right things. The associated risk and cost is relatively low. Offering free wi-fi to guests, having tea-coffee appliances, voice-mail and wake-up call systems in rooms, and using standardized complaint and suggestions forms for guest feedbacks are some examples of Level 1 innovations.
- Level 2 innovations involve efficiency. This step is a little more complex than Level 1 innovations and is related to doing the right things right. Not only offering a free wi-fi to guests but providing fast and secure free wi-fi to consumers is a type of Level 2 innovations. These type of innovations are a bit harder than Level 1 ones but they are much better for hotels as they are related to productivity, thus impact the profitability and created value much more.
- Level 3 innovations consist of improving the hotel services. They are related to doing things better. Sustainability and quality training of hotel staff are Level 3 innovations.

- Level 4 innovations are related to cutting. The procedure is about doing away with things. Getting rid of unnecessary hotel procedures; making processes leaner, shorter, and faster; reducing the waste are some examples of Level 4 hotel innovations.
- Level 5 innovations involve the implementation and adaptation of the hospitality changes and improvements. They consist of doing things other people are doing. The imitation of best hotel cases, benchmarking applications are Level 5 type of hotel innovations and they help hotels to keep up with the trends in the hospitality industry.
- Level 6 innovations relate to being unique and different. They constitute doing things no one else is doing. Launching a totally new service to the market or opening up the first global underwater hotel in the world are examples for Level 6 innovations. This step requires inventions and very high levels of creativity. Level 6 innovations makeup and shape the international hospitality industry trends instead of following them. Level 6 innovations are the most expensive and risky investments but when successful, also the most profitable and sound ones.
- Level 7 innovations are almost impossible to achieve at the present time. They are related to doing things that can't be done. Level 7 is the hardest step which is about doing the impossible for today, like launching a space hotel.

Success Factors and Characteristics That Leads International Hotels to Innovation

The innovation success, level of innovation application degree, and the types of applied innovations depend not only on the type and size of the hotel establishment but also on the country and culture the hotel operates within. In this regard, it is found that international hotels are more successful in implementing innovations due to their global network connections, global connectivity, human resources capacity in terms of having qualified staff, superior knowledge, co-production knowledge capacity and tendency to use of high technology and know-how (Williams and Shaw, 2011). Some of the major factors affecting the success of hospitality innovations are stated below:

- Customer and guest involvement: The involvement of customers in the innovation process is important for the development of ground-breaking services and products because very often customers make substantial contributions through the articulation of their ideas, wishes, and needs (Pechlaner et al., 2006).
- Internal marketing: In addition to customer involvement, employee involvement also has a high share in the success of international hospitality applications. It is found that "*hospitality innovation projects that are supported by strategic human resource management (SHRM) approach achieve higher financial results*" (Ottenbacher, 2007, p. 441). Internal marketing, employee understanding, motivation, and commitment issues should be supported by management if new hospitality innovations are going to result in better staff and customer relationships (Hon and Lui, 2016).
- Strategic human resources management is vital for positive outcomes (Ottenbacher and Gnoth, 2005)

To run a formal well-planned process and to be successful in hospitality innovation, leadership style and know-how need to be the focus. The successful process is created from a clean, well-communicated strategy and vision, by managers who support the project strongly.

(Gyurácz-Németh et al., 2013, p. 647)

- The capacity of the hotel's innovativeness: Some hotels have an organizational tendency for innovativeness; their organizational structure with qualified staff is more open to engaging innovations and changes. As they implement innovations, they gain strategic advantages accordingly (Kessler et al., 2015). The higher the hotels' innovativeness capacity, the higher is the hotels' success possibility.

- Quality management: As hospitality services are highly heterogeneous and hard to standardize, it is important to have a proper quality positioning and provide tangible quality cues to guests (Ottenbacher and Gnoth, 2005) with the help of service, technologic and soft innovations.
- Glocalization: Global operations focusing on local culture and tastes are found to be quite successful in their innovation implementations because glocalization of the hospitality processes and services seems to reduce the *"tension which exists between standardization and localization"* (Williams and Shaw, 2011, p. 34). Culture innovation in hotels *"combines local culture to enhance innovation value"* (Horng et al., 2017, p. 45).
- Size of the hotel and affiliation/membership relation: *"innovation capacity is positively influenced by firm size, small firms' managerial systems are not adequate to support innovations and employees in small firms have low competencies"* (Gomezelj, 2016, p. 540). Large hotels with affiliations and members of franchises or management contracts have a better chance of succeeding innovations. The affiliation availability of resources encourages hotel's innovation investment. Also, affiliations like being a chain member or a franchisee help distribution of the innovation risks, as well as supplying co-branding, know-how, and other technical benefits (López-Fernández et al., 2011).
- Institutional leadership, openness to organizational changes, and organizational strength are also important factors for successful hospitality innovation applications.
- Seasonality is also an important issue for successful international hospitality innovations. Research indicates that all year open hotels' staff is more creative and more innovative when compared to seasonal hotels' employees (Erdem et al., 2011).
- Information technology communication (ICT): *"ICT development is important for innovation and the use of information communication technology contributes to efficiency, productivity and improvements in innovation processes"* (Gomezelj, 2016, p. 543).
- The technical and digital capacity of a hotel to implement innovation and the ability to access the technological resources are vital aspects for success.
- Qualified staff and training of employees: For innovational success, employing qualified staff with multiple skills and continuous employee training on multiple skills is important (Gomezelj, 2016; Ottenbacher and Gnoth, 2005).
- Appealing to customers' senses: Experience, cultural, local, unique, and sustainable elements in innovation are important in influencing the hotel's attractiveness for the consumer.
- Emphasizing sustainable green innovations through energy-water conservation and waste reduction: Green innovations are related to *"green practices which are a value-added utility for hospitality operations, and they provide benefits to hospitality businesses in the operational domains of finance and marketing, as well as to the environment"* (Kim et al., 2017, p. 235). Green innovations, like installation of occupancy sensors to turn on or turn off lights in unused areas or installation of rooftop solar water heating systems (Prakash and Shashidhar, 2016), decrease the negative environmental impacts of the hotels resulting in a cost reduction in a short time period (del Rosario and René, 2017). Providing the necessary environmental training for all employees is also important.
- Using measurement criteria to evaluate the service innovation's success (Akbaba, 2006): R&D expenses, new service development expenses, committed financial or human resources are some common examples of innovation input metrics. The number of new services launched, the financial returns, incremental gains in profits, indirect outcomes, positive increases in customer satisfaction, and number of repeat customers as a measure for loyalty are other examples of innovation output metrics.

- Implementing a mix of appropriate innovation types: All types of innovations are important for hotels for competitive advantage (De la Peña et al., 2016), and utilizing the proper mix of soft and hard technological and different types of product, process, marketing and organizational innovations are vital for satisfactory outcomes.

Trends in the Innovations of International Hospitality Industry

Some of the popular and increasing spheres and implementation areas of innovations in the international hospitality industry are as follows:

- Using integrated information systems and advanced analytics to provide simulation, prediction, and optimization in hospitality managerial issues
- Sustainable, eco-friendly, and green certification like ISO 14001 (Tavmergen and Meric, 1999) or LEED (Kim et al., 2017), for responsible and eco-conscious guests' recognition, because usually although not majority yet, green customers are willing to spend more if the hotel is a green one and they are more satisfied (Dimara et al., 2015)
- Sustainability as a means for cultural innovation and corporate social responsibility (Horng et al., 2017)
- Green innovations and green practices such as water and energy reduction programs and waste reduction systems (Kim et al., 2017)
- Recycling and renewable energy optimization for sustainability (Prakash and Shashidhar, 2016)
- Using organic food and organic material in the hospitality services
- Active involvement in social media and mobile marketing
- Smart hotels and tech-savvy rooms with in-room iPads and Wi-Fi access (Salazar, 2018)
- Customization of hotel services, tailor-made plans and programs for guests for maximum satisfaction
- Rising concerns for personal data protection and security (Salazar, 2018)
- Dynamic marketing packaging (adaptable packages instead of standard packages)
- Following online global hospitality review, evaluation, and rating platforms and WEB sites
- Sharing economy leading to sharing competence and knowledge, and the ability to combine different perspectives and approaches. Increasingly often, innovations are created on the interfaces of various competence areas (Tou et al., 2018)
- Technology enhancements for a guest experience through virtual and augmented reality, digital-smart – AI and cloud computing – applications (Buhalis and Leung, 2018)
- E-innovation applications and using Internet provided electronic services like online promotions, online reservations, online check-in and check-outs, real-time messaging apps, automation in front-office, rooms, and F&B services (Salazar, 2018).

Conclusion and Recommendations

International hospitality innovation is a process of new or altered products, services, ideas, behaviors, organization, and managerial or operational processes for better and more valuable outcomes as cost reduction, better organizations, new markets, added value, improved benefits, effective marketing, efficient management, and better performance through focusing on creativity, differentiation, and uniqueness. Innovation is essential for sustainable profitability and competitive differential advantage for all the international hospitality firms regardless of the size.

The innovation areas or types for international hotels are quite complex and it is hard to find a common classification scheme for international hospitality innovation types. Although this is the case, taking into consideration the most common categorization bases for innovation types in literature, it is logical to group them under four headings as: fieldwork of hospitality innovation application and the innovation areas, relation to hospitality technology, adaptation levels of innovation and the place, and scale of the hospitality innovation application.

There are many different areas of innovations in the international hotel industry. Most popular ones are about green and sustainable innovation applications focusing on energy / water saving and waste reduction, strategic human resources management, employee and guest involvement in innovations, soft innovations including design, artistic, intellectual, and aesthetic aspects of hotels, technological and digital improvements, marketing operations for higher guest satisfaction, brand loyalty, and organizational improvements. Although there are various types of hospitality innovations, it is important to implement the optimal and suitable blend for better services, sustainable operations, increased efficiency, better performance, and higher profits.

References

Akbaba, A. (2006), "Measuring service quality in the hotel industry: A study in a business hotel in Turkey", *International Journal of Hospitality Management*, Vol.25, No.2, pp.170–192, doi:10.1016/j.ijhm.2005.08.006.

Bandyopadhyay, R. (2016), "Challenges to implement innovative ideas and practices: A case of ITC Welcome Group's Fortune Park Centre Point Jamshedpur (India)", *Worldwide Hospitality and Tourism Themes*, Vol.8, No.4, pp.490–495, doi:10.1108/WHATT-04–2016–0017.

Buhalis, D. and Leung, R. (2018), "Smart hospitality—Interconnectivity and interoperability towards an ecosystem", *International Journal of Hospitality Management*, Vol.71, pp.41–50, doi:0.1016/j.ijhm.2017.11.011.

Carvalho, L. and Costa, T. (2011), "Tourism innovation–A literature review complemented by case study research", *Tourism & Management Studies, International Conference on Tourism & Management Studies Book of Proceedings*, Algarve, Vol.I, pp.23–33.

De la Peña, M.R, Núñez-Serrano, J.A, Turrión, J., and Velázquez, F.J. (2016), "Are innovations relevant for consumers in the hospitality industry? A hedonic approach for Cuban hotels", *Tourism Management*, Vol.55, pp.184–196, doi:10.1016/j.tourman.2016.02.009.

Del Rosario, R.S.M. and René, D.P. (2017), "Eco-innovation and organizational culture in the hotel industry", *International Journal of Hospitality Management*, Vol.65, pp.71–80, doi:10.1016/j.ijhm.2017.06.001.

Dimara, E., Manganari, E., and Skuras, D. (2015), "Consumers willingness to pay premium for green hotels: Fact or Fad?", *Proceedings of International Marketing Trends Conference*, 14th IMTC, 22–24 January 2015, Paris, pp.1–16.

Dogan, H., Nebioglu, O., Aydın, O., and Dogan, I. (2013), "Architectural innovations are competitive advantage for hotels in tourism industry?: What customers, managers and employees think about it?", *Procedia-Social and Behavioral Sciences*, Vol.99, pp.701–710, doi:10.1016/j.sbspro.2013.10.541.

Drucker, P.F. (1994), *Innovation and Entrepreneurship*, Elsevier Publishers, New York, NY.

Drucker, P.F. (1998), "The discipline of innovation", *Leader to Leader*, Vol.9, pp.13–15, doi:10.1002/ltl.40619980906.

Dzhandzhugazova, E.A., Blinova, E.A., Orlova, L.N., and Romanova, M.M. (2016), "Innovations in hospitality industry", *International Journal of Environmental and Science Education*, Vol.11 No.17, pp.10387–10400, ISSN: EISSN-1306–3065.

English, F.W. and Ehrich, L.C. (2015), "Innovatus interregnum: waiting for a paradigm shift", *International Journal of Educational Management*, Vol.29, No.7, pp.851–862, doi:10.1108/IJEM-05–2015–0055.

Erdem, B., Gokdeniz, A., and Met, O. (2011), "Yenilikcilik ve isletme performansı iliskisi: Antalya"da etkinlik gösteren 5 yıldızlı otel isletmeleri ornegi", *Dokuz Eylul Universitesi Iktisadi ve Idari Bilimler Fakultesi Dergisi*, Vol.26, No.2, pp.77–112.

García-Villaverde, P.M., Elche, D., Martínez-Pérez, Á., and Ruiz-Ortega, M.J. (2017), "Determinants of radical innovation in clustered firms of the hospitality and tourism industry", *International Journal of Hospitality Management,* Vol.61, pp.45–58, doi:10.1016/j.ijhm.2016.11.002.

Gomezelj, D.O. (2016), "A systematic review of research on innovation in hospitality and tourism", *International Journal of Contemporary Hospitality Management*, Vol.28, No.3, pp.516–558, doi:10.1108/IJCHM-10–2014–0510.

Gray, B.J., Matear, S.M., and Matheson, P.K. (2000), "Improving the performance of hospitality firms", *International Journal of Contemporary Hospitality Management*, Vol.12, No.3, pp.149–155, doi:10.1108/09596110010320643.

Gyurácz-Németh, P., Friedrich, N., and Clarke, A. (2013), "Innovation in special hotels–as a key to success", *Proceedings of the Management, Knowledge and Learning International Conference 2013*, 19–21 June, Zadar, Coratia, pp.643–653.

Hjalager, A.M. (1997), "Innovation patterns in sustainable tourism: An analytical typology", *Tourism Management*, Vol.18, No.1, pp.35–41, doi:10.1016/S0261–5177(96)00096-9.

Hjalager, A.M. (2002), "Repairing innovation defectiveness in tourism", *Tourism Management*, Vol.23, No.5, pp.465–474, doi:10.1016/S0261–5177(02)00013-4.

Hon, A.H. and Lui, S.S. (2016), "Employee creativity and innovation in organizations: Review, integration, and future directions for hospitality research", *International Journal of Contemporary Hospitality Management*, Vol.28, No.5, pp.862–885, doi:10.1108/IJCHM-09–2014–0454.

Horng, J.S., Liu, C.H., Chou, S.F., Tsai, C.Y., and Chung, Y.C. (2017), "From innovation to sustainability: Sustainability innovations of eco-friendly hotels in Taiwan", *International Journal of Hospitality Management*, Vol.63, pp.44–52, doi:10.1016/j.ijhm.2017.02.005.

Hu, M.L.M., Horng, J.S., and Sun, Y.H.C. (2009), "Hospitality teams: Knowledge sharing and service innovation performance", *Tourism Management*, Vol.30, No.1, pp.41–50, doi:10.1016/j.tourman.2008.04.009.

Jacob, M., Tintoré, J., Aguiló, E., Bravo, A., and Mulet, J. (2003), "Innovation in the tourism sector: results from a pilot study in the Balearic Islands", *Tourism Economics*, Vol.9, No.3, pp.279–229, doi:10.1177/135481660300900303.

Kaynak, R. and Maden, M.O. (2012), "Expansion of boundaries on innovation: Open innovation", *The International Journal of Economic and Social Research*, Vol.8, No.1, pp.31–47, ISSN:1306–2174.

Kessler, A., Pachucki, C., Stummer, K., Mair, M., and Binder, P. (2015), "Types of organizational innovativeness and success in Austrian hotels", *International Journal of Contemporary Hospitality Management*, Vol.27, No.7, pp.1707–1727, doi:10.1108/IJCHM-03–2014–0150.

Kim, S.H., Lee, K., and Fairhurst, A. (2017), "The review of "green" research in hospitality, 2000–2014: Current trends and future research directions", *International Journal of Contemporary Hospitality Management*, Vol.29, No.1, pp.226–247, doi:10.1108/ijchm-11–2014–0562.

Konovalova, T. and Jatuliavičienė, G. (2015), "Innovation development perspectives in a hotel industry by example of Radisson hotel chain in Ukraine", *Regional Formation and Development Studies*, Vol.15, No.1, pp.73–85, doi:10.15181/rfds.v15i1.981.

Leung, R. (2019), "Smart hospitality: Taiwan hotel stakeholder perspectives", *Tourism Review*, Vol.74, No.1, pp.50–62, doi:10.1108/TR-09–2017–0149.

López-Fernández, M.C., Serrano-Bedia, A.M., and Gómez-López, R. (2011), "Factors encouraging innovation in Spanish hospitality firms", *Cornell Hospitality Quarterly*, Vol.52, No.2, pp.144–152, doi:10.1177/1938965510393723.

Martínez-Ros, E. and Orfila-Sintes, F. (2009), "Innovation activity in the hotel industry", *Technovation*, Vol.29, No.9, pp.632–641, doi:10.1016/j.technovation.2009.02.004.

Martin-Rios, C. and Ciobanu, T. (2019), "Hospitality innovation strategies: An analysis of success factors and challenges", *Tourism Management*, Vol.70, pp.218–229, doi:10.1016/j.tourman.2018.08.018.

Martin-Rios, C., Demen-Meier, C., Gössling, S., and Cornuz, C. (2018), "Food waste management innovations in the foodservice industry", *Waste Management*, Vol.79, pp.196–206, doi:10.1016/j.wasman.2018.07.033.

Nagy, A. (2012), "A Review of Tourism and Hospitality Innovation Research", *Annals of the University of Oradea, Economic Science Series*, Vol.21, No.2, pp.364–370.

Nicolau, J.L. and Santa-María, M.J. (2013), "The effect of innovation on hotel market value", *International Journal of Hospitality Management*, Vol.32, pp.71–79, doi:10.1016/j.ijhm.2012.04.005.

Nieves, J., Quintana, A., and Osorio, J. (2014), "Knowledge-based resources and innovation in the hotel industry", *International Journal of Hospitality Management*, Vol.38, pp.65–73, doi:10.1016/j.ijhm.2014.01.001.

Orfila-Sintes, F. and Mattsson, J. (2009), "Innovation behavior in the hotel industry", *Omega*, Vol.37, No.2, pp.380–394, doi:10.1016/j.omega.2007.04.002.

Ottenbacher, M. and Gnoth, J. (2005), "How to develop successful hospitality innovation", *Cornell Hotel and Restaurant Administration Quarterly*, Vol.46, No.2, pp.205–222, doi:10.1177/0010880404271097.

Ottenbacher, M.C. (2007), "Innovation management in the hospitality industry: Different strategies for achieving success", *Journal of Hospitality & Tourism Research*, Vol.31, No.4, pp.431–454, doi:10.1177/1096348007302352.

Pechlaner, H., Fischer, E., and Hammann, E.M. (2006), "Leadership and innovation processes—development of products and services based on core competencies", *Journal of Quality Assurance in Hospitality & Tourism*, Vol.6, No.3–4, pp. 31–57, doi:10.1300/J162v06n03_03.

Peters, M. and Pikkemaat B. 2006, "Innovation in Tourism", *Journal of Quality Assurance in Hospitality & Tourism*, Vol.6, pp. 3–4. doi:10.1300/J162v06n03_01.

Pirnar, I., Bulut, C., and Eris, E.D. (2012), "Improving the performance and competitiveness of tourism establishments by means of innovation: Trends and applications", *Proceedings of IRAT Enlightening Tourism "Conference*, Naples, Italy, Vol.1, No.1, pp.133–143.

Prakash, M. and Shashidhar, C. (2016), "Innovations in green practices in hospitality sector", *ISBR Management Journal*, Vol.1, No.2, pp.29–52, ISSN:2249-2496.

Presenza, A., Petruzzelli, A.M., and Sheehan, L. (2019), "Innovation trough tradition in hospitality. The Italian case of Albergo Diffuso", *Tourism Management*, Vol.72, pp.192–201, doi:10.1016/j.tourman.2018.11.020.

Rajapathirana, R.J. and Hui, Y. (2018), "Relationship between innovation capability, innovation type, and firm performance", *Journal of Innovation and Knowledge*, Vol.3, No.1, pp.44–55, doi:10.1016/j.jik.2017.06.002.

Rodgers, S. (2007), "Innovation in food service technology and its strategic role", *International Journal of Hospitality Management*, Vol.26, No.4, pp.899–912, doi:10.1016/j.ijhm.2006.10.001.

Salazar, A. (2018), "Hospitality trends: Opportunities and challenges", *Worldwide Hospitality and Tourism Themes*, Vol.10, No.6, pp.674–679, doi: 10.1108/WHATT-07–2018–0047.

Schumpeter, J.A. (1935), "The analysis of economic change", *The Review of Economics and Statistics*, Vol.17, No.4, pp.2–10, doi: 10.2307/1927845.

Schumpeter, J.A. (2000), "Entrepreneurship as innovation", *Entrepreneurship: The Social Science View*, pp.51–75, available at: SSRN: https://ssrn.com/ (accessed 05 January 2019).

Sipe, L.J. and Testa M. (2009), "What is innovation in the hospitality and tourism marketplace? A suggested research framework and outputs typology", *International CHRIE Conference-Refereed Track*, available at: https://scholarworks.umass.edu/cgi (accessed 15 January 2019).

Stoneman, P. (2010), *Soft Innovation: Economics, Product Aesthetics, and the Creative Industries*, Oxford University Press, Oxford, UK.

Tajeddini, K. and Trueman, M. (2012), "Managing Swiss hospitality: How cultural antecedents of innovation and customer-oriented value systems can influence performance in the hotel industry", *International Journal of Hospitality Management*, Vol.31, No.4, pp.1119–1129, doi:10.1016/j.ijhm.2012.01.009.

Tavmergen, I.P and Meric, P.O. (1999), "Cevre korumasina yonelik turizm uygulamalari: yesil otelcilik, doga turizmi ve ISO 14000", *Turizmde Secme Makaleler*, TUGEV, Istanbul, Vol.33, pp.19–38.

Tou, Y., Moriya, K., Watanabe, C., Ilmola, L., and Neittaanmäki, P. (2018), "Soft innovation resources: enabler for reversal in GDP growth in the digital economy", *International Journal of Managing Information Technology*, Vol.10, No.3, pp.9–27, doi:10.5121/ijmit.2018.10302.

Turker, M.V. (2012), "A model proposal oriented to measure technological innovation capabilities of business firms–a research on automotive industry", *Procedia-Social and Behavioral Sciences*, Vol.41, pp.147–159, doi:10.1016/j.sbspro.2012.04.019.

Varis, M. and Littunen, H. (2010), "Types of innovation, sources of information and performance in entrepreneurial SMEs", *European Journal of Innovation Management*, Vol.13, No.2, pp.128–154, doi:10.1108/14601061011040221.

Victorino, L., Verma, R., Plaschka, G. and Dev, C. (2005), "Service innovation and customer choices in the hospitality industry", *Managing Service Quality: An International Journal*, Vol.15, No.6, pp.555–576, doi:10.1108/09604520510634023.

Williams, A.M. and Shaw, G. (2011), "Internationalization and innovation in tourism", *Annals of Tourism Research*, Vol.38, No.1, pp.27–51, doi:10.1016/j.annals.2010.09.006.

25

SUCCESS FACTORS OF SME HOTEL MANAGEMENT COMPANIES IN CHINA

A Revisit

Arthur S.R. Wang

Introduction

By the year 2020, China will be the world's number-one tourist destination, with annual arrivals exceeding 140 million visitors and 5.5 billion domestic trips (DiscoverChina.com, 2019). China's increasingly affluent population will travel even more within the country, based on eased governmental policies regarding the number of working days and annual holidays, thereby adding to the country's massive leisure-tourism movement (Pine and Qi, 2004). This is fueling the need for new hotels (Cai et al., 2000). Moreover, China's dynamic economic growth over the past three decades has attracted international business and investment interests in accommodation properties. Pine (2002) indicated that China's stock of hotels will need to expand and upgrade significantly in order to serve its potentially massive market in line with the expected growth of international and domestic leisure and business arrivals. This includes an upgrade of service standards to international levels (Yu and Gu, 2005). Lew et al. (2003) expected intensified competition from international developers and operators, thus posing significant challenges for domestic hotel operations in China. According to Aliouche and Schlentrich (2011) and Gu and colleagues (2012), many of China's domestically owned hotels perform far behind internationally managed properties. There are several reasons for this, for example, management inefficiencies, inadequate corporate governance, or inferior service quality. Those shortcomings provide international corporate giants as well as small-to-medium-sized hotel management companies unprecedented opportunities to capture a substantial share of the hotel management market, as long as hotel management companies are equipped with international expertise and experience as a need for performance upgrade already exists. Furthermore, the hospitality industry in China is a diverse composite of ownership patterns, varying management structures, and varieties of services offered (Timothy and Teye, 2009). However, in today's business scene, it is becoming imperative for every player in the hotel industry to work strategically toward achieving and maintaining differential positioning based on professional standards in all aspects, while "me-too" players will suffer from diminishing returns.

The above-noted facts lead to the question of how small-to-medium-sized hotel management companies and/or individual hotels can successfully increase market share in China and sustain their position in this extremely competitive market.

A Look through the Theoretical Lens: Success Factors from Literature

Literature in the triangle of hospitality, entrepreneurship, and strategic management has been reviewed to gain a general overview of what has been done in the past regarding success factors for small- and medium-sized enterprises (SMEs). Based on an adaption of Wong's work (2005), segmentation regarding factors and elements that lead to business success is displayed in Table 25.1. As

Table 25.1 Previous research topics and thematic clusters

Success/Sustainability factor	Author (Year)
Management and leadership support Characteristics of leadership, the owner(s), the executives and/or the management; entrepreneurs' orientation	Huang et al. (2011), Clarkin and Swavely (2006), Kazem and van der Heijden (2006)
Culture Corporate culture, empowerment culture, cross-cultural/ intercultural management	Huang et al. (2011), Cunill and Forteza (2010), Okoroafo et al. (2010), Aliouche and Schlentrich (2009), Sheth and Sisodia (2005), Aung (2000)
Performance criteria and measurement Business scope, scale and scope effects, size of firm, business tenure, service standards, service quality, profitability, sales, revenue, ROI, quick payback, financial health, net worth, financial performance, CSR	Avcikurt et al. (2011), Harvie (2010), Okoroafo et al. (2010), Cunill and Forteza (2010), Ihua (2009), Mak (2008), Xiao et al. (2008), Cohen and Winn (2007), Tang et al. (2007), Ruzzier and Konecnik (2006), Kilic and Okumus (2005), Wong (2005), Yu and Gu (2005)
Strategic management and purpose Localization, international experience, customization, company strategy, planning, source of competitive advantage, firm reputation, reliability, product quality, innovation and creativity, location/proximity and market/ niche, segment, market orientation, ownership, control and integration, own property, business background, stakeholder orientation, communication, value propositions, business model, family business, risk taking, branding	Huang et al. (2011), Cunill and Forteza (2010), Harvie (2010), Okoroafo et al. (2010), Aliouche and Schlentrich (2011), Gunaratne (2009), Lv and Zhao (2009), Xiao et al. (2008), Abrahamsson (2007), Liu (2007), Tang et al. (2007), Cohen and Winn (2007), Altinay (2006), Ruzzier and Konecnik (2006), Ruzzier et al. (2006), Sheth and Sisodia (2005), Vachani (2005), Wong (2005), Zhang et al. (2005), Pine and Qi (2004), Cai et al. (2000), Connell (1999)
Organization and structure Organization, project management, portfolio, corporate governance, transparency, franchising capability, barriers and fencing, purchasing power, hotel management capability, resources, experience, core competencies, CRS, (de)centralization of decision-making, market control, brand protection, business ethics, crisis management, supply-chain handling, pre-opening expertise, decision support system, flexibility, business intelligence, strategic thinking, network building, supply chain management, accounting, policies and procedures, taxation, exchange-rate management, revenue management, inventory control, capital management, government regulations and legal affairs	Avcikurt et al. (2011), Huang et al. (2011), Cunill and Forteza (2010), Okoroafo et al. (2010), Harvie (2010), Aliouche and Schlentrich (2011), Gunaratne (2009), Ihua (2009), Lv and Zhao (2009), Xiao et al. (2008), Green and Malik (2007), Liu (2007), Whitla et al. (2007), Harrington and Kendal (2006), Carter et al. (2005), Selmer (2005), Sheth and Sisodia (2005), Yu and Gu (2005), Pine and Qi (2004), Harrison (2003), Peng (2003), Zhang (2003), Littrell (2002), Oboh (2002), Peng and Shenkar (2002), Epstein and Wisner (2001), Nath and Raheja (2001), Aung (2000), Cai et al. (2000), Pine et al. (2000), Rangone (1999), Ekeledo and Sivakumar (1998)

Success/Sustainability factor	Author (Year)
Processes and activities Business tradition and environment, operational management, operation efficiency, operational discipline, maintenance system, booking service, build cost advantage, marketing skill and expertise, access to distribution channel, knowing and meeting customer needs/trends, knowing potential market, corporate communication, advertising, media/public relation support	Avcikurt et al. (2011), Cunill and Forteza (2010), Okoroafo et al. (2010), Aliouche and Schlentrich (2011), Ihua (2009), Gunaratne (2009), Mak (2008), Baloglu and Pekcan (2006), Kazem and van der Heijden (2006), Sheth and Sisodia (2005), Vachani (2005), Wong (2005), Yu and Gu (2005), Bell et al. (2004), Brotherton (2004a, 2004b), Brinders et al. (2003), Peng (2003), Suarez-Ortega (2003), Tracey and Clark (2003), Buhalis and Main (1998)
Information and communication technology Technology adoption, technological innovation, technological advantages	Cohen and Winn (2007), Liu (2007), Ruzzier et al. (2006), Sheth and Sisodia (2005), Pine and Qi (2004)
Talent acquisition and management HRM, language, education, age, build skilled workforce, HR pool, internal HR, employee retention, emotional bond with employees, employee attitude, psychological profiles, industry tenure, employee satisfaction, creative and positive thinking, training and development activities	Avcikurt et al. (2011), Lv and Zhao (2009), Aliouche and Schlentrich (2011) Harvie (2010), Gunaratne (2009), Presley et al. (2007), Ruzzier and Konecnik (2006), Aung (2000), Selmer (2004), Hambrick and Mason (1984), Xiao et al. (2003), Clarkin and Swavely (2006), Xiao et al. (2008), Abrahamsson (2007), Yusof and Aspinwall (1999), Liu (2007), Chau and Pederson (2000), Liu (2007), Huang et al. (2011)
Resources Hardware, business network, affiliation with entrepreneurs, network, informal business contacts, friendship/*guanxi*, strategic alliance and partnership, alliance/chain affiliation, friends and family, angels/private investors, venture capitalists, internal and external finance resources, government relations and policy support	Huang et al. (2011), Cunill and Forteza (2010), Harvie (2010), Okoroafo et al. (2010), Ihua (2009), Gandolfi and Bekker (2008), Liu (2007), Tang et al. (2007), Ruzzier and Konecnik (2006), Dickson et al. (2006), Grangsjo and Gummesson (2005), Yu and Gu (2005), Wong (2005), Peters and Buhalis (2004), Brinders et al. (2003), Chathoth and Olsen (2003), Ritter et al. (2003), Bamforth and Brookers (2002), Holsapple and Joshi (2000), Sivadas and Dwyer (2000)

shown, the cluster of success factors retrieved from the literature includes management and leadership support, culture, performance criteria and measurement, strategic management and purpose, organization and structure, process and activities, information and communication technology, talent acquisition and management, as well as resources. Table 25.1 delineates the substructure of those success factors in detail.

A Snapshot of China's Hotel Industry

China has the second-largest hotel-development pipeline in the world after the United States, according to industry sources reported in CBRE Research Asia's April 2009 issue. Hotel operators, particularly international hotel chains, have been active in getting involved in these hotel developments, while new domestic players have been aggressively building up their hotel networks. The rapid expansion of international hotel chains and the entry of new players, coupled with the global economic downturn, have made the market more competitive (CBRE Research Asia, 2009). But based on a long-term outlook of the hotel industry, hotel operators in China have increasingly new opportunities in a more sophisticated marketplace. Here, domestic and international operators are effectively in business side-by-side in a country where there is still much opportunity for the hotel industry to grow and mature.

Related to the lifestyle changes in Mainland China and the rapid development of the real estate sector over the last 20 years, China's demand drivers for the hotel market have altered significantly. As China's economy enjoyed successive years of strong, positive growth and people had more disposable income after purchasing necessary goods and services, Chinese citizens accumulated greater wealth, allowing them to adopt lifestyles that included luxury and leisure spending. This leisure economy evolved as the growing Chinese middle class took full advantage of the previously mentioned government-sanctioned national holidays. At the same time, improvements in transport infrastructure including airports, railways, and highways increased the population's mobility. These three factors – greater wealth, increased leisure time, and improved transport networks – came together to nurture the expansion of the nation's mushrooming tourism industry as well as its hotel industry (CBRE Research Asia, 2009).

From the entry of the first privately run hotel in the 1980s, when the market was dominated by state-owned operators, to the real estate boom leading to the completion of a large number of hotels serving different markets, China's market-oriented hotel industry has had a relatively short development history of about 30 years (Cai et al., 2000). Although its rapid growth in the past few years has raised concerns about oversupply, the industry is still considered less mature than its counterparts in established global cities in terms of market penetration and sophistication of products and services. Cai et al. (2000) elaborated that a period of consolidated growth is expected but with sound fundamentals. From this basis, the market will continue to grow and shift with changes in the industry based on demand patterns. Since the early 1990s, China has experienced a real estate boom with mixed-use development as a model used in abundance. The hotel element is seen as being at the heart of the mixed-use model, creating a premium identity for the whole project. High-end hotels operated by well-known international brands can be found in most major Chinese cities. Domestic players dominate the fragmented mid-range hotel market and economy/budget sector. Fundamentally, each sector has its niche market.

Increasingly, international players identify expansion into the Chinese market as a key strategy for their growth and value creation (Aliouche and Schlentrich, 2011). However, this increased market opportunity does not come without risk. Foreign markets are, in general, much riskier than the home market, with a larger possibility of loss and failure (Han and Diekmann, 2001). The spectacular growth in the number of hotels in China over the past few years has inevitably led to concerns about the risk of oversupply, especially in first-tier cities like Shanghai and Beijing. However, the consensus is that the overall fundamentals remain sound, that any oversupply situation would be short-term, and that the markets would be able to absorb new properties and stabilize. Indeed, most operators have continued expansion plans in China and maintained their roll-out of new hotels (Aliouche and Schlentrich, 2011). Nowadays, market entry is anticipated to become increasingly difficult as the industry matures and becomes more competitive. Finding a well-located project to manage would become tougher, although, with the myriad of brands at their disposal, there is a certain amount of flexibility when choosing sites. International and domestic hotel operators have remained aggressive in developing their businesses using different branding, especially in the mid-tier market, which was viewed as less affected by the rapidly shrinking number of foreign travelers. However, large international players still hold a competitive advantage in brand recognition over local players as customers might prefer international-branded, lower-cost alternatives to 5-star hotels rather than paying more for an upscale domestic brand. Local players aiming to raise their competitiveness would have to implement more-comprehensive branding strategies. In addition, the competition was set to move beyond the traditional first- or second-tier cities and major tourist destinations to lower-tier cities in order to tap domestic demand. Xiao et al. (2008) indicated that multinational franchisors are actively seeking growth in the expanding Chinese market and have launched businesses in dramatic numbers month by month.

What Are Small-to-Medium-Sized Enterprises in China?

Small-to-medium-sized enterprises in China have achieved rapid and sustainable growth in recent decades. Such growth has increasingly contributed to China's economic development. Overall, SMEs make up 99.7% of the total number of companies operating in China (Liu, 2007). As in other economies, SMEs are an important foundational layer underpinning both domestic and international commerce and are critical to the operation of nearly all industries. High-quality SMEs generate good-paying jobs and new innovations for fueling China's goal of creating an advanced manufacturing and service economy. This position gives SMEs an important role to play in employment generation. Large enterprises employ 18.11% of the total workforce; medium enterprises take 30.76% of the share; and small enterprises have 51.13% (National Bureau of Statistics of China, 2007). To establish a common understanding, a clear definition of SMEs within the Chinese context has to be established. The Interim Categorizing Criteria on Small-to-Medium-Sized Enterprises (SMEs), published in 2003 and based on SME Promotion Law of China, set the guidelines for classifying SMEs (SME Promotion Law of China, 2003).

As shown in Table 25.2, the guidelines cover mainly payroll, revenue, and total assets of enterprises. Specific criteria apply to the industrial sector, construction, transportation, wholesale and retail businesses, and hotels and restaurants. SMEs commonly employ 100–500 people, but the large share, comprising around 70%, employ five people or fewer or are run by self-employed individuals. Most SMEs usually operate in a formal manner from fixed premises, are owner-managed, and have always been known to play a vital role in job creation and economic development. In the context of this contribution, SME hotel management companies are defined following the SME

Table 25.2 SME classification in the P.R. China

Size/category	Industries	Employment base	Total assets	Revenue (RMB)
Small	Industry	<300	<40 million	<30 million
	Construction	<600		<30 million
	Wholesale	<100		<30 million
	Retail	<100		<10 million
	Transport	<500		<30 million
	Post	<400		<30 million
	Hotel and restaurant	<400		<30 million
Medium	Industry	300–2,000	40–400 million	30–300 million
	Construction	600–3,000		30–300 million
	Wholesale	100–200		30–300 million
	Retail	100–500		10–150 million
	Transport	500–3,000		30–300 million
	Post	400–1,000		30–300 million
	Hotel and restaurant	400–800		30–150 million

Note: SME should meet one or more of the conditions; ME should meet three conditions, otherwise SE.
Source: SME Promotion Law of China (2003).

Promotion Law of China (2003) as having an employee base of fewer than 800, an asset base of less than 400 million Yuan, and business revenue totaling less than 150 million Yuan a year, with hotel management, operations, and related businesses in China.

Methodological Framework and Design

A qualitative approach has been chosen to explore small-to-medium-sized hotel management companies in China and their current and future market success and outlook. A purposive sampling technique has been adopted for generating the primary data as part of a larger study. Jankowicz (2005) suggested that this involves selecting people whose views are relevant, important, and particularly worth obtaining for the research, i.e., the key informant technique of selecting people with specialized knowledge. The data collection has been performed as individual, focused panel interviews with senior executives from different hotel management companies according to the criteria mentioned above. The expert panel consisted of 22 key decision-makers in the hotel industry who have had market experience in China. Among the panel members, all were top executives having worked in China in businesses that fit the definition of small-to-medium-sized companies targeted in this study, with backgrounds in either international chain, a local chain, or small-to-medium-sized hotel management companies. One executive is from a US-based hotel management company; two are from Singapore; three executives are from a Swiss-based hotel management company; and four others are from companies based in Hong Kong. Four executives are from companies operating out of Taiwan, and eight executives represent companies based in Mainland China.

The focused panel interviews have been conducted with a semi-structured, open-ended questionnaire based on Wong's (2005) methodology, to collect and derive specific insights and opinions from the experts selected. The advantage of the chosen method is its focused approach, centering the topic on success factors of small-to-medium-sized hotel management companies in China but leaves informants adequate space through its open-ended structure to elaborate on the topic, thereby creating a rich corpus for further contextual analysis.

The methodological process evades the limitations mentioned by Garrod (2002) regarding expert interviews and their opinions about complex issues or problems. In contrast to a Delphi technique, the deduction of results from the data is not based on the consensus of the experts but the researcher. The interview method chosen produced a richness of personal experience that cannot be subjected to quantitative analysis. Interviews were tape-recorded and subsequently transcribed to enable a thorough exploration of ideas raised. At various times during the analysis, preliminary interpretation was revealed to participants for their verification and future disclosure.

Success Factors of SME Hotel Management Companies in China

After conducting and transcribing the interviews and performing content analysis and clustering, the following results could be retrieved regarding the success factors of small- and medium-sized hotel management companies in China. It is not surprising that, in an East Asian context, which is highly focused on efficiency, output, and results as well as driven by numbers, a certain array of factors is regarded as granting success for hotel management companies. In addition, it needs to be understood that, in a market like China's, which is currently the largest in the world, large and state-owned companies are very much dominating not only the market but also according to their reputations.

Senior executives see the financial performance and profitability of the enterprise as the most important factor. This is especially true in the Chinese market, with its vast growth potential, because financially adept operating companies can accelerate their development and roll out new projects. The second factor named was leadership. Strong and efficient leadership is especially seen as a virtue in the power distance in East Asia. Employees, stakeholders, investors, and government officials are looking up to those leaders. As a third factor, revenue has been named, which includes a property's performance, its occupancy rate, and the revenue achieved per available room. Here, at the end of the day, sales is the only word that counts in a rapidly expanding or supply-driven market. This is definitely a highly significant difference compared to other Western and mature markets. In the fourth position, the financial health of the enterprise and its net worth are important. This is based on the investors in a booming market, who are looking carefully into the growth rate and margin of the investment, which could easily be allocated to any other of the booming sectors. Closely related to leadership but ranked at the fifth position, the personality traits and characteristics of managers are important because leadership has to be accurately and loyally executed. This relies on effective business operation and the performance of the team and is especially interwoven with a society whose social and business principles are based on its Confucian roots. Efficiency, loyalty, and team play are important; no team member wants to stick out, stay out, or stay an individual. Giving face to each colleague and the company, and especially to the leadership, is an important principle. It is not surprising that the corporate culture of the company is ranked number 7. However, in an East Asian context, corporate culture may have a different connotation than in Western countries. It is about the above-mentioned loyalty toward the team and an almost paternal attitude toward leadership. In the context of the service industry, in general, and the hospitality business, in particular, an important factor for SME hotel management companies is how they define and execute superior customer service and quality control of this service. Here, service needs to be above average because, for most of those smaller companies and lesser-known brands, reputation is missing, while reputation and a famous brand are very strong signals for attracting customers in the Chinese market. This links to the ninth position, which is brand value and reputation.

Here, small- and medium-sized hotel management companies are striving to improve their brand and reputation in the market. In markets where a larger share of the population now has enough spending power and excess money to spend on luxury goods, travel, and tourism, the demand is directed by social media toward famous or en vogue brands. At the end of the top 10, the capabilities of managing hotels, resources, and related experiences in the industry are considered important. This is a typical characteristic for growing markets and a situation where top management can currently rely on importing experienced general hotel management expertise from Western specialists. In the future, such foreign expertise will be substituted step-by-step by a new generation of domestic and homegrown hotel managers (Table 25.3).

Linking back to the clusters found in the literature, the current results regarding critical success factors provide feedback for the results displayed in Table 25.4. Regarding management and leadership support, leadership and the manager's characteristics and personality are important. Regarding culture, the corporate culture, as well as the agility, the entrepreneurial spirit, and the willingness to change and adjust to the demands of the internal and external environment are highlighted. Regarding performance criteria and measurement, the financial performance and profitability of the enterprise were named as well as revenue, performance occupancy rate, and the revenue per available room. The brand value and the reputation of the hotel management company, as well as its strategy, planning, and management have been put forward for the cluster of strategic management and purpose. Regarding organization and structure, the capability of the hotel manager, the human resources, as well as the experience related to those talents have been rated as important together with core competencies in human resources, operations, and marketing. For the cluster of processes and activities, management skills regarding operational efficiency as well as the ability to conduct effective business operations and the performance of the team have been named as important.

Table 25.3 Ranked critical success factors for SMEs

Ranking	Critical success factor
1	Financial performance and profitability
2	Leadership
3	Sales revenue (performance, occupancy, and REVpar)
4	Financial health of company and net worth
5	Manager's characteristics and personality
6	Effective business operations and performance of the team
7	Corporate culture of the company
8	Superior customer service/service quality control
9	Brand value and reputation
10	Hotel management capability, resources, and experience

Table 25.4 Important (critical) key success factors for SMEs

Cluster	Key success factor
Management and leadership support	Leadership
	Manager's characteristics and personality
Culture	Corporate culture of the company
	Agility, entrepreneurial spirit, and willingness to change and adjust
Performance criteria and measurement	Financial performance and profitability
	Sales revenue (performance, occupancy, and REVpar)
Strategic management and purpose	Brand value and reputation
	Company strategy, planning, and management
Organization and structure	Hotel management capability, resources, and experience
	Core competencies in human resources, operations, and marketing
Process and activities	Management skills (operation efficiency)
	Effective business operations and performance of the team

Note: The cluster's information and communication technology, talent acquisition and management as well as resources have been not listed.

Interestingly, based on informant-based data, success factors in the cluster of information and communication technology, talent acquisition, and management as well as resources have not been named explicitly.

Implications and Conclusion

Due to China's rapid economic growth, tourism and particularly the hotel business have grown tremendously. Chinese local enterprises have been working hard to meet the demand and have begun to adopt standard international hospitality practices combined with selective cultural adjustments to achieve growth (Okoroafo et al., 2010). At the same time, international players consider expansion into the Chinese market as a key strategy for their growth and value creation (Aliouche and Schlentrich, 2011). Under the above-mentioned circumstances, small-to-medium-sized enterprises with skills and advantages such as flexibility, customization, localization, and better services have significant opportunities to play an important role in China's hospitality industry.

However, SMEs have distinct disadvantages too. Their challenges include weak linkages with and know-how about the external market, weak or insufficient technological innovation, and most importantly, inadequate financing with little room to cover business risks. This has limited the growth of small-to-medium-sized companies in China (Liu, 2007). In accordance with Harvie (2010), SMEs will find that the competitive environment is looking at size, and reputation is linked with size. In addition, as an SME, there are disadvantages in regard to the acquisition of a skilled workforce, the acquisition and cost of financing, a burdensome and complex bureaucracy, and economic and social instability. As Blees et al. (2003) initially found, SMEs are still suffering from more barriers to conducting business than large companies. Not being a state-owned star and blue-chip firm, barriers are related to advertising, communication, branding, and reputation. The structural disadvantages include capital requirements, higher costs of operating abroad, higher wages to compensate for being an SME, research and market intelligence capabilities, and selling expenses and commissions, all of which are less restrictive for larger companies.

SMEs comprise the largest proportion of businesses all over the world. Hospitality SMEs in China that equipped themselves with the necessary strengths to overcome their challenges in each environment play tremendous roles in employment generation, provision of services, and contributions to better living standards, especially in remote areas.

China currently offers a huge market potential for the international hotel management industry. As a result, the competition within the industry arises not only from local operators but also from international ones, and SMEs' competitors are not only other SMEs but also commercial chains. To be successful in China's hotel management field is the most important task – even a survival game – for all players in the market but especially for SMEs, which often lack a scale of economies and funding.

However, there is space for further analysis regarding a comparison between small- and medium-sized companies as well as large companies in addition to a cross-comparison between China and other, more mature markets like Europe or North America.

References

Ali, A.J. (2000), *Globalization of Business: Practice and Theory*, Haworth Press, Binghamton, NY.

Aliouche, E.H. and Schlentrich, U. (2011), "A model of optimal international market expansion: The case of US hotel chains expansion into China", in *New Developments in the Theory of Networks*, Physica, Heidelberg, pp.135–154.

Altinay, L. (2005), "Factors influencing entry mode choices: Empirical findings from an international hotel organization", *Journal of Hospitality and Leisure Marketing*, Vol.12, No.3, pp.8–9.

Altinay, L. (2006), "Selecting partners in an international franchise organization", *International Journal of Hospitality Management*, Vol.25, No.1, pp.108–128.

Altinay, L. and Wang, C. (2006), "The role of prior knowledge in international franchise partner recruitment", *International Journal of Service Industry Management*, Vol.12, No.5, pp.430–443.

Arinaitwe, S.K. (2006), "Factors constraining the growth and survival of small scale business: A developing countries analysis", *Journal of American Academy of Business*, Vol.8, No.2, pp.67–179.

Ashmos, D.P., Duchon, D., Mcdaniel, R.R., and Huonker, J.W. (2002), "What a mess! Participation as a simple managerial rule to "complexity" organizations", *Journal of Management Studies*, Vol.39, No.2, pp.189–206.

Aung, M. (2000), "The Accor multinational hotel chain in an emerging market: Through the lens of the core competency concept", *The Service Industries Journal*, Vol.20, No.3, pp.43–60.

Bader, E.E. (2005), "Sustainable hotel business practices", *Journal of Retail and Leisure Property*, Vol.5, No.1, pp.70–77.

Bamforth, S. and Brookers, N.J. (2002), "Incorporating the voice of multiple customers into product design", *Journal of Engineering Manufacture*, Vol.216, No.B, pp.809–813.

Baum, J.A.C. and Havenman, H.A. (1997), "Love the neighbor? Differentiation and agglomeration in the Manhattan hotel industry", *Administrative Science Quarterly*, Vol.42, pp.304–338.

Begley, T. and Tan, W.L. (2001), "The socio-cultural environment for entrepreneurship: A comparison between East Asian and Anglo countries", *Journal of International Business Studies*, Vol.32, No.3, pp.537–554.

Bell, J., Crick, D., and Young, S. (2004), "Small firm internationalization and business strategy: An exploratory study of "knowledge-intensive" and "traditional" manufacturing firms in the UK", *International Small Business Journal*, Vol.22, No.1, pp.23–56.

Blees, J., Kemp, R., Maas, J., and Mosselman, M. (2003), "Barriers to entry: Differences in barriers to entry for SMEs and large enterprises", in Blees, J., et al. (Ed.), *Scientific Analysis of Entrepreneurship and SMEs*, EIM, Amsterdam, pp.143–150.

Brotherton, B. (2004a), "Critical success factors in UK corporate hotels", *The Service Industries Journal*, Vol.24, No.3, pp.19–42.

Brotherton, B. (2004b), "Critical success factors in UK budget hotel operations", *International Journal of Operations & Production Management*, Vol.24, No.9, pp.944–969.

Brotherton, B. and Shaw, J. (1996), "Towards an identification and classification of critical success factors in UK hotels plc", *International Journal of Hospitality Management*, Vol.15, No.2, pp.113–135.

Brouthers, K. and Brouthers, L. (2001), "Explaining the national cultural distance paradox", *Journal of International Business Studies*, Vol.32, No.1, pp.177–189.

Cai, L.A., Zhang, L., Pearson, T.E., and Bai, X. (2000), "Challenges for China's state-run hotels: A marketing perspective", *Journal of Hospitality Marketing & Management*, Vol.7, No.1, pp.29–46.

Campbell, N.M. (2005), *Correctional Leadership Competencies for the 21st Century: Executives and Senior-Level Leaders*, National Institute of Corrections, U.S. Department of Justice, Washington, DC.

Capizzi, M.T. and Ferguson, R. (2005), "Loyalty trends for the twenty-first century", *Journal of Consumer Marketing*, Vol.22, No.2, pp.72–80.

Carter, L., Ulrich, D., and Goldsmith, M. (2005), *Best Practices in Leadership Development and Organization Change: How the Best Companies Ensure Meaningful Change and Sustainable Leadership*, John Wiley & Sons, San Francisco, CA.

CBRE Research Asia. (April, 2009), "Hotel operators in China: New opportunities in a more sophisticated marketplace", available at: http://www.cbreindia.com/inet_newsmanager/newsfiles/Hotel%20Operators'%20Opportunities%20in%20China_Eng.pdf> (accessed June 2019).

Chathoth, P.K. and Olsen, M.D. (2003), "Strategic alliances: A hospitality industry perspective", *International Journal of Hospitality Management*, Vol.22, No.4, pp.419–434.

Chu, R.K.S. and Choi, T. (2000), "An importance-performance analysis of hotel selection factors in the Hong Kong hotel industry: a comparison of business and leisure travelers", *Tourism Management*, Vol.21, No.4, pp.363–377.

Clarkin, J.E. and Swavely, S.M. (2006), "The importance of personal characteristics in franchisee selection", *Journal of Retailing and Consumer Services*, Vol.13, No.2, pp.133–142.

Cohen, L., Manion, L., and Morrison, K. (2003), *Research Methods in Education*, Routledge Falmer, New York, NY.

Cohen, B. and Winn, M. (2007), "Market imperfections, opportunity, and sustainable entrepreneurship", *Journal of Business Venturing*, Vol.22, No.1, pp.29–49.

Connell, J. (1999), "Diversity in large firm international franchise strategy", *Journal of Consumer Marketing*, Vol.16, No.1, pp.86–95.

Crane, A. and Matten, D. (2006), *Business Ethics: Managing Corporate Citizenship and Sustainability in the Age of Globalization*, Oxford University Press, Oxford, UK.

Day, G.S. (2000), "Managing market relationships", *Journal of the Academy of Marketing Science*, Vol.28, No.1, pp.24–30.

Dickson, K., Janjuha-Jivraj, S., Primrose, P., and Woods, A. (2006), "Clustering and networking among small independent hotels: Developments over ten years", paper presented to International Small Business and Enterprise Conference, 2-5 November, Cardiff, UK, pp.1-15.

Dwyer, L., Edwards, D., Mistilis, N., Roman, C., and Scott, N. (2009), "Destination and enterprise management for a tourism future", *Tourism Management*, Vol.30, No.1, pp.63–74.

Ekeledo, I. and Sivakumar, K. (1998), "Foreign market entry mode choice of service firms: A contingency perspective", *Journal of the Academy of Marketing Science*, Vol.26, No.4, pp.274–292.

Epstein, M. and Wisner, P. (2001), "Using a balanced scorecard to implement sustainability", *Environmental Quality Management*, Vol.11, No.2, pp.1–10.

Evans, M.R. and Chon, K.S. (1989), "Formulating and evaluating tourism policy using importance performance analysis", *Hospitality Education and Research Journal*, Vol.13, 203–213.

Evans, N. (2001), "Alliances in the international travel industry: Sustainable strategy options?", *International Journal of Hospitality & Tourism Administration*, Vol.2, No.1, pp.1–26.

Fernandez, J.I.P. (2009), "Measuring tourism sustainability: Proposal for a composite index", *Tourism Economics*, Vol.15, No.2, pp.277–296.

Gale, D. (2009), "World's largest hotel companies: Corporate 300 chart", *Hotel Business*, Vol.20, No.3, pp.34–36.

Gandolfi, F. and Bekker, C.J. (2008), "Guanxi: The art of finesse and relationship building when conducting business in China", *Regent Global Business Review*, Vol.2, No.1, pp.5–11.

Garrod, B. (2002), "Defining marine ecotourism: A Delphi study", in Garrod, B. and Wilson, J.C. (Eds.), *Marine Ecotourism: Issues and Experiences*, Channel View Publications, Clevedon, UK, pp.17–36.

Geller, A.N. (1985), "Tracing the critical success factors for hotel companies", *Cornell Hotel and Restaurant Administration Quarterly*, Vol.25, pp.76–81.

Go, F. and Pine, R. (1995), *Globalization Strategy in the Hotel Industry*, Routledge, London, UK.

Grangsjo, Y. and Gummesson, E. (2005), "Hotel networks and social capital in destination marketing", *International Journal of Service Industry Management*, Vol.17, No.1, pp.58–75.

Gu, H., Ryan, C., and Yu, L. (2012), "The changing structure of the Chinese hotel industry: 1980–2012", *Tourism Management Perspectives*, Vol.4, pp.56–63.

Gu, Z. (2003), "The Chinese lodging industry: Problems and solutions", *International Journal of Contemporary Hospitality Management*, Vol.15, No.7, pp.386–392.

Gunaratne, K.A. (2009), "Barriers to internationalization of SMEs in a developing country", in Luxton, S. (Ed.), 2009 *ANZMAC Annual Conference*, Australia and New Zealand Marketing Academy, Melbourne, Australia.

Hambrick, D.C. and Mason, P.A. (1984), "Upper echelons: The organization as a reflection of its top managers", *Academy of Management Review*, Vol.9, No.2, pp.193–206.

Han, S.H. and Diekmann, J.E. (2001), "Approaches for making risk-based go/no-go decision for international projects", *Journal of Construction Engineering and Management*, Vol.127, No.4, pp.300–308.

Harrington, R.J. (2004), "The environment, involvement, and performance: Implications for the strategic process of food service firms", *International Journal of Hospitality Management*, Vol.23, No.4, pp.317–341.

Harrington, R.J. (2005), "The how and who of strategy making: Models and appropriateness for firms in hospitality and tourism industries", *Journal of Hospitality & Tourism Research*, Vol.29, No.3, pp.372–395.

Harvie, C. (2010), "SMEs and regional production networks", *ERIA Research Project Report*, pp.19–45.

Heung, V.C.S., Zhang, H., and Jiang, C. (2008), "International franchising: Opportunities for China's state-owned hotels?", *International Journal of Hospitality Management*, Vol.27, No.3, pp.368–380.

Holsapple, C.W. and Joshi, K.D. (2000), "An investigation of factors that influence the management of knowledge in organizations", *Journal of Strategic Information Systems*, Vol.9, No.2/3, pp.235–261.

Huang, H., Bruzga, K., and Wang Y. (2011), "Business key success factors in China and the West", *African Journal of Business Management*, Vol.5, No.22, pp.9363–9369.

Ihua, U.B. (2009), "SMEs key failure-factors: A comparison between the United Kingdom and Nigeria", *Journal of Social Sciences*, Vol.18, No.3, pp.199–207.

Jankowicz, A.D. (2005), *Business Research Projects*, Thomson Learning, London, UK.

Kazem, A. and van der Heijden, B. (2006), "Exporting firms' strategic choices: The case of Egyptian SMEs in the food industry", *SAM Advanced Management Journal*, Vol.71, No.3, pp.21–33.

Lew, A.A., Yu, L., Ap, J., and Zhang, G. (2003), *Tourism in China*, The Haworth Hospitality Press., New York, NY.

Li, J.T., Xin, K., and Pillutla, M. (2002), "Multi-cultural leadership teams and organizational identification in international joint ventures", *International Journal of Human Resource Management*, Vol.13, No.2, pp.320–337.

Littrell, R.F. (2002), "Desirable leadership behaviors of multi-cultural managers in China", *Journal of Management Development*, Vol.21, No.1, pp.5–74.

Liu, J. and Mackinnon, A. (2001), "Comparative management practices and training – China and Europe", *Journal of Management Development*, Vol.21, No.2, pp.118–132.

Liu, X. (2007), "SME development in China: A policy perspective on SME industrial clustering", in Lim, H. (Ed.), *ERIA Research Project Report*, Jakarta, Indonesia, No. 5, pp.37–68.

Lv, B. and Zhao, L. (2009), "The evolution of international competence of Chinese hotel corporations and its implications", *Asian Social Science*, Vol.5, No.9, pp.93–97.

Mak, B. (2008), "The future of the state-owned hotels in China: Stay or go? *International Journal of Hospitality Management*, Vol.27, No.3, pp.355–367.

Magnini, V. (2009), "An exploratory investigation of the real-time training modes used by hotel expatriates", *International Journal of Hospitality Management*, Vol.28, No.4, pp.513–518.

Man, T.W.Y., Lau, T., and Chan, K.F. (2002), "The competitiveness of small and medium enterprises: A conceptualization with focus on entrepreneurial competencies", *Journal of Business Venturing*, Vol.17, No.2, pp.123–142.

Martorell, O., Mulet, C., and Rossello, M. (2008), "Valuing growth strategy management by hotel chains based on the real options approach", *Tourism Economics*, Vol.14, No.3, pp.511–526.

Mathews, V.E. (2000), "Competition in the international hotel industry. *International Journal of Contemporary Hospitality Management*, Vol.12, No.2, pp.114–118.

O'Donnell, A., Gilmore, A., Cummins, D., and Carson, D. (2001), "The network construct in entrepreneurship research: A review and critique", *Management Decision*, Vol.39, No.9, pp.749–760.

Okoroafo, S.C., Koh, A., Liu, L., and Jin, X (2010), "Hotels in China: A comparison of indigenous and subsidiaries strategies", *Journal of Management Research*, Vol.2, No.1, pp.1–10.

Palmeri, C. and Balfour, F. (2009), "Starwood is blanketing China", *Business Week*, Vol.4145, pp.56–57.

Peng, J.F. (2003), "Top ten marketing challenges in China in 2002", *China Marketing* (in Chinese), Vol.1, No.1, pp.26–29.

Peng, M.W. and Shenkar, O. (2002), "Joint venture dissolution as corporate divorce", *Academy of Management Executive*, Vol.16, No.2, pp.92–105.

Peng, W. and Littlejohn, D. (2001), "Organizational communication and strategy implementation – A primary inquiry", *International Journal of Contemporary Hospitality Management*, Vol.13, No.7, pp.360–363.

Pine, R. (2002), "China's hotel industry: Serving a massive market", *The Cornell Hotel and Restaurant Administration Quarterly*, Vol.43, No.3, pp.61–70.

Pine, R. and Phillips, P. (2005), "Performance comparison of hotels in China", *International Journal of Hospitality Management*, Vol.24, No.1, pp.57–73.

Pine, R. and Qi, P. (2004), "Barriers to hotel chain development in China", *International Journal of Contemporary Hospitality Management*, Vol.16, No.1, pp.37–44.

Pine, R., Zhang, H.Q., and Qi, P. (2000), "The challenge and opportunities of franchising in China's hotel industry", *International Journal of Contemporary Hospitality Management*, Vol.12, No.5, pp.300–307.

Pizanti, I. and Lerner, M. (2003), "Examining control and autonomy in the franchisor-franchisee relationship", *International Small Business Journal*, Vol.21, No.2, p.131.

Presley, A. and Meade, L. (2002), "The role of soft systems methodology in planning for sustainable production", *Greener Management International*, Vol.37, pp.101–110.

Rangone, A. (1999), "A resource-based approach to strategy analysis in small-medium sized enterprises", *Small Business Economics*, Vol.12, No.3, pp.233–248.

Ritchie, B. and Riley, M. (2004), "The role of the multi-unit manager within the strategy and structure relationship: Evidence from the unexpected", *International Journal of Hospitality Management*, Vol.23, No.2, pp.145–161.

Ruzzier, M., Hisrich, R.D., and Antoncic, B. (2006), "SME internationalization research: Past, present, and future", *Journal of Small Business and Enterprise Development*, Vol.13, No.4, pp.476–497.

Ruzzier, M. and Konecnik, M. (2006), "The internationalization strategies of SMEs: The case of the Slovenian hotel industry", *Management: Journal of Contemporary Management Issues*, Vol.11, No.1, pp.17–35.

Saunders, M.N.K., Lewis, P., and Thornhill, A. (2009), *Research Methods for Business Students*, Prentice Hall, London, UK.

Selmer, J. (2004), "Psychological barriers to adjustment of Western business expatriates in China: Newcomers vs long stayers", *International Journal of Human Resource Management*, Vol.15, No.4, pp.794–813.

Selmer, J. (2005), "Cross-cultural training and expatriate adjustment in China: Western joint venture managers", *Personnel Review*, Vol.34, No.1, pp.68–84.

Siu, W. S. (2000), "Marketing and company performance of Chinese small firms in mainland China: A preliminary study", *Journal of Small Business and Enterprise Development*, Vol.7, No.2, pp.105–122.

Siu, W.S., Fang, W.C., and Lin, T.L. (2004), "Strategic marketing practices and the performance of Chinese small and medium-sized enterprises (SMEs) in Taiwan", *Entrepreneurship and Regional Development*, Vol.16, No.2, pp.161–178.

Sivadas, E. and Dwyer, F.R. (2000), "An examination of organizational factors influencing new product success in internal and alliance-based processes", *Journal of Marketing*, Vol.64, No.1, pp.31–49.

SME Promotion Law of China. (2003), Beijing, China.

Suarez-Ortega, S. (2003), "Export barriers: Insights from small and medium-sized firms", *International Small Business Journal*, Vol.21, No.4, pp.403–441.

Szarka, J. (1990), "Networking and small firms", *International Small Business Journal*, Vol.8, No.2, pp.10–22.

Tang, Y.M., Wang, P., and Zhang, Y.L. (2007), "Marketing and business performance of construction SMEs in China", *Journal of Business & Industry*, Vol.22, No.2, pp.118–125.

Timothy, D.J., and Teye, V.B. (2009), *Tourism and the Lodging Sector*, Elsevier, Oxford, UK.

Tracey, P. and Clark, G.L. (2003), "Alliances, networks, and competitive strategy: Rethinking clusters of innovation", *Growth and Change*, Vol.34, No.1, pp. 1–16.

Tsang, N. and Qu, H. (2000), "The service quality in China's hotel industry: A perspective from tourists and hotel managers", *International Journal of Contemporary Hospitality Management*, Vol.12, No.5, pp.316–326.

Vachani, S. (2005), "Problems of foreign subsidiaries of SMEs compared with large companies", *International Business Review*, Vol.14, No.4, pp.415–439.

Vanhonacker, W. (1997), "Entering China: An unconventional approach", *Harvard Business Review*, Vol.75, No.2, pp.130–140.

Westhead, P., Wright, M., and Ucbasaran, D. (2001), "The internationalization of new and small firms: A resource based view", *Journal of Business Venturing*, Vol.16, No.4, pp.333–358.

Westhead, P., Wright, M., and Ucbasaran, D. (2002), "International market selection strategies by "micro" and "small" firms", *The International Journal of Management Science*, Vol.30, No.3, pp.51–68.

White, M., Haire, J., Rex, J., and King, J. (2003), "Managing stakeholder "push back", an exploratory investigation into dealing with negative cross cultural communication in a global environment", in Kennedy, R. (Ed.), *ANZMAC Annual Conference*, Adelaide, Australia, pp.1533–1539.

Whitla, P., Walters, P.G.P., and Davies, H. (2007), "Global strategies in the international hotel industry", *International Journal of Hospitality Management*, Vol.26, No.4, pp.777–792.

Wickham, P.A. (2006), *Strategic Entrepreneurship*, 4th ed., Prentice Hall, Essex, UK.

Wong, K.Y. (2005), "Critical success factors for implementing knowledge management in small and medium enterprises", *Industrial Management & Data Systems*, Vol.105, No.3, pp.261–279.

Xiao, Q., O'Neill, J.W., and Wang, H. (2008), "International hotel development: A study of potential franchisees in China", *International Journal of Hospitality Management*, Vol.27, No.3, pp.325–336.

Xiao, Z., Xiao, Q., and Wang, H. (2003), *The Pattern of Transforming State-Owned into Joint-Stock in the Hospitality Industry*, China Travel and Tourism Press, Beijing.

Yang, S. (2001), *Franchise: Good and Bad*, Tourism Press, Beijing.

Yu, L., and Gu, H. (2005), "Hotel reform in China: A SWOT analysis", *Cornell Hotel and Restaurant Administration Quarterly*, Vol.46, No.2, pp.153–169.

Yu, R. (2005), "Western hotel chains build on China's change", *USA Today*, Money Section, 4b.

Zhang, H., Pine, R., and Lam, T. (2005), *Tourism and Hotel Development in China*, The Haworth Hospitality Press and International Business Press, New York, NY.

Zhou, Y., Lu, L., and Jiang, B. (2005), "Study on staff management practice of multinational company affiliates in China", *Management Decision*, Vol.43, No.4, pp.516–522.

Zimmerer, T.W., and Scarborough, N.M. (2005), *Essentials of Entrepreneurship and Small Business Management*, Pearson Prentice Hall, Upper Saddle River, NJ.

PART V

International Challenges and Perspectives

A Case Study Approach

26

KNOWLEDGE REPLICATION AND ADAPTATION IN THE INTERNATIONAL GROWTH OF HOSPITALITY FIRMS

The Case of Paulaner

Desiderio J. García-Almeida, Laura Schmidt, and Burkhard von Freyberg

Introduction

As firms grow and try to increase the market share or to cover new geographical markets in their core business, they usually set up new units (acquired firms, intra-firm agreements, or start-ups). This way to grow can be followed by many organizations which want to set new production, distribution, or research centers in geographical zones where they already have a presence or in new ones. Such organizations often open many subsidiaries, outlets, and facilities worldwide every year. The literature on internationalization proposes that the expansion process can be implemented by companies following two different, opposite paths: one where the organization attempts to adapt its new operations to the local conditions, and another where the company tries to impose corporate standards in the new unit.

Desiring to take advantage of the knowledge that guides the management processes and operations, firms can attempt to transfer their business practices to the new units. So, one of the strategic options which these organizations can try to follow is to achieve that the new units operatively resemble the organization's other existing units in the closest possible way, by attempting to transfer the management and operational knowledge and practices that characterize their operations. The premise that underpins this approach is related to getting the highest appropriation of rents from their knowledge assets, replicating the formula to succeed that these firms have used or think they can achieve. Regarding the hospitality industry, when a hotel or gastronomy chain incorporates a new unit in its structure, it has, on the one hand, the possibility of transferring internally the knowledge that the firm uses in some other organizational parts. The conceptual foundations that justify this process could be drawn from growth and internationalization literature and the resource- and knowledge-based views of the firm (e.g., Barney, 1991; Bartlett and Ghoshal, 1989; Grant, 1996; Hedlund, 1994; Kogut and Zander, 1992, 1993; Penrose, 1959). In this sense, it is essential to consider the knowledge of tourism organizations as a resource that can be of high importance for its performance and long-term survival (García-Almeida and Yu, 2015). On the other hand, the opposed strategy would consist of providing a high degree of independence to the new units. Under this strategic perspective, the corporate headquarters would reject the knowledge transfer option on the basis of the need to adapt to local conditions.

When a hospitality firm integrates a new unit (or units) in its portfolio, it has several options to relate that unit to the whole company. It can keep the new unit with no market relationship with the rest of the chain units by assigning a name with no relationship to the chain, it can develop a new brand for the new units, or it can relate the new unit to an existing brand (García-Almeida, 2009). Many hospitality companies adopt this last option in their internationalization strategy in order to take advantage of their brand image and the core resources of their strategy. According to Kwun and Oh (2007), hotel firms have used brand strategies in their expansion and routinely differentiated their products and services through branding. Because brand associations help consumers process, organize, and retrieve information to assist them in making purchase decisions (Kwun and Oh, 2007), lodging firms usually face their internationalization process by adding hotels to their existing brands and further extending their global strategy. However, the internationalization strategy also fosters the increase of brands/products/concepts, due to the identification of opportunities outside the usual market boundaries where the firm has been competing. A parallel discussion regarding this is the alternative routes that a firm can follow to obtain and develop brands: It can build and develop them, or it can acquire companies or assets that possess them (Doyle, 1990).

In the following sections, we review the theoretical foundations to understand the knowledge replication and adaptation needs of hospitality firms when they grow internationally. We illustrate the challenges of this knowledge replication and adaptation efforts with the example of a German food and beverage company (Paulaner Bräuhaus) and its expansion in Singapore.

Standardization or Adaptation to Local Context

Adaptation of operations, managerial practices, and structural aspects to new situations have been addressed in the management literature. One of the most prominent discussion lines about this topic is the contingency theory. The contingency approach has exerted a powerful influence on organization theory and strategic management (García Falcón, 1995). Consequently, its premises have oriented many research projects. From this theoretical line, managerial practices should fit the context where they are implemented. It questions the universal validity of the managerial knowledge in order to be applied in every context. Moreover, it casts some doubts about the general validity of the knowledge in the intraorganizational level: Is the successful knowledge generated or used in a subunit valid for some other subunits embedded in different contexts? In a widely recognized work, Lawrence and Lorsch (1967) emphasized that organizations and its subunits develop the best structures to adapt to the requirements of the different environments they face. To delve into this idea, Lawrence and Lorsch (1967) indicate that adjustment between an organization and its environment has two levels: on the one hand, the structural features of the subunits should be adapted to the specific environments they face; and on the other hand, the organizational differentiation and integration should be globally adapted to the general environment.

In the area of the multinational corporation management, the debate about the convenience of adaptation to local contexts has been present as well. Classical work in this field is the one by Perlmutter (1969) on managers' attitudes. This author addresses managers' attitudes/mental schemes regarding the international operations of their corporations and describes three basic types of attitudes: ethnocentric, polycentric, and geocentric. The ethnocentric attitude is observed when the manager believes that the best work approaches are those of the headquarters or the home country market, which is linked to the presence of home country managers in foreign subsidiaries. The polycentric attitudes are associated with the emphasis on total adaptation to local markets and they are based on the belief that managers in the host country know the best work approaches and practices for running the business there. The geocentric attitude is based on a world-oriented view and focuses on using the best approaches and peoples from around the world.

Another important theoretical pillar in the analysis of knowledge adaptation, whose origin lies in Perlmutter's work (1969), is provided by the available strategic orientations to manage the international operations. Ghoshal and Westney (1993) review the contributions on this topic under the framework integration/responsiveness. According to it, they suggest that strategy and structure in the multinational corporation are defined by the answers to two factors: global integration and national differences.

In order to improve the organizational capabilities of the multinational corporations and increase their global competitiveness, Bartlett and Ghoshal (1989) stress different needs: the need to learn (while fostering global innovation), the need to be efficient (providing arguments for the global integration), and the need to be sensitive to the markets where they operate (supporting local differentiation). Supporting global integration, Levitt (1983) argues that the needs and preferences of the people in the world are increasingly homogeneous. This trend allows for global product standardization and prompts the achievement of scale economies to remain competitive. Opposite to it, one of the key barriers to globalization is the structural market differences and consumer preferences from the different countries where the firm operates (Bartlett and Ghoshal, 1989). This aspect poses some problems to the ideas of total homogenization and fosters adaptation and sensibility to "local" circumstances. Therefore, two opposite strategic orientations appear to manage international operations: the global strategy and the multi-domestic strategy. They attempt to emphasize efficiency and local responsiveness, respectively. Global strategy is often related to activity centralization in the home country (or at least few countries), because it is more efficient and units in other countries work as distribution channels. Nevertheless, firms can set up units with more implication in the value chain but under strong guidance (plans, directives) from the headquarters (Pla Barber et al., 1999), as can be seen in several service firms. Some authors have recognized the relevance of mixing both perspectives (Ghoshal and Westney, 1993), and have outlined a more holistic approach which is called a *transnational* organization in Bartlett and Ghoshal's terminology (1989) or *heterarchy* in Hedlund's (1993).

Bonache (2000) performs an interesting analysis regarding the transfer of human resource practices in multinational corporations. He compares the need to standardize to relativist approaches which stand for adaptation to local demand and needs. Following this author and Rosenzweig and Singh (1991), the advantages of adapting to local conditions must be weighed against the benefits derived from standardizing in every part of the multinational organization. Several ideas support the standardization argument: the belief that practices are the basis for sustaining the organizational competitive advantage, the high degree of unit interdependence, the need for internal consistency and equity, and the opinion that homogeneous operations ease knowledge and information flows.

In line with this discussion, Zaheer (1995) analyzes the convenience for foreign subsidiaries to face the liabilities of foreignness (unfamiliarity of the environment, cultural, political, and economic differences, etc.) by importing the capabilities embodied in the organizational practices from the headquarters or by imitating local firms. This author's findings display that foreign subsidiaries can achieve better outcomes by using imported routines when the firm's main source of specific advantage lies in the organizational capabilities. In that situation, that option is better than attempting to copy local practices that the company has not developed.

For some authors (e.g., Foss and Pedersen, 2000; Pedersen et al., 2000), transferring knowledge is not replicating the source's knowledge exactly in a new outlet, because this process is often associated to changes for the specific context. From this view, what organizations transfer are problem solutions (understood as knowledge applications) and not the underlying knowledge. The interaction between sources and recipients is frequently critical to the transfer success because it shows the existence of a "customized market" (Leonard-Barton and Sinha, 1993). Thus, the transfer should include some adaptation processes to recontextualize knowledge as is advised under the *international* strategy, according to Bartlett and Ghoshal (1989). In addition, this approach also recommends that both the source and recipient participate in the adaptation of the knowledge to be transferred (McArthur, 1998). In this sense, some works explicitly outline that the outcomes of knowledge transfer processes imply the development of new knowledge (e.g., Armistead, 1999; Pedersen et al., 2000).

At this point, it is interesting to review the literature to find out some evidence about the used strategies in this domain. Reddy and Zhao (1990) study a wide sample of works on international technology transfer and they conclude that most multinational corporations do not adapt knowledge when they transfer it. Moreover, this work addresses the reasons why companies show this non-adaptation behavior, and the authors conclude that firms seldom perform this contextualization processes due to costs or possible dysfunctions. This conclusion is reinforced with the theoretical argument of superior knowledge that lies beneath the existence of multinational organizations.

Regarding hospitality management, Ramón Rodríguez (2002) outlines the important role that knowledge and knowledge-based resources play in organizational competitiveness of international hospitality firms in global expansions. In the tourism industry, many firms grow globally by using strategies based on the transfer of knowledge resources (García-Almeida and Yu, 2015). Some authors have indicated that the strategic orientation towards operational homogeneity belongs to the past and at the same time define the adaptation strategy as a new emphasis (Alexander and Lockwood, 1996; Litteljohn, 1997) or as a need (Jones et al., 1998). However, Ingram and Baum (1997, p. 72) asserted that "the strategy of hotel chains can be described with one word, standardization." This opinion was confirmed by García-Almeida (2009), who found that 82% of Spanish hotel chains that had grown domestically and internationally had substantially transferred their systems to their new units. The exception to this trend could be hotel conversions where the hotel under the former management showed good performance (García-Almeida and Bolívar-Cruz, 2007), that is, integrating a hotel that already functioned and had profitable performance in a hotel chain.

Process and Content Adaptation in Knowledge Replication Success in New Units

As we have mentioned, knowledge replication can be very relevant when facing growth processes. As some authors express it, technology transfer lies at the heart of the issue of the growth of firms, domestically and internationally (Kogut and Zander, 1993), because, as Nelson and Winter (1982) suggest, the replication of assets and capabilities is related to the growth and profitability of a firm. Winter and Szulanski (2002) see replication as the implementation of practices or routines in new settings that are quite similar to the original routine in significant aspects. A factor to consider when transferring knowledge to new organizational units successfully is the adaptation of that knowledge and the transfer process to fit the new units' context and characteristics. Generally speaking, the question is whether the firm needs to "personalize" the knowledge to transfer and the way to transmit it or the company should just repeat the practices that operate in some other organizational parts. This can be a success factor for the whole process and, as García-Almeida and Yu (2015) note, success in the knowledge transfer processes should be addressed after assuming that many hospitality chains opt for that alternative in their growth strategy abroad.

According to the concept of knowledge replication, the knowledge to transfer to new units is deemed valid and can generate competitive advantages in the new locations. Tourism, in particular, is a people-oriented service business and, consequently, effective knowledge transfer from the corporate office to the unit property in the host country is essential to ensure service consistency, guest satisfaction, and brand loyalty. These factors are fundamental in the hospitality industry

(Olsen et al., 1992; Pizam, 2007). As observed after discussing the ideas of the contingency approach, standardization and relativism advantages, and the strategic orientations for multinational corporations, there exists a whole body of knowledge to understand the conceptual bases of adaptation to new organizational units in the hospitality industry.

From his study on international technology transfer, McArthur (1998) observes managed adaptation as a jointly managed process with strategies to adapt technology to the recipient unit, to mobilize that technology, and to adapt methods and provide training to the recipient unit. Therefore, a flexible replication system can influence the transfer content and process. Another approach to this topic is provided by Leonard-Barton and Sinha (1993). These authors consider adaptation as system improvement so that it fits users' specific needs as well as work process redesign in order to take advantage of the new system benefits. As told above, for some authors (e.g., Foss and Pedersen, 2000; Pedersen et al., 2000) transferring knowledge is not an accurate knowledge replication in a new location, that is, the sources cannot replicate their knowledge in different settings. This aspect is especially relevant when considering knowledge tacitness. Many practices in the tourism industry are characterized by high levels of tacitness because the underlying knowledge has been developed through expertise and contacts with customers and other stakeholders. For Attewell (1992), transferring knowledge with a high degree of complexity and causal ambiguity requires its reconstruction and adaptation in the recipient unit. One of the advantages linked to the employment of rich communication mechanisms in tacit knowledge transfers is their ability to adapt this knowledge to the new settings with a higher degree of accuracy.

With regard to the interest and importance of adaptation when attempting to transfer knowledge, the departure point is Reddy and Zhao's work (1990) where they showed that multinational corporations seldom adapt. However, Leonard-Barton (1988) documents the existence of failures when technical system developers or users are not willing or are unable to adapt it. In a later work, Leonard-Barton and Sinha (1993) review some situations where adaptation in knowledge transfers takes place, whether because the technology is reinvented by users in order to meet their needs or because it is adapted to the workplace through worker training, changes in rewards, creation of new labor roles, or organization changes. Regarding the operatives in adaptation, McArthur (1998) prefers to adopt technology and methods to the recipient unit than to adapt that unit to the new technology, although the author recognizes the need to change some recipient abilities. In fact, in 13 out of the 15 cases he studies, McArthur (1998) finds out training situations and significant changes in recipient unit's workers. Leonard-Barton and Sinha (1993) also conduct an empirical approach and conclude that technology or workplace adaptation has got a significant influence on the new system efficiency; they measure efficiency with the user assessment on productivity gains. Their empirical findings suggest that modifications jointly created by system developers and users are more critical than the initial adjustment between the new system to implement and the recipients' context.

In the same line, Dixon (2000) asserts that knowledge cannot be used until it is customized due to the source and recipient's different contexts. This author goes on to qualify that the higher the knowledge tacitness, the higher the translation effort to be exerted. On the other hand, Winter and Szulanski (2002) conduct a case study research where they analyze a successful, admired knowledge replication strategy implemented by a bank. They emphasize how a generic body of knowledge is provided to the new units and later each unit customizes it within the given framework. In the hospitality industry, small (or not so small) changes and variations in the product and in the process of a new chain outlet or unit abroad can also be detected in comparison with the chain or central units in the home country of the company.

As shown above, the need to adapt/translate conceptually stems from differences between the source unit and the recipient one (context, features). In his research guided by the principles of grounded theory, McArthur (1998) observes how transfers are more troublesome in some situations where unexpected differences in the national, corporate, unit or personal aspects associated to the task arise. Those differences call for process, content, or method adaptation in order to achieve smooth operations in units following headquarters guidelines. The causal conditions to trigger the adaptation processes which this author identifies rely on differences on infrastructure and culture in the geographical area of the recipient unit, on technical, economic, and national models that the participating agents have got, and on recipient agent abilities regarding those of the source. This last aspect referring to the concept of absorptive capacity, which refers to the previous knowledge that individuals possess, is widely discussed by Cohen and Levinthal (1990). Many hotel and food and beverage chains with growth strategies also face these differences in the context of the home and host countries, which pose challenges in the transfer process.

The question of who should participate in the adaptation process is an interesting topic to address. After studying some organizations which are leaders on the knowledge transfer domain, Dixon (2000) asserts it is irrelevant who performs that adaptation. That is, the adaptation could be performed by the recipient team (translating into their context) or by the source agents (analyzing the situation of the recipient unit). Of course, several agents may participate and be critical to success in knowledge transfer projects (headquarters, external consulting firms, etc.). However, the literature on knowledge and technology transfer focuses on the essential role that source and recipient play (which can be multiple and very complex). For Leonard-Barton (1988), the internal implementation of new technology must be a mutual adaptation process. In the same discussion line, McArthur (1998) defends that the best outcomes in technology transfer are achieved when source and recipient units are active throughout the process. He goes on to outline that if one of the two parties involved leads to a process that requires adaptation and information to perform that adaptation, the made decisions show a lower degree of quality. Therefore, these contributions seem to suggest that adaptation displays better outcomes when the recipient unit is involved in the transfer process. For hospitality firms, it implies the need for listening to local partners and employees to fine-tune the knowledge that the headquarters want to bring to the new setting abroad. This process can be even more necessary in the case of converted hotels and restaurants because there is an established way of doing things and a shared cultural framework in those new chain outlets.

Regarding new product technical systems, Leonard-Barton and Sinha (1993) review the effects of user involvement in new product development. They stress that user implication could increase product and process quality and their motivation to adopt the new technology, but the empirical test of those hypotheses did not display convincing results. Two additional aspects of this study are relevant here: according to the authors, there seems to be a turning point in the positive gains of user involvement, and users do not always want to participate. Leonard-Barton and Sinha (1993) find that even though high-involvement projects show the highest level of employee satisfaction, dissatisfaction is only caused by very low user involvement. Moreover, we must bear in mind that the knowledge recipient's involvement can vary along the transfer process: in fact, Leonard-Barton and Sinha (1993) distinguish between the initial and final stages.

Nevertheless, McArthur (1998) reminds us that adaptation is not a sole recipient role because the source unit is the one that starts the process. In his analysis, this author finds that at the beginning of the transfer the source unit has got more technical abilities (technically privileged) than the recipient unit, but lack the knowledge about the recipient's internal and external aspects, and vice versa. After the transfer, these positions could have been corrected. From a normative point of view in search of effectiveness and efficiency, McArthur (1998) recommends that transfers should start with the changes proposed by the source agents, as they could boost those technical modifications with their expertise. The final part of the adaptation process should be led by the specific changes regarding the recipient's context, whose authors would be recipient unit agents and expatriates.

A note on the key role of the knowledge replication project manager is required because his/her decisions are critical to the existence and modes of adaptation in a given project. Adaptation strategies are carried out based on managers' perceptions and assessments about the transfer implementation and obstacles (McArthur, 1998). A related line on this issue is rooted on Perlmutter's ideas (1969) about managerial attitudes, as those views could be paramount for transfer planning and problem solution. The responsible manager for that in many hospitality firms for this knowledge and adaptation processes is the business development manager, the area manager, the corporate product manager, the new general manager of the unit, or some other corporate staff or even external consultants.

Diverging from Perlmutter's perspective (1969), McArthur (1998) focuses on the transfer project manager's role in adaptation processes. According to this last author, those managers usually assess the specific difficulties of a certain project in several fields: distance, communication and cultural barriers, technical novelty, knowledge and familiarity with the geographical area, and capability differences. Besides that analysis, the manager assesses how fast the recipient unit is learning the technical system required to adapt and operate with the transferred knowledge. As a consequence of that assessment, the manager classifies the project as *on-course* or *off-course* (McArthur, 1998). Off-course transfers require additional strategies to be implemented in order to correct the situation.

As a corollary, Von Krogh and Cusumano (2001) analyze knowledge *duplication* in a context of growth. They consider that in a replication context, it is important to get a trade-off between standardization and adaptation. Therefore, a new subsidiary should learn the local conditions and apply that knowledge in the adaptation of products, marketing, and operations.

García-Almeida and Yu (2015) analyzed in the hospitality industry that employees in foreign units must assimilate and accept the transferred knowledge because this is critical to maintaining the desired level of service standards. In order to increase the satisfaction of the recipient employees, the cultural compatibility between the knowledge and their cultural background, and the motivation of the employees who are responsible for transferring the knowledge seem to be key (García-Almeida and Yu, 2015).

The Case of Paulaner Franchise & Consulting

Olsen et al. (1998) indicated that the internationalization of hospitality chains had been a relevant trend. The theoretical discussion of the standardization and adaptation strategies in the growth orientation and the adaptation of processes on knowledge transfer is complemented by a case study on the internationalization efforts of a Munich-based firm, following next to beer brewing the distribution of a beer-oriented gastronomy concept.

This firm initially used a decentralized approach regarding knowledge concerning operational duties by leaving freedom to its international partners, but possible negative outcomes and the potential damage to the brand reputation forced it to implement a replication strategy of its German practices abroad. Nevertheless, some adaptation in the organizational knowledge was required to meet satisfaction standards of local customers.

Background

Paulaner is one of the oldest and most famous beer brewing companies, located in Munich, the capital of Bavaria, in Germany. Its name refers to the Paulaner fraternity, founded by Franz von Paola, whose image can be found on the Paulaner logo nowadays. The monks of the Paulaner fraternity had been brewing beer for their own usage since 1634. On feast days of the founder, the beer was also being served to the public. Due to the abolishment of the cloister in 1799, the brewery was handed over to business people. For many decades the Paulaner beer was being brewed on the famous Nockherberg, which today is part of the Munich district "Au." Today, the Paulaner brewery is owned by the Paulaner Brauerei Gruppe; 70% of it belongs to the Schoerghuber Unternehmensgruppe, 30% belongs to the Dutch company Heineken International. The Paulaner Brauerei Gruppe itself is the owner of different breweries such as Hacker-Pschorr or Fuerstlich Fuerstenbergische Brauerei.

The popularity of Paulaner beer extends far beyond the city limits of Munich. More than 2 million hectoliters leave the brewery each year – traveling from Munich-Langwied (the new brewing location) to over 70 countries (Paulaner, n.d., www.paulaner.com/us/brewery/portrait). The beer is being sold through different distribution channels, like wholesalers, supermarkets, liquor stores, beer tents of fairs (like the Oktoberfest in Munich), and several F&B outlets (restaurants, bars, beer gardens) worldwide.

One of the distribution channels are Paulaner licensed restaurants. With their microbreweries and very own Paulaner master brewers, Paulaner Bräuhaus restaurants offer a unique combination of Bavarian tradition and Munich lifestyle. A prominent eye-catching feature among the Bräuhaus locations are the copper brewing kettles with their pipes and fittings (Paulaner, n.d.; www.paulaner-brauhaus-worldwide.com/de/unser-bier/hausbrauerei).

In total there exist 28 Bräuhaus restaurants (by February 2019): 1 in Munich, 6 in Russia, 19 in China, 1 in Azerbaijan, and 1 in Singapore. The first Bräuhaus with a microbrewery opened in 1989 in the city center of Munich. The first international Bräuhaus with 280 seats opened in the Kempinski Hotel in Beijing in 1992, followed by Bangkok (Figure 26.1).

Locations World Wide

China		Russia	Singapore	Azerbaijan
Beijing (1992)	Shenzhen Sea World (2014)	St. Petersburg Pulkovskaya (2002)	Singapore (1996)	Baku (2018)
Shanghai Xintiandi (2001)*	Changsha (2014)	St. Petersburg Nevsky (2010)*		
Shanghai Binjiang (2003)*	Guiyang (2014)	Moscow Paveletsky (2013)	Taiwan	Germany
Shanghai Expo (2010)	Beijing (HP) (2015)	Petrozavodsk (2013)	Taipei I (2009)	Munich Kapuzinerplatz (1989)
Chengdu (2004)	Beijing Yanqi Lake (2015)	Yaroslavl (2013)*	Taipei University Campus (2009)*	Dresden (1997)**
Shenyang (2004)	Fuzhou (2015)	Chelyabinsk (2014)	Taipei Urban City (2010)*	Zwickau (2001)**
Dalian (2005)	Xi'an (HP) (2015)	Sochi (2014)*		Regensburg (HP) (2005)
Nanjing (2007)	Zhengzhou (2015)*	Novokuznetsk (2015)	Indonesia	Leipzig (2006)**
Suzhou (2009)	Changchun (2016)	Novosibirsk (2015)	Jakarta (2010)	Munich Nockherberg (2018)
Yinchuan (2010)	Hangzhou (2016)	Volgograd (2015)		
Chongqing (2012)	Kunming (2016)	Moscow Olimpic (2016)		
Tianjin (2012)*	Shanghai (HP) (2017)*			
Xiamen (2012)	Shanghai Raffles (2017)*			
Taiyuan (2013)	Yiwu (2017)*			

Figure 26.1   Locations of all Paulaner restaurants (including Paulaner Wirtshaus and Hacker Pschorr Bräuhaus restaurants).

Notes: As of September 2018. HP= Hacker-Pschorr; *Wirtshaus; **other brands.

Problems and Change of Strategy

The Paulaner Bräuhaus restaurants have all been opened by local partner companies on the basis of a License & Consulting Agreement with Paulaner (back then with the sub company Paulaner Bräuhaus Consult GmbH). This agreement consists of the following important rights and duties:

- The local partner is allowed to use the rights in terms of the name "Paulaner" and the brand. Paulaner sells to the partner advertising material such as mugs and T-shirts.
- Paulaner assures "protection of the location," meaning that Paulaner does not sell another license to someone else for the specified region unless the partner agreed.
- The partner is only allowed to sell Paulaner beer in bottles, cans, or barrels, which is imported from Paulaner or locally brewed according to Paulaner standards. A brewing plant is provided by Paulaner.
- Paulaner offers a holistic project development (location check, concept development)

In the framework of the consulting agreement, the partners were given useful information concerning all aspects of the marketing mix (for example food offers, prices, furnishing & decoration, processes), leading to a knowledge transfer. However, the result of the collaboration was not what was expected by the Paulaner brewery. A consistent brand image and a high product quality at every customer touchpoint could not be guaranteed.

- On the one hand, the local partners accepted and used the information and help given at the beginning of the collaboration. Recommendations were implemented. These suggestions, however, vanished over time. The local partners partly introduced their own ideas and started managing their restaurants differently, hoping they could increase sales. This especially applied to the food offers and the guest entertainment which differed from what was seen as original Bavarian and from what Paulaner expected. A high level of uncontrolled adaptation done by the recipient, the local partner, was apparent.
- On the other hand, the partners were facing many questions, which, due to the big distance, often remained unanswered or were for both sides laborious, such as: where can equipment be bought? How can the kitchen be set up? What further trainings would make sense? Where can the ingredients for the food be ordered? A high desire for additional support of the source unit was observable.

As mentioned earlier by Von Krogh and Cusumano (2001) in a replication context it is important to get a trade-off between standardization and adaptation. Regarding Paulaner this trade-off was at this time imbalanced. Finally, two aspects made Paulaner introduce changes to improve the current situation:

- In respect of how the different restaurants were being managed, Paulaner was afraid to risk a wrong perception of the brand and of the brand's promises to its customers which would in turn damage the brand reputation and image. In order to guarantee that the restaurants promote Paulaner in Asia and worldwide, they had to introduce a system to ensure quality and the representation of the brand.
- Chinese law protects license contracts only to a certain extent.

On the one hand, Paulaner wanted to guarantee a clear appearance of its brand in foreign countries. On the other hand, the company wanted to ensure faster growth of the Paulaner gastronomy

	Paulaner Bräuhaus	Paulaner Wirtshaus	Paulaner Bierhaus
Location	addition: name of the city / top locations; 1 per city (major cities possibly >1)	addition: name of the district; >1 per city / top locations	locations with lots of transit (city, traffic, trade); >1 per city
Micro brewery	yes	no	no
Size	around 1,200 sqm inside / around 200 sqm outside	around 700 sqm inside / around 200 sqm outside	around 200 sqm inside/ around 40 sqm outside
Capacity	>350 seats	>150 seats	<150 seats
Sales per year	3.3 - 4.5 Mio €	1.6 - 2.2 Mio €	700,000 - 800,000€
Sales mix	55% food / 45% drinks	60% food / 40% drinks	40% food / 60% drinks
Franchise fee (Royalty)	up to 7.5 % of the net sales (for all concepts)		
Need for capital	around 3,000€/sqm	around 2,800€/sqm	around 2,500€/sqm

Figure 26.2 Detailed franchise manuals were developed, which are the knowledge basis for the multiplication.

outlets. Therefore, the Paulaner Franchise & Consulting GmbH (Successor of the Paulaner Bräuhaus Consult GmbH) was founded, aiming at the development of a franchise concept. The franchise contracts should replace license contracts. Furthermore, they should be offered to new partners. The franchise fee is based on net sales. The concept was based on the goal of being a contemporary Munich restaurant, which offers the opportunity to experience beer with all senses and to enjoy authentic Bavarian cuisine. The practices and knowledge acted as a template to replicate overseas, but with a certain degree of adaptation in the foreign outlets. In order to make the concept compatible for different locations and accommodations, three variations were introduced: a small outlet with around 200 m^2 (Paulaner Bierhaus), a middle one with around 700 m^2 (Paulaner Wirtshaus), and a big one with around 1,200 m^2 (Paulaner Bräuhaus) (Figure 26.2).

Implementation and Adaptation of the Strategy: The Example of the Singapore Outlet

Since 1996 a license contract had existed for the outlet in Singapore. However, the restaurant did not meet the economic expectations and became insolvent. Therefore, in 1999, the Paulaner Franchise & Consulting GmbH had the opportunity to buy the operating company from the licensee. The new Paulaner Bräuhaus Singapore was about to become a prototype for franchise brew houses of the future. The new furnished and rebuilt Singapore Bräuhaus opened in May 2017.

From the beginning, Paulaner was paying a lot of attention to how the guests reacted to the concept in order to analyze weak points and improve them. Therefore, Paulaner deployed mystery guests that checked and reviewed the food and the drinks as well as the service and the experience during a visit. Amongst others, a group of students from the Munich University, department of tourism, was involved. The group visited the Bräuhaus for lunch and dinner on specific days in May 2018 and rated the visit on the basis of the experienced customer journey. Especially the seven "Ps" of the marketing mix were being examined. For example, the following findings resulted from the test:

- Product:
- High beer quality; Very good quality of the food; partially the portion sizes were too big, especially during lunch; Quantity and quality of the merchandise could be improved
- Price: Prices for food and drinks are above average; however, in respect of the portion size and in comparison to other local restaurants they are acceptable
- Processes: Service processes demand improvement; Celerity of the service team is mostly given

- Place and Promotion: The brewhouse is not easily accessible due to the infrastructure in front of the building; A lot of advertising material is being used and partially even distributed to other companies (for events)
- People: Missing knowledge of food and drinks; Training needs concerning upselling and cross-selling; Partially, technical mistakes were made; Missing leadership
- Physical Evidence: The outer appearance of the building is not ideal, as it looks a lot like an office building; Good atmosphere at the bar, rather cold atmosphere in the restaurant on the first floor

The mystery test acted as a proof of concept and based on the key findings, an action plan was developed and additional adaptations on the concept were made in order to maximize local success. For example, using fewer spices and adjusting the service culture. Those aspects are emphasized on McArthur´s research (1998), where adaptation is not a sole recipient role because the source unit is the one that started the process in this case. Especially in the case of the specific Singapore restaurant, the unit manager plays a special role because his decisions are critical.

Conclusion

In this work, we have reviewed the academic literature of an interesting aspect that affects international hospitality firms when they set or acquire/manage new units abroad: the decisions about the mobilization of knowledge from the headquarters or template/model units to these new recipient units. The strategy to transfer significant, key parts of the underlying knowledge about managerial and operational decisions and practices tends to be prevalent in international hospitality firms. However, this knowledge replication requires adaptation due to the differences between the context where the knowledge was originally developed and the context of the country and the specific characteristics of the new unit. The participation of the members of the recipient unit can also be very helpful, and the key role of the manager responsible for the knowledge transfer and adaptation is highlighted.

A conclusion can also be drawn from the case of the expansion process of the firm that we have studied to illustrate these aspects. The initial strategy to extend the restaurant chain abroad was mainly based on an emergent transnational strategy. Although there were significant knowledge transfers of the concept and operations in the home country to the new outlets, it did not translate into a major replication concept that aimed to set up cloned outlets abroad. Apart from some dynamics in the headquarters, this situation was probably due to the format for the expansion chosen by the internationalizing firm, which was based on license and consulting agreements with local partners in the host country that regulated the relationship and how it was enforced. This format allowed for having local managers without hierarchical links to superiors in the home country, but related to the internationalizing firm through just commercial ties. The results of the approach with a comparatively loose collaboration caused some dissatisfaction in the headquarters because a high level of an uncontrolled adaptation done by the recipient was evident as well as their continuous lack of information in different important questions.

This aspect originated a change in the internationalization strategy of the focal company, which became a more global orientation and was based in a knowledge replication concept. Mainly in order to strengthen quality and brand in the future, the firm started to implement a clear and stricter franchising concept. In the first new unit (in Singapore) the concept was tested. The results showed that adaptation of the concept is preferred in these circumstances and a supporting action plan was needed in order to maximize local success and satisfaction in the headquarters.

References

Alexander, N., and Lockwood, A. (1996), "Internationalisation: a comparison of the hotel and retail sectors", *Service Industries Journal*, Vol.16, No.4, pp.58–473.

Armistead, C. (1999), "Knowledge management and process performance", *Journal of Knowledge Management*, Vol.3, pp.143–154.

Attewell, P. (1992), "Technology diffusion and organizational learning: The case of business computing", *Organization Science*, Vol.3, pp.1–19.

Barney, J.B. (1991), "Firms resources and sustained competitive advantage", *Journal of Management*, Vol.17, pp.99–120.

Bartlett, C.A. and Ghoshal, S. (1989), *Managing Across Borders: The Transnational Solution*. Harvard Business School Press, Boston, MA.

Bonache, J. (2000), "The international transfer of an idea suggestion system. Against radical relativism in international human resource management", *International Studies of Management and Organization*, Vol 29, pp.24–44.

Cohen, W. and Levinthal, D.A. (1990), "Absorptive capacity: A new perspective on learning and innovation", *Administrative Science Quarterly*, Vol.35, pp.128–152.

Dixon, N. (2000), *Common Knowledge: How Companies Thrive by Sharing What They Know*, Harvard Business School Press, Boston, MA

Doyle, P. (1990), "Building successful brands: The strategic options", *Journal of Consumer Marketing*, Vol.7, No.2, pp.5–20.

Foss, N.J. and Pedersen, T. (2000), "Transferring knowledge in MNCs: The role of sources of subsidiary knowledge and organizational control", paper presented at the 26th EIBA Annual Conference in Maastricht, The Netherlands. 10–12 December 2000.

García-Almeida, D.J. (2009), *La transferencia de conocimiento en la expansión de las cadenas hoteleras*, Editorial Centro de Estudios Ramon Areces SA, Madrid, Spain.

García-Almeida, D.J. and Bolívar-Cruz, A.M. (2007), "La integración de hoteles en las cadenas hoteleras", in Parra López, E. and Calero García, F. (Eds.) *Situación actual, implicaciones y perspectivas futuras del turismo en Canarias*, Vol. 2, Ayuntamiento de Adeje, Adeje, Spain.

García-Almeida, D.J. and Yu, L. (2015), "Knowledge transfer in hotel firms: Determinants of success in international expansion", *International Journal of Hospitality & Tourism Administration*, Vol.16, pp.16–39.

García Falcón, J.M. (1995), *Dirección estratégica. Fundamentos*, C.I.E.S, Las Palmas de Gran Canaria, Spain.

Ghoshal, S. and Westney, D.E. (1993), "Introduction and overview", in Ghoshal, S. and Westney, D.E. (Eds.), *Organization Theory and the Multinational Corporation*, St. Martin's Press, New York, NY.

Grant, R.M. (1996), "Toward a knowledge-based theory of the firm". *Strategic Management Journal*, Vol.17, pp.109–122.

Hedlund, G. (1993), "Assumptions of hierarchy and heterarchy, with applications to the management of the multinational corporation", in Ghoshal, S. and Westney, D.E. (Eds.), *Organization Theory and the Multinational Corporation*, St. Martin's Press, New York, NY.

Hedlund, G. (1994), "A model of knowledge management and the N-form corporation", *Strategic Management Journal*, Vol.15, pp.73–90.

Ingram, P. and Baum, J.A.C. (1997), "Chain affiliation and the failure of Manhattan hotels, 1898–1980", *Administrative Science Quarterly*, Vol.42, pp.68–102.

Jones, C., Thompson, P., and Nickson, D. (1998), "Not part of the family? The limits to managing the corporate way in international hotel chains", *The International Journal of Human Resource Management*, Vol.9, pp.1048–1063.

Kogut, B. and Zander, U. (1992), "Knowledge of the firm, combinative capabilities, and the replication of technology", *Organization Science*, Vol.3, pp.383–397.

Kogut, B. and Zander, U. (1993), "Knowledge of the firm and the evolutionary theory of the multinational corporation", *Journal of International Business Studies*, Vol.24, pp.625–645.

Kwun, D.J.W. and Oh, H. (2007), "Consumers' evaluation of brand portfolios", *International Journal of Hospitality Management*, Vol.26, No.1, pp.81–97.

Lawrence, P.R. and Lorsch, J. (1967), *Organization and Environment*, Irwin, Homewood, IL

Leonard-Barton, D. (1988), "Implementation as mutual adaptation of technology and organization", *Research Policy*, Vol.17, pp.251–267.

Leonard-Barton, D. and Sinha, D.K. (1993), "Developer-user interaction and user satisfaction in internal technology transfer", *Academy of Management Journal*, Vol.36, No.5, pp.1125–1139.

Levitt, T. (1983), "The globalization of markets", *Harvard Business Review*, Vol.83, No.5&6, pp.92–102.

Litteljohn, D. (1997), "Internationalization in hotels: Current aspects and developments", *International Journal of Contemporary Hospitality Management*, Vol.9, pp.187–192.

McArthur, D.N. (1998), "A grounded theory of international technology transfer within multinationals", UMI Dissertation Services.

Nelson, R. and Winter, G. (1982), *An Evolutionary Theory of Economic Change*, Belknap Press, Cambridge, MA.

Olsen, M.D., Tse, E.C., and West, J. (1992), *Strategic Management in the Hospitality Industry* (1st ed.), Van Nostrand Reinhold, New York, NY.

Olsen, M.D., Tse, E.C., and West, J. (1998), *Strategic Management in the Hospitality Industry*, 2nd ed., Van Nostrand Reinhold, New York, NY.

Paulaner. (n.d.), *Hausbrauerei*, available at: https:// www.paulaner-brauhaus-worldwide.com/de/unser-bier/ hausbrauerei (accessed 4 February 2019).

Paulaner. (n.d.), *Portrait*, available at: https:// www.paulaner.com/us/brewery/portrait (accessed 4 February 2019).

Pedersen, T., Petersen, B., and Sharma, D. (2000), "Means of knowledge sourcing and transfer mechanism in the internationalization process", paper presented at the 26th EIBA Annual Conference in Maastricht, The Netherlands. 10–12 December 2000.

Penrose, E. (1959), *The Growth of the Firm*, Basic Blackwell, New York, NY.

Perlmutter, H.V. (1969), "The tortuous evolution of the multinational corporation", *Columbia Journal of World Business*, Vol.4, No.1&2, pp.9–18.

Pizam, A. (2007), "Does the tourism/hospitality industry possess the characteristics of knowledge-based industry?", *International Journal of Hospitality Management*, Vol.26, No.4, pp.759–763.

Pla Barber, J., León Darder, F., and Dasí Coscollar, M.A. (1999), *Dirección de empresas multinacionales: teoría y práctica*, Promolibro, Valencia, Spain.

Ramón Rodríguez, A. (2002), "Determining factors in entry choice for international expansion. The case of the Spanish hotel industry", *Tourism Management*, Vol.23, No.6, pp.597–607.

Reddy, N.M. and Zhao, L. (1990), "International technology transfer: A review", *Research Policy*, Vol.19, pp.285–307.

Rosenzweig, S. and Singh, J. (1991), "Organizational environments and the multinational enterprise", *Academy of Management Review*, Vol.16, pp.340–361.

Von Krogh, G. and Cusumano, M.A. (2001), "Three strategies for managing fast growth". *MIT Sloan Management Review*, Vol.43 (Winter), pp.53–61.

Winter, S.G. and Szulanski, G. (2002), "Replication of organizational routines: Conceptualizing the exploitation of knowledge assets", in Choo, C.W. and Bontis, N. (Eds.), *The Strategic Management of Intellectual Capital and Organizational Knowledge*, Oxford University Press, New York, NY.

Zaheer, S. (1995), "Overcoming the liability of foreignness", *Academy of Management Journal*, Vol.38 pp. 341–363.

27

THE SPECIAL ROLE OF 'HOSPITABLENESS' FOR CUSTOMER SATISFACTION IN SOUTH TYROL (ITALY)

Anja Marcher, Philipp Corradini, Harald Pechlaner, and Michael Volgger

Introduction

Customer satisfaction or dissatisfaction is essential to determine the quality of a product or service within a tourism destination and happen to be an effective mean of promotion (Pizam et al., 2016). Satisfaction within the domain of services derives from a complex combination of tangible (objects) and intangible elements (e.g., relational aspects) also depending on the context (servicescape). Existing research offers a broad range of service satisfaction measurement tools (Scuttari et al., 2017). Moreover, research on relational aspects of tourism services often focuses on host-guest relationships and its genuine elements, known as *hospitableness* (Kayed, 2007; Tasci and Semrad, 2016; Telfer, 2001). These relational and inter-personal aspects in accommodation settings and their impact on customer satisfaction have gained importance (Ariffin et al., 2013; Lashley et al., 2007; Tasci and Semrad, 2016). Hospitableness is one central aspect of quality in hospitality and tourism best described as a system of values and relationships characterized by helpfulness, kindness, and an inner attitude that goes beyond professional service quality (Pechlaner et al., 2017a).

As these aspects of hospitality are critical for a comprehensive tourism management strategy in a tourism destination, this chapter focuses on the following research questions: How important is a genuine welcoming behavior (*hospitableness*) from a customer point of view? In which way do perceptions regarding hospitableness differ between customer segments? In order to investigate these research questions, a survey with domestic and foreign tourists was conducted during the Northern hemisphere spring and summer seasons in 2017 in different areas of the region of South Tyrol, an Alpine tourism destination in Northern Italy (*n=579*). The findings indicate that the most important reasons for choosing the destination were its landscape and weather or climate. The third most important reason was hospitableness. The analysis of specific aspects of hospitableness shows differences between their importance for guests and guest satisfaction with the respective performance.

Theoretical Background

Customer Satisfaction

Customer satisfaction is not only the leading criterion to determine the quality of a product or service, but it is essential for corporate survival, as it notably contributes to the reinforcement of the positive attitudes towards a brand and, more generally, customer loyalty (Hallowell, 1996; Pizam and Ellis, 1999; Pizam et al., 2016). Moreover, it reduces price elasticity, increases cross-buying attitudes, and contributes to the willingness of the generation of positive word-of-mouth (Matzler et al., 2004). Within highly competitive markets, the achievement of customer satisfaction becomes a vital strategy, which must also consider the shift from a product-centric towards a service-centric and finally an experience-centric customer approach (Maklan and Klaus, 2011). In service-based industries, this shift can be conceived as somehow less arduous than in product-based industries, as the service "product" manifests per definition a higher concentration of intangible elements. Customer satisfaction is connected to the expectations, which customers built on previous experiences and during any interaction with tangible and intangible elements of services (Nichols et al., 1998). While the importance of customer satisfaction measurement has been widely covered within the marketing and management literature, a general consensus on how to perform the measurement itself has not yet been found (Gilbert and Veloutsou, 2006). For instance, the time between the consumption and the measurement of the satisfaction needs to be considered as recent research showed that the judgment of satisfaction changes over time (Pizzi et al., 2015).

In the tourism industry, for several reasons customer satisfaction is regarded to be highly important. These comprise considerations of destination competitiveness, generation of repeat visits by increasing the probability of return through customer satisfaction and the triggering of positive word-of-mouth recommendations (Buhalis, 2000; Hultman et al., 2015; Swarbrooke and Horner, 2007). The last aspect has considerably increased in importance due to the technological developments, and in particular due to the advent of new means of communication, which boosted customers' influence as co-creators of valuable information (Vermeulen and Seegers, 2009). Moreover, regarding social media, it has been observed, that most of the information created and shared was during the post-trip phase of the travel, followed by the phase of actual stay within the tourism destination. The consumption of information seems to be mostly located within the pre-trip phase, during which social media also has a certain level of influence regarding both destination and accommodation choice (Fotis et al., 2012).

Individual service encounters are one fundamental component of customer satisfaction, influencing both the transaction-specific and the overall satisfaction (Jones and Suh, 2000; Wilkins, 2010). Hereby the overall satisfaction can be regarded as a cumulative construct, which emerges through the summation of the satisfaction concerning specific services of organizations. In case of tourism destinations, the overall satisfaction includes the satisfaction with the connection between the different tourism products and the performance of the different service providers integrated towards a comprehensive tourism experience originating from a multitude of interactions (Buhalis, 2000; Garbarino and Johnson, 1999; Swarbrooke and Horner, 2007). Overall satisfaction is usually more stable than transaction-specific satisfaction, which varies based on the different service encounters (Auh et al., 2003).

One of the most widely used concepts for the analysis of customer satisfaction is Kano's three-factor theory, which comprises three types of product or service attributes: basic, performance, and excitement factors (Kano et al., 1984). The basic factors are considered to be essential attributes referring to the functionality of the product or service and are therefore taken for granted by the customer. Performance factors represent product requirements, which are expected and requested by the customer and thus proportional to the customer satisfaction, resulting in satisfaction if fulfilled and dissatisfaction if not fulfilled. Finally, excitement factors are attributes, which are not explicitly requested by the customer and, if provided, help to exceed customer expectations. Their provisioning leads to high customer satisfaction, while, at the same time, their absence does not necessarily result in the dissatisfaction of the customer. A basic strategy aiming to ensure customer satisfaction can follow the following approach: fulfillment of the basic factors, competitiveness regarding the performance factors, and differentiation through excitement factors (Berger et al., 1993; Brandt, 1988; Lai and Hitchcock, 2015; Matzler et al., 2004). Excitement factors are not expected by the customer or guest and may increase the overall service. Excitement represents, according to Pechlaner et al. (2017a), one central starting point for a successful positioning and differentiation of the tourism product or destination on the market (Figure 27.1). Unexpected levels of attention (excitement factor) and the relational quality between guest and hosts (*hospitableness*) may play an increasingly important role for future guests but can also be perceived as basic factors for regular guests.

The Meanings of Hospitality and Hospitableness

Historically, *hospitality* means giving protection to a guest in a foreign context without anything in return (Kayed, 2003) and also includes the way in which foreigners and guests are welcomed (traditional hospitality). Nowadays, it describes a *"temporary reception, service, or accommodation, for strangers as well as for members of the own group"* (Kayed, 2007, p. 31). In academic research, diverse disciplines studied the historic and present definition and meaning of hospitality and its relation to the encounter and treatment of strangers (Pechlaner et al., 2018). Some researchers applied the concept of hospitality to the arrival and treatment of migrants, such as Friese (2014). In the tourism industry, *hospitality* is usually defined as an economic activity, as "a cluster of service sector activities associated with the provision of food, drink, and accommodation" (Lashley, 2001, p. 2). In the

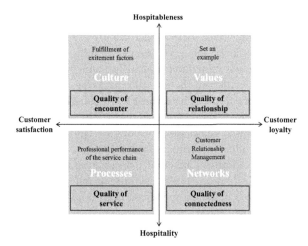

Figure 27.1 Relationship between customer satisfaction, customer loyalty, hospitality and hospitableness. The figure was adapted and reprinted by permission from Springer Nature: Springer eBook, Hospitality Management ist mehr als Service Management: Skizzen eines umfassenden Qualitätsansatzes by Pechlaner, Volgger, and Nordhorn, p.143, copyright (2017).

last decades, within hospitality management research, a discussion of *hospitality* and *hospitableness* in a broader social setting started, where we can identify different strands of literature. Some authors do not distinguish between the two terms and generally focus on host and guest relationships (Ariffin et al., 2013; Lashley et al., 2007). Other authors differentiate *hospitableness* and see it as part of a broader construct of *hospitality* and as one important aspect to increase consumer satisfaction. In this context, the "umbrella term" *hospitality* refers to professionalism in service performance and *hospitableness* is an "*element of the human component [...] what makes the product special*" (Tasci and Semrad, 2016, p. 30). In this sense, *hospitableness* is interpreted as a trait possessed by hospitable people (Telfer, 2001).

The meaning and definition of hospitality and hospitableness vary across different languages and cultures. German literature on hospitality management is strongly influenced by the discussion about host-guest interpersonal relationships as a distinctive feature between hospitality and service (Kayed, 2007; Pechlaner and Raich, 2007a; Perathoner, 2000). In this context, the term *hospitableness* – in German *Gastfreundschaft* – often refers to the quality of the guest-host relationship (*Gast* = guest, *Freundschaft* = friendship). It focuses on the appropriate behavior at this specific relational level (Pechlaner et al., 2017a). Therefore, *hospitality* can be defined as the professional service quality (*Gastlichkeit*) (Pechlaner and Raich, 2007b). The combination of hospitality and hospitableness represents therefore a promising overall strategy to enhance the service quality in tourism, as they are strongly related to customer satisfaction and loyalty (Figure 27.1) (Pechlaner et al., 2017a).

Lashley (2001) proposed the analysis of three different hospitality activities by distinguishing between a "social/cultural," "private/domestic," and "commercial" domain, which represent aspects of hospitality provisions that are independent and at the same time overlapping. The social domain "*considers the social settings in which hospitality and acts of hospitableness take place with the impact of social forces on the production and consumption of food/ drink/ and accommodation*" (ibid., p. 5). The private domain relates according to Lashley (2015a, p. 4) "*to the meaning of hospitality, hosting and "hospitableness,"*" where the act of hospitality involves people that are not members of the household. In contrast to the first two domains, hospitality-related activities connected to the commercial domain, are driven by the surplus value generated from the service interaction, a commercial imperative that creates tensions and contradictions (ibid.). However, commercial hospitality should include aspects of the social and the private domain, to add value to the customer experience with intangible elements that may be "*dependent on a 'unique' encounter for each guest*" (Lashley, 2015b, p. 160). Research shows that *hospitality* as a concept to explain host-guest-relationships is often used in a comprehensive manner to include *hospitableness* and a system of values and relationships characterized by helpfulness, kindness, and an inner attitude which influence the relationship quality at the interface between guests and hosts (Marcher et al., 2017). This type of tourism hospitality goes beyond mere service quality, rejects a complete standardization of the tourism product, and focuses on relational quality (Ariffin et al., 2013; Lashley, 2007; Pechlaner et al., 2017a).

The Conceptual Framework of Hospitality

As part of a research project, the Lucerne University of Applied Sciences and Arts developed a conceptual framework of "hospitality" (Stettler et al., 2016, 2017, 2018), defining hospitality as a quality feature characterizing the relationship between guests and hosts and as competitive advantage. Within the "Lucerne framework," *hospitality* contains two different perspectives, a traditional and a commercial one (Stettler et al., 2017): (1) Traditional hospitality refers to the culturally conditioned and grown hospitality in a destination. It is strongly influenced by culture, identity, and tourism awareness of the hosting population. Traditional hospitality has a decisive influence on the experience quality of guests in a destination (see also Thiem, 2001) and can also be called "hospitableness." (2) Professional hospitality, instead, is defined as a central component of tourism service quality covering, in particular, the service encounter and host-guest relationship in a professional and commercial setting. Commercial hospitality becomes traceable at the service provider level and is demonstrated by the competence in dealing with guests (Pechlaner and Raich, 2007b; Pechlaner et al., 2017a).

The conceptual framework of hospitality developed in Stettler et al. (2017, 2018) distinguishes three different dimensions of hospitality (Figure 27.2): (1) the socio-cultural level as general dimension including cultural identities, values, norms, traditions, and other aspects of the society; (2) the organizational and/or destination level including supporting dimensions, such as visual appearance, cleanness, or architecture; and (3) the level of (personal) host-guest interaction represented by different core dimensions of hospitality and hospitableness. The latter comprises elements such as service and professional expertise, communication skills, openness to other cultures, empathy, authenticity, friendliness, cordiality, generosity, attention, reliability, appreciation and respect, helpfulness as well as interest and openness (Stettler et al., 2016).

In this contribution, we refer to those core aspects of the third dimension as "elements of hospitableness." The second and third level is embedded in the socio-cultural context; it means that commercial hospitality is connected to the traditional hospitality within a destination. It represents a comprehensive understanding and definition of commercial hospitality.

Method

In order to analyze elements of hospitableness, i.e., core elements of hospitality (Figure 27.2), a quantitative research approach was applied, using a questionnaire developed in collaboration with the Lucerne University of Applied Sciences and Arts including importance and performance measurement items. The questionnaire is based on the comprehensive hospitality framework presented in Figure 27.2. The questionnaires' hospitableness items have been identified through a mix of qualitative and quantitative methods (Stettler et al., 2018). With the help of the questionnaire,

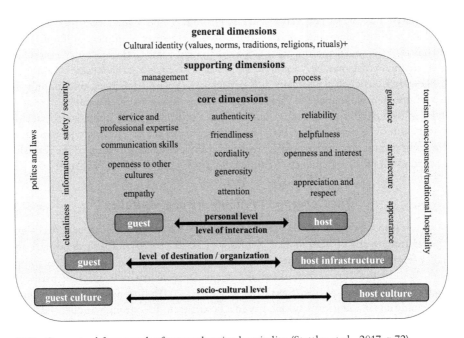

Figure 27.2 Conceptual framework of comprehensive hospitality (Stettler et al., 2017, p.72).

we identified the tourists' visiting reasons, evaluated their importance, and explored visitors' perceptions of elements of hospitableness in a destination. A 5-point Likert Scale was used to rate importance and satisfaction, and an importance-performance matrix of hospitality elements was plotted. Comparisons were based on the mean values of the obtained importance and performance scores. In addition, socio-demographic information was collected.

Study Area

The Autonomous Province of Bolzano-Bozen, also called South Tyrol, is located in the Alps in the Northeast of Italy and represents an interesting study area, because of the growing importance of tourism for the regional economy (Kofler et al., 2018). Tourism accounts for 13.8% of the regional value-added (ASTAT, 2018) and 13.5% of the region's employment (Department for labor market observation, 2018). According to the statistical yearbook on tourism of the European Union (Eurostat, 2014), the province is one of the top 20 European regions regarding nights spent in hotels and other accommodations and the tourism sector "*is considered an important business driver because of its cross-sectoral character*" (Kofler et al., 2018, p. 71).

In 2017, the region registered more than 7.3 million arrivals and about 32 million overnight stays. Visitors came mainly from Germany (48.7%), Italy (31.8%), Switzerland and Liechtenstein (4.9%), and other European source countries (14.7%) (ASTAT, 2018). The highest shares of overnight stays were registered in 3-star hotels (34.6%) and 4-star hotels (22.6%), followed by tourist apartments (9.1%) and farm stays (8.3%). The average length of stay was 4.4 days.

Data Collection and Sample

In 2017, 579 tourists were surveyed in different areas within the destination South Tyrol. The survey was conducted by two interviewers in the low season in spring (March and April) and during the peaking summer season (August). Both seasons were covered in order to reach a diverse group of guests and because it is conceivable that tourism service quality may differ between the seasons.

Table 27.1 summarizes the guest characteristics of our sample, as demographic characteristics of consumers can affect quality expectations (Stettler et al., 2018; Webster, 1989) and therefore, also service quality perceptions in tourism. All participants stayed more than one night in South Tyrol. The sample has an equal share of domestic and international guests: 49.7% were domestic (i.e., Italian) tourists and 50.3% international tourists (33.7% were from Germany), reflecting the overall patterns of inbound tourism to the region. A high share of guests was older than 44 years (67.2%), more than 50% had a high level of education and more than 75% stayed in a hotel.

Empirical Evidence

The Role of Hospitableness

To better understand the role of hospitality and hospitableness, survey participants were asked to rank the importance of ten different reasons for visiting South Tyrol. Table 27.2 illustrates the suggested reasons to visit, which have been ranked from 1 'least important' to 10 'most important.' Considering all surveyed visitors in a comprehensive manner, the landscape appears to be the main attractor, followed by weather and/or climate and hospitableness (hospitable behavior). These results indicate thus that hospitableness affects the tourists' booking decision and destination choice, and hence confirm prior research (Pechlaner et al., 2017b).

Table 27.1 Guest characteristics

		Number	*Percentage*
Gender	Male	287	49.6
	Female	291	50.3
	Prefer not to say	1	0.2
Age	15–24 years	8	1.4
	25–44 years	178	30.7
	45–64 years	307	53.0
	65 years and older	82	14.2
	Missing	4	0.7
Highest level of education	Secondary (compulsory) education	21	3.6
	Post-secondary vocational education	34	5.9
	Post-secondary non-tertiary education	208	35.9
	University degree	314	54.2
	Other	2	.3
Country of origin	Domestic	288	49.7
	International	291	50.3
City size	City	209	36.1
	Medium town	252	43.5
	Small town	69	11.9
	Village	49	8.5
Accommodation type	Hotel	445	76.9
	Budget hotel	*40*	*6.9*
	Medium-priced hotel	*253*	*43.7*
	Premium/luxury hotel	*152*	*26.3*
	Other (youth hotel, holiday flat, B&B, camping)	134	23.1

Table 27.2 Ranking of visiting reasons for South Tyrol

Reasons	*Mean*	*Rank*
Landscape	7.1	1
Weather/climate	6.6	2
Hospitableness (hospitable behavior)	6.3	3
Food	6.3	4
Accommodation	5.7	5
Local culture	5.4	6
Price	5.0	7
Local activities and attractions	4.9	8
Accessibility of the destination	4.1	9
Sustainability	3.6	10

If different customer segments (domestic and international tourists) are considered separately, it becomes apparent that the visiting reasons differ slightly between groups. While the first three

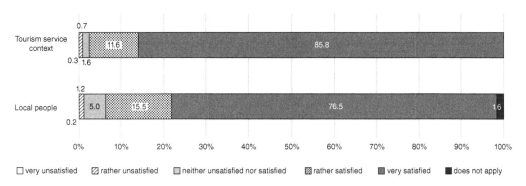

Figure 27.3 Overall satisfaction with South Tyrol's hospitableness.

reasons for visiting the region among domestic (Italian) tourists were the same as for the totality of the survey participants, the ranking of visiting reasons differed slightly for international tourists. In the international tourist group, for example, the culinary aspect is seen as being more important than hospitableness for visiting the region of South Tyrol.

Given the overall relevance of the hospitableness element, a more detailed analysis of the importance as well as performance of its constituting factors is warranted. Figure 27.3 shows that the surveyed guests were highly satisfied with the South Tyrolean hospitableness. More than 85.0% declared to be 'very satisfied' and 11.6% 'rather satisfied' with the hospitableness shown in a tourism service context (commercial hospitality). A slightly lower (but still high) share of the participants (76.5%) indicated that they were 'very satisfied' with the hospitableness of the local people in South Tyrol. Considerably, 15.5% were 'rather satisfied' and 5% 'neither unsatisfied nor satisfied.' The share of tourists with a higher dissatisfaction level was small. The overall performance of the destination South Tyrol in terms of hospitality and hospitableness thus seems to be very good, but to get a deeper understanding, it is necessary to look at the different elements of hospitableness.

An Importance-Performance Analysis of Hospitality Core Elements

Obtained importance and satisfaction scores for the previously defined core elements of hospitableness are illustrated in Table 27.3 (whole sample). The data helps to identify over- and under-performance regarding the central hospitableness dimensions. The numbers generally show high degrees of importance as well as high levels of satisfaction for each aspect of hospitality, although there are some differences between importance and performance.

Importance scores with a high rating have a small standard deviation and the actual values thus are close to the mean of the data. On the contrary, satisfaction scores have a greater spread in the data, even if all standard deviations remain below 1. The satisfaction rating for the hospitableness element "generosity" is the item with the highest variation and is the only one with a spread below 4.

Importance-performance analyses consider customer expectations be met or exceeded when the level of satisfaction is equal to or higher than the level of importance (De Nisco et al., 2015). Table 27.3 illustrates that none of the elements met or exceeded the customers' expectations (i.e., the average satisfaction rating was below the average degree of importance), but the importance-performance differences were very small (see also Figure 27.4). All average values were above 4.5 on a scale from 1 "not important/satisfied" to 5 "very important/satisfied." The

Table 27.3 The average degree of importance and satisfaction and standard deviation for elements of hospitableness

Dimensions of 'hospitableness'	Importance			Satisfaction		
	Average degree	*Ranking*	*Standard deviation*	*Average degree*	*Ranking*	*Standard deviation*
Reliability	4.92	1	0.364	4.79	3	0.532
Appreciation and respect	4.90	2	0.350	4.76	7	0.601
Friendliness	4.89	3	0.374	4.83	2	0.516
Authenticity	4.88	4	0.438	4.78	4	0.557
Cordiality	4.87	5	0.404	4.75	8	0.574
Interest and openness	4.87	5	0.419	4.72	9	0.611
Service and professional experience	4.86	7	0.447	4.83	1	0.744
Communication skills	4.86	7	0.449	4.68	12	0.476
Helpfulness	4.84	9	0.458	4.76	5	0.537
Generosity	4.84	9	0.511	4.58	13	0.846
Level of attention	4.81	11	0.520	4.70	11	0.637
Empathy	4.79	12	0.587	4.76	6	0.553
Openness towards other cultures	4.73	13	0.678	4.72	10	0.588

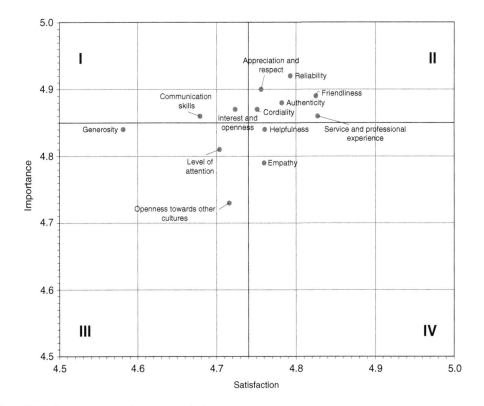

Figure 27.4 Importance–performance analysis.

importance-performance analysis (IPA) illustrated in Figure 27.4 includes data-centered quadrants (Lai and Hitchcock, 2015) using the average importance (= 4.85) and satisfaction values (= 4.74) as distinctive features.

The importance-performance grid presented in Figure 27.4 illustrates four quadrants, where the upper right quadrant (Section II) indicates very good performance and highlights the attributes where no improvement is necessary (Lai and Hitchcock, 2015, p. 243). Lower satisfaction ratings on highly important elements indicate a high improvement priority (Section I) and less important features with a high level of satisfaction show that the resources would be better employed elsewhere (Section IV) (De Nisco et al., 2015). So, each element of hospitableness *"can be analyzed by locating the quadrant in which it falls"* (Joppe et al., 2001, p. 256). Therefore, the most important and best-performing hospitableness elements were reliability, appreciation and respect, friendliness, authenticity, cordiality as well as service and professional experience (see Section II). The two-dimensional grid highlights that guests' satisfaction with social competencies such as friendliness, reliability, appreciation and respect, but also authenticity, cordiality, interest and openness, and helpfulness are perceived to be high in South Tyrol (Sections II and IV). However, features rated as important, such as communications skills, interest and openness, were below the average satisfaction rating and did not fully meet guests' expectations (Section I). Section I highlights those elements of hospitable behavior on which South Tyrol as tourism destination should focus its improvements. Other aspects with improvement margins (but less important and thus of lower priority) are illustrated in Section III: "openness towards other cultures," "level of attention," and "generosity."

The same analytical approach was applied to the two previously differentiated customer segments in order to compare the indicated levels of importance and customer satisfaction for domestic (Italian) and international (mostly German and other European) visitors (Figures 27.5 and 27.6). Figure 27.5 shows the evaluations for the elements of hospitableness distinguishing between domestic and international tourists. The two graphs illustrate a slight difference between the two groups. The level of importance and satisfaction of international tourists is relatively even, with a maximum difference between the values of 0.15. The satisfaction ratings for the items "empathy," "openness towards other cultures," and "service and professional experience" were higher than the mean value of the hospitality importance ratings. By contrast, domestic (Italian) tourists' satisfaction did not meet the importance they attributed to these features. With the subgroup of domestic tourists, there is therefore room for improvement in areas such as "generosity," "communications skills," "interest and openness," "cordiality," and "appreciation and respect." Figure 27.6 shows the importance-performance analysis divided by the two groups.

The comparison between domestic (Italian) and international visitors in Figure 27.6 shows clear and consistent differences between the two segments. The grid is divided based on the overall importance and satisfaction means to facilitate identification of elements of hospitableness that may help to enhance the destinations' competitiveness. There are clear differences between the two customer segments in the IPA-grid. International tourists, mainly from Germany, were much more satisfied with most of the hospitableness elements of the destination than Italian tourists (see Section IV, Figure 27.6). Most of the elements rated by domestic visitors were below the overall satisfaction rating of the whole sample (Section II). Hospitableness elements, such as communication skills, interest and openness, cordiality or appreciation and respect, represent very important service aspects for national tourists. The importance of these elements was rated higher in the group of domestic tourists than in the group of international tourists and shows therefore a clear cultural difference in expectations.

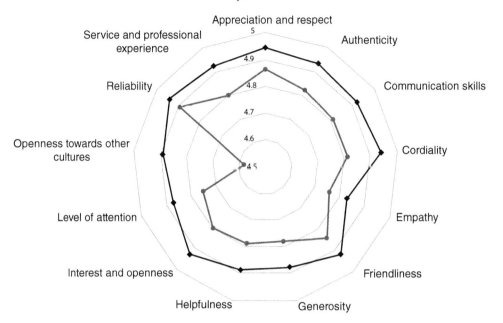

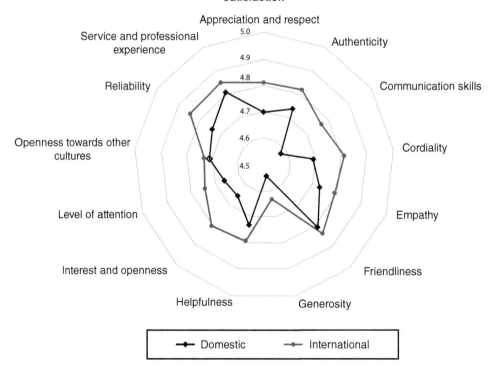

Figure 27.5 Importance and satisfaction of hospitality dimensions for international and domestic visitors.

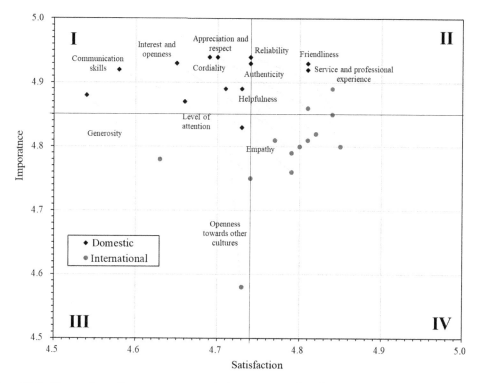

Figure 27.6 Comparison of customer segments in importance and performance.

Tourists' perception differs in relation to guest characteristics. Domestic (Italian) tourists seem therefore to be more critical than international guests, as their expectations, in terms of importance ratings, are higher than their satisfaction with all elements of hospitableness.

Conclusion

Hospitableness as an "enhanced service," going beyond the mere professional fulfillment of the hospitality service itself and including encounters with the local population, seems to be an essential part of the tourism product and also expected by the customer (Smith, 1994; Stettler et al., 2016). Considering that this study finds high importance attributed to the hospitable behavior by surveyed visitors (overall rank 3 among all suggested items), it can be indicated as a central performance factor for the analyzed destination, although further analysis is necessary to generalize this interpretation. Nevertheless, hospitableness or hospitable behavior is a central aspect that customers take into consideration when choosing a destination, but some of its dimensions need improvements, like communication skills and interest and openness. South Tyrol should "keep up the good work" regarding hospitableness elements such as reliability, appreciation and respect, friendliness, authenticity, cordiality as well as service and professional experience (high priority and satisfaction).

The segmentation of findings between domestic (Italian) and international (predominately German) tourists revealed that the perceived importance and satisfaction highly depend on different (cultural) backgrounds. For instance, results indicated slightly higher expectations and lower satisfaction of domestic tourists in contrast to international tourists. The implication for practitioners in the destination is, when dealing with domestic (Italian) tourists, to strive for a generalized improvement of communication skills, generosity, appreciation and respect, cordiality, level of attention, helpfulness, interest and openness towards its guests as well as towards other cultures. The consistency of this finding across several dimensions of hospitableness emphasizes the impact of cultural backgrounds on expectations and thus underscores the need to consider cultural differences. These insights resonate, for example, with other studies, where perception of the destination varies according to the visitors 'origin' (Joppe et al., 2001).

Study Limitations and Outlook

The present contribution focused on elements of hospitableness of the Lucerne hospitality framework, without considering other measurement tools. The implementation of other hospitableness elements within the study may have the potential to understand aspects of hospitableness on a destination level. The results give insights into the importance and satisfaction from a customer point of view but need further analysis. A detailed analysis of socio-demographic characteristics may provide additional insights to improve host-guest interactions regarding the different range of customer segments. In addition, Stettler et al. (2018) highlight some general limiting factors, like the non-solvable situational impact on hospitableness. Furthermore, there are other variables that may influence customers' perception of hospitableness, such as income, travel experience, or number of previous visits. Therefore, further research is warranted.

Although the satisfaction of tourists regarding the hospitableness of the local population (or traditional hospitality) is high in the studied destination, it is still slightly lower than the perceived hospitableness within the tourism service context (or commercial hospitality). Future research distinguishing between different seasonal impacts on the hospitableness perceptions as well as influences of tourism intensity would be important.

References

Ariffin, A.A.M., Nameghi, E.N., and Zakaria, N.I. (2013), "The effect of hospitableness and servicescape on guest satisfaction in the hotel industry", *Canadian Journal of Administrative Sciences*, Vol.30, No.2, pp.127–137. https://doi.org/10.1002/cjas.1246.

ASTAT. (2018), *Database*, Provincial Statistics Institute, Autonomous Province of Bolzano-Bozen, available at: https://astat.provinz.bz.it/de/datenbanken-gemeindedatenblatt.asp (accessed 12 December 2018).

Auh, S., Salisbury L.C., and Johnson, M.D. (2003), "Order effects in customer satisfaction modelling", *Journal of Marketing Management,* Vol.19, No.3–4, pp.379–400. https://doi.org/10.1362/026725703321663700.

Berger, C., Blauth, R. E., and Boger, D. (1993) "Kano's Methods for Understanding Customer-defined Quality", *Center for Quality Management Journal*, pp. 3–35.

Brandt, R.D. (1988), "How service marketers can identify value-enhancing service elements", *Journal of Services Marketing*, Vol.2, No.3, pp.35–41. https://doi.org/10.1108/eb024732.

Buhalis, D. (2000), "Marketing the competitive destination of the future", *Tourism Management*, Vol.21, No.1, pp.97–116. https://doi.org/10.1016/S0261-5177(99)00095-3.

De Nisco, A., Riviezzo, A., and Napolitano, M.R. (2015), "An importance-performance analysis of tourist satisfaction at destination level: evidence from Campania (Italy)", *European Journal of Tourism Research*, Vol.10, pp.64–75.

Department for labor market observation. (2018), *Arbeitsmarktdaten [database]*, Autonomous Province of Bolzano-Bozen, available at: http://www.provinz.bz.it/arbeit-wirtschaft/arbeit/statistik/arbeitsmarktdaten-online.asp (accessed 12 December 2018).

Eurostat. (2014), *Eurostat Regional Yearbook 2014: Tourism*, European Union, available at: https://ec.europa.eu/eurostat/publications/statistical-books (accessed 12 December 2018).

Fotis, J., Buhalis, D., and Rossides, N. (2012), "Social media use and impact during the holiday travel planning process", in Fuchs, M., Ricci, F., and Cantoni, L. (Eds.), *Information and Communication Technologies in Tourism 2012*, Springer, Vienna, pp.13–24.

Friese, H. (2014), *Grenzen der Gastfreundschaft: Die Bootsflüchtlinge von Lampedusa und die europäische Frage*, Transcript, Bielefeld.

Garbarino, E. and Johnson, M. (1999), "The different roles of satisfaction, trust and commitment in customer relationships", *Journal of Marketing,* Vol.4, pp.70–87. http://dx.doi.org/10.2307/1251946.

Gilbert, G.R. and Veloutsou, C. (2006), "A cross-industry comparison of customer satisfaction", *Journal of Services Marketing*, Vol.20, No.5, pp.298–308. https://doi.org/10.1108/08876040610679918.

Hallowell, R. (1996), "The relationships of customer satisfaction, customer loyalty, and profitability: an empirical study", *International Journal of Service Industry Management*, Vol.7, No.4, pp.27–42. https://doi.org/10.1108/09564239610129931.

Hultman, M., Skarmeas, D., Oghazi, P., and Beheshit, H.M. (2015), "Achieving tourist loyalty through destination personality, satisfaction, and identification", *Journal of Business Research,* Vol.68, No.11, pp.2227–2231. https://doi.org/10.1016/j.jbusres.2015.06.002.

Jones, M. and Suh, J. (2000), "Transaction specific satisfaction and overall satisfaction: an empirical analysis", *Journal of Services Marketing*, Vol.14, No.2, pp.147–159. https://doi.org/10.1108/08876040010371555.

Joppe, M., Martin, D.W., and Waalen, J. (2001), "Toronto's image as a destination: A comparative importance-satisfaction analysis by origin of visitor", *Journal of Travel Research*, Vol.39, No.3, pp.252–260. https://doi.org/10.1177/004728750103900302.

Kano, N., Seraku, N., Takahashi, F., and Tsuji, S. (1984), "Attractive quality and must-be quality", *Journal of The Japanese Society for Quality Control*, Vol.14, No.2, pp.147–156. https://doi.org/10.20684/quality.14.2_147.

Kayed, C. (2003), *Gast sein: ein Lesebuch*. Athesia Tappeiner Verlag, Bolzano-Bozen.

Kayed, C. (2007), "Gastfreundschaft und Philosophie", in H. Pechlaner and F. Raich (Eds.), *Gastfreundschaft und Gastlichkeit im Tourismus: Kundenzufriedenheit und -bindung mit Hospitality Management*, ESV, Berlin, pp.31–36.

Kofler, I., Marcher, A., Volgger, M., and Pechlaner, H. (2018), "The special characteristics of tourism innovation networks: The case of the regional innovation system in South Tyrol", *Journal of Hospitality and Tourism Management*, Vol.37, pp.68–75. https://doi.org/10.1016/j.jhtm.2018.09.004.

Lai, I.K.W. and Hitchcock, M. (2015), "Importance-performance analysis in tourism: A framework for researchers", *Tourism Management*, Vol.48, pp.242–267. https://doi.org/10.1016/j.tourman.2014.11.008.

Lashley, C. (2001), "Towards a theoretical understanding", in Lashley, C. and Morrison, A. (Eds.), *In Search of Hospitality*, Routledge, London and New York, pp.1–17. https://doi.org/10.4324/9780080508566.

Lashley, C. (2007), "Discovering hospitality: Observations from recent research", *International Journal of Culture, Tourism and Hospitality Research*, Vol.1, No.3, pp.214–226. https://doi.org/10.1108/17506180710817747.

Lashley, C. (2015a), "Hospitality and hospitableness", *Research in Hospitality Management*, Vol.5, No.1, pp.1–7. https://doi.org/10.1080/22243534.2015.11828322.

Lashley, C. (2015b), "Hospitality experience: An introduction to hospitality management" [Book review], *Journal of Tourism Futures*, Vol.1, No.2, pp.160–161. https://doi.org/10.1108/JTF-12-2014-0008.

Lashley, C., Lynch, P., and Morrison, A.J. (Eds.) (2007), *Hospitality: A Social Lens*, Elsevier, Amsterdam and Boston.

Maklan, S. and Klaus, P. (2011), "Customer experience: Are we measuring the right things?", *International Journal of Market Research*, Vol.53, No.6, pp.771–772. https://doi.org/10.2501/IJMR-53-6-771-792.

Marcher, A., Pechlaner, H., Kofler, I., and Innerhofer, E. (2017), "Ospitalità e accoglienza: Il turismo e l'immigrazione straniera", in A. Membretti, I. Kofler, and P.P. Viazzo (Eds.), *Per forza o per scelta: L'immigrazione straniera nelle Alpi e negli Appennini*, Aracne, Rome, pp.187–198.

Matzler, K., Bailom, F., Hinterhuber, H.H., Renzl, B., and Pichler, J. (2004), "The asymmetric relationship between attribute-level performance and overall customer satisfaction: a reconsideration of the importance-performance analysis", *Industrial Marketing Management*, Vol.33, pp.271–277. https://doi.org/10.1016/S0019-8501(03)00055-5.

Nichols, J.A.F., Gilbert, G.R., and Roslow, S. (1998), "Parsimonious measurement of customer satisfaction with personal service and the service setting", *Journal of Consumer Marketing*, Vol.15, No.3, pp.239–253. https://doi.org/10.1108/07363769810219116.

Pechlaner, H., Nordhorn, C., and Marcher, A. (Eds.) (2018), *Flucht, Migration und Tourismus – Perspektiven einer "New Hospitality"*, Lit-Verlag, Münster.

Pechlaner, H. and Raich, F. (Eds.) (2007a), *Gastfreundschaft und Gastlichkeit im Tourismus: Kundenzufriedenheit und -bindung mit Hospitality Management*, ESV, Berlin.

Pechlaner, H. and Raich, F. (2007b), "Wettbewerbsfähigkeit durch das Zusammenspiel von Gastlichkeit und Gastfreundschaft", in Pechlaner, H. and Raich, F. (Eds.), *Gastfreundschaft und Gastlichkeit im Tourismus: Kundenzufriedenheit und -bindung mit Hospitality Management*, ESV, Berlin, pp.11–24.

Pechlaner, H., Volgger, M., and Nordhorn, C. (2017a), "Hospitality Management ist mehr als Service Management: Skizzen eines umfassenden Qualitätsansatzes", in Pechlaner, H. and Volgger, M. (Eds.), *Die Gesellschaft auf Reisen – Eine Reise in die Gesellschaft*, Springer, Wiesbaden, pp.139–161.

Pechlaner, H., Volgger, M., Demetz, M., Scuttari, A., Innerhofer, E., Lun, L.M., Erschbamer, G., Bassani, R., Ravazzoli, E., Maier, R., and Habicher, D. (2017b), *Zukunft Tourismus Südtirol 2030*, Eurac Research, WIFO, Bolzano-Bozen.

Perathoner, G. (2000), *Gastfreundschaft im Tourismus: Eine Tugendethik aus der Sicht des Gastgebers*, Lit-Verlag, Münster.

Pizam, A. and Ellis, T. (1999), "Customer satisfaction and its measurement in hospitality enterprises", *International Journal of Contemporary Hospitality Management*, Vol.11, No.7, pp.326–339. https://doi.org/10.1108/09596119910293231.

Pizam, A., Shapoval, V., and Ellis, T. (2016), "Customer satisfaction and its measurement in hospitality enterprises: A revisit and update", *International Journal of Contemporary Hospitality Management*, Vol.28, No.1, pp.2–35. https://doi.org/10.1108/IJCHM-04-2015-0167.

Pizzi, G., Marzocchi, G.L., Orsingher, C., and Zammit, A. (2015), "The temporal construal of customer satisfaction", *Journal of Service Research*, Vol.18, No.4, pp.484–497. https://doi-org/10.1177%2F1094670515584752.

Scuttari, A., Pichler, S., and Bonelli, A. (2017), "La soddisfazione dei turisti in Alto Adige: valutazioni comparative nell'ambito turistico e dei trasporti", in Pechlaner, H. and Streifeneder, T. (Eds.), *Regionen, Standorte und Destinationen entwickeln: Perspektiven der Beziehung von Raum und Mensch / Lo sviluppo di regioni, luoghi e destinazioni: prospettive sulle relazioni tra uomo e territorio*, Athesia, Bolzano-Bozen, pp.78–91.

Smith, S.L. (1994), "The tourism product", *Annals of Tourism Research*, Vol.21, No.3, pp.582–595. https://doi-org/10.1177/004728759403300240.

Stettler, J., Amstad, O., and Taufer, B. (2016), "Gastfreundschaft in der Zentralschweiz: Ergebnisse einer Anbieterbefragung", in Bieger, T., Beritelli, P., and Laesser, C. (Eds.), *Gesellschaftlicher Wandel als Herausforderung im alpinen Tourismus: Schweizer Jahrbuch für Tourismus 2015/2016*, ESV, Berlin, pp.159–172.

Stettler, J., Rosenberg-Taufer, B., and Amstad, O. (2017), "Die effektivsten Massnahmen zur Stärkung der Gastfreundschaft in der Zentralschweiz", in Bieger, T., Beritelli, P., and Laesser, C. (Eds.), *Markt- und Branchenentwicklungen im alpinen Tourismus: Schweizer Jahrbuch für Tourismus 2016/2017*, ESV, Berlin, pp.71–81.

Stettler, J., Steffen, A., and Huck, L. (2018), "Hospitality in Switzerland: An empirical analysis for effective improvement", paper presented at Conference of the International Association of Scientific Experts in Tourism (AIEST conference), 26–30 August 2018, Treviso, Italy.

Swarbrooke, J. and Horner, S. (2007), *Consumer Behaviour in Tourism*, 2nd ed., Butterworth-Heinemann, Amsterdam and London.

Tasci, A.D.A. and Semrad, K.J. (2016), "Developing a scale of hospitableness: A tale of two worlds", *International Journal of Hospitality Management*, Vol.53, pp.30–41, https://doi.org/10.1016/j.ijhm.2015.11.006.

Telfer, E. (2001), "The philosophy of hospitableness", in Lashley, C. and Morrison, A. (Eds.), *In Search of Hospitality*, Routledge, London and New York, pp.38–55.

Thiem, M. (2001), "Tourismus und kulturelle Identität", in Belwe, K. (Ed.), *Tourismus*, Aus Politik und Zeitgeschichte, Vol.47, Bundeszentrale für politische Bildung, Bonn, pp.27–31. available at: http://www.bpb.de/apuz/25889/tourismus-und-kulturelle-identitaet (accessed 13 December 2018).

Vermeulen, I.E. and Seegers, D. (2009), "Tried and tested: The impact of online hotel reviews on consumer consideration", *Tourism Management*, Vol.30, No.1, pp.123–127, https://doi.org/10.1016/j.tourman.2008.04.008.

Webster, C. (1989), "Can consumers be segmented on the basis of their service quality expectations?", *Journal of Services Marketing*, Vol.3, No.2, pp.35–53, https://doi.org/10.1108/EUM0000000002485.

Wilkins, H. (2010), "Using importance-performance analysis to appreciate satisfaction in hotels", *Journal of Hospitality Marketing & Management*, Vol.19, No.8, pp.866–888. https://doi.org/10.1080/19368623.2010.514554.

28

KEYS TO SUCCESS

Connective Structures for Educational Innovations in the Hotel Industry

Hartwig Bohne

Introduction

The steps of operational human resources management, which are coordinated for the company's needs and at the same time in the interests of the employees, are brought together in the concept of a strategic human resources policy. In the 1980s, the Harvard Business School developed the "Human Resource Management Approach" as a basis for this, in which the strategic importance of the "employee" factor is brought to the fore. Various elements of both traditional and modern human resources theories merge in these application-oriented approaches to modern human relation management. The approach is to be seen as a process along the development stages of an employee, i.e., from the orientation phase after hiring, through training and further education, and potential assessment including the development plan to remuneration and leaving the company, so that a so-called "Employee relations journey" is created (Meier, 2015; Vahs and Schäfer-Kunz, 2015).

This changed prioritization and recognition of human relation management as an identical influencing factor for economic success and securing the company's existence also leads to an adjusted perception among applicants and other actors. In addition, the strategic importance of well-trained and sufficient numbers of existing employees also influences the development of changing framework conditions. In this respect, three closely linked key functions for successful and continuous human relation management can be identified. Positive value-bound positioning of the company as an attractive employer is the basis for being present in the labor market and asserting oneself. The optimal use according to their qualifications secures the commercial use for the enterprise underuse of suitable abilities and skills of the employees. In order to keep them loyal and motivated, committed and performance-oriented, adequate employee participation and individual personnel support also play a decisive role (Institut der Deutschen Wirtschaft e. V., 2014; Schuhmacher and Geschwill, 2009).

Consequently, an attractive company can be identified by the fact that its employees describe it as "their" company and thus express their degree of loyalty. This creates the ideal conditions for optimized staff recruitment and development, as well as sustainable employee motivation, representing the company's internal and external positioning (Krauthammer and Hinterhuber, 2003; Schuhmacher and Geschwill, 2009) (Figure 28.1).

Building on this, in order to call up the maximum performance potential of employees and at the same time treat them with respect, elements that integrate them into a distinctive participation philosophy are just as important as sensible instruments for controlling movements, i.e., planned procurement, resource-saving deployment, and socially and image-compatible redundancies. A

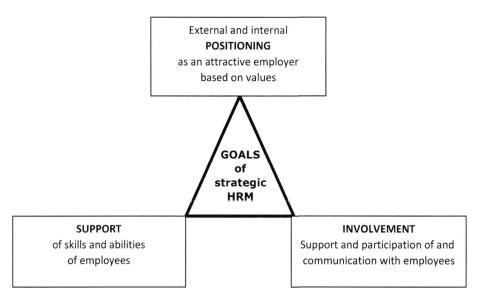

Figure 28.1 Three main goals of strategic HR Management (Bohne, 2019).

graduated reward system (salaries and bonuses) can sharpen the bond and optimize it in line with the organization of work as well as performance and qualifications. Embedded in the strategic management level of a company, this comprehensive personnel-focusing approach is influenced both by the actors involved, e.g., executives, and also by external, mostly situational factors, e.g., current and forecast economic development or the anticipated effects of technological and demographic change. This holistic approach enables a targeted, individual and market-driven employee focus, in which the needs of the employees are on the same level as those of the company as a whole. All internal and external reference groups can be adequately considered so that an overall coordinated concept of sustainable human relation management can be achieved (Von Freyberg and Zeugfang, 2014). Cooperative structures have strong impacts on such a concept in a value-enhancing, long-term successful overall strategy that is profitable for both, the entrepreneur and his employees. In this context different development and design processes of such networks as well as differentiable features and legal forms and operating phases and criteria have to be analyzed.

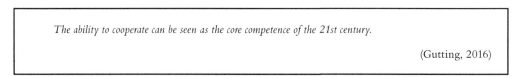

The ability to cooperate can be seen as the core competence of the 21st century.

(Gutting, 2016)

The extensive diversity of target levels and categories leads to conflicting objectives and loss of efficiency. Clear decision-making structures and balanced set of priorities are of great importance for economically meaningful but at the same time employee-oriented coordination (Bartscher et al., 2012).

The changes in employee management also become clear when looking at the development phases of operational human resource management. In the 1950s, the bureaucratic management of existing staff to implement personnel policy decisions dominated. As a result of sufficient employee potential, companies limited themselves to hiring and personnel management. This administrative character was favored by quiet markets with constant growth and a sufficient supply of skilled workers. In most cases, the responsibility was with the commercial management and not with a separate HR manager. In the 1960s, professionalization began in the direction of structured institutionalization and specialization, which in large companies was also accompanied by the establishment of central personnel departments (Vahs and Schäfer-Kunz, 2015).

Initial rationalization measures within the framework of socialization concepts and increasing complexity also led to a lack of specialist qualifications and the introduction of strategic planning instruments (Winter, 2008). Since 1970, it has been possible to derive an adjustment of the organizational structures, also oriented to the needs of the employees, with the aim of a more intense people development and activation (Thommen and Achleitner, 2016). These accommodation concepts also included the more intensive involvement of employee participation.

For this reason, this decade is also referred to as the "humanization of personnel work." Increased strategic value creation through more efficient and structured personnel work became more important from 1980 onwards. This "economization of human resources work" was also characterized by an increase in the economic orientation towards key figures within the framework of a decentralized and generalizing human resources policy (Bartscher et al., 2012). In the 1990s and 2000s, extreme market developments were discernible in terms of the availability of junior staff and skilled workers. This led to increased pressure on dynamic processes in human resources (so-called "entre- and intrapreneuring" of human resources work (Wunderer, 1992), an increase in value for conceptual personnel work and the stronger consideration of employee expectations (Meier, 2015). The "Human Resource Management" with strategic importance emerged from an economized HR management. Value creation through good employee administration and support has been recognized as well as the advantages of long-term personnel recruitment, retention, and development for the economic security of companies. The role of employees changed into that of "co-entrepreneurs" (Thommen and Achleitner, 2016). Consequently the economic and financial value of employees started to be reflected in the human capital accounting instrument, which underscores the development of human capital management. In this context, the acceptance as an equivalent strategic component of successful corporate management is nowadays analogous to non-monetary and financial capital, so that human resources is anchored as the third relevant pillar of a company structure (Stotz and Wedel-Klein, 2013).

As a consequence of this change in perception, the perspective of "Employee Relationship Management" emerges in order to take account of the adapted distribution of roles between company managers and employees. The self-conception of the personnel department as a strategic partner and service provider emphasizes the importance of the employees for the company as well as the changed terminology. The integration and participation in decision-making processes, interdisciplinary work forms and a stronger consideration of individual competencies and needs lead to the fact that the employee area is recognized as an integrative component of a cooperative corporate strategy and thus upgraded (Brysch, 2014). This shows the economic and political situation in which the company has to operate and to approach its employees. At the same time, it shows approaches and response options for current and predictable developments and business issues. There is a trend towards higher demands on the working environment of employees and applicants, so that companies' efforts to find and retain employees have to be adapted. Within a reliable framework, the characteristics of individual aspects as well as influencing factors and dependencies have to be taken into account (Meier, 2015).

At the beginning, employers and employees have to analyze the operational and socio-economic environment. The change in values, the development of the population structure, and the technologization as well as the internationalization of working conditions form the cornerstones of a constantly changing working environment in which the flexibility of the employees increases and the companies are required to react appropriately to the same extent.

Political influences and instruments of participation complete the picture of the spectrum of expectations and design of today's HR challenges (Meier, 2015). The complexity of today's requirements in terms of professional qualifications, personal structure, and social action entails an extensive process of communication and coordination both for employees and for companies in order to combine as many interests as possible. A profound and lasting cultural change leads to a stronger emphasis on family, leisure, environmental protection, and health among applicants and employees as well as to stronger prioritization of the demands for self-fulfillment and participation (Michel and Breisig, 2016).

Rigid hierarchies, obedience, and fulfillment of duties make employers and job profiles unattractive, whereas participation, adequate, emotional recognition, as well as respect and appreciation of commitment are regarded as reasons for a decision in favor of or against an employer. In addition, the effects of structural changes in the quantity and quality of the labor supply are just as noticeable as the further development of jobs offered as a result of internationalization, digitization, and flexibilization. These new challenges in human relation management entail the need to adapt the instruments to the future competition for talented employees (Bartscher et al., 2012; Olfert, 2015; Vereinigung der Bayerischen Wirtschaft e. V., 2015).

For an adequate weighting of the individual components, it is necessary to classify them into one of the six typical human resources decision categories. These include the transfer of learning and knowledge, the efficiency of personnel measures, especially in the areas of training, education and further training, the motivation of the workforce and employees, the identification effect and influence of the industry as well as the development of the feeling to belong to a group (Matiaske, 2009). In the second step, after a fundamental analysis of the environment and allocation of the complex and at the same time dynamic challenges, the development of a sustainable employer marketing takes place. The focus is on the long-term development and positioning of a brand that summarizes the values and performance promise of the employer, both internally and externally. The impact of a brand that has been created is primarily shown to advantage in the process of recruiting and retaining people (Gruner, 2008).

This strategy therefore serves both to identify with the company and as a basis of trust for the loyalty of a workforce. Building on this, the third stage is effective personnel planning and recruitment, which anticipates and mitigates distortions in the changing supply of skilled workers. Differentiated selection systems and people development based on targeted support and encouragement play key roles here. Appropriate participation and incentive systems as well as training and education opportunities for employees also improve selection options and development opportunities (Hillitzer and Spinnler, 2014). The intermeshing of suitable procurement channels, consistent internal and external brand communication, the maintenance of an applicant database, and the structured selection of applicants ensure the supply of the required number of suitably trained and professionally qualified employees (Olfert, 2012). A successful selection also facilitates the loyalty of employees. This is all the more important because their willingness to change is more pronounced and the supply of skilled workers is continuously declining.

In addition, different elements of individual development mean that an employer is seen not only as a provider of a job but also as an option for personalized training and additional professional qualifications (Michel and Breisig, 2016). Applicants and skilled workers interested in changing jobs also use the characteristics of such offers as a criterion for comparing attractive employers, so that the pressure on companies to position themselves in this way increases (Ringlstetter and Kaiser, 2008). For companies, binding measures are sensible instruments for reducing or avoiding fluctuation. From the employee's point of view, false expectations, lack of identification and social integration are the main reasons for a change of job or company. In this respect, companies can achieve positive economic effects through targeted promotion and transparency in these areas (Meier, 2015).

Focus on Co-operation

As a result of these basic assumptions, it is necessary to concentrate on one focus of economic activity: "the ability to cooperate and its deployment options." The reason for entering into co-operation is an effort or a necessity to professionalize and strategically design business processes. This involves the resource-saving use of own capacities and the meaningful integration of external solutions and offers. Modern approaches to corporate management interpret cooperations as advantageous constructions of entrepreneurial actions in order to optimize management systems, improve problem-solving behavior, and respond more flexibly and specifically to environmental changes (Friese, 1998; Siller and Peters, 2014).

The need for coordination that arises also leads to the reflection of activities and previous processes as well as to a more precise assessment of success potential (Schertler, 1998). Cooperation can be manifold; the terms "alliance," "network," and "cooperation" are mostly used synonymously in the relevant literature, also for linguistic reasons. The core is the same for all concepts: a form of voluntary cooperation with another company or with an education provider is described, and different motives and objectives of cooperation models can be derived. Collaborative structures are primarily used to develop the most efficient organizational form and thus to secure the company's existence. To understand the complexity of the economic environment and to be prepared properly for crises as well as to seek allies within the framework a holistic view of market events is important in order to secure one's existence. This applies in particular to small- and medium-sized enterprises, which often do not want to merge, but are willing to cooperate. Cooperative structures then affect both the corporate culture and technological foundations as well as the organizational structures of partner companies (Friese, 1998; Laux and Soller, 2012; Rahn, 2015; Siller and Peters, 2014). Such an economic model also makes sense if either a required resource is not (any longer) sufficiently available in the company, or a decline in the supply of the required resource is assumed in the long run, or a new resource source is to be tapped (Bea and Haas, 2009). A harmonious balance between own achievements and profits as well as those of the partner is essential, whereby the adaptation processes to changes in an economy are just as much a part of the requirements of cooperation as the response to the mutual relations between the alliance partners (Gutting, 2016). The flexible and cooperation-specific design of networks becomes a core element of adaptability within the framework of "multistability" (Schertler, 1998).

Kempinski Hotels and the Neoma Business School/Reims Management School were early players in the field of educational cooperation partners and founded a bilateral EMBA program to empower the General Managers of Kempinski Hotels. The aim was to give a clear signal to the owners of Kempinski properties as well as to the stakeholder of Kempinski that the professionalization of internal leaders and future managers is one of the most important priorities for the success of an international hotel chain. Following the tough competition among luxury hotel brands the strict educational strategy of Kempinski was a role model also for other hotel groups to follow (Knipper, 2018).

The objective of cooperation can be developed from a broad range of motives. This includes aspects of risk minimization as well as the increase of profitability or the expansion of a power position within an existing market to displace competitors or increase market shares or to facilitate entry into a new market (Friese, 1998; Gutting, 2016; Wöhe, 2000). Securing patent rights or similar intangible assets, as well as access to customer data or increasing the credibility of the company, can also be initial factors for building up the cooperation. The goals of an alliance can also be a joint market presence in order to present the economic position better than it is, to impress competitors, to support a brand family, or to intensify lobbying work. Many of the motives and objectives are difficult to differentiate from one another or are the result of active cooperation. In the consequence of such cooperation both sides profit from a fair "giving and taking" of the competences brought into the network so that a mutual improvement in the market can be achieved (Freiling, 2005).

Particularly in the area of innovation and knowledge distribution and exchange, cooperation can achieve added value and thus contribute to securing a long-term existence (Brass, 2004). The emergence of synergies through the sharing of knowledge resources, as well as a related response to technological change and the consequences of digitization, also reduces operational uncertainties. The resulting concentration on core competencies can also sharpen the company's profile, enabling new markets to be opened up more efficiently. The market-oriented strategy of a company is of great relevance for all operational and cultural concerns of a company (Gutting, 2016; Krauthammer and Hinterhuber, 2003; Schuh et al., 2005; Theling and Loos, 2004). This leads to improved credibility and a stronger relationship of trust among peripheral actors in company activity, e.g., banks or suppliers. Especially against the background of a broader distribution of entrepreneurial risks and the pressure of globalization as well as the volatility of sales markets, the implementation of a resilient network leads to a stronger positioning. The opportunities for mutual learning and a lively cultural, linguistic and mentality-related exchange should not be underestimated because the previously separate design of business processes is brought closer together by an alliance, so that both can gain insights into the partner's behavior and structures – and in turn, benefit from them (Bamford et al., 2003; Schuh et al., 2005; Theling and Loos, 2004).

The dynamics of the overall economic development, political influences, and the lowering of trade borders, e.g., the free movement of goods and employees, also make it necessary to optimize the operational risk structure. This also leads to a broadening of one's own perspective and opens the way to adjustment modalities that a company alone would not or could not represent. This results in a multiplication of the possibilities to optimize the own competitive situation and internal structures (Schuh et al., 2005). Especially during a period of internationalization and expansion of a company, cooperation can be helpful and reduces the skepticism of potential customers towards new market participants (Berghoff and Sydow, 2007; Gutting, 2016; Wöhe, 2000).

Cooperation, however, does not exist on its own but depends on active partners. Personal relationships between executives promote the vitality of cooperation and lead to mutual economic benefits. A "well thought-out" cooperation strategy and transparent and realistic expectations of the purpose and content of cooperation play a decisive role. It is precisely the operative design of the "day-to-day cooperation" that determines the longevity and success of the chosen model (Bamford et al., 2003; Rahn, 2015).

The big companies are merging, the small companies have to cooperate.

(Becker et al., 2005)

An impressive model for international educational cooperation is the "Executive Master in Hospitality Management" program, which has been offered in a trilateral cooperation between the Falkensteiner Michaeler Tourism Group, the Free University of Bozen/Bolzano, and the Cornell School of Hotel Administration since the summer semester 2014. This offer of university education and training for employees is unique in international comparison. The hotel chain has an influence on the content of the studies in order to ensure practical relevance. As a result, four main topics have been identified:

1   Organizational and Human Resource Management
2   Strategic and Marketing Management

3   Financial management
4   Decision, Risk, and Operations Management

The contents of the course are taught and examined as a block event in Bruneck/South Tyrol on a total of 60 attendance days. Graduates have the opportunity to pursue a career in the executive area of Falkensteiner Hotels. The close combination of operational requirements with modern management skills covers a broad spectrum of current management topics. This model is therefore a good instrument for retaining and developing managers and for increasing the attractiveness of both the company and the participating universities (Bohne, 2017).

The objectives in setting up cooperative structures are characterized by the guiding principle of achieving competitive advantages, because the required competencies and resources do not have to be developed by the company itself, but can be temporarily integrated by experienced partners. In the case of manufacturing companies, the focus is also on expanding capacities and competencies; all partners willing to cooperate attach great importance to reducing costs due to the hitherto isolated economic activity. The aim is also to achieve benefits through more effective management and administration as well as a reduction in transaction costs. The bundling of previously separate activities, e.g., recruiting as well as people training and development, is another aspect of network planning (Bundesministerium für Wirtschaft und Technologie, 2011; Dyer and Singh, 1998).

The range of people development extends from self-designed internal courses to external training courses offered to employees. Companies pursue the goal of retaining employees over the long term and improving their professional qualifications. Also important are the development of personal competencies and social skills, which are intended to ensure the continuity of internal processes and communication (Olfert, 2015). People training is understood as a basic function of people development and the focus is on company-specific training, e.g., orientation days for new employees or specialist seminars on operational processes or certain company products. The additional support measures within the framework of people development already represent a supplementary offer, e.g., seminars from areas which are not related to the own position and for which external trainers may also be appointed. The most comprehensive interpretation is personnel development in the broadest sense, in which employees are offered participation in organizational changes, e.g., in the course of a quality team to redesign work processes (Kirschten, 2017; Müller-Vorbrüggen, 2016). In this way, in particular, an employer's esteem and commitment intentions can be expressed in a sustainable manner. These diverse options also offer companies willing to receive sufficient support opportunities to successfully position themselves as cooperative employers in the challenging market of talents (Table 28.1).

Table 28.1 Motives for establishing co-operative structures (Bohne, 2019)

Motives for co-operative structures		
Synergy effects through know-how transfer	Access to new markets and new target groups	Positive effects of cultural differences
Advantages due to digitalization	Time efficiency	Adaption of processes
Focus on core business	Fewer risks	Informational framework
Reduction of uncertainty	Reduction of costs and empty capacities	Successful co-operation as benchmark
Effects of globalization and volatile markets	Better evaluation for banks and investors	Preparation of closer relations/joint-venture or more
Technological developments	Diversification of products and services	Reliability
Technical reference	**Economic reference**	**Organization reference**

For the partners involved, the benefit should be greater than acting as single companies. This is associated with the demand for a significant increase in revenue and optimized utilization of the company's own infrastructure. The intention to jointly implement innovations faster and also to achieve non-economic goals more easily, e.g., to gain prestige, makes the importance of a collaborative framework comprehensible, especially for small market players (Becker et al., 2005; Olfert, 2012).

In this context, characteristic features and forms of joint action in the market emerge. These are structures involving at least two enterprises or one enterprise and one educational institution. The voluntary participants remain economically and legally independent, establish their own clear and transparent decision-making rules, and commit themselves to the uniform introduction of content and the establishment of structures. The objectives and the time dimension are set out in writing in order to facilitate the structured exchange of competences and performance reserves for mutual benefit. The extent of the cooperation, i.e., local, regional, national to international, is also determined, as is the intensity of the commitment, i.e., which business areas are covered by the cooperation, what level of decision-making depth is sought, and whether institutional cooperation management is appropriate. The origin of the partners and the commitment, i.e., written or oral form, personnel and financial integration and clarification of the temporal structure (frequency/rhythm, deadline/period) are relevant for this. And such cooperation also and especially depends on the number of partners (Bundesministerium für Wirtschaft und Technologie, 2011; Theling and Loos, 2004; Von Freyberg and Zeugfang, 2014).

The complexity can also be seen in the fact that it is already a challenge to determine the appropriate number of partners. This depends on the scope of the cooperation, the competence of the partners, the required and existing qualification as well as the business relations (Breisig, 2015; Wöhe, 2000). A bilateral (two partners), trilateral (three partners), or simple (many partners with a centralized decision-making structure/also "hub-and-spoke architecture") or complex (many partners with a multilateral contact structure) target identity influences the subsequent coordination effort considerably. A distinction must also be made between the intentions and needs of the partners. If there is an agreement to compensate for the same weaknesses by pooling resources, this is a redistributive cooperation (also known as "Y-Alliance" or "Critical Mass Alliance"). If the partners want to achieve different goals because they assume that the partner will optimally compensate their own weaknesses, because both have different weaknesses, a reciprocal cooperation (also called "X-Alliance," "Closing Gap-Alliance") is formed (Freiling, 1998; Killich, 2005; Rotering, 1993).

The decisive factor is the style of relationships between the previously individually operating companies. In the case of horizontal cooperation, competitive relationships have existed so far because both have offered similar products. If a vertical cooperation is sought, a transaction relationship is to be assumed, because it was primarily a supplier-to-customer relationship or vice versa. This starting point determines the employment relationship and the subsequent process steps. Diagonal networking opens up new options because neither the products nor the processes were previously connected to each other or offered on the same markets. The trust between the partners and their integrity are of decisive importance for the course of the new alliance. This must be accompanied by a determination of the direction in which the cooperation is to work. A horizontal cooperation means that competitors work together at the same level of the value chain, e.g., form a purchasing cooperation (Friese, 1998; Gutting, 2016; Laux and Soller, 2012).

The aim can be to achieve better conditions or to eliminate other competitors by increasing market power or setting a benchmark. In a vertical network, upstream or downstream production partners form an alliance, differentiating between forwarding cooperation (e.g., with the customer) and backward cooperation (e.g., with a supplier). As a third variant, the establishment of a diagonal (also lateral, conglomerate, complementary) cooperation may be necessary and meaningful. In such a structure, partners at different levels of the value chain come together. These non-competing areas of different companies in different sectors conclude cooperation to bundle common interests, e.g., they share the investment costs for a large purchase, but use the device for different products. Or they invest in an object with mixed-use, without cannibalizing themselves, e.g., a cinema and a university jointly build a lecture hall, which is used during the day for teaching purposes as a lecture hall and in the evening for film screenings (Killich, 2005; Theling and Loos, 2004; Von Freyberg and Zeugfang, 2014).

The wide range of cooperation models that have developed between companies is characterized by the changing degree of economic and legal integration. While an informal cooperation suggests a very weak connection, the working and interest communities are already characterized by the cooperation for at least one project. A research community often offers the breeding ground for a spin-off, i.e., a spin-off from a scientific enterprise for the commercial exploitation of relevant research results. A strategic alliance plays a role above all in expansive business plans because it comprises a contractual basis for mutual support in improving the competitive situation (Gutting, 2016; Killich, 2005; Sydow, 2005).

With the joint venture, the partners agree on the establishment of a new subsidiary, whereas the takeover entails the integration of one partner into the structures of the other. The merger, on the other hand, represents the merger of two legally and economically independent companies for the purpose of jointly founding a new company (Breisig, 2015; Rahn, 2015).

In the hotel industry, the acquisition of Ritz-Carlton Hotels by the Marriott hotel group or those of the Fairmont hotel groups with the Swissôtel, Raffles, and Fairmont brands as well as 25h by the European hotel group Accor Hotels are examples that have an impact on the market, also the purchase of Six Senses by IHG is a significant example. Synergy effects are created by merging distribution channels, for example. Economic advantages also result from stronger market power vis-à-vis suppliers and access to larger guest files as a basis for the expansion of profitable loyalty programs (Rahn, 2015; Theling and Loos, 2004; Wöhe, 2000).

Co-operations under Operation

These differentiation options for cooperation types show that a meaningful strategy is needed to develop the appropriate character of cooperation and to be successful in the long term because the emergence of cooperation follows the change of traditional organizational forms and as a reaction to strong changes in competition and market concentration (Bundesministerium für Wirtschaft und Technologie, 2011).

The choice of partners is therefore of decisive importance for the strategy, course, and yield of cooperations. A similar corporate culture and tradition, as well as comparable values and leadership styles, facilitates cooperation, as does a solid financial and human capital base for all parties involved. A balanced relationship between performance and expectations as well as the readiness for honest evaluation and transparent controlling goes hand in hand with a coordinated strategic orientation and the equally high prioritization of the network agreement (Laux and Soller, 2012).

Cooperation management is a clear management task based on fairness and trust. This also results in the necessity of a coordinated cooperation strategy. Above all, the advantages to be expected compared to the previous unique position must be analyzed and compared with the chances of using or exploiting the cooperation effects. In order to ensure the involvement of management and all employees, comprehensible decision-making structures as well as incentives for innovation must be developed. By connecting to the management levels of the actors now linked in partnership, models and visions can be adapted and optimized on the one hand, and communication difficulties can be avoided on the other. This is accompanied by openness to the further development of such cooperation and sensitization to new competitive situations and market changes (Bamford et al., 2003; Bundesministerium für Wirtschaft und Technologie, 2011; Dyer and Singh, 1998) (Table 28.2).

Table 28.2 Quartet of co-operative strategies (Bohne, 2019)

Design of co-operations	*Establishing own co-operative abilities*
• Reason • Advantages for all partners • Targets • Structure and circumference • Criteria for partners • Negotiation strategy • Cooperation structure • Distribution of responsibilities • Decision-making structures	• Communication and implementation of the idea of cooperation • Determination of internal coordination and responsibility for cooperation matters • Clarification of informal or formal discussion culture • Centralized or decentralized organization of cooperation issues • Avoidance of skepticism or fear of outflow of competence and capital
Implementation of co-operations	*Management of co-operative structures*
• Relationship between several cooperation models and partners • Reaction to different visions and working styles • Dealing with competitive situations • Openness for further development or commitment to a rigid model	• Activity plan for the first six months • Decision-making paths and methods • Weighting of strategic and operational issues • Evaluation criteria • Incentive criteria

Co-operations as Role Models for Success

The strategy of a network includes both an activity plan and a schedule for the first phase as well as the entire project duration, or at least for a realistic time window. Seven phases of cooperation can be distinguished from each other. After an idea, an initial spark (usually also as a result of personal contacts between managers), the network can be set up and subsequently constituted. This is followed by the daily routine of practical cooperative action. The sense and purpose of the co-operation become clear in this phase, the good preparatory work and a conscientious formulation of a strategy become noticeable. The roles of the partners and the results are evaluated regularly in the course of a close cooperation or on the occasion of an agreed deadline. Each actor weighs his own advantages and his participation in the idea of cooperation. This is followed by a discussion between the partners on maintaining the structures, further development, or the need to adjust. The result can be both the termination of the cooperation, e.g., the splitting up of merged companies and the continuation with known rules and the same leadership. The course of cooperation is determined by many determinants, so that the design of the seven phases also takes place in varying degrees of detail. This also depends on the prioritization of a successful cooperation in the management of participating companies (Bundesministerium für Wirtschaft und Technologie, 2011; Flocken et al., 2001; Howaldt and Ellerkmann, 2005).

Obstacles and difficulties can also arise in the course of cooperation if realistic objectives are adhered to. "Outlearning" (mutual learning and competitive cooperation are neglected) and the "lock-in effect" (excessive specialization of cooperation leads to the formation of weak points and inflexibility) represent major risks. As soon as the opportunistic behavior of the partners prevails and the character of the company is dominated by a self-centered and resource-oriented leadership perspective, the partnership model can be damaged or broken (Schramm-Klein, 2005). Uncertainty about an outflow of know-how without adequate consideration getting into mutual dependency is a risk that can only be countered internally by communicating the cooperation components and advantages. The disregard for the performance of the partner attributable to the persons acting or the lack of interest among decision-makers can only be counteracted by a process of communication and the emergence of a corporate culture willing to cooperate. The high coordination effort required to enable economically meaningful controllability should not be underestimated as an obstacle.

Also, a wrong prioritization and the exclusive concentration on the daily business paired with too little market knowledge with responsible management persons must be taken into account and mitigated from the outset. The role of company management and other internal role models is decisive for the success of cooperation. Especially in companies without cooperation experience and culture – where skepticism and complexity due to virtuality, digitalization, and market development, are usual – structuring guidelines must be developed and credibly exemplified. Because a network focuses on processes rather than results, professional conflict management is also very important. The speed and responsiveness of a network organization are threatened to decrease the larger the group of partners is. A transparent and reliable coordination of the network is therefore just as important as the awareness that cooperation does not replace an internal strategy. Moreover, cooperation with partners should not be interpreted as compensation for management weaknesses or restructuring aid, as the partners expect active participation. A one-sided withdrawal of services and relying on the advantage of bringing in the other partners will not fertilize cooperation but diminish positive effects. It therefore represents only a slight reduction in the individual entrepreneurial risk. The design of cooperative structures and the avoidance of risks therefore also depends on the number and competence of the "programers," i.e., role models in all partner companies (Berghoff and Sydow, 2007; Bundesministerium für Wirtschaft und Technologie, 2011). Cooperative business models are the most complex variants of entrepreneurial leadership challenges. There is neither a guarantee of success for their course nor a blueprint for the number of partners, the appropriate legal structure, and many other design criteria (Figure 28.2).

However, three pairs of criteria have emerged as key factors for a good start to a successful course and a satisfactory conclusion of a corporate cooperation: trust in the partners and legitimacy for the establishment of cooperation, information about the partners and to employees combined with the openness for the beginning of a learning process, and finally the intensive motivating support for the coordinating executives but also between the partners in order to keep the communication and the basis of trust alive. The effects of cooperation can also be seen in the internal working environment and in the satisfaction of employees with their employer. Due to

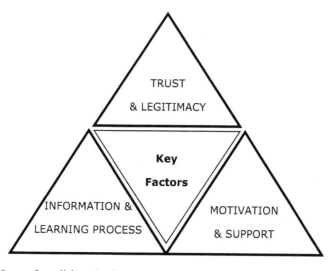

Figure 28.2 Key factors for collaborative business structures (Bohne, 2019).

the higher market value and better positioning, employees feel that they are in a more professional environment (Siller and Peters, 2014). Ultimately, the question is no longer whether cooperation between the hotel industry and educational institutions makes sense or is advantageous, but simply who makes the best use of it. Both the hotel industry and educational institutions can benefit – and they should.

References

Bamford, J., et. al. (2003), *Mastering Alliance Strategy*, Wiley, San Francisco, CA.

Bartscher, T., et. al.. (2012), *Personalmanagement*, Munich, Germany.

Bea, F.X. and Haas, J. (2009), *Strategisches Management*, Stuttgart, Germany.

Becker, T., et. al. (2005), *Netzwerke – praktikabel und zukunftsfähig*, in Becker, T., et al. (Eds.), *Netzwerkmanagement. Mit Kooperation zum Unternehmenserfolg*, Berlin, Germany.

Berghoff, H. and Sydow, J. (2007), *Unternehmerische Netzwerke-Theoretische Konzepte und historische Erfahrungen*, in: Berghoff, H. and Sydow, J (Eds.), *Unternehmerische Netzwerke*, Stuttgart, Germany.

Bohne, H. (2017), "Interdependenzen und Erfolgsfaktoren von Kooperationsmodellen zwischen Hochschulen und Hotelketten in Deutschland", Dissertation, Trier, Germany.

Bohne, H. (2019), *Kooperationsorientiertes Personalmanagement für die Hotellerie*, Munich, Germany.

Brass, D. (2004), "Taking stock of networks and organizations: A multilevel perspective", *Academy of Management Journal, Ausgabe*, Vol.47, No.6, pp.795–817.

Breisig, T. (2015), *Betriebliche Organisation*, Herne, Germany.

Brysch, A. (2014), "Personalmanagement im Umbruch", in Gardini, M.A. and Brysch, A. (Eds.), *Personalmanagement im Tourismus*, Berlin, Germany, pp.3–34.

Bundesministerium für Wirtschaft und Technologie. (2011), *Kooperationen planen und durchführen*, Berlin, Germany.

Dyer, J. and Singh, H. (1998), "The relational view: Cooperative strategy and sources of interorganizational competitive advantage", *The Academy of Management Review*, Vol.23, No.4, pp.660–679.

Flocken, P., et al. (2001), *Erfolgreich im Verbund – Die Praxis des Netzwerkmanagements*, Eschborn, Germany.

Freiling, J. (1998), *Kompetenzorientierte strategische Allianzen, Management*, Vol.67, pp.23–29.

Freiling, J. (2005), "Die Einordnung des Netzwerkgedankens in die Ressourcentheorie", in Stahl, H. and von den Eichen, S. (Eds.), *Vernetzte Unternehmen – wirkungsvolles Agieren in Zeiten des Wandels,* Berlin, Germany.

Friese, M. (1998), *Kooperation als Wettbewerbsstrategie für Dienstleistungsunternehmen*, Wiesbaden, Germany.

Gutting, D. (2016), *Interkulturelles Management, Diversity und internationale Kooperation*, Herne, Germany.

Gruner, A. (2008), *Management Lexikon Hotellerie & Gastronomie*, Frankfurt, Germany.

Hillitzer, R. and Spinnler, A. (2014), *Personalmanagement in der Hospitality-Industrie*, Berlin, Germany.

Howaldt, J. and Ellerkmann, F. (2005), "Entwicklungsphasen von Netzwerken und Unternehmenskooperationen", in Becker, T, et al. (Eds.), *Netzwerkmanagement: Mit Kooperation zum Unternehmenserfolg*, Berlin, Germany.

Institut der Deutschen Wirtschaft e. V. (2014), *Lebensphasenorientierte Personalpolitik*, Cologne, Germany.

Killich, S. (2005), "Kooperationsformen", in Becker, T., et al. (Eds.), *Netzwerkmanagement: Mit Kooperation zum Unternehmenserfolg*, Berlin, Germany.

Kirschten, U. (2017), *Nachhaltiges Personalmanagement*, Munich, Germany.

Knipper, T. (2018), *Wir brauchen keine Heuchler*, available at: www.karriere.de/interview-mit-reto-wittwer-wir-brauchen-keine-heuchler/23043734.html (accessed 17 December 2019).

Krauthammer, E. and Hinterhuber, H.H. (2003), "Selbstverständlichkeiten als Wettbewerbsvorteile. Wie führen wir unser Hotel in die Einzigartigkeit?", in Matzler, K., et al., *Unternehmertum in der Hotellerie*, Bozen, Italy.

Laux, S. and Soller, J. (2012), "Kooperationsbildung als Erfolgsstrategie für touristische Unternehmen", in Soller, J. (Ed.), *Erfolgsfaktor Kooperation im Tourismus*, Berlin, Germany.

Matiaske, W. (2009), "Typische personalwirtschaftliche Fragestellungen und ihre theoretische Fundierung:, in Matiaske, W. (Ed.), *Personalwirtschaftliche Theorien*, Hamburg, Germany.

Meier, H. (2015), *Unternehmensführung*, Herne, Germany.

Michel, M. and Breisig, T. (2016), "Personalentwicklung", in Breisig, T. (Ed.), *Personal*, Herne, Germany, pp.237–280.

Müller-Vorbrüggen, M. (2016), "Struktur und Strategie der Personalentwicklung", in Müller-Vorbrüggen (Ed.), *Michael: Handbuch Personalentwicklung*, Stuttgart, Germany.

Olfert, K. (2012), *Lexikon Personalwirtschaft*, Herne, Germany.

Olfert, K. (2015), *Personalwirtschaft*, Herne, Germany.

Rahn, H.J. (2015), *Unternehmensführung*, Herne, Germany.

Ringlstetter, M. and Kaiser, S. (2008), *Humanressourcen-Management*, Munich, Germany.

Rotering, J. (1993), *Zwischenbetriebliche Kooperation als alternative Organisationsform: ein transaktionstheoretischer Erklärungsansatz*, Stuttgart, Germany.

Schertler, W. (1998), *Unternehmensorganisation*, Munich, Germany.

Schramm-Klein, H. (2005), "Wettbewerb und Kooperation in regionalen Branchenclustern", in Zentes, J., et al. (Eds.), *Kooperationen, Allianzen und Netzwerke*, Berlin, Germany, pp.550–561.

Schuh, G., et.al. (2005), *Kooperationsmanagement*, Munich, Germany.

Schuhmacher, F. and Geschwill, R. (2009), *Employer Branding*, Wiesbaden, Germany.

Siller, L. and Peters, M. (2014), "*Grenzübergreifende Kooperationen als Werkzeug für die Regionalentwicklung: Der Netzwerkgedanke am Beispiel eines kulturtouristischen Festivals*", in Pechlaner, H. and Jochmann, J. (Eds.), *Grenzüberschreitende Kooperationen im Tourismus*, Berlin, Germany, pp.123–139.

Stotz, W. and Wedel-Klein, A. (2013), *Employer Branding*, Munich, Germany.

Sydow, J. (2005), *Strategische Netzwerke*, Wiesbaden, Germany.

Theling, T. and Loos, P. (2004), *Determinanten und Formen von Unternehmenskooperationen*, Mainz, Germany.

Thommen, J.P. and Achleitner, A.K. (2016), *Allgemeine Betriebswirtschaftslehre*, Wiesbaden, Germany.

Vahs, D. and Schäfer-Kunz, J. (2015), *Einführung in die Betriebswirtschaftslehre*, Stuttgart, Germany.

Vereinigung der Bayerischen Wirtschaft e. V. (2015), *Arbeitslandschaft 2040*, Munich, Germany.

Von Freyberg, B. and Zeugfang, S. (2014), *Strategisches Hotelmanagement*, Munich, Germany.

Winter, K. (2008), "Die Entwicklung der Personalarbeit", in Hänssler, K.H.(Ed.), *Management in der Hotellerie und Gastronomie*, Munich, Germany, pp.201–202.

Wöhe, G. (2000), *Einführung in die Allgemeine Betriebswirtschaftslehre*, Munich, Germany.

Wunderer, R. (1992), "Das Personalwesen auf dem Weg zu einem Wertschöpfungscenter", *Personal-Zeitschrift für Human Resource Management*, Vol.44, No.4, p.148.

29

OWNER-MANAGERS' INTERPRETATIONS OF DIGITALIZATION IN SME MANAGEMENT PROCESSES

A Qualitative Study of the Hospitality Industry

Robert Eller, Mike Peters, and Tatijana Pantovic

Introduction

Digital technology allows firms to analyze, communicate, and reach more customers than ever. Digitalization is defined as the socio-technical process of applying digital technologies to a broader social and institutional context and is a pathway to existing incumbent firms (Tilson, Lyytinen, and Sørensen, 2010; Warner and Wäger, 2019). Small and medium-sized enterprises (SMEs) face a number of challenges such as low funding (Han et al., 2014; Sohn and Kim, 2013), increased barriers in strategic planning efforts (O'Regan and Ghobadian, 2002), and identifying proper business value (Meske and Stieglitz, 2013). They are characterized by a low propensity for new product and service development (Camisón and Monfort-Mir, 2012). Moreover, the increase of agile internet companies and changed consumer behavior force SMEs to adjust their strategic orientation to survive in the digital age (Jamil et al., 2018; Valdez-Juárez et al., 2018).

SMEs are characterized by criteria such as owner-manager ages, organizational size, and entrepreneurial orientation. All of these influence businesses' ability and willingness to manage change (Chrisman et al., 2015; Gray, 2002). Recent studies highlight SMEs' reluctance towards new technology adoption, a result of everyday business dominating and preventing strategic planning efforts (Myrna, 2012; Peters and Buhalis, 2004; Taiminen and Karjaluoto, 2015). In contrast, SMEs who undertake innovation activities, employ well-educated workers, decentralize decision-making, and who are led by a visionary owner-manager have increasing levels of new technology adoption (Banerjee, 2004; Giotopoulos et al., 2017; Quinton et al., 2018).

How owner-managers perceive technological change and manage digitalization has to date been under-researched. Recent research suggests that owner-managers need to respond to digitally induced environmental change, even when its outcome is uncertain (Brady et al., 2002; Mikalef and Pateli, 2017). For example, owner-managers must be willing to adopt digital marketing technologies although they lack the necessary knowledge and resources, while an unpredictable return on investment prevents owner-managers from adopting digital marketing solutions (Alford and Page, 2015).

Digital technologies can be viewed as a combination of information, computing, communication, and connectivity technologies (Bharadwaj et al., 2013; Warner and Wäger, 2019). Recent research has found that digital technologies transform business strategies, business processes, firm capabilities, products, and services. They also enable firms to interact with stakeholders, customers, suppliers, and partners more efficiently (Barba-Sanchez et al., 2007; Bharadwaj et al., 2013; Kenney et al., 2015).

In this study, we examine owner-managers' perceived attitudes, as well as factors of the digitalization process, information technology adoption behavior, and their impact on SMEs' businesses. We ask: "How do owner-managers in tourism SMEs perceive and manage the adoption and impact of digitalization?" This research contributes to a better understanding of digitalization in SMEs, showing that it is mainly associated with social media utilization in an effort to improve marketing efficiency. Previous literature has displayed limitations in explaining owner-managers' perceptions of digitalization, which is why this study will attempt to contribute to a deeper understanding of owner-managers' perceptions of digitalization in tourism SMEs.

Theoretical Background

The literature advises businesses to innovate products and services in combination with information technologies to stay competitive and leverage organizational performance (Barba-Sanchez et al., 2007). However, research also indicates that innovation efforts and especially business model innovation often fail; the underlying reasons for this continue to remain unexplored (Geissdoerfer et al., 2018).

The increase in new digital technologies and capabilities such as cloud computing, analytics, and big data capabilities fundamentally transform business strategies, business processes, firm capabilities, products, and services. These are essential for future innovations (Bharadwaj et al., 2013; Kenney et al., 2015; Pappas et al., 2018). Information technology is mandatory for digitalization efforts, and is defined as a combination of computer hard- and software to enable computing, communication, and connectivity capabilities (Boaden and Lockett, 1991).

This means that information technology can be viewed as a subset of digital technologies to increase firms' capability to develop new products and services, and in addition enable knowledge exchange within the firm (Dedrick, Gurbaxani, and Kraemer, 2003; Roberts, 2000). In a broader context, digitalization is defined as "a socio-technical process of applying digitizing techniques to broader social and institutional contexts that render digital technologies infrastructural" (Tilson et al., 2010, p. 749). The literature describes digital technology adoption within a strategic renewal of business goals (Warner and Wäger, 2019).

Digital technologies leverage a firm's capability to enhance products and services, improve processes, increase or gain a new competitive advantage, increase customer relationships, and impact firms' profitability (Gnyawali et al., 2010; Lee et al., 2003; Majumdar et al., 2018; Shahiduzzaman et al., 2018). In addition, organizational factors such as firm size, information technology experience and capabilities, employee training, and financial and managerial resources influence the adoption behavior of an organization (Hugill and Helfat, 2018). Furthermore, factors such as an owner-managers' overall attitude towards new technologies, an innovative mindset, a general enthusiasm about new technologies, and an experimental spirit positively influence adoption processes in SMEs (Bruque and Moyano, 2007; Dahnil et al., 2014; Mehrtens et al., 2001). Literature has found that owner-managers' perceived benefits of information technology adoption include reduced costs, increased process efficiency, and improved communication capabilities (Barba-Sanchez et al., 2007). However, the implementation of new technology (e.g., self-service technologies) is not always embraced by customers, and can even lead to negative outcomes (Bitner et al., 2000).

Recent studies show that social media platforms enable SMEs to access new customer segments and positively influence the export performance of SMEs (Bouwman et al., 2018;

Prasad et al., 2001). Managers face three hurdles to increasing customer relationships with social networks: organizational readiness, over-expectation, and project management failings (Woodcock et al., 2011). In spite of these, social media platforms let SMEs promote products and services and instantly respond to customer needs and complaints; enable the ability to provide immediate and constant support; allow the creation of communities; and create access to potentially new customers (Zeiller and Schauer, 2011). The ability to target specific groups of customers and learning about customer needs are the main perceived benefits of social media (Roberts, 2000). Supporting customers via a social network in the best case turns customers into loyal repeat business who develop a preference for products and services via continual patronage and the willingness to spread positive word of mouth about the company (Dick and Basu, 1994; Rosman and Stuhura, 2013). These kinds of customers are called loyal advocates who want to share their opinion with friends and families without expecting a reward in return (Duffy, 1998).

The loyalty of customers can be enhanced using different digital channels to improve the relationship and especially the value of social media (Rosman and Stuhura, 2013). The utilization of social networks allows an improvement in companies' internal communication and knowledge-sharing processes, well-maintained relationships with customers, and even market research (Kim et al., 2013). In establishing customer relationships, certain strategies should be adopted as an appropriate incentive for customers to stay committed to the company (Berry, 2002). To understand how owner-managers in SMEs interpret the challenges of digitalization, we will examine the factors influencing social media adoption and drivers in the following.

Methodology

We chose a qualitative approach to gain deeper insights into owner-managers' perception of digitalization in SMEs (Creswell and Poth, 2018; Marshall, 1996). A semi-structured interview guideline was developed consisting of five sections: (1) influence of owner-managers on information technology adoption, (2) perceived benefits and drivers of digitalization, (3) perceived barriers, (4) external influences, and (5) information and its effect on customer loyalty (Hu et al., 1999; Rauniar et al., 2014; Renzi and Klobas, 2008; Riemenschneider et al., 2003; Vogelsang et al., 2013; Yu and Tao, 2009). All interview questions were supported with sub-questions to achieve deeper insight into the respective topic (Mayring, 2010).

We conducted a total of 15 in-depth interviews in SMEs from the Western Austrian tourism industry, including apartment houses, hotels, and restaurants. A saturation point was reached after 15 interviews, with no new and relevant information added to the topic after this (Dworkin, 2012). Western Austria is a region characterized by the dominance of SMEs, particularly in the tourism and hospitality industries. About 95% of all businesses in tourism are small or medium-sized firms (Peters, 2017). Table 29.1 shows the data sample of the conducted interviews.

Table 29.2 shows the distribution of participating businesses in the data sample.

Sixty percent of all businesses are micro businesses with less than 10 employees, 27% employ 10–50 employees, and 13% employ between 51 and 250 employees. The interview length ranged from 25 to 70 minutes (average 35 minutes). The interviews were held in German and audio recorded. All audio files were transcribed into text and analyzed using MAXQDA software for qualitative data analysis (Bell et al., 2019). In the first step, meaningful text segments were assigned to code as first-order topics. After this, all similar codes were merged to a second-order topic representing the meaning of the corresponding text fragment (Saldaña, 2015). Unclear or contradicting codes were discussed until all of the researchers agreed on them.

Table 29.1 Participating firms

Firm	Age	Position	Size (full-time employees)	Year of founding
A.K.	26	Founder	2	2014
N.R.	29	Restaurant Manager	8	2013
PH.W.	23	Founder	6	2016
F.L.	33	Founder	24–30	2016
F.S.	28	Manager	20	2018
M.B.	32	Founder	25	2016
D.L.	39	Destination Manager	120–130	2000
M.E.	39	Founder	4	2009
M.M.	51	Founder	24	2010
J.M.	35	Founder	3	2011
D.S.	28	Manager	10	2011
M.G.	25	Founder	2	2016
C.K.	29	Founder	2	2013
S.I.	44	Founder	1	2016
Q.M.	28	Marketing Manager	50	Information not provided

Table 29.2 Distribution of firms

Employees	Count	Distribution (%)
51–250	2	13
10–50	4	27
Less than 10	9	60
Total	15	100

Results

The findings and abstraction that emerged revealed five issues: owner-manager–related factors, perceived benefits, perceived barriers, environmental factors, and loyalty.

Owner-Managers

The findings show that all 15 owner-managers have used information technology and social media in the past, with all of them deciding to adopt social media for business purposes. All 15 owner-managers had used a private Facebook account before setting up a business account. All interviewees perceived Facebook as a beneficial tool for marketing and promoting their business (AK, NR, PH, FL, FS, FL, MB, DL, ME, MM, JM, DS, MG, CK, SI, QM).

> *I was using it for private reasons. (…) I knew that you could create advertisements for a very low price or even for free throughout this network.*

> *(JM)*

The respondents reported that connecting friends from their private Facebook accounts let them promote their own business through existing channels, creating more awareness as a result (CK, JM, MB, MM).

The biggest benefits are definitely the connections (...). It's very important to have a certain network in place before starting a business because without help this is impossible.

(JM)

Eight participants (CK, FS, FL, JM, ME, MG, QM) reported negative attitudes regarding social media use and using the same account for private and business. Along with the perceived benefits of social media use, the participants reported customer pressure from social media, and the negative attitudes created about social media usage. Five participants (DL, FL, JM, MB, QM) argued that owner-managers aged 50 and older do not fully recognize, understand, or exploit the full benefits of social media.

They did not know really about the potential of social media advertisement and communication.

(JM)

However, older owner-managers delegate social media marketing to more experienced and educated employees who are familiar with the technology and can help the business benefit from social media.

So, if I present an idea and I try to explain how I envision what we should do with this technology throughout the digital channels, he trusts me and gives me enough money to work on it.

(QM)

Perceived Benefits

Cost Reduction: The majority of participants' SMEs focus on marketing activities through social media channels. They perceive these channels as inexpensive (AK, CK, DL, FS, FL, JM, MB, NR).

You do not need a big budget, that's the first thing. You can do marketing with a hundred Euros. If you think about a printed brochure, we are talking about thousands of Euros.

(DL)

Four participants reported no additional expenses for marketing activities besides social media platforms (FS, MB, MG, PH). Some owner-managers even use existing connections on social media to reach customers. Owner-managers perceived social media as a benefit for promoting their business in the critical startup phase (CK, DL).

For companies that don't have any financial capital or any start-up funding, like we had, we were still able to advertise, and target customers affordably, and that's how we built our business.

(CK)

Speed: Several firms mentioned how instant customer feedback through social media allows faster reactions to changing consumer needs, prompting them to effectively adapt their services and products (AK, CK, DL, DS, MB, NR).

One more thing that is useful is speed. So, things that would have taken a long time in the past can be done faster with technology.

(AK)

Promotion: Social media platforms allow users to be tracked and targeted, enhancing promotion capabilities. A large user base and a large number of social media friends are perceived as very powerful (CK, DL, DS, FS, FL, JM, MG, NR, SI).

> *If you post a cool event and you promote it (...), everyone can see it immediately. I think it's a huge improvement that information technology and social media and the Internet bring us.*
>
> *(DS)*

Ease of Use: All participants reported a distinct character of social media platforms.

> *It's not perfect, but it's relatively cheap and definitely simple to use. I think if you have any basic knowledge about how to use a computer, which most people in our generation have, you are able to run and update your website in an hour.*
>
> *(AK)*

Perceived Barriers

Skills: An unusable website, Facebook page, or Instagram account negatively influences digital presence. A lack of statistical analysis skills and underdeveloped photo and video editing skills are the most dominant barriers. Moreover, creating engaging, high-quality posts and articles is perceived as a major challenge for successful social media marketing (CK, DL, FL, JM, MB, QM).

> *This is a huge challenge because you always have to be innovative, post high-quality pictures, and high-quality videos, which is hard for a small firm like us.*
>
> *(QM)*

In addition, changing algorithms and user interfaces on social media sites lead to difficulties for owner-managers to keep their knowledge up to date (AK, CK, FL, JM, QM, PH).
Time: All 15 participants mentioned time constraints as a major barrier. Owner-managers' report that using digital technologies is very time consuming and remains a major challenge for SMEs. The owner-managers mentioned strict timetables preventing the management of social media channels (AK, CK, FL, JM, M, PH, QM).

> *This is why I get a team member to help me with social media. We are already in negotiation with a candidate [to take this over] because I can't do it anymore (...) otherwise I'll die.*
>
> *(JM)*

Digital Marketing Competition: Today, access to digital marketing solutions is simple, with many firms adopting them to reach new customers. However, this makes online platforms be perceived as increasingly overcrowded, making it difficult to set their own company apart from the competition. Strong online competition is challenging and promoting unique marketing content and campaigns is becoming more difficult (CK, DL, MB, MG, PH).

> *There are so many brands and so many companies and so many different things. Even if I sell a pretty unique product, there are still plenty of other options similar enough to the product, and it only takes five to ten minutes to search for them all.*
>
> *(CK)*

Creating a unique image and differentiated product is getting more difficult for owner-managers (DS, MG, PH).

> *We always try to differentiate from our competitors and structure our events differently. We always have our own style, and no one else uses this style and that's pretty important for us. And we compare ourselves on social media with our competitors and look at how they design their posts, what they are doing, and then we say ok: let's do it differently.*
>
> *(DS)*

Control: Consumer ability to post comments about SMEs' services and products is perceived as both a benefit and a risk. Posts from anonymous users can negatively impact a firm's image and reputation. The lack of control over misleading posts might even discourage SMEs from using social media channels (CK, FL, NR, QM).

> *Everyone is able to write a negative comment. Sometimes these customers were never even in contact with the company, they just don't like me. There's no control over it.*
>
> *(NR)*

Lack of Resources: Two firms invest in different digital technologies to improve business performance (DL, QM).

> *Digital technology is expensive. Those digital sign screens, each of them was about €30,000. The VR project was €50,000. The online shop costs a yearly fee of about €50,000 to €60,000. So, it's pretty expensive, but we try to get the maximum out of it and earn more.*
>
> *(QM)*

Lack of financial resources, in some cases implies the inability of firms to hire well-educated employees:

> *The second thing is that my previous colleague was not a good marketing manager. You start with a really low salary, and you don't get really well-educated employees.*
>
> *(QM)*

External Influences

Competitors, Consumers, Partners: Most owner-managers argue about our society is highly digitized. Neglecting digital technology adoption leads to a competitive disadvantage (AK, CK, MG, PH), meaning that the adoption of digital technologies is perceived as mandatory (AK, MG, CK, DL, DS, QM, FL, PH).

> *I think the customer has changed in recent years, the whole society has totally digitized, and therefore all the industries have to adopt because these so-called 'digital natives' live in their digital world and you want to get into business with them. You have to use the digital channels and you have to use digital technologies to reach them.*
>
> *(QM)*

Publicly available information about competitors provides SMEs with important information about future events and the chance to respond accordingly (DS, FL, MB). Owner-managers reported using competitors' newsletters as a source to adapt their own sales and pricing strategies

(AK, CK, DS). Today, social media networks are deeply embedded in business processes, and they are expected to have their own profile to participate in cross-posting activities with different partners (DL).

> *We also have strong partners. For example, this morning I had a meeting with A and with B. They share our content and we share their content.*
>
> *(DL)*

Loyalty

Communication: Building customer loyalty depends on communication quality and online availability (ME, FL, MB, NR). Social media forces owner-managers to stay online most of the time, as customers can contact SMEs around the clock. Owner-managers feel the need to respond very quickly to avoid losing customers. In addition, communication from customers via social networks increases a firm's response rates (DL, MB, NR). Social media networks here become the primary communication tool with customers (AK, CK, DS, ME, FL, FS, JM, MB, MG, NR, SI, QM).

Customization: The ability to track customers' online behavior (AK, CK, QM), reading their needs, and analyzing likes, complaints, feedbacks, and comments (AK, DL, DS, FL, FS, JM, SI) allow owner-managers to optimize marketing communication. The participants reported that they categorize consumers via targeting, tracking, and recognition technologies such as Google Analytics or Facebook Analytics.

Relationship: Several respondents personalize their business profiles on social networks through likes, comments and appreciating users' posts (CK, FL, FS, DL, DS, MB, QM). Owner-managers believe firms are perceived as individuals and ascribe a certain personality to firms (CK, JM, FS, MB).

> *On digital media, especially social media, and those travel sites we attempt to be active as individuals, not just as a company.*
>
> *(QM)*

Owner-managers' report that the number of likes allows them to identify high-value customers. Likes are used as an indicator to build closer relationships by offering certain discounts and informing about marketing activities (AK, CK, QM). Some owner-managers (DL, MB) use social networks as a customer database to interact with them on a personal level.

> *We try to engage with every review if they write something. If someone rewards us with stars, we like it. When someone has written a review, we always engage with it and if it is a good review, we appreciate it.*
>
> *(MB)*

Trust: SMEs use live videos and social network profiles to produce more personal, authentic, and exclusive content showing insights into their firms (JM, FS):

> *We can even make a live video showing us pressing 50 liters of lemon juice.*
>
> *(FS)*

Social networks encourage this transparency. Comments, stories, and photos increase trust and the authenticity of the products or services (AK, JM, ME, MB, QM, PH, CK).

> *You have immediate feedback and the entire world can see that you are a real and authentic business.*
>
> *(AK)*

Discussion and Conclusion

This study reveals owner-managers' perceptions of social media, and their positive attitude towards new digital technologies (Alford and Page, 2015; Cragg and King, 1993; Mehrtens et al., 2001). Even if the owner-manager's perception is not always positive, the benefit for the businesses is still often perceived as such (Alford and Page, 2015). Furthermore, owner-managers with a less digital mindset or those who neglect the opportunities of digitalization still take the responsibility of fostering digitalization processes by delegating tasks to the respective employees (Bruque and Moyano, 2007). Social media's perceived usefulness and ease of use lead to technology adoption (Davis et al., 1989; El-Gohary, 2010; Venkatesh et al., 2003). The increased speed of business processes, cost reduction in marketing, and enhanced promotional capabilities through social media adoption is perceived as very useful for owner-managers (Barba-Sanchez et al., 2007; Dal Fiore et al., 2014; Konstantinou, 2016).

The perceived advantages indicate that digital technologies are beneficial for SMEs and increase a firm's competitiveness, closing the gap between larger companies and SMEs as a result (Barba-Sanchez et al., 2007; Lee et al., 2016). For instance, joining a social media platform provides a fully developed website and is available at a reasonable price for SMEs. Furthermore, tracking of user interests and online behavior, and the ability to respond to user comments enable SMEs to adjust their products and services while targeting potential new customers (Barba-Sanchez et al., 2007; Konstantinou, 2016; Lee et al., 2016).

As supported by previous studies, the barriers to digitalization include a lack of skills, time constraints, and strong digital marketing competition (Alford and Page, 2015; Brady et al., 2002; Cragg and King, 1993; Dahnil et al., 2014). Social media platforms have low (if any) access barriers, fostering their adoption and use by rival owner-managers. Special skills are however needed to create high quality and engaging content, as well as analyze the data generated and optimize marketing spending (Jones et al., 2015; Leeflang et al., 2014). This suggests that owner-managers adopt social media platforms as a marketing tool to engage with users in a first step while producing high quality and unique content later on, which impedes owner-managers from optimizing marketing strategies and spending. Furthermore, and as seen in previous studies, time constraints are perceived as a major hurdle (Bruque and Moyano, 2007; Cragg and King, 1993; Dahnil et al., 2014; Konstantinou, 2016).

The majority of participants argued that a digital online presence is necessary to gain a competitive advantage (Durkin et al., 2013; Mehrtens et al., 2001). Owner-managers perceive social media platforms as a tool to improve promotion, service, and communication with customers, increasing their trust and loyalty as a result (Anderson and Srinivasan, 2003; Woodcock et al., 2011). Additionally, owner-managers are able to identify loyal customers and constantly communicate and interact with high-value customers via social networks (Woodcock et al., 2011).

Interestingly, owner-managers use social media primarily for marketing purposes to engage with customers and strengthen the business relationship. A second emphasis is competitor observation and differentiation of the own SME among the market. Opportunities to expand the business internationally or reach international customers were not reported.

Improved communication, relationships, and trust through transparency and authenticity, as well as the customization of products and services positively influence loyalty from the perspective of owner-managers (Woodcock et al., 2011).

Although the interviewees were asked to reflect upon the entire range of digitalization impacts and benefits, it was surprising that the majority of SMEs mainly focused on social media or online communication. Along with marketing, the digitalization of businesses affects not only process and product/service innovation, but other SME business functions as well such as human resource management, knowledge management, or logistics. There are far fewer findings of these significant benefits digitalization can generate. Quinton et al. (2018) defines digital orientation as a combination of technology, knowledge, and an entrepreneurial mindset which is needed to re-think traditional analogous business models. We assume that SMEs rarely reflect upon all of these digitalization dimensions at one single time, and as a result, might even misinterpret the complex impacts of this phenomenon.

References

Alford, P. and Page, S.J. (2015), "Marketing technology for adoption by small business", *The Service Industries Journal*, Vol.35, No.11–12, pp.655–669. https://doi.org/10.1080/02642069.2015.1062884.

Anderson, R.E. and Srinivasan, S.S. (2003), "E-satisfaction and e-loyalty: A contingency framework", *Psychology and Marketing*, Vol.20, No.2, pp.123–138. https://doi.org/10.1002/mar.10063.

Banerjee, B. (2004), "Environmental policy and technological innovation: Why do firms adopt or reject new technologies?", *Technovation*, Vol.24, No.7, pp.595. https://doi.org/10.1016/j.technovation.2004.03.008.

Barba-Sanchez, V., del Pilar Martinez-Ruiz, M., and Jimenez-Zarco, A.I. (2007), "Drivers, benefits and challenges of ICT adoption by small and medium sized enterprises (SMEs): A literature review", *Problems and Perspectives in Management*, Vol.5, No.1, pp.103–114.

Bell, E., Bryman, A., and Harley, B. (2019), *Business Research Methods*, 5th ed., Oxford University Press, Oxford.

Berry, L.L. (2002), "Relationship marketing of services perspectives from 1983 and 2000", *Journal of Relationship Marketing*, Vol.1, No.1, pp.59–77. https://doi.org/10.1300/J366v01n01_05.

Bharadwaj, A., El Sawy, O.A., Pavlou, P.A., and Venkatraman, N. (2013), "Digital business strategy: Toward a next generation of insights", *MIS Quarterly*, Vol.37, No.2, pp.471–482. https://doi.org/10.25300/MISQ/2013/37:2.3.

Bitner, M.J., Brown, S.W., and Meuter, M.L. (2000), "Technology infusion in service encounters", *Journal of the Academy of Marketing Science*, Vol.28, No.1, pp.138–149. https://doi.org/10.1177/0092070300281013.

Boaden, R. and Lockett, G. (1991), "Information technology, information systems and information management: Definition and development", *European Journal of Information Systems*, Vol.1, No.1, pp.23–32. https://doi.org/10.1057/ejis.1991.4.

Bouwman, H., Nikou, S., Molina-Castillo, F.J., and de Reuver, M. (2018), "The impact of digitalization on business models", *Digital Policy, Regulation and Governance*, Vol.20, No.2, pp.105–124. https://doi.org/10.1108/DPRG-07-2017-0039.

Brady, M., Saren, M., and Tzokas, N. (2002), "Integrating information technology into marketing practice – The IT reality of contemporary marketing practice", *Journal of Marketing Management*, Vol.18, No.5–6, pp.555–577. https://doi.org/10.1362/0267257022683703.

Bruque, S. and Moyano, J. (2007), "Organisational determinants of information technology adoption and implementation in SMEs: The case of family and cooperative firms", *Technovation*, Vol.27, No.5, pp.241–253. https://doi.org/10.1016/j.technovation.2006.12.003.

Camisón, C. and Monfort-Mir, V.M. (2012), "Measuring innovation in tourism from the Schumpeterian and the dynamic-capabilities perspectives", *Tourism Management*, Vol.33, No.4, pp.776–789. https://doi.org/10.1016/j.tourman.2011.08.012.

Chrisman, J.J., Chua, J.H., de Massis, A., Frattini, F., and Wright, M. (2015), "The ability and willingness paradox in family firm innovation", *Journal of Product Innovation Management*, Vol.32, No.3, pp.310–318. https://doi.org/10.1111/jpim.12207.

Cragg, P.B. and King, M. (1993), "Small-firm computing: Motivators and inhibitors", *MIS Quarterly*, Vol.17, No.1, pp.47. https://doi.org/10.2307/249509.

Creswell, J.W. and Poth, C.N., (2018), *Qualitative Inquiry and Research Design: Choosing Among Five Approaches*, 4th ed., Sage, Los Angeles, CA.

Dahnil, M.I., Marzuki, K.M., Langgat, J., and Fabeil, N.F. (2014), "Factors influencing SMEs adoption of social media marketing", *Procedia – Social and Behavioral Sciences*, Vol.148, pp.119–126. https://doi.org/10.1016/j.sbspro.2014.07.025.

Dal Fiore, F., Mokhtarian, P.L., Salomon, I., and Singer, M.E. (2014), " 'Nomads at last'? A set of perspectives on how mobile technology may affect travel", *Journal of Transport Geography*, Vol.41, pp.97–106. https://doi.org/10.1016/j.jtrangeo.2014.08.014.

Davis, F.D., Bagozzi, R.P., and Warshaw, P.R. (1989), "User acceptance of computer technology: A comparison of two theoretical models", *Management Science*, Vol.35, No.8, pp.982–1003. https://doi.org/10.1287/mnsc.35.8.982.

Dedrick, J., Gurbaxani, V., and Kraemer, K.L. (2003), "Information technology and economic performance", *ACM Computing Surveys*, Vol.35, No.1, pp.1–28. https://doi.org/10.1145/641865.641866.

Dick, A. S. and Basu, K. (1994), "Customer loyalty: Toward an integrated conceptual framework", *Journal of the Academy of Marketing Science*, Vol.22, No.2, pp.99–113. https://doi.org/10.1177/0092070394222001.

Duffy, D.L. (1998), "Customer loyalty strategies", *Journal of Consumer Marketing*, Vol.15, No.5, pp.435–448. https://doi.org/10.1108/07363769810235910.

Durkin, M., McGowan, P., and McKeown, N. (2013), "Exploring social media adoption in small to medium-sized enterprises in Ireland", *Journal of Small Business and Enterprise Development*, Vol.20, No.4, pp.716–734. https://doi.org/10.1108/JSBED-08-2012-0094.

Dworkin, S.L. (2012), "Sample size policy for qualitative studies using in-depth interviews", *Archives of Sexual Behavior*, Vol.41, No.6, pp.1319–1320. https://doi.org/10.1007/s10508-012-0016-6.

El-Gohary, H. (2010), "E-marketing – A literature review from a small businesses perspective", *International Journal of Business and Social Science*, Vol.1, No.1, pp.214–244.

Geissdoerfer, M., Vladimirova, D., and Evans, S. (2018), "Sustainable business model innovation: A review", *Journal of cleaner production*, Vol.198, pp.401–416. https://doi.org/10.1016/j.jclepro.2018.06.240.

Giotopoulos, I., Kontolaimou, A., Korra, E., and Tsakanikas, A. (2017), "What drives ICT adoption by SMEs? Evidence from a large-scale survey in Greece", *Journal of Business Research*, Vol.81, pp.60–69. https://doi.org/10.1016/j.jbusres.2017.08.007.

Gnyawali, D.R., Fan, W., and Penner, J. (2010), "Competitive actions and dynamics in the digital age: An empirical investigation of social networking firms", *Information Systems Research*, Vol.21, No.3, pp.594–613. https://doi.org/10.1287/isre.1100.0294.

Gray, C. (2002), "Entrepreneurship, resistance to change and growth in small firms", *Journal of Small Business and Enterprise Development*, Vol.9, No.1, pp.61–72. https://doi.org/10.1108/14626000210419491.

Guest, G., Bunce, A., and Johnson, L. (2006), "How many interviews are enough?", *Field Methods*, Vol.18, No.1, pp.59–82. https://doi.org/10.1177/1525822x05279903.

Han, L., Benson, A., Chen, J.J., and Zhang, S. (2014), "The use and impacts of bank support on UK small and medium-sized enterprises", *International Small Business Journal*, Vol.32, No.1, pp.61–80. https://doi.org/10.1177/0266242612455008.

Hu, P.J., Chau, P.Y.K., Sheng, O.R.L., and Tam, K.Y. (1999), "Examining the technology acceptance model using physician acceptance of telemedicine technology", *Journal of Management Information Systems*, Vol.16, No.2, pp.91–112. https://doi.org/10.1080/07421222.1999.11518247.

Hugill, A. and Helfat, C.E., (2018), "Managerial resources and capabilities", in Augier, M. and Teece, D.J. (Eds.), *Living Reference Work. The Palgrave Encyclopedia of Strategic Management*, Vol.14, pp.1–5, Palgrave Macmillan, London, UK. https://doi.org/10.1057/978-1-349-94848-2_604-1.

Jamil, G.L., Pinto Ferreira, J.J., Pinto, M.M., Magalhães Pessoa, C.R., and Xavier, A., (2018), *Strategic Innovation Management for Improved Competitive Advantage, A Volume in the Advances in Business Strategy and Competitive Advantage (ABSCA) Book Series*, Business Science Reference, Hershey, PA.

Jones, R., Alford, P., and Wolfenden, S. (2015), "Entrepreneurial marketing in the digital age: A study of the SME tourism industry", in *Global Research Symposium on Marketing and Entrepreneurship*, Bournemouth University, Bournemouth, UK.

Kenney, M., Rouvinen, P., and Zysman, J. (2015), "The digital disruption and its societal impacts", *Journal of Industry, Competition and Trade*, Vol.15, No.1, pp.1–4. https://doi.org/10.1007/s10842-014-0187-z.

Kim, H.D., Lee, I., and Lee, C.K. (2013), "Building Web 2.0 enterprises: A study of small and medium enterprises in the United States", *International Small Business Journal*, Vol.31, No.2, pp.156–174. https://doi.org/10.1177/0266242611409785.

Konstantinou, J.K. (2016), "Digitization of European SMEs in tourism and hospitality: The case of Greek hoteliers", [Advance online publication], available at: https://doi.org/10.5281/zenodo.1124259.

Lee, S.-C., Barker, S., and Kandampully, J. (2003), "Technology, service quality, and customer loyalty in hotels: Australian managerial perspectives", *Managing Service Quality: An International Journal*, Vol.13, No.5, pp.423–432. https://doi.org/10.1108/09604520310495886.

Lee, V.-H., Foo, A.T.-L., Leong, L.-Y., and Ooi, K.-B. (2016), "Can competitive advantage be achieved through knowledge management? A case study on SMEs", *Expert Systems with Applications*, Vol.65, pp.136–151. https://doi.org/10.1016/j.eswa.2016.08.042.

Leeflang, P.S.H., Verhoef, P.C., Dahlström, P., and Freundt, T. (2014), "Challenges and solutions for marketing in a digital era", *European Management Journal*, Vol.32, No.1, pp.1–12. https://doi.org/10.1016/j.emj.2013.12.001.

Majumdar, D., Banerji, P.K., and Chakrabarti, S. (2018), "Disruptive technology and disruptive innovation: Ignore at your peril!", *Technology Analysis & Strategic Management*, Vol.30, No.11, pp.1247–1255. https://doi.org/10.1080/09537325.2018.1523384.

Marshall, M.N. (1996), "Sampling for qualitative research", *Family Practice*, Vol.13, No.6, pp.522–525. https://doi.org/10.1093/fampra/13.6.522.

Mayring, P. (2010), *A Companion to Qualitative Research* (repr, Vol.1), SAGE, London, UK.

Mehrtens, J., Cragg, P.B., and Mills, A.M. (2001), "A model of Internet adoption by SMEs", *Information & Management*, Vol.39, No.3, pp.165–176. https://doi.org/10.1016/S0378-7206(01)00086-6.

Meske, C. and Stieglitz, S. (2013), "Adoption and use of social media in small and medium-sized enterprises", *Practice-Driven Research on Enterprise Transformation*, Vol.151, pp.61–75. Springer Berlin Heidelberg. https://doi.org/10.1007/978-3-642-38774-6_5.

Mikalef, P. and Pateli, A. (2017), "Information technology-enabled dynamic capabilities and their indirect effect on competitive performance: Findings from PLS-SEM and fsQCA", *Journal of Business Research*, Vol.70, pp.1–16. https://doi.org/10.1016/j.jbusres.2016.09.004.

Myrna, J.W. (2012), "A rolling stone gathers no moss: prevent your strategic plan from stagnating", *Business Strategy Series*, Vol.13, No.3, pp.136–142. https://doi.org/10.1108/17515631211225297.

O'Regan, N. and Ghobadian, A. (2002), "Effective strategic planning in small and medium sized firms", *Management Decision*, Vol.40, No.7, pp.663–671. https://doi.org/10.1108/00251740210438490.

Pappas, I.O., Mikalef, P., Giannakos, M.N., Krogstie, J., and Lekakos, G. (2018), "Big data and business analytics ecosystems: Paving the way towards digital transformation and sustainable societies", *Information Systems and e-Business Management*, Vol.16, No.3, pp.479–491. https://doi.org/10.1007/s10257-018-0377-z.

Peters, M. (2017), "Familienunternehmen im Tourismus: Forschungserkenntnisse und Besonderheiten", in Bußjäger, P. and Gsodam, C. (Eds.), *Schriftenreihe des Instituts für Föderalismus: Band 124. Tourismus und Multi-Level-Governance im Alpenraum*, Vol.124, Nap New Academic Press, Wien, pp. 191–209.

Peters, M. and Buhalis, D. (2004), "Family hotel businesses: Strategic planning and the need for education and training", *Education + Training*, Vol.46, No.8/9, pp.406–415. https://doi.org/10.1108/00400910410569524.

Prasad, V.K., Ramamurthy, K., and Naidu, G.M. (2001), "The influence of internet–marketing integration on marketing competencies and export performance", *Journal of International Marketing*, Vol.9, No.4, pp.82–110. https://doi.org/10.1509/jimk.9.4.82.19944.

Quinton, S., Canhoto, A., Molinillo, S., Pera, R., and Budhathoki, T. (2018), "Conceptualising a digital orientation: Antecedents of supporting SME performance in the digital economy", *Journal of Strategic Marketing*, Vol.26, No.5, pp.427–439. https://doi.org/10.1080/0965254X.2016.1258004.

Rauniar, R., Rawski, G., Yang, J., and Johnson, B. (2014), "Technology acceptance model (TAM) and social media usage: an empirical study on Facebook", *Journal of Enterprise Information Management*, Vol.27, No.1, pp.6–30. https://doi.org/10.1108/JEIM-04-2012-0011.

Renzi, S. and Klobas, J. (2008), "Using the theory of planned behavior with qualitative research", available at: https://researchrepository.murdoch.edu.au/id/eprint/23550/ (accessed 12 December 2019).

Riemenschneider, C.K., Harrison, D.A., and Mykytyn, P.P. (2003), "Understanding it adoption decisions in small business: integrating current theories", *Information & Management*, Vol.40, No.4, pp.269–285. https://doi.org/10.1016/S0378-7206(02)00010-1.

Roberts, J. (2000), "From know-how to show-how? Questioning the role of information and communication technologies in knowledge transfer", *Technology Analysis & Strategic Management*, Vol.12, No.4, pp.429–443. https://doi.org/10.1080/713698499.

Rosman, R. and Stuhura, K. (2013), "The implications of social media on customer relationship management and the hospitality industry", *Journal of Management Policy and Practice*, Vol.14, No.3, pp.18–26.

Saldaña, J., (2015), *The Coding Manual for Qualitative Researchers*, 3rd ed., SAGE, Los Angeles, CA.

Shahiduzzaman, M., Kowalkiewicz, M., and Barrett, R. (2018), "Digital dividends in the phase of falling productivity growth and implications for policy making", *International Journal of Productivity and Performance Management*, Vol.67, No.6, pp.1016–1032. https://doi.org/10.1108/IJPPM-02-2017-0050.

Sohn, S.Y. and Kim, Y.S. (2013), "Behavioral credit scoring model for technology-based firms that considers uncertain financial ratios obtained from relationship banking", *Small Business Economics*, Vol.41, No.4, pp.931–943. https://doi.org/10.1007/s11187-012-9457-5.

Taiminen, H.M. and Karjaluoto, H. (2015), "The usage of digital marketing channels in SMEs", *Journal of Small Business and Enterprise Development*, Vol.22, No.4, pp.633–651. https://doi.org/10.1108/JSBED-05-2013-0073.

Tilson, D., Lyytinen, K., and Sørensen, C. (2010), "Research commentary —digital infrastructures: The missing is research agenda", *Information Systems Research*, Vol.21, No.4, pp.748–759. https://doi.org/10.1287/isre.1100.0318.

Valdez-Juárez, L.E., García-Pérez-de-Lema, D., and Maldonado-Guzmán, G. (2018), "ICT and KM, drivers of innovation and profitability in SMEs", *Journal of Information & Knowledge Management*, Vol.17, No.01, pp.1850007. https://doi.org/10.1142/S0219649218500077.

Venkatesh, V., Morris, M.G., Davis, G.B., and Davis, F.D. (2003), "User acceptance of information technology: Toward a unified view", *MIS Quarterly*, Vol.27, No.3, pp.425–478. https://doi.org/10.2307/30036540.

Vogelsang, K., Steinhueser, M., and Hoppe, U. (2013), "A qualitative approach to examine technology acceptance", in *Proceedings of the* 34. International Conference on Information Systems, December 15-18, Milan, Italy, pp.1-16.

Warner, K.S.R. and Wäger, M. (2019), "Building dynamic capabilities for digital transformation: An ongoing process of strategic renewal", *Long Range Planning*, Vol.52, No.3, pp.326–349. https://doi.org/10.1016/j.lrp.2018.12.001.

Woodcock, N., Green, A., and Starkey, M. (2011), "Social CRM as a business strategy", *Journal of Database Marketing & Customer Strategy Management*, Vol.18, No.1, pp.50–64. https://doi.org/10.1057/dbm.2011.7.

Yu, C.S. and Tao, Y.H. (2009), "Understanding business-level innovation technology adoption", *Technovation*, Vol.29, No.2, pp.92–109. https://doi.org/10.1016/j.technovation.2008.07.007.

Zeiller, M. and Schauer, B. (2011), "Adoption, motivation and success factors of social media for team collaboration in SMEs", in Lindstaedt, S. (Ed.), *Proceedings of the 11th International Conference on Knowledge Management and Knowledge Technologies*, ACM, New York, NY, p. 1, available at: https://doi.org/10.1145/2024288.2024294 xx.

30

SPORTS STADIUM HOSPITALITY AND CATERING

A Global Perspective

Thorsten Merkle and Philippa Golding

Introduction

Spectator sports play an important economic role in many countries, with revenues of more than 63 billion dollars in North America alone in 2015 (PwC, 2017). The sports industry contributed an estimated 245 billion Euros in 2014 to the European economy (European Commission, 2018). While much research has been conducted on various aspects of spectator sports, sports stadia hospitality and catering services have received relatively little attention.

The literature reveals that practitioner literature (non-peer-reviewed) plays a far more important role in sports catering than academic literature does. While there is much literature dealing with general Food and Beverage Management, there is little relevant literature available about sports stadium spectator catering. Scholars mainly work in the contexts of the United States of America, the United Kingdom, Greece, Australia, New Zealand, and Germany.

This chapter discusses different aspects of sports stadia catering services in an academic and practitioner-oriented context:

- Food and Beverage Concessions Operations
- Branding and Brand Associations
- Health and Public Health
- Service Quality and Customer Satisfaction
- Stadium Hospitality Programs

Any good discussion starts by clarifying terminology. Organizations managing sports stadia often refer to "Hospitality and Catering" for the department dealing with all food- and beverage-related issues. The term Catering in this environment typically includes Public Catering, Media Catering, and Staff Catering. Public Catering refers to Food and Beverage concessions (Clemes et al., 2011), where the public are provided with foods and beverages. Concessions are structures (permanent or temporary) within the stadium perimeter where food and beverages are sold to spectators (FIFA, 2012). The Public Catering program is therefore also referred to as the Concessions program. For public catering, football clubs (or stadium operators) usually appoint concessionaires and then financially participate through a revenue-share agreement. The concessionaires then usually operate at their own risk.

Often, separate Food and Beverage services are provided for Media representatives, especially at large events (Media Catering). Food and Beverage services provided for athletes, officials, as well as employees working on-site are part of the Staff Catering program. The term Hospitality usually includes areas where specific groups of guests are hosted on-site or in adjacent hospitality villages. Stadium Hospitality includes VIP Hospitality, Sponsor Programs as well as Commercial Hospitality Programs. Guests in these areas can enjoy refreshments and meals before, during, and after the event. Many stadiums operate multi-tier purchase systems of hospitality or exclusive facilities (FIFA, 2011).

For commercial hospitality operations, football clubs (or marketing agencies appointed by them) sell hospitality packages. These packages typically involve a catering service provider for the food and beverage component. Catering in the hospitality areas is often organized as a service (Merkle and Lewis, 2016b). The caterer provides service to the expected number of guests beforehand and will then invoice the club (or an appointed marketing agency) subsequently. After this terminology clarification, this chapter subsequently concentrates on Public Catering (Concessions).

Food and Beverage Concessions Operations

Food and beverages not only play an important role in the stadium environment and in the experience for the spectators of a sporting event (Sukalakamala et al., 2013), they also provide stadium operators and sports clubs an opportunity to add value and to gain additional revenues.

Attendance and Expenditure

Exploring demand for attendance at professional Football and Baseball sporting events in the United States, Coates and Humphreys (2007) used a data set including ticket cost and an index reflecting other aspects associated with attendance. They showed that attendance demand is relatively price inelastic, i.e., changes in ticket prices have little influence on ticket demand (Coates and Humphreys, 2007; Krautmann and Berri, 2007). Coates and Humphreys (2007) furthermore show that demand for auxiliary goods, such as food and beverage concessions, is more price elastic. Overall, food and beverage concession demand tends to fall when entrance ticket prices rise above the inelastic region of demand. Krautmann and Berri (2007) support Coates and Humphreys' findings (2007) by showing that it is plausible for owners and clubs to price tickets in the inelastic region of demand to maximize revenue on food and beverage concessions.

Operations

While spectators prefer food they can eat quickly, concession operators need to consider logistics and handling, preferring food which is fast and easy to prepare. Both tend towards food that can be eaten quickly by hand (Sukalakamala et al., 2013). Operationally, concessions service in stadiums faces unique challenges compared to traditional contexts. Service periods are not consistent, with very low demand following peaks, depending on the sport played. Whisenant et al. (2013) claim that 80% of concession sales occur by the conclusion of halftime, and only 20% occur after halftime. In European Football, for example, the halftime break lasts only 20 minutes (Merkle and Lewis, 2016b). As early as 1997, Motsinger et al. (1997) conducted a comparative study on Food and Beverage Concession operations in different sport facilities in North Carolina, the United States of America. Besides aspects of speed and quality of service, Motsinger et al. (1997) highlighted the commercial importance of the operation for the stadium operator and discussed approaches to maximize sales. From a concessions operations point of view, the following critical issues were identified: cash handling, concessions design, pricing, as well as the sale of alcohol.

Concessions Design and Pricing

Fuhrmeister (2018) reports that requests from fans for affordable concessions in NFL stadiums have resulted in the Atlanta Falcons announcing their "Fan-First Pricing" in 2016, which offered premium items alongside a range of food and beverages for under $10. This step, however, did follow the announcement of a price increase in tickets (Fuhrmeister, 2018). This decrease in prices still resulted in a 16% overall increase in concessions revenue in 2017. Several benefits have been observed following this new pricing system: The Falcons were ranked within the top three teams for overall game-day experience and a family-friendly environment. Furthermore, they ranked first in the NFL in security screenings as fans were entering the stadium earlier because of cheaper food and drinks, which resulted in a 90% increase in merchandise sales from 2016. Following the success of the program, several other clubs both in the NFL and other sports have made similar announcements (Fuhrmeister, 2018). In addition to new pricing strategies, stadiums in the United States of America have also been introducing new "premium concessions": local and known chefs create items for quick service to improve the food experience and service quality (Fuhrmeister, 2018).

Hygiene and Food Safety

Handling and preparation of food items have certain inherent risks that need to be managed to guarantee consumers' health and safety. This is achieved by employing food safety management systems based on the codex Alimentarius, a collection of internationally recognized standards relating to food safety (Alimentarius, 2014). Food safety management systems aim at preventing any food contamination with (micro-) biological, chemical, or physical agents. Because contamination may occur at any point, food safety management systems need to holistically integrate all the production processes and assess potential hazards of various types. One of these measures is based on the principles of Hazard Analysis and Critical Control Points also referred to as HACCP (Alli, 2003). The HACCP system has seven principles grounded in the concept of critical control points in a production process where potential hazards might be controlled or eliminated (Mortimore and Wallace, 2013). Elaborating and implementing a food safety management system is only the starting point. More importantly, all employees need to be trained on the system; compliance with its rules needs to be ensured at all times (Merkle and Lewis, 2016a).

Logistics and Food Production

The process of producing stadium food for both Public Catering as well as Concessions is highly specialized and includes a high level of division of labor. Planning usually involves using menu-planning systems, forecasting the amounts of each item that needs to be prepared, and aggregating them into an integrated production plan. Based on the system of Food and Beverage standards (Davis et al., 2018), the production process and the raw materials required are then forecast.

Central production kitchens and widely distributed sales outlets throughout the venue pose special challenges to on-site logistics. Once the venue is opened for spectators, possibilities for internal goods transports are very limited; caterers need to adhere to a strict temporal logistical plan. Whilst distribution of food and beverage items, as well as equipment and similar items, needs to be completed before gates open to spectators, concessionaires need to prepare for cash disposal as well. Although more and more stadia use proprietary cashless (card) payment systems, cash payments remain important in many stadia. Often the provision of float, disposal of cash receipts as well as their handling is outsourced to specialized cash handling companies so concession employees can concentrate on the core task: producing and selling food and beverage items.

Staffing and Human Resources

Most venues have league events only every other week, meaning that the whole operation needs to be activated and shut down repeatedly. Whilst a small core management crew often is employed full-time, hundreds of employees are required for event days only. This challenging situation for stadium caterers typically is solved using casual labor (e.g., students) as well as labor brokers (Merkle and Lewis, 2016b). With a high division of labor in the food production process, workers can feel estranged from the final product, leading to lower levels of employee motivation.

Security

A number of events have highlighted the need for security strategies in sports stadia. Ninety-six casualties were reported and 766 spectators were injured in the 1989 Hillsborough disaster, following poor crowd management and unfortunate stadium design and layout (Sawer, 2017). As Hall (2010) states, English Football stadiums use new designs to control the spaces in and around the stadiums and integrate command centers into the stadiums that can monitor turnstiles, fire alarms, and Closed Circuit Television (CCTV). The creation of security command centers has subsequently been the case in most countries for professional sports stadia. This is not only due to spectator behavior, as sports facilities are nowadays considered tempting targets for terrorist attacks (Galily et al., 2016). European football's governing body UEFA subsequently identified several key factors for a safe environment including crowd management training for stewards, encouraging the police to interact with the crowds.

Waste Management

Due to security, as well as operational reasons, disposable cups are often used in Public Catering. Due to environmental issues and increased awareness of sustainable development, this practice is increasingly questioned by consumers. Waste separation typically is the minimum measure taken, and more and more stadia have started to use reusable cups that come with a deposit to incentivize spectators to return the cups. Bayern München, the German top football club, has admitted to having discovered the importance of reusable cups only very late. It has subsequently, however, been high on the agenda, and the club is now playing a leading role in sustainability movements in the German league (Wildmann, 2018).

Service Quality and Customer Satisfaction

The delivery of the spectator sport experience is a service, and therefore, can be understood by the general characteristics of services, such as inseparability and intangibility (Fliess and Kleinaltenkamp, 2004). According to Clemes et al. (2011), two streams of research are useful for managers wanting to improve spectators' experience: Dimensions of service quality as well as factors influencing spectator satisfaction.

Service Quality

A multitude of aspects such as *concession design* (Fodness and Murray, 2007), *employee-related attributes* (Heung et al., 2002), *price, speed of service, location, quality of food,* or *cleanliness* (Mason et al., 2013) have been found to influence perceived service quality, which can thus be understood as a multidimensional construct. Several approaches have been developed to assess it. One of the most commonly applied is the SERVQUAL model developed by Parasuraman et al. (1988). Based on the dimensions of the SERVQUAL instrument, McDonald et al. (1995) elaborated the TEAM-QUAL instrument in conjunction with a Major League Baseball team. TEAMQUAL is based on five service dimensions, namely *Tangibles, Reliability, Responsiveness, Assurance,* and *Empathy*. Studies in the U.S. context using this approach have identified that the dimension *Tangibles*, followed by *Reliability*, had the overall highest weight and importance for the NFL (National Football League), NBA (National Basketball Association), and MLB (Major League Baseball) fans as well as spectators at professional basketball games in Greece (Theodorakis et al., 2001). It can be argued that spectator Food and Beverage services fall under the *"Tangibles"* dimension. Also in the NFL context, Larson and Steinman (2009) applied the SERVQUAL model in order to determine fans' satisfaction and return intentions within concession service quality. They find that the dimensions *Assurance* and *Empathy* predict neither overall concession stand experience nor intent to return to a concession stand.

Customer Satisfaction

Evaluations of the service(s) received are finalized in the post-consumption stage (Babin and Harris, 2011; Fliess, 2009; Hoffmann and Turley, 2002; Lovelock and Wirtz, 2011; Solomon, 2015). The construct of (post-consumption) customer satisfaction has traditionally been investigated as a key factor influencing loyalty and re-patronage intentions (Bowden, 2009). The relationship between customer satisfaction and loyalty has received considerable attention in research (Babin and Harris, 2011; Davis et al., 2008; Fliess, 2009; Lovelock and Wirtz, 2011). This research has traditionally been achieved through a model including customer satisfaction as an antecedent of behavioral intentions (such as positive word-of-mouth and re-patronage intentions).

The historically dominant customer satisfaction model is based on the rational choice paradigm, comparing received service deliveries (as perceived by the customers) and contrasting them with a priori expectations. Positive disconfirmation of expectations leads to customer satisfaction, whereas negative disconfirmation leads to customer dissatisfaction (Bruhn and Georgi, 2006; Fliess, 2009; Grönroos, 2001; Lovelock and Wirtz, 2011). This utility-oriented approach is based on disconfirmation theory (Kivela, Inbakaran, and Reece, 1999). Several authors acknowledge the importance of team game performance on customer satisfaction (Van Leeuwen et al., 2002; Whisenant et al., 2013); however, the top priorities regarding value offered to fans by NFL, NBA, and MLB teams, as ranked by fans, are not related to the team and its performance, but instead reflect concerns such as arena/stadium comfort (McDonald et al., 1995). Kelley and Turley (2001) agree, claiming that food and beverage concessions do affect the perceived service quality at sporting events.

Van Leeuwen et al. (2002), in their Sport Spectator Satisfaction Model, consider a so-called "peripheral service dimension," which includes food and beverage concessions. Extending said model, Ko et al. (2011) developed a model to measure event quality in major spectator sports, based on research conducted in the MLB context. Besides acknowledging the importance of game performance, Ko et al. (2011) split the peripheral service dimension into further sub-dimensions to include both the *availability of wide ranges of food and beverage* as well as *interactions with personnel* as part of the interaction quality dimension. Greenwell et al. (2007) found that food prices in a professional spectator sport setting may qualify as a dissatisfying aspect, i.e., they may cause dissatisfaction if too high but will not lead to customer satisfaction if set at the right level. Clemes et al. (2011), calling for an integrated approach, consider the provision of food and beverage as part of interaction quality. Their findings show that food and beverage service contributes positively to interaction quality and also that interaction quality positively contributes to overall service quality.

Financial and Contractual Aspects

The stadium operator or sports club (or a marketing agency on their behalf) usually initially holds the catering rights and then transfers them to a Food and Beverage Concessionaire, often by means of a tender process (Merkle and Lewis, 2016b). In the Western European and U.S. context, a number of concessionaire systems are common.

- Master Concessionaire: The master concessionaire model sees the operations of all concessions awarded to one master concessionaire who then operates those outlets in the respective stadium, and is usually also involved in developing the concessions.
- Prime Operator: In a prime operator model, the airport leases packages of locations to two or more operators, each operating more than three locations within the venue.
- Direct Leasing: As in other contexts, in the direct leasing model, the stadium catering rightsholder leases individual locations or small groups of concessions (no more than three) directly to the operators (ACI, 2014).

There are also mixed forms and operational concepts where e.g., the master concessionaire is owned by the stadium operator (as was e.g., the case in Munich's Football stadium). Concessionaires then usually pay a fee to the rightsholder (stadium operator or club), often based on the Food and Beverage revenues attained in a given period. Caterers typically forecast revenues using key indicators such as the number of spectators, the incident rate (percentage of spectators that consume) as well as the Average Guest Check (average amount per transaction (Davis et al., 2008)). Instead of agreeing on a royalty fee as a percentage of Food and Beverage revenue, some caterers pay a fixed amount per spectator entering the stadium to the rightsholder.

Innovations

A number of innovative approaches to service and operations have been discussed. Motsinger et al. (1997) suggested at-seat service (hawking), an approach to maximize sales whilst evening out demand peaks during breaks that is mainly used for products that are pre-packaged and can easily be transported such as beverages, ice cream, or popcorn. Hawkers, however, may obstruct the view for other spectators and distract from the action on the field. Consequently, many stadium operators do not allow Hawkers to enter the stands during match time.

Whilst concessions are usually fixed structures with certain production and sales equipment, temporary concessions (mainly for beverages or snack foods), as well as mobile units (pushcarts selling beverages, popcorn, or other snacks), are often used to better serve crowds at peak times (FIFA, 2011). Innovative catering concepts such as the inclusion of well-known food brands or on-site specialty restaurants that are open also on non-match-days are part of the commercialization of sports stadia. The availability of franchises and well-known food brands is primarily in the context of the United States rather than Europe, possibly due to a larger presence of franchise businesses in North America in general (Gillard and Merkle, 2015).

Process innovations, such as central beer distribution systems are found mainly in newly built stadia (Oldenkotte, 2008). Advantages include reduced process times (pouring of draft beer) as well as improved management of beer quality and temperature. Efficient automated systems allow for simpler, more economical and hygienic cleaning of the beer lines. On the other hand, those systems involve higher efforts and costs for pipe cleaning and breakdowns on Match Days have more severe consequences, which needs to be considered during risk management.

Customer Preference/Food Offers

Whilst typical stadium foods such as hamburgers, French fries, and other fast-food style offers still attract customers, there is a growing demand for healthier options (Sukalakamala et al., 2013). Motsinger et al. (1997) identified rising demand for lighter and healthier food in sports stadia in the 1990s. Interestingly, the explanation given for this rise in demand is the growing attendance of women spectators in baseball stadia, as well as the generally increasing health consciousness and preference for healthier foods globally. Research by Mulherin (1997) in the context of Australia as well as the United States suggests that female spectators ask for a wider food and beverage offering in sports stadia. This claim is supported by Ireland and Watkins (2010) who investigated spectators' attitudes towards food and drinks available in the English Premier League. They found that women tended to ask for healthier food choices, and were not satisfied with the choices of either food or alcohol available. Most of the men, however, were happy with the choices available. Both men and women agreed in one point only: that the quality of food and beverages available in the stadium was unsatisfactory.

In general, food offered at a stadium should reflect the demands of the customers (Emery et al., 2016) and should be able to be eaten quickly and easily so that fans can return to their seats without delay (Sukalakamala et al., 2013). Consumers' increasing demand for healthier, higher-quality food and drink choices shows potential revenue opportunities lie in more varied concessions offers.

Branding and Brand Associations

Sporting events such as football league matches are tradable goods, and as such linked to value generation in various fields. The four main sources of marketing-related income for the clubs are stadium visits, sponsoring, broadcast rights, and the sale of merchandise (Swieter, 2002). Besides ticketing revenues, income generated from food and beverage concessions falls under the category of stadium visit, as do revenues from Commercial Hospitality Programs. Brand associations are an individual's thoughts regarding a particular service. In light of sporting events, Ross et al. (2006) developed a model using a set of 11 different factors that play a role in sports team brand associations and concluded that, besides factors such as team play, commitment, and social interaction, Food and Beverage concessions are important for creating sports team brand association for fans.

In the context of the German Fussball-Bundesliga (first division of the German professional football league), Swieter (2002) describes the value-generating mechanisms in a professional football league. Recently, a growing number of football clubs have concentrated their operational business in limited companies (limited liability companies, public limited companies, and associations limited by shares). Furthermore, a growing number of football clubs have sold marketing rights to sport marketing agencies, which sees the club receive a fee in exchange for their marketing rights (TV broadcasting, merchandising, and advertising rights) from the sport marketing agency for a specified period of time (Swieter, 2002). Considering that an average of 43,879 fans visited each of the 306 matches of the first division of the German Bundesliga in the season 2017/2018 (Deutscher Fussball-Bund, 2018), the revenue potential from food and beverage concessions is substantial.

Sponsoring agreements are another aspect of income generation that impacts food and beverage concessions. Traditionally, sponsors obtain various rights such as the use of the club's brand in public communication and advertising, along with various rights to conduct certain activities with the club and its players. In exchange, sponsors pay a certain sponsoring fee to the clubs (Swieter, 2002). For sponsors involved in food and beverage industries (such as soft drink producers, breweries, or snack producers), it is common for their products to be sold exclusively on-site in the respective product category as part of a sponsoring agreement. This, in turn, affects the concessionaire and their supply chain (Merkle and Lewis, 2016b).

Spectator Sports and Public Health

Health and Public Health

Health and public health issues are mainly of importance in the context of stadium food and beverage concessions from an academic perspective. The main body of research in this field is carried out on alcohol consumption and its consequences.

Concessions stands typically sell food and drinks that are nutrient-poor, high-calorie, and high in fats and sugars (Sukalakamala et al., 2013) as they are perceived as easy to prepare and serve and therefore cheaper to supply than fresh food (Donaldson et al., 2019; Eime et al., 2008). Ireland and Watkins (2010) correctly point out that the quality and types of food and drinks available in sports stadia often present a contradictory message to the health messages associated with professional sports, especially to children.

Consuming alcohol is often central to the match experience for spectators (Pearson and Sale, 2011), and many stadiums advertise alcohol sold both by hawkers as well as at concessions (Lenk et al., 2010). Collin and MacKenzie (2006) question the relation between the health-promotion component of professional sports and partnerships with alcohol producing companies, namely breweries. Whilst advertisement and partnerships between professional sports and tobacco companies no longer exist in developed countries (Collin and MacKenzie, 2006), breweries hold a big stake in international professional sports, especially football. The majority of football governing bodies such as FIFA, UEFA, the FA as well as the German football association (DFB) all have breweries among their sponsors and partners (Deutscher Fussball-Bund, 2018; FIFA, 2018; The Football Association, 2018; UEFA, 2018). In 2015, Anheuser-Busch InBev (the rightsholder of the beer brand Bud Light, amongst others) committed to a $1.4 billion sponsorship deal as the official beer sponsor of the NFL (National Football League) until the 2022 Superbowl (Roberts, 2015).

Alcohol consumption and issues connected to it also need to be seen in the light of stadium safety, security, and hooliganism. Hall (2010) points out that restricting alcohol distribution and encouraging responsible consumption can reduce public drunkenness and unruly behavior. This is especially important as these issues can extend beyond the stadium, as an incident that occurred in the United States in 2005 illustrates. Food and beverage concessions operator Aramark was ordered to pay USD 75 million in punitive damages after a beer vendor in the New York Giants stadium employed by Aramark had accepted a bribe, violated an alcohol serving policy, and continued to serve beer to an obviously intoxicated fan, who then caused a traffic accident, paralyzing one person (Leong and Hom, 2005).

Sale of Alcohol

The sale and consumption of alcoholic beverages is governed by laws differing from country to country or even state to state. In the United States of America, most states prohibit the sale of alcohol to people under 21 and people that seem intoxicated (National Institute on Alcohol Abuse and Alcoholism, 2012). New Zealand requires that premises licensed to serve alcohol, including stadia, also provide and promote low-alcohol and non-alcoholic drinks (Lyne and Galloway, 2012). Additionally, the conditions for sale of alcoholic beverages in sports stadia can further be tightened by cities, municipalities, authorities, clubs, and associations.

Toomey, Erickson et al. (2008) researched the likelihood of illegal alcohol sales in stadia in the United States of America through pseudo-underage and pseudo-intoxicated attempts to purchase alcohol at hockey, basketball, baseball, and football stadia. They determined that pseudo-intoxicated sales are generally very likely (74%), with little difference between sales at concessions and sales that take place in the stands (hawking). They further found that pseudo-underage sales were less likely than pseudo-intoxicated sales with 18%; however, there was a big difference between pseudo-underage sales in the stands (30%) and at concession booths (13%), despite little variance in pseudo-underage and pseudo-intoxicated alcohol sales between the different spectator sports.

Lenk et al. (2010) found that most stadia do have an alcohol serving policy (mostly that no more than two alcoholic beverages can be sold per transactions and that patrons' ages are to be checked if they appear younger than e.g., 30). They also found that about one third of stadia designate certain sectors as alcohol-free. An unexpected result of their study was that almost half of stadia (46%) allowed employees under the legal drinking age of 21 to sell and serve alcohol to patrons. Most states within the United States stipulate a minimum age of 18 for the sale and serving of beer (National Institute on Alcohol Abuse and Alcoholism, 2012). Results show that first, regulations preventing the sale of alcohol to intoxicated persons are not applied effectively and second, vendors of alcoholic beverages (especially beer hawkers) need to be better trained regarding the sale of alcohol to underage fans.

Several strategies to reduce the problems caused by intoxication are mentioned in the literature. Most commonly, the requirement of servers and service managers to attend training courses, checking the age of patrons who appear younger than 30, and supervision of younger and less experienced servers (Lenk et al., 2010). Prohibiting intoxicated patrons from entering the stadium, discouraging heavy alcohol consumption before the game, and creating alcohol-free sections were less common strategies (Lenk et al., 2010). Both, however, can reduce the number of intoxicated patrons, encourage a more family-friendly environment, and provide space for people and families away from intoxicated or rowdy patrons (Lyne and Galloway, 2012). Toomey et al. (2008) even suggest banning alcohol in professional sports stadia. This suggestion may have far-reaching consequences, considering the importance of sponsorship deals that could be lost.

Alcohol and Aggression

Violent spectator behavior is a global problem across all types of sports. Damage to property, injury, and even loss of life have been attributed to spectators' alcohol consumption. Because, in most cases, drinking does not lead to violent behavior, the issue is more complex (Ostrowsky, 2014). Nevertheless, Australian researchers noted a spike in assaults (70%) and domestic violence (40%) in New South Wales on the nights of State of Origin rugby games, to which the consumption of alcohol may contribute (Livingston, 2018). They also found an increase in domestic violence incidents reported by British police in relation to the English team fixture during the 2018 World Cup, most of which were attributed to alcohol (BBC, 2018). This aligns with findings presented by Crawford et al. (2001) who analyzed consultations with crowd doctors at Glasgow Celtic football club about the relevance of alcohol consumption, discovering that excessive alcohol consumption contributed to the condition at hand in 20% of cases.

Alcohol is even an important factor for poor behavior by sport spectators in venues where alcohol is not sold, because some spectators consume large amounts of alcohol prior to entering the venue (Nicholson and Hoye, 2005). Nepomuceno et al. (2017) found the sale and consumption of alcohol inside sports stadia had little influence on fans' violent behavior when comparing the occurrence of hooliganism during periods of alcohol legalization and prohibition inside football stadia in Brazil. Pearson and Sale (2011) agree, claiming that alcohol bans inside football stadia in the United Kingdom have little impact on alcohol-related violence, even worsening disorder as fans rushed to consume large quantities of alcohol before entering the grounds.

Bormann and Stone (2001) researched the effects of eliminating alcohol in a college stadium in Colorado, United States of America. Of the non-renewing season ticket holders, 29% reported that the ban of alcohol was a motive for their non-renewal, but only 6% stated that the ban was the "one biggest reason" for their non-renewal. Bormann and Stone (2001) report that whilst the ban of beer has been made permanent in the general stands and concession areas, hospitality areas and skyboxes can still serve alcoholic beer to their patrons.

Chupp et al. (2007) examined the connection between alcohol availability and baseball attendance regarding the legalization of alcohol sales on Sundays in a Minor League Baseball team in the United States of America. Whilst alcohol availability in the venue had little impact on spectator attendance, legalizing Sunday beer sales led to an increase in consumption amongst the spectators.

Conclusion

The review of relevant literature shows that spectator catering services in professional spectator sports have been approached from several different angles. Most research has been carried out on service quality and public health issues in the context of the United States of America, with alcohol sales and their consequences being a major topic of discussion. Operational issues are mainly covered in practitioner literature and less in academic journals, although some research covers aspects of attendance, product demand relations, and branding issues. Whilst there is literature covering the Catering side of stadium Food and Beverage operations, VIP, Commercial and Sponsor Hospitality Programs have not yet received much attention from academia.

Food and beverage concessions in professional spectator sport settings serve several purposes: providing customer service and maximizing revenues for the club or the owner. It is noteworthy that different models and scenarios for the operation of concessions (own operations versus outsourcing to a concessionaire) have not been researched. This represents an opportunity for further research, such as identifying advantages and disadvantages between outsourcing and in-house operations and developing an 'ideal' model for food and beverage concessions operations.

It is furthermore interesting to note that issues relating to alcoholic beverages, mainly beer, have proven significant from several perspectives. Studies focusing on health and public health, food and beverage concessions operations as well as branding and attendance issues deal with alcohol in sports stadia, although from different angles. It is surprising that the availability of alcoholic beverages has not yet been subject to service-quality and customer satisfaction–related research. The field of spectator catering services in professional spectator sports stadia certainly shows potential for further research.

References

ACI. (2014), *2014 ACI-NA Concessions Benchmarking Survey Summary Results*, available at: http://www.aci-na.org/sites/default/files/2014-concessionsbenchmarking-results.pdf (accessed 7 July 2014).

Alli, I. (2003), *Food Quality Assurance: Principles and Practices*, CRC Press, Boca Raton, FL.

Babin, B.J. and Harris, E.G. (2011), *CB3*, Cengage South-Western, Boston, UK.

BBC. (2018), *World Cup 2018: Rise in Domestic Abuse Reports, Say Police*, available at: https://www.bbc.com/news/uk-england-45453062 (accessed 28 May 2018).

Bormann, C.A. and Stone, M.H. (2001), "The effects of eliminating alcohol in a college stadium: The Folsom Field beer ban". *Journal of American College Health*, Vol.50, pp.81–88. doi: 10.1080/07448480109596011.

Bowden, J. (2009), "Customer engagement: A framework for assessing customer-brand relationships: The case of the restaurant industry", *Journal of Hospitality Marketing and Management*, Vol.18, pp.574–596. doi: 10.1080/19368620903024983.

Bruhn, M. and Georgi, D. (2006), *Services Marketing: Managing the Service Value Chain*, Pearson Education, London, UK.

Chupp, A., Stephenson, F.E., and Taylor, R. (2007), "Stadium alcohol availability and baseball attendance: Evidence from a natural experiment", *International Journal of Sport Finance*, Vol.2, pp.36–44.

Clemes, M.D., Brush, G.J., and Collins, M.J. (2011), "Analysing the professional sport experience: A hierarchical approach", *Sport Management Review*, Vol.14, pp.370–388. doi: 10.1016/j.smr.2010.12.004.

Coates, D. and Humphreys, B.R. (2007), "Ticket prices, concessions and attendance at professional sporting events", *International Journal of Sport Finance*, Vol.2, pp.161–170.

Collin, J. and MacKenzie, R. (2006), "The World Cup, sport sponsorship, and health", *Lancet*, Vol.367, pp.1964–1966. doi: 10.1016/S0140–6736(06)68862-4.

Crawford, M., Donnelly, J., Gordon, J., MacCallum, R., MacDonald, I., McNeill, M., and West, G. (2001), "An analysis of consultations with the crowd doctors at Glasgow Celtic football club, season 1999–2000", including commentary by Maclean JA, *British Journal of Sports Medicine*, Vol.35, pp.245–250. doi: 10.1136/bjsm.35.4.245.

Davis, B., Lockwood, A., Pantelidis, I., and Alcott, P. (2008), *Food and Beverage Management*, Routledge, London and New York.

Deutscher Fussball-Bund. (2018), *Deutscher Fußball-Bund e.V,* available at: http://www.dfb.de/index.php?id=57 (accessed 21 November 2018).

Donaldson, A., Reimers, J., Brophy, K., and Nicholson, M. (2019), "Barriers to rejecting junk food sponsorship in sport – A formative evaluation using concept mapping", *Public Health*, Vol.166, pp.1–9. doi: 10.1016/j.puhe.2018.09.021.

Eime, R.M., Payne, W.R., and Harvey, J.T. (2008), "Making sporting clubs healthy and welcoming environments: A strategy to increase participation", *Journal of Science and Medicine in Sport*, Vol.11, pp.146–154. doi: 10.1016/j.jsams.2006.12.121.

Emery, P., Westerbeek, H., Schwarz, E.C., Liu, D., and Turner, P. (2016), *Managing Sport Facilities and Major Events*, Routledge, London and New York.

European Commission. (2018, 21.01.2014), *European Commission*, available at: http://europa.eu/rapid/press-release_MEMO-14-35_en.htm (accessed 21 November 2018).

FIFA. (2011), *Football Stadiums – Technical Recommendations and Requirements*, FIFA Fédération Internationale de Football Association, Zurich.

FIFA. (2012), *Invitation to Tender for the Rights of the FIFA Food and Beverage Concessionaire Programme Phase II*, Fédération Internationale de Football Association, Zurich.

FIFA. (2018), *2018 FIFA World Cup Russia Marketing*, Available at: https://de.fifa.com/worldcup/organisation/partners/ (accessed 21 November 2018).

Fliess, S. (2009), *Dienstleistungsmanagement: Kundenintegration gestalten und steuern*, Springer, Wiesbaden.

Fliess, S. and Kleinaltenkamp, M. (2004), "Blueprinting the service company: Managing service processes efficiently", *Journal of Business Research*, Vol.57, pp.392–404. doi: 10.1016/S0148–2963(02)00273-4.

Fodness, D. and Murray, B. (2007), "Passengers' expectations of airport service quality", *Journal of Services Marketing,* Vol.21, pp.492–506. doi: 10.1108/08876040710824852.

Fuhrmeister, C. (2018), "Stadium food is suddenly getting cheaper", available at: https://www.eater.com/2018/8/29/17785134/stadium-food-fan-friendly-prices-atlanta-falcons-texas-longhorns (accessed 1 June 2018).

Galily, Y., Yarchi, M., Tamir, I., and Samuel-Azran, T. (2016), "Terrorism and sport: A global perspective", *American Behavioral Scientist*, Vol.60, pp.1039–1042. doi: 10.1177/0002764216632839.

Gillard, E. and Merkle, T. (2015), "Promotions in Franchises: Do the Inter-Organizational Agreements Influence Firm Internal Labour Market?", paper presented at the European Council on Hotel, Restaurant, and Institutional Education, 14–16 October, 2015, Manchester.

Greenwell, T.C., Janghyuk, L., and Naeger, D. (2007), "Using the critical incident technique to understand critical aspects of the minor league spectator's experience", *Sport Marketing Quarterly*, Vol.16, pp.190–198.

Grönroos, C. (2001), *Service Management and Marketing* (Vol.2), Wiley, New York, NY.

Hall, S.A. (2010), "An examination of British Sport security strategies, legislation, and risk management practices". *Sport Journal*, Vol.13, No.2, available at: https://www.cabdirect.org/globalhealth/abstract/20103132444.

Heung, V.C.S., Wong, M.Y., and Qu, H. (2002), "A study of tourists' satisfaction and post-experience behavioral intentions in relation to airport restaurant services in the Hong Kong SAR", *Journal of Travel and Tourism Marketing*, Vol.12, pp.111–135. doi:10.1300/J073v12n02_07.

Hoffman, K.D. and Turley, L.W. (2002), "Atmospherics, service encounters and consumer decision making: An integrative perspective", *Journal of Marketing Theory and Practice*, Vol.10, No.3, pp.33–47, doi: 10.1080/10696679.2002.11501918.

Ireland, R. and Watkins, F. (2010), "Football fans and food: a case study of a football club in the English Premier League", *Public Health Nutrition*, Vol.13, pp.682–687. doi: 10.1017/S1368980009991765.

Joint FAO/WHO Codex Alimentarius Commission. (2014), "Codex alimentarius". *Rome, Food and Agriculture Organization of the United Nations*, available at: www.codexalimentarius.org.

Kelley, S.W. and Turley, L.W. (2001), "Consumer perceptions of service quality attributes at sporting events", *Journal of Business Research*, Vol.54, pp.161–166. doi: 10.1016/S0148–2963(99)00084-3.

Kivela, J., Inbakaran, R., and Reece, J. (1999), "Consumer research in the restaurant environment. Part 2: Research design and analytical methods", *International Journal of Contemporary Hospitality Management*, Vol.11, pp.269. doi: 10.1108/09596119910281766.

Ko, Y.J., Zhang, J., Cattani, K., and Pastore, D. (2011), "Assessment of event quality in major spectator sports", *Managing Service Quality*, Vol.21, pp.304–322. doi:10.1108/09604521111127983.

Krautmann, A.C. and Berri, D.J. (2007), "Can we find it at the concessions? Understanding price elasticity in professional sports". *Journal of Sports Economics*, Vol.8, pp.183–191. doi: 10.1177/1527002505275093.

Larson, B.V. and Steinman, R.B. (2009), "Driving NFL fan satisfaction and return intentions with concession service quality", *Services Marketing Quarterly*, Vol.30, pp.418–428. doi: 10.1080/15332960903199430.

Lenk, K.M., Toomey, T.L., Erickson, D.J., Kilian, G.R., Nelson, T.F., and Fabian, L.E.A. (2010), "Alcohol control policies and practices at professional sports stadiums", *Public Health Reports*, Vol.125, pp.665–673. doi: 10.1177/003335491012500508.

Leong, B. and Hom, A. (2005), "Aramark loses in legal battle", *Risk Management (00355593)*, Vol.52, pp.8–9.

Livingston, M. (2018), "The association between state of origin and assaults in two Australian states", *Centre for Alcohol Policy Research, School of Psychology and Public Health*, available at: http://fare.org.au/wp-content/uploads/The-association-between-State-of-Origin-and-assaults-in-two-Australian-states-noEM.pdf (accessed 21 November 2018).

Lovelock, C.H. and Wirtz, J. (2011), *Services Marketing: People, Technology, Strategy*, 7th ed., Prentice Hall, Boston, UK.

Lyne, M. and Galloway, A. (2012), "Implementation of effective alcohol control strategies is needed at large sports and entertainment events", *Australian and New Zealand Journal of Public Health*, Vol.36, pp.55–60. doi: 10.1111/j.1753–6405.2011.00813.x.

Mason, K., Jones, S., Benefield, M., and Walton, J. (2013), "Consumer perceptions of quick service restaurants", *Journal of International Business and Economics*, Vol.13, pp.109–116. doi: 10.18374/JIBE-13–4.8.

McDonald, M.A., Sutton, W.A., and Milne, G.R. (1995), "TEAMQUAL ™: Measuring service quality in professional team sports", *Sport Marketing Quarterly*, Vol.4, pp.9–15. doi: 10.1080/14783360600588190.

Merkle, T. and Lewis, R.A. (2016a), "LSG Sky Chefs Sao Paulo: Managing food safety in airline catering in an emerging market", *Journal of Hospitality and Tourism Cases*, Vol.5, No.2, pp.21–23.

Merkle, T. and Lewis, R.A. (2016b), "RB Leipzig: A novel approach to sport stadium hospitality", *Journal of Hospitality and Tourism Cases*, Vol.5, pp.1–5.

Mortimore, S. and Wallace, C. (2013), *HACCP: A Practical Approach*, Springer, Wiesbaden.

Motsinger, S.E., Turner, E.T., and Evans, J.D. (1997), "A comparison of food and beverage concession operations in three different types of North Carolina sport venues", *Sport Marketing Quarterly*, Vol.6, pp.43–52.

Mulherin, M. (1997), "Not everybody wants a meat pie!", *Cyber-Journal of Sport Marketing*, Vol.1, pp.1–3.

National Institute on Alcohol Abuse and Alcoholism. (2012), "Alcohol policy information system", available at: http://www.alcoholpolicy.niaaa.nih.gov/ (accessed 6 November 2012).

Nepomuceno, T.C.C., de Moura, J.A., e Silva, L.C., and Costa, A.P.C.S. (2017), "Alcohol and violent behavior among football spectators: An empirical assessment of Brazilian's criminalization", *International Journal of Law, Crime and Justice*, Vol.51, pp.34–44. doi:10.1016/j.ijlcj.2017.05.001.

Nicholson, M. and Hoye, R. (2005), "Contextual factors associated with poor sport spectator behavior", *Managing Leisure*, Vol.10, pp.94–105. doi: 10.1080/13606710500146175.

Oldenkotte, G. (2008), "Efficient distribution", *Panstadia International*, Vol.15, pp.40–47.

Ostrowsky, M.K. (2014), "The social psychology of alcohol use and violent behavior among sports spectators", *Aggression and Violent Behavior*, Vol.19, pp.303–310. doi: 10.1016/j.avb.2014.05.001.

Parasuraman, A., Zeithaml, V.A., and Berry, L.L. (1988), "SERVQUAL: A multiple-item scale for measuring consumer perceptions of service quality", *Journal of Retailing*, Vol.64, pp.12–40.

Pearson, G. and Sale, A. (2011), " 'On the Lash'–revisiting the effectiveness of alcohol controls at football matches", *Policing and Society*, Vol.21, No.2, pp.150–166. doi: 10.1080/10439463.2010.540660.

PwC. (2017), *PwC Sports Outlook*, available at: https://www.pwc.ch/en/publications/2018/2017%20Sports%20Outlook_FINAL.pdf (Accessed 24 October 2017).

Roberts, D. (2015), *Bud Light Will Remain NFL's Official Beer Until 2022*, available at: http://fortune.com/2015/11/04/bud-light-nfl-deal/ (accessed 13 October 2015).

Ross, S.D., James, J.D., and Vargas, P. (2006), "Development of a scale to measure team brand associations in professional sport", *Journal of Sport Management*, Vol.20, pp.260–279. doi: 10.1123/jsm.20.2.260.

Sawer, P. (2017), "What happened at Hillsborough in 1989?" *The Telegraph*, available at: https://www.telegraph.co.uk/news/0/happened-hillsborough-1989/ (accessed 2 August 2017).

Solomon, M.R. (2015), *Consumer Behavior: Buying, Having, and Being*, 11th ed., Pearson Education, Harlow, UK.

Sukalakamala, P., Sukalakamala, S., and Young, P. (2013), "An exploratory study of the concession preferences of generation Y consumers", *Journal of Foodservice Business Research*, Vol.16, pp.378–390. doi: 10.1080/15378020.2013.824278.

Swieter, D. (2002), *Eine ökonomische Analyse der Fussball-Bundesliga*, Duncker and Humblot, Berlin.

The Football Association. (2018), *Commercial and Charity Partners of the FA*, available at: http://www.thefa.com/about-football-association/partners (accessed 26 June 2018).

Theodorakis, N., Kambitsis, C., and Laios, A. (2001), "Relationship between measures of service quality and satisfaction of spectators in professional sports", *Managing Service Quality*, Vol.11, No.6, pp.431–438. doi: 10.1108/09604520110410638.

Toomey, T.L., Erickson, D.J., Lenk, K.M., and Kilian, G.R. (2008), "Likelihood of illegal alcohol sales at professional sport stadiums", *Alcohol Clinical Experiment Research*, Vol.32 No.11, pp.1859–1864. doi:10.1111/j.1530-0277.2008.00770.x.

UEFA. (2018), *UEFA Official Sponsors and Partners*, available at: https://www.uefa.com/partners/ (accessed 25 July 2018).

Van Leeuwen, L., Quick, S., and Daniel, K. (2002), "The sport spectator satisfaction model: A conceptual framework for understanding the satisfaction of spectators", *Sport Management Review (Sport Management Association of Australia and New Zealand)*, Vol.5, No.2, pp.99–128. doi:10.1016/S1441–3523(02)70063-6.

Whisenant, W., Dees, W., Bollling, M., and Martin, T. (2013), "Concession sales: The examination of novelty effect and consumer mood", *International Journal of Education and Research*, Vol.1 No.4, pp.1–10.

Wildmann, M. (2018), *FC Bayern München ist Mehrweg-Meister*, available at: https://www.cleanenergy-project.de/gesellschaft/helden-der-nachhaltigkeit/fc-bayern-muenchen-ist-mehrweg-meister/ (accessed 17 July 2018).

31

HOTEL MARKET ANALYSIS
The Case of Beijing, China

Jichul Jang, Misun (Sunny) Kim and Hyunghwa Oh

Introduction

During the past 20 years, the tourism industry in China has grown rapidly domestically and internationally. In 2017, the number of overseas visitors reached 139 million and tourism-related earnings exceeded $123 billion, increases of 7.46% and 58.14%, respectively, compared to the data from 2013 (National Bureau of Statistics of China, 1999~2018).

China's tourism industry accounted for 11% of the country's GDP in 2017, or a total of $1.35 trillion (China National Tourism Administration, 2017). The state council forecast that China would be the world's most popular tourist destination by 2030, after many major sporting events, including the 2022 Winter Olympic Games. The reasons why the tourism industry has been booming in China can be explained in a threefold way. First, China's government has been actively engaged in the tourism industry with various policy initiatives (Zhang et al., 1999). The government is acting as an operator, regulator, coordinator, and educator, all contributing to the rapid development of tourism (Zhang et al., 1999). Second, China has been experiencing a rapid economic growth rate of double digits, or close to that, in GDP. As economic development usually leads to tourism expansion in Asian countries (Kim and Chen, 2006; Oh, 2005), China's explosive economic growth could be a crucial factor. Third, from a social perspective, the strong growth of the middle-class population is a significant factor in increasing the prosperity of the tourism and hotel industries in China. This increasing middle-class population and their changes in consumerism are raising leisure spending, thereby boosting tourism and the hotel industry (Zeng and Ryan, 2012). China's lodging industry has closely reflected the government's regulations and the country's economic transition (Gu et al., 2012). Such strong growth in inbound tourism has expanded the hotel industry in China. According to an increasing demand, this industry has grown dramatically. In 2016, the number of star-rated hotels reached 11,685, up 66.09% from 1999.

After an open-door policy was in place in the late 1970s, China appealed for foreign hotel investment to overcome a lack of local capital. Between 1979 and 1988, about $47.7 billion of foreign investment was made (Tisdell and Wen, 1991). However, the Chinese government put too much emphasis on the quantitative aspects of hotel development with this influx of foreign investment in such a short period (Tisdell and Wen, 1991). One of the side effects of rapid growth and the long domination of state-owned hotels was that China's hotel industry was unable to have enough time to foster skilled professionals (Alon and Ferreira, 2008). As a result, the industry is still struggling with this shortage of qualified staff, especially at the managerial level (Alon and Ferreira, 2008). To develop competent human resources and take the next step, China hotel industry calls for systematic training programs. Furthermore, China experienced a small step-back after 2010 due to the oversupply of hotel rooms (Zheng and Gu, 2011).

After experiencing problems caused by the lack of sufficient preparation for such rapid quantitative growth, the government sought innovative changes to solve the problems and advance the hotel industry (Guillet et al., 2011). The key and first action that the Chinese government took in order to improve the hotels' performance was the establishment of a star rating system (Liu and Lu, 2011). These ratings are from 1 to 5 stars based on facilities, equipment, maintenance, cleaning, hygiene, service, quality, and guest satisfaction (Pine and Phillips, 2005). This system standardized the hotel industry, made it more professional and started its fast-tracking. Hosting of the Beijing Olympics in 2008, the Shanghai World Expo in 2010, and the Asian Games in Guangzhou in 2010 also played a significant role in the hotel industry's development (Guillet et al., 2011).

Although the economy of China is undergoing major structural adjustments, China's hotel industry is still enjoying its popularity as a travel destination both for outbound and inbound travelers. In particular, many smaller cities such as Nanjing, Wuhan, Xi'an, Chongqing, and Chengdu are attracting various industries, including electronics, pharmaceutical, and retail. With the full support of the central government regarding infrastructure, these cities are now attracting more business. However, neighboring countries, such as Thailand and Japan, are catching up with their double-digit growth rates (World Tourism Organization, 2018). In such competitive situation, China's hotel industry needs to seize the opportunity and service the skyrocketing increase in domestic travelers. The middle-class segment can pay for leisure activities and is rapidly increasing, and their emergence is keeping China's lodging industry on a promising path (Barton et al., 2013).

In this chapter, we focus on Beijing market because Beijing, the capital city of China, has been playing a leading role in the development of China's hotel industry as an attractive destination for companies and tourists. This mega-city has the greatest number of *Fortune Global 500* companies. The Beijing International Airport – the world's second largest – handled over 100 million passengers in 2018.

Our analysis is based on data from Smith Travel Research (STR) for 1,533 hotels with 239, 594 rooms in the Beijing market. In terms of the types of hotels, the "independent hotel" (44.16%) and "economy hotel" (42.14%) account for 86.3% of all hotels. Recently, the market share of economy hotels has grown 8.81%, and 27 "luxury hotels" comprise 0.26% of the total. The ratio of independent hotels is exceptionally high because of China's unique politics.

In terms of having a parent company, Wyndham Worldwide, an international hotel and resort chain based in the United States, has 218 "Super 8" – the largest hotel brand in Beijing. Wyndham Worldwide is the top international company in China, followed by 7 Days Inn, Homeinns Hotel Group, GreenTree Inns, Huazhu Hotels Group, Jinjiang Holdings, and Beijing Capital Tourism.

Not only are these domestic chain organizations growing quantitatively, but they have also succeeded quantitatively. Their positioning strategy of targeting the budget hotels to differentiate them from international luxury brands has worked out well (Gu et al., 2012). For example, Jinjiang International Hotel Development Co. Ltd., the largest Chinese hotel management company, developed its local brands: Jinjiang Hotel, Peace Hotel, Park Hotel, and Metropole Hotel, depending on their respective targets.

There are three main types of management – chain management, franchise, and independent hotels – in China's hotel industry. Independent hotels have the largest number of hotels (44.16%), followed by franchise hotels (36%) and chain management hotels (19.84%). Figures 31.6 and 31.7 presents hotel properties by type of operations.

Hotels with less than 150 rooms account for the majority at 58.8% of all properties. In contrast, Hot Spring Leisure City, with its 1,800 rooms, has the greatest number of rooms in Beijing.

Even after a few decades of phenomenal growth, Beijing's hotel industry is still growing. Table 31.1 shows the core indicators of hotel operations as of July 2018. All indicators rose,

Table 31.1 Current statistics in Beijing market

Variables	Value	% change
Hotels	1,533	1.93
Rooms	239,594	0.93
Room supply	87,056,791	1.25
Room demand	66,846,066	3.45
ADR (CNY)	618.5	7.30
REVPAR (CNY)	474.9	9.65
Room revenue (CNY)	41,345,045,945	11.01

especially room revenue, up 9.65% and RevPAR up 11.00%. Because unprofitable operations have been considered as a weakness of the industry (Yu and Huimin, 2005), these results reflect how the financial situation is improving.

Looking at the numbers more closely, ADR and RevPAR are going up slowly, despite a small slowdown in 2014. This upturn can be attributed to reducing inbound demand, the changing real estate market situation, and declining inflation (InterContinental Hotels Group, 2014). In contrast, during the same period, the annual occupancy rate has had steep growth. The annual occupancy rate was less than 65% in 2010, but by 2018, this figure had increased to 76.8%, which might signal the enhanced vigorousness of China's hotel industry. The results are shown in Figures 31.1 and 31.2.

During the year of 2010 to 2018, occupancy rates show the lowest in February indicating 54% on average while March through November shows higher occupancy rates ranging from 74% to 73.0% on average. This fluctuating occupancy rates could be affected by air pollution in Beijing. Beijing is one of the most important tourism destinations in China with 7 UNESCO heritage sites, 99 key cultural sites, 5 national geological parks, and 15 national forest parks and 151 registered museums (UNWTO-WTOF, 2017). Although Beijing is popular tourist destinations in China, Beijing becomes one of the most polluted cities in China (Zhang et al., 2015). Zhang et al. (2015) found that the peak seasons of haze pollution in January, February, March, November, and December are negatively associated with average monthly tourist arrivals from 2011 to 2013 in Beijing (Figure 31.3).

In particular, the occupancy rate is continuously growing from January 2016 to December 2018 regardless of the day of the week. In general, weekday's occupancy rate (76.3%) is higher than weekend's occupancy (72.4%) in Beijing. Peak ADR rate is on Wednesday or Thursday in Beijing hotels. On average, between January 2016 and December 2018, weekday average ADR is ¥589.70 and Weekend Avg. = ¥573.94 (Jan 2016–Dec 2018). Peak RevPAR is on either

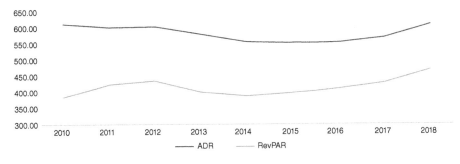

Figure 31.1 Annual ADR and RevPAR in Beijing.

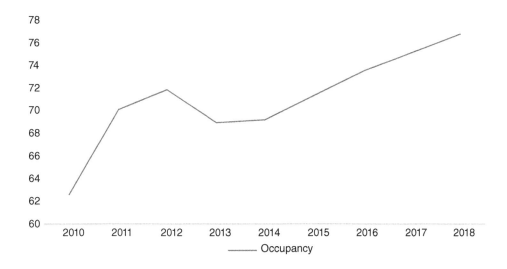

Figure 31.2 Annual occupancy rate in Beijing.

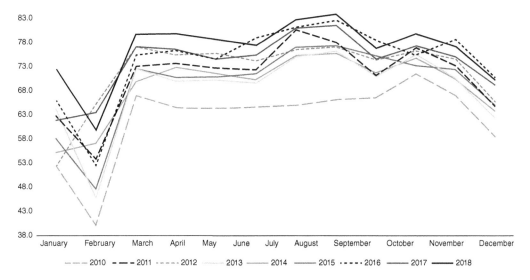

Figure 31.3 Occupancy and seasonality during the year of 2010–2018.

Wednesday or Thursday. Weekday (i.e., from Sunday to Thursday) has higher RevPAR (¥450.85) than Weekend (i.e., Friday and Saturday) RevPAR (¥415.33) in general. Therefore, no significant difference among key performance indicators was identified between weekday and weekend in Beijing (Figures 31.4 and 31.5).

The luxury class had the highest ADR (¥1203.19) which is about 5.6 times more than Economy class ADR (¥214.26). In addition, Luxury Class shows the highest RevPAR (¥758.62) while Economy class shows the lowest RevPAR (¥167.27). The midscale class shows the highest occupancy rate (78%) while luxury class shows the lowest occupancy rate (63%). In addition, the midscale class shows the most significant RevPAR percent change (12%) while the upper midscale class shows the lowest RevPAR percent change (4%). Midscale Class shows the highest ADR

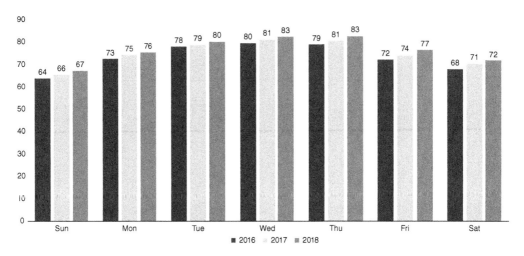

Figure 31.4 Actual occupancy rate by day of the week.

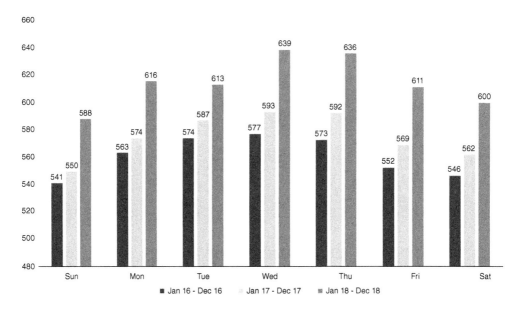

Figure 31.5 Actual ADR by day of the week.

percent change (3.78%) and occupancy rate percent change (8%). Upscale Class (−0.04%) and Upper Upscale Class (−0.41%) shows minus ADR percent change. Thus, the lower tier class such as the economy class and the midscale class shows higher key performance indicators in general. As such, UNWTO-WTOF (2017) reported that budget hotels are most welcomed by tourists in Beijing which were found based on the Beijing Tourism Commission's survey from 2007 to 2014 by contacting 128,000 Beijing residents. Specifically, 39.3% of respondents preferred to stay in budget hotels the most followed by the medium price hotels (2-Star and 3-Star) for 21.7%, and luxury hotels for 2.2% in Beijing (UNWTO-WTOF, 2017) (Figures 31.6 and 31.7).

Revenue has gradually increased by 14% since 2011 in spite of minus revenue percent change (−4.9%) in 2013 (see Figure 15). This 14% revenue increase from the period from the Year 2011 to the Year 2018 is significantly lower compared to 180% revenue increase during the period from

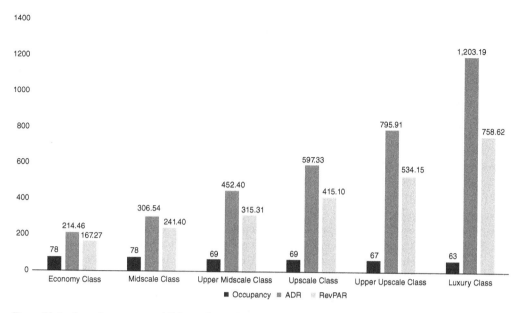

Figure 31.6 Actual occupancy, ADR, and RevPAR by class in Beijing.

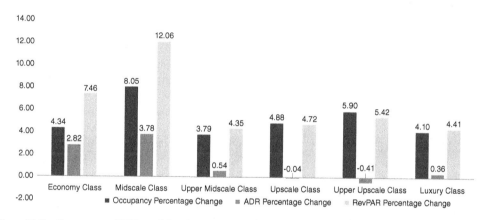

Figure 31.7 Occupancy, ADR, and RevPAR percentage change by class in Beijing.

2000 to 2009 in China (Yang and Cai, 2016). The lower revenue increase (14%) from the period from the Year 2011 to the Year 2018 may indicate the Beijing hotel market is getting more competitive. Indeed, Yang and Cai (2016) pointed out over-supplied hotels in China, which partially made one key hotel performance indicator (i.e., RevPAR) decreased by 2.8% in 2013 compared to the Year 2012.

In 2013, demand percent change decreased by −0.8% (2,900,187 room nights) while supply percent change increased by 3.5% (3,406,137 room nights) (see Figure 16). One of the potential reasons for decreased demands in 2013 was air pollution (Mudallal, 2015; Zhang et al., 2015). In 2013, the average "haze days" in Beijing was six times more than the average in China (Zhang et al., 2015). China's badly polluted air received close attention via worldwide news which affected significantly slowing inbound tourism to China (CBSNEWS, 2013). Beijing's tourism arrival growth from 2012 to 2013 was −10.1% followed by Shanghai (−6.5%), Hangzhou (−4.6%), Shenzen (−3%), Guangzhou (−3%), and Zhuhai (−3%) (Mudallal, 2015) due to the air pollution. This decreased demand affected revenue percent change by −4.9% ($265,841,429). However, since 2013, Chinese government has had strict anti-pollution policy forcing companies in Beijing to reduce the 50% of coal consumption between 2013 and 2018 (Parker, 2018). As a result, particulate matter (PM), defined as a mixture of solid particles and liquid droplets found in the air, was significantly reduced by 45% in the fourth quarter of 2017 compared to the same quarter in 2016 (Parker, 2018). Chinese government efforts to reduce air pollution may affect the demand percentage change positively which, in turn, increases revenue percent change after 2013.

Room supply shows higher than room demand regardless of the class. Upper Midscale Class shows the highest supply (25,310,754) and demand (17,612,505), while Midscale Class shows the lowest supply (3,598,266) and demand (2,854,476) (see Figure 17).

In particular, demands in Beijing South and West Suburban submarket are higher than Beijing central business district and Beijing Capital Airport submarket. This higher demand in outlying submarket than Beijing central area may be due to the central and municipal governments' efforts to disperse Beijing-centered populations, which cause air pollution, high population density, high costs of living, high traffic jams, and more. They have been trying to shift Beijing's non-capital functions to Tianjin and Hebei, which are located near Beijing West and Beijing South (UNWTO-WTOF, 2017).

Figure 20 summarizes information regarding pipeline report. According to pipeline report in STR (Jan, 2019), there are 7,400 rooms in 35 hotel projects under Contract in Beijing, China. More specifically, projects presently under construction are at 18 projects with 3,488 rooms, while projects expected to start construction within one year are at nine hotel projects with 1,794 rooms. Very early projects in the planning stage in Beijing are at 8 projects with 2,118 rooms.

During the year of 2018, Beijing market has opened 29 new hotels with 2,216 rooms. Among 29 new hotels, majority hotels consist of economy and independent hotels, representing 75.8% of new hotels in Beijing market in 2018. Increasing domestic demand plays a vital role in boosting the hotel industry in Beijing market although overall growth of China's GDP has slowed down in recent years.

In particular, Hampton by Hilton is one of the fastest growing hotel brands in China due to partnership between Hilton and China's Plateno Hotel Group in 2014. After that, Hilton and Plateno Hotel Group have opened 47 Hampton by Hilton hotels and have aggressive plan to continue to build Hampton by Hilton across China. Two Hampton by Hilton hotels with 270 rooms are under construction in Beijing market.

Conclusions

Future Opportunities 1: Emerging Sub-Markets (South and West Suburban) in Beijing Market

Beijing has shown consistently increasing revenues since 2011 except for slight dip (−4.9%) in 2013. However, the increased revenue in percentage between 2011 and 2018 (14%) is almost 13 times less than the increased revenue in percentage between 2000 and 2009 (180%). In other words, Beijing hotel market became saturated with over-supplied hotels. Yang and Cai (2016) stated that overly supplied hotels in Beijing contribute to decreasing hotel performance. However, demands in Beijing South and West Suburban submarket is getting more attractive areas for the domestic travelers to stay. Perhaps, the efforts to disperse Beijing-centered populations to outlying areas by building more sound infrastructures allowing people to travel from outside to the center of Beijing may contribute to the higher demand increase in Beijing South and West Suburban submarket than Beijing CBD. Furthermore, due to the Beijing government's policy regarding strictly controlling the increase in commercial properties in the urban areas, the pace of new hotel supply slowed significantly compared to a few years ago. Given that average daily rate (ADR) in South and West Suburban submarket is pretty lower than ADR in Central Business District (CBD), building new hotels in South and West Suburban areas is attractive to potential hotel developers with increasing domestic demands.

Future Opportunities 2: Mid-scale Hotel Segment
Will Grow in Next Few Years

While traditionally, China's hotel market is largely driven by international tourism, now, domestic tourism that is significantly influenced by middle-class and growing per capita income is the main growth driver of hotel market in China and is expected to continue to grow. Unlike China' upscale hotel segment, which may suffer from oversupply, mid-scale hotel segments are projected to grow in Beijing market. With the economic downturn and declined growth in the real estate market in China, hotel investors in China have paid more attention to the investment cost of hotel and thus have shifted their interests to select-service hotel products.

Future Opportunities 3: New Types of Hotels to Meet
Sophisticated Customers' Needs

Another type of hotels that have attracted interest in China are the boutique hotels being developed. While major international hotel brands such as Marriot, Sheraton, Hyatt, Hilton, and Intercontinental have had a presence across China, there is lack of unique boutique hotels. Given that China' hotel industry has a relatively high number of independent hotels with less than 150 hotel rooms, lifestyle or boutique hotel properties are growing in popularity for meeting sophisticated customers' needs. As travelers are looking for engaging more with the local communities they are visiting, China's hotel industry has had to shift gear to meet these new desires, and no sector of the hotel industry has utilized better than boutique hotels. Boutique hotels provide customers with a memorable and unique experience that lacks the vastness of a chain hotel. Furthermore, boutique hotels have a focus on connecting local culture, stylish design, and gourmet cuisine. Given the benefits of boutique hotels, we expect that boutique hotels are a fast-growing model in Beijing, China.

References

Alon, I. and Ferreira, T. (2008), "Human resources challenges and opportunities in China: A case from the hospitality industry", *International Journal of Business and Emerging Markets*, No.2, pp.141. doi:10.1504/ijbem.2008.020866.

Barton, D., Chen, Y., and Jin, A. (2013), "Mapping China's middle class", *McKinsey Quarterly*, Vol.3, pp.54–60.

CBSNEWS. (2013, August 13), "Air pollution takes toll on China's tourism", *CBSNEWS*, available at: https://www.cbsnews.com/newsair-pollution-takes-toll-on-chinas-tourism/

China National Tourism Administration. (2017), *The Yearbook of China Tourism Statistics*, China Tourism Publishing House, Beijing, China.

China National Tourism Administration. (1979–2009), *The Yearbook of China Tourism Statistics and Supplement*, NTAPRC, Beijing, China.

Gu, H., Ryan, C., and Yu, L. (2012), "The changing structure of the Chinese hotel industry: 1980–2012", *Tourism Management Perspectives*, Vol.4, pp.56–63. doi:10.1016/j.tmp.2012.02.001.

Guillet, B.D., Zhang, H.Q., and Gao, B.W. (2011), "Interpreting the mind of multinational hotel investors: Future trends and implications in China", *International Journal of Hospitality Management*, No.2, pp.222–232. doi: 10.1016/j.ijhm.2010.10.005.

InterContinental Hotels Group PLC. (2014), "Intercontinental hotels group annual report", *InterContinental Hotels Group PLC*, available at: https://www.ihgplc.com/files/reports/ar2014/index.asp.

Kim, H.J. and Chen, M.H. (2006), "Tourism expansion and economic development: The case of Taiwan", *Tourism Management*, No.5, pp.925–933. doi: 10.1016/j.tourman.2005.05.011.

Liu, S. and Lu, K. (2011), "The development & management of China tourism hotel industry: Review of the 11th five year and outlook for the 12th year", *The Yearbook of China Hotel*, China Tourism Press, Beijing, China.

Mudallal, Z. (2015, January 27), "China's air pollution is driving away international tourists",. *QUARTZ*, available at: https://qz.com/333787/chinas-air-pollution-is-driving-away-international-tourists/

National Bureau of Statistics of China. (1999~2018), *China Statistical Yearbook*, China Statistics Press, Beijing, China.

Oh, C.O. (2005), "The contribution of tourism development to economic growth in the Korean economy", *Tourism Management*, No.1, pp.39–44. doi: 10.1016/j.tourman.2003.09.014.

Parker, J. (2018, January 25), "How China cut its air pollution", *The Economist Explains*, available at: https://www.economist.com/the-economist-explains/2018/01/25/how-china-cut-its-air-pollution

Pine, R. and Phillips, P. (2005), "Performance comparisons of hotels in China', *International Journal of Hospitality Management*, No.1, pp.57–73. doi: 10.1016/j.ijhm.2004.04.004.

Tisdell, C. and Wen, J. (1991), "Investment in China's tourism industry: Its scale, nature, and policy issues", *China Economic Review*, No.2, pp.175–193. doi:10.1016/1043–951x(91)90003-q.

World Tourism Cities Federation. (2017), "UNWTO-WTCF city tourism performance research Beijing case study", *UNWTO-WTOF*, available at: http://cf.cdn.unwto.org/sites/all/files/docpdf/beijingcase-study.pdf

World Tourism Organization. (2018), *UNWTO Tourism Highlights: 2018 Edition*. [Online], available at: https://www.e unwto.org/doi/pdf/10.18111/9789284419876 (accessed 21 April 2019).

Yang, Z. and Cai, J. (2016), "Do regional factors matter? Determinants of hotel industry performance in China", *Tourism Management*, Vol.52, pp.242–253. doi: 10.1016/j.tourman.2015.06.024.

Yu, L. and Huimin, G. (2005). "Hotel reform in China: A SWOT analysis", *Cornell Hotel and Restaurant Administration Quarterly*, No.2, pp.153–169. doi: 10.1177/0010880404273892.

Zeng, B. and Ryan, C. (2012), "Assisting the poor in China through tourism development: A review of research", *Tourism Management*, No.2, pp.239–248. doi: 10.1016/j.tourman.2011.08.014.

Zhang, H.Q., Chong, K., and Ap, J. (1999), "An analysis of tourism policy development in modern China", *Tourism Management*, No.4, pp.471–485. doi:10.1016/s0261–5177(99)00020-5.

Zhang, A., Zhong, L., Xu, Y., Wang, H., and Dang, L. (2015), "Tourists' perception of haze pollution and the potential impacts on travel: Reshaping the features of tourism seasonality in Beijing, China", *Sustainability*, No.3, pp.2397–2414. doi:10.3390/su7032397.

Zheng, T. and Gu, Z. (2011), "Overcapacity in Shanghai's high-end hotel sector: Analysis based on an inventory model", *Journal of Convention & Event Tourism*, No.4, pp.253–270. doi: 10.1080/15470148.2011.621585.

32

A REGIONAL APPROACH TO ATTRACTING AND RETAINING EMPLOYEES

A Chance for Small and Medium-sized Hotels?

Celine Chang and Katrin Eberhardt

Introduction

Employers in the hospitality industry increasingly face challenges when it comes to attracting and retaining skilled employees. There are multiple reasons that contribute to this phenomenon: Skills shortages due to the demographic change, incongruence between changes in work-related values in society and the work characteristics of the industry, decrease of the number of people who decide to pursue vocational training, and the trend for higher education, to name but a few key trends (cf. Barron, 2008; bsw, 2014; Ameln and Wimmer, 2016; Immerschitt and Stumpf, 2019). In addition, the majority of employers are small and medium-sized enterprises (SMEs), most of which are not well known outside of their region. They find it hard to compete with national and international hotel chains that increasingly expand into local markets (Henschel et al., 2018; Warnecke, 2019). In more rural destinations, SMEs suffer even more from the migration of staff to urban areas (FMEAE, 2013). Consequently, SMEs struggle to fill open positions or are forced to hire staff that lack critical skills and qualifications needed for their respective jobs. Thus, existing staff members have to work overtime, which is a driver to leave the industry entirely (Bieger et al., 2005).

It becomes clear that the competitive capability is increasingly depending on the Human Resource (HR) dimension (Bohne, 2018). The dilemma for SMEs is that they usually do not have a strategic HR management (HRM) in place. They lack the expertise and the resources for strategic HRM (bsw, 2014). Most do not employ HR professionals. However, SMEs are forced to find solutions in the wake of skills shortage in order to be able to operate their businesses. Besides investing in their HRM, we propose that SMEs join efforts and share costs by forming regional HR alliances.

This case study presents key results of EU-funded research on this topic in three tourism destinations in Austria and Bavaria (Germany). Based on the example of health tourism, our objective was to develop a concept for a regional HR approach. The research looks into current HR challenges, the strategies that are being pursued, as well as the extent to which collaboration with other organizations already exists. Besides empirical results, the chapter presents a concept for a regional HR approach that includes three levels of action, i.e., the enterprise or employer level, the regional level, and the cross-regional level. It argues that a regional HR approach based on an

HR alliance of employers is a promising strategy that not only helps attract potential employees but also enables SMEs to professionalize their HRM through sharing knowledge and costs.

Because the case study focuses on one Austrian and two Bavarian tourism regions close to the Austrian-German border, the following sections on the labor market, HRM, and the situation of SMEs address the situation in both countries; however, international applicability is assumed in similar markets.

The Skilled Labor Situation: The Status Quo

Due to the demographic change, the number of people in the workforce is continuously decreasing. In Germany, since 2013, more people retire than enter the workforce. The labor force potential will shrink from 49 million in 2013 to 38 million in 2060. Until the year 2030, approximately 4 million workers are predicted to be missing in the service industries (Bohne, 2018). Hence, the skilled labor situation in the tourism industry has become tenser in the past years. For instance, it is often impossible to fill job vacancies or to fill them adequately. According to a representative study in Germany, 45% of employers in tourism that have job vacancies cannot fill these positions. In the hospitality industry, every other employer is affected (bsw, 2014). The situation in Austria is similar: 62% of Austrian tourism enterprises say they are affected by the shortage of skilled staff, and three-quarters of the enterprises are currently looking for staff (Kapferer et al., 2018).

The term "skilled" refers to professionals that have completed a formalized vocational training (usually 2–3.5 years) or have a recognized academic qualification (*Fachkräfte*). Austria and Germany have a long-standing tradition of a dual vocational education and training system for apprenticeships, which means that training takes place at two "learning venues" (Deissinger, 2015). One venue is the company that employs the apprentice and provides training on the job throughout the apprenticeship, while the other venue is the part-time vocational school (*Berufsschule*) where the apprentice studies both general and specific subjects related to the vocation. Usually, the apprentice spends either two days at the vocational school and the rest of the week with the company or longer periods at either venue before switching. The collaboration is regulated by law (FMER, 2019) with the regional chambers playing a key role in ensuring that occupational standards are fulfilled (Deissinger, 2015). In Germany, for example, candidates can complete a formal apprenticeship in six vocations in the hospitality area (DEHOGA, 2018a), such as chefs and hotel clerks. The majority of people working in the industry in Austria and Germany are skilled and were trained through this system (IAB, 2018; Schmee and Biehl, 2017).

However, there has been a strong general decline in the number of apprentices in recent years across all industries. This drop has been mainly attributed to the trend for higher education and to the demographic change (Deissinger, 2015). Whereas in 2008, 103,578 apprentices were working in the German hotel and restaurant industry, this number had declined to 52,285 in 2018 (DEHOGA, 2018b). Austria also saw a decline in apprenticeships: the number of apprentices in the hospitality industry dropped from 11,840 in 2011 to 8,905 in 2017 (WKO, 2018). Within the hospitality industry, a large number of apprenticeship positions remain open each year. In Germany, hotel and restaurant jobs are among the top 10 vocations for which most apprenticeship positions remain unfilled. In addition, apprenticeships like chef and hotel clerk have a high dropout rate and a high rate of changes of employers (FMER, 2017). At the same time, the number of study programs in hospitality management at universities in the German-speaking area increases. There are about 4,000 graduates each year (Bohne, 2018). However, not all of them stay in the industry. For example, a survey among alumni of the department with the highest number of students in Tourism and Hospitality in the German-speaking area (Chang, 2018), showed that at the mean age of 31 years, only 34.3% were still working in the industry. The main reasons for leaving the industry were higher salaries and better career development opportunities.

Therefore, in addition to the demographic change and the trend for higher education, employers face the challenge of migration of skilled labor to other industries. This can be attributed to unattractive working conditions and a poor image of the industry for employment (e.g., bsw, 2014; cf. Gardini, 2014). Employers in the tourism industry even consider the latter to be one of the main reasons for their staffing problems (bsw, 2014). The development outlined in this section shows that implementing a comprehensive and strategic HR management has become even more crucial.

Human Resources Management in the Hospitality Industry

Even though the strategic importance of HRM in tourism is widely acknowledged in both the academic debate and among practitioners, it is also widely acknowledged that the industry still lags behind (e.g., Baum, 2007, 2015; Gardini, 2014; Kusluvan et al., 2010). This lag behind seems incomprehensible, given that the positive correlation between staff competence, service quality, and customer satisfaction has been proven many times (cf. Gardini, 2014), and HRM practices link positively to company performance (cf. Madera et al., 2017). Because competent employees are the key to success in the service industry, this is even another rationale to engage in strategic HRM. Many employers in the hospitality industry would agree. In a study conducted among hoteliers and HR managers in Germany (Verlemann et al. 2013), 87% agreed that HRM needs to become more professional in the industry.

It is important, however, to differentiate between large multinational hotel chains and SMEs when looking at the degree of professionalism in HRM. While professional HRM is noticeable in large companies, in SMEs there is hardly any change in that direction. In SMEs, especially in hotels and restaurants, "many things have not changed over the past 20 years – productivity remains stubbornly low, working conditions are poor, and remuneration levels are well below national averages in many countries" (Baum, 2007, p. 1384).

In Germany, 99.9% of the companies in the hospitality industry are SMEs and 90.7% of the employees in the hotel and restaurant industry work in SMEs (FSO, 2018a, 2018b). In Austria, this is true for 99.8% of the companies and 94% of the employees (Austrian Institute for SME Research, 2019). In Germany, 80% of the hotels and restaurants employ ten employees or less (bsw, 2014). This situation is similar in Austria (WKO, 2019). It is thus not surprising that most companies do not have a strategic HRM in place. Eighty-eight percent of the hotels and restaurants are led by the owner who would also be in charge of HR issues. Because such leaders are responsible for a large range of topics and are strongly involved in day-to-day operations, there is little opportunity for strategic reflections (bsw, 2014). Therefore, it is not surprising that most employers do not offer much more to their employees than participation options, consideration of individual requests for work schedule planning, and compensation for overtime (ibid.). The prevalence of HR practices also depends on the size of the company. One example is training/further education. While 84% of the employers with more than 50 employees invest in employee development, only 44% of the small employers with up to five employees do so. Generally, employers do not consider training and further education as overly important, especially in the catering industry (ibid.). This is dangerous, given that training and further education are key factors for employer attractiveness (Lohaus et al., 2013) and employee retention (Qayed Al-Emadi et al., 2015).

An explanation of the lack of interest in investing in cost-intensive HR practices such as training can also be drawn from theory. Ferrary (2015, p. 1008) points out that, from a resource-based view, "human capital resources are related to individual employees and pertain to their knowledge, training, experience, judgment, intelligence, and relationships." Moreover, according to human capital theory, human capital is transferable, which creates a risk for employers when the employee moves to another employer before there was any return in investment. For large companies with a sizeable internal job-market, the investment in transferable HR is justifiable. By investing in HR the firm creates a competitive advantage through building strategic knowledge and by providing job security and other incentives to stay with the employer. For SMEs, in contrast, investing in transferable HR is not attractive: "The small sizes of their internal labor markets do not generate the economy of scale necessary to invest in training, and they do not provide enough job security and career opportunities to attract and retain talented people" (Ferrary, 2015, p. 1012). The question about the reasons and ways SME employers (should) invest in strategic HR under these circumstances thus requires further investigation. Academic literature has not addressed this topic sufficiently yet (ibid.).

In conclusion, most employers in the industry are small. Such companies typically do not employ HR experts (Festing et al., 2013). Instead, the person responsible for HR has several different roles to fulfill, among which HRM is not a priority. HRM tends to be viewed as administrative work (labor laws, payroll, etc.) rather than a strategic management function (ibid.). Issues are rather solved ad hoc. SMEs lack the resources and the knowledge for strategic HRM (Liebhart and Nungesser, 2017) and do not invest in HR development (Panagiotakopoulos, 2011). However, in view of the realities of the labor market which sees more jobs than job seekers, adopting a more professional approach to HRM is critical for SMEs if they want to stay in the market.

A Regional HR Approach Through HR Alliances

The current state of the labor market and HRM in the hospitality industry raises the question of what SMEs can do to find and retain qualified staff. Apart from shifting priorities and investing in their HRM, it makes sense for SMEs to join efforts and to form HR alliances, either on a regional or cross-regional level. In this chapter, we will look into a regional concept, because we argue that such concepts are easier and less costly to implement. In addition, a regional HR alliance enables SMEs to engage in regional employer branding. By "regional employer branding" we understand that principles of employer branding are applied to a whole region. The term "employer branding" usually comprises all activities a company carries out to position itself as a unique and attractive employer among potential and actual employees by communicating their employer brand to specified target groups (e.g., Immerschitt and Stumpf, 2019). The employer brand can be defined as the unique image of a company as an employer (Stotz and Wedel, 2009). Investing in regional employer branding implies establishing an image of the region as a unique place of residence for (potential) employees where it is worthwhile to live and work. Marketing the regional employer brand to potential employees, especially from outside the region, could create a competitive advantage to other regions.

The research presented in this chapter had the objective to conceptualize a regional HR approach for three rural destinations adjacent to the Austrian-German border. This topic, however, is hardly reflected in academic literature. Comprehensive research in both general as well as tourism and hospitality-related literature databases, with approximately 40 different key words, did not yield satisfactory results. The main reasons are that HR literature mainly focuses on the organizational and management perspective (Baum, 2015) and on large, multinational companies (Festing et al., 2013). We found very few sources on HR alliances (other words used in literature are "networks," "cooperation," and "collaboration") and hardly any publications on regional HR approaches.

Generally, HR alliances offer numerous advantages, especially for SMEs. HR alliances can share resources and costs, companies can learn from each other and thus have a high potential for synergies and economies of scale (Festing et al., 2011, 2013). Disadvantages can be the time-consuming set-up and coordination processes, strong dependencies, or the spread of sensible firm data (ibid.). From an employee perspective, HR alliances are beneficial, because they offer more career opportunities and increase job security (Ferrary, 2015). However, in their study of SMEs in

Germany, Festing et al. (2011) reported that only 25% of companies work together with others on HR topics within a network or alliance. In such alliances, SMEs mainly collaborated with other companies (59%), and less with universities, or other public institutions (27%), or firm networks / clusters (14%). There was also evidence that the likelihood to cooperate is higher with larger SMEs. As for the hospitality industry, an early study on family hotel businesses in Austria (Peters and Buhalis, 2004) confirmed that cooperation with other firms was generally low. It showed that family businesses wanted to keep control of the business within the family. However, the study highlighted that the willingness to cooperate correlated positively with the size of the company. In addition, businesses that cooperated with other companies had significantly higher profit growth rates than other companies in the sample. The authors concluded, "family hotels still do not understand their need to collaborate with other firms and to establish long-term partnerships" (Peters and Buhalis, 2004, p. 410).

In his notable conceptual paper, Ferrary (2015) argues that an HR alliance creates value for SMEs by providing them with access to strategic knowledge and sharing human resources. Alliances create an "inter-organizational internal labor market" (p. 1009) from which the employer can source qualified staff. The author conceptualizes the alliance as an entity with two stakeholders, employer-provider and employer-user. The employer-provider is responsible for recruiting, training, and deployment of staff to employer-users that need staff with specific competencies (ibid.). In order for the alliance to work, the individual employee's interests have to be taken into account. The alliance is set up long-term based on a contract that specifies the ways of staff deployment.

However, making such alliances work requires that all partners involved be committed to contributing to the "collaborative venture" (Ferrary, 2015, p. 1014). Employees need to be prepared to be deployed to different employers. The chapter does not discuss, however, how to ensure that these requirements are being met. According to the study, there should not be more than one hotel per geographical region (p. 1020). We assume the author introduces this condition to avoid the increase of competition among local businesses. Another reason might be the fear that private information could be conveyed to other businesses in the same market that might use that information to their advantage. As for the required mobility, the risk is that this model mainly works for a specific group of employees, namely professionals, who are single and have no children (cf. Strack et al., 2018). Generally, the willingness for job mobility has been declining in recent years. In addition, the willingness to relocate for the job varies by country. Employees in Germany and Austria are less mobile than employees in many other countries (Strack et al., 2018).

There are some arguments in favor of establishing HR alliances on a regional level. Regions can be characterized by various criteria, such as geography, homogeneity, culture, social, and political factors. Another key characteristic is the interdependent relationships between stakeholders that are similar to networks (Bachinger and Pechlaner, 2011). In regional networks, geographical proximity allows for face-to-face interaction, and stakeholders are part of a social context that shares a common language, culture, and established structures for interaction. Bachinger and Pechlaner (2011) argue that regional core competencies lie in these social structures, which generate resources in terms of social capital. They point out that inherent to the network is the collective regional knowledge and the building of specific knowledge through interaction of the members network. The members of regional networks are mainly SMEs of various industries, which can reach competitive advantages through their adaptive capabilities, knowledge sharing, and activities to reach a win-win situation for both the individual company and the network (ibid.).

Service providers in tourism destinations usually are part of a regional network that frequently follows a joint tourism strategy, creates joint service offerings or packages along the value chain, and invests in destination marketing coordinated by the respective destination marketing organizations (DMOs). It thus makes sense to conceptualize HR alliances for SMEs on a regional level. For a regional and tourism-specific HR approach to work, it is important to embed it in the regional tourism strategy in order to make sure that suitable activities to attract and retain skilled labor are chosen (FMEAE, 2013). In order to draft a regional HR approach, we propose to consider three dimensions.

1   *The employer level*: Even though HR alliances can take over some HR tasks, each employer still needs to manage their key HR tasks themselves. Therefore, a regional HR approach does not take away the responsibility of employers to reflect on their HR strategy and to invest in specific HR practices. Even if an HR alliance is in place to cover specific HR areas such as training, each company still has to carry out certain tasks in that area (e.g., selecting training participants).
2   *The regional level*. When joining efforts and resources in an HR alliance, tasks, roles, responsibilities, and operating procedures such as membership requirements and financial issues need to be defined. In addition, it needs to be decided whether cooperation should be only for employers of a specific industry or whether it should be cross-sectional. In order to increase the attractiveness of each employer in the alliance and of the alliance itself, HR marketing and even employer branding of the alliance, the industry and the region are questions that need to be addressed.
3   *The cross-regional level*: HR cooperation should be complemented by cross-regional activities. On this level, a wide range of activities can take place, ranging from sourcing in a specific area abroad and building networks with professional educational institutions such as universities to employee exchanges between summer and winter destinations. It also includes the acquisition of public funding or grants on a state, national, or international level, which can promote actions in HR management (cf. Panagiotakopoulos, 2011).

Research Questions

The main objective of the study presented in this chapter is to conceptualize a skilled labor concept for selected tourism destinations. Due to the lack of literature on this topic, an exploratory approach was chosen to address the following research questions.

(1) Employer level:

- What challenges do employers in hospitality and tourism face in terms of their human resources management?
- How do employers deal with these challenges? What HR practices do they use to attract, develop, and retain skilled employees?

(2) Regional level:

- What is the as-is situation on regional cooperation in HR management?
- What do stakeholders in the industry think about a regional HR concept?
- Are there best practices for regional HR alliances in the industry?
- How do employees perceive the region as a living environment? What factors do employees find important?

(3) Cross-regional level:

- What is the as-is situation on cross-regional cooperation?
- Are there best practices for cross-regional cooperation?

Methodology

The research questions were analyzed using the cases of three close-boarder rural tourism destinations in Bavaria (Tegernsee and Bad Reichenhall) and Austria (Abtenau/Tennengau). Most tourists visit these regions for their natural resources, such as mountains and lakes, and to do sports like hiking and skiing. The regions are not far from the major cities of Salzburg and Munich. The research was part of an EU-funded project[1] that mainly looked at the effects of a health-focused holiday (here balneotherapy and moderate mountain hiking) on elderly tourists (Prosegger et al., 2019) and, based on the results, on the development of new service offerings in health tourism. All destinations have in common that they have specific geothermal water that is already used or planned to be used for balneotherapy. Therefore, our focus was on skilled labor in health tourism, which meant that, in addition to the "traditional" jobs and employers in tourism we also looked at professions and employers that provide services in health-related areas such as baths and clinics.

In order to increase external validity, we investigated the research questions from the perspective of various stakeholders and used a mixed-methods approach (cf. Kuckartz, 2014) following four steps. First, we conducted semi-structured interviews with $N = 54$ experts (90% face-to-face) from the tourism industry (DMOs, selected employers, associations), employment agencies, chambers of commerce, politics, education, and diverse other labor market protagonists in Austria and Bavaria. The objective was to develop a comprehensive picture of the research topic. The interviews were transcribed and analyzed with a qualitative content analysis based on Mayring (2015) using the software MAXQDA (Kuckartz and Rädiker, 2019).

Based on the findings, we developed two questionnaires, one for employers and one for employees, which were then used for anonymous online surveys. The objective of the survey for employers was to validate the as-is HR situation and HR practices. The employee survey intended to include the view of the target group in focus because employers and employees might have different views on the research topic. The surveys mainly consisted of questions with closed answer options, such as multiple-choice answers and Likert scales. They each took approximately 10–15 minutes to complete. The DMOs of the respective destinations compiled a mailing list with all employers involved in health tourism in their destination. The mailing list mainly included hotels and restaurants, but also service providers in health tourism and medical institutions, where available. The project partners also sent out the emails with the invitations to participate. The invitation to participate in the survey for employees was sent out through the same list. Thus, employees could only be reached if their employers forwarded the email.

As the response rate was unsatisfactory, additional employers in (health) tourism were contacted through various associations; however, this did not substantially increase the number of participants. In the end, a total of 106 usable online questionnaires for evaluating the employer responses were received, of which 60% came from the hospitality industry, 28% from the health sector, and 6% from the tourism industry (remainder: others). In the project regions, the response rate for the employer survey was 64%. The response rate across all employers contacted was 37%. The response rate for the employee survey was also low. A total of 95 questionnaires were found suitable for evaluation. Ninety-five percent of the employees surveyed work in SMEs. Eighty-four percent work in the hospitality and tourism industry, the rest work for medical institutions or for health service providers.

The data collected from the questionnaires were analyzed using IBM SPSS Statistics (Statistical Package for the Social Sciences). Because there were no significant differences between regions and employers in the health sector and employers in tourism for both questionnaires, the data analysis was conducted across all cases respectively. In parallel, an analysis of best practices was carried out. Best practices were identified through the interviews as well as desktop research.

Based on the results, it was possible to derive six strategic fields of action for a regional HR concept for skilled labor. For each field of action, relevant measures and recommended actions for implementation on a company, regional, and cross-regional level were laid down. The concept was validated in a workshop together with the project partners from the regions.

Results

Key Challenge: Skills Shortage

"We lack service personnel, chambermaids, cooks. We lack people who simply love the hospitality industry and love serving and looking after guests." This quote of one of the experts summarizes the key challenge employers are facing. Overall, 57% of employers say they sense the skills shortage. For 53%, it has become more difficult to fill vacancies. Fifty-three agree that the number of applications has decreased in recent years, and according to 56%, the quality of the applicants' profiles has declined. Twenty-six percent agree and 26% partially agree that the skills shortage affects their competitive ability.

The migration of skilled labor also presents a challenge to companies. Seventy percent say that the migration of skilled staff to other industries is a problem. Thirty-six percent reported movements of regional skilled employees to the cities as problematic. Among the most frequently named reasons for staff handing in their notice were better job alternatives (46%), the possibility to acquire new experience working for other employers (44%) and a lack of attractiveness of the respective region as a working and living environment (29%).

Ninety-six percent of the participating employers are small and medium-sized enterprises. Thirty percent have up to 9 employees, 37% up to 49 employees, and 29% up to 249 employees. Only 20% have their own human resources experts. Many do not have the time (55%), the personnel (40%), or financial resources (29%) for implementing professional HR management. Eighty-seven percent of the respondents agree, however, that good HR management increases staff competence and thus satisfaction among their guests. Hence, the need for action in this field has indeed been recognized, but employers have not yet taken sufficient action.

Results on Company, Regional, and Cross-regional Level

Results relating to the research questions are presented along the six strategic fields of actions that were identified as important for a regional HR concept (see Figure 32.1), based on the dimensions – employer, regional, and cross-regional level. On the employer level, the key HR areas every employer needs to deal with professionally, especially in times of skills shortage, are recruiting, learning, and development as well as retention of staff. On a regional level, the HR alliance comes into place where joint activities in key HR areas are organized. Besides employers, regional stakeholders, such as regional development agencies, DMOs, and regional politicians, will play a role in the successful implementation. Another strategic field of action refers to the region as a living environment. This takes into account the role the region plays in the decision for a specific employer as well as the question of what a region needs to offer in order for an employee to decide to move or to stay there respectively. On a cross-regional level, the focus is on additional cooperation, e.g., with institutions such as employment agencies, chambers of industry and commerce, federal-state organizations as well as universities.

Employer Level: Recruiting

Sixty-six percent of the employers had job vacancies during the survey period. As reported above, the majority finds them difficult to fill. For 47%, it has also become increasingly difficult to hire apprentices. About 61% offer apprenticeship positions. Finding candidates is particularly difficult

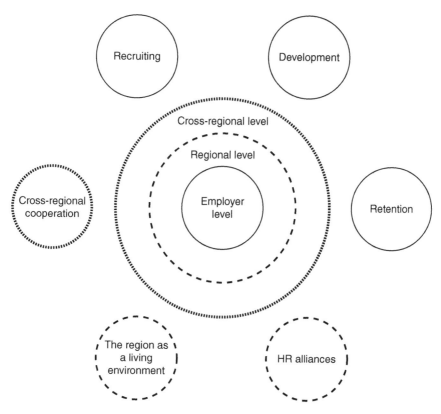

Figure 32.1   Six strategic fields of action for a regional HR concept. Types of lines indicate which level (employer, regional, cross-regional) this strategic field is mainly allocated to in terms of responsibilities.

for service, cook, and kitchen roles. For positions related to health tourism, notably masseurs and physiotherapists are difficult to hire. Regarding the recruiting channels used most frequently, more employers still publish their job vacancies in print media (73%) than on online job portals (58%), and only 55% on their own website. Forty-three percent use external support through services provided by federal employment agencies (which is free of charge). Cooperation with secondary schools, professional schools, or universities as a recruiting channel is not widely common yet (29%).

A surprising finding is that 70% of the enterprises do not have a "careers" section on their website and thus fail to convey to potential candidates what the company stands for as an employer and why candidates should choose them over other companies. Careers pages and the company website, however, are among the most important sources of information for job seekers (Seng et al., 2012).

In the interview study, some examples of recruiting abroad were mentioned, e.g., in Spain. These initiatives mainly developed through personal connections of business owners or managers. However, experts pointed out the high investments that are required (recruiting abroad, language training, accommodation, etc.). Especially in a market with a majority of German-speaking tourists, German language skills are a key selection criterion to them. Therefore, skilled labor from abroad is highly welcomed when candidates speak the language. Most employers have skilled staff from neighboring countries, especially Eastern-European countries such as the Czech Republic, Slovakia, Hungary, the Balkans, or Bulgaria.

Employer Level: Development

Personnel development is an important HR area when it comes to attracting and retaining employees. It mainly comprises training, further development, career planning, and performance appraisal (Lee-Ross and Pryce, 2010). The employee survey revealed that career prospects and opportunities for development are among the top five motivating factors for staff in their current jobs. Furthermore, for better development and career prospects 51% of respondents would consider a change of employer. Appraisal interviews (66%) and the opportunity to participate in shaping the company (44%) are also very important to the respondents.

As regards the employers, 75% of the companies on one hand said that they offer internal and external further education and training courses for their staff in equal measure. On the other hand, only 35% offer a comprehensive range of education and training courses as well as a systematic staff and management development program. Forty-one percent of companies spend on average €100 up to a maximum of €300 per year on employee on further training. Twenty percent of the employers in the project regions believe that insufficient development and career prospects are one of the most frequent reasons for staff handing in their notice.

Employer Level: Employee Retention

In order to retain qualified employees and to reduce undesirable fluctuation rates, it is important to understand which factors motivate employees to stay in their current jobs. The top five motivating factors mentioned by the surveyed employees out of a list of 12 items were (1) the tasks themselves, (2) job atmosphere, (3) job security, (4) contact with guests/clients, (5) a good relationship with the superior, and (6) fair working hours.

Development opportunities were not among the top 5, but on rank 6. Results also show that, once most employees have opted for the tourism/hospitality industry, they consider staying in the industry. In the sample, 74% of the employees stated that they could imagine working in the industry until they retire. Sixty-three percent said that, if they handed in their notice, they would only change their employer but not the industry. The main reasons for changing the employer are to gain experience (57%), an increase in salary (57%), and to carry out new and interesting tasks (53%).

Employees were also asked which HR practices or activities are most important to them and which were already in place at their company. Table 32.1 shows the top 5 most important HR

Table 32.1 Ranking of personally most important and the most frequently implemented HR measures from the employees' point of view (*N* = 95).

HR practices important to employees	HR practices most frequently offered by employers
1 Appraisal interviews	1 Team events
2 Flexible organization of working time	2 Appraisal interviews
3 Comprehensive range of training and further education opportunities	3 Flexible organization of working time
4 Monetary incentives	4 Involvement opportunities to shape the company
5 Involvement opportunities to shape the company	5 Non-monetary benefits
6 Team events	6 Comprehensive range of training and further education opportunities
7 Salary above industry average	7 Measures to promote health
8 Promotion of individual career goals	8 Promotion of individual career goals
9 Measures to promote health	9 Salary above industry average
10 Promotion of study programs	10 Monetary incentives

practices and the five most frequently offered HR practices in the company. It is evident that the measures only partly coincide with what is important to the employees. In particular, employers seem to underestimate the importance of monetary incentives.

Regional Level: HR Cooperation

Employers were asked to what extent they already cooperate with other stakeholders in the field of HR. As shown in Figure 32.2, the majority of companies do not cooperate on HR issues and have no plans to do so. A smaller percentage are planning cooperation on HR issues. In most cases, employers cooperate with associations, external consultants, and trainers as well as with educational institutions. Thirty-four percent work together with other tourism enterprises in their region, 24% with tourism enterprises outside the region. Only a few consider cooperation with non-tourism enterprises in the region to be relevant and see the chances that lie in the cooperation to provide more benefits to staff, such as reduced fares for leisure activities.

The experts interviewed also considered regional cooperation in HR issues to be a sensible field of action. They were skeptical as to its feasibility as the urge to compete would lower the willingness to cooperate. It was recommended to begin with a few "strong enterprises" that support the idea and that the example might attract other employers to join the alliance.

As for HR alliances, research for best practices of HR alliances also did not yield many significant results. Out of a handful of examples, three cases qualified as best practice examples based on the following criteria: sustainable concept, several years in place, very good results, outstanding example and role-model for the industry, award-winner. Table 32.2 gives an overview of the three best practice examples. In-depth interviews were then conducted with responsible contacts of each alliance. The following success factors for HR alliances were identified by the interview partners.

- Clear responsibilities: Successful alliances require leadership. Such leadership can be assumed by members of the hotelier network/tourism board or an external coordinator. An external and neutral coordinator might be helpful to build trust among members to share internal information on HR topics.

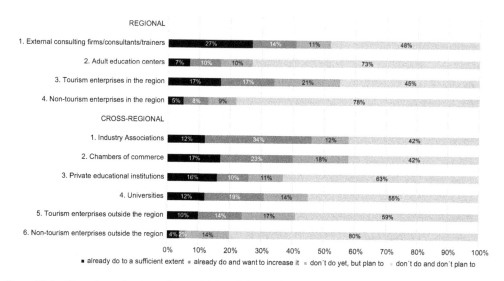

Figure 32.2 Overview of cooperation activities of the employers in HRM (*N* = 106).

- Common basis: There needs to be a shared understanding and clear rules for the cooperation to create commitment and trust among members.
- Long-term perspective: Investing in an alliance is a significant financial commitment that does not yield immediate results. It may take several years until the investment pays off and results become visible.
- Budget: Members need to be committed to their financial investment. Therefore, they need to understand the business case behind.

Table 32.2 Description of three best-practice examples of HR alliances in the industry

		YOURGSTAAD.CH	
Overview	The Frankfurt Hotel Alliance is a group of 60 hotels that represents the political and commercial interests of the hotel industry in Frankfurt (Germany). Within that alliance, there is a group of members that focus on the work of HR topics ("HR Ressort").	YOURGSTAAD is an online platform hosted by the Hoteliers Association of Gstaad Saanenland (Switzerland) that bundles a job website for open positions in Gstaad with information on working and living in Gstaad and Switzerland as well as regional employer branding ("Why Gstaad?"). In addition, YOURGSTAAD offers trainings and a discount card for shops, hotels, and restaurants.	"Work for us" is an alliance in the district of Zell am See (Austria). All members are employers in tourism, most of which are hotels. Founded in 2008 as an EU-funded training alliance ("Qualifizierungsverbund"), it is now funded by its members. The alliance not only offers high-quality trainings and other benefits to their employees, but also promotes jobs in Tourism to secondary school students.
Founded	2013	2007	2008
Number of members	60	38	29
Main objectives	• Enhance the image of jobs in the hospitality industry • Market Frankfurt as an attractive city to work in	• Advertise the destination as an attractive place to work • Establish an effective recruiting and joint employer branding	• Promote the professional and personal development of their employees • Offer an attractive working environment
Fields of HR in focus	• Employer Branding • Training • HR politics	• Employer Branding • Recruiting • Training • Benefits	• Employer Branding • Recruiting inland and abroad (Spain, Croatia, Germany) • Training • Benefits

	FRANKFURT HOTEL ALLIANCE	YOURGSTAAD.CH	WORK FOR US
Main activities	• Regular HR meetings: build task forces, discuss results, lectures by external speakers • Host annual graduation ceremony for apprentices after successful completion of their apprenticeship • Branding and recruiting projects, e.g., lectures at secondary schools, job fairs, marketing materials • Collaboration with vocational training school: exam preparation for apprentices, additional trainings on demand	• Maintain platform • Social media activities (e.g., facebook) • Trainings open to all employees • Staff events and parties • Member meetings to further develop platform (twice/year) • Discount card	• Joint training program (ca. 50 trainings/year) • Discount card (selected shops, service providers) • Discounts for rooms and dining at member hotels • Job website • Apprenticeship promotion days • Collaboration with secondary schools (lectures) • Representation of members at job fairs
Specific characteristics / differentiators	• Strong focus on apprentices • Tribute to apprentices with high-profile graduation ceremony and ball • Intensive collaboration with CCI★, DEHOGA★★, employment agencies & vocational schools	• Potential applicants find all relevant information on one website • All local hotels/restaurants can promote themselves as employers • Application can either be sent in response to a job posting or application can be uploaded to reach all hotels	• Independent coordinator for the alliance (part-time) • Trainings with trainers that are well-known in the industry • Alliance was established out of an EU-funded project
Success factors	• Consistent efforts of dedicated people who established the network • HR professionals of member hotels are included and invited to work in the HR group, not only General Managers	• Clear responsibilities and commitment of the Hoteliers Association • All local hotels and restaurants are featured on YOURGSTAAD • Funded through the Hoteliers Association (member fees) • Platform can easily be promoted through staff	• Independent coordinator important to build trust among members • Coordinator funded through member fees, costs for trainings split per participant • Well-known alliance with comprehensive concept

(Continued)

	FRANKFURT HOTEL ALLIANCE	YOURGSTAAD.CH	WORK FOR US
Achievements	• Primary contact and established partner for federations and other institutions • Increased HR competence of members • Hospitality HR Award 2018★★★	• Volume of website-based applications and number of application recipients have increased • All open positions for the season can be filled • Platform has around 2,200 visitors per month, ¾ of which are new visitors • Hospitality HR Award 2018	• Increasing number of applications • Increase in employee loyalty • Concept workshops and think tank for owners • Cost savings for trainings • Increase in trust and collaboration among members • Hospitality HR Award 2016 • HR Award 2018 (Austria)
Website	https://frankfurt-hotel-alliance.com [in German]	https://yourgstaad.ch/ [in German, English, French]	https://www.workforus.at/ [in German]

Notes:
* CCI: Chamber of Commerce and Industry.
** DEHOGA: Deutscher Hotel- und Gaststättenverband (German Hotel and Restaurant Association).
*** The Hospitality HR Award is an established prize in the German speaking area for excellent and innovative HR practices.

• Industry focus: All three alliances stressed the importance of the industry focus. Members are either only or mainly hotels. This would ensure a clear profile both internally and externally.

Regional Level: The Region as Living Environment

Both employers and employees were asked about their perceptions of the region as a living space. In general, both employers and employees consider their regions to be attractive places to live and work in. All three project regions offer a wide range of sporting activities as well as leisure and medical facilities and services. However, housing is expensive compared to salary level. Only a few companies are able to offer housing for staff in Bavaria, while this is more widely offered in Austria.

The employees see room for improvement in particular with regard to the development of the local public transport system, affordable housing and family-friendly services (e.g., childcare facilities). The findings from the employer survey confirm this assessment. In addition, employers see a need for improvement as regards collaboration between the players on the services provider side and the marketing of the region to skilled employees.

Marketing a region to (potential) skilled staff in and in particular outside of the region is not widely common yet. Similar to a company's career website, the information should provide answers to any questions potential staff might have ("know why"), e.g., about regional characteristics, infrastructure, quality of life, employers, and employment. A website on living and working can thus help build a regional brand for employment and employers respectively. A best practice example is the marketing of the region Allgäu in Bavaria (www. allgaeu.de), which is targeted not only to tourists but also to qualified employees. The greater objective is to position the Allgäu as an attractive place to live and work. The website includes all relevant information for potentially interested employees. Moreover, it features a welcome guide and good reasons why the Allgäu is an attractive region to live in (https://standort. allgaeu.de/karriere).

Cross-regional Level: Cooperation

Figure 32.2 also shows the as-is cooperation of employers with stakeholders that mostly are located in another region. Cooperation is mainly sought with industry associations such as the hotel and restaurant association as well as chambers of commerce that offer advisory services and training programs. Cooperation with universities is less popular. One reason might be that the traditional educational path in the industry is the apprenticeship. The number of university graduates working in the industry is much lower, but slowly increasing (Bohne, 2018). Cross-regional cooperation with tourism enterprises outside the region seems to be relevant for only some companies. Here, some employers see the potential in employee exchange for different seasons. As one Austrian employer put it: "*[There should be] better cooperation on a country level, better promotional programs for exchanging apprentices. When companies at the Baltic Sea close in winter-time, employees could come to Austria and work in the winter sports resorts.*" In this area, we found a best practice example with the platform jobs2share (www.jobs2share.ch/en). The platform posts jobs of two destinations in Switzerland, one being a summer and the other a winter season destination. Once a candidate finds a position for both seasons respectively, the two employers involved sign a contract of collaboration. This gives the candidate a longer employment perspective and each employer has the chance to rehire good employees in the following year.

Cooperation with non-tourism enterprises outside the region does not seem to be relevant for most employers, however. Although the regions are located in a border-area (Bavaria/Austria), cross-border cooperation on HR topics has only been pursued by 21% of the employers so far.

Discussion

The study confirms that the situation in terms of skilled labor in the tourism industry is already tense. Employers are fully cognizant of the need for taking action to manage this challenge. However, the majority of the type of employers investigated still do not assign strategic HR management the priority it requires. Regional cooperation on HR issues has hardly been taken into consideration to date. Key obstacles for companies seem to be the lack of resources, but also the barrier of cooperating with other companies that are viewed as regional competitors (cf. Panagiotakopoulos, 2011). In addition, establishing cooperation is a long-term endeavor that requires the commitment of all stakeholders involved.

When looking at the results it becomes evident that, in addition to focusing on effective recruiting strategies, employers need to concentrate on their existing employees and adopt suitable measures to develop and retain them. To do so, it is important for employers to understand what motivates their employees as well as which development goals and career aspirations they have. Moreover, HR development and retention activities, when jointly realized in an HR network, create prospects that are even more attractive for the employees. Based on the results a number of recommended action steps were identified that are summarized in Table 32.3 along each strategic field of the HR concept. The objective of the employer-based measures is to professionalize HR management. Regional measures aim at making the region more attractive as a working and living environment and to establish regional cooperation in the HR field. Finally, the measures on a cross-regional level are intended to create a suitable framework for implementing employer-based as well as regional measures. The cooperation with policy-makers and access to funding might facilitate the barrier of investing in HRM, especially training and development (cf. Panagiotako-poulos, 2011).

Table 32.3 Recommended actions to implement a regional HR concept

Level	Strategic field of action	Stakeholder	Recommended actions	Expected benefits
Employer	**Recruiting**	Employer	• Create a meaningful careers page which includes "know-why information" (Why should someone work for us?) • Create individual employer brand • Increase online and social media presence • Define and use target-group specific recruiting channels	• Increased distribution of employer information • Professional employer information is more convincing to job applicants
	Development	Employer	• Develop training and further education opportunities tailored to requirements • Create individual development and career prospects • Work together with other employers to provide a wider range of further education and training courses	• Qualified staff • Retention of qualified staff • Further training of staff for new tasks and positions
	Retention	Employer	• Tailored staff retention through retention measures geared to staff requirements • Integration of staff in decision-making processes in order to increase empowerment and involvement • Provision of housing solutions	• Higher job satisfaction • Lower staff fluctuation • Committed and motivated employees • Higher employee loyalty

Level	Strategic field of action	Stakeholder	Recommended actions	Expected benefits
Regional	**HR cooperation / alliance**	Employer	• Establishing regional HR networks • Cooperation in particular in training and further education for employees • Defining rules for the cooperation (e.g., no poaching of employees)	• Bundling of resources and cost savings • Creation of development perspectives for employees • Increased attractiveness of the employer and the region
		Regional stakeholders	• Support in the setting up and execution • Support an independent coordinator	
	The region as living and working environment	Employer DMO / Regional marketing Politicians / Community administration	Provision of housing options Bundling of information on living and working in the region Improvement of the infrastructure, i.e., provision of housing, development of the local public transport system, provision of places in child day-care centers	• Increased promotion of the region as an attractive place to work and live • To make it easier to attract skilled labor from outside the region • To increase the attractiveness of the region through improved infrastructure
Cross-regional	**Cooperation**	Employers & regional stakeholders	• Cooperation with other tourism regions (e.g., exchange of skilled staff for changing seasons) • Capitalize on cross-border offerings (e.g., further education and training courses offered) • Cooperation with employment agencies as regards applications for support/funding, recruiting from abroad, information on instruments for SMEs (piloting function) • Cooperation with universities on applied research projects and recruiting channels	• Create synergies and bundle resources • Regional, national, or international support programs help to start initiatives and minimize financial risks • Knowledge transfer and external perspective add-value to own approach

The components of a regional HR concept with a strong focus on cooperation are a first step towards a holistic approach to attract and retain skilled employees in the region. The characteristic feature of the concept is its multi-level perspective and it illustrates the importance of cooperation on HR issues, in particular for SMEs. The basic conditions for setting up a successful HR cooperation scheme are, on the one hand, that the partners in the network show their willingness to pursue the same goals by working together instead of independently. On the other hand, the partners should benefit from pooling existing competencies and resources and agreeing on what common measures they want to carry out, what entities can participate and what role they can play (FMEAE, 2013). Establishing an HR network takes time as mutual trust has to be built first (Möhring-Lotsch and Spengler, 2009). Questions to be decided upon refer to the coordinator (internal vs. external), the industry (sectional vs. cross-sectional), and funding. If an industry-specific HR alliance is set up, the DMO or hoteliers association may take up the role of the coordinator. Moreover, it has to be clarified what role the location marketing and business promotion agencies should assume. Further research should also investigate the different scales of structure and formalization HR alliances can have (ranging from loose networks to formalized alliances with detailed requirements for membership) in relation to success.

In the HR approach presented in this chapter, cross-regional cooperation has a supportive function to the regional focus of the HR approach. However, in case a regional approach is not feasible to realize, a cross-regional HR alliance might be a suitable option for individual employers. While in this case, employers would not access regional competences and benefits, they would have the advantage that there is less or no competition between members of the alliance and that they can offer different regional experiences to their employees for staff exchange, training, and other joint HR activities. One option would be to implement HR alliances within hotel alliances. Hotel alliances mainly focus on joint sales and marketing activities; cooperation in the HR area still seems to be rare (Chang and Konzack, 2016). This option also needs further investigation especially concerning challenges and success factors.

Because the results presented were from selected destinations in Austria and Bavaria (Germany), the question arises in how far the results are internationally relevant. We argue that in regions with a majority of SMEs and similar HR challenges, the drafted HR concept is applicable and that HR alliances are one serious solution strategy to meet the challenges successfully.

Limitations

In order to obtain a valid overview of the research matter, we pursued a triangulation of methods and perspectives (employer, employees, and experts) within an exploratory research design. The small samples sizes of the questionnaire studies are a limitation, however. Only very limited inferential-statistical data analysis was possible and so results are of descriptive nature. A larger database should be used in future studies, with the objective of generating knowledge on relationships between variables and influencing factors on the success of HR alliances. We recommend cooperation with a larger number of project regions and the inclusion of multipliers to promote the research to the target groups. The willingness of the employers to take part in the study seemed to be low, even though their respective DMO addressed them directly. Therefore, additional promotion through various stakeholders seems necessary. Another critical point is the dependence on employers when recruiting employees for the study. This can lead to a positive bias in case only employers with a professional HR management or attractive employers forward the request for participation to their employees. Additional channels to reach skilled employees should be evaluated in further research.

Another aspect to look at critically is the composition of the samples. Even though no differences were found between employer types, and the samples predominately consisted of hotels and employees of hotels, the studies did include a few service providers in health tourism due to the project context. For the sole view of employers in the hotel and restaurant business, different samples should be used in further studies.

In addition, the rather broad approach adopted in the project has its disadvantages. Although it did provide a comprehensive perspective, a more in-depth research is needed in some subject areas. Further explanatory studies should now build on the results of this study. In the process, the employees' viewpoint should also be taken into consideration. Generally, further research on HR networks and HR cooperation schemes in tourism destinations are necessary.

Conclusion

The skills shortage that employers face will become even more pronounced in the near future (e.g., Prognos, 2012). Thus, the tourism industry, and the hospitality industry in particular need to find solutions for a challenge that will affect their competitive capabilities. Regional HR concepts to attract, develop, and retain skilled employees in the region would contribute considerably to the competitiveness of tourism destinations. However, in order to form effective HR alliances, some obstacles need to be overcome, mainly on the employers' side. Given that the majority of alliance members would be SME who lack the necessary resources, it might make sense to think about installing the role of an independent "regional HR manager" in a destination. This role would drive the alliance and raise awareness on the importance of the activities on the employers' side. In addition, the regional HR concept needs to be aligned with the tourism strategy (FMEAE, 2013).

Overall, the presented draft of a regional HR concept provides a framework for action for the tourism industry. We hope that it initiates further projects with scientific evaluation. This topic requires further attention from both the industry and the academic world. In the end, no regional tourism strategy and no employer's HR strategy can be implemented effectively if there are not enough employees with the right skillset available.

Note

1 EU-Interreg Program Austria-Bavaria 2014–2020, project "Trail for Health Nord" (AB40), project duration: 09/2015-12/2018; project partners: Paracelsus Medical University (Salzburg), Ludwig-Maximilians-Universität München, Munich University of Applied Sciences, Innovations- und Technologietransfer Salzburg GmbH, Tegernseer Tal Tourismus GmbH, Bayerisches Staatsbad Kur-GmbH Bad Reichenhall/Bayerisch Gmain, Verein Gästeservice Tennengau.

References

Ameln, F. v. and Wimmer, R. (2016), "Neue Arbeitswelt, Führung und organisationaler Wandel (New working environment, leadership and organizational change)", *Gruppe Interaktion Organisation (Group Interaction Organization)*, Vol.47, pp.11–21 [online], available at: doi: 10.1007/s11612-016-0303-0 (accessed 29 July 2019).

Austrian Institute for SME Research. (2019), *SME Data* [Online], available at: www.kmuforschung.ac.at/facts-and-figures/kmu-daten/?lang=en (accessed 29 July 2019).

Bachinger, M. and Pechlaner, H. (2011), "Netzwerke und regionale Kernkompetenzen: der Einfluss von Kooperationen auf die Wettbewerbsfähigkeit von Regionen", in Bachinger, M. Pechlaner, H., and Widuckel, W. (Eds.), *Regionen und Netzwerke. Kooperationsmodelle zur branchenübergreifenden Kompetenzentwicklung*, Gabler, Wiesbaden, pp.3–28.

Barron, P. (2008), "Education and talent management: implications for the hospitality industry", *International Journal of Contemporary Hospitality Management*, Vol.20, No.7, pp.730–742 [online], available at: http://dx.doi.org/10.1108/09596110810897583 (accessed 29 July 2019).

Baum, T. (2007), "Human resources in tourism: Still waiting for change", *Tourism Management*, Vol.28, No.6, pp.1383–1399 [online], available at: doi: 10.1016/j.tourman.2007.04.005 (accessed 29 July 2019).

Baum, T. (2015), "Human resources in tourism: Still waiting for change? – A 2015 reprise", *Tourism Management*, Vol.50, pp.204–212 [online], available at: http://dx.doi.org/10.1016/j.tourman.2015.02.001 (accessed 23 November 2018).

Bieger, T., Laesser, Ch., and Boksberger, P.E. (2005), "Fluctuation and retention factors of tourism professionals: Cross-industry mobility in Switzerland", *Tourism*, Vol.53, No.1, pp.17–32.

Bohne, H. (2018), "Innovative Netzwerke für erfolgreiche Personalarbeit in der Hotellerie. Kooperationen zwischen Hotelketten und Hochschulen", in Ehlen, T. and Scherhag, K. (Eds.), *Aktuelle Herausforderungen in der Hotellerie. Innovationen und Trends*, Erich Schmidt, Berlin, pp.283–300.

bsw/Bildungswerk der Sächsischen Wirtschaft. (2014), *Projektbericht Arbeitsmarkt- und Fachkräfteanalyse Tourismus* [online], available at: www.tourismus-fachkraefte.de/BSW/ documents/tourismus/140829-Projektbericht_final.pdf (accessed 13 July 2018).

Chang, C. (2018), "Persönliche und berufliche Entwicklung im Studium. Ergebnisse einer Alumnibefragung", *Tourismus Management Passport*, Vol.2, pp.70–72.

Chang, C. and Konzack, S. (2016), *Mit Menschen gewinnen. Human Resources Management in der Hotellerie. Best Practices*, B&L Mediengesellschaft, Munich.

DEHOGA Bundesverband. (2018a), *Ausbildungsberufe (Apprenticeships)* [online], available at: www.dehoga-bundesverband.de/ausbildung-karriere/ausbildungsberufe/(accessed 23 November 2018).

DEHOGA Bundesverband. (2018b), *DEHOGA Zahlenspiegel II/2018* [online], available at: www.dehoga-bundesverband.de/fileadmin/Startseite/04_Zahlen_Fakten/07_Zahlen-spiegel_Branche-berichte/Zahlenspiegel/180921_Zahlenspiegel_2._Quartal_2018.pdf (accessed 26 November 2018).

Deissinger, T. (2015), "The German dual vocational education and training system as "good practice"?", *Local Economy*, Vol.30, No.5, pp.557–567 [online], available at: doi: 10.1177/0269094215589311 (accessed 13 July 2018).

FSO/Federal Statistical Office. (2018a), *Anteil der Beschäftigten in KMU an allen Beschäftigten in Deutschland nach Wirtschaftszweigen im Jahr 2016* [online], available at: de.statista.com/statistik/daten/studie/731946/ umfrage/anteil-der-beschaeftigten-in-kmu-an-allen-beschaeftigten-in-deutschland-nach-wirtschaftsz-weigen/ (accessed 29 July 2019).

FSO/Federal Statistical Office. (2018b), *Anteil der KMU in Deutschland an allen Unternehmen nach Wirtschaftszweigen im Jahr 2016* [online], available at: de.statista.com/statistik/daten/studie/731918/umfrage/anteil-der-kmu-in-deutschland-an-allen-unternehmen-nach-wirtschaftszweigen/ (accessed 29 July 2019).

Ferrary, M. (2015), "Investing in transferable strategic human capital through alliances in the luxury hotel industry", *Journal of Knowledge Management*, Vol.19, No.5, pp.1007–1028 [online], available at: doi: 10.1108/JKM-01–2015–0045.

Festing, M., Schäfer, L., Massmann, J., and Englisch, P. (2011), *Talent Management im Mittelstand – Mit innovativen Strategien gegen den Fachkräftemangel*, Ernst & Young, Essen.

Festing, M., Schäfer, L., and Scullion, H. (2013), "Talent management in medium-sized German companies: an explorative study and agenda for future research", *The International Journal of Human Resource Management*, Vol.24, No.9, pp.1872–1893 [online], available at: http://dx.doi.org/10.1080/09585192.2013.777538 (accessed 18 February 2019).

FMEAE/Federal Ministry of Economic Affairs and Energy. (2013), *Tourismusperspektiven in ländlichen Räumen. Kurzreport Fachkräfte* [online], available at: www.bmwi.de/Redaktion/DE/Publikationen/Tourismus/tourismusperspektiven-in-laendlichen-raeumen.html (accessed 12 February 2019).

FMER/Federal Ministry of Education and Research. (2017), *Berufsbildungsbericht 2017* [online], available at: www.bmbf.de/pub/Berufsbildungsbericht_2017.pdf (accessed 26 November 2018).

FMER/Federal Ministry of Education and Research. (2019), *The German Vocational Training System* [online], available at: https://www.bmbf.de/en/the-german-vocational-training-system-2129.html (accessed 27 November 2018).

Gardini, M.A. (2014), "Personalmanagement im Tourismus zwischen theoretischen Anforderungen und betrieblicher Realität: Eine kritische Bestandsaufnahme (Human resources management in tourism between theoretical requirements and operational reality: a critical appraisal)", *Zeitschrift für Tourismuswissenschaft*, Vol.6, No.1, pp.57–73 [online], available at: doi: 10.1515/tw-2014–0106 (accessed 27 November 2018).

Henschel, K.U., von Freyberg, B., and Gruner, A. (2018), *Hotelmanagement*, 5th ed., Oldenbourg De Gruyter, Berlin.

IAB/Institut für Arbeitsmarkt- und Berufsforschung (Institute for Employment Research). (2018), *Berufe im Spiegel der Statistik. Tourismus-, Hotel- und Gaststättenberufe* [online], available at: http://bisds.iab.de/ Default.aspx?beruf=BHG63&region=1&qualifikation=0 (accessed 15 March 2019).

Immerschitt, W. and Stumpf, M. (2019), *Employer Branding für KMU: Der Mittelstand als attraktiver Arbeitgeber* (2nd. ed.), Springer Gabler, Berlin.

Kapferer, A., Breyner, B., and Rudigier, J. (2018), *Tourismusbarometer 2018. Eine Studie von Deloitte Tirol und ÖHV* [online], available at: www2.deloitte.com/content/dam/Deloitte/at/Documents/consumer-business/at-tourismusbarometer-2018.pdf (accessed 23 November 2018).

Kuckartz, U. (2014), *Qualitative Text Analysis: A Guide to Methods, Practice & Using Software*, Sage, London, UK.

Kuckartz, U. and Rädiker, S. (2019), *Analyzing Qualitative Data with MAXQDA. Text, AUDIO, VIDEO*, Springer, Cham, UK.

Kusluvan, S., Kusluvan, Z., Ilhan, I., and Buyruk, L. (2010), "The human dimension: A review of human resources management issues in the tourism and hospitality industry", *Cornell Hospitality Quarterly*, Vol.51, No.2, pp.171–214.

Lee-Ross, D. and Pryce, J. (2010), *Human Resources and Tourism. Skills, Culture and Industry*, Channel View Publications, Bristol, UK.

Liebhart, U. and Nungesser, S. (2017), "Sozial nachhaltiges Personalmanagement in mittelständischen Hotelbetrieben – wie Hotelkooperationen unterstützen können", in Lund-Durlacher, S., Fifka, M.S. and Reiser, D. (Eds.), *CSR und Tourismus. Handlungs- und branchenspezifische Felder*, Springer Gabler, Berlin, pp.83–99.

Lohaus, D., Rietz, C., Haase, S. (2013), "Talente sind wählerisch – was Arbeitgeber attraktiv macht", *Wirtschaftspsychologie aktuell*, Vol.3, pp.12–15.

Lohaus, D. and Rietz, C. (2015), "Arbeitgeberattraktivität. Der Stellenwert von Bekanntheit und Labels in der frühen Rekrutierungsphase", *Zeitschrift für Arbeits- u. Organisationspsychologie*, Vol.59, No.2, pp.70–84 [online], available at: https://doi.org/10.1026/0932-4089/a000175 (accessed 27 November 2018).

Madera, J.M., Dawson, M., Guchait, P., and Belarmino, A.M. (2017), "Strategic human resources management research in hospitality and tourism: A review of current literature and suggestions for the future", *International Journal of Contemporary Hospitality Management*, Vol.29, No.1, pp.48–67 [online], available at: https://doi.org/10.1108/IJCHM-02-2016-0051 (accessed: 23 July 2019).

Mayring, P. (2015), *Qualitative Inhaltsanalyse. Grundlagen und Techniken*", 12th revised ed., Beltz, Weinheim and Basel.

Möhring-Lotsch, N. and Spengler, T. (2009), "Bildungsnetzwerke optimal gestalten. Ein Leitfaden für die Netzwerkarbeit", *Berufsbildung in Wissenschaft und Praxis*, Vol.2, pp.32–35.

Panagiotakopoulos, A. (2011), "Barriers to employee training and learning in small and medium-sized enterprises (SMEs)", *Development and Learning in Organizations: An International Journal*, Vol.25, No.3, pp.15–18 [online], available at: https://doi.org/10.1108/14777281111125354 (accessed 18 February 2019).

Peters, M. and Buhalis, D. (2004), "Family hotel businesses: Strategic planning and the need for education and training", *Education + Training*, Vol.46, No.8/9, pp.406–415 [online], available at: https://doi.org/10.1108/00400910410569524 (accessed 23 July 2019).

Prognos AG, Vereinigung der Bayerischen Wirtschaft e.V. (2012), *Studie Arbeitslandschaft 2035* [Online], available at: www.prognos.com/uploads/tx_atwpubdb/121218_Prognos_Studie_vbw_Arbeitslandschaft_2035.pdf (accessed 15 March 2019).

Prosegger, J., Huber, D., Grafestätter, C., Pichler, C., Weisböck-Erdheim, R., Iglseder, B., Wewerke, G., and Hartl, A. (2019), "Effects of moderate mountain hiking and balneotherapy on community-dwelling older people: A randomized controlled trial", *Experimental Gerontology*, Vol.122, pp.74–84 [online], available at: https://doi.org/10.1016/j.exger.2019.04.006 (accessed 20 November 2019).

Qayed Al-Emadi, A.A., Schwabenland, C., and Wei, Q. (2015), "The vital role of employee retention in human resources management: A literature review", *The IUP Journal of Organizational Behavior*, Vol.14, No.3, pp.7–32.

Schmee, J. and Biehl, K. (2017), *Tourismus in Wien. Lage und Entwicklung unter besonderer Berücksichtigung des Arbeitsklimas und der Tourismusförderung* [online], available at: www.forschungsnetzwerk.at/downloadpub/Stadtpunkte_24.pdf (accessed 15 March 2019).

Seng, A., Fiesel, L., and Krol, B. (2012), "Erfolgreiche Wege der Rekrutierung in Social Networks", *KCS Schriftenreihe*, Vol.4, MA, Akademie Verlags- und Druck-Gesellschaft, Essen.

Stotz, W. and Wedel, A. (2009), *Employer Branding. Mit Strategie zum bevorzugten Arbeitgeber*, Oldenbourg, München.

Strack, R., Booker, M., Kovacs-Ondrejkovic, O., Antebi, P., and Welch, D. (2018), *Decoding Global Talent* [online], available at: http://media-publications.bcg.com/Decoding-Global-Talent/BCG-2018-Jun-2018-R.pdf (accessed 15 February 2019).

Verlemann, I., Kipker, I., Westermann, A., Chang, C., and Gruner, A. (2013), *GVO-Studie. HR-Trends in Hotellerie & Gastronomie. Impulse für zukünftiges Personalmanagement*, GVO, Osnabrück.

Warnecke, T. (2019), *Hotelmarkt Deutschland 2019,* Edited by German Hotel Association, IHA-Service, Bonn.

WKO/Wirtschaftskammer Österreich. (2018), *Tourismus und Freizeitwirtschaft in Zahlen* [online], available at: www.wko.at/branchen/tourismus-freizeitwirtschaft/tourismus-freizeitwirtschaft-in-zahlen-2018.pdf (accessed 26 November 2018).

WKO / Wirtschaftskammer Österreich. (2019), *Hotellerie: Branchendaten.* Abteilung für Statistik.

INDEX

Note: **Bold** page numbers refer to tables; *italic* page numbers refer to figures and page numbers followed by "n" denote endnotes.

Printed in the United States
by Bookmasters